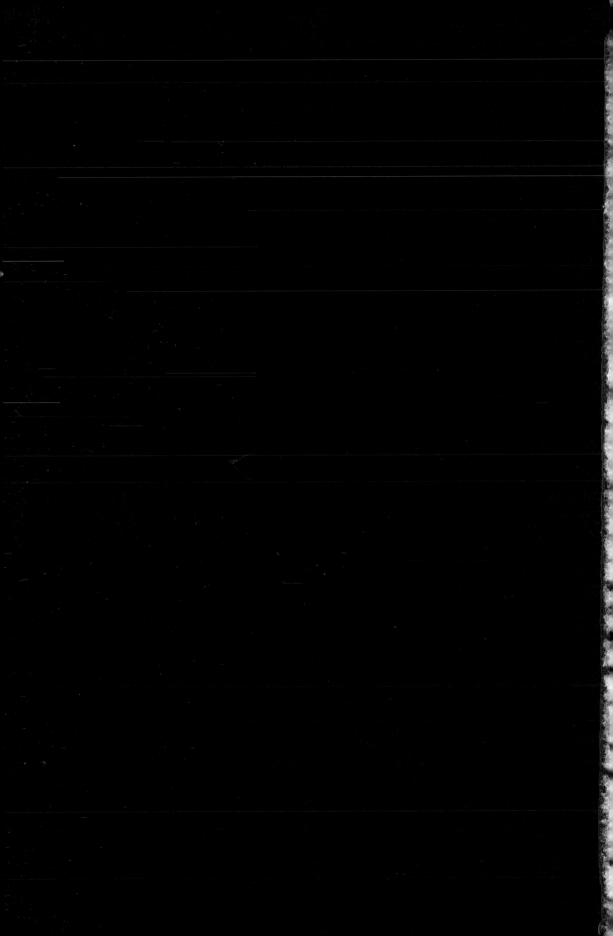

COLLECTED WORKS OF ERASMUS

VOLUME 16

Erasmus, after Hans Holbein the Younger, c 1530
By permission of the Parma Gallery / Anderson-Giraudon

THE CORRESPONDENCE OF
ERASMUS

LETTERS 2204 TO 2356

August 1529–July 1530

translated by Alexander Dalzell

annotated by James M. Estes

University of Toronto Press

Toronto / Buffalo / London

The research and publication costs of the
Collected Works of Erasmus are supported by
University of Toronto Press.

© University of Toronto Press 2015
Toronto / Buffalo / London
Printed in the U.S.A

ISBN 978-1-4426-4749-7

Printed on acid-free paper

Library and Archives Canada Cataloguing in Publication

Erasmus, Desiderius, –1536
[Works. English]
Collected works of Erasmus.

Includes bibliographical references and indexes.
Contents: v. 16. The correspondence of Erasmus, letters 2204 to 2356
ISBN 978-1-4426-4749-7 (v. 16)

1. Title.

PA8500 1974   199'.492   C740-06326X

University of Toronto Press acknowledges the financial assistance
to its publishing program of the Canada Council for the Arts
and the Ontario Arts Council, an agency of the Government of Ontario

Canada Council   Conseil des Arts
for the Arts   du Canada

ONTARIO ARTS COUNCIL
CONSEIL DES ARTS DE L'ONTARIO
an Ontario government agency
un organisme du gouvernement de l'Ontario

University of Toronto Press acknowledges the financial support
of the Government of Canada through the Canada Book Fund
for its publishing activities

Collected Works of Erasmus

The aim of the Collected Works of Erasmus
is to make available an accurate, readable English text
of Erasmus' correspondence and his
other principal writings. The edition is planned
and directed by an Editorial Board, an Executive Committee,
and an Advisory Committee.

Contents

Illustrations
ix

Preface
xi

Map showing the principal places mentioned in volume 15
xxvi

LETTERS 2204 TO 2356
1

Erasmus' Illness in 1530
409

Table of Correspondents
414

Works Frequently Cited
418

Short-Title Forms for Erasmus' Works
421

Corrigenda for CWE 15
426

Index
427

Illustrations

Erasmus
frontispiece

Clement VII
39

More family portrait
41

Antoine, duke of Lorraine
52

The siege of Vienna
80

William Roper and Margaret More
88

Thomas More
126

Catherine of Aragon
137

Pieter Gillis
147

Jacopo Sadoleto
191

Balthasar Merklin
219

Title-page of Geldenhouwer's unauthorized edition of Erasmus'
Epistola contra pseudevangelicos
237–8

Pero Mexía
263

Title-page of Martin Bucer's *Epistola apologetica*
294

Johann Bugenhagen and Erasmus
301

Moritz von Hutten
321

Nicolaus Olahus
361

Philippus Melanchthon
371

Preface

This volume comprises Erasmus' surviving correspondence for the period 9 August 1529–31 July 1530. He was now living in Freiburg im Breisgau, having moved there in April 1529 rather than remain in Basel after the banning of Catholic doctrine and worship in that hitherto hospitable city.[1] Freiburg had many advantages to offer: imperturbable allegiance to the old church, the presence of a 'not undistinguished university,' the use of a splendid house, the protection and patronage of the powerful sovereign of the Breisgau (Ferdinand of Hapsburg), the presence of good friends (including a number of fellow refugees from Basel), and close proximity to Basel and the Froben press. Nonetheless, Erasmus was not yet completely resigned to remaining there and was still considering the advisability of moving further away. This had less to do with the high cost of living and the general lack of excitement in Freiburg (as compared to Basel) than with the fear that the town was not safely distant from the expected violent consequences of political and religious strife in Switzerland and Germany.[2] On the other hand, all the other alternatives to Basel had one or more fatal drawbacks: too close to a princely court and its politics; too close to the scene of warfare; too full of old enemies; too far away for an old and often ill man to contemplate the journey.[3] And, for the time being at least, no thought could be given to returning to Basel where, as Bonifacius Amerbach reported with dismay and disgust, the preachers had mounted a 'tyrannical' campaign to require all residents to participate in the reformed celebration of the Lord's Supper or face severe penalties, including exclusion from public office and exile.[4] As a result, Erasmus would remain in Freiburg until the summer of 1535, by

* * * * *

1 See CWE 15 xi–xiii and Epp 2209:35–47, 2211:58–69, 2217:31–9, 2328:11–25.
2 See CWE 15 xiii and Epp 2215 n10, 2256:24–8, 2295 n4, 2308:30–2.
3 See Epp 2222:7–29, 2328:55–63, 2330:20–4, 2353A:73–9, and cf CWE 15 x–xi.
4 Epp 2248:16–19, 2267:27–38, 2312:6–17, 2321:43–52

which time the city fathers of Basel were prepared to welcome him back on his own terms.

It is difficult to find a single, dominant theme in the letters of the twelve months covered by this volume. The closest thing to it is Erasmus' nagging anxiety, always present but not always at the forefront of discussion, about the conflicts and disorders of Europe and Germany. In Italy, the emperor's decisive defeat of French forces in the summer of 1529 had led to the Peace of Cambrai (5 August 1529), which brought a cessation of the seemingly interminable conflict between Francis I and Charles V that had begun in 1521. The 'peace' was in fact only a truce that left major issues unsettled, but it would last until 1536.[5] While coming to terms with Francis I, Charles had also concluded the Treaty of Barcelona (29 June 1529) with Pope Clement VII, who had paid dearly for siding with Francis I in the recent conflict.[6] The news of these developments elicited from Erasmus expressions of regret that peace between the monarchs had not been made much earlier and that the pope was involved in politics at all.[7] Moreover, given the history of treachery and betrayal in relations between Charles and Francis, and between the pope and both monarchs, there could be no confidence that an era of peace and stability had opened in western Europe.[8]

While the situation in the West thus remained troubling, that in the East was menacing. In May 1529 the Ottoman Turks, who had occupied most of Hungary in 1526, launched a drive westward that culminated in the siege of Vienna in September–October.[9] News of these events reached Freiburg slowly. At the end of November 1529 Erasmus still did not know of the siege of Vienna, and at the end of January 1530 he still did not know that the Turks had raised the siege and retired into Hungary. Under the circumstances, fears of a long and terrible war remained, and Erasmus fretted about the reluctance of the imperial diet to vote adequate funds to support King Ferdinand in his struggle against the Turkish invaders.[10] Meanwhile, the question of war against the Turks had become the topic of a lively debate in which, as we shall see, both Luther and Erasmus would become involved.

If the spectre of war with the Turks haunted Germany at this time, so too did that of an armed conflict between the increasingly bellicose alliances

* * * * *

5 Ep 2207 n5
6 Ep 2211 n14
7 Epp 2211:48–57, 2217:14–17, 2230:27–32
8 Ep 2209:29–31
9 Ep 2211 nn9–10
10 Epp 2211:32–5, 2215:11–17, 2217:17–21, 2222:12–15, 2226:2–6, 2230 n7, 2261 n10

of Catholic and Lutheran princes and cities that had been forming since 1526.[11] At the Diet of Speyer (March–April 1529) the Catholic majority, angered and frightened by the spread of heresy despite its having been outlawed by the Edict of Worms in 1521, decreed an end to all further religious 'innovations' pending a council. The evangelical princes and cities, who had formed a united front in preparation for the diet, responded with the famous 'protestation' that gave birth to the term 'Protestant.' In it they declared that in matters of God's honour and the salvation of souls they were answerable to God alone and not to the majority decisions of diets. Saxony and Hessen then took the lead in efforts to form a defensive alliance capable of offering armed resistance to any attack on any of its members because of their religion.[12] In furtherance of these efforts, Philip of Hessen summoned a colloquy of Lutheran and Zwinglian theologians at Marburg (October 1529), in an (unsuccessful) effort to resolve the disagreement over the question of the Real Presence that stood in the way of a united Protestant front – Lutheran princes on the one hand, predominantly Zwinglian imperial cities on the other – in the face of Catholic hostility (a division that would not be bridged until 1536).[13] Early in 1530, however, the return of Emperor Charles v to the Empire after an absence of nine years raised hopes of a peaceful settlement of the conflict between Catholics and Protestants in Germany.

The Peace of Cambrai, the Treaty of Barcelona, and the retreat of the Turks from Vienna had rendered the emperor free at last to deal in person with urgent business in Germany. On 22 March 1530, shortly after having been crowned Holy Roman Emperor by the pope in Bologna, he set out for Germany.[14] On 15 June he arrived in Augsburg, where the imperial estates had already gathered several weeks earlier in response to his summons (21 January 1530) to a diet. In that summons the emperor had announced that all parties to the religious conflict were to present their views in preparation for an amicable settlement of their differences under his benevolent leadership.[15] The main political business of the diet was aid against the Turks and the election of Ferdinand of Austria as King of the Romans (ie designated successor to the emperorship), but the Protestants insisted that the religious issue had to be dealt with first. In attendance at the diet were many friends

* * * * *

11 Epp 2215:38–9, 2249:22–7 with n7, 2253A:38–41, 2328:102–19
12 See Epp 2107 n1, 2215 n11, 2219 n10.
13 See Ep 2219:36–7 with n12.
14 Epp 2240 n8, 2294 n7
15 Ep 2261:31–2 with n7

and supporters of Erasmus, including the papal legate Lorenzo Campeggi, who expected him to come to the diet or at least to submit to it a memorandum with his proposals for healing the religious breach.[16] Erasmus, however, insisted that he would not consider attending the diet unless invited by the emperor, and (rumours to the contrary notwithstanding) no such invitation ever arrived. He stated further that, were he to receive an invitation, he would turn it down on grounds of poor health.[17] As for the requested memorandum, he felt that he had already outlined his programme for dealing with the religious schism in a book that he had published in December 1529,[18] and there are good grounds for suspecting that he sent a copy of the passage in question to Campeggi in Augsburg.[19] On 31 July, the date of the last letter in this volume, the diet was still in session and would remain so until 19 November. The Lutheran *Confessio Augustana* had been read out in the presence of the emperor on 25 June,[20] and the Catholic *Confutatio* was almost ready for presentation (3 August). Still to come were the long and laborious attempts at a negotiated settlement and, after they failed, the adoption by the Catholic majority of a recess that harshly condemned the 'adherents of the Augsburg Confession' as outlaws and rebels and threatened them with suppression by force, thus giving new life and urgency to their attempts to form a defensive alliance. Most of the story of Erasmus and the Diet of Augsburg will therefore be dealt with in CWE 17.

When Erasmus wrote that poor health would prevent him from attending the diet, he was not exaggerating or making lame excuses. In 1529 he reported that the move from Basel to Freiburg had been good for his health,[21] and in early 1530 he responded to a critic's depiction of him as mentally and physically decrepit with an indignant assertion of his mental and physical vigour.[22] But in mid-June 1530, when the diet in Augsburg was finally getting down to business, Erasmus was in the final weeks of a mysterious, painful, and debilitating illness that had begun in March, taken a turn for the worse in mid-April, and would persist until near the end of June.[23] It was an illness for which he had no name. It was not the 'English

* * * * *

16 Ep 2328 with n17
17 Ep 2339 n6
18 The *Epistola contra pseudevangelicos*; see Ep 2308:13–19 and cf n39 below.
19 See Ep 2341:18–20 with n7.
20 Ep 2333
21 See Ep 2151 n1, and cf Epp 2209:46–7, 2211:74.
22 Ep 2275:24–37
23 See Ep 2320 n1.

sweat,' which in 1528–9 had made it to the continent for the first time,[24] nor was it the stone, a frequent affliction but not one that disabled him.[25] Much less was it 'the French pox,' concerning which alarming reports were circulating.[26] Characterized by acute gastrointestinal distress and strange abdominal lumps that formed 'a huge abscess,' the illness was like nothing else in Erasmus' experience. Both it and the remedies prescribed by the doctors caused him such pain and distress and so disrupted his work that for a time he feared for his life. The crucial stage of the illness appears to have been 6–24 June, a period for which no letters by Erasmus survive. When on the twenty-fourth a physician lanced the abscess, the symptoms abated and the slow process of recovery began.[27]

Given the seriousness and the duration of his illness, it is not surprising that virtually all the works of Erasmus that made it into print in the months covered by this volume were published in the period before its onset, December 1529–March 1530. Literary effort resumed after recovery had commenced in late June, but the results did not make it into print until the period that will be covered in CWE 17. For convenience' sake the works in question can be grouped, somewhat arbitrarily in certain cases, under two headings: controversial writings and literary publications.

The controversy unleashed by the publication of the *Ciceronianus* in 1528 had now quieted down and moved from centre stage. Erasmus was nonetheless still mending fences with friends who had felt slighted by being omitted from the roster of good Latin stylists included in the work, and he was eager to know whether Guillaume Budé, the butt of a jest in the book that had backfired badly, had said anything about him, friendly or unfriendly, in his latest book.[28] Similarly, the old feud with Heinrich Eppendorf was now on the back burner, though it would erupt once again briefly in 1531.[29] More important than these essentially personal quarrels were Erasmus' battles with the two principal groups of his theological antagonists: the Catholic critics who saw in him the source of Luther's heresies and were angry that he would not admit his guilt and recant; and the reformers of Switzerland and southwestern Germany, who thought that his views

* * * * *

24 Ep 2209 n31
25 See Ep 2260 n74.
26 Ep 2209 n40
27 For more details, see the appendix, 'Erasmus' Illness in 1530,' 410–11 below.
28 Epp 2221 n7, 2223:2–6, 2224:1–10, 2249:8–13, 2261:59–72, 2291:61–73, 2302:2–9, 2340:82–98
29 Epp 2216:19–30, 2294:2–11, 2324:13–16, 2333:48–50, 2344:22–5

led logically to their 'evangelical' reforms and could not understand his obstinate refusal to break with the church whose abuses he had so severely criticized.

On the Catholic side, there was currently a lull in the old controversy with Noël Béda and the Paris faculty of theology, but it would have one last flare-up in 1531–2.[30] There was a similar hiatus in the more recent controversy with Alberto Pio, which would also come to life again briefly in 1531.[31] The dispute with the religious orders in Spain, which had begun 1527, would have ended with the publication of Erasmus' *Apologia adversus monachos quosdam Hispanos* in 1528 if Erasmus had not decided to extend it into 1529 by publishing a second edition of that work. In February 1529, while he was working on that second edition, Erasmus learned of a new Spanish antagonist, the Franciscan Luis de Carvajal, who had published at Salamanca in 1528 and again at Paris at the beginning of 1529 a work defending the religious orders against Erasmus' criticisms of them over the years: *Apologia monasticae religionis diluens nugas Erasmi.* The advice of Erasmus' Spanish friends that Carvajal was someone of too little importance to be worthy of a reply arrived too late to keep him from publishing the *Responsio adversus febricitantis cuiusdam libellum* (March 1529), in which he referred to Carvajal as 'Pantalabus' (after the buffoon in Horace's *Satires*).[32] To this Carvajal responded by publishing at Paris his *Dulcoratio amarulentiarum Erasmicae responsionis,* a copy of which seems to have reached Erasmus by late February 1530. Meanwhile, another Franciscan antagonist, Frans Titelmans of Louvain, had entered the lists against Erasmus.

Titelmans was an ardent defender of the Vulgate against its humanist critics. In 1527 Erasmus learned from friends in Louvain that Titelmans was attacking him in his lectures and wrote him a letter warning him to desist. Titelmans responded with a defence of his views and then wrote *Collationes quinque super epistolam ad Romanos,* in which he attacked Erasmus, Lefèvre d'Etaples, and Lorenzo Valla (long since deceased). Manuscript copies of the work were in circulation by May 1528, but it was not until May 1529 that Titelmans managed to get it published at Antwerp.[33] Erasmus found the twenty-seven-year-old Titelmans so insufferably arrogant in his attitude towards the eminent seniors criticized in his book that he referred to him derisively as a 'young teacher of old men' and replied to Titelmans with

* * * * *

30 Ep 2213 n8
31 Epp 2261:75–7, 2280 n2, 2311:17–23, 2328:41–54
32 See CWE 15 xvi–xvii, Ep 2205:241–60.
33 See Ep 2206 introduction.

Responsio ad Collationes cuiusdam iuvenis gerontodidascali (October 1529), an early draft of which was sent as a letter to Johann von Botzheim (Ep 2206) and published as the last letter in the *Opus epistolarum*. A further reply to the *Collationes* was included in Ep 2260 (28 January 1530), which was published in February as an addendum to Erasmus' edition of Xenophon's *Hieron*. Meanwhile, Titelmans had published two further works in the first weeks of 1530: *Epistola apologetica pro opere Collationum* and *De authoritate libri Apocalypsis*.

Unwilling to reply directly to Carvajal's *Dulcoratio* or engage in further direct controversy with Titelmans, Erasmus chose to respond indirectly in an open letter of general reproach to the Franciscans, who seemed to him to have replaced the Dominicans and Carmelites as his principal antagonists among the religious orders.[34] The letter was published as a pamphlet (c February–March 1530) under the title *Epistola ad gracculos* (Letter to the Jackdaws).[35] In it Carvajal and Titelmans are both denounced with vehement abuse, though neither is referred to by name. Both, however, are named as well as derided at length in letters to Cristóbal and Pero Mexía in Seville that were published in the *Epistolae floridae* in 1531.[36] Neither Carvajal nor Titelmans chose to respond to these attacks.

Less easily dealt with were the 'false evangelicals,' that is, the reformers of southwestern Germany and Switzerland, who by 1529 had long since parted company with Luther over the question of the Real Presence and become leaders of a form of evangelical Christianity distinct from that of Luther and his supporters. The members of this group – Huldrych Zwingli in Zürich, Johannes Oecolampadius in Basel, Martin Bucer in Strasbourg, and more besides – had come to the Reformation via Erasmian humanism and had once enjoyed cordial relations with Erasmus. Since 1523, however, when they offered their support to the likes of Ulrich von Hutten and Otto Brunfels,[37] relations with them had grown ever more tense, with communication becoming rare or (in the case of Zwingli) ceasing altogether. Erasmus took particular exception to their habit of describing themselves and their reforms as 'evangelical,' that is, 'in conformity with the gospel (*evangelium*),' and missed no opportunity to decry that description as false.[38] The

* * * * *

34 See Ep 2205:180–3.
35 Ep 2275
36 Epp 2299–2300
37 See CWE 10 xiv–xv.
38 In a letter of 2 April 1524 he called them 'not evangelicals but diabolicals' (Ep 1437:112). Cf Ep 2338:56–7.

tension was made worse by the persistent claim of the so-called evangelicals that they were completing the work that Erasmus had begun, and by their annoying habit of suggesting that he should join their number. By the summer of 1529, after Erasmus had left Basel rather than live in a city with an evangelical church order devised by Oecolampadius, the time must have seemed ripe for a public settling of accounts with the supposed evangelicals. The *casus belli* was supplied by Gerard Geldenhouwer of Nijmegen, a one-time friend who had now settled in Strasbourg and allied himself with its reformers.

In 1529, as part of a campaign against the death penalty for heretics, Geldenhouwer published three pamphlets featuring an excerpt from the *Apologia adversus monachos quosdam Hispanos* in which Erasmus had urged civil authorities to exercise caution and clemency in their treatment of heretics. In two of these pamphlets Geldenhouwer included letters of his own to Charles v and others, making his case against the death penalty.[39] He probably thought that he was making appropriate use of the renowned Erasmus' ideas in support of a good cause, but Erasmus saw it as a dishonest attempt to associate him with a movement of which he thoroughly disapproved. His response was the *Epistola contra pseudevangelicos*, which was in print by early December 1529.[40] Although cast in the form of a letter to Geldenhouwer, whom Erasmus addresses as 'Vulturius Neocomus' (a punning parody of the Latin form of his name, Gerardus Noviomagus),[41] the *Epistola* is much more than a settling of scores with him. The real target of Erasmus' wrath is Martin Bucer and his fellow pastors in Strasbourg, together with the entire roster of 'false evangelicals' in southwestern Germany and Switzerland. He accuses them of craft and deceit in the pursuit of their goals, of having departed from the path of the apostles, of destroying everything good in the church, and of having provoked endless tumult and disorder.[42] Geldenhouwer himself countered by publishing at Strasbourg in March 1530 an unauthorized edition of the *Epistola contra pseudevangelicos* that included 'scurrilously abusive' annotations (*scholia*) by himself.[43] To this 'worthless trash' and 'womanish tirade' Erasmus responded with a letter to the magistrates of Strasbourg, pointing out that the book had been published without the indication of printer and place of publication required by the city's law and

* * * * *

39 Ep 2219 nn4–5
40 See Ep 2219 n5.
41 See Ep 2238 n1.
42 Cf cwe 78 216.
43 Epp 2289 n2, 2321:26–7

demanding action against the printer.[44] Meanwhile, Bucer had responded to Erasmus' attack with his *Epistola apologetica*, a detailed defence of the evangelical cause that was published in the name of all the Strasbourg reformers in May 1530.[45] Erasmus' response to this 'load of prosy trash' was the *Epistola ad fratres Inferioris Germaniae*, which had been completed by 1 August 1530 and was in print by September.[46]

Erasmus' determination not to be perceived to be in agreement with any of the reformers carried over into his public statements at this time on war against the Turks. The first of these was the treatise *De bello Turcico* (March 1530), excerpts from which Allen published as Ep 2285. The second was a letter of 20 June 1530 to Duke George of Saxony, which Erasmus published in 1531 in the *Epistolae floridae*.[47] Both statements were written against the background of a public squabble over Luther's views on war with the Turks. In 1518, in a discussion of the limits of papal authority, Luther had observed in passing that for the pope to call for war against the Turks was 'to oppose God,' in whose hands the Turks were a lash for the chastisement of human sins. Ripped from its context, this was widely misunderstood and harshly condemned as a rejection of all armed resistance to the Turks.[48] To counter this misunderstanding, Luther published in the spring of 1529 his treatise *On War Against the Turks*. In it he reaffirmed his opposition to papal crusades against 'infidels' in defence of Christendom, but he also made clear his view that the emperor and other Christian princes had both the right and the duty to defend their subjects against unjust attack. To Luther's enemies, this was just another example of his talent for self-contradiction and insincere retraction, and Johannes Cochlaeus published a parody of the work in which he contrasted Luther's presumed original position with his subsequent 'palinodes' (retractions).[49] Erasmus, who probably knew Luther's treatise only via Cochlaeus' parody of it,[50] had to be careful what he said about it. The problem was that, as Erasmus and Luther both knew, their positions on war against the Turks were virtually identical: they shared their long-standing opposition to crusades against the Turks as well as their current acknowledgment of the justice of resistance

* * * * *

44 Ep 2293
45 See Ep 2312 n2.
46 Epp 2321:29–31, 2324 n2
47 Ep 2338
48 See Ep 2285:134–7 with n35.
49 Ep 2338 n14
50 Ep 2279 n1

to them. In neither case had either man really changed his mind about anything. But Erasmus, with his conservative critics eager to pounce on any sign of agreement with Luther, felt it necessary to distance himself from Luther on this question as well as on others. This he did by finding fault with the view that Luther had supposedly expressed in 1518, by following Cochlaeus in his characterization of *On War Against the Turks* as a laughable 'palinode,' and by offering arguments in support of resistance to the Turks while ignoring those that Luther had advanced. Accordingly, *De bello Turcico* was addressed to two sets of adversaries: those who wrongly advocated a crusade against the Turks and those (that is, Luther) who wrongly opposed making war on the them.[51] By 1530, however, the controversy had died down, with the result that *De bello Turcico* attracted little attention, pro or con, and never made it onto anyone's list of Erasmus' more important writings.

Also to be listed among Erasmus' efforts to distance himself from the reformers, particularly the 'evangelical brethren' who denied the Real Presence, was his edition (March 1530) of the treatise *De veritate corporis et sanguinis Dominici in Eucharistia* by the medieval theologian Alger of Liège.[52] Alger (d c 1131) was one of the principal defenders of the Real Presence against his older contemporary Berengar of Tours, whose arguments against it anticipated those of Zwingli and the other 'sacramentarians' of the sixteenth century.[53] These latter-day deniers of the Real Presence were wont to claim that their views were taken from the writings of Erasmus,[54] and Erasmus himself had written that if one were guided by Scripture alone and not bound by the consensus of the church, one could easily conclude that the Eucharist was nothing more than a memorial meal in which the body and blood of Christ were not truly present in the bread and wine.[55] What better way to affirm his allegiance to the consensus of the church and distance himself from the violators of that consensus than to publish, with approving commentary, a cogent statement of the church's traditional position that refuted the standard arguments against it? It helped that Alger was a pre-scholastic theologian who appealed to Scripture and the early Fathers and wrote more elegantly than the scholastics with their slavish devotion to Aristotle.

* * * * *

51 Ep 2338 n17
52 Ep 2284
53 Ep 2284 n12
54 See for example Ep 2204 n4.
55 See Ep 2175:24–9.

So much for Erasmus' dealings with his adversaries in the period August 1529–July 1530. Turning to his scholarly endeavours in the same period, one finds that the most elaborate project by far was the five-volume Froben edition of St John Chrysostom in Latin translation. Famous as a preacher and biblical exegete, Chrysostom was the kind of theologian whom humanists like Erasmus found particularly appealing. In recent years Erasmus had devoted much attention to the search for manuscripts of Chrysostom and had published a variety of his works in the original Greek as well as, in some cases, Latin translation.[56] Into these efforts to make Chrysostom better known and more easily accessible Erasmus had recruited the French humanist Germain de Brie,[57] to whom he held out the future prospect of a 'splendid [Latin] edition' of Chrysostom to be published by Froben.[58] The opportunity for such an edition arrived in the autumn of 1529, when Hieronymus Froben, who had kept seven presses busy until early September printing the ten-volume edition of St Augustine (Ep 2157), needed a new major project. Work on Chrysostom appears to have begun immediately.[59] In early January 1530 Erasmus reported that the edition would be published in the autumn, in the same 'splendid format' as the Augustine.[60] At the end of the month he complained about the slowness of the contributing translators.[61] By the end of March the project was so far advanced that the printers could not wait for Brie's promised translation of the *Monachus*.[62] For that work, and several others, Froben had to make use of translations, some of them already published, by Johannes Oecolampadius, whose defects as a translator had drawn the criticism of Brie and others.[63] Owing, moreover, to a breakdown in communication with prospective translators, Chrysostom's Homilies on Romans had to be omitted from the edition and were published separately in 1533.[64] The nearly complete edition appeared on schedule in the autumn of 1530, with a dedicatory letter dated 5 August.[65] It is noteworthy that in the new catalogue of his works that was included in Ep 2283, Erasmus did not include Chrysostom among the Fathers that he had edited.

* * * * *

56 Ep 1661 n2
57 Ep 1733 introduction
58 Ep 1736
59 Ep 2226:65–7
60 Ep 2253:18–19
61 Ep 2263:44–6
62 Ep 2291:5–6
63 Epp 2052:4–5, 2062:26–9, and cf Epp 2226:67–75 (from Tunstall), 2239:51–5.
64 Ep 2258 n6
65 Ep 2359

Instead he merely listed the works of Chrysostom that he had translated.[66] As Allen observed, this indicates that Erasmus probably contributed to the project only his name and his efforts to secure needed translations, and that he did not take on heavier editorial responsibilities.[67]

In the meantime, during the months when he was not ill, Erasmus was able to publish a number of smaller literary works, here listed in the order in which they are mentioned in the letters.

1 / *Opus epistolarum*, the largest collection of Erasmus' letters to be published in his lifetime, with Ep 2003 (the final letter in CWE 15) as its preface. In press since May 1529, it was in print by early September and copies were being sent to friends.[68] The first three letters in this volume (Ep 2004–6), dated 9, 13, and 19 August, were the last to be included in it.

2 / *In psalmum 22 ennaratio triplex* (February 1530), written at the request of Thomas Boleyn, Viscount Rochford, who as the father of Anne Boleyn was a supporter of the attempt of Henry VIII to divorce Catherine of Aragon. Erasmus, who was devoted to Queen Catherine, yielded to the request because there was nothing in the psalm (number 23 in Protestant Bibles) that required him to discuss marriage.[69]

3 / A translation of Xenophon's *Hieron* (The Tyrant) that Erasmus had made some years earlier and now published (February 1530) with a dedication to the Augsburg banker Anton Fugger, who had sent him a valuable gold cup.[70]

4 / *De civilitate* (March 1530), a little textbook for boys on the rules of civility, dedicated to Henry of Burgundy, the youngest son of Erasmus' patron Adolph of Burgundy, lord of Veere. An immediate and huge success, the book went through at least twelve editions in 1530 alone.

One can add to this list two works of Erasmus that were published at the instigation of others. One was *Adagiorum aureum flumen*, a selection of Erasmus' adages published at Antwerp in February 1530 by the otherwise unknown Theodoricus Cortehoevius, with the aim of satisfying the needs of those who could not afford to purchase the large volume of the complete work.[71]

* * * * *

66 Ep 2283:174–83. Cf Ep 2283:241, where Erasmus notes that he had edited Augustine 'with infinite toil.'
67 See Allen Ep 2359 introduction.
68 Ep 2214:1–2
69 Ep 2266
70 Epp 2273, 2307
71 Ep 2265

Erasmus' reaction, if any, is not known. But he reacted with indignation to the other publication, Alaard of Amsterdam's unauthorized first edition of the *Paraphrasis in Elegantias Vallae,* which Erasmus had composed around 1489 and then forgotten.[72] In addition to being offended at not having been consulted or asked for his permission, Erasmus was dismayed at what he thought was the thoroughly inept job that Alaard had done in preparing the text for publication. His own edition of the work would appear at the beginning of 1531.[73]

As always, a number of the letters in this volume deal with Erasmus' financial affairs, chiefly the regular collection and payment of the income from his livings in England and the Netherlands. In this connection it is noteworthy that one of the letters provides the first clear evidence that the archbishop of Canterbury, William Warham, had provided Erasmus with pensions from not one but two livings in England, one at Aldington and another at an unknown location.[74] Another letter, from Erasmus' friend in Louvain Conradus Goclenius, documents a painfully embarrassing episode caused by Erasmus' misunderstanding of the receipts for sums deposited with Goclenius and Jan de Neve in 1521–2. Despite his chronic anxieties about money and his impatience with those who owed it to him,[75] Erasmus now enjoyed financial security, thanks primarily to the good offices of his friend Erasmus Schets, the Antwerp banker who had assumed responsibility for the collection and prompt remittance of his income from England and the Netherlands.[76]

Finally, one letter in this volume stands out from the others because of its bibliographical importance. Addressed to Hector Boece in Aberdeen and published with *De bello Turcico,* it includes a 'List of All the Works of Erasmus of Rotterdam.'[77] It is the first updating of the list of Erasmus' publications included in the second edition of the *Catalogus lucubrationum* in 1524.[78] A comparison of the two lists shows that in 1530 Erasmus followed the same basic division into *ordines* as that used in 1524, with the first five as well as the eighth and ninth *ordines* being the same in both cases. In the 1530 list,

* * * * *

72 Epp 2259A, 2260:70–134
73 Ep 2416
74 Ep 2332:49–51 with n10
75 See Ep 2239.
76 Epp 2270, 2286, 2325
77 Ep 2283:43–242
78 See Ep 1341A:1500–1639.

however, the number of *ordines* was reduced from ten to nine, though it was not yet the final list of nine that would be used from 1540 onwards in editions of the *Opera omnia*.[79]

Of the 156 letters in this volume, 96 were written by Erasmus, 58 were addressed to him, and a further 2 were written by others to a third party at Erasmus' request. These surviving letters include 82 references to letters that are no longer extant. Since a few of these references are to an unspecified number of letters, no exact total of letters known to have been written during the period covered by this volume can be determined, but 250 would be a cautious estimate. Of the surviving letters, 61 were published by Erasmus himself. Of these, 3 appeared in the *Opus epistolarum* of 1529 and 46 in the *Epistolae floridae* of 1531. Another 4 were prefaces to works or editions by Erasmus, 3 were addenda to such publications, two were prefaces to works by other scholars, and 3 were works written by Erasmus in epistolary form and included by Allen (in whole or in part) for that reason. The remaining letters were published by a variety of scholars in the period from 1529 to 1988. Thirty of them were first published by Allen. To allow the reader to discover the sequence in which the letters became known, the introduction to each letter cites the place where it was first published and identifies the manuscript source if one exists.

Except for Ep 2259A, which was translated by Charles Fantazzi, the letters in this volume were translated by Alexander Dalzell. Allen's text and his numbering of the letters have been followed. In consequence of shrewd questions raised by Timothy Wengert, two letters, Epp 2315 and 2355, have been assigned new dates and appear here as Epp 2312A and 2353A. Four letters that were unknown to Allen appear here as Epp 2233A, 2253A, 2259A, and 2350A.

All of Erasmus' correspondents and all of the contemporaries of Erasmus who are mentioned in the letters are referred to by the version of their name that is used in CEBR. Wherever biographical information is supplied in the notes without the citation of a source, the reader is tacitly referred to the appropriate article in CEBR and to the literature there cited. The index to this volume contains references to the persons, places, and works mentioned in the volume, following the plan for the Correspondence series in CWE. When that series of volumes is completed, the reader will also be supplied with an index of topics, as well as of classical, scriptural, and patristic references.

* * * * *

79 See Ep 2283 nn8, 15–17, 19.

As with all the other volumes in this series, P.S. Allen's edition of the *Erasmi epistolae* is the basis for translation and the annotation of the text. In those cases where Allen's work as annotator needed to be corrected, updated, or expanded, I was able to rely on the advice and assistance of distinguished colleagues here in Toronto and elsewhere. The great majority of the classical and patristic references that were not identified by Allen were supplied by the translator, Alexander Dalzell. Timothy J. Wengert, Charles Fantazzi, and Willis G. Regier read the entire manuscript and suggested many important corrections and other improvements. Dominic Baker-Smith, James K. Farge, Paul Grendler, Erika Rummel, Hans Trapman, Heinz Scheible, and Ari Vanderlaan patiently and generously responded to my requests for information about difficult matters of history or bibliography. The notes on coinage, which had been drafted by John H. Munro before his death in December 2013, were revised for publication by Lawrin Armstrong. Mary Baldwin once again earned her reputation as copyeditor without peer. The book was typeset by Lynn Browne and Philippa Matheson.

As always, two libraries were of particular importance in the preparation of this volume: that of the Centre for Reformation and Renaissance Studies at Victoria College in the University of Toronto, and that of the Pontifical Institute of Mediaeval Studies on the campus of St Michael's College in the University of Toronto. To Stephanie Treloar, Assistant to the Director of the Centre for Reformation and Renaissance Studies (2008–11), to her successor Amyrose McCue Gill (2011–12), and to William Edwards, reference librarian of the Pontifical Institute, I am indebted for generous and unstinting support and assistance.

JME

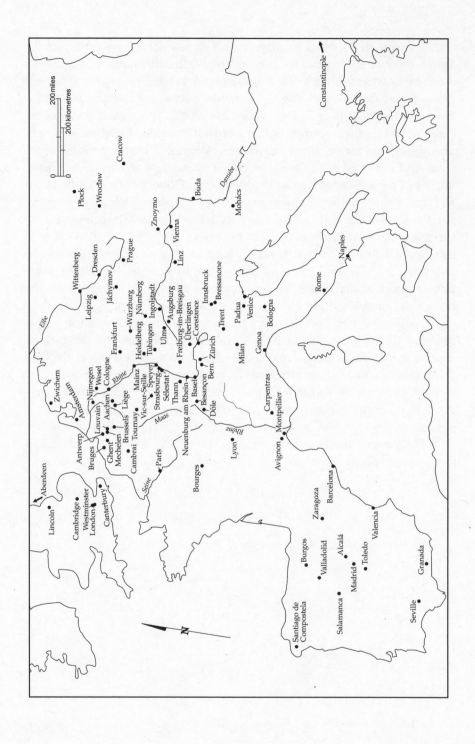

THE CORRESPONDENCE OF ERASMUS

LETTERS 2204 TO 2356

2204 / To Janus Cornarius   Freiburg, 9 August 1529

This letter was among the very last (along with Epp 2205–6) to be included in the *Opus epistolarum*, the printing of which had been under way since May (Ep 2161:53). By early September the volume would be in circulation. See Ep 2203 introduction.

Janus Cornarius (Johann Hainpol) of Zwickau, c 1500–1558, studied at Leipzig under Petrus Mosellanus (BA in September 1518) and then at Wittenberg, where he received his MA in January 1521 and his licence in medicine in December 1523. He spent the next five years wandering through much of northern Europe, visiting Livonia, Sweden, Denmark, England, France, Germany (Mecklenburg), and the Netherlands, where he lived for a time at Louvain in the home of Simon Riquinus (Ep 2246:13–21). In 1528 he visited Strasbourg, where Heinrich Eppendorf gave him a letter of introduction to Bonifacius Amerbach. In September of that year Cornarius, who had by then made a thorough study of Greek medicine, turned up in Basel, looking for employment. Although Cornarius made a good impression and gave a few lectures at the university, Amerbach was unable to secure him employment either at Basel or, via letter of recommendation to Udalricus Zasius, at Freiburg (AK Epp 1296–7). Cornarius did, however, establish close and enduring contact with the Basel printers, who were to publish most of his prodigious output of editions and translations of Greek medical and patristic authors. In 1530, Cornarius returned to his native Zwickau, where he established a medical practice. He subsequently practised medicine in Nordhausen (1535–7) and Frankfurt am Main (1538–42) before moving to Marburg (1543), where he became professor of medicine in 1545. In 1546 he returned to Zwickau as town physician, and in 1557 he was appointed to a chair in medicine at Jena.

During his sojourn in Basel, Cornarius became acquainted with Erasmus, who formed a good opinion of him. In this letter, which was evidently written on the eve of Cornarius' departure for Zwickau, Erasmus encourages him to continue in his scholarly labours. No further correspondence between Cornarius and Erasmus has survived

ERASMUS TO JANUS CORNARIUS, PHYSICIAN OF ZWICKAU, GREETING

Your outstanding gifts, most honoured Cornarius, have earned you the right to my deep affection and to be accorded every possible attention. It is, in fact, entirely natural for me to love and admire men like you. 5 But, among other distractions, the constant – I almost said the excessive – demands of my work are turning me into a Scythian towards everyone

alike.[1] So I have all the more reason to admire your courtesy; for although
you might complain of my incivility, you actually express your gratitude
for what you call the many great kindnesses shown to you by Erasmus.   10

It is my hope that you will continue to pursue your work on Hippocrates, the prince of medicine,[2] a task you have begun with such meticulous attention and, I am sure, with great success.[3] You have intelligence,
training, a strong constitution, and a lively mind. In short, you lack none of
the qualities that seem essential for success in this field, difficult though it   15
is. Indeed I would be urging you to undertake it, had I not seen you moving
rapidly in this direction some time ago.

If you return to Wittenberg, be sure to convey my greetings to Melanchthon.[4] As for Luther, I have no idea how things stand between him

* * * * *

2204
1 Scythians were proverbial for their cruelty; *Adagia* IV ix 85.
2 By this time, Cornarius had already published three works dealing with Hippocrates: *Quarum artium, ac linguarum cognitione medico opus sit. Praefatio ante
  Hippocratis Aphorismorum initium ... Aphorismi Hippocratis, graece ...* (Johann
  Setzer: Haguenau c 1527); *In divi Hippocratis laudem praefatio ante eiusdem prognostica, per Ianum Cornarium Zuiccauien habita Basiliae* (Basel: Froben, December
  1528); *Hippocratis Coi De aere, aquis, & locis libellus. Eiusdem de flatibus graece et
  latine ...* (Basel: Froben 1529). Later Cornarius would be a major contributor
  to the great Basel edition of Hippocrates in Greek and Latin (*Hippocratis Coi
  medici vetustissimi ... libri omnes* (Froben 1538).
3 In the preface to his Latin Hippocrates of 1546, Cornarius proudly cited this
  sentence as evidence of Erasmus' support of his early scholarly efforts. See
  Hippocratis Coi ... Opera quae ad nos extant omnia (Basel: Froben), *3 recto.
4 Although Erasmus and Philippus Melanchthon maintained civil relations with
  one another that were based on their mutual respect as humanist scholars,
  Melanchthon's long-standing disapproval of the older man's theology (cf Ep
  1496 n18) persisted. Indeed, just days before Erasmus wrote this letter, Melanchthon had given sharp new expression to that disapproval in a letter to
  Joachim Camerarius (24 July 1529). Melanchthon complained that nowhere
  in Erasmus' works was there 'one word worthy of a Christian' concerning justification or the duty of magistrates to remove papal abuses. Even worse, Erasmus was the source of all the Zwinglian errors concerning the Real Presence
  that were at the root of the lamentable sacramentarian controversy between
  Wittenberg and Zürich. See MBW Ep 807 T 3 550:31–551:39. Melanchthon subsequently claimed that at the Marburg Colloquy (Ep 2219 nn11–12) Zwingli
  himself told him that his view of the Lord's Supper had originally been taken
  from the writings of Erasmus. See MBW Ep 830 T 3 612:7–9 (12 October 1529).
  The claim was not without merit. Erasmus himself had recently written that,
  were the doctrine of the Real Presence not anchored in the 'consensus of the

and me, since, it appears, he cannot stand anyone who disagrees with 20
him.[5]

I wish you all the success your remarkable abilities deserve. You will
ask no favour of me in vain, provided that it is within my power to grant
it. Farewell.

Freiburg im Breisgau, 9 August 1529 25

2205 / To Johann von Botzheim   Freiburg, 13 August 1529

This letter was first published in the *Opus epistolarum* (cf Ep 2204 introduction).
In his complaints about the Franciscans (lines 214–68), Erasmus repeats much
of what he had said in Ep 2126. For the reply of Frans Titelmans (line 232 with
n38) in defence of his order, see Ep 2245.

On Botzheim (1480–1535), who was canon of the cathedral chapter at Constance and a devoted friend and correspondent of Erasmus, see Ep 1285.

DESIDERIUS ERASMUS OF ROTTERDAM TO JOHANN VON BOTZHEIM,
GREETING

I do not think, my dear Botzheim, that you are the sort of person to assess a
friendship by the number of letters received; and I am not one whom even
death, let alone an interruption in a familiar association, would put dear 5
friends such as you out of mind. But from the time I received your two
or three letters,[1] there was no one available to go to Überlingen, your new
domain;[2] and furthermore I thought that since, during this sadly unsettled
period, you are acting as vice-dean, you would almost never be free to read
a pointless letter or one devoted to some banal subject. Sometimes it is un- 10
helpful to send a word of greeting, while to be silent is helpful. To burden

* * * * *

church,' he could easily have concluded on the basis of scriptural testimony
alone that the Eucharist was simply the memorial meal that Zwingli and his
followers imagined it to be. See Ep 2175:24–9 with n9, and cf Ep 2284:180–3.
5 On the controversy between Erasmus and Luther over the subject of free will,
see CWE 76 xi–cvi. After replying to Erasmus' *De libero arbitrio* (1524) with his
De servo arbitrio (1525), Luther had fallen silent, viewing Erasmus' responses
to his treatise, *Hyperaspistes* 1 and 2 (1526, 1527), as unworthy of rebuttal.

2205
1 One of them was Ep 2117; another one is mentioned in Ep 2206:2–3.
2 Following the triumph of the Reformation at Constance in 1527, Botzheim
had moved with the chapter to Überlingen (on the northern shore of Lake
Constance), where he remained for the rest of his life.

a friend with a frivolous letter is discourteous; to write a serious one is not safe.

But, you will say, 'just as when friends are together they joke with one another in an amicable way, so when they are apart they do the same by letter.' True – in tranquil times. But 'a tale told out of season is like music in a house of mourning.'³ Perhaps you were expecting a letter of consolation from me; but at that time such was the state of affairs that I needed a physician myself. Finally, I was aware how that truly noble and truly Christian mind of yours could always rise above every blow of fortune. Until now Fortune has struck only at the least part of your happiness: she has just eaten away at your income; your reputation and your life remain unharmed.

'But,' you say, 'what I am experiencing is a kind of exile.' Suppose it is: yet it is not a harsh exile, and perhaps it will not last long. Is there a person alive who is so consistently favoured by Fortune as never to suffer anything unpleasant? It may be impossible to avoid or dispel misfortune, yet much of the pain will be eased if we bear it graciously. That will happen if each person says to himself (as is in fact the truth) that it is the hand of God that is scourging us for a time, not to destroy us but to correct us. If we calmly accept the blows of our physical parents, even sometimes when their rage is unreasonable, how much more calmly should we bear the hand of the Almighty, who is the father not only of our bodies but of our souls? How far we still are from the standard set by blessed Job!⁴ The Babylonian exile afflicted the Israelites for seventy years, and they were restored to their temple as soon as it seemed good to the Lord.

Among all the remedies for sadness that speakers commonly devise, I know of nothing more effective than to reflect on these words: 'It is the Lord: let him do what seems good in his eyes.'⁵ We have deserved harsher treatment; he is no less merciful when he strikes than when he comforts. He alone knows what is good for us. Let him even kill us if he wishes, for he can only want what is best. Often he saves by destroying and destroys by saving. If we have received so many blessings from the hands of our beneficent Father, why are we troubled by afflictions that come from that same Father, when we deserve to suffer even more? He is open to our prayers; he will not keep his anger forever;⁶ he will not send

* * * * *

3 Ecclus 22:6; cf Ep 39:140–1.
4 See, for example, Job 1:21.
5 1 Sam 3:18
6 Micah 7:18

troubles beyond our strength to bear,[7] but even as he chastens, he remembers mercy,[8] measuring out the comfort of the Spirit in proportion to the pain. If that comfort is present, neither death nor torments more cruel than death destroy the spirit of the righteous; if it is absent, we are laid low even 50 by the slightest misfortune. Remember too that in this world he tempers our transient afflictions with the plentiful comfort of the Spirit, and in the world to come he requites us with everlasting joy. Furthermore, we have it within ourselves both to alleviate these misfortunes and to shorten them, but we must first reflect on how we have misused our blessings, acknowl- 55 edge the righteousness of God, sincerely confess our sins and beg for his mercy, and we must not inflict punishment on others before we have punished ourselves. If we first punish ourselves, he will become our protector rather than our persecutor, our healer rather than our destroyer. Let us cry unto the Lord, not to one prince or another nor to regiments of armed 60 men. Let us cry unto the Lord, I say, and he will shorten the days of our tribulation.[9]

But alas! Christian morals have sunk to the point where almost no one knows what it means to 'cry unto the Lord,' although this is almost the sum and substance of the Christian faith. One man looks to the power of 65 cardinals and bishops, another to the military might of princes, a third to the confederate ranks of theologians and monks. But what are these, I ask you, but the expedients of men? What do we expect from them? Not to see Christian piety flourishing again, but to be restored to our former wealth and pleasures as to a lost kingdom. It was for this very reason that God 70 unleashed upon us those cruel and arrogant chastisers, to shake into sobriety a world that was drunk with its pleasures and dozing over its earthly riches, so that we may despise all that in our folly we loved before and turn our hearts to better things.

Certain people have given no small encouragement to these distur- 75 bances;[10] they have stretched the rope beyond its limit, preferring to break it rather than slacken and preserve it.[11] The Roman pontiff, as head of the whole church, holds the greatest authority and correspondingly deserves the

* * * * *

7 1 Cor 10:13
8 Hab 3:2
9 Deut 26:7; Matt 24:22
10 Literally 'given a handle to these disturbances'; see *Adagia* I iv 4.
11 For the rope stretched to the breaking point see *Adagia* I v 67. The image is sustained in the following paragraphs.

greatest respect. But those who have exalted his power beyond measure, if
they have not snapped the cord, have certainly frayed it. When papal in-   80
dulgences were kept within bounds, the people received them with proper
respect. But when monks and redemptors introduce them with incredible
ceremony for their own profit,[12] when they promote them without restraint
and push their sale in the most greedy manner, when every single church
has its cross and its red chest, when the pope's arms and the triple crown   85
are set up on every column, when some people are even bullied into pur-
chasing indulgences (as, we are told, is more or less the case in Spain), these
men have come close to breaking this cord also.

Again, when they turn the invocation and veneration of the saints into
a superstition or exalt these things beyond measure, this cord too is nearly   90
broken. It was a beautiful practice to adorn our churches with pictures and
statues either for decoration or as a memorial of those whose example could
inspire in us a zeal for holy living; but when churches display tasteless pictures on every wall and when we slip into an almost idolatrous and super-
stitious respect for such things, we have made it likely that this cord too   95
will break.

It is both an old practice and a sacred duty to praise God in 'hymns
and spiritual songs';[13] but when music is heard in the churches that is more
suitable for feasts and weddings than divine service, when the sacred words
are obscured by the unnatural roar of voices or, worse still, when silly hu-   100
man compositions take the place of the sacred, when one hears nothing in
church but an incessant chanting, here too the cord begins to be in danger.[14]
Is there anything more holy than the mass? But when shabby and unedu-
cated priests learn perhaps three masses and celebrate them with no more

* * * * *

12 The sale of indulgences to the accompaniment of great pomp and ceremony
   was a common and much abused practice in late medieval and early modern
   times. But the reference here to 'redemptors' (*redemptores*) presumably indicates that Erasmus has in mind the Order of Trinitarians, who were particularly active in France and Spain. One of their principal activities was the ransom (or redemption) of Christians held captive in Muslim lands, particularly
   in North Africa. To raise the necessary money, the Trinitarians sold indulgences, doing so to the accompaniment of elaborate theatrical presentations
   designed to move hearts and open purses.
13 Col 3:16
14 Erasmus frequently expressed his dislike of the noisy extravagance of contemporary church music. See, for example, Ep 1756:107–16, and cf *Paraphrase on
   Ephesians* CWE 43 345 n30.

thought than a cobbler brings to his craft, when those who repeatedly ap- 105
proach the table of the Lord live openly sinful lives, when this mystery is
performed without proper reverence, when so sacred a rite is turned into a
public market, they have all but broken this cord too.

Now what can be more beneficial than private confession? Yet when
they bind it with too many rules, when they make it an anxious ordeal,[15] 110
when they use it as a pretext to chase after the money of simple folk or plot
against the virtue of young women or commit other unspeakable outrages,
when they turn confession, which was intended for the healing of souls, into
a means of exercising tyrannical control, have they not given ample cause
for the cord to break? 115

As long as there is no end or limit to human regulations, as long as
many introduce new regulations for their own power and profit or distort
those previously introduced, this cord too is in danger. For similar reasons
perhaps, priests who fail to live a life that deserves respect while demanding
to be treated with inordinate deference have come to be despised by many. 120
Again, when monks court the favour of the people not by the integrity of
their lives and character but relying on wealth, numbers, conspiracy, and
other evil schemes to crush those whom they cannot deceive by trickery,
when they ascribe to the habit the power to drive out diseases, to restore
good fortune to the house, and to provide protection against demons, what 125
else have they accomplished except to make those who were once esteemed
as divine seem hardly to qualify as decent human beings?

I do not mention these matters, my dear Botzheim, to defend people
who defame things that are good in themselves because of the sins of those
who misuse them and who prefer to tear down a fine practice rather than 130
mend it. My aim is partly to make us endure more patiently a state of affairs for which we ourselves are responsible and partly to show how we can
calm the present storm. For as we look at people's present state of mind, I
am afraid that, on whatever side the dice falls, things will be no better for
those who genuinely love the glory of Christ and the beauty of his house.[16] 135
Those who pride themselves on the name of the gospel[17] generally behave
as though their goals were depravity, or wealth, or anarchy, or an untram-
melled freedom to do anything they desire. Certainly no one is being made

* * * * *

15 Cf Ep 1211:146–7, 533–5. Cf also *Exomologesis* LB V 155D; *Apologia adversus monachos* LB IX 1063F.
16 Cf Ps 26 (25 Vulgate):8.
17 Ie those who call themselves 'evangelicals.' Erasmus probably has the 'false
evangelicals' in mind; cf Ep 2219 n5.

better and very many become much worse. The other side, which demands
to be seen as Catholic, includes a number of people who feel so strongly that   140
nothing should be lost from tradition that they even add much that is su-
perstitious and pharisaical. Some on that other side curse Luther with their
lips but reproduce his ideas on many subjects – if indeed he ever taught
such doctrine. They neglect to observe the canonical hours and never pray
at all. They neglect the fasts prescribed by the laws of the church, even din-   145
ing more sumptuously on those days than on others. They show a profound
contempt for the decrees of the Roman pontiffs on the immunity of ecclesiastical persons,[18] on avoiding simony, on not laying hands on a clergyman,[19]
on and many other matters, so that I do not know if anyone is doing more to
undermine papal decrees than those who profess to be staunch protectors   150
of the church.

There is a rumour, too persistent to be regarded as completely empty,
that an agreement has been patched up between the emperor and the king of
France,[20] on what terms is not yet clear, and that the present mobilization of
forces and levying of taxes were not intended for war but for the ceremonies   155
in connection with the receipt of the imperial crown from the pope. It seems
that the emperor, being a man of great piety, wishes to fulfil all the proper
requirements. Whether the story is true or not I do not know, for there are
rumours on the other hand about a most frightful war – though rumours
are preferable to war itself. Certainly it is nothing new to have the most   160
awful threats of war, conscription of soldiers, stationing of garrisons, and
imposition of taxes at the very moment when a secret agreement has been
reached among the kings. However, if it is not an idle rumour and if a
happy agreement has indeed been reached by the emperor, the pope, the
king of France, the king of England, and the rest of the princes, then we   165
must earnestly pray that they will turn their minds to restoring the vigour
of gospel piety. For there is no doubt that this settlement will cause a lot
of pressure for reform. And it is not enough to pray that our rulers be so
minded unless we try also to deserve it, for often it is our fault when they
run amok.   170

* * * * *

18 Ie the *privilegium fori*, the right of clergymen charged with civil or criminal
    offences to be tried in an ecclesiastical court
19 Ie the *privilegium canonis*, the personal inviolability of clergymen. Canon law
    prescribed that anyone who laid malicious hand on a clergyman or monk
    automatically incurred anathema, the raising of which was reserved to the
    pope.
20 See Ep 2207 n5.

If you want news of my own situation, never have Béda and his cronies had such a triumph. They succeeded in burning Louis Berquin.[21] Neither his face nor his cause was known to me except that, in refusing to abandon his unrealistic hopes or obey the advice of his friends, he inflamed much hostility towards me and brought about his own destruction (at least as far 175 as his physical survival is concerned), to the great sorrow of all who favour humane studies. Those who were closely acquainted with him maintain that he was a man of the utmost integrity. What destroyed him was simply his outspokenness (which goes with a good conscience) and his self-confidence.

Up to this point many Dominicans and Carmelites did everything they 180 could to make trouble for me.[22] Now I have no more bitter foes than the progeny of Francis, especially those members of the fraternity who for some reason are known to the people as 'Observants.'[23] Friesland has given us a Dominican called Laurens Ruffus,[24] who is now, they tell me, prior of Groningen, a tough fellow with a loquacious tongue. When he was pursuing 185 a doctorate at Louvain he tried to curry favour with some of the theologians by attacking the author of the *Moria* month after month in his sermons before the people.[25] It reminded me of the Old Comedy, for it seemed as though he had smeared himself with dirt and was speaking from a cart rather than proclaiming the message of the gospel from the sacred pulpit.[26] But this 190 man vented his fury only within the walls of his monastery.

* * * * *

21 See Epp 2158, 2188. Contrary to what Erasmus says here (and elsewhere), the execution of Louis de Berquin was not the doing of Noël Béda or his 'cronies' at the Paris faculty of theology; see Ep 2188 n30.
22 For Erasmus' antagonists among the Dominicans, who included Vincentius Theoderici (n28 below) and Laurens Laurensen (n24 below), see Rummel I 128–35. The best known of his Carmelite opponents was Nicolaas Baechem, called Egmondanus (Ep 1254 n6); see Rummel I 135–44.
23 The Observants were those members of the Franciscan Order who claimed to 'observe' exactly the Rule of St Francis, in contrast to the Conventuals, whom they regarded as too worldly and lax. In 1517, at a general chapter of the order summoned by Pope Leo x, the Observants were formally separated from the Conventuals and declared to be the true Order of St Francis. On Erasmus' view of the Observants, cf Ep 2094:4–28.
24 This is clearly Laurens Laurensen (Ep 1166 n6), but it is not clear where 'Ruffus' comes from.
25 Epp 1164:5–12, 1166:25–33, 1173:111–17, 1581:423–6, 1582 n8
26 Erasmus is referring to an early form of Greek comedy in which the actors, their faces smeared with wine lees (the yeasty residue of fermentation), were taken around in carts, from which they uttered offensive remarks at the expense of any convenient target; see *Adagia* I vii 73.

Another and much tougher member of the same fraternity appeared, who in St Peter's church raved for a whole hour against Erasmus with such impudent scurrility that several people left the sermon and returned home.[27] There were murmured protests even from those who did not know me. Are 195 you surprised at the man's gall? Well, first of all he was a Dominican, then he was a visitor, and he had hardly finished a good meal before he left for somewhere else. And there was no shortage of theologians present who connived quite willingly at this behaviour.

Next came four chosen champions of the church, who joined forces to 200 have a little book printed at Antwerp in defiance of a public ruling by the authorities – and, God help us, what a book![28] It was stuffed full of solecisms, lies, insults for which 'scurrilous' would be too mild a term, and other mad and foolish nonsense. One of those responsible was the great Doctor Ploughboy,[29] another was a bachelor of theology shortly to be promoted *baccalarius* 205 *formatus*.[30] Johannes Faber, at one time prior of the monastery at Augsburg, had previously been highly complimentary towards me in person;[31] he had also blurted out intolerably insulting remarks about the pope and Cardinal

* * * * *

27 Erasmus appears to be retelling the episode described in Ep 1342:131–50. There, however, he identifies Laurensen (n24 above) as the culprit.

28 *Apologia in eum librum quem ab anno Erasmus Roterodamus de confessione edidit*, published at Antwerp on 21 March 1525. The author named on the title-page was 'Godefridus Ruysius Taxander,' which, as Erasmus eventually learned, was the collective pseudonym for four Dominicans whose ringleader was Vincentius Theoderici (Ep 1196). See Epp 1571 n14, 1581A introduction.

29 Erasmus' derisive nickname for Vincentius Theoderici (see preceding note) was 'Bucenta,' which he derived from the rare Greek word βουκέντης (*boukentes*, literally 'ox-goader') because of the obvious pun on Vincentius. The translation of 'Bucenta' as 'Ploughboy' is the invention of Roger Mynors; see Ep 1342:157 (where, in n40, unwarranted doubt is cast on Allen's correct identification of Bucenta as Theoderici).

30 On the meaning of this term (literally 'formed bachelor'), for which there is no English equivalent, see CWE 40 782 n19. The bachelor in question was possibly Walter Ruys, who appears to have been a student at Louvain in 1524 and was a member of the Taxander quartet that produced the *Apologia* against Erasmus (n28 above).

31 On Johannes Faber, OP see Ep 1149 introduction. In earlier years, relations between Faber and Erasmus had been friendly. Together they wrote the anonymously published *Consilium cuiusdam* of November 1520, which recommended an independent commission of inquiry and arbitration as the means of a peaceful settlement of the Luther question. Later, however, Faber turned against both the Reformation and humanism and, as the following sentence indicates, Erasmus came to believe that Faber had denounced him at Rome.

Cajetanus[32] and had even extorted from me several letters of reference.[33] But as soon as he reached Rome, he began an outspoken attack on me, think- 210 ing in this way to win the approval of his fellows. Spain has among many others the tough-minded Pedro, preacher at Burgos and instigator of the whole uproar against me.[34]

But when it seemed that the Dominicans were becoming more tem- perate, the Franciscans began their fierce opposition. At the beginning they 215 attacked me only surreptitiously, quietly removing from their libraries any- thing by Erasmus. Soon in their public lectures they began an organized assault on my reputation, though they avoided putting anything on paper, since it is easy to deny the spoken word and very difficult to refute it. At this point, if the rumour is true, Jean Gachi moved into action in Savoy.[35] Then 220 there was Petrus de Cornibus, who is responsible for that slogan popular among the Franciscan clans: 'You shall tread upon the lion and the adder,'[36] Luther being the lion and Erasmus the adder – though one might just as easily interpret the whole verse as applying to the four orders of mendi- cants: 'You shall tread upon the asp and the basilisk,' that is, on the evil 225 Carmelite and the worse Augustinian, and 'you shall tread upon the lion and the adder,' meaning the ferocious Dominican and the false Franciscan. Any woman could use Scripture in this way to blacken a reputation. Yet how often this tasteless joke has been applauded by the Franciscan cohorts, especially in their cups! God help us, they even thought this witty remark 230 worthy of a painting![37]

* * * * *

32 On Tommaso de Vio, known as Cajetanus, general of the Dominicans and Rome's most formidable theological champion of the papacy against Luther, see Ep 891:26n.
33 Epp 1149–52
34 On the basis of sketchy information from his Spanish supporters, Erasmus had come to the conclusion that his most vehement and influential critic at the Val- ladolid conference in 1527 (Ep 2094) had been a Dominican named Pedro de Vitoria, brother of Francisco de Vitoria, the illustrious Dominican theologian at Salamanca. This identification is, however, open to serious question. Indeed it is far more likely that it was Francisco rather than his brother who spoke against Erasmus at Valladolid. For a more detailed analysis of this matter, see Epp 1836:23–36 with nn8–12, 1902:93–7 with n20, and 1908:22–40 with n8.
35 See Ep 1891.
36 Ps 91 (90 Vulgate):13. Cornibus (Ep 2126 n37) was warden of the Franciscan convent at Paris. Erasmus is the only source for the allegation that Cornibus had applied this passage to him and Luther. See James K. Farge *Biographical Register of Paris Doctors of Theology 1500–1536* (Toronto 1980) 111 (item 115).
37 The painting has not been identified.

Louvain has a young teacher of old men,[38] hardly old enough, I am told, to have a beard. I only wish his complement of learning was large enough to win for his industry the general approval of the learned, and that he possessed sufficient skill at promoting piety to equal his apparent 235 ambition and his self-confidence. Antwerp has given us a certain Matthias,[39] a man with a loud voice and good lungs, especially when addressing the people. He brandishes his tongue like a javelin against Erasmus and stirs up his fellow combatants to take up their pens. England has Standish, now a bishop and, in comparison with the others, a less bitter enemy.[40] 240

But no region harbours tougher opponents than Salamanca in Spain. There a certain Carvajal released a book (and, good God, what a book!) a worthy offering for a follower of Francis![41] As soon as it appeared, it was nailed to the public gibbet, the usual fate of something that has been condemned.[42] The Franciscans had this splendid tract published in Paris in 245 contravention of a public edict, but with some sections removed in which the writer had paid the emperor such toadying compliments as would have given grave offence to the French; for they wanted it to be accepted as a divine right that there should be a single monarch for the whole world, just as there is a single sun.[43] They dedicated this work to their cardinal to 250 let the whole world know that the descendants of the humble Francis, who could not be forced even into taking priestly honours, now have a cardinal.[44] The author rattles away about logic and physics and metaphysics as if he were the only authority on these matters. All this, I suppose, he had learned

* * * * *

38 The word here translated as 'teacher of old men' is the Greek γεροντοδιδάσκαλος, or *gerontodidaskalos* in its Latinized form. The word, which appears to have originated with Plato (*Euthydemus* 272C), was used by Varro as the title of one of his satires. See *Adagia* I ii 60: *Senis doctor* 'A teacher of the old.' Here Erasmus uses the word in conjunction with *iuvenis* 'young' to describe his Franciscan critic in Louvain, Frans Titelmans (b 1502). For further details, see Ep 2206 introduction and n1.

39 Matthias Weynsen (Ep 1188 n5), warden of the Franciscan monastery at Antwerp since 1518. He was a forceful preacher and an inveterate foe of Luther. Cf Ep 2245:10–53.

40 On Henry Standish, bishop of St Asaph, see Ep 608:15n.

41 Luis de Carvajal *Apologia monasticae religionis diluens nugas Erasmi* (Salamanca 1528; Paris 1529; n pr in either case). Erasmus replied with *Responsio adversus febricitantis cuiusdam libellum* (Basel: Froben, March 1529). On this controversy and its subsequent development, see Epp 2110 n10, 2126, 2198, 2275.

42 See Ep 2163:126–31.

43 For Erasmus' more detailed complaints about the French edition, see Ep 2126.

44 Francisco de Quiñones (Ep 2126 n3)

from Francis! He defines a monk so broadly that Christ, the Blessed Virgin,   255
and the apostles qualify as monks.[45] He said that anyone who does not live
according to the gospel rule is not a monk, thus evidently absolving me of
a serious calumny. For I always make an exception for good monks and
never attack any but bad monks;[46] so since according to him such people
are not monks at all, then no monk has any cause to be angry with me.   260
Hungary and Poland and perhaps Italy have men like these, but my friends
have not thought fit to write down their names.[47] Where now are those who
fear for the church's ruin when it has people to defend it by such tactics![48]
Their only hope lies in the stupidity of the people. The Franciscans want to
make a name in the world, but in my opinion they would do better to seek   265
fame in other ways. If the authority of the princes has made no headway, or
certainly very little, against the new sects, how much less will be achieved
by the scurrilous buffoonery of the mendicants!

Here, I think, is a good-sized letter; after this you will not be able to
complain about my silence or make remarks like 'I wonder if you can have   270
forgotten your friend Botzheim.' That you always think of Erasmus in the
midst of disaster, I can well believe, though I should prefer it if Erasmus
came to mind when everything is peaceful. But to hold the rudder straight
in a storm rather than in a calm sea is at least more creditable, if it is not so
pleasant. Farewell, dear Botzheim, first among my loyal friends.   275

Freiburg im Breisgau, 13 August 1529

2206 / To Johann von Botzheim   Freiburg, 19 August 1529

This letter to Botzheim (Ep 2205 introduction) is in fact one of Erasmus' *apologiae* against his critic Frans Titelmans, Franciscan of Louvain (Epp 1823 introduction, 2205:232–6). Like his teacher Jacobus Latomus (Ep 934), Titelmans
was an ardent defender of the Vulgate against its humanist critics. In 1527,
having learned from friends that Titelmans had criticized him sharply in his
lectures, Erasmus admonished him to desist (Ep 1823). The friar responded
with a letter defending his views (Ep 1837A), and then set to work on a book

* * * * *

45 Cf Ep 2300:124–5, with n36.
46 See Ep 2275:16–18, 70–1.
47 Though this statement occurs several times in Erasmus' letters, there is no
    evidence anywhere in his surviving correspondence of Franciscan hostility
    in Hungary or Poland. Cf Epp 1823:17–18 with n5, 2126:179. Nor does there
    appear to be any evidence of problems with Franciscans in Italy.
48 Cf Ep 2201:98–9.

attacking Erasmus (as well as Lorenzo Valla and Lefèvre d'Etaples). By May 1528, friends of Erasmus had seen manuscript copies of the book (Epp 1994, 1994A). Although the faculty of theology at Louvain, acting in response to recent injunctions from the papal curia and the imperial court (Ep 1823 n2), had attempted to prevent publication of the work (Ep 2089:2–6), Titelmans managed to have it printed at Antwerp by W. Vorsterman in May 1529: *Collationes quinque super epistolam ad Romanos*.

While at work on his reply to Titelmans' *Collationes*, Erasmus received from Botzheim a request to see samples of it (lines 2–3 below). Erasmus complied with this letter, which he quickly published as the last item in the *Opus epistolarum* before expanding it into the more substantial *Ad Collationes cuiusdam. Opus recens* (usually referred to as the *Responsio ad Collationes*), which was printed at Antwerp by P. Sylvius in October 1529. Titelmans responded to this letter (and Ep 2205) as well as to the *Opus recens* in two works: *Epistola apologetica pro opere Collationum* ... (Antwerp: W. Vorsterman, January 1530) and *De authoritate libri Apocalypsis* (Antwerp: M. de Keyser 1530); cf Epp 2245 and 2417. In February 1530 Erasmus denounced Titelmans without naming him in the open letter to the Franciscans (Ep 2275) that was soon printed at Antwerp by M. de Keyser under the title *Epistola ad gracculos*. In March 1530 Erasmus denounced Titelmans by name in a letter to Pero Mexía that was not published until 1531 (Ep 2300:29–43). To these attacks Titelmans chose not to reply.

We have followed Allen's example by printing only the opening section and the final sentence of the *Opus epistolarum* text.

ERASMUS OF ROTTERDAM TO JOHANN VON BOTZHEIM, GREETING
I see you were not as swamped with business as I imagined, since you want me to send you a sample of my *Gerontodidaskalos*.[1] You know that at the moment the presses are rattling away at full speed.[2] I did, however, take a cursory glance at several pages and indicated in a word or two what reply 5 could be made if I thought this helpful to scholarship. I am enclosing a few pages of the work so that you can judge if I was right in thinking it better to be silent than to get involved in the laborious task of replying with very little profit to the cause of letters. There are many aspects of his writing

* * * * *

2206
1 Greek in the text. Erasmus found the young Titelmans (b 1502) so self-important and confident in his criticism of older scholars (Epp 2126:177–9, 2205: 232–3, and lines 117–40 of this letter) that he now referred to him derisively as *iuvenis gerontodidascalus* 'young teacher of old men'; see Ep 2205 n38.
2 In preparation for the September book fair in Frankfurt

that seem to point to human vanity. He tells us repeatedly that he lectures   10
on Scripture in a famous university,[3] although even mature scholars often
complain of being compelled, on orders from their elders, to undertake a
task beyond their powers. If it is simply a case of ambition, this is a curable
weakness in a young person, although it is hardly seemly in a Franciscan.
But if falseness lurks underneath, the malady is incurable. There are, indeed,   15
occasional indications of something rotten under the surface. But God alone
knows the heart;[4] it is not for me to judge another man's spirit. If he were
a very dear acquaintance of mine, I would have advised him not to rush
into publication but first to train his mind by a long course of reading. The
evidence is clear enough that he does not have a good command of Latin.   20
As far as I can see, he has only a reading knowledge of Greek. But now for
my sample.

In the long-winded preface that he prefixed to the work he storms with
rage at those who curse the Old Translator,[5] spit on him, hiss at him, kick
and trample him. At the beginning of his 'discussion' he singles me out for   25
a drubbing: apparently it is my doing that the Translator is so badly treated.
None of this is at all relevant to me; nor as yet do I see any evidence that
the old version has been trampled underfoot, since it is read everywhere in
churches and universities; nor can he get it through his head[6] that I have
simply presented what is in the Greek manuscripts without prejudice to the   30
use of the Vulgate for public reading.

To ascribe a solecism to the Translator is, in his view, an appalling insult, although he admits there are solecisms even in the writings of the apostles; but if these are reproduced by the Translator, he does not believe that
an error has been committed. He appears not to understand, or at any rate   35
to consider, that the language in which the apostles proclaimed the gospel
message was not that of the learned, but the everyday speech of ordinary
people – cobblers, sailors, weavers both men and women, and indeed of
pimps and madams (for the gospel was written for them too). If at that time
the Greek language had been as corrupt as it is today and the corrupt form   40
had been as widely used as Greek was then, I believe the apostles would

* * * * *

3 Louvain
4 Acts 1:24
5 Ie the anonymous translator of the Vulgate New Testament, not Jerome, whom
  Erasmus considered to be merely the reviser of the older Latin version. See
  Ep 2172 nn2 and 5.
6 Literally 'keep it in his mind' (*meminisse*), which is the word found in the
  Opus epistolarum text. Allen substituted the rather improbable *eam minuisse* for
  meminisse, giving the meaning 'nor can our having presented the reading of
  the Greek manuscripts ... have diminished it [the Vulgate].'

have adopted it, just as Christ did not speak a pure Hebrew but Syriac,[7] a language evidently corrupted by contact with other tongues. So the Latin Translator, who in my opinion was the earliest,[8] adopted the language that was then common to men, women, and children, and to the lowest ranks of society, but could nevertheless be understood by the educated on account of its familiar use. If at that time the Latin language had been as corrupted as it is now in France, Spain, and Italy, the Translator would probably have used the popular idiom in spite of its degeneracy, just as today those who preach the gospel in French or Spanish or Italian are using a language that, in comparison with Latin, is greatly debased. So it is not surprising if, in the opinion of those who speak correctly, the Translator makes mistakes, since he wanted to be understood by ordinary people rather than by the educated, who were particularly resistant to the gospel. Furthermore, my critic refuses to regard it as a solecism when, for pious reasons, the rules of correct speech are disregarded. This is an argument I have never heard before. I do not deny that a solecism may be excused for a pious reason. But anyone who excuses a solecism is admitting there is one. Moreover, the writings of Augustine, Cyprian, and Ambrose are not free from error, especially when they cite Scripture. I too am often guilty of solecisms of this sort.

My critic collects several passages that appear in the Vulgate in the form corrected by Jerome, but is silent about those that differ from the reading Jerome approved. 'But,' he says, 'Jerome may later have obtained better manuscripts from which he restored the reading in certain cases.'[9] But he had said that the earlier recension was produced under the inspiration of the Spirit. So does the Spirit babble too? And if it was a case of supernatural inspiration, what need was there for manuscripts?

He is fierce in his anger, and not without reason, against those who turn up their noses at the sacred texts for their lack of meretricious embellishments, sesquipedalian words, and overblown and inflated expressions.[10] I too condemn such people. My only aim has been to convey what is found in the Greek manuscripts in a more elegant yet simple and clearer style.

He is remarkably complimentary about the Translator, praising him for his excellence, sanctity, wisdom, and learning, as a man inspired by the Holy Spirit. He may well have been so. But if we were to press our eulogist, he

* * * * *

7 'Syriac' (*Syriaca lingua*) is the name that Erasmus customarily applied to Aramaic.
8 See n5 above.
9 As Allen points out, Erasmus is referring to folio b verso in Titelman's *Collationes* but not quoting it literally.
10 The language here echoes Horace *Ars poetica* 97.

would not be able to say whether the Translator was a Jew, a pagan, or a Christian, a heretic or a believer, a cobbler or a soldier, a youth or a veteran, a man or a woman. If we did owe our New Testament to a pagan, it would carry all the more weight with us, since the translation would have been made by one who was a stranger to the gospel. But there is no need   80 to worry overmuch about the Translator, since the sources are extant. The church approved the result; it does not know the author. No one can interpret the Scriptures correctly unless inspired by that same Spirit who is the author of Scripture. But there are two kinds of 'interpretation.'[11] It is one thing to translate the Scriptures from one language to another, and quite   85 something else to interpret the spiritual meaning. There are likewise two forms of inspiration: the inspiration by which Holy Scripture was first produced cannot be attributed with certainty to any but the original authors. Nevertheless, while we may say perhaps that some measure of inspiration was necessary to translate the Old Testament – just as no one will easily   90 make a correct translation of the writings of the philosophers unless he has a fair acquaintance with the subject – in the New Testament the language is so simple that any ordinary person could have produced a version such as this translator did.

I believe that the inspiration of the Spirit was present in some way to   95 all the recognized Doctors of the church, yet it is not uncommon for them to slip into errors, even heretical errors. St Jerome translated and interpreted the prophets yet often admits that he does not understand the meaning. So it is possible to translate what one does not fully comprehend. Translation is a lesser art than exposition. But if, as my opponent claims, it is unac-   100 ceptable for the Translator to depart even from the tropes and figures of the original, then Jerome is guilty of impiety, for in the Old Testament he boldly removed almost all of the Hebrew tropes despite Augustine's protestations.[12] If everything the Translator wrote comes from the inspiration of the Spirit, then it was wrong for Jerome to change even a word. Yet he was   105 not afraid to do so. I find it amusing that every time something in Jerome is plainly contrary to my opponent's view, his response is that Jerome is writing rhetorically.

Scripture will not automatically become a human artefact if the translator uses the human powers of his mind to translate what he reads, for   110 Scripture exists in the meaning, not in the words; or if Scripture does exist

* * * * *

11 The argument in this passage depends on the two senses of the Latin verb *interpretari*, which can mean both 'translate' and 'interpret.'
12 Augustine Ep 71

in the words, then the integrity of the words resides in the original language, not in the translation. If, however, he wants to blame all awkwardness of language on the carelessness of copyists, then as far as I am concerned, he is free to do so, but I am afraid he will find no one to believe   115
him.

So much for his preface. Someone else would perhaps fault him for having the dead and the living talk together in his *Collationes*.[13] I can readily overlook the fact that he makes me sound like himself. Since, moreover, he acts the part of the young *gerontodidaskalos*,[14] casting himself in the role of   120
the censor, criticizing three old men, often correcting and chastising them in a severe and confident manner, I admit that the Holy Spirit once manifested his power through the young Daniel, and I would not be ashamed to learn something worth knowing even from a child. Certain things he approves, some he allows and condones, some he rejects and condemns, rather   125
heatedly. But a young man should have something excellent to offer if he decides to take the cane to three veterans, who, with the possible exception of myself, are men of no ordinary learning. Then he plays the characteristically juvenile trick of offering peace and harmony if we agree to be friends of the truth – as if it were impossible that he could be mistaken   130
himself. Certainly he would have made his book more marketable if he had treated the subject more succinctly. But by rehearsing what Lorenzo said, what Jacques Lefèvre said, what Desiderius said,[15] by explaining all this in his own words, with preambles and personal attacks, by citing what was read by Cyprian, Ambrose, Jerome, Augustine, Sedulius, and Hesychius   135
(which proved nothing against me, since my concern is with the Greek text and with purity of language), by inserting prefaces and interjections, by extending the discussion with a concluding flourish, by adding much that neither supports the translator nor works against me, he lays a heavy burden on the reader.   140

I am afraid this may be more than enough for you. But you should blame yourself, for it was you who insisted on my sending it. Farewell, dearest friend of my heart.

Freiburg im Breisgau, 19 August 1529

* * * * *

13 Titelmans represented himself in conversation with Lorenzo Valla (d 1457) and Lefèvre d'Etaples (d 1536) as well as Erasmus.
14 Greek in the text; see n1 above.
15 Throughout the *Collationes*, Titelmans refers to Valla as Lorenzo and Erasmus as Desiderius.

2207 / From Johann von Botzheim Überlingen, 20 August 1529

The autograph of this letter, which was first published as Ep 110 in Förstemann / Günther, was in the Burscher Collection at Leipzig (Ep 1254 introduction). On Botzheim, see Ep 2205 introduction.

Greetings. It seems, my distinguished patron, that all thought of Botzheim
has vanished from your mind, for I have received no letter from you in
Freiburg all the time you have been there.[1] I cannot be sure if you have
formed a grudge against me, though I am certainly not aware of having
given you any cause. Nothing is more pleasing to me or more important 5
that the name of Erasmus, nor will all the philistine hordes of suffragans[2]
and monks and sophists tear me away from you. But I must not allow my
pen to run on like this.

A fresh rumour reached us yesterday from Trent, straight from the
oracle of Apollo,[3] that it was as certain as could be that on the seventh day 10
of August the emperor Charles reached the port of Monaco in Italy and
on the following day entered Genoa with a more than royal retinue,[4] and
that the peace concluded between the emperor Charles and King Francis of
France and King Henry of England (which, I hope, will turn out for the best)
was proclaimed again on the fifth day of August.[5] I want to let you know 15

* * * * *

2207
1 Cf Ep 2205:6–8.
2 In English, 'suffragan' usually refers to an auxiliary bishop but, correctly used,
the Latin term *suffraganeus* means a diocesan bishop who is subject to an archbishop as the metropolitan of the province. Botzheim's use of 'suffragans'
where one would expect 'bishops' (*episcopi*) was probably intended to be pejorative. At all events the sense of the passage is that neither bishops nor monks
nor theologians ('sophists') will succeed in undermining Botzheim's devotion
to Erasmus.
3 *Adagia* I vii 90
4 Charles had in fact reached Monaco on 4 August and entered Genoa on the
twelfth; cf Ep 2208 n12.
5 The Peace of Cambrai, called the 'Ladies' Peace' because it was negotiated by
Louise of Savoy, the mother of Francis I, and Margaret of Austria, the aunt of
Charles V. The treaty left Charles in firm command of Italy while conceding to
Francis the possession of Burgundy. Although it was only a temporary pause
in the Hapsburg-Valois wars, which would resume in 1536, the Peace of Cambrai gave Charles the opportunity to settle the affairs of Italy and have himself
crowned Holy Roman Emperor by the pope (24 February 1530) before returning to Germany, where he hoped to bring an end to the religious divisions

this in case you have not heard, for this gives us hope that deliverance will soon come to Germany.

Write back if you remember your friend Botzheim and let me know the reason for your silence towards me. The parish priest of Freiburg,[6] if you cannot make other arrangements, can bring me a letter on almost any 20 day. Farewell.

From exile in my cave at Überlingen, 20 August 1529

Your most devoted friend Johann von Botzheim

To the incomparable champion of true theology and the humane arts, Desiderius Erasmus of Rotterdam, his most beloved teacher and mentor. In 25 Freiburg im Breisgau

2208 / From Juan Luis Vives   Bruges, 30 August 1529

This letter was first published in volume 2 of Vives' *Opera* (Basel: Episcopius 1555). On Vives see Ep 927 introduction.

VIVES TO ERASMUS

When I was in Antwerp in June, I wrote you about the revision of my Augustine and arranged for the letter to be delivered to you. Afterwards I received a letter from you, which had been a long time on the way;[1] it was sent from Freiburg, to which, you said, you had moved from Basel. I hope 5 this will work out for the best. I wish you had come closer, but I know that the state of your affairs is a persuasive argument against this. I have almost finished revising Augustine.[2] I shall give the completed text to Franz before

* * * * *

that had taken root since his last visit there in 1521. See Knecht 219–20. As for Henry VIII, he had done what he could to keep the war between Emperor Charles and King Francis going so as to prevent the unity between pope and emperor that would frustrate his hope for a papally sanctioned divorce from Queen Catherine, who was the emperor's niece (cf Ep 1993 n2). Deprived of this hope by the success of the negotiations at Cambrai, Henry gave his assent to the peace at the last moment. See Scarisbrick 232–3.
6 Georg Keck of Hechingen (d 1547), curate of the minster at Freiburg 1519–32, later a member of the faculty of theology

2208
1 Neither of these letters is extant.
2 The decision not to reprint the first version of Vives' edition of the *City of God* (1522) in the new ten-volume Froben edition of Augustine on the ground that there were too many unsold copies of the expensive volume still in the warehouse (Ep 1889:19–21) was still in effect in September 1528 (Ep 2040:31–4).

October.[3] He assured me that if I handed it over even as late as the first of
November, that would be soon enough. If I had received your letter earlier,   10
or if X had mentioned the matter to me,[4] Froben would have had the book
long ago.

The archbishop of Toledo has been gravely ill.[5] There was a general impression throughout Spain that he was dead;[6] some were even so informed
by letter. But he recovered, and was appointed by the emperor before he   15
left to assist the empress in the administration of the affairs of Spain.[7] To
these two were added the duke of Alba and the Master of the Horse,[8] who
lost his father recently, but these three men have more the role of advisers
and consultants; the empress is in control of everything.

Your mentioning me in the preface to the Augustine[9] pleases me greatly   20
because the compliment comes from you and was inspired by our mutual
affection. Otherwise I care little for fame or the mention of my name.[10]

* * * * *

It seems that over the summer of 1529 Vives, doubtless encouraged by Erasmus' hints about needed revisions (Ep 1889:22–3), had worked on a revised
edition. Whether he ever got the completed text to Froben is not clear. But
when the first sets of the new Froben edition were sent out in the autumn,
volume 5, the *City of God*, was missing (Ep 2227:16–22), and when it did appear at the end of the year, it contained only the bare text without Vives' introduction or commentary. Vives' revised edition of the work was first published
by Claude Chevallon at Paris in 1531 as part of the edition of Augustine's
Opera omnias. Cf Ep 2157 introduction; and see also Charles Fantazzi 'Vives'
Text of Augustine's *De civitate Dei*' in *Neulateinisches Jahrbuch* 11 (2009) 19–33,
especially 20–1.

3 Franz Birckmann (Ep 258:14n), the Antwerp bookseller who had long been
   involved in the distribution of Erasmus' works
4 Allen suggests that 'X' was probably Birckmann (see preceding note), though
   it is not clear why Vives would name him in one sentence and then conceal
   his identity three lines further on.
5 The archbishop was Alonso de Fonseca (Ep 1748), the dedicatee of the Froben
   Augustine (Ep 2157).
6 Cf Epp 2253:70–2, 2253A:1–8.
7 During his many absences from Spain, Charles entrusted its governance to
   Isabella of Portugal (1503–39), whom he had married in 1526 (cf Ep 1647 n6).
8 The (second) duke of Alba was Fadrique Alvarez de Toledo (c 1460–1531). The
   Master of the Horse (head of Empress Isabella's household) was Francisco de
   Zúñiga (d 1538), third count of Miranda. His appointment was in effect by 10
   October 1528.
9 Ep 2157:554–6
10 On this cf Ep 2061:76–9.

Nothing is more empty or tainted with more bitter gall than fame. Even if the whole world were to idolize and applaud me like an actor in the theatre, I do not imagine myself made one whit the better or more fortunate; in fact I should often be more miserable and wretched, for the excitement takes me out of myself and I cannot turn my eyes and my thoughts within since they are fixed on the applauding crowd. At one time I worshipped fame and sought it when it was seen from afar, but now that it has come near, almost within my grasp, I realize that it is an empty thing and that those who court it are emptier still. If I could do something to improve the character of men, I would consider that a solid achievement, one that was likely to last. I have said this so that you won't keep holding out before me the prospect of fame as some sort of encouragement. You should know that I have no interest in this and am not more influenced by it than by a mere puff of wind. You will have more effect on me by pointing to things that have public value. I imagine that you take more delight in such things than in reputation and widespread fame, a fame that has come to you deservedly. If those two things are separated, merit and success, I should much prefer the first to the second.

The archbishops' gift is small when one considers his affection for you and his profound admiration.[11] He will send more some day, but I know that you place less value on the gift itself than on its origins, that is, the strong feelings of good will that it manifests.

I believe you have heard that the emperor set sail from Barcelona with a well-equipped fleet consisting of forty galleys, seventy cargo ships, and ten light vessels carrying, besides members of the court and the flower of the young Spanish nobility, up to ten thousand naval ratings, an elite force selected from the whole of Spain. They write from Marseille that the fleet was sighted on the fifth of August skirting the French coast. Some add that on the seventh of that month it had reached Genoa and disembarked there, but this is not certain.[12] May the Lord Jesus keep the emperor safe and bestow on him the means and the desire to restore Christendom to a healthier state!

Bruges, 30 August 1529

* * * * *

11 In 1528 Archbishop Fonseca (n5 above) had sent Erasmus 200 ducats in support of his work on the edition of Augustine. The gift reached Erasmus in March 1529. See Epp 2004:38–41, 2133:63–7.
12 The fleet set sail from Barcelona on 27 July. It reached Savona on 7 August and Genoa on the twelfth. See Allen's note.

2209 / To Karel Uutenhove   Freiburg, 1 September 1529

On Karel Uutenhove of Ghent, see Ep 2001 n7. After a brief period as a member of Erasmus' household (summer 1528–February 1529) he was now in Italy completing his studies.

This letter was printed at the end of the volume containing the revised editions of *De recta pronuntiatione* and the *Ciceronianus* (Basel: Froben, March 1530); cf Epp 1948–9. Here again, as in Ep 2188, Erasmus selects Uutenhove as the recipient of a long, discursive letter.

DESIDERIUS ERASMUS OF ROTTERDAM TO THE DISTINGUISHED
YOUNG KAREL UUTENHOVE, GREETING

Your letter reached me rather late,[1] my dear Uutenhove, but gave me much pleasure on several counts: first because your journey, which several people predicted would turn out badly, brought you safely to Italy, the destination 5 of your dreams, and you suffered no harm to person or property; then you found there the University of Padua with its illustrious professors and its distinction in every branch of learning; finally you had the good fortune not just to know and see and talk to two of the brightest lights of this age, Battista Egnazio and Pietro Bembo,[2] but to be admitted to their intimate 10 circle and received into the inner sanctum of their friendship. A most elegant and generous letter from Bembo revealed what a high opinion he has of your abilities. The expressions used in that letter sound like criticism of the testimonial I wrote for you as being too tentative and reserved.[3] For all this I acknowledge the deep debt I owe to this unique person, but it is 15 no small debt I owe to you too, for I did not take much trouble over my recommendation, but you, by your kindness and good sense, commended your commender much more effectively to one to whom he was just as eager as you to be commended. It is dangerous to commend some people, a duty to commend others, while there are some whom it is highly profitable to 20 commend. So I congratulate myself as well as you because through you I have been fortunate to gain something that I always deeply wanted. You have no reason, therefore, to thank me. If I did you any service, you have repaid it with interest. You yourself have become even dearer to me now

* * * * *

2209
1 The letter is not extant. There is a reference to it in Ep 2249:1.
2 Erasmus had given Uutenhove letters of introduction to both men: Ep 2105–6.
3 Ep 2144:48–55

that you have won the respect of men like that, whose judgment I regard as 25
much more perceptive than my own. I am confident you will never repent
of going to Italy, which will send you back to us with the fine finish of a
liberal education.

You write that your part of the world is a peaceful place for study – I
hope it may always be so. But I fear that the end of the French war may be 30
the first step on the way to another.[4] When you invite me to join you there,
I don't know whether you are serious or joking. Certainly, now that I am
weighed down with the burden of years, there is no place I would rather be
than where you are, particularly since I know from experience that the climate is not injurious to me. But to bring you up to date on my situation, I 35
have left the Rauric lands[5] to become a resident of the Breisgau. Alarmed
by the endless upheavals,[6] I moved to Freiburg, which is a city under the
jurisdiction of Ferdinand, a day's journey from Basel.[7] It has a not undistinguished university, illumined by the presence of the great Zasius,[8] who
is famed as much for his wise eloquence as for his knowledge of the law. 40
Many young scholars are developing under his care who will one day reflect the excellence of their master.[9] King Ferdinand, who was then residing
in Speyer,[10] invited me once more to Vienna, promising a magnificent income.[11] But I did not trust this poor body of mine; indeed it was with great
trepidation that I left the nest to which I had grown accustomed for so many 45
years. It turned out, however, that I was not in any danger, for my health
here has begun to improve.[12]

* * * * *

4 The Peace of Cambrai had brought to a temporary halt the warfare in Italy
   between Charles v and Francis i. The conflict would resume in 1536. See Ep
   2207 n5.
5 The Raurici were the ancient tribe that lived in the area of Basel.
6 Ie the upheavals accompanying the victory of the Reformation in Basel; see Ep
   2097 n1.
7 Freiburg was the capital of the Breisgau, a territory in Anterior Austria under
   the rule of the emperor's brother, Ferdinand. The move took place in April
   1529; see Ep 2149 introduction.
8 Udalricus Zasius (Ep 303), professor of law at Freiburg since 1506
9 Bonifacius Amerbach was one of his students.
10 Presiding over the imperial diet; cf Ep 2107 n1.
11 For the earlier invitation, see Epp 2000, 2005. The letter with the renewed
   invitation does not survive; cf Ep 2090 introduction.
12 For the effects on Erasmus' health of the move from Basel to Freiburg in April
   1529, see Ep 2151:1–2 with n1, and cf Epp 2211:74, 2215:27–31, 2217:37–9,
   2250:11–12, and 2253A:43–5.

Who, I wonder, spread the melodramatic rumour in Italy about my misfortunes and my terrible illness?[13] The same people, I suppose, who are forever killing me off.[14] Why is there such perversity in men who profess a 50 perfect piety? When I lived in Basel, they used to cry that I support the sect they describe as worse than heretical. If I had suffered some painful blow from that sect, they ought to have seen it as a kind of martyrdom. Now they show well enough how they would react when, in the absence of any real misfortune, they invent horrible rumours so that they can have something 55 to cheer about. If God will implant a sound mind in these people, I shall consider it a greater miracle than if he turned a viper into a man. But they gain nothing except an ever worsening reputation throughout the world for intrigue. Here you see the mysterious workings of the eternal deity.

For a month and a half I mulled over in my mind the idea of quitting 60 Basel. During this period I was invited to various places by kings, princes, bishops, and scholars, and offered the most flattering terms.[15] Some sent travel money, others even offered favours, such as the promise of perpetual support. I left on a brilliant day; even those with whose ideas I openly disagreed were sad.[16] If I think of returning, I shall be made welcome, if not 65 by everyone, at least by all the best people. Here in Freiburg I am shown every kindness both by the council and the university. Now Omaar and your friend Ammonius have written most eloquent letters inviting me to your native Flanders and promising a generous welcome.[17] Your relative, Karel Sucket, has left Dôle and gone to Bourges,[18] attracted by the reputation of 70 Andrea Alciati, who teaches jurisprudence there at a high salary and with even higher status.[19] The sweet allure of Alciati's name has drawn several excellent young men there. But if the rumour is true, I am afraid they will not be able to enjoy him for long, for I am told that the plague is rampant

* * * * *

13 Cf Epp 2144:2–5, 2154:1–3, 2174:8–9, 2324:11–13.
14 Cf Ep 1518, where Erasmus complains at length of the 'priests and monks and grandchildren of Dominic and Francis' who forever spread rumours that he has died a gruesome death.
15 See Ep 2159:12–24, and cf Epp 1875:195–201, 2029:98–104.
16 The leader of the Reformation in the city, Johannes Oecolampadius, had urged him not to leave; see Ep 2147 introduction.
17 The letter from Omaar van Edingen inviting Erasmus to settle in Ghent does not survive; but in Ep 2197:83–130, Edingen's friend Levinus Ammonius argues at length that Erasmus should accept the invitation.
18 Ep 2191
19 In the spring of 1529 Alciati (Ep 1250) had taken up a royal appointment at the University of Bourges (Epp 2168:27–31, 2194:14–16), where he would remain until returning to Italy in 1533 to teach at Pavia.

there.[20] Among friends I used to say that Alciati's fortune did not match 75
his excellent qualities. Yet I think that it is not really a misfortune, but the
hand of destiny, causing one man to inspire many with a love of honourable
studies and to lend distinction to many universities.

A premature death has robbed us and the scholarly world of Jacobus
Ceratinus. He had already gained equal competence in both languages. He 80
had won a position that suited him perfectly. Adolph, lord of Veere, had
invited him to be his younger son's tutor at a salary generous enough to
cause some to envy him.[21] But Ceratinus, to use Paul's phrase, held his treasure in an earthen vessel,[22] as is often the case with true-born men of letters.
His delicate constitution could not stand the severity of Zeeland's weather. 85
Dorp too was taken from us recently,[23] just when, after those theatrical diatribes of his,[24] he was set to become a real theologian. Many regret that
so much midnight oil was wasted. Such people seem to me no wiser than
the woman who lamented that her husband died an innocent man; she received the sensible reply that it was better to die innocent than guilty.[25] We 90
could justifiably reply to Dorp's critics that it is better to die learned than
ignorant, better to die a human being than a beast. What more honourable
course could there be than that which he followed? Surely one cannot regard as blessed those who passed their lives in luxury, sleep, and idleness?
No one complains in their case about the hardships and the many sleepless 95
hours they wasted, for they did nothing in life, and by the very fact that
they accomplished nothing, their whole life was a waste. I see little cause to
mourn those who were already dead before they died. Rather it was their
life that we should mourn, a life that was in no way different from death.

I feel very sad that Megaera,[26] who has wrought dreadful havoc on 100
the state of public affairs and on religion, is now sending her snakes into
the world of learning and, contrary to nature, is causing division between

* * * * *

20 Cf Epp 2219:6, 2225:4–5.
21 The source of this false report of the death of Ceratinus (Ep 622:34n) was
doubtless Ep 2197:73–4. Ceratinus seems to have left Veere at just about this
time and gone to Louvain, where he died on 20 April 1530.
22 2 Cor 4:7
23 Maarten van Dorp, Erasmus' best friend among the Louvain theologians, had
died on 31 May 1525, at about forty years of age; see Ep 1584.
24 This appears to be a reference to Dorp's early attempts to defend scholastic
philosophy and theology against the criticisms of humanist scholars (eg Ep
347), before yielding to the arguments of Erasmus and Thomas More.
25 The reference is to Xanthippe, wife of Socrates, who mourned that her husband
died an innocent man; see Diogenes Laertius 2.5.35.
26 Megaera, one of the Furies, was the cause of jealousy and envy.

the Graces and the Muses. I have to regret the lack of candour among some
Frenchmen.[27] They suborn a few second-rate versifiers,[28] while they themselves are of course too mighty to be angry with Erasmus. The same trick   105
was resorted to by those who made trouble for Alciati.[29] I would not object if France entered into competition with Italy and Germany over the first
place in scholarship, provided it was without bitterness: 'Strife of that sort
is good for mortals.'[30]

     After so many upheavals in the world, so many battles, massacres, dis-   110
sensions, after so many plagues, after scarcity and rising prices, a new and
deadly evil has arisen, which for almost forty years was confined to England.[31] When it first began its attack, it was something new and unknown;
medical science could offer no relief. So many people were carried off by
it in England that one can scarcely believe the island contained so many in-   115
habitants. And once it arrived, it never let up. However severe the winter,
although this plague may from time to time die down to a mere flicker, it
constantly flares up, sparing no one. This terrible scourge has not yet got a
name, nor so far as I know has medical science yet found an effective relief.
Up to now it kept to its island home, attacking the natives there more than   120
foreigners. Now it has travelled up the Rhine and moved into Germany,
within a few days leaping incredibly rapidly from Cologne to Strasbourg.
Everyone is naturally worried it may spread farther. There has never been
a more horrible or contagious affliction than this. Whatever home it enters,
it leaves hardly anyone unaffected. It makes no distinction of age or sex,   125
unlike other plagues, which are selective in those they attack; some spare
young children and the old, some do not affect women. It has this, however, to be said for it that it does not torture its victims with prolonged
agony; within twelve hours, sometimes less, it either carries a person off or

* * * * *

27 Cf the opening paragraph of Ep 2223, where it is made clear that Erasmus is
   here referring to Guillaume Budé and the uproar over the *Ciceronianus* (Ep
   2021 introduction).
28 Janus Lascaris and Jacques Toussain; see Epp 2027:25–8, 2077:10–16, 2119,
   2223:6–9.
29 Here again Erasmus puts the blame on Budé; cf Epp 2223:8–9, 2329 n14.
30 Hesiod *Works and Days* 24, cited in Greek
31 Erasmus is referring to the disease known as 'the sweating sickness' or 'the
   English sweat,' which first appeared in England in 1485. Only the fourth of its
   six outbreaks, in 1528–9, appears to have spread widely on the continent, and
   then only in the lands bordering on the North and Baltic seas. See Ep 1593
   n14 and, for the current outbreak, see lines 120–2 below and Epp 2220:8–9,
   2223:13–35, 2225:5–7, 2240:1 and 17, 2249:37–42, 2253A:58–62, 2254:14–22.

offers clear prospect of survival. They also claim that it is an easy death – 130
like that which is said to follow the bite of an asp. But it has this unpleasant
characteristic, that it returns to its prey again and again. John Colet was afflicted three times within a single period and survived all three, but when
his body had been weakened by the plague, an attack of dropsy followed,
and this carried him off to heaven, a man who deserved a better life.[32]   135

    As generally happens in such cases, the remedies that were tried first
actually proved fatal. The disease causes sweating, but a fiery sweating that
produces a most obnoxious stench – you would think it came up from the
river Phlegethon.[33] It makes the nails particularly painful; it constricts the
arms so that you cannot raise them even if you wanted to, which is just as   140
well, for to uncover the arms is fatal. So, as a rule, those who could not stand
the heat and let in too much cool air perished immediately. On the other
hand, those who had noticed the disastrous effect that this produced on several patients went to the opposite extreme and suffered the same fate. For by
closing up all the cracks and stoking up a big fire and covering themselves   145
with blankets in the hope of producing a bigger and healthier sweat, they
suffocated from the heat. Admitting the cold, however, brings on a swifter
death. In the end a happy medium was found and many more survived the
illness than died. The principal method of treatment is to put the sick person to bed, then gradually to pull the sheet, soaked with smelly sweat, from   150
beneath the patient without disturbing the blankets and covers or letting the
breeze touch the body, then in the same careful manner to insert fresh clean
linen that has been thoroughly dried before the fire. This has to be done
several times. Some people boast of having discovered an effective cure for
the disease. But what it is, I have not yet been able to discover – certainly   155
this swift-acting plague does not respond to the remedies commonly prescribed by the doctors. The English place their hopes of a full recovery in
the treatment I have just described.

    I learned these facts from the reports of those who suffered from the
disease more than once. I myself was never present during the illness – I say   160
this to the praise of our Saviour Christ, and I hope Nemesis is not listening.[34]
As far as I know, no one has yet clearly explained the source and cause

* * * * *

32 See Epp 106 introduction, 1211:411–15.
33 Phlegethon, which means 'flaming' in Greek, was a sulphurous river of the
    Underworld.
34 There was an ancient belief that those who are excessively fortunate become
    hubristic: the Greek goddess Nemesis had the function of restoring equilib-
    rium by punishing such arrogance. Cf *Adagia* ii vi 38.

of this disease. It is highly probable that it arises from a concentration of
poisonous humours. It is thought that this explains why those who indulge
in excessive drinking are in greater danger. Relying on this fact, Andrea 165
Ammonio, an Italian with more sobriety than one expects from an Italian,[35]
had no fear of the infection. But his confidence betrayed him. He deserved
a long, long life, but caught the disease and perished.[36]

It is my opinion that England would be less subject to this plague if
they covered the floors of their houses with wood rather than rushes and 170
had more windows that could be opened when the weather is conducive
to good health and closed when it is overcast and stormy.[37] At present a
good part of their walls consists of glass but with scarcely a tiny window
large enough to put one's head through to see the view. As a result there
is hardly any ventilation to scatter the mould produced by the decaying 175
rushes. The plague is more virulent in marshy places and close to river
banks, so it is evident that damp air is the material on which the epidemic
feeds. Pliny tells us that a not dissimilar disease used to be produced by
poisoned honey, which is found particularly in Heraclea in the Pontus. He
mentions a white herb, which gets its name *aegoletros* 'goat's bane' from the 180
effect it produces.[38] Bees take in a deadly poison from its flower. This does
not happen at any season, but only during spring when rot sets in as a result
of excessive moisture. At other times it is eaten without a problem. Those
who have tasted it fling themselves on the ground in an attempt to cool
themselves, since they are not only overheated but are made miserable by 185
sweating. In the same Pontic region there is another type of honey, which
produces madness and hence is called *maenomenon*.[39] The poison is gathered
from the flower of the rhododendron. Pliny reveals many remedies for this
problem.

Now for many years the world has been seized by another kind of 190
plague, as yet without a name,[40] whose treatment is neglected to everyone's

* * * * *

35 Cf Ep 2157:106–7, where Erasmus refers to traditional Italian sobriety.
36 See Ep 623:12–19.
37 For more on Erasmus' view of the disease-inducing defects of houses in England, see Epp 1489:5–16, 1532.
38 *Naturalis historia* 21.74–7
39 Greek in the text; the word means 'raving.'
40 The reference is to syphilis, which did not acquire that name until the publication in 1530 of the didactic poem in three books *Syphilis sive morbus gallicus*
(Syphilis, or The French Disease) by the Italian physician and poet Girolamo
Fracastoro. The poem relates the tale of a shepherd boy named Syphilis who,
because he insulted Apollo, was punished with the horrible disease. It was

loss. By constantly sending us so many new plagues, God is calling us to amend our lives, yet we do not change one whit for the better. The Egyptians were visited long ago by fewer disasters. According to the Greek proverb, it takes blows to mend a Phrygian.[41] We are harder than any Phrygian, and in   195
spite of all our many afflictions, so long and severe and without precedent, our hearts do not melt in repentance, but as though we are now inured to pain by the remedies that have been applied to us,[42] we grow even more stubborn in our opposition to God, who is our healer. If anyone should ask me for a remedy, I would have nothing better to suggest than that each man   200
choose to live his life as if each day were his last. If no disaster happens, it will be a blessing to have been afraid. If something does happen, it will not find the victim unprepared. If your fear is unjustified, then there will be this on the plus side, that you are still completely well; if not, you have wisely taken care that our better part is free from danger. Farewell.   205

Freiburg, 1 September 1529

2210 / From Viglius Zuichemus   Bourges, 1 September 1529

On Viglius Zuichemus (Wigle van Aytta van Zwichem, 1507–77), who would become a distinguished legal scholar and (from 1540) a high official in the Hapsburg government of the Netherlands, see Ep 2101 introduction. At this time he was studying law with Andrea Alciati (Ep 1250) in Bourges.

This letter was first published as Ep 7 in *Viglii ab Aytta Zuichemi Epistolae selectae = Analecta Belgica* 2/1. The surviving manuscript is a late sixteenth-century copy of unknown provenance in the University Library at Ghent (MS 479 page 77).

TO ERASMUS OF ROTTERDAM
I knew, most learned Erasmus, that you would not read without a shudder the letter I wrote recently from Lyon about my travels,[1] but I was carried away by the extraordinary respect I have for you, which drove me to this

* * * * *

more commonly known as the French (or Spanish, or whatever) pox. Cf Epp 1593:93–7, 2285:24–8.
41 *Adagia* I viii 36; cf Epp 2249:42–3, 2285:16–18.
42 'Remedies' in this rather obscure sentence refers to the plagues sent by God to cure human perversity.

2210
1 Ep 2168

serious lapse. For after I pledged to you my complete devotion and you in   5
turn generously received me into your favour, I thought it my duty to keep
you informed about any new plans I made.

My life here at Bourges is very much as I would wish. I greatly enjoy
and benefit from the learning and good will of Andrea Alciati. I have nothing to report about him, except to say how delighted I am by the daily com-   10
pliments he pays to the excellence of your incomparable genius. He mentions no one more frequently or more respectfully than 'our Erasmus.' With
these words he associates himself with you and, so to speak, enlists as a
soldier under your command.

You are familiar with the old grumbles of the French nation here. They   15
try everything short of issuing an interdict to keep Guillaume Budé's *Annotations on the Pandects* from Alciati,[2] as though Budé had a prescriptive
right to the whole field, leaving no room for our friend to win acclaim. It
appears, however, that there is now a truce, although some people are still
stirring up the French professors to rob the Italian of his glory. Recently,   20
one of their countrymen, Petrus Stella of Orléans,[3] has been issuing grave
threats and giving notice of legal action, but Alciati crushed him so effectively that the Frenchman does not dare to jump a second time even onto
his own dunghill.[4] It is surprising that so few people here are ready to let
in the light of liberal studies. There are even some who have the effron-   25
tery to make Alciati's purer diction into a fault, although – and this is like a
miracle to me – in his public lectures he can speak the language of Bartolo
so well that you would think he had been trained in the same school.[5] In

* * * * *

2 Budé's *Annotationes in xxiv Pandectarum libros* (Paris: Bade 1508) was the first of
the works of scholarship that established his reputation as the greatest French
humanist of his day. Cf Ep 403 introduction.

3 Petrus Stella (Pierre Taisant de l'Estoille, 1480–1537) was the leading member
of the faculty of law at Orléans and a disciple of Budé. When in 1518 the German jurist Udalricus Zasius (Ep 2209 n8) criticized Budé's interpretation of
a pair of passages in the Digest, Stella published a polemical retort, thus in-
augurating a controversy in which several others, including Alciati, became
involved. When in 1528 Stella enlarged his attack on Zasius to include Alciati,
the latter replied in a book that Bonifacius Amerbach arranged to be published by Froben at Basel in 1529. The dispute, which continued until 1532,
contributed to the antagonism between French legal scholars and those from
other nations. For more details, see Allen's note and CEBR III 284.

4 *Adagia* IV iv 23

5 Bartolo da Sassoferrato (1313–56), the greatest of the medieval commentators
on Roman law. His works were still vital to the teaching of law, although
Renaissance scholars like Lorenzo Valla found fault with his Latin style.

private, however, his language is so pure that he seems to have wet his lips
in the nag's spring.[6] He is a great admirer of your divine writings; there   30
could have been no more discriminating reader of your *Chiliads*.[7]

How much he values your judgment I lately discovered from a 'response' of his, if I may speak in lawyers' slang. A schoolmaster at Dôle, not
accepting your opinion,[8] wanted to alter the reading *pontificium* in Aulus
Gellius[9] – he had argued that the correct reading was *officium*. So to avoid   35
the penalty for being proved wrong, he recently consulted Alciati also on
the same problem. Alciati gave a neat reply, couched in legal language: 'I
must not dissent from an opinion that was accepted by Erasmus. He is my
Lydian stone.'[10] With these words he confounded the pedantic schoolmaster, confirming the accepted reading by citing a constitution of Constan-   40
tine on maternal property in the Theodosian Code, where we read *fruendi
pontificium*.[11]

I have gone on too long, but I want to tell you these things to give
you an account of my studies. They seem to go much better under a teacher
who, like me, recognizes you as the true prince in every branch of learning   45
and respects and loves and reveres you. I recently learned from Sucket how
constant is your affection for me.[12] Although nothing more welcome could
have happened to me, I am, nevertheless, deeply worried as to how I am to
live up to such a generous gesture by so great a man. You decided recently
to give public witness to your affection for me and to immortalize me by the   50
lasting honour of a letter from yourself.[13] I cannot help being exceedingly

* * * * *

6 The 'nag's spring' is Hippocrene, the fountain of the Muses, whose waters, according to legend, were struck from the earth by the hoof of the winged horse
Pegasus. Viglius is quoting the first line of the prologue to Persius' *Satires*.
7 Ie the *Adagia*, which, starting with the second edition of 1508 (*Adagiorum chiliades*), were arranged in 'chiliads' (thousands) and 'centuries' (hundreds). Erasmus himself often referred to the *Adages* as his *Chiliads*; see eg Ep 2305:39–47.
8 We have not been able to determine where Erasmus expressed this opinion.
9 Gellius 1.13.1; Gellius discusses the question whether one should fulfil a given
commission to the letter or change one's orders if it becomes clear that a different course would be to the benefit of one's employer. The reading *pontificium* 'authority' was challenged because an ecclesiastical term seemed out of
place in the context. But the word can carry the ordinary sense of 'authority'
and the text can stand.
10 Ie standard of accuracy and good judgment; see *Adagia* I v 87.
11 *Codex Theodosianus* 8.18.1.1: *ut fruendi pontificium habeant* 'that they may have
the authority to enjoy'
12 On Sucket, see Ep 2191.
13 Ep 2111

pleased at this; still I blush to owe you so much, which I cannot hope to repay however long I live. I am very much afraid that my eyes are still dazzled by the bright rays of your sun, and that when scholars, who are the most avid readers of your letters, recognize me, they will toss me from the 55 nest as a false and parasitic nestling (whose eyes would not bear the light of immortality) and will not permit me to stand in your list of honoured names. Perhaps they will say, 'Recently he was an inarticulate child: has he just now suddenly wakened from a dream of bursting on the scene as a poet?[14] Does he dare to insert this letter of his like a rough pebble among 60 Erasmian pearls? 'What a cancerous growth the desire to write is!'[15] But there is no need to rehearse the whole range of their reproaches – how, beguiled by the rashness of youth, I dared to intrude upon the greatest man of our age with a letter of mine, and a silly letter too, written by an ignoramus. 65

So, Erasmus my learned friend, unless you defend your poor protégé now, he will certainly be hissed off the stage on which you have launched him. You got me into this, so please don't let me take the blame. As for the fact that I deliberately worked my way into your friendship, others may blame me for this, but I shall never regret it. However, I should not like 70 any responsibility to be attached to me for the publication of my letter in your collection.[16] Of course, I should be less afraid of its falling into the hands of critics like Laelius, since it was approved by you, my Persius;[17] yet just as you excel others in learning, so you surpass them in kindness and

* * * * *

14 In this passage Viglius conflates two lines from Persius: one from *Epilogue* 6.3, and the other from *Satires* 6.10–11.
15 Juvenal 7.52
16 Ep 2101
17 Not Persius (AD 34–62) the Stoic satirist (cf nn6 and 14 above), but Persius the learned orator of the second century BC, who was famed for his great intelligence. His contemporary, the satirist Lucilius, wrote that he did not want to be read by Persius, whose learning he feared because it was greater than his own. Although Lucilius' works are lost, the remark about Persius is recorded more than once by Cicero (*De oratore* 2.25, *De finibus* 1.3.7, *Brutus* 26.99) as well as by Pliny the Elder (*Naturalis historia* pref 7). 'Laelius' is presumably Gaius Laelius Sapiens, a distinguished political and military figure of the second century BC and a brilliant orator, whom Horace praised for his 'gentle wisdom' (*Satires* 1.72) and Cicero made the main speaker in *De amicitia*. It is strange that he should be made the symbol of people of inferior intelligence. One wonders if perhaps Viglius had someone else in mind and pulled the wrong name from his memory. In any case, his point is clear, namely, that if he has the approval of so brilliant a critic as Erasmus, he need not fear the attacks of lesser men.

generosity. Since this was how you wished to show your feelings towards   75
me, I promise I shall always remember your kindness – I would not want
you to think it was wasted on a reluctant subject. And since by this gesture
you thought perhaps you could spur me on to aim for greater things in my
studies, I shall concentrate on my work so that, by making good progress in
it, the service you have done me may every day become more and more evi-   80
dent. Farewell, Erasmus, the matchless glory of our age and the outstanding
patron of all true lovers of learning.

Bourges, 1 September 1529

2211 / To Thomas More   Freiburg, 5 September 1529

> This letter was first published in the *Epistolae floridae*. The surviving manu-
> script is an autograph rough draft in the Royal Library at Copenhagen (MS
> GKS 95 Fol, folio 229). For More, see Ep 999.

TO THOMAS MORE

Cordial greetings. Dear Thomas More, best of friends, the longer and more
agonizing the wait for peace between the most powerful monarchs in the
world, the greater our present joy that this deadly conflict has ended.[1] Indeed even now we hardly dare to trust our good fortune, but the story per-   5
sists – we read about it in letters from many people, and we hear it from
many reliable sources. But it still seems like a voice in a dream, the sort of
thing that happens when, after a very painful attack, everything suddenly
changes dramatically for the better, or like a scene in a tragedy when some
god unexpectedly appears from the machine. Nor have people failed to no-   10
tice that we owe much of this relief to the invincible King Henry the Eighth
of England. He showed great wisdom and persistence and did not rest until he had turned what looked like an incurable dissension into the peace
we had long hoped for.[2] It remains for us to appeal to the gods in all our
prayers that they may be pleased to make the gift of peace permanent, or   15
if nothing in this mortal life is permanent, at least to make it continue for
a long time. If it is at all possible, I shall most gladly make known to fu-

* * * * *

2211
1 With the Peace of Cambrai, 5 August 1529; see Ep 2207 n5. More had been a
  member of the English delegation present at the signing of the peace (LP 4 no
  5744).
2 This undeserved praise for King Henry (cf Ep 2207 n5) is repeated in Ep
  2215:18–22.

ture generations in some work of mine the truly pious and Christian mind of this outstanding peacemaker.[3]

I would think myself very happy, my dear More, if King Ferdinand enjoyed the success that his exceptional piety deserves. He seems to me a man endowed by nature with every virtue. He so warmly supports Erasmus that I could not wish for a better friend.[4] Two years ago he invited me to Vienna at a salary of four hundred florins on the sole condition that I reside there.[5] Recently I had sent a brief note to the bishop of Trent, the king's chancellor, commending a certain tippler for a place in the cavalry escort.[6] The king immediately gave him a place, saying 'What would I not do for my master Erasmus?'[7] I have never done anything to deserve this. I wonder what he would do if I had really done him some service, since, as it is, he misses no opportunity to show me his favour? But Fortune has not yet matched the excellent qualities of this very fine prince.

Lately, as you know, there was a meeting of the princes at Speyer.[8] Help was sought against the Turks, who are threatening Hungary.[9] The sum

* * * * *

3 Erasmus never fulfilled this pledge. As Allen points out, Henry's determined pursuit of a divorce from Queen Catherine (Ep 1932 n11) may have moved Erasmus to conclude that silence was the prudent course for someone so dependent on the favour of Charles v, who was the nephew of Queen Catherine (cf n14 below).

4 Ever since Ferdinand's generous reaction (Ep 1343) to Erasmus' dedication to him of the Paraphrase on John (Ep 1333), Erasmus had felt himself to be in secure possession of the prince's favour.

5 The offer had actually been made a little over a year earlier; see Epp 2005–6.

6 Felix Rex's own report to Erasmus (Ep 2130:58) indicates that Ferdinand had made him an archer.

7 On Erasmus' commendation and the king's response, see Ep 2130:59–65.

8 The imperial diet at Speyer, 15 March–22 April 1529, at which Ferdinand presided as regent for the emperor

9 Although the diet is remembered largely because of the famous 'protestation' of the evangelical estates against the hostile recess of the Catholic majority (see Ep 2107 n1), the main business on Ferdinand's mind had been the securing of the support of the imperial estates against the Turks, who were allied with John Zápolyai, his rival for the control of Hungary (cf Ep 2100 introduction). In September 1527 Ferdinand had defeated John decisively at Tokaj and was for a time king of all Hungary. But then Sultan Suleiman I accepted John as his vassal, recognized him as king of Hungary, and launched an invasion of Hungary in May 1529, capturing Buda in early September. On 20 September he laid siege to Vienna, but on 15–16 October had to raise the siege and withdraw. Ferdinand was left in control of 'Royal Hungary,' which constituted approximately thirty per cent of what had been the late-medieval kingdom of

of money offered was so small that he preferred to thank them for their
intentions rather than be indebted for their gift. Everyone knows what hap-   35
pened to Mary, the emperor's sister, and to her husband Louis.[10] Now the
Turk has invaded Hungary again and ravaged a large part of it. Mary, to
whom I dedicated my *Widow*,[11] left out of fear for a city in Moravia commonly called Znojmo, not feeling sufficiently secure even in Vienna. The
Turk fears the ever-growing power of the emperor and would rather have   40
had John as his neighbouring king than Ferdinand.[12] Perhaps someone will
say in this case too that it would have been preferable to accept a half instead of the whole.[13] But I think the divine will is aiming in another direction. I have no doubt that the eternal deity in his goodness will bring everything to a happy conclusion if we turn our hearts to the things that please   45
him.

If you ask what these things are, it is not so much that I do not know
as that I do not want to say. Would that the emperor had patched up his
quarrel earlier with the king of France and come in time to assist his brother
and sister! I fear that Italy and the embrace of the pope will delay him too   50
long, though given the religious character of the man, I have no doubt he
will show the pope all the respect that a son owes a father.[14] I wish the pope

* * * * *

Hungary. After a few more years of conflict, Ferdinand had to sign a truce
(1533) with the sultan in which he renounced any claim to rule beyond the
borders of Royal Hungary.
10 In August 1526, the Hungarian army was annihilated by the Turks at Mohács,
   and King Louis II of Bohemia and Hungary lost his life in the battle. His
   widow, Mary of Austria (usually referred to as Mary of Hungary), was the
   sister of Emperor Charles V and Archduke Ferdinand of Austria. She helped
   Ferdinand establish his claim to the Hungarian crown, which was, however,
   contested by John Zápolyai (see preceding note).
11 Ep 2100
12 On the 'ever-growing power,' cf Epp 2225:9–10, 2230:26–7, 2249:33–4, 2328:100–
   101.
13 The meaning is presumably that it might have been better for Ferdinand and
   his rival to divide the spoils rather than fight over them.
14 Early in the latest phase of the warfare between Charles V and Francis I in Italy,
   1526–9, relations between Charles and Pope Clement VII had been severely
   strained by the latter's having frequently changed sides from Charles to Francis and back again. Following the sack of Rome in May 1527, the pope was
   for a time the emperor's virtual prisoner in Rome. He fled Rome in December 1527, and not until October 1528 were relations between him and the emperor such that he could return. Cf Ep 1935 n11. Given the overwhelming victory of imperialist forces over the French in the summer of 1529, the pope
   had no choice but to become the emperor's ally once again, and he did so by

would ascribe to Christ all the glory that men shower on him because of
Christ! I have no doubt, however, that this present Clement will do this.
That the pope should become involved in treaties made by a prince seems   55
to me expedient neither to the pope nor to Christendom.[15] He is too great
to be bound by any treaty – that at least is my opinion.

If I had remained in Basel, the theologians would have blazoned it
abroad that I was in sympathy with the things that are going on there.[16]
Now they brag that I left because I was afraid. In fact my departure caused   60
general disappointment, even among those whose teaching I frankly and
openly detested.[17] Certainly I was reluctant to leave the nest where I had
settled for so many years, and my health was such that I felt it would not
stand any move at all. Nor was I unaware of the costs I would incur by
moving. But I preferred to risk my life rather than appear to approve a   65
programme like theirs. There was some hope of a return to moderation. But
two monks, one a preacher in the cathedral, the other a preacher in his own
order, the Dominicans, stirred up a great agitation against me.[18] It is true
they have decamped, but others are affected by the same disease. George,
duke of Saxony, is engaged in the same kind of vexatious controversy with   70
Luther as mine with Eppendorf.[19] I told him to let the fellow alone and not
inflame a man who was fierce enough as it was. Now Luther is enjoying his
triumph, since he is stirring up trouble for so great a prince.

* * * * *

agreeing to the Treaty of Barcelona on 29 June. In return for the restoration of
the rule of his Medici kinsmen in Florence (whence they had been expelled
in May 1527) and the return to the papal states of a number of territories lost
in the wars, Clement agreed to crown Charles emperor and to grant absolution to all those responsible for the sack of Rome. As a direct consequence
of this treaty, Clement, on 16 July, decided to dismiss Henry VIII's suit to be
granted a divorce from the emperor's niece, Queen Catherine of Aragon, thus
precipitating the series of events that led ultimately to England's break with
Rome.

15 An apparent reference to the Treaty of Barcelona (see preceding note)
16 Ie the victory of the Reformation and the banning of Catholic worship; see Ep
2097 n1.
17 Johannes Oecolampadius, the leader of the Reformation at Basel, had visited
Erasmus and urged him not to leave the city; see Ep 2147.
18 On seeing this letter in print in 1532, Ambrosius Pelargus (Ep 2169) concluded with good reason that the reference was to him and Augustinus Marius (Ep 2321) and complained bitterly to Erasmus about it (Ep 2721). Erasmus
protested his innocence (Ep 2722), but relations between the two remained
cool for some time.
19 For Erasmus' controversy with Heinrich Eppendorf, see Ep 1934 introduction.
For the most recent of the several controversies between Duke George and
Martin Luther, see Ep 2338:11–43.

Pope Clement VII
Sebastiano del Piombo
Museo e Gallerie Nazionali di Capodimonte, Naples

So far the move has benefited my health, something I did not expect.[20]
The summer here has been particularly agreeable, but I fear the autumn.   75
Half the town is surrounded by mountains that overlook it, so hardly a
day passes without cloud and mist. The council assigned me a truly regal
mansion,[21] built originally for the emperor Maximilian but left unfinished
and more suited to summer than winter. I only wish that, while I am still
alive, I could see the friends who are so dear to me! I have seen them in a   80
manner of speaking in a picture that Holbein showed me,[22] which gave me
very great pleasure. My best wishes to you and all who are most dear to you.

Freiburg im Breisgau, 5 September 1529

2212 / To Margaret Roper   Freiburg, 6 September 1529

This letter was first published in the *Epistolae floridae*.

Margaret Roper (*née* More) was the eldest and brightest of the children of
Thomas More and a formidably learned woman. Erasmus admired her greatly
but, apart from Ep 1404 (the dedication to her of the commentary on Pruden-
tius' hymns for Christmas and Epiphany), only this letter and Ep 2233 survive
from their correspondence.

ERASMUS OF ROTTERDAM TO MARGARET ROPER, GREETING
I could scarcely find the words, dear Margaret Roper, glory of your beloved
Britain, to express the delight I felt in my heart when the painter Holbein brought your whole family before my eyes so felicitously that I would
hardly have enjoyed a better view if I had been among you.[1] Often a great   5
longing comes over me that once more before my final hour I may have the
good fortune to look upon that little society that is so dear to me. To it I
owe a good part of such success and renown as I have had, nor are there
any other persons to whom I would so happily acknowledge my debt. The
painter's skilful hand has answered a considerable part of my prayer. I rec-   10
ognized everyone, no one more clearly than you. I imagined I was looking
beyond the lovely exterior into the brilliant and even lovelier mind within.

* * * * *

20 See Ep 2209 n12.
21 See Ep 2112 n4.
22 Cf Ep 2212:2–5. Erasmus may be referring to the Holbein drawing of the
family of Thomas More that is now in the Kunstmuseum Basel.

2212
1 See Ep 2211:80–81 with n22.

Study for a portrait of the More family by Hans Holbein the Younger, 1526
Kunstmuseum Basel, Kupferstichkabinett

I congratulate you all on your good fortune, but especially your excellent father.

So that you may have no reason to regret your devotion to learning, 15 I am sending you a letter from a most worthy man who holds the office of preacher to Mary, the emperor's sister and former queen of Hungary.[2] It was she to whom I dedicated the *Christian Widow*,[3] which I believe you have read. From this letter you will understand with what enthusiasm this noble lady embraces the liberal arts. She is now discovering the truth of those 20 words of Marcus Tullius, that reading is an enhancement of prosperity and a consolation in adversity,[4] although she, more than most people, deserved an unbroken prosperity. But since the fortunes of men ebb and flow alternately like the tides of the Euripus,[5] one should fortify one's mind against every turn in fortune with the bulwark of philosophy.   25

I write this when absolutely swamped with business and in poor health to boot. So be kind enough to convince all your sisters that this is an ordinary letter and that it is addressed to them individually as well as to you.[6] Please give my greetings to your mother, the estimable Dame Alice,[7] and commend me to her warmly and sincerely. I give her portrait a hearty kiss 30 since I cannot embrace her in person. I pray your brother John More may have every success.[8] But also give my greetings to your worthy husband Roper,[9] who is very dear to you as he deserves to be. May the Lord keep you all safe and well and be pleased to prosper everything you do with his omnipotent favour.   35

Freiburg im Breisgau, 6 September 1529

2213 / To Pierre Du Chastel   Freiburg, 7 September 1529

The only known manuscript of this letter is a sixteenth-century copy in the Bürgerbibliothek Bern: Cod 450.48 (no 64) folio 133 recto. It was first published

* * * * *

2 Mary of Hungary's preacher was Johann Henckel (Ep 1672). The letter in question may have been the one answered by Ep 2110.
3 Ep 2100
4 Cicero *Pro Archia* 16
5 The tides of the strait of Euripus were proverbial for their prodigiously rapid ebb and flow; see *Adagia* I ix 62: *Euripus homo* 'Man's a Euripus.'
6 More had three daughters, Margaret, Elizabeth, and Cecily (Ep 999 n28).
7 Alice Middleton (Ep 999 n29), a widow whom More married in 1511, was his second wife and the stepmother of his children.
8 John was More's youngest child and only son (Ep 999 n28). Ep 1402 is the dedication to him of Erasmus' commentary on Ovid's *Nux*.
9 William Roper (Ep 1404 n3)

by Johann Rudolph Sinner in his *Catalogus codicum mss. bibliotecae Bernensis annotationibus criticis illustratus* III (Bern: Brunner & Haller 1772) 247–8.

Pierre Du Chastel (Ep 1894 n3) lived with Erasmus for several months in 1527 while working at the Froben press. When he left Basel, Erasmus gave him a letter of introduction to Michel Boudet, bishop of Langres (Ep 1894). Du Chastel was now at Bourges, studying law under Andrea Alciati (Epp 2168 n2, 2218–20, 2224, 2356). At Bourges he met Louis de Husson, bishop-designate of Poitiers, who in the autumn of 1530 took him into his service (Ep 2388). In 1531 the bishop took Du Chastel with him to Paris where at the royal court he became secretary to François de Dinteville, bishop of Auxerre and French ambassador to Rome. Before following his master to Rome, Du Chastel matriculated at the University of Freiburg (8 June 1532) and for a few months was once again in personal contact with Erasmus (Epp 2719–20). After some months in Italy, he reportedly visited the Holy Land, returning via Constantinople. By November 1534 he was in Metz, not yet sure where his future lay (Ep 2974). By the beginning of 1537 he had returned to the French court, where he embarked upon a distinguished administrative and ecclesiastical career in the service of Francis I and Henry II. In 1540 he succeeded Guillaume Budé as the royal librarian and became an important patron of humanist scholars. In 1544 he was made bishop of Mâcon, in 1548 Grand Almoner, and in 1551 bishop of Orléans. He died in 1552 shortly after leaving the court and settling in his new diocese.

Sent to Bourges

TO THE MOST LEARNED MASTER PIERRE DU CHASTEL
FROM ERASMUS OF ROTTERDAM, CORDIAL GREETINGS
When you pile on the rhetoric over my changed attitude to you, Du Chastel, my learned friend, I recognize your devotion to me and I sincerely admire 5
your learning and your enthusiasm. Where would I have got the idea that I should distance myself further from you? You should know, however, that none of the letters you mention reached me. I think Anton[1] did not visit your brother,[2] although he had already gone broke in Paris and had left rich only in bad and in good, as the saying goes.[3] When I entrusted Anton with 10

* * * * *

2213
1 The courier Anton Bletz (Ep 1784 n1)
2 Pierre's brother Emeric, about whom virtually nothing is known
3 The phrase 'in bad and in good' (*bonis malis*) comes from Pliny *Naturalis historia* 18.39. Erasmus cites it at the end of the adage *Necessarium malum* 'A necessary evil' (*Adagia* I v 26), ie something or somebody that is bad but nonetheless necessary to the general good. Pliny says that profitable farming consists of turning something poor (cheap land) into something good by hard work. The suggestion here appears to be that in Emeric's case, going

my most recent letters before his departure for Paris,[4] I gave him a gold crown. He smiled but did not let on that he was not returning there. I also gave him four additional crowns to take to someone. He, however, attended faithfully to all these things by delegating them to others.

I do not know what influence I have with the queen of Navarre.[5] I have never had any dealings with her except that once or twice at the instigation of others I addressed her by letter.[6] She replied with nothing more than a formal greeting. I wish I could be helpful to you, my dear Pierre. There is no one I would more willingly oblige, and your character and good qualities deserve such support. I am glad to be indebted to the bishop of Bourges[7] – and there are several others of his temper. But Béda and his crew are raving mad.[8] If your letter, which was delivered by Hieronymus Froben, had arrived four days earlier, there was a reliable messenger here by whom I sent a letter to Karel Sucket,[9] who wanted me to commend him to Alciati.[10] You too would have received a letter from me by the same courier. As it is, I do not know when this will reach you.[11] I have no recollection of having

* * * * *

broke had somehow or other proved to be a 'necessary evil' that led to good fortune.

4 None of these survive. Allen speculates that they may have been concerned with the uproar in Paris over the *Ciceronianus* (Ep 1948), which was still troubling Erasmus.

5 Margaret of Angoulême, sister of Francis I

6 Epp 1615, 1854

7 François de Tournon (Ep 1319)

8 Noël Béda (Epp 1571, 1943 n5, 2082 n56), syndic of the faculty of theology at Paris, was still Erasmus' most implacable critic in France. From 1519 he waged a relentless campaign to prove that Erasmus and other humanist scholars were secret supporters of Luther. The long and increasingly bitter correspondence between Béda and Erasmus ended in 1527, but their controversy continued all through 1528 and into 1529. For the moment, things were quiet, but there would be a final exchange of denunciations in 1531–2; see CWE 14 xvi, CWE 15 xviii. Erasmus seldom referred to Béda and his allies without calling them 'raving mad.'

9 The letter is not extant. It must have been fairly recent: on 1 September Erasmus knew that Sucket, having already declared his intention to leave Dôle (Ep 2191:54), had settled in Bourges to study with Alciati (Ep 2209:69–72).

10 Erasmus had written to Alciati on 2 September, but the letter, which is not extant, did not reach Alciati until January 1530 (AK Epp 1400:68–72, 1409:38–9). Alciati answered on 1 March 1530 with Ep 2276.

11 Erasmus sent the letter to Bonifacius Amerbach in Basel for forwarding to Bourges; see Epp 2218:2–3, 2219:1–2. Bonifacius took the precaution of sending another copy of the letter to Frankfurt in the expectation that someone would be found at the fall book fair to deliver it to Bourges; Ep 2220:4–6.

discouraged you from writing; for what could you not achieve in whatever sphere you chose to use your splendid talents? Farewell.

Freiburg im Breisgau, on the eve of the Nativity of the Virgin 1529

You will recognize Erasmus from his bad handwriting.   30

2214 / To Willibald Pirckheimer   Freiburg, 7 September 1529

This letter (= WPB Ep 1242) was first published in the *Pirckheimeri opera*. For Pirckheimer see Ep 318.

Cordial greetings, illustrious Willibald. I asked Hieronymus[1] to send you a copy of my *Letters*.[2] You will find among them one in which I thank you for the bowl you gave me.[3] This gift was no less pleasing to me than if it weighed a talent in gold,[4] since I took it as a pledge of your unchanging good will towards me, and this is something I consider not the smallest part   5 of my good fortune.

As for the Greek manuscript,[5] I know you will be kind enough to pardon me for breaking my promise. I am beginning to collate it in preparation for the fair, but the further I go into the work, the more monstrosities I encounter. Sometimes whole lines are omitted, and there is much   10

* * * * *

2214
1 Hieronymus Froben
2 The newly published *Opus epistolarum*; see Ep 2203.
3 Ep 2196
4 A talent was a measure of weight generally said to equal c 26 kilograms. Here the meaning is simply 'a pile of gold.'
5 It is not clear what manuscript Erasmus is referring to here. On 8 September he sent a manuscript of the letters of St Basil the Great to Levinus Ammonius, asking him to copy it; see Epp 2258:3–6 and 98–9, 2270:18–22. In May 1528 Erasmus had asked Pirckheimer to arrange for Vincentius Opsopoeus to send Erasmus his manuscript copy of the letters of Basil and Gregory Nazianzen, if indeed he had one; see Ep 1997:5–14. Three months later, in August 1528, Erasmus reminded Pirckheimer of the request; see Ep 2028:1–3. Allen, in his annotation for Ep 1997:12 (faithfully echoed by CWE in Ep 1997 n8), concluded from the absence of any mention of an Opsopoeus manuscript in the introduction to Erasmus' 1532 edition of Basil (Ep 2611) that Pirckheimer had not been able to fulfil the request. Here, however, Allen says that the manuscript sent to Ammonius was probably the one borrowed through Pirckheimer in 1528 and cites Epp 1997 and 2008. This seems unlikely, given that Erasmus was not likely to send to Ammonius for copying a manuscript on which he was currently working. So the identity of the manuscript and its owner (lines 13–14), as well as the nature of the promise made to Pirckheimer concerning it (lines 7–8), remain a mystery.

that is altered, deliberately I think. Many letters have been omitted. Finally, over a third of the text is missing. The collation is finished, but I have begun to copy the missing parts. Don't worry about the manuscript: it will be kept safe for its owner. Perhaps I shall have my version printed.   15

I cannot write more at present, for time presses, and autumn has, rather unkindly, greeted me with a severe abscess in my teeth accompanied by a fever. I hope you are in top form, dear patron and friend beyond compare.

Freiburg im Breisgau, 7 September 1529

Erasmus of Rotterdam, hurriedly, in his own hand   20

To the distinguished Master Willibald Pirckheimer, counsellor to his imperial Majesty

2215 / To William Blount, Lord Mountjoy   Freiburg, 8 September 1529

This letter was first published in the *Epistolae floridae*. The surviving manuscript, an autograph rough draft, is in the Royal Library at Copenhagen (GKS 95 Fol, folio 192). On Blount, fourth Baron Mountjoy and Erasmus' great friend and patron, see Ep 79.

ERASMUS OF ROTTERDAM TO WILLIAM MOUNTJOY,
ENGLISH BARON, GREETING

Most generous Maecenas,[1] the gift sent by her most serene Majesty was highly gratifying,[2] although her kind thoughts were enough for me without a gift. I am so impressed by the lady's piety and learning, which is a   5 reproach to our indolence and corrupt morals, that I consider it a benefit to myself if I can do anything to please her. She has a niece very like herself, Mary the former queen of Hungary, to whom I dedicated my *Christian Widow*.[3] How she felt about the book and with what interest she read it you will discover from the letter I sent to More's daughter, Margaret.[4]   10

If the affairs of King Ferdinand were prospering, Erasmus would be a very happy man. No one is more friendly or more genuine than he is.

* * * * *

2215
1 The name of Maecenas, confidant of Emperor Augustus and the patron of Virgil and Horace, became (and remains) the byword for a generous and enlightened patron of the arts.
2 A belated gift from Queen Catherine of Aragon in return for the dedication of the *Institutio christiani matrimonii* to her (Ep 1727); cf Ep 1960 introduction and lines 74–7.
3 Ep 2100
4 Ep 2212:15–20

Although I have done nothing to deserve it, he is so truly on my side that not only does he willingly do anything I ask, but even anticipates anything he thinks would be helpful to me. But the Turk has penetrated so far into 15 Hungary that there are fears also for Austria, Poland, and the neighbouring regions,[5] and perhaps even for Italy. I hear that peace has been agreed on between the kings[6] – I only wish this had happened earlier. A good part of this happy outcome we owe to your king, who with great persistence and equal good sense did not rest until he had cemented an agreement between 20 the most powerful kings in all Europe.[7] May Heaven be pleased to make this blessed state permanent!

I know you will be good enough to forgive me for deciding to make my *Adages* the joint property, so to speak, of you and your son Charles. It seemed a good idea to add the youth's name to stimulate his interest in his 25 studies.[8]

As long as there was hope, I stayed in Basel. When all hope was lost, I moved to Freiburg, a town within Ferdinand's domain, despite the drain on my resources and the serious risk to my health.[9] I hardly expected that my poor body would stand such a change of circumstances, since it has been so 30 battered that a change of wine or any other minor upset puts it in jeopardy. I preferred, however, to risk my life rather than appear to approve what is happening there.

Everything here is very expensive;[10] moreover I have now lost the splendid advantages that the Froben press offered me. But I must spend the 35 winter here. If I enjoyed reasonable health, I would not lack money or respect. But as your Highness used to say, 'Nowadays Fortune offers food to the toothless.' I sadly fear that the gospel may involve us in a deadly war, so readily do men rush to arms.[11]

* * * * *

5 See Ep 2211 n9.
6 The Peace of Cambrai between Francis I and Charles V; see Ep 2207 n5.
7 This is a repetition of the unwarranted praise of Henry VIII found in Ep 2211:10–14.
8 The new, enlarged edition of the *Adagia* published in 1528 included, following the preface 'To the Reader,' a second prefatory letter addressed to Charles Blount, William's son and heir; see Epp 2022–3.
9 See Ep 2209 n12.
10 A frequent comment in the letters of this period; see Epp 2192:116–17; 2201:81–2, 2249:35–6, 2295:4–5, 2325:9–10.
11 This fear was well founded. Relations between the German princes and cities that adhered to the Reformation, led by Electoral Saxony and Hessen, and the Catholic princes, led by Emperor Charles and King Ferdinand, had been deteriorating steadily since 1526 and had taken a turn for the worse at the Diet of Speyer in the spring of 1529. Although the war that Erasmus feared would

The complete Augustine has come out.[12] It almost killed me. I wish that   40
certain theologians had a better attitude, for while they try in their clumsy
way to heal the situation, they make the problem worse by their hysterical
agitation. I am tired of suffering the fate of Hercules, always having to fight
with monsters. I believe there has never been a more turbulent age since
the beginning of the world, so heated are the conflicts that are breaking out   45
everywhere. Now the Ciceronians are stirring up a new fuss over nothing
because I want good writing to speak of Christ rather than of Romulus or
Jupiter Optimus Maximus.[13]

If her serene Majesty has not read *The Christian Widow*, ask her to be
kind enough to do so, for she is mentioned there several times.[14] Will you   50
please be my substitute for a letter to her?[15] I would greatly like to write,
but neither my health nor the constraints of time allow it.[16] Amid such
distressing problems my heart swells with joy when I hear that you, the
oldest of my patrons and my incomparable friend, are flourishing. I hope
Cardinal Campeggi has long since dispelled that little cloud (you know   55
what I mean).[17] We are in the hand of God. May he keep you all safe and
well.

Freiburg im Breisgau, 1529, on the Nativity of the Virgin Mother

2216 / From Petrus Plateanus   Jáchymov, 8 September 1529

The autograph of this letter, which was first published as Ep 111 in Förstemann / Günther, was in the Burscher Collection at Leipzig (Ep 1254 introduction).

* * * * *

not come until 1546, the two sides were already forming alliances against one
another; see Ep 2107 n1.
12 Ep 2157
13 Ep 1948
14 Not surprisingly, the references are highly flattering; see CWE 66 188, 195, 257.
15 This is a striking evasion of duty on the part of someone who had just ac-
    knowledged receipt of a gift from the queen (lines 1–2 above).
16 Cf Ep 2214:16–18.
17 In 1528, Pope Clement VII had sent Lorenzo Cardinal Campeggi (Ep 961) to
    England to deal with the problem of Henry VIII's wish to divorce his wife,
    Queen Catherine (Ep 1932 n11). After failing to persuade the queen to solve
    the problem by entering a convent, Campeggi in due course joined with Car-
    dinal Wolsey in presiding over an extraordinary legatine court to hear King
    Henry's suit. The court convened on 18 June 1529, but it was adjourned on 31
    July, after news arrived that Clement had transferred the case to Rome. See
    Scarisbrick 213–15, 224–7. Erasmus had evidently not yet heard of the unhappy
    outcome of Campeggi's mission.

Petrus Plateanus (d 1551) was born near 's-Hertogenbosch and received his early education at the school of the Brethren of the Common Life in Liège. He studied at the Collegium Trilingue in Louvain and then, in 1525, matriculated at Wittenberg. On the recommendation of Melanchthon, he was appointed rector of the town school at Jáchymov (Joachimsthal) in Bohemia. There Plateanus became friendly with Georgius Agricola (Ep 1594 n23), a physician whose interest in metallurgy he shared. In 1531, when Agricola left Jáchymov to become town physician at Chemnitz, Plateanus decided to go to the University of Marburg for further study. In March 1533 he visited Erasmus at Freiburg (Ep 2782). In 1535, on Agricola's recommendation, Plateanus was appointed rector of the Latin school at Zwickau in Saxony. He enjoyed great success in reorganizing the school, improving its quality, and increasing its enrolment. In 1547 he left Zwickau, which had suffered badly in the Schmalkaldic war (Ep 2219 n10), and ended his days as pastor and superintendent in Aschersleben.

Greetings. For many years now I have had no dearer wish than to see our Erasmus face to face and to talk to him, or if my guiding spirit,[1] who generally brings me little luck, should deny me this pleasure, at least to address him by letter (I say 'our Erasmus,' for you will never be able to break free and claim you do not belong to us).[2] So when I decided that I should first 5 send to you the dialogue on metallurgy by Georgius Agricola the physician,[3] who is very devoted to you, and then pass it on to Basel for printing, I thought I should not miss the opportunity to write to you, as I had long wished to do. There was also this consideration, that I felt the work itself would not be published if it were not first presented to you.[4] About 10

* * * * *

2216
1 The Latin word here is *genius*, ie the attendant spirit which, according to Roman mythology, was allotted to every person at birth to accompany him through life, govern his fortunes, and determine his character. The word 'genius' can also have that meaning in English.
2 Lines 34–5 below make clear that Plateanus is addressing Erasmus as a fellow Dutchman.
3 In the autumn of 1526, Agricola (Ep 1594 n23) was appointed town physician and apothecary in Jáchymov, which was the at the centre of one of the most prosperous silver-mining areas in Europe. He spent much time treating the ailments of the miners and smelters, and in the process acquired an excellent knowledge of mining and metallurgy. The first fruit of this interest was the dialogue *Bermannus sive de re metallica dialogus*. See *Complete Dictionary of Scientific Biography* 1 (Detroit 2008) 77–8.
4 Erasmus arranged for the dialogue to be published by Froben (1530) and added his own preface (Ep 2474). The book's success made Agricola a well-known author.

the book, I judge it superfluous to say anything in its praise, especially to
you. Agricola himself, because of his special affection for you and his general concern for all good and learned men, has earned your good opinion.
Physicians are in his debt not just for the work he did in Venice some years
ago when he corrected many passages in Hippocrates and in several books   15
of Galen,[5] as that edition, which was rushed into print, made clear, but some
day they will owe him a much greater debt when he completes his work on
metallurgy and publishes a few other important pieces that he has in hand.[6]

The humour in your colloquies, no less polished than it is pointed,
is greatly admired by learned men, but they are especially taken by 'the   20
Knight from Como.'[7] The knight, with the help of his followers, has now
spread the rumour that if he had not pardoned you in response to the pleas
of mutual friends, you would have been publicly chastised by the magistrate for slander; but that you were required to pay an indemnity, which he,
to let you see what a generous knight he is, refused to take and gave the   25
money to a beggar; finally that you were then forced to recant, seemingly
at his dictation.[8] All this triumphalist self-glorification is simply laughed at
by decent people. Some time ago I was invited to a party and when I got
there, I spotted his egregious brother and Thraso himself.[9] I left, since I was
offended by the brother's disloyalty to you.   30

The affection I feel for you compelled me to write this note to you
in recognition of your great services to all scholars, or perhaps for another,

* * * * *

5 Towards the end of a sojourn in Italy (1523–5) to complete his medical education, Agricola had been a member of the editorial team that prepared texts
  for the Aldine editions of Galen and Hippocrates.
6 During the remaining quarter century of his life, Agricola published many
  works on political, economic, and scientific topics, but the work for which he
  is chiefly remembered is his De re metallica, which was published in 1556, four
  months after his death in November 1555.
7 The reference is to the colloquy Ἱππεὺς ἄνιππος, sive Ementita nobilitas 'The
  Knight Without a Horse, or Faked Nobility' (CWE 40 880–90), which was first
  published in the March 1529 edition of the Colloquia. The fake knight Harpalus
  von Como is a satirical portrait of Erasmus' despised antagonist Heinrich Eppendorf and his dubious claim to noble status. On the origins of the controversy between Erasmus and Eppendorf, see Ep 1437:10–113. On the revival
  and continuation of the controversy in 1528, see CWE 14 xi–xii and Ep 1934
  introduction.
8 For the rumours of Eppendorf's 'triumph' over Erasmus and the latter's response, see Ep 1992.
9 Erasmus often referred to Eppendorf as 'Thraso,' the braggart soldier in Terence's Eunuchus. On Eppendorf's brother, about whom nothing is known, cf
  Ep 1377:9–10.

not unimportant, reason – what I might call a sort of familial relationship
– namely that you come from Rotterdam and I was born not far from 's-
Hertogenbosch. Lucas Scuppegius, who is burgomaster here, a man of un- 35
usual industry and considerable learning and a great supporter of yours,
shuns as a public pest anyone who disparages you. If you write back to me
(as I hope you will do), please add a word of greeting to him.[10] Farewell.

Jáchymov, 8 September 1529

Petrus Plateanus 40

I hope to get hold of the works of Paulinus of Nola.[11] Unless they have
already been printed, I shall send them to you to publish as soon as I have
had them copied out, if you think this would be worth your while.

To Master Erasmus of Rotterdam, easily the prince of theologians

2217 / To Jean de Lorraine [Freiburg, September 1529]

This letter was first published in the *Epistolae floridae*. Allen assigned the conjectural date on the basis of the reference in lines 13–15 to the Peace of Cambrai
(Ep 2207 n5), which indicates that the letter must have been written 'not long
after Epp 2211, 2215.' In Ep 2211, the news of the peace had just arrived and
was scarcely believed, and in both letters, as in this one, Erasmus expresses
the wish that it had been concluded earlier.

Jean de Guise, bishop of Metz and cardinal of Lorraine (Ep 1841), was a
trusted adviser of Francis I and a generous patron of humanist scholarship. In
1527 Erasmus had appealed to him to help prevent the condemnation of his
works by the Paris faculty of theology (Ep 1911). This is the last of the five
surviving letters in the correspondence between the two men.

ERASMUS OF ROTTERDAM TO JEAN, CARDINAL OF LORRAINE,
GREETING

Out of your kindness you have so weighed me down with the heavy burden
of your generosity that not only am I unable to think of a way in which I
might repay some part of what I have received, but I am embarrassed to 5

* * * * *

10 Lucas Scuppegius (documented 1521–34) served several terms as burgomaster
of Jáchymov. Erasmus' response to this letter, if there was one, is not extant,
but in later letters to Georgius Agricola (Epp 2529, 2918) Erasmus did send
greetings to Scuppegius.
11 St Paulinus (c 353–431) was bishop of Nola and a friend of such figures as St
Martin of Tours, St Ambrose, and St Augustine. Many of his letters and poems
survive. Plateanus was apparently trying to obtain a manuscript of Paulinus
that Erasmus would publish, but no such edition ever appeared.

Antoine, duke of Lorraine
Hans Holbein the Younger
Staatliche Museen zu Berlin, Gemäldegalerie

thank you; for according to the general practice one gives thanks for moderate acts of kindness. I am not now speaking only of your splendid and
truly royal gift,[1] but much more of the exceptional devotion and good will
that inspired it. I cannot but admire such generosity in so great a prince,
and would admire it even if it had been of no use to me. For exceptional   10
goodness is attractive and lovable in itself. All I can do for the present is
proclaim your kindness and my good fortune, until an opportunity comes
along to free myself before the world from the suspicion of ingratitude.

The patching up of friendship between the emperor and the French
king calls for hearty congratulations to both men; I only wish it had taken   15
place earlier – and on somewhat milder terms. Time, however, which heals
and soothes every wound, will readily cause this scar to fade. But, as I see
it, trouble follows trouble. Even supposing all our efforts against the Turk
succeed, I foresee inevitably a long and dreadful war;[2] and if victory comes,
I fear it may be what is known as a Cadmean victory, in which the victor   20
will weep as many tears as the vanquished.[3] But since the outcome of war
rests in the hand of the supreme deity, we must pray to him for a result
that, if not happy, at least promises a healthier outcome.

The bearer of this letter[4] is most eager to be commended to your Eminence and through you to your brother, the most illustrious duke of Lor-   25
raine;[5] he hopes that, if there is a vacancy, the duke will admit him to an
honourable position in his household. His father is a man of influence and
he is blessed with exceptional good sense and honesty – his position in society is the least part of his distinctions.[6] This young man is very like his
father.   30

* * * * *

2217
1 Possibly the 200 écus mentioned in Ep 2027:17–19
2 Cf Ep 2211 n9. Erasmus knew that the Turks had invaded Hungary in May
   1529 (Ep 2211:36–7) but the news of the siege of Vienna in September would
   not yet have reached him.
3 *Adagia* II viii 34
4 Johann Egli Offenburg (d after 1560) was the son of Henmann Offenburg,
   burgomaster of Basel and commander of the Basel contingent at the battle
   of Marignano in 1515. In 1514 Egli matriculated at the University of Basel,
   where he studied under his future brother-in-law Henricus Glareanus (cf line
   43 below). In 1525 he became a member of the Great Council. Because of
   his firm opposition to the Reformation, he accompanied his father-in-law, the
   burgomaster Heinrich Meltinger, on his flight from Basel on the night of 8–9
   February 1529; cf Ep 2112 n17.
5 Antoine de Guise (1489–1544), since 1508 duke of Lorraine
6 See n4 above.

Everyone is aware of the storms that have for some time now been battering the city of Basel.[7] One convulsion follows after another. That was the reason why so many of its distinguished citizens left and imposed a sort of voluntary exile upon themselves, preferring to lose their material possessions rather than forego the pious observance of their beliefs, for they   35 regard nothing as secondary to the Christian faith. I myself belong to this number. I left the nest to which I had grown accustomed for so many years, not just at some considerable financial cost to myself, but at serious risk to my life.[8]

I hope that this young man will commend himself to your Eminence   40 by his own qualities. He is competent and ready to serve in any capacity, whether there are tasks to be done in the domestic sphere or the times call for a stout warrior. Moreover his sister is the wife of Henricus Glareanus,[9] whom I think your Highness knows as a man of wide erudition who has given excellent service to the cause of learning. So any assistance you give   45 this young man will make two people who are already very devoted to you, Erasmus and Glareanus, much more devoted still. I do not doubt that this young man's disposition will carry the greatest weight with you and with your brother the prince, given his deep attachment to Christian piety, for although he could live among his own people not just comfortably but also   50 with respect, he prefers to abandon the advantages of home rather than profess beliefs that he is convinced are inconsistent with the true doctrine of the Christian faith, especially since the preliminary moves in this conflict seem to thinking persons to portend a bloody outcome.[10] May God bring all things to a peaceful conclusion, and may he long keep your Highness safe and well!   55

2218 / To Bonifacius Amerbach   [Freiburg, c 25 September 1529]

This letter (= AK Ep 1379) was first published in the *Epistolae familiares*. The autograph is MS AN III 15 11 in the Öffentliche Bibliothek of the University of Basel. Amerbach's answer is Ep 2219.

* * * * *

7 Ie the tumultuous victory of the Reformation in the winter and spring of 1528–9; see Ep 2097 n1.
8 See Ep 2209 n12.
9 The marriage of Glareanus (Ep 440) and Anna Offenburg took place in November 1522; see Ep 1316:42–7.
10 It seems that neither the cardinal nor his brother could find a position for Offenburg, for in the same year he was working as the steward of the bishop of Basel.

If you and yours are well, I have good reason to be delighted. I, thank
Heaven, am fairly well. If you find anyone to take a letter to Alciati, please
give him the enclosed for Pierre Du Chastel,[1] who is living in Bourges. See
that you take good care of yourself and of all those dear to you. I do not
want this request to worry you. It is of no great importance.   5

To the very distinguished Doctor Bonifacius Amerbach. In Basel

2219 / From Bonifacius Amerbach   Basel, 27 September 1529

First published by Allen, this letter (= AK 1380) is Bonifacius' answer to Ep
2218. There are two autograph rough drafts in the Öffentliche Bibliothek of the
University of Basel: MSS C VI a 54 22 and 73 371, the former being more than
twice as long as the latter. Allen reproduced the longer text but incorporated
a few readings from the other. Erasmus' answer is Ep 2220.

†

Greetings. I received your letter, Erasmus, my illustrious friend, along with
the one you want me to send on to Pierre Du Chastel;[1] but did you need to
ask a favour when rightfully you could and should command me? I shall do
this gladly and see that it is taken to Bourges by the first available courier,
that is, if you still think it should be sent, for I have learned that Alciati   5
has fled from Bourges because of the plague that has taken hold there.[2]
It is hardly likely that Du Chastel remained behind.[3] There are not many
Frenchmen who would risk facing such an imminent danger. So please write
again and let me know what you want done with the letter.

Your strictures on heretics, excerpted from somewhere in your writ-   10
ings, have been published in Latin and German at Strasbourg on the initiative of Nijmegen.[4] I do not understand what this fine fellow hopes to gain by

* * * * *

2218
1 Ep 2213

2219
1 See Ep 2218:2–3.
2 Cf Epp 2209:74–5, 2225:4–5. In Ep 2010, written from Bourges by Viglius Zuichemus, there is no mention of the plague.
3 Alciati and Du Chastel were both still in Bourges.
4 This reference, concerning which Erasmus made no comment in his reply
to this letter, is difficult to pin down. In 1529 Gerard Geldenhouwer of Nijmegen (Ep 487), in cooperation with the press of Christian Egenolff at Strasbourg, published no fewer than three pamphlets featuring an excerpt from

such a favour to you; I am afraid his action is hardly distinguishable from an attack.[5] That he acted with the intention of leading you into the new sect,

* * * * *

the *Apologia adversus monachos quosdam Hispanos* (1528) in which Erasmus had argued that the civil authorities should exercise caution and clemency in their treatment of heretics. This was done to bolster with the authority of Erasmus Geldenhouwer's own argument that civil authorities had no right to put heretics to death. To two of these pamphlets Geldenhouwer added letters of his own on the treatment of heretics, and two of them were also published in German translation. The best known of the pamphlets, published in the autumn of 1529, bore the title *D. Erasmi Roterodami Annotationes in leges pontificias et caesareas de haereticis. Epistolae aliquot Gerardi Noviomagi.* Allen identified it as the work referred to here, but this can hardly be the case. For one thing, Bonifacius makes no mention of any letters of Geldenhouwer in the volumes he saw. Furthermore, the German translation of the *Annotationes* did not appear until December 1529, published by Alexander Weissenkorn at Augsburg: *Verzeychnung Erasmi Roterodami über Bäpstliche vnnd Kaiserliche Recht von den Ketzern. Etlich Sendtbrieff Gerardi Noviomagi.* Equally out of the question is a similar pamphlet that had been published in the spring of 1529 and did not appear in German. No longer extant, it is known only by the title that Erasmus gave it when referring to it in the *Epistola contra pseudevangelicos* (see following note), ie *Epistola Erasmi.* Erasmus had seen the pamphlet in Basel while he was preparing to move to Freiburg. These two pamphlets having been ruled out, one is left with the third, which survives only in the German version. It carried the title *Ejn Antwort des D. Erasmi von Roterdam, die ersuchung und verfolgung der Ketzer betreffend, disser zeyt allen Fürsten, Herren, Ratherren, Richter und allen gewalthabern fast nötig zu wissen,* and was published in the autumn of 1529 without indication of printer or place of publication. Bonifacius' information that it and the Latin text had been printed at Strasbourg at the instigation of Geldenhouwer could well have come from the booksellers. The German text is an exact translation of a large chunk of *Responsio* 22, entitled 'Contra sanctam haereticorum inquisitionem,' in the *Apologia adversus monachos* (= all but one sentence of LB IX 1054C [Quoties]–1057E [inutiliter]). None of Geldenhouwer's own letters were appended. For the meticulous examination of the sparse and often confusing evidence leading to the conclusions summarized here, see Augustijn 147–53.

5 Erasmus and Geldenhouwer had once been good friends, but the latter was now allied with the Strasbourg reformers and their leader, Martin Bucer, with whom Erasmus' once cordial relations had also cooled in recent years. Geldenhouwer's unauthorized publication and use of material from one of Erasmus' works in support of his own views was but the latest example of the penchant of the reformers of the Zürich-Strasbourg-Basel school for claiming him as the inspiration for their religious innovations. Having started out as Erasmians, they were convinced that their views were logical developments of his own and that he really belonged on their side. In this conviction that they were good Erasmians and that Erasmus should acknowledge this, the Strasbourgers

I cannot believe.[6] Nothing could be written so prudently and carefully and,   15
I may add, so truthfully which, if repeated out of context, will not pile up
abuse for the author and arouse prejudice among the people. Now, if ever,
the people, as the poet says, are divided into two opposing factions.[7] The
odour of suspicion smells different on one side and the other. One man accuses you of having joined this side, another denies it, but only ...[8] I am   20
not sending you a copy, for within a short space of time the bookseller here
sold off absolutely everything he had.

As for our situation, I do not know what Enyo is hatching.[9] Unless I
am mistaken, she is about to pile affliction upon the afflicted. In the past
the gospel had nothing to do with wars. Now no one is more eager for   25
vengeance or readier to take to war than these people who under the impulse
of the spirit make their voices heard and want to be regarded as standard-
bearers among the evangelicals[10] – or should I call them 'the enthusiasts'?

* * * * *

and their allies were in agreement with Erasmus' conservative Catholic critics
like Noël Béda and Alberto Pio. It is no wonder then that Erasmus, who had
spent years vigorously defending his Catholic orthodoxy and distancing himself from Luther, felt constrained to defend himself against the claims of the
'false evangelicals' and distance himself from them. His opening salvo against
them took the form of a letter addressed to Geldenhouwer: *Epistola contra quosdam qui se falso iactant evangelicos*, which came to be known as the *Epistola contra pseudevangelicos* (cf Ep 2287 n4). Completed and dated on 4 November 1529
(see CWE 78 253), the work was in print by early December (Freiburg: Johann
Faber Emmeus); cf Ep 2238. Far more than just a settling of scores with Geldenhouwer, the *Epistola* takes aim at Bucer and the entire roster of 'false evangelical' reformers in southwestern Germany and Switzerland, accusing them
of using craft and deceit in the pursuit of their goals, discrediting the cause
of true reform, destroying everything good in the church, and undermining
the peace of Christendom. Geldenhouwer would respond by publishing an
unauthorized edition of Erasmus' *Epistola* with his own annotations (Ep 2289
n2), but the really important response would be Bucer's *Epistola apologetica* (Ep
2312 n2).

6 In the manuscript, this sentence was written in between the year-date and the
   signature, with no indication of where it was meant to be inserted into the
   text.
7 Virgil *Aeneid* 2.39
8 This incomplete sentence was added in the margin.
9 Enyo was a Greek goddess of war, known to the Romans as Bellona.
10 At the diet at Speyer (15 March–22 April 1529), the Catholic majority, led by
   King Ferdinand, had adopted a harshly anti-evangelical recess aimed at halt-
   ing the spread of the Reformation. The evangelicals had responded with a
   formal protestation, thus becoming 'the protesting estates,' or 'protestants'
   for short. In the wake of the diet, the princes and cities that had lodged the

But we commend these matters to God. Now that I know that you are well I
feel much better. I pray again and again to our Saviour Christ that you can   30
continue in good health for a very long time to come. Farewell, Erasmus,
best of men.

In haste, Basel, 27 September 1529

You will recognize the handwriting of one who is truly and sincerely
yours.   35

I am sure you know that Oecolampadius and Zwingli have set out for
Marburg[11] – with the intention, I imagine, of subduing Luther.[12] Here we
are preparing to celebrate victory.

* * * * *

protest, whom Bonifacius here calls 'standard-bearers among the evangelicals,' launched a concerted effort to find security in an armed alliance. The
final outcome of this effort would be the formation, in 1530–1, of the League
of Schmalkalden for the purpose of the armed defence of the Protestant estates should any of the Catholic princes, including the emperor himself, make
war on them because of their religion. Cf Ep 2107 n1. The leading members
of the league were Electoral Saxony and Hessen. War did not in fact come until 1546–7, but the fear of war and preparations for it were a constant theme
of German history through the whole of the intervening period.

11 Zwingli arrived in Basel on 5 September en route to the Marburg Colloquy
(see following note). On the following day, he and Oecolampadius departed
by boat for Strasbourg (Zw-Br Epp 915–17), where Martin Bucer joined them
for the remainder of the journey to Marburg.

12 Landgrave Philip of Hessen (Ep 2141 n6) was the foremost champion of the
idea that all the Protestant princes and cities of Germany and Switzerland
should come together in a grand alliance. Of the several barriers to the achievement of this goal, the most intractable was the division between Lutherans
and Zwinglians over the question of the Real Presence in the Eucharist. On
the Lutheran side were North German princes, led by Saxony, as well as
Nürnberg and a few other cities in Franconia. On the Zwinglian side were
the cities of southwestern Germany and neighbouring Switzerland: Constance,
Strasbourg, Basel, Zürich, and others. The Wittenberg theologians, Melanchthon as much as Luther, thought that Zwingli's denial of the Real Presence was
patently unbiblical and represented a contempt for the sacraments which, if
accepted, would slam the door on any possibility of reconciliation with Rome.
They were thus inclined to characterize Zwingli and his followers as 'fanatics'
(Schwärmer), a category that included Anabaptists and other radicals. Landgrave Philip, who cared little about the Real Presence but much about Protestant unity against Catholics and Hapsburgs, took it upon himself to bring together the leading representatives of both sides – Luther and Melanchthon
on the one; Zwingli, Oecolampadius, and Bucer on the other – so that they
could negotiate an end to their differences. At the colloquy, which took place
in Marburg on 1–4 October 1529, Luther and Zwingli managed to agree on

To Master Erasmus of Rotterdam, prince of theologians and father of
sound learning, our incomparable mentor and patron. In Freiburg   40

2220 / To Bonifacius Amerbach   Freiburg, 27 September 1529

This letter (= AK Ep 1381), Erasmus' reply to Ep 2219, was first published
in the *Epistolae familiares*. The autograph is MS AN III 15 7 in the Öffentliche
Bibliothek of the University of Basel. Bonifacius' answer is Ep 2221.

Greetings. I received a letter written on 24 August from Bourges,[1] in which
everything, it seemed, was going well for Alciati. If he has left, he must have
left recently.[2] It distresses me that the man's luck bears so little relationship
to his merits. Will Enyo allow me to put aside my worries about you?[3] Don't
trouble yourself about the letter to Du Chastel;[4] it is of no importance, and   5
I have sent another copy to Frankfurt.[5] I trust that, with your usual good
sense, you will take precautions against coming to any harm. As for me, I am
still, thank Heaven, very well. The British plague, which is more frightening
than any of the others, has crept into Germany.[6] We belong to God; let him
do with us whatever he wills. My best wishes to you, Bonifacius, truest of   10
friends, and to all who are dear to you.
Freiburg, 27 September 1529

* * * * *

fourteen articles of faith, but on the fifteenth, the Lord's Supper, they could
not agree on the matter of the Real Presence. Already before the colloquy,
the Wittenbergers had declared that this error of the Zwinglians made them
unacceptable as partners in any alliance in defence of the faith. So, at the end of
the colloquy, Luther declared that Zwingli and his followers were 'of another
spirit' and rejected the Zürich reformer's offer of his hand in fellowship. The
Swiss were henceforth excluded from alliance with the German Lutherans.
In the 1530s, on the other hand, Bucer and Melanchthon would negotiate an
agreement (the Wittenberg Concord of 1536) that won Luther's approval and
opened the door to membership in the League of Schmalkalden for the cities
of southwestern Germany.

2220
1 Possibly Ep 2210
2 See Ep 2219:5–6.
3 Cf Ep 2219:23. Erasmus appears here to be worried about the course of the
  First Kappel War in Switzerland; see Ep 2221:3–5.
4 Ep 2213
5 Ie to the fall book fair, where someone would be found to carry it to Bourges
6 Ie 'the sweating sickness'; see Ep 2209:110–68 with n31.

Your friend, Erasmus
To the eminent doctor of laws Bonifacius Amerbach. In Basel

2221 / From Bonifacius Amerbach   Basel, 30 September [1529]

This letter (= AK Ep 1382) is Bonifacius' answer to Ep 2219. It was first published by Allen, using the autograph in the Öffentliche Bibliothek of the University of Basel (MS C V a 73 168). Erasmus' reply is Ep 2223.

I have your letter to thank, dear Erasmus, my most distinguished friend,
for the good news that all is well with Alciati.[1] His learning and his rare
warmth of feeling certainly entitle him to a happier fate. The war among
the Swiss has been settled,[2] an outcome that I attribute to the absence of
certain people,[3] for the Swiss are not giving up hope of peace. I would have   5
no doubts about a lasting peace, if only the so-called heralds of the gospel
would allow them to live in peace with us.

Wattenschnee[4] has only one copy of Budé's *Notes on the Greek Language,*[5]
but he keeps such a close watch over it that he hardly allows anyone to look
at it.[6] Since the short time allowed me hampered a thorough inspection, I   10
was unable to find anything that specifically concerns you.[7] What do you

* * * * *

2221
1 See Ep 2220:1–2.
2 The so-called First Kappel War, between the Catholic and evangelical cantons
   in Switzerland (Ep 2173 n10) had come to an end in June without any fighting
   having taken place. The First Peace of Kappel, signed on 25 June, was ratified
   at Baden on 22 September; see Burckhardt Ep 45 n3.
3 An apparent reference to Zwingli, who was at this time on his way to attend
   the Marburg Colloquy; see Ep 2219:36–7.
4 A name frequently applied to Johann Schabler (d c 1540), a citizen of Basel
   who owned bookstores in Basel, Paris, and Lyon and was a major figure in
   the distribution of the output of the Froben press.
5 Ie the *Commentarii linguae graecae,* which had just been published; see Ep 1812 n1.
6 Cf Epp 2223:2–6, 2224:1–6.
7 In 1527 Erasmus had called to Guillaume Budé's attention that the fourth edition of the New Testament with Annotations (Basel: Froben, March 1527) included 'highly complimentary references' to him and expressed the wish that
   he would respond with some indication of good will towards Erasmus in one
   of his major works; see Ep 1794:11–24. In August 1528 Gervasius Wain reported from Paris that Budé had a book on Greek and Latin style in press
   with Bade and that there were rumours that Erasmus was mentioned in it; Ep
   2027:31–3. By September 1528, at the height of the furore over the slighting
   comment about Budé in the *Ciceronianus,* Erasmus had heard that the rumoured

think about the British scourge?[8] May the gods save us from such a plague! If only, when the disease was confined to its home, we had sent money to the needy and to those who bore the burden of every kind of illness besides!

Luther has translated the New Testament into Latin;[9] this, as they say, is like writing about the Trojan war after Homer![10] Because I thought it was important for you to know this, I determined to inform you as soon as possible by adding a word or two to the present letter even though the courier was just about to set out. You need not worry about the letter you sent me: I shall see that it is conveyed to Dôle.[11] I pray that Christ will keep you safe for a very long time both for the sake of learning and for our sakes, dear Erasmus, best and most learned of men. Your health is of great concern to me.

Basel, in haste, 30 September

2222 / To Johann von Vlatten   Freiburg, 2 October 1529

This letter was first published in LB III/2 1742 *Appendix epistolarum* no 350. No other source for it survives.

Johann von Vlatten (Ep 1390) was an old friend and correspondent who in 1524 had become councillor to the duke of Cleves. The address shows that Vlatten, who had attended the imperial diet at Speyer earlier in the year (see Ep 2146), was in Speyer again, perhaps to conduct business before the Reichskammergericht (Imperial Supreme Court).

* * * * *

comments on him in Budé's work were 'not very flattering,' though by December he was expressing doubts about this; see Epp 2052:7–9, 2077:66–70. Erasmus had evidently asked Bonifacius to have a look at the book as soon as it became available. As it turned out, Budé did not mention Erasmus at all.
8 See Ep 2220:8–10.
9 Although the translation of the Bible into German was one of Luther's greatest achievements, he continued to use the traditional Latin text for academic purposes. In so doing, however, he felt obliged to correct what he deemed to be the philological and theological errors in it. In 1529, after six years of work in collaboration with Melanchthon, he published a revised version of the Vulgate New Testament together with the Pentateuch, Joshua, Judges, and 1–4 Kings (Wittenberg: Nicolaus Schirlentz). Bonifacius had doubtless seen a copy of the volume containing the New Testament by itself that Johann Setzer published at Haguenau in the same year. See WA-DB 5 xxiv–xxvi.
10 Ie it was preposterous to make a another Latin translation after Erasmus had published his.
11 Probably Ep 2213, which was evidently to go to Bourges via Dôle; see Ep 2213 n11.

ERASMUS OF ROTTERDAM TO THE HONOURABLE MASTER
VON VLATTEN, SCHOLASTER OF AACHEN, CORDIAL GREETINGS
To Speyer
Dear Vlatten, most honoured sir, the summer here has suited me well
enough, but I fear that autumn and winter will not be so kind to this   5
poor body of mine. I am preparing a nest in someone else's house, but
at my own expense.[1] Before I left Basel, Anton Fugger sent his personal
messenger with an offer of one hundred florins for travelling expenses
and a yearly stipend of the same amount if I agreed to go to Augsburg.[2] I
thanked him and made my excuses.[3] Soon afterwards, on receiving my let-   10
ter, he sent me a very elegant gilt cup, worth, if I am not mistaken, forty
florins.[4] I have always had negative feelings about Vienna,[5] and I see that
Ferdinand's situation is precarious and unsettled. I was assured he was
preparing a royal gift for me, but the present commotion has quashed the
plan.[6] Mary, King Ferdinand's sister, to whom I dedicated *The Christian*   15

* * * * *

2222
1 When he moved to Freiburg in April 1529 Erasmus was given the use, rent-
   free, of the second floor of the house 'zum Walfisch' in the Franziskanergasse
   as his residence; see Ep 2112 n4. By Christmas 1529, however, he had been
   notified that he would henceforth have to pay rent. By mid-January 1530 he
   knew that the owners wanted the house for themselves and that he would
   have to move; see Epp 2256:32–34, 2330:24–7. In March 1531 he was ordered
   to vacate the house by 24 June, but the move to the new house 'zum Kind Jesu'
   in the Schiffgasse did not take place until September. For detailed account of
   the rather confusing history of this move see Allen Ep 2462 introduction.
2 See Epp 2145, 2159, 2191–2.
3 In Ep 2145
4 For the gift, see Ep 2192:58–60 with n9. Erasmus is presumably referring to the
   current Rhenish gold florins. According to Conradus Goclenius, writing from
   Louvain in July 1530, this florin was then worth 56d groot (28 stuivers), which
   had been its official value in the Hapsburg Low Countries from 1500 to the eve
   of Charles v's coinage ordinance of February 1521. Though that ordinance, in
   issuing new gold coins (réal, demi-réal, Carolus florin) with enhanced values
   for their gold contents, should have raised the value of the Rhenish florin
   proportionately, to 59d groot, it also stipulated that all current gold coins,
   both Hapsburg and foreign, were to retain their former, pre-1521 rates – rates
   verified in Goclenius' letter to Erasmus. See Ep 2352:53–5; CWE 12 578–9, 650
   Table 3D. Forty florins at the rate of 56d groot (£9 6s 8d groot) was equivalent
   in value to the money wages of Antwerp master masons/carpenters for 253
   days (1.2 years' income), at 9.05d per day (CWE 12 691 Table 13).
5 Where Ferdinand had invited him to settle; see Epp 2005–6.
6 Erasmus knew that the Turks had invaded Hungary in May 1529 and were
   rapidly moving west (Epp 2211 n9, 2217 n2), but he would not yet have known
   about the siege of Vienna in September and October.

Widow,[7] had the same idea in mind, but she withdrew to Moravia out
of fear of the Turks.[8] I do not see what I could do in Brabant.[9] I hate
castles – people would think I feared for my life if I shut myself up in
any castle.[10] I am told that not even Cologne is very peaceful and that
the theologians there have lately begun to grunt their disapproval of me   20
because of their confidence, I believe, that peace has been patched up
between the kings.[11] If this rumour is true, I am afraid we may come
to the conclusion that this peace is a heavier cross to bear than war.
Just think of those horrible monks and theologians who will jump at our
heads!   25

I am very grateful for your offer of a house,[12] but I hate coal,[13] and I
don't know if it would be wise for me to have the cardinal of Liège as so
close a neighbour. He is a real Carthaginian![14] I have decided to remain here

* * * * *

7 Ep 2100
8 See Ep 2211:37–9.
9 Margaret of Austria, regent of the Netherlands, had made the payment of
   Erasmus' imperial pension dependent on his return to Brabant (Ep 2192:97–
   104), and when he made clear his intention to leave Basel, Erasmus' friends
   in the Netherlands entertained high hopes that he would return to his native
   land (Ep 2196:154–8). But unhappy memories of conflicts with the Louvain
   theologians, combined with the fear of becoming entangled in the affairs of
   the imperial court, ultimately defeated whatever temptation there was to 'go
   home' (Epp 2196:158–61, 2328:57–62).
10 The Latin here is arces, which means 'castles,' 'fortresses,' 'citadels,' etc. It is
   not clear what Erasmus intends to say. Our best guess is that he is not referring
   specifically to Brabant but rather to his general reluctance to be tied to any
   royal or noble court and thus be forced to become a partisan or defender of
   its dynastic, political, or other policies.
11 If the Cologne theologians did indeed harbour such confidence, it was perhaps because Charles v, having concluded the Peace of Cambrai with Francis
   I in August 1529 (Ep 2207 n5), was eager to return to Germany to restore religious unity. In the spring of 1529 the cardinal-archbishop-elector of Cologne,
   Hermann von Wied, had invited Erasmus to settle there; see Ep 2137:33–49.
   Erasmus, of course, had many memories of the hostility to him of the Cologne
   theologians, especially Jacob of Hoogstraten (Ep 1006).
12 Although most of the relevant correspondence is lost, we know that Erasmus
   had been invited to settle in the domains of the duke of Cleves; see Ep 2146.
   This passage shows that the provision of a house was part of the offer.
13 Jülich-Cleves was an area of coal mining, and Erasmus appears to be saying
   that he feared stoves that burned coal. On Erasmus' dislike of German stoves
   (as opposed to open fireplaces) see Epp 1248 n5, 1258 n18, 1399:4–7, 2055 n7,
   2112:4 and 23–4, 2118:45–6.
14 The Carthaginians were proverbial for treachery; see Adagia I viii 28. The
   cardinal of Liège was Erard de la Marck (Ep 738). Over the years the

this winter, but I am ready to fly with the swallows wherever God calls me. I am sorry about your broken leg (Dilft told me about it),[15] but am glad that it has mended. 30

This messenger of mine, Quirinus, I am sending again to Britain, since nothing has been sent me from there for some time.[16] I dedicated a little work of mine to William, prince of Jülich.[17] Please give Quirinus the benefit of your advice as to how best he may present it. From him you can get a full 35 account of my affairs. Your letter did not come to hand while I was writing this.[18] Farewell.

Freiburg, 2 October 1529

* * * * *

originally cordial relations between him and Erasmus had been marred by mistrust, misunderstanding, and suspicions of betrayal, but in the period 1527–30 they had re-established tolerably good relations with one another (see Epp 2054 introduction, 2082). All the same, Erasmus was evidently disinclined to live in too close proximity to the cardinal. The final breach between him and Erard did not come until 1531, when the Dominican Eustachius van der Rivieren dedicated to the cardinal a pamphlet sharply attacking Erasmus' *Enchiridion* (see Allen Ep 2522:77–92) and Erasmus refused to take seriously either the cardinal's claim that he had had nothing to do with the book or his assurances of continued good will.

15 Frans van der Dilft (Ep 1663) had now returned from his unsuccessful journey to Spain in search of employment (see Ep 2109:1–24) and was once more staying with Erasmus; cf Ep 2243:40–1. Later he volunteered to go to Besançon to fetch Erasmus' supply of Burgundy wine; see Epp 2225:16–17, 2241–2. In January 1530 he once again set out for Spain, with letters of recommendation from Erasmus (Epp 2252–5).

16 In addition to the book for William of Cleves (see following note), Quirinus Talesius carried Epp 2211–12, 2215, a letter to Cuthbert Tunstall (Ep 2226:1–2), a letter to John Longland (Ep 2227:3), a letter to Simon Riquinus (Ep 2246:1), and a letter dated 8 September that reached Levinus Ammonius at Ghent via Erasmus Schets and Omaar van Edingen on about 18 October; see Epp 2214 n5, 2258:3–6, 2270:18–22. Ep 2227 shows that Quirinus was charged with the distribution of the copies of the Froben Augustine (Ep 2157) that had been sent as gifts to friends and patrons in England. In London by 24 October, he there received for delivery to Erasmus Epp 2226–8, 2232–3, and 2237. Leaving London in late November, he made his way home via Tournai (Ep 2239), Antwerp (Ep 2243), and possibly Mechelen (Ep 2244), arriving in Freiburg in early January (Ep 2253:40–1).

17 Erasmus had dedicated *De pueris instituendis* and two short works attributed to St Ambrose to young William v of Cleves, son and heir of the reigning duke, John III; see Epp 2189–90.

18 The letter is not extant.

2223 / To Bonifacius Amerbach　　　　　　　Freiburg, 4 October 1529

> This letter (= AK Ep 1384), which answers Ep 2221, was first published in the
> *Epistolae familiares*. The autograph is MS AN III 15 8 in the Öffentliche Bibliothek
> of the University of Basel. Bonifacius' reply is Ep 2224.

Cordial greetings. Good God! What sort of gospel is this we have now, not
just lascivious and gluttonous, but militant and grasping. I do not doubt
that it was Konrad's trickery that prevented Budé's new work from reaching me.[1] I can easily believe that Budé is not sharpening his pen against me
– I only wanted to see the book so that I might learn something from it.　5
Now because of Konrad's doing I shall have to wait for Easter.[2] Budé, being the grand personage he is, does not stoop to deal with ordinary folk;
but just as he suborned some pitiful versifiers, one of whom was Jacques
Toussain,[3] to attack me, so he has put up some wretched lawyers to ma-
lign Alciati,[4] to whom, as to myself, he wishes no good. You will learn　10
part of the story from a letter sent me by Viglius,[5] a young man of great
promise.

　　If the British plague has moved to Germany, no disease is more deadly
nor more contagious than this one.[6] It started in Britain almost forty years
ago and has never ceased, although from time to time its attacks become　15
more severe. You would hardly believe there were as many people in England as have died, for the virulence of the disease was previously unknown. It causes a fiery sweat, which within eight hours or a little longer
either carries the victim off or offers hope of recovery. Those who cannot stand the heat and let in cold air suffocate immediately; those who　20

*　*　*　*　*

2223
1 Cf Ep 2221:8–12. Konrad Resch (Ep 330:15n) was the nephew of Johann Schab-
　ler (Ep 2221 n4). He had managed the latter's store in Paris from 1515 until
　1526, when he settled in Basel and became the acknowledged head of Schab-
　ler's bookstore there. Erasmus was indebted to him for the publication at Paris
　of a number of his works as well as for the conveyance to France of many
　letters. As is made clear in Ep 2224:1–7, Resch had refrained from importing
　Budé's work from Paris because he wanted to publish an edition of it in Basel.
2 Easter in 1530 fell on 17 April. Erasmus means that he would have to wait
　until the spring book fair to acquire a copy.
3 See Ep 2209:103–5.
4 See Ep 2209:105–6.
5 See Ep 2210:15–20.
6 See Ep 2209:110–68 with n31.

close everything up and stoke up a great fire in the bedroom also suffocate. If in changing the sheets a little breeze touches the body, it is all over, especially if they open their arms, though the disease itself constricts the arms so tightly that even if they wished they could not open them. So sheets that are fetid with sweat are removed gradually without disturbing the covers, and fresh sheets are gradually inserted while keeping out the draught. As a result of this moderate treatment many fewer people have died. But it attacks a person again and again with a new infection. They say that an effective remedy has been found by the doctors, but what kind it is, I have so far been unable to discover. I believe that in England scarcely one person in thirty has escaped the disease. In More's large family it left no one untouched except More himself and his wife. However, so far as I know, it killed none of them. How many scourges has God sent to warn us! Yet we do not mend our ways.

If ever you want to refresh your spirits by a change of scene for a fortnight, there will be a room and a fairly comfortable bed here for you and you will be to me a most welcome guest.[7] I have made myself a fairly comfortable nest here at my own expense. I only wish I could obtain a supply of good wood, at whatever the cost! There is no need for you to consider the expense. I shall count it pure gain if I have the privilege of your erudite company.

Give my greetings to Basilius and your wife.[8] I wish you yourself all the best.

Freiburg, 4 October 1529
You will recognize the hand.
To the honourable Doctor Bonifacius Amerbach. In Basel

2224 / From Bonifacius Amerbach   Basel, 18 October [1529]

This letter (= AK 1386), which answers Ep 2223, was first published by Allen, using the autograph rough draft in the Öffentliche Bibliothek of the University of Basel (MS C VI a 73 310).

* * * * *

7 Bonifacius had paid Erasmus a visit in Freiburg in August 1529 (AK Ep 1375 introduction), and Erasmus was now longing for his return. Not until after Christmas was Bonifacius free to travel to Freiburg; see Epp 2231:1–3 and 58–9, 2235:16–20, 2236:21–4, 2248:1–6, 2280:9–15.
8 Basilius was Bonifacius' older brother. Bonifacius' wife was Martha Fuchs of Neuenburg; see Ep 2151 nn6–7.

You guessed correctly, Erasmus, my distinguished friend. Konrad has arranged to have Budé's *Commentary on the Greek Language* printed here,[1] having, by some devious means, got hold of his prize from the Ascensian press while the ink was still wet on the page, and, unless I am mistaken, using the same deviousness to prevent copies of the Paris edition from reaching   5
us. I am sending you a sample from the beginning of the work as it is being printed here. I shall send you more before long if you let me know that you would welcome this, for Bebel, who has the contract, is such an obliging person that I am sure there will be no trouble in getting hold of it.   10

    This is how we live here, dear Erasmus: we use the gospel as a pretext to cover the hunt for profit even if it means a loss for someone else. There is nothing now that the liberty of the gospel does not allow or require. You are aware, I believe, that contrary to everyone's expectations our men returned;[2] it is unclear what they gained by their disputation. Yester-   15
day Zwingli preached a sermon to the people on the proper organization of the state,[3] in which he argued that the commonwealth has two pillars, prophecy and the sword. He maintained that a state would be successful if the primary place were assigned to the prophets (by this he meant the preachers), provided that the sword, namely the magistrates, listened to the   20
preachers and enforced everything they ordered or prohibited. Some people were saying that he was preparing to give to our prophets dictatorial rule, something that he had not just aspired to for himself in Zürich, but might even have obtained.[4] But whether this is so or not is nothing to me.

* * * * *

2224
1 The Paris edition of Budé's *Commentarii linguae graecae* had been published by Josse Bade (Ascensius) in September 1529. The Basel edition, which was a close reprint of Bade's text, was published by Johann Bebel in March 1530.
2 Ie Oecolampadius and Zwingli arrived back in Basel sooner than expected from the colloquy at Marburg (Ep 2219 nn11–12)
3 According to the Basel chronicler Peter Ryff, Oecolampadius and Zwingli arrived on Saturday, 16 October, and Zwingli preached in the minster on Sunday; see *Basler Chroniken* ed Wilhelm Vischer et al 1 (Leipzig 1872) 105.
4 Zwingli's view of the proper relationship between secular magistrates and clergy – or in his terms, magistrates and prophets – was fundamentally the same as that of all the 'magisterial' reformers as well as of Catholic thinkers, and reflected the influence of Erasmus' views on the subject. For Zwingli, Zürich (or any other sovereign political entity) was a Christian commonwealth governed jointly by magistracy and prophecy (ie the clergy), which were co-responsible for ordering society in accordance with the will of God as revealed in Scripture. The magistrates, whose sphere of responsibility was

You give a frightening account of the English sickness.[5] I wish you   25
could have obtained that highly effective remedy you wrote about. I have
no doubt you would have passed it on, being the generous man you are.
Now I use the common preventatives against the plague. Let the Lord's
will be done! I wish to stand or fall in accordance with his will. Unless the
rumour is false, we have seen the seeds of this new disease in one or two   30
cases, though they have been quite moderate, for exactly as you describe,
those who were protected by blankets against any harm from draughts have
survived.

As for the offer of your home if I should wish to revive my spirits by
a change of place,[6] that, dear Erasmus, is typical of your exceptional gen-   35
erosity, from which flow kindnesses of every sort as from an inexhaustible
cornucopia. Though I would not presume to meet you on equal terms, I
wish I could at least give evidence of a grateful heart that would gladly return measure for measure if it were possible. I sent your letter to Pierre
Du Chastel in Bourges.[7] My best wishes to you, who bring unequalled dis-   40
tinction to every branch of learning. And spare a thought for your humble
servant.

Basel, 18 October

2225 / To Ludwig Baer   Freiburg, 22 October 1529

This letter was first published by Allen, using the autograph that was part of
the Radowitz collection of the former Prussian State Library in Berlin. Since
World War II the manuscript has been part of the collection of Erasmus auto-
graphs at the Bibliotheka Jagiellońska in Cracow.

* * * * *

human righteousness, were responsible for the proper ordering of public life,
which included the public exercise of religion. The prophets, who were the
competent interpreters of Scripture, and whose sphere of responsibility was
divine righteousness, were to instruct the magistrates concerning the will of
God for church and society. Zwingli's view of society was thus 'theocratic' in
the sense that it was subject to the 'rule of God' by magistrates and clergy, but
he did not believe in 'dictatorial rule' by the clergy. At the time, however, and
many times since, Zwingli was accused of blurring the distinction between
magistracy and prophecy by his personal intervention in the government of
Zürich. See Robert C. Walton *Zwingli's Theocracy* (Toronto 1967) chapter 12.

5 See Ep 2223:13–35.
6 See Ep 2223:36–41.
7 Ep 2213

Ludwig Baer (Ep 488), until recently professor of theology and cathedral canon at Basel, was a trusted friend whom Erasmus had often consulted on matters of theology. Like Erasmus, he decided to leave Basel because of the triumph of the Reformation there, but he did so in January 1529, about three months before Erasmus' own departure. Baer seems to have gone first to Thann in Upper Alsace, where he owned a house and was a canon; see Ep 2087. The first paragraph of this letter, which is addressed to him at Thann (line 29), appears to indicate that he was now preparing to move to Freiburg, where he would spend the rest of his life. The first surviving references to his presence in Freiburg are in Epp 2321–2 of 22–3 May 1530.

Cordial greetings. I think my last letter has reached you.[1] You have the good sense to decide for yourself what is most likely to serve your interests. The arrangements for your welcome here are as I explained in my letter.

In France the plague romps through the land in the most appalling way;[2] the deadly sweat ravages Brabant and Flanders and reaches as far as 5 Strasbourg.[3] While it strikes terror into everybody, it carries off few of its victims. In this city one hears nothing of this scourge – let this be said to the glory of Christ (and I hope Nemesis is not listening).[4] The Turk occupies most of Hungary, sparing no one.[5] He realizes how far the power of Charles and Ferdinand extends[6] – I only wish that our Christian princes also did 10 not fear it! For what is done through fear cannot last. Nothing surprises me more than that despite so many plagues and such horrendous disasters, no one is mending his ways. Rome is more wicked than it was. Who among the dissolute canons has separated from his mistress? Who, having repudiated his pleasures, has taken to the study of Holy Scripture? But I must not write 15 more now, for I may waste my efforts if my dear Dilft,[7] who has kindly agreed to do this errand for me, should not pass your way.

* * * * *

2225
1 The letter is not extant.
2 Cf Ep 2219 n2.
3 See Ep 2209:110–68 with n31.
4 See Ep 2209 n34.
5 See Ep 2222 n6.
6 See Ep 2211 n12.
7 In the absence of Quirinus Talesius (Ep 2222 n16), Frans van der Dilft had offered to go to Besançon to fetch wine for Erasmus (see Ep 2222 n15) and was evidently intending to pass through Thann on his way. He did not return until about 10 December; see Epp 2241–2.

The archbishop of Rossano, who is the new papal legate at Ferdinand's court,[8] has given orders for a *diploma gratiarum* to be sent to me.[9] They write that he is very devoted to me. Farewell in the Lord, dear mentor and my special patron.

I am beginning to tackle a work 'On preaching,'[10] but my mind, once released from its chains, keeps changing shape, like Proteus, so as to avoid being captured.[11] I shall, however, conquer it. I am not sorry that the pope's

* * * * *

8 Vincenzo Pimpinella (d 1534), member of the curia and archbishop of Rossano in Calabria, had taught at the University of Rome, where he lectured on the Greek New Testament and Latin classical authors. In the period 1529–32 he served as Clement VII's nuncio to the court of King Ferdinand.

9 *Diploma gratiarum* is not found in glossaries of canonical or legal terms. By the sixteenth century, Renaissance scholars had (erroneously) come to the conclusion that *diploma* was the correct classical word for any kind of charter. As for *gratiarum*, it could mean either 'of thanks' or 'of graces/favours.' If the former sense was intended here, Erasmus was expecting a 'diploma of thanks,' ie a formal letter of thanks or appreciation from the papal legate for some unspecified service or services to the church. The second meaning, however, is the more likely one. The word *gratia* calls to mind the *Signatura gratiae*, which was part of the Apostolic Penitentiary in the Roman Curia. 'The Signatura gratiae regulated requests for grace of an extraordinary nature and was empowered to bypass the established law that could nullify the requested favour'; see John F. D'Amico *Renaissance Humanism in Papal Rome: Humanists and Churchmen on the Eve of the Reformation* (Baltimore and London 1983) 21–4. In this case, Erasmus would have requested a 'diploma of graces,' ie a document granting or renewing privileges or exemptions of the sort that can come only from the pope. Popes Julius II and Leo X had granted him several; see CWE 12 538–9. Allen, echoed by CEBR III 85, speculated that the diploma in question might have been the renewal of the permission to eat meat in Lent granted to Erasmus (and up to three guests at his table) by Clement VII in Ep 1542. But a privilege that had been granted less than five years earlier by the still-reigning pope and did not include a time limit would scarcely have needed to be renewed. On the other hand, there is no indication in the surviving correspondence that Erasmus had at this time requested any other special 'graces' from the pope. Whatever the nature of the document, the essential point here is Erasmus' satisfaction that the new legate at the court of King Ferdinand was 'very devoted' to him.

10 Ie the often promised but seemingly never finished *Ecclesiastes sive de ratione concionandi*, which would not be published until 1535; see Ep 1932 n25.

11 Proteus was a minor deity who possessed prophetic powers but would answer questions only if captured, a fate that he avoided by constantly changing his shape.

legate is in France.[12] He will moderate Béda's intemperance.[13] Those people 25
realize that such backbiting only makes things worse. Farewell again.

Freiburg, 22 October 1529

You will recognize your humble servant's hand and heart.

To the outstanding theologian Master Ludwig Baer. In Thann

2226 / From Cuthbert Tunstall London, 24 October 1529

> The autograph of this letter, which was first published as Ep 112 in Förste-
> mann / Günther, was in the Burscher Collection at Leipzig (Ep 1254 introduc-
> tion).
>
> Cuthbert Tunstall (Ep 207:25n), now bishop of London, had been Erasmus'
> loyal friend and supporter since 1516. This is the last of Tunstall's surviving
> letters to Erasmus, whose reply is Ep 2263.

Cordial greetings. There is no happy news in your letter except that you
have moved safely from Basel to Freiburg.[1] I understood how many reasons you have for gloom, given the turbulent nature of the times, when the
noble land of Germany, torn apart by these new sects, faces a common enemy within its boundaries who is much too powerful for any king, however 5
strong, to drive away.[2] Its power has now been so much increased by the
conflicts among Christians that we have every reason to fear that with its
immense wealth and the extent of its empire, strengthened already by the
capture of Hungary, it will, God permitting, exact a heavy penalty on us for
our squabbling. 10

 I am deeply distressed over the ruin of the famous city of Basel, for
what else can I call it but 'ruin' when it attaches itself to those detestable
and insane heresies and defects from the true faith?[3] You write that, at

* * * * *

12 Either Giovanni Salviati, whose appointment had expired on 6 August (cf Ep
  2066 n22) or his successor, Cesare Trivulzio, bishop of Como (d 1548), who was
  appointed legate on 28 September and arrived in Paris c 2 November 1529.
  See *Actes de François I* IX 125–6.
13 On Béda, see Ep 2213 n8.

2226
 1 The letter is not extant. It would have been delivered by Quirinus Talesius;
  see Ep 2222 n16.
 2 The Turks, who had just raised their siege of Vienna; see Ep 2211 n9.
 3 See Ep 2097 n1.

the instigation of certain persons, many monks, especially Franciscans, have
been stirred up against you;[4] however, if you return insult with insult, there   15
will never be any end to the discord, since you are contending with thousands of opponents. Fire is not extinguished by fire,[5] but made to burn more
fiercely. Against annoyances of that sort it is safest to follow Paul's advice:
'If your enemy hungers, feed him, if he thirsts, give him something to drink,
for in so doing you will heap coals of fire upon his head.'[6] And what could   20
be safer than to hold firmly to the anchor of our faith and stick to the true
church, as you say you will do? And if any of your views that have drawn
criticism offend the church, it is better to correct them yourself than face the
censure of others; you should also open all the rest of your ideas to the judgment of the church. For when you are gone, the church will pass its own   25
judgment on you, as it has done heretofore on all who have lived before
you. At that time no defence will be possible if you yourself, while you
were still alive, did not value the judgment of the church over your own,
as is the general practice of many learned and saintly Fathers. Did Augustine not put his works back on the anvil[7] when he was already quite an old   30
man?[8] Did Jerome too not correct many of his works? Clearly, they did not
maintain the same opinion throughout their lives, for they wrote one thing
when, in the heat of argument, they were bent on refuting their adversaries,
and something quite different when they were quietly attempting to interpret a passage of Scripture. If you follow their example, you will both shut   35
the mouths of your critics and make a number of your works eternal; otherwise they risk having several passages that offend learned readers. This is
my advice on how to deal with the trouble your opponents are causing you.

A while ago you translated some fragments of Origen on Matthew,
which contain passages that the learned find offensive, even if they really   40
are the work of Origen.[9] They express a different view of the Lord's bread
(if by that term he really means the Eucharist) from any ever held by the
church or the ancient Fathers. Even if the view expressed is genuinely that
of Origen and not something added by his imitators, all the old authorities
reject it. I would have preferred that you had left it untranslated rather than   45

* * * * *

4 The missing letter (see n1 above) must have included a passage similar to Ep
    2215:40–3.
5 *Adagia* iii iii 48
6 Rom 12:20
7 Ie correct them; *Adagia* i v 92
8 In his *Retractationes* (AD 426–7)
9 See Epp 1835:14–17, 1844:40–78.

give the impression, by translating it, that you approve it, especially in these times when there is so much controversy among these new sects over the Eucharist. For what is written there seems to apply more to the bread that is blessed and commonly distributed to the people by a priest after mass on the Lord's day than to the majesty of the Lord's body.[10] So I would urge you 50 to make clear in your writings that your opinion on the issue agrees with that of the church and not to give posterity any reason to suspect your orthodoxy as a result of translations you made some time ago. Many of Origen's writings displeased the ancient Fathers. If this work had not been one of these, some orthodox scholar, I think, would have translated it before now. 55

I advised you earlier about cleaning up the *Colloquies*.[11] There are passages in them that offend many people who are not without learning – certainly passages on fasting, ceremonies, the decrees of the church in the Ἰχθυοφαγία,[12] on pilgrimages, on the invocation of the saints in times of peril – where because of your sneering tone they charge you with sniping at these 60 doctrines. You could easily correct problems of this sort and so remove all excuse for disparaging your work.

You have translated some of Chrysostom on the Acts of the Apostles.[13] I wish you would complete the whole work – that is, if texts are available – for you could not spend your time in any better way. You tell me in your 65

* * * * *

10 Tunstall thinks that Origen was referring to the (usually leavened) bread that was blessed by the priest at the offertory and distributed after mass to non-communicants, ie those who had not received the consecrated (unleavened) bread of the sacrament. Except at Eastertide, this was normally everybody but the priest himself. This custom of distributing 'blessed bread' (*panis benedictus*), which represented Christ's body in a purely symbolic way, originated in ancient times in the eastern churches, but by the sixth century it had spread to Europe, and it survived until recently in France, Switzerland, and Quebec. See Joseph A. Jungmann, sj *The Mass of the Roman Rite* trans Francis A. Brunner II (St. Louis 1955; repr Westminster, Md 1986) 452–4; Amy Nelson Burnett 'The Social History of Communion and the Reformation of the Eucharist' *Past and Present* 211 (2011) 77–119, especially 87–9, 94. In Ep 2263 Erasmus will argue that Origen was probably referring to a different rite of the early church.
11 In 1526 Erasmus had written to English patrons to defend his *Colloquies* against critics in England; see Epp 1697, 1704, 2037. But Ep 1697:81–4 suggests that Tunstall had not at that time expressed any disapproval.
12 Ἰχθυοφαγία 'A Fish Diet' is the only colloquy mentioned by name. The others alluded to are *Peregrinatio religionis ergo* 'A Pilgrimage for Religion's Sake,' *Naufragium* 'The Shipwreck,' and *De votis temere susceptis* 'Rash Vows.' For Erasmus' defence of the colloquies in question, see *De utilitate Colloquiorum* CWE 40 1098:25–1100:9 with especially nn11 and 19; 1107:23–4 with n85.
13 See Ep 1801.

letter that, now that the Augustine is complete,[14] the Froben press is tackling Chrysostom.[15] One should be careful above all not to follow Oecolampadius.[16] Apart from the fact that the margins of the work are stuffed with Lutheran notes, they[17] have corrupted the old text by making additions of their own. Moreover, scholars here who are highly competent in Greek have   70 discovered that anything translated by Oecolampadius, apart from being generally suspect, is so inaccurate that they wonder that he took on the task of translating when he has such a poor command of the language.[18] So publish nothing that has been translated by him: it could make the rest less saleable. We have in the university a huge volume of Chrysostom's homilies   75 on the First Epistle to the Corinthians, translated by Francesco Aretino.[19] Farewell.

London, 24 October 1529

Cuthbert, bishop of London, a brother and friend who loves you deeply

To the most learned Master Erasmus of Rotterdam, doctor of sacred   80 theology. In Freiburg

2227 / From John Longland   London, 28 October [1529]

This letter was first published as Ep 76 in Enthoven. The manuscript, in a secretary's hand but signed by the bishop, is in the Rehdiger Collection of the University Library at Wrocław (MS Rehd 254.99). Allen assigned the year-date on the basis of the arrival of the Froben edition of Augustine (Ep 2157) in London; see lines 8–15.

* * * * *

14 It had been published in the summer of 1529; see Ep 2157.
15 On the five-volume Froben edition of Chrysostom (1530), see Ep 2359.
16 Oecolampadius had edited volumes 5 and 6 of the Cratander Latin edition of Chrysostom (Basel 1522 and 1525); see Staehelin nos 68, 104.
17 Ie Oecolampadius and the translators
18 Cf Epp 1817:44–54, 2016:95–102, 2052 n2, 2062:26–9, 2082:316–32 and 350–5, 2239:53–4, 2263:44–50, Allen Ep 2379:48–51.
19 Francesco Griffolini of Arezzo, more commonly known as Francesco Aretino (1420–after 1465), studied with (among others) Lorenzo Valla and became an industrious translator of Greek works into Latin. For the Froben edition of Chrysostom Erasmus used a manuscript of Aretino's translation of the first 29 of the 44 homilies on 1 Corinthians lent to him by John Fisher, bishop of Rochester; see Allen Ep 2359:52–7. Allen, thinking it 'very likely' that the manuscript described in this letter was the one that Erasmus used, and knowing that Fisher's university association was with Cambridge – Tunstall's was more with Oxford, and there were no others – concluded that the university referred to here was Cambridge.

On John Longland (1473–1547), bishop of Lincoln, distinguished preacher, and friend of Erasmus, see Ep 1535.

JOHN LONGLAND, BISHOP OF LINCOLN, TO HIS FRIEND
MASTER ERASMUS OF ROTTERDAM, CORDIAL GREETINGS
Your man Quirinus brought me a letter,[1] which, coming from Erasmus, was most welcome. In it you thank me warmly for writing to you, but I should be constantly thanking you most warmly for your frequent and kindly replies. 5
And you are not content simply to write, but you send me gifts as well; so I feel that I lack nothing that a friend could ever expect.

Your most recent gift is exceptional on two counts: first because it is the work of a most accomplished author, Augustine, and of a meticulous editor, Erasmus. The burning desire that I felt to see these works as soon as 10 they were released from the press was surpassed by the joy I experienced when they arrived. When Quirinus, in handing over your letter, announced that he had brought the work with him, you cannot imagine the excitement that flowed over me. I could not rest until it was handed over and I could finally look inside. When I examined the volumes in order, to my surprise I 15 came upon one bearing the name of Juan Vives.[2] I set it aside as something I had already seen and read, a sort of unexpected extra. Then, returning to my new and hidden treasure, I became aware that volume five was missing. I was puzzled and could not think of any explanation other than that Quirinus had dropped it. So I inquired of your friend Aldridge[3] if he had 20 happened to discover anything more about it from Quirinus. 'How is it,' I said, 'that in our case the fifth volume is missing?' He was unable to set my mind at ease. So I called back Quirinus, who solved the puzzle, assuring me that the Vives volume was the one we were so anxiously seeking, and he pointed to the explanation given in the index. He settled my doubts on 25 the subject, but did not satisfy my mind. For I was all agog to see Erasmus' splendid annotations, especially on the *City of God*. God will yet grant you the strength to undertake this mighty task.

What Vives has produced is certainly clever and erudite, but anything that has come from Erasmus' pen has a certain quality not matched by other 30

* * * * *

2227
1 Not extant. See Ep 2222 n16.
2 Erasmus had sent a copy of Vives' 1522 edition of the *De civitate Dei* (Ep 1309 introduction) because the new abridged version without Vives' notes was not yet ready; see Ep 2208 n2. Cf lines 31–3 below.
3 Ep 1656

writers. Your servant told me that Vives' work was included with yours so that something that was hardly publishable on its own could be offered for sale along with yours. All who are devoted to learning are willing enough to purchase both, but they are unhappy to be deprived of your work where there is something of his. I imagine I can hear urgent appeals rising from all 35 the most learned scholars. As your devoted friend, whom you generously allow to speak his mind on anything he wishes and to ask you any favour, I beg and implore you, or perhaps I should say that Augustine himself is imploring you, that when you have time, you take your file to his work,[4] brush up the text, and clarify obscure and recondite points in your notes. 40 You will plead your weak health, saying that it would no longer stand up to such an undertaking. We are painfully aware that old age is an increasing burden to you and that illness is wearing you down. If, however, the thing could be done without injury to your health, we shall hope to have from you what, if you refuse, we do not expect to receive from anyone else. 45

I am delighted that Seneca has been carefully revised and freshly edited by you.[5] I am grateful and I thank you for this immense labour, which I can in no way repay. The person, whoever he was, who ruined the earlier edition was an ungrateful and disloyal wretch.[6] However, what he did was not altogether unhappy in its outcome, since we see such a perfect 50 and beautiful result.

Farewell, beloved Erasmus, and continue for the rest of your life, as you have begun, to illuminate the Sacred Scriptures. Never forget the promise 'They that explain me shall have everlasting life.'[7]

I have given my usual gift to Quirinus for you.[8] Be good enough to 55 accept it, and know that I am at your service in any way I can. Quirinus informed me that you received what I gave Birckmann around Christmas for you.[9] I was very pleased about that too.

London, 28 October

Your friend John, bishop of Lincoln   60

To the most erudite of scholars and my very dear friend, Master Erasmus of Rotterdam. In Freiburg

* * * * *

4 *Adagia* i v 58
5 See Ep 2091.
6 Wilhelm Nesen, whom Erasmus blamed for the careless first edition; see Epp 1341A:451–8, 2091:33–8.
7 Ecclus 24:31 (Vulgate; Douay Version)
8 Fifteen angels; see Ep 2072:4–6.
9 Franz Birckmann (Ep 1931 n6)

2228 / From Thomas More   [Chelsea], 28 October [1529]

This letter, which was first published as Ep 113 in Förstemann / Günther, is
More's reply to Ep 2011. The autograph was in the Burscher Collection at
Leipzig (Ep 1254 introduction). Allen assigned the year-date on the basis of the
clear reference in the first paragraph to More's appointment as lord chancellor.

Cordial greetings. Although I have long been contemplating retirement, even
sighing for it, I suddenly find myself plunged into affairs of the most demanding and important nature.[1] What these are you will hear from your
man Quirinus.[2] Some of my friends are very excited and heap congratulations upon me. But you are always a wise and prudent judge of human   5
affairs; so you will perhaps pity me for this turn in my fortune. I am adapt-
ing myself to the situation, and I take delight in the extraordinary favour
and good will that our excellent prince has shown me. I know that in intelligence and in other qualities I am quite unequal to the task, but I shall try
hard to measure up to the great hopes he has placed in me by acting con-   10
scientiously and to the best of my ability, or at any rate by showing loyalty
and good will.
     You will hear the rest of my news from Quirinus, whom I have care-
fully briefed on everything. I pray for your success, my dear Erasmus, more
fervently than for my own inasmuch as I recognize that your work is the   15
more important for Christendom. Farewell, my dear Erasmus, more than
half my soul.[3]
     From my country house, 28 October
     Yours with all my heart, Thomas More   20
     To the excellent and erudite Master Erasmus of Rotterdam. In Freiburg

2229 / To Johannes Erasmius Froben   Freiburg, 2 November 1529

This letter was first published in the *Epistolae floridae*. On Johannes Erasmius Froben, youngest son of Johann Froben and godson of Erasmus, see
Ep 635:36n. In 1522 Erasmus had dedicated the new edition of the *Familiarum
colloquiorum formulae* to him (Ep 1262). Following Erasmus' move to Freiburg in

* * * * *

2228
1 On 25 October More had been appointed to succeed Thomas Wolsey as lord
  chancellor.
2 See Ep 2222 n16.
3 The phrase used by Horace (*Odes* 1.3.8) of his friend Virgil

April 1529, Erasmius lived with him until the beginning of November, when his elder half-brother Hieronymus Froben fetched him back to Basel to make provision for his further education. As will be seen in Epp 2231, 2233A, 2235, and 2236, this would produce a squabble with the Froben family in which Erasmus became extremely (but briefly) angry at Hieronymus.

ERASMUS OF ROTTERDAM TO JOHANNES ERASMIUS FROBEN,
GREETING

I am returning the short letter that I wrote you,[1] which you left here, I imagine, by an oversight; you said that you wanted to preserve it among your most precious souvenirs. I am also sending my *Colloquies*, complete with ties.[2] If you pick them up frequently, that will mean that although we are separated one from the other, we shall enjoy a kind of colloquy.

Before you leave Basel,[3] do write to me and let me know how you got on with the ride and what kind of auspicious welcome you received from your native city on your return. If you don't regret the move, I shall bear your loss more easily. And if you live a more lively and profitable life elsewhere than you lived here with us, I shall congratulate you on your good fortune, for we let you go only on the assumption that you would lead a more satisfying and productive life in some other place. If that happens, I shall derive more pleasure from your gain than distress from your absence. If not, remember that when we sent you away it was on the understanding that you would return here until a better prospect offers. So write me as soon as you can and write frankly. If a more reliable messenger does not turn up, you can safely convey any message you wish through Bonifacius Amerbach. I assure you that no letter of mine will reach you empty-handed. Farewell, my dearest Erasmius.

Give my greetings to all your family. Haio sends his good wishes.[4] Kan,[5] I imagine, plans to write himself.

Freiburg im Breisgau, 2 November 1529

* * * * *

2229
1 Not extant
2 The Froben *Colloquia* of March and September 1529 were such thick volumes that cloth ties were specially useful.
3 Various plans had been considered for sending Erasmius to Lyon, Paris, or Louvain to study. In the end he was sent, largely at the insistent urging of Erasmus, to Louvain. He lived first with Karl Harst (on whom see Ep 2231 n4) and then in the Collegium Trilingue, where Conradus Goclenius found him to be a poor student; see Epp 2231, 2235–6, 2352:292–304.
4 Haio Cammingha (Ep 2261 n1)
5 Nicolaas Kan (Ep 1832); cf Ep 2236:12–14.

2230 / To Johann Henckel   Freiburg, 2 November 1529

This letter was first published in the *Epistolae floridae*. For Johann Henckel, court preacher and confessor to Queen Mary of Hungary see Ep 1672, and cf Epp 2011, 2100.

ERASMUS OF ROTTERDAM TO JOHANN HENCKEL, GREETING
This at least can be said for our friend Bellerophon: he has faithfully carried out my orders.[1] Now he writes that he needs only twelve gold pieces to buy a horse and a set of armour to fight the Turks,[2] for he is calling down curses on their head.   5

My dear Henckel, I could scarcely find the words to describe the pleasure I felt at the enthusiastic welcome given to my *Widow*[3] by that excellent and gallant lady, who is much more distinguished for her piety than her connection to a long line of kings and emperors. I again feel embarrassed and upset that neither the argument nor my treatment of it comes up to my   10 hopes or the lady's merits. And was there any reason, my good friend, for you to thank me on your own account for such a small service? I was rather afraid that a modest man like you would be offended. It is my opinion that you and the queen have heaped on me an enormous load of thanks, when in fact I am in debt to both of you – to you for prodding me when I was   15 being lazy,[4] and to her for being so generous in her judgment of my little gift. So there is no reason for you to be worried about this. However, if the present troubles will allow her to send me in return some little memento that will do honour to the recipient and not inconvenience the giver, I shall receive it, whatever it is, with the same warm feelings with which   20 both of you embraced my little work.[5] You are hearing the voice of vanity, not greed!

* * * * *

2230
1 A clear reference to Felix Rex, nicknamed Polyphemus, the messenger whom Erasmus had dispatched in March 1529 to carry letters and copies of *De vidua christiana* to King Ferdinand at Speyer and Mary of Hungary at Znojmo in Moravia; see Ep 2130 introduction. For Bellerophon as letter-carrier see *Adagia* II vi 82.
2 Rex had received from Ferdinand appointment as an archer, which required him to keep a horse and arm himself (Ep 2130:58, 129–32).
3 Ep 2100
4 See Ep 2100:26–9.
5 It seems that Queen Mary could not afford to send money as a memento, so she later expressed her appreciation in a handwritten letter of thanks; see Epp 2309:11–16 with n3, 2345.

The siege of Vienna, 1529–30
Detail from a woodcut by Nikolaus Meldemann
Staatliche Graphische Sammlung, Munich

There are some who think we ought not to have provoked that thrice-
savage boar.[6] However, now that this has happened (for, in my opinion, God
willed it so) I am all the more delighted that, under Ferdinand's command,   25
the first stage has gone well.[7] I hope that the joint might of the two brothers
will break, or at least weaken, the enemy's violence.[8] I only wish that the
rift between us and France had not lasted so long, and that this matter had
been taken up earlier.[9] But a different course was our due reward and was
perhaps more expedient for Christendom. For myself, I place considerably   30
more hope in the godly character of the emperor and of Ferdinand than in
their wealth, troops, and arms.

I am sorry you are having a bad time with gout. But is there anything
in this world that is totally happy?[10] I beg you most earnestly to commend
me diligently to your illustrious patron. Farewell.   35

Freiburg im Breisgau, 2 November 1529

2231 / To Bonifacius Amerbach   Freiburg, 4 November 1529

The autograph of this letter (= AK Ep 1389), which was first published by Allen,
is in the Öffentliche Bibliothek of the University of Basel (MS AN III 15 9). It is
the first of four letters concerning the brief but heated quarrel between Erasmus and the family of his beloved godson, Erasmius Froben, over plans for
the boy's education. The other three letters are Epp 2233A, 2235 (Bonifacius'
response to this letter), and 2236.

Greeting. I wish Hieronymus Froben had not tossed me headlong into a

* * * * *

6 The Turk. The word 'thrice' in 'thrice savage' (Greek in the text) was a proverbial way of adding emphasis, as in once-common English expressions like
  'thrice (ie greatly) blessed.' Cf Adagia II ix 5.
7 Here Allen notes that the siege of Vienna by the Turks had been raised on 15–
  16 October 1529. But there is no evidence that Erasmus knew anything about
  the siege at this early date. By the end of January 1530, he will have heard
  that 'King Ferdinand has lost Vienna' (Ep 2261:35–6), which indicates that he
  still did not know that Vienna had not fallen to the Turks. So Erasmus is here
  simply repeating his earlier reports of the deceptively successful 'first stage'
  (1527–8) of Ferdinand's attempt to establish his control of Hungary. See Epp
  1935 nn5 and 8, 1977:48–9, 2090:14–18 and 34–7, 2211 n9.
8 See Ep 2211 n12.
9 Ie it would have been better if the Peace of Cambrai between Charles V and
  Francis I (Ep 2207 n5) had been concluded earlier; cf Epp 2215:17–21, 2222:
  21–2.
10 See Horace Odes 2.16.27–8: 'There is nothing that is totally happy.'

false state of happiness by giving me hope of your return here.[1] There is plenty of room in this house.

We parted with our dear Erasmius.[2] In case you think that this happened against my will, let me say that I have long been working to the same end, although the boy was unaware of it. But listen to this tale of deceit. My advice has always been that he should go to Louvain and not be removed completely from his studies until he had clearly reached maturity, though in fact he is already mature.[3] Louvain is a place of elegance, it has a large university with many public lectures, even free lectures. Karl Harst is there; he boards several distinguished young men in his house and has a wife who is admirably suited to provide the attention that boys sometimes require.[4] Association with boys of rank, some of them princes, would have had a settling effect on Erasmius' character. Moreover, all the professors there are in my debt and would do anything for me. These are the reasons why I concluded that such educated company and the happy association with good people might remove the hostility and distaste that he feels towards liberal studies, something that he imbibed from his early years from that pack of torturers.[5] On this subject you will hear some surprising things from his own mouth. The advice I gave never satisfied them. This, however, need not trouble me overmuch since it is nothing new; in fact whenever we discussed the boy's education, they took anyone's advice in preference to mine. They had already decided to send him to Lyon to perish from the chill in Melchior's shop[6] and be so changed by a long and degrading servitude that he would never recover his spirits.

* * * * *

2231
1 See Ep 2223 n7.
2 See Ep 2229.
3 Cf lines 52–4 below.
4 On Karl Harst, Erasmus former famulus, who had settled down as a teacher in Louvain and would soon join the circle of Erasmian councillors at the court of the duke of Cleves, see Epp 1215 introduction, 1768, 1778, 1788, 2352:278–83.
5 The principal 'torturer' was Johann Herwagen; cf the reference in Ep 2236:4 to 'Herwagen's torture chamber,' and cf also lines 26–7 in the same letter. Herwagen (1497–c 1558), a successful Strasbourg printer who had published many works by Luther and other reformers, moved to Basel in 1528 and married Johann Froben's widow, Gertrud Lachner, thus becoming young Erasmius' stepfather. At first Herwagen was a partner in the Froben firm, but in 1531 he went into business for himself; cf Ep 2033 n24.
6 Ie in the shop of the Lyon printer Melchior Trechsel (Epp 2083 n1, 2133 n2). The word here translated as 'chill' is *frigus*, which can mean 'cold' in the literal sense or, metaphorically, 'coldness' or 'lack of affection.' The second meaning is doubtless the one intended here.

When these plans were in the air, Hieronymus came here to take Erasmius away.[7] I drew him aside and asked what had been decided. He said the whole plan had changed; it was decided that Erasmius should go to Paris, and that he would not be withdrawn completely from his studies. He let drop a number of other suggestions, indicating the possibility that in the   30
meantime Erasmius might spend the winter in Basel. Although I put forward many arguments to dissuade him, I was concentrating on other things and did not see through their chicanery clearly enough. But further reflection overnight made the whole thing transparent. I am told that Oecolampadius has dealings with the family (Chrysostom furnished the excuse).[8] They   35
had consulted him also about the boy. He advised them that he should stay in Basel as a pupil of Cyrenaeus.[9] They hate letters,[10] so they created a thick smokescreen of noble declarations, but their aim was partly financial and partly to confirm an innocent boy in their own heresy. They are suspicious of me because I have a habit of turning my friends away from allegiances   40
of this sort.

In the morning they had already hired a horse for Erasmius. I revealed my suspicions to Hieronymus; I said, along with much else, that the plan was in my opinion the worst possible, yet I had cause to bear it more lightly. When he asked what this was, I said 'It will help me to get over my feelings   45
for Johann Froben, which up to now even the man's death could not diminish.' I have no doubt that George, who is pushing this scheme forward, is in Basel.[11] They are afraid the boy may not turn out a good enough heretic.

* * * * *

7 At the beginning of November; see Ep 2229.
8 In the preparation of their 1530 edition of Chrysostom, the Froben press had had to make use of some translations by Oecolampadius, despite the poor opinion of them held by Erasmus and others; see Allen Ep 2359 introduction, and cf Ep 2226 n18.
9 This is clearly a nickname for Simon Grynaeus (Ep 1657), professor of Greek at Basel, a close associate of the Froben press, and a supporter of Oecolampadius. The nickname is an allusion to Simon Cyrenaeus (Simon of Cyrene) in the New Testament (Matt 27:32, Mark 15:21).
10 'They' are presumably the family, Hieronymus and Herwagen, together with Oecolampadius and Grynaeus. Hatred of letters is a strikingly odd charge to level at two scholarly publishers and two learned humanists. The real point is revealed in the rest of the sentence: keeping Erasmius in Basel would deny him the fine Catholic education at Louvain that Erasmus wanted for him, thus saving the family money and, at the same time, making it easier to hound the boy into a becoming a heretic.
11 George was the messenger who had carried letters back and forth between Erasmus and his Polish friends and then gone to work for the Froben press. Earlier in the year he had tried to extort money from Erasmus; see Ep 2173 n11.

Since he is an innocent by nature and all too ready to follow any lead, he
has been tormented for years by a pack of torturers to the point of destroy-   50
ing his mind. Now they are at it again, blunting what is left of his mind by
their boorishness and keeping him a child forever. Unless I am mistaken,
he has reached his sixteenth year; Hieronymus keeps asserting that he has
not yet passed fourteen.[12] There is nothing odd in a cuckoo's egg, dropped
surreptitiously into another's nest, hatching out a chick that is destined to   55
devour the genuine offspring.[13] Nor need we be surprised if he takes no
interest in the son when he always treated the father as a joke.[14]

　　We can talk more about this matter if you come, which I hope you will
do as soon as is conveniently possible.[15] Meanwhile I would like you to do
me this little favour: will you quietly sniff out what they are doing about   60
Erasmius and what George is up to? I believe that Carinus is there too.[16]
Talk to the boy and try to find out if he is happy about leaving Freiburg
and what his feelings are towards me. I do not think he is bright enough
to distinguish between those who serve his interests and those who don't.
Even if he had ten fathers, they would not treat him more lovingly that he   65
was treated by me. There is no bigger hypocrite than that awful Hieronymus. After showing a most unfilial contempt for his father, and forming an
alliance with a wife like that, he has now pushed her into an unspeakable
marriage.[17] All that remains is to ruin Erasmius. Oh that some deity would

* * * * *

12 The exact date of Erasmius' birth is uncertain. It took place before 16 October
　　1515, when he is first mentioned in a letter of his father, but after the end of
　　August 1514, when Erasmus arrived in Basel; see AK Ep 538 n5.
13 The 'cuckoo' is presumably the 'he' of the next sentence, ie Hieronymus Froben;
　　see following note. The image makes a certain amount of sense in the light of
　　Johann Herwagen's place in the Froben family. See n17 below.
14 Lines 66–9 below make clear that this is a reference to Hieronymus Froben.
　　Erasmus is saying that Hieronymus, who had 'unfilial contempt' for his own
　　father, Johann, had no interest in his half-brother, Erasmius, the younger son
　　of Johann.
15 See n1 above.
16 Ludovicus Carinus (Ep 1799), a former friend with whom Erasmus had had a
　　falling-out in the summer of 1528; see Ep 2111 n2.
17 Since 1524 Hieronymus Froben had been married to Anna Lachner, the sister
　　of his stepmother, Gertrud Lachner, who was the mother of his half-brother
　　Erasmius. Moreover, Hieronymus was now the brother-in-law, as well as the
　　business partner, of Johann Herwagen (see n5 above), who in 1528 had mar-
　　ried Gertrud Lachner, thus becoming the stepfather of Erasmius. In his anger
　　over the perceived plan to keep Erasmius in Basel to save money and make
　　him a heretic (see lines 34–6 above), Erasmus sees the 'unspeakable marriage'

rescue the world from this accursed gospel, which gives birth to nothing   70
but real monstrosities.

I have spoken too frankly and for your ears alone, for you understand
what to say and when to be silent. If you postpone your visit and can find a
reliable person to carry a letter, give me news of these mysterious goings-on.
Farewell.   75

Freiburg, 4 November 1529. I have not read over this.

You will recognize the hand of your friend Erasmus.

Someone should correct Budé's work.[18] If I am not mistaken I discovered a number of errors.

Column 1, line 12: I think one should write κατήγορος.   80

Column 13, 6 lines from the bottom: I think the reading should be
βουλῇ.

Column 18, line 16: ἐκείνος is wrong.[19]

Column 19, 11 lines from the bottom: For εἴκους read οἴκους.

If you approve, let Bebel know.[20]   85

To the distinguished doctor of laws Bonifacius Amerbach. In Basel

2232 / From Gerard of Friesland   [Westminster], 4 November 1529

The autograph of this letter, which was first published as Ep 114 in Förstemann / Günther, was in the Burscher Collection at Leipzig (Ep 1254 introduction). It was doubtless delivered by Quirinus; see Ep 2222 n16.

Nothing is known about Gerard of Friesland apart from what can be learned
from this letter and Ep 2815, that is, that he was a Frisian, that he had studied
with Gerardus Listrius (line 26), that he had at some point met Erasmus, and
that he made his career in royal service in England. This precludes his being
identified with the Frisian Gerard of Ep 2311:26–7, who had been in the service
of Alberto Pio.

* * * * *

of Herwagen to the widow of Hieronymus' father as something engineered
by Hieronymus so that he could 'ruin' Erasmius with the help of Herwagen,
Oecolampadius, and Grynaeus. So if he is the cuckoo of lines 54–6, it is in the
sense of deliberately having deposited Herwagen in the Froben 'nest' where
he would devour Erasmius.
18 The Basel edition of Budé's *Commentary on the Greek Language*, published by
   Johann Bebel in March 1530; cf Ep 2224:1–2 with n1.
19 The correct reading is ἐκεῖνος.. As Allen points out, in all except the fourth
   example, the errors are in accentuation.
20 Cf n18 above.

JESUS MARIA

TO ERASMUS OF ROTTERDAM FROM GERARD OF FRIESLAND
THE YOUNGER, GREETING

You have in England, my beloved Erasmus, your Zoiluses and your Mae-
cenases.[1] The former are killing themselves with their own swords; the   5
latter are doing all they can to share with others the fine product of
that divine mind. My master Viscount Rochford,[2] by far the most accomplished expert in affairs of state, appeals to you by the great love he
has for your kindly self that you employ all your skill and cleverness
to open up for us in all its aspects the famous psalm 'The Lord ruleth   10
me and I shall want nothing.'[3] I beg you, dear Erasmus, to accede to
his request.[4] Apart from doing a service to others as well as to him, I
know how much more closely you will bind the man to you and how
many of his Majesty's other councillors will be won over to become your
friends. He would have written himself to your good self, but was un-   15
able to do so because of the pressing claims of public business. Farewell.
If there is anything you would like us to take care of here, just say the
word.

From the English court.[5] 4 November 1529

I pray yow gyff credyt to thys, and pardon me thow I wryt nat at thys   20
tyme to yow my selff.

Yowr own asseurydly

T. Rocheford

This was signed in English by Thomas Boleyn, Viscount Rochford, secretary to my lord the king, a man of great learning, especially in divinity.   25
Farewell again. Do not be too hard on a pupil of Listrius![6]

To Master Erasmus of Rotterdam. In Germany

* * * * *

2232

1 For Zoilus as the archetype of the biting critic see *Adagia* II v 8; Maecenas was
   the enlightened and generous patron of both Virgil and Horace.
2 On Thomas Boleyn, Viscount Rochford and influential courtier to Henry VIII,
   see Ep 2266 introduction.
3 Gerard is quoting the Vulgate text of Psalm 23 (22 in the Vulgate numbering):
   'Dominus regit me et nihil mihi deerit.'
4 Erasmus did so promptly; see Ep 2266.
5 King Henry was at this moment residing in Cardinal Wolsey's mansion at
   Westminster in order to attend the opening of parliament; see LP 4 nos 6043,
   6214, and page 2708.
6 Gerardus Listrius (Ep 495)

2233 / From Margaret Roper   [Chelsea], 4 November [1529]

This is the reply to Ep 2212. The autograph of the letter, first published in LB
III/2 1743–4 *Appendix epistolarum* no 352, is in the Rehdiger collection of the
University Library at Wrocław (MS Rehd 254.129).

MARGARET ROPER TO THE MOST LEARNED MASTER ERASMUS
OF ROTTERDAM, CORDIAL GREETINGS
How often it happens that we find most satisfaction in some happy circumstance if it comes suddenly and unexpectedly! Recently I had a perfect example of this, most learned of men, when your man Quirinus brought me   5
your elegant and affectionate letter,[1] which bore unmistakable evidence of
your devotion to my father and to his whole family. The more unexpected
its arrival, the greater the pleasure I naturally felt, for I could not have hoped
or anticipated that someone as busy as you are with so many important literary projects, constantly shaken by painful maladies, and worn down by the   10
discomforts of old age, would ever have written to me. I shall never deserve
the honour to which you have thought fit to raise me by the favour of a letter
from your hand. I am sure that whenever I show it to someone else, it will
give a considerable boost to my reputation. No other kind of acclaim could
have had such an effect as your letter, for what could compare with the hon-   15
our that was done me when one who is the glory of the whole world judged
me deserving of a personal letter? Your kindness, you see, has conferred a
distinction on me far beyond my merits; and by the same token I confess
myself quite incapable of thanking you properly for such a splendid tribute.
        You say that the arrival of the picture gave you such pleasure because   20
it brought you a painted likeness of both my parents and of us all. We gladly
acknowledge this and we thank you for it. We have no more fervent wish
than that some day we may see you in person and converse with you; for
you, an old and faithful friend of my father, have been our mentor, and
it is to your learned labours we owe whatever acquaintance we may have   25
gained with humane letters. Farewell.
        My lady mother sends you her sincere good wishes, likewise my hus-
band, who is your devoted admirer, and my brother. Both my sisters send
you cordial greetings.[2]

        * * * * *

2233
1 See Ep 2222 n16.
2 For all these members of Margaret Roper's family, see Ep 2212.

William Roper and Margaret More
Hans Holbein the Younger
Metropolitan Museum of Art, New York
Rogers Fund, 1950

4 November 30
To the most distinguished and learned theologian, Master Erasmus of Rotterdam. In Freiburg.

2233A / To Bonifacius Amerbach Freiburg, 6 November 1529

This letter was unknown to Allen and the editors of AK. The manuscript, a copy in the hand of Basilius Amerbach, the older brother of Bonifacius, was found by Jean-Claude Margolin in a Paris collection whose owner insisted on remaining anonymous. Margolin published the letter in 1970; see 'Du nouveau sur Érasme: un billet inédit de l'humaniste hollandais' *Bibliothèque d'Humanisme et Renaissance* 32 (1970) 107–13 (Latin text on page 109).

TO MASTER BONIFACIUS AMERBACH, EMINENT DOCTOR OF LAWS, GREETING

I sent you a letter yesterday by my carrier.[1] You can get this young woman[2] to take back any reply you wish to write – unless, as I very much hope, you are planning to give me the pleasure of your company soon.[3] But I 5 would not want this to happen if it caused you a lot of inconvenience. If you are coming, wring letters out of our friends, especially Hieronymus and Episcopius.[4] There is plenty of room in the house and we have a place for the horses, if that is necessary. I am very anxious to know what Borus is doing.[5] I hope you and yours are in the best of health. 10

Freiburg, 6 November 1529
Yours sincerely, Erasmus

* * * * *

2233A
1 Ep 2231?
2 Unidentified.
3 See Ep 2223 n7.
4 Nicolaus Episcopius (Epp 1714, 2202) was the friend, business partner, and brother-in-law of Hieronymus Froben, whose sister Justina he had married in the summer of 1529.
5 Nowhere else in the correspondence is there any mention of 'Borus.' The reference could be to Martin Borrhaus (also known as Martinus Cellarius) of Stuttgart (1499–1564), whose book *De operibus Dei* (Strasbourg: n pr 1527) had attracted attention in Basel and Zürich because of its criticism of infant baptism and other tenets held dear by everyone save Anabaptists and other radicals. From 1527 Borrhaus lived in Strasbourg and on a private estate in Lower Alsace, but in 1536 he moved to Basel, where he received academic appointments as a teacher of rhetoric and the Old Testament.

2234 / From Duke William of Cleves   Büderich, 10 November 1529

> This is the response of Duke William to the dedication to him of *De pueris
> instituendis* (Ep 2189). The manuscript, written by a secretary but signed by
> the duke, is in the Rehdiger collection of the University Library at Wrocław
> (MS Rehd 254.81). The letter was first published in LB III/2 1744 *Appendix
> epistolarum* no 353.

WILLIAM THE YOUNGER, DUKE OF JÜLICH, CLEVES, AND BERG,
COUNT ETC, TO ERASMUS OF ROTTERDAM, THEOLOGIAN
Greeting. There are no words to describe, most learned Erasmus, how much
pleasure we derived from your latest offspring, the work that you dedicated to us; it is not just that it will bring us undying glory among future   5
generations, but it seems to deal with the well-being of the state, which we
are destined one day to administer, however unequal to the task we may
be. Who would not be proud to be celebrated and befriended by one whose
writings benefit not only us but the whole world? Dionysius used to say
that he cultivated the learned so that through them he might win the ad-   10
miration of the world;[1] we shall do what we can to ensure that the learned,
whose friendship it is our pleasure to enjoy, will make us a fit governor of
the Sparta that has fallen to our lot.[2] And let us reflect that the old saying
handed down by our elders is relevant here too, that either the state should
be ruled by philosophers themselves or that those who rule it should engage   15
philosophers as councillors.
    I am sending you a cup with the inscription 'Here's to good luck!'[3]
I intend it only as a memento and a pledge of friendship so auspiciously
begun;[4] it will serve for the time being until I have an opportunity to reward your labours with a more generous gift. You will learn the rest of our   20
news (if there is anything to learn) from our friend Heresbach.[5] Farewell.

* * * * *

2234
1 Plutarch *Moralia* 176c *Regum et imperatorum apophthegmata*
2 *Adagia* II v 1
3 Cited in Greek in the text; Ἀγαθοῦ δαίμονος 'Here's to good luck!' or 'A blessing on it!' was a common toast among the ancient Greeks; see *Adagia* I vi
   53.
4 On 3 March 1530 the cup had not yet arrived; see Ep 2277:6–7. But it is in
   the 1534 inventory of Erasmus' belongings and was bequeathed to Conradus
   Goclenius; see Sieber 7 and 18, Major 42 and 49.
5 On Konrad Heresbach, see Ep 1316. No letter from him to Erasmus at this
   time survives.

Blessings on you, my dear friend, and may you continue with your untiring labours to advance the cause of letters and the public good.

From our castle at Büderich,[6] 10 November 1529

By my own hand, Wilhm

To the erudite Erasmus of Rotterdam, theologian, my very dear friend

2235 / From Bonifacius Amerbach   [Basel, November 1529]

This letter (= AK Ep 1391) is Bonifacius' reply to Ep 2231. The autograph rough draft is in the Öffentliche Bibliothek of the University of Basel (MS C VI a 73 309 verso). Allen reports that on folio 311 verso there are four other autograph drafts of the letter, the longest of which goes only as far as line 9. Erasmus' reply is Ep 2236.

With regard to the business you wrote me about – of secretly sniffing out events – I am very pleased to tell you, illustrious Erasmus, that the Frobens have changed their plan. The day after I received your letter, they talked to me about sending the boy to Paris and, unless I am deceiving myself, they were ready to listen to my opinion.[1] I urged them to consult you since   5
you loved the boy like a father, and now I have learned from Episcopius[2] that they followed my suggestion and will pay attention to your advice. He added that, after receiving your letters of recommendation,[3] he would set out within a week for Louvain.[4] Whether this really happens, events will show. In the meantime I shall continue my spying and keep you informed   10
about everything. When I chanced to run into the boy on a bridge, I asked him how he was and why he had left Freiburg; he replied that he would gladly have stayed there but for the fact that you had advised Hieronymus and other members of his family that he be placed elsewhere. Certainly, as far as I could see, he gave every sign of warm feelings towards you.   15

* * * * *

6 A small town now incorporated into the city of Wesel in North Rhine-West-phalia.

2235
1 In one of the other drafts, Bonifacius identified 'they' as Hieronymus himself.
2 Ep 2233A n4
3 See Epp 2231:14–15, 2236:19–20.
4 In addition to the letters of recommendation, Episcopius carried with him a manuscript of Chrysostom for Goclenius (Epp 2258 n6, 2352:329–39), and doubtless also Erasmus' letter of 11 November to Levinus Ammonius (Ep 2258 n5).

Whatever happens, you will be told about it in my next letter. I am prevented from visiting you for the moment, first because of those domestic complications by which I, as a new parent, am kept constantly on the run, and secondly by my public responsibilities as a teacher. Unless you tell me otherwise, I shall come to see you at Christmas,[5] for there is nothing in my   20
domestic or my public life that is so arduous or demanding that I would not feel obliged to abandon it if you, my bulwark and the sweet pride of my life,[6] wanted my help, for small though my efforts may be, they are always at your disposal wherever you are. Farewell, Erasmus, my eminent friend.

2236 / To Bonifacius Amerbach   Freiburg, 18 November 1529

This letter (= AK Ep 1392), which answers Ep 2235, was first published in the *Epistolae familiares*. The autograph is in the Öffentliche Bibliothek of the University of Basel (MS AN III 15 10).

Greeting. I did not stand in the way of the boy's going to Paris, although I would have preferred him to go to Louvain. What I objected to was his staying on in Basel, swelling the numbers in the Evangelical school, and being dragged back into Herwagen's torture chamber.[1] It is certainly true that his departure took place on my advice.[2] But I wonder where the boy   5
found that out, for I had given instructions that it be kept secret. I had taken him in out of affection: I sent him away as a matter of judgment. I loved him with a father's love. I hoped that, through living here, he would come to develop a love of learning. The boy was very keen to come here. Even so I would not have been disposed to admit him, had I not been swayed by pity.   10
He was living with the prior as his sole pupil and was beaten regularly.[3] He had to serve at table, for there were six residents but no servant. Nor would I have sent him away if Nicolaas had treated him as I wished.[4] Nicolaas has an inflexible attitude, and unless I fall in with his whims, he is intolerable.

* * * * *

5 See Ep 2223 n7.
6 Horace *Odes* 1.1.2; these words are used to describe Horace's patron Maecenas.

2236
1 Cf Ep 2231 nn5, 10, 17.
2 Ie his departure from Erasmus' household in Freiburg; see Ep 2235:11–15.
3 Unidentified. Allen assumed without warrant that the prior in question lived in Freiburg and suggested that he might have been Andreas Rösslin, prior of the Dominicans, who lectured on divinity at the university.
4 Nicolaas Kan; see Ep 2229:23.

I am surprised that the boy has not written since he left, as he promised 15
to do; he has not even asked that a greeting be included in someone else's
letter. If this was the result of embarrassment or a boy's thoughtlessness,
it is forgivable. But if it is ingratitude, I am afraid I have not invested my
affection and assistance very wisely; I almost regret burdening Goclenius
with such a detailed recommendation.[5]   20

There is no reason for you to come here if it causes you any bother.[6]
I wanted to enjoy your company, but only if a visit would be welcome to
you and convenient. When you come, we have a room ready for you and a
fairly commodious stable, but no fodder.

Continue to act as my spy, although I imagine those people have left 25
by now. For my own gratification I would like to know if the boy was beaten
by Herwagen before he left. I shall be surprised if the fellow was able to
keep his hands off him.

France is shattered, Italy is completely devastated,[7] the Turks are in
control of Hungary.[8] I fear that this storm will spread to the whole world, 30
and before long too. I am sorry that you are tormented by domestic cares,
which not infrequently trouble me too. But we must brace our spirits to face
whatever comes. Farewell, dearest of mortals.

Freiburg, the octave of St Martin's day 1529[9]

You will recognize the hand.   35

To the distinguished doctor of laws Master Bonifacius Amerbach. In
Basel

2237 / From Zacharias Deiotarus   London, 21 November 1529

This letter, delivered by Quirinus Talesius (see Ep 2222 n16), was first published as Ep 115 in Förstemann / Günther. The autograph was in the Burscher
Collection at Leipzig (Ep 1254 introduction). On Zacharias Deiotarus of Friesland (d 1533), a former servant-pupil of Erasmus who was now in the service
of William Warham, archbishop of Canterbury, see Ep 1909 introduction.

Cordial greetings. The arrival here of your man Quirinus was as welcome
to me as his return will be to you, for he will go back to you as a cherished

* * * * *

5 One of the letters carried by Episcopius; see Ep 2235 nn3, 4.
6 See Ep 2223 n7.
7 In consequence of the wars between Francis I and Charles V; see Ep 2207 n5.
8 See Ep 2211 n9.
9 St Martin's day is 11 November; so the date of this letter is 18 November.

friend, laden with wealth. He is such a warm-hearted person and so charming that, far from considering him a burden or a nuisance, I would love to
have such a guest here always. There is no reason for you to worry about   5
the expense to me; my fortune (thank God!) is not so meagre that I feel the
effect of having Quirinus in my house. Whatever I have done for him, or
am doing, is nothing, and if it does amount to something, I count it as profit,
not loss or expense. Moreover, is there anything I do not owe to you, my
teacher and master? I was and am your beneficiary, and I remain your slave   10
and servant. So let me hear no more remarks like 'If Quirinus is worthy of
your hospitality,' 'Do not allow yourself be burdened by the expense.' Just
order me, give me your instructions and commands, and set me any task
you wish; and do please accept the fact that everything I own is at your service. I say this in all sincerity, so much so that I am ready to be thought a   15
liar and a fraud if ever in your life you find it otherwise. Farewell, my most
respected teacher and mentor, to whom I owe all that I am.

London, 21 November 1529

Quirinus and I have purchased for you one and a quarter ells of the
best quality purple cloth at two angelets, five groats, and two pence, also five 20
white skins at one angelet and thirteen groats, and a cap for twelve groats.[1]
You will hear our news from Quirinus himself. He will tell you about the
play of Fortune;[2] I see many indications of where her cruelty and injustice
will lead. May God change everything for the best. Farewell again.

Your Excellency's servant, Zacharias Deiotarus   25

To my most respected master and teacher Erasmus of Rotterdam. In
Freiburg

2238 / To Gerard Geldenhouwer   Freiburg, 3 December 1529

This very short letter is Erasmus' response to a letter from Geldenhouwer that
is no longer extant. Erasmus' *Epistola contra pseudevangelicos*, his reaction to

* * * * *

2237
1 The gold angelet (a half angel-noble) was then worth 45d sterling (CWE 14 476
  Table 3); the silver groat, 4d; and the silver penny, 1d. The purple cloth (1.25
  ells) was therefore worth 112d (or 9s 4d) sterling (equivalent in value to 18.67
  days' wages for a Cambridge master mason); the five white skins, 97d (or 8s
  1d) sterling (16 days' wages); the cap, 48d (or 4s) sterling (8 days' wages).
2 The fall of Wolsey in consequence of his failure to procure papal approval for
  the divorce of King Henry from Queen Catherine. Thomas More had already
  been appointed to replace him as lord chancellor. See Scarisbrick 233–7, and
  cf Ep 2228:1–3.

Geldenhouwer's unauthorized publication and tendentious interpretation of passages from the *Apologia adversus monachus quosdam Hispanos*, was now in press and about to be published. See Ep 2219 nn4–5.

The letter was first printed on the verso of the title-page of Geldenhouwer's unauthorized, annotated edition of Erasmus' *Epistola contra pseudevangelicos* published at Strasbourg in March 1530; see Epp 2289:1–3 (with illustration on pages 337–8), 2293:1–2, 2321:26–7. For some reason the letter was not included in the 1540 Basel *Opera omnia*, but the LB editors found it and placed it above the title of their text of the *Epistola* (x 1573–4).

ERASMUS OF ROTTERDAM TO GERARD OF NIJMEGEN, GREETING
I am sorry that your letter reached me late. They were already printing my *Epistola*, in which I attempt to dispel the hostility stirred up against me by those books, though I refrained from using your family name, which I have given in an altered form.[1] I wonder who are responsible for playing this 5 game. Farewell.

Freiburg, 3 December 1529

2239 / From Pierre Barbier   Tournai, 7 December 1529

The manuscript of this letter, in a secretary's hand but signed by Barbier, was in the Burscher Collection at Leipzig (Ep 1254 introduction). On Pierre Barbier, who was now dean of Tournai, see Epp 443, 1294, 1862 n2.

Cordial greetings. My greatly revered father in Christ, if Barbier's fortune matched his intentions or the hopes he once entertained, not only would we quickly come to an agreement, but I would go even beyond anything you prayed for. But the fact is that I have such a large family of orphaned nephews that there is hardly enough black bread to eat.[1] I admit that I owe 5

* * * * *

2238
1 In the *Epistola contra pseudevangelicos* Erasmus addresses Geldenhouwer, whose name in Latin was Gerardus Noviomagus (Gerard of Nijmegen), as 'Vulturius Neocomus.' 'Vulturius' is a pun on Geldenhouwer's first name, the first sylla-ble of which sounds like the Dutch word *gier* 'vulture.' 'Neocomus' is an ap-proximation in Latinized Greek of the Romano-Celtic *noviomagus* 'new market.'

2239
1 Although Barbier had served as chaplain and secretary to the imperial chan-cellor Jean Le Sauvage and then to Pope Adrian VI, both had died before mak-ing adequate provision for his financial security. The income of the deanship

that half-yearly pension (it amounts to eleven pounds groot or thereabouts),[2] and I propose to pay it as soon as I can to the person who, either during your lifetime or after your death, brings back the present letter with your signature and a clear indication of that person's name.[3] With regard to that further amount that my erstwhile patron Le Sauvage had instructed me to   10 pay,[4] I never received it, and therefore I shall continue to maintain that

* * * * *

at Tournai was inadequate to cover Barbier's family expenses and other costs, with the result that monies owed to others tended to be paid tardily or not at all. This was a sore point with Erasmus, to whom Barbier was responsible for payment of the annuity from St Mary's church in Courtrai. See Epp 1862:8–16, 2015:8–12, 2356:17–18.

2 In a note on a letter written in 1516, Allen deduced from Erasmus' later corre-spondence with his banker Erasmus Schets that the annual value of this Courtrai annuity or pension was 130 florins (Allen and CWE Ep 436:6n). These were not gold florins but the commonly used Burgundian-Hapsburg money-of-account, also known as the *livre* of 40 gros and thus equal in value to one sixth of the pound groot (CWE 1 347 Appendix E, 3). In May and July 1528, Erasmus Schets clearly stated that the half-yearly value of this Courtrai pension was 65 'florins' (of account); see Epp 1993:50–2 and n13, 2014:44–5. That amount was equal to £10 16s 8d groot (gros) – just slightly less than the amount mentioned here, 'eleven pounds groot (gros) or thereabouts.' Confirmation of the value of the Courtrai pension can be found in several letters to and from Erasmus Schets in 1530 (Ep 2286:10–11, Allen Epp 2364:6–8, 2403:5–9, 2413:16–19). In 1529–30, this sum would have been the equivalent of 281 days' wages, at 9.25d groot per day, for an Antwerp master mason (1.338 years' money-wage income). For a list of the pensions and other incomes that Erasmus received in 1526 and their values, see 'Money, Wages, and Real Incomes in the Age of Erasmus' in CWE 12 697–9 Table 17. Unfortunately the entry for this Courtrai pension, dated 15 December 1526, errs by indicating that the amount is in Rhenish florins (worth 56d groot, rather than 40d for the money-of-account); but this error is due to Erasmus' own statement, in his letter to Schets, that a sum of money owed to him 'I think – amounts to 130 Rhenish florins,' and that 'the same sum will come due on the Feast of Purification from my Courtrai annuity' (Ep 1769:3–5). But one can hardly blame Erasmus for being confused in having to deal with such a wide variety of florins, both in coins and in moneys-of-account.

3 Allen speculates here that Barbier was falling in with Erasmus' earlier request that he devolve the living at Courtrai to a younger person so that the pension would continue to be paid to Erasmus without interruption should Barbier die; cf Epp 1458:16–45, 1740:32–8. But the language of the text suggests only that Barbier was proposing to pay the sum mentioned to a person whom Erasmus would designate to receive it.

4 In the winter of 1516–17, Barbier had been instrumental in gaining for Eras-mus an advance on the unpaid balance of the imperial pension that Chan-cellor Le Sauvage had procured for him. Barbier was authorized to receive

I do not owe it. However, my love and affection for Erasmus is such that, if God should make good what I now lack, I would hand over a generous payment either to Nicolaas Kan[5] or to anyone else whom you named in a certificate or affidavit, and the sum would perhaps be more than you, as an honest and fair-minded man, would wish to exact from me. If fortune, which once seemed to smile favourably upon me, had come up to my hopes and prayers, you would have nothing to complain about in this affair. Even now, if my less trustworthy debtors were to pay me not just what I might hope for but what they rightfully owe, Erasmus would not find me wanting in good faith or slow in keeping my promises. But enough on this subject.

I had written to your Excellency on the instructions of the archbishop of Palermo that you would be most welcome at our court.[6] I do not know if my letter was delivered. Do consider the matter if your mind is not averse to returning here, and write and tell us what you decide, for the archbishop seems to have wonderful things in mind. But it is not for me to advise you; you must be your own counsellor. I should not fail, however, to do what a good and faithful servant ought to do for his master, so I beg and implore you by your avowed devotion to the truth and to the purity of the gospel that in future, when you are urged and prodded by someone to send to the printers some ancient or recent author's work for publication, you not only examine it carefully, but judge it in relation to the tradition of the sacred Fathers and the church.

I feel impelled to say this because two years ago you were responsible for publishing Bishop Faustus' treatise on free will, to which you added a letter addressed to Ferry de Carondelet, archdeacon of Besançon.[7] You were

* * * * *

the money and then transfer it to Erasmus. But Barbier did not receive the full amount that Erasmus had been promised and remitted a disappointingly small sum (40 florins instead of 100). The balance was still unpaid. See Ep 611 introduction.

5 Ep 1832

6 The letter is not extant; it may have been written in response to the wish expressed by Erasmus in Ep 2055:13–17. Jean (II) de Carondelet, archbishop of Palermo (Epp 2055), served as one of the highest officials at the Hapsburg court in Mechelen during the regencies of Margaret of Austria and Mary of Hungary. From 1531 to 1540 he was president of the privy council. He was a loyal friend, to whom Erasmus had dedicated his edition of Hilary (Ep 1334) and to whom he had frequently turned for help in the collection of his imperial pension and in the struggle against his critics. This attempt to induce Erasmus to return to the Netherlands would not be his last; see Epp 2689, 2784, 2912.

7 Ep 2002

under the impression that this Faustus was not the person suspected in the
distant past of heretical views on free will.[8] But if you had read the little
work of Maxentius (who is known also as 'the Servant of God') in which
he replies to the letter that the Roman pontiff Hormisdas wrote to Bishop   40
Possessor attacking the Scythian monks,[9] and if you had considered the arguments which that good father[10] adduces and compared the passages that
he cites from Faustus against Faustus in the preface and in chapters 1, 7,
and 17 of book one,[11] you would quickly have gathered that this Faustus
was indeed the man who was suspected of this type of heresy not just in our   45
day but in those times also and was responsible for the very works that you
sent to the printer. When you get to the work of Maxentius himself, look
carefully at the chapters that I indicate here,[12] for in the work itself there
are occasional printing errors. You will find Maxentius' work, along with
the writings of St Fulgentius, in a volume published at Cologne in 1526.[13]   50

* * * * *

8 It was more a matter of Erasmus' confusion over the proper form of the name
  than of the identity of Faustus, bishop of Riez; see Ep 2002:47–50. Faustus'
  treatise *De gratia Dei*, which was an attack on the heresy of Pelagianism, was
  itself condemned as 'semi-Pelagian' and declared heretical by the Synod of
  Orange in 529; see Ep 2002 nn9, 15.
9 Joannes Maxentius, an archimandrite (abbot of a monastery or group of monas-
  teries) in Scythia Minor, is documented in the period of the reign of Pope
  Hormisdas (514–23). For his 'little work,' see n11 below.
10 Ie Maxentius
11 *Responsio Maxentii Iohannis Servi Dei adversus epistulam quam ad Possessorem a Ro-
  mano Episcopo dicunt haeretici destinatam*; see *Corpus Christianorum, Series Latina*
  85A (Tournhout 1978) 123–53, here pages 143–52. Allen emended this passage, changing *ex Fausto contra Faustum* 'from Faustus against Faustus' to *ex
  Augustino contra Faustum* 'from Augustine against Faustus,' but in so doing
  missed the point of what Barbier is saying. It is true that Maxentius cites
  Augustine repeatedly in his denunciation of the 'heretical' views of Faustus,
  but it is not those passages from Augustine to which Barbier wishes to direct Erasmus' attention. Barbier simply wants Erasmus to compare the citations from Faustus in Maxentius with the text of Faustus' *De gratia Dei* that
  he had published, in order to remove any doubt that *his* Faustus was the one
  that Maxentius had accused of heresy.
12 There are no chapters in Maxentius' work. Barbier doubtless means to say that,
  when reading Maxentius, Erasmus should pay careful attention to his citations
  from the indicated chapters in book one of Faustus' treatise.
13 Identified by Allen as a volume published in July 1526 by Hero Alopecius
  (Hero Fuchs). It was a reprint of an earlier edition (Haguenau: T. Anshelm
  1520) in which Fulgentius was edited by Willibald Pirckheimer and Maxentius
  by Johannes Cochlaeus.

Your good man Quirinus[14] reported that you are now at work on a
translation of Chrysostom and Theophylact.[15] Everyone is very interested
in this, for people are holding off from reading these great authors because of Oecolampadius' 'shavings' (I shall not call them his 'offscourings').[16]
They promise to devour them rapidly as soon as you have purged them of   55
error.

I should like to write more, but this obdurate carrier is eager to steal
Quirinus from us, who in any case is hurrying back to you by his own
choice.

Tournai, 7 December 1529   60

P. Barbier, your Reverence's humble servant

To the excellent and most learned Master Erasmus of Rotterdam, man
of letters and theologian, his most esteemed patron

2240 / From Claudius Cantiuncula   [Vic-sur-Seille], 7 December [1529]

This letter is Cantiuncula's response to one from Erasmus that is not extant. The
autograph, which was first published as Ep 117 in Förstemann / Günther, was
in the Burscher Collection at Leipzig (Ep 1254 introduction). Allen assigned
the year-date on the basis of the reference to the fall of Wolsey; he chose the
conjectural place of writing on the ground that many of Cantiuncula's letters
of this time were written from his principal residence at Vic-sur-Seille.

In 1524 Cantiuncula (Epp 852:85n, 1616 and 1636 introductions, 1674 n18,
1732 n18, 1841 n3, 2062 n18) resigned his professorship of civil law at the
University of Basel because of his distaste for the growing strength of the
Reformation in the city. After a brief interlude as syndic and legal consultant
to the council of his native city of Metz, he entered the service of Jean de
Guise, cardinal of Lorraine and bishop of Metz (Epp 1841, 2009), becoming
his chancellor in 1527. Vic-sur-Seille was the seat of the administration of the
diocese.

* * * * *

14 Ep 2222 n16
15 For the edition of Chrysostom see Ep 2359. Erasmus published no translations
   of Theophylact, but Oecolampadius published one of his *Enarrationes* on the
   Gospels (Basel: Cratander, March 1524; repr 1525, 1527–8); see Staehelin nos
   93, 108, 138, 159.
16 Oecolampadius had published a volume of translations of short works by
   Chrysostom under the title *Chrysostomi Psegmata* (Shavings of Chrysostom);
   see Ep 2052 n2. Barbier mischievously puns on *psegmata* by referring to the
   work as *peripsemata* 'offscourings.' On Oecolampadius' poor reputation as a
   translator of Chrysostom, cf Ep 2226:70–4 with n18.

Greeting. I am not so afraid of the disease,[1] dear sir, as of the behaviour of our countrymen, for if they find out that for around six months I had been in a place where there was no danger nor even a hint of danger,[2] and had returned to the prince's court,[3] they will accuse me of an accursed crime. The same rumour about the cardinal of York has been gaining ground among   5
us to the delight of the people,[4] even those who have never set eyes on the man or heard of him before this, so that I feel sure that if a vote were to be taken in Christian lands for his ostracism, the cardinal would face a general call for his expulsion and get the dreaded vote from everyone. He forgot Ausonius' warning: 'Treat Fortune with great respect' – you know the   10
rest.[5] But there is also this saying: 'God is a just judge, strong and patient, etc.'[6]

I have heard nothing about the bishop of Trent.[7] Not all rumours about the emperors' arrival in Bologna are quite accurate, particularly about his kissing the most blessed feet.[8] This particular rumour is not believed by   15
those who would likely have been the first to know of it. I am much more afraid of this than of the epidemic, for I worry that in this and other more important matters the Spanish mass-priests, those 'dedicated ceremonialists'

* * * * *

2240
1 Probably a reference to the 'English sweat,' which was now widespread on the continent; see Ep 2209 n31.
2 Cantiuncula's surviving correspondence gives no clear indication of his movements in 1529. He is known to have attended the imperial diet at Speyer (15 March–22 April 1529) as a member of the delegation from Lorraine, but that alone would not have accounted for six months.
3 The prince was the cardinal of Lorraine.
4 Evidently a reference to early reports of the fall of Thomas Wolsey on 25 October 1529; see Ep 2237 n2 and cf Epp 2241:3–5, 2243:5–7, 2253:25–30.
5 Ausonius *Epigrams* 8.7; the rest of the couplet reads: 'you who rise from a humble position to great wealth.'
6 Ps 7:12 (Vulgate; Douay Version)
7 Possibly a reference to false rumours that Bernhard von Cles, King Ferdinand's chancellor (Epp 1357, 2007), had retired from the court; cf Ep 2295:10–12.
8 Charles arrived in Bologna on 5 November 1529; Pope Clement had arrived on 21 October. When formally received by the pope, the emperor did indeed kneel and kiss his foot, hand, and forehead. See Pastor 10 78, 80, 82. Charles and Clement then devoted several months to settling their remaining differences and arranging the affairs of Italy before Charles departed on his journey to Germany on 22 March. In the meantime, on 24 February, Clement had crowned Charles Holy Roman Emperor. Charles was the last German emperor who would seek and receive coronation at the hands of the pope. See Pastor 10 82–99.

(if you will permit the phrase),[9] may take advantage of the prince's natural kindness. The cities of the Empire who hold to their own gospel are meeting   20
these days in Esslingen.[10] It is not yet known what they have done, but they are said to be hatching something monstrous, especially since their delegates were detained for several days in an inn because of illness.[11]

I would like you, dear sir, if an opportunity offers, to send a letter of recommendation to the abbot of Murbach[12] on behalf of my relative Henry,   25
whom he has removed from his studies with Glareanus.[13] I have sent greetings on your behalf to my lord of Hildesheim, carefully adding his title of honour as you request.[14] I know this man is a great supporter of yours, and I have often heard him say so himself. Farewell, my dear friend.

On the eve of the Conception of Mary   30

Always your humble servant, Claudius Cantiuncula

To Master Erasmus of Rotterdam, his master and mentor, who has earned his respect in many ways. In Freiburg

* * * * *

9 The Latin is *ceremoniatissimi*, meaning presumably people devoted to ceremonies in the Erasmian sense of obstinate traditionalists who defend any and all ceremonies against any and all criticism of them in the interest of greater emphasis on interior piety.

10 From time to time, the German imperial cities held *Städtetage* (diets or conferences of city delegates) to discuss their common interests and decide on appropriate action. There was such a diet in Esslingen (on the Neckar, about nine miles southeast of Stuttgart) in November 1529. It was called primarily to consider the best response to the Turkish threat (Ep 2211 n9) but the delegates also discussed ways to deal with the division between Lutheran and Zwinglian cities (cf Ep 2219 n12), which weakened the common front against their traditional foes, the imperial princes. See Georg Schmidt *Der Städtetag in der Reichsverfassung: eine Untersuchung zur korporativen Politik der freien und Reichsstädte in der ersten Hälfte des 16. Jahrhunderts* (Stuttgart 1984) 35, 163, 371, 468.

11 There is no evidence for Allen's statement that the illness was the English sweat.

12 From 1512 the abbot of the Benedictine abbey of Murbach in Upper Alsace, near Guebwiller (Gebweiler), was George of Masevaux (Masmünster), d 1542. During his years as abbot, the abbey's library provided important manuscripts for Basel humanists and printers, including the edition of Jerome that brought Erasmus to Basel in 1514.

13 This sentence contains all that is known of 'Henry.' Since Glareanus (Ep 440) was now living in Freiburg, Henry must have been studying with him there.

14 Balthasar Merklin (Epp 1382 n8, 2123 introduction), since 1527 bishop of Hildesheim and coadjutor bishop of Constance, had become bishop of Constance in January 1529, when the reigning bishop, Hugo von Hohenlandenberg, resigned.

2241 / To François Bonvalot Freiburg, 10 December 1529

This letter was first published in the *Epistolae floridae*. On François Bonvalot, canon of Besançon and treasurer of the chapter, see Ep 1534 n10.

ERASMUS OF ROTTERDAM TO FRANÇOIS, TREASURER OF BESANÇON, GREETING

I had sent one of my two servants to England and am anxiously awaiting his return,[1] for I desperately want to know if there is any truth in what is no longer a new rumour, that the great cardinal of England has been thrown 5 into prison and is even in danger of losing his life.[2] How like Euripus are the affairs of men![3]

My servant has been absent now for three months and is expected hourly. So since only one remained with me, Dilft,[4] with his customary good nature, begged for this commission; indeed he almost forced it out 10 of me. More than once I repented of saddling him with this assignment, since the weather was so unpleasant and continued to be so. But his return changed all my fears into joy, since the expedition had gone so well. When I was preparing to sympathize with him, he promptly replied that he counted himself lucky to have gone to Besançon for many reasons, but in particu- 15 lar because he had got to know and to become friends with such wonderful men. He brought back your gift with as much care as if the kegs had been stuffed with gems, and he did not cost me much more than that scoundrel of a carrier who upset your generous intentions got for his services.[5] I have always admired that young man's character, and now he has become much 20 dearer to me because of your commendation and the good turn he has done me. You have challenged me so often by your generosity; it remains for me to think of some way by which I may escape the charge of ingratitude. Brunus sent me his greetings in verse;[6] I replied to him in trochaics,

* * * * *

2241
1 Quirinus Talesius; see Ep 2222 n16.
2 See Ep 2240:4–12.
3 Ie how like a shifting tide; see Ep 2212 n5.
4 See Epp 2222 n15, 2225 n7.
5 Ep 2141:9–11 seems to indicate that Bonvalot had generously prepaid the carrier's fee for transporting an earlier consignment of wine, and that the carrier had then managed to get a second fee from Erasmus, thus spoiling Bonvalot's generous gesture.
6 'Brunus' is unidentified. Allen suggests that the name was possibly a misprint for *Gruerius*, ie Léonard de Gruyères, another canon of Besançon and friend of Erasmus (Ep 1534).

though concealing the fact that it was verse. I would like you too to hide   25
this from him for the fun of seeing if he realizes it is verse without being
told.

I had received the copies of the letters from Spain,[7] with the sole exception of the letter from Mercurino, who is now a cardinal.[8] However, this
letter was particularly precious to me, for it was written in a most affec-   30
tionate style; I wonder where it has got to. I wrote briefly to Italy.[9] There is
nothing in particular to write about just now. If anything should turn up,
there are frequent couriers going back and forth on this route. However, I
am very grateful for the assistance you have offered. The emperor is celebrating his triumph in Italy;[10] Ferdinand is sick at heart.[11] I have scarcely   35
ventured to write this note since I feel weak as a result of a passing fever.
Otherwise I would pester you with a load of books, if I thought this would
not be unwelcome. Farewell.

Freiburg im Breisgau, 10 December 1529

2242 / To François Bonvalot [?]   Freiburg, 10 December 1529

This letter was first published in the *Epistolae floridae*, where it immediately
follows Ep 2241. The two letters resemble one another so closely that this one
is perhaps to be considered either as an earlier draft of the former or, as Allen
speculated, a letter sent in duplicate. Alternatively, it is possible that the address in the *Epistolae floridae* is incorrect, in which case the intended addressee
might have been Léonard de Gruyères (Ep 1534), another friend in Besançon
to whom Erasmus was indebted for shipments of wine (Ep 2139). If that is so,
however, Gruyères cannot have been the 'Brunus' with whom Erasmus exchanged messages in verse (Ep 2241:24 with n6), for this is not the trochaic
reply mentioned there.

ERASMUS OF ROTTERDAM TO FRANÇOIS, TREASURER OF BESANÇON,
GREETING
Our friend Dilft most carefully and conscientiously delivered your kind gift.
More than once I regretted my decision to let him go, since the weather

* * * * *

7 Apparently duplicates of a packet of letters from friends in Spain
8 The letter is not extant. Mercurino Gattinara (Ep 1150) had been created cardinal in August 1529.
9 Presumably to Spanish friends who were with the emperor in Italy. None of
   the letters survive.
10 See Ep 2240 n8.
11 Because of his troubles with the Turks; see Ep 2211 n9.

was so unpleasant. But it turned out better than I feared, for he counted 5
himself lucky to have won the friendship of such fine men, and the kegs
were delivered with as much care as if they had been full of gems. Although
this young man has always been very dear to me, he came back dearer still
because of your commendation and the good turn he has done me. I am
ashamed to be thanking you so often. I would prefer to be doing something 10
for you in return, if an opportunity came my way. May the Lord keep you
safe and well, most honoured friend.

Freiburg im Breisgau, 10 December 1529

2243 / From Erasmus Schets   Antwerp, 13 December 1529

> This letter was first published by Allen, using the autograph preserved in the
> Öffentliche Bibliothek of the University of Basel (ms Scheti epistolae 20). It
> answers a letter carried by Quirinus Talesius.
>
> Since 1525 the Antwerp banker Erasmus Schets (Epp 1541, 1931), had man-
> aged Erasmus' financial affairs in England and the Netherlands and had done
> much to assure the reliable flow of income from his various pensions and
> annuities.

Cordial greetings. In the month of July I replied to the letters I had received
from you up to that date,[1] congratulating you both on your departure from
Basel and your arrival in Freiburg. Now it remains for me to reply to the
letter brought by your man Quirinus,[2] who has come back from England
and is now preparing to return to you. The archbishop of York, I hear, is in 5
trouble there, for the wheel has turned and he who had long sat at the top
is now clinging to the bottom.[3]

As you will see from the statement of monies received from England, I
got from Quirinus what amounts in our money to 791 florins and 2 stuivers.[4]
If these are added to the 733 florins and 3 stuivers that you asked me to 10
retain for the time being, the total amounts to 1,524 florins and 5 stuivers in

* * * * *

2243
1 The replies are not extant. Ep 2159 is one of the letters received.
2 Not extant. On Quirinus' journey, see Ep 2222 n16.
3 See Ep 2040:4–12.
4 Presumably the Carolus florin, introduced in 1521 and valued at 42d *groot*
  Flemish. This was equivalent in value to the money wages of Antwerp master
  masons/carpenters in 1526–30 for 17.48 years at 9.05d per day (CWE 12 649–50,
  691 Tables 3C–D, 13).

our money;[5] I have paid this sum to your man Quirinus, as you asked me
to do. He will deal with it according to the instructions you gave him.

From Master de Hondt I have not been able to recover anything this
year.[6] He told me he was not required to pay anything further. Quirinus   15
went to see him in Courtrai. He will explain the reason de Hondt gave for
refusing.

As for your reminder to inquire into the pension that was paid last
year to Pieter Gillis by the Italians on behalf of the archbishop of Canterbury,[7] I looked into this but could find nothing anywhere. The Italians main-   20
tained that they owed nothing beyond what was indicated in their document.
Whether they received more can hardly be discovered without asking Canterbury himself, which it was not appropriate for me to attempt.

It annoys me greatly that you have received neither a gift nor a note of
thanks from Portugal.[8] My friend João Brandão, whose good faith I could   25
count on there in the past, died two years ago.[9] If death had not carried him
off, I know you would have received a more generous response from that
quarter.

You would hardly credit how much I suffered from the fading of my
hopes that you might come back here to us, even though I know from the   30
many arguments you gave me that you are living a quieter life where you
are.[10] In my opinion, however, there are grave reasons to fear serious con-
vulsions in the German world as long as there are so many sects and factions
of the different parties massing against one another; and I can hardly see
how they could be settled or suppressed without violence and bloodshed.[11]   35
May God direct all things for the best!

* * * * *

5 Equivalent to the wages of Antwerp artisans in 1526–30 for 16 years at 9.05d
    per day (CWE 12 691 Table 13). The total of 1,524 florins 5 stuivers represented
    a very considerable sum.
6 For the role of Jan de Hondt in the payment of Erasmus' Courtrai pension,
    see Ep 1993 n11. In 1528 he had been late with his payment; see Ep 2015:7–11.
7 See Epp 1965:29–57, 1993:56–72, 1999:1–9, 2014:1–59.
8 In return for the dedication to John III of Portugal of the *Chrysostomi lucubra-*
    tiones (Ep 1800), an undertaking that Schets had repeatedly urged upon Eras-
    mus. Erasmus subsequently learned that the book had never been presented
    to the king because his courtiers feared that he would be offended by Eras-
    mus' strictures on monopoly and profiteering in the letter of dedication. See
    Epp 1681 n8, 1800 introduction, and Allen Ep 2370:8–12.
9 João Brandão (d 1527) was the factor of the Portuguese Indiahouse in Antwerp
    from 1509 to 1514 and then again from 1520 to 1525.
10 See Epp 2159:1–9; 2193:1–4.
11 Cf Ep 2219 n10.

Meanwhile do please remember that here you have your own Erasmus, who, for what he is worth, is totally at your command. Always feel free to avail yourself of whatever help I can provide, for nothing gives me greater pleasure than serving you and complying with your wishes. Please give my 40 greetings to Frans van der Dilft, if he is still with you.[12]

Farewell, from Antwerp, 13 December 1529

Erasmus Schets, your devoted friend

† To the most excellent and learned Erasmus of Rotterdam, your most sincere friend. In Freiburg   45

2244 / From Adriaan van der Kammen   Mechelen, 26 December 1529

The autograph of this letter was in the Burscher Collection at Leipzig (Ep 1254 introduction). Adriaan van der Kammen of Mechelen (d 1540) studied at Louvain, where he received a licentiate in civil and canon law. He subsequently became pensionary (legal consultant) to the town of Mechelen. Otherwise nothing is known of him except that he wrote this letter to Erasmus.

ADRIAAN VAN DER KAMMEN TO MASTER ERASMUS,
CORDIAL GREETINGS

If, most worthy Erasmus, I have been more presumptuous in writing to you than is proper for one who is known to you neither by face nor by name, the explanation lies in that warm heart of yours, with which you embrace 5 everyone most generously. Besides, your servant bolstered my courage,[1] for when he saw how distressed I was at not knowing you and that I could not imagine that, if I obtruded upon you with my foolish nonsense, you would dignify me with even a single line of reply, he convinced me that it was as certain as anything could be that you would be glad to receive a letter from 10 me. As a result I could not restrain myself from handing him a letter to take to you. If it tells you nothing else than that there are many people here who are devoted to you and to your writings, and that at Mechelen there is a certain Adriaan who has at last given in to a long-standing desire to write to you, I have no doubt that it will give you some small degree of pleasure 15

* * * * *

12 Ep 2222 n15

2244
1 Quite possibly Quirinus Talesius, who was now returning to Erasmus from England via the Netherlands; see Ep 2222 n16.

and that you will not scoff at my silly efforts; for those who are embroiled
in the rough and tumble of civic affairs and in the noisy confrontations of
the courts, where for some time I have been pushing against the rock of
Sisyphus,[2] have scant leisure to devote to polite letters.

Farewell, most learned and distinguished Erasmus. Be assured that if   20
there is any way in which I could be of service to you, I would (as the saying
goes) leave no stone unturned to bring it about. If you are prevented from
replying to me by the heavy tasks with which you are occupied, I hope at
least for this, that if you had the leisure, you would be very glad to reply.
Farewell again.   25

From Mechelen, the morrow of the birthday of our Lord 1529

To Erasmus of Rotterdam, theologian and leader in every form of learning, my most respected master. In Freiburg

2245 / From Frans Titelmans   Louvain, December 1529

> This letter consists of Allen's selections from Frans Titelmans' *Epistola apologe-*
> *tica pro opere Collationum . . . ad Desyderium Erasmum Roterodamum . . .* (Antwerp:
> W. Vorsterman, January 1530). In the *Epistola apologetica* Titelmans replies to
> Erasmus criticisms of him in Epp 2005–6 and the recently published *Opus*
> *recens*. For the history of the controversy between Erasmus and Titelmans, see
> Ep 2006 introduction.

TO MASTER ERASMUS OF ROTTERDAM, PRIEST AND THEOLOGIAN,
FROM FRANS TITELMANS OF HASSELT, CORDIAL GREETINGS
Erasmus, my very dear brother, I recently received your *Opus recens*, printed
at Antwerp. In this work you reply to my *Collations on the Epistle to the Ro-*
mans,[1] which I published last summer in defence of the old church ver-   5
sion.[2] I have read your book and carefully compared the proofs I adduced
in support of the authoritativeness of that translation with those which you

* * * * *

2 Sisyphus was a king whom the gods punished by compelling him to spend
  all eternity rolling a huge boulder up a hill, only to watch it roll back down
  again. 'Rolling the rock of Sisyphus' became proverbial for spending one's
  life in useless toil. See *Adagia* II iv 40.

2245
1 For both the *Opus recens* and Titelmans' *Collationes*, see Ep 2206 introduction.
2 Ie the Vulgate

attempt to adduce in this 'recent work' in defence of your criticisms and alterations.

Moreover, that Matthias, whom you like to slander in front of your devo- 10
tees as though he were one of your antagonists, is perhaps not so hostile
as you wrongly imagine.[3] You are extremely credulous, particularly where
the glory of your name is concerned. As for your statement that he brandishes his tongue like a javelin against Erasmus, I spent the whole of eighteen months under his instruction, but could never detect any hint of that. 15
And although, during that period, as part of his duties as warden, he often
addressed words of counsel to the brothers, I do not remember hearing anything from his lips during those eighteen months that was directed against
you, not even the smallest little word. Nor have I ever heard him mention
you in his public sermons. In fact it was he who carefully arranged for sev- 20
eral of your books on theological themes to be placed in the public library
of the friars and treated with respect, given decent bindings, placed in a
good position, and provided with impressive titles – I am thinking of all the
volumes of your revision of Jerome and your edition of the New Testament
along with the Annotations and Paraphrases. These things do not show him 25
as ill-disposed to you as you wrongly seem to imagine.
    I am aware of course that sometimes in meetings of the friars he likes
to impress upon his hearers, as he is obliged to do by the duties of his office, that they should not interest themselves in the latest trash from modern writers but attend to their studies and not waste the most precious days 30
of their lives on such things or inquire into pedantic irrelevancies. Nowadays many people are doing this, and they attract a number of eager followers, even among those who would be better employed devoting themselves
to more serious studies. It is now the normal and customary thing to give
the name 'Erasmians' to those who apply their energies to such things, pre- 35
sumably because they regard you as the leader, patron, and restorer of such
studies; so it is possible that when occasionally someone is heard to speak
out against these 'Erasmians,' he is believed to be 'brandishing his tongue
like a javelin against Erasmus.' I have sometimes heard him deliver a sermon to the friars against these people, for he feels responsible for the care 40
of his flock, as one who will render an account for their souls.[4] Clearly his
aim is to turn the minds of simple men away from the example of these

* * * * *

3 Matthias Weynsen, warden of the Antwerp Franciscans; see Ep 2205:236–9 with
  n39.
4 Heb 13:17

people so that they are not lured by their artifice and led unawares into error.

But Antwerp, which, as you say, has given him to us, has a very different 45
view of the exceptional talents of this man; as a result of his talents, many of
the inhabitants of this city acknowledge that life ought to be something of
the spirit, not the body. Above all they appreciate his zeal for truth, thanks
to which, as Antwerp recognizes, the city has been largely preserved among
the elect from the poison of pernicious dogma. You yourself are not unaware 50
of this, since you were here in Antwerp at the time when he was assiduously
denouncing that fugitive deserter, Jacob Proost, the condemned leader of the
heretics.[5]

These are the points I wished to make, brother Erasmus, after reading
through your little work in reply to mine. 55

And if you decide to reply to this new work of mine on the authority of the
Apocalypse (which I am sending to you along with this letter),[6] I ask this
one favour from you, that you say whatever you wish to say as truthfully as
you can without the sort of fabrications and deceptions that I noticed in your
earlier response and that (if our good Lord wills) I hope to illustrate more 60
clearly at an opportune moment. May you abound in God, most honoured
priest, and love me with a good heart, since I love you too with a true
affection.

Louvain, December 1529

* * * * *

5 Jacob Proost (Ep 1254 n4) became prior of the Augustinian house at Antwerp in 1518. In 1519 Erasmus praised him to Martin Luther as 'a genuine
Christian,' a devoted follower of the Wittenberg reformer, and 'almost the
only' Augustinian friar 'who preaches Christ.' At some point Proost went
off to Wittenberg to study, returning to Antwerp in the summer of 1521
with a licentiate in theology. When he preached Luther's doctrines he was
denounced by the Inquisition and forced to make a public recantation in
February 1522. In October 1521, on the eve of his departure for Basel (28
October), Erasmus spent several days in Antwerp 'harvesting' his imperial
pension (Epp 1302:28–9, 1342:100–2). This would appear to have been his
only chance to hear (or hear oral reports of) the denunciations of Proost by
Weynsen.
6 De authoritate libri Apocalypsis, presumably sent to Erasmus in manuscript. At
some point in 1530 the book was published by M. Hillen at Antwerp, with an
undated dedicatory letter to Erasmus (Ep 2417).

2246 / From Simon Riquinus [?], 1 January 1530

The autograph of this letter, which was first published as Ep 119 in Förstemann / Günther, was in the Burscher Collection at Leipzig (Ep 1254 introduction). The letter appears to have been written from the ducal court of Jülich-
Cleves, which would preclude Allen's conjectural choice of Cologne as the location (cf n11). But the duke and his entourage could have been in any number
of places in the United Duchies. Like the letter of Riquinus to Hermann von
Neuenahr mentioned in n10, this one could have been written from Benrath
(now part of the city of Düsseldorf), where the dukes had a castle.

Simon Riquinus (cf Ep 2077 n23) was probably born around 1502 and is
documented until 1547/8. He studied at Cologne for six years (1519–25), receiving his MA in 1522 and probably making a start in the study of medicine
as well. From 1525 to 1528 he was the headmaster of a school at Diest in Brabant. He next settled in Louvain, where he cultivated contacts with the faculty
of the Collegium Trilingue and presumably completed his medical education.
By September 1529 he had become the personal physician of Duke John III of
Jülich-Cleves. Although he and Erasmus may have known one another since
the latter's visit to Cologne in 1520, Riquinus is first mentioned in Erasmus'
correspondence in 1528 (Ep 2077), and the present letter is the first of the two
that constitute their surviving correspondence. The other is Ep 2298.

Cordial greetings. Your letter, delivered by Quirinus,[1] brought me both joy
and sorrow. You are wondering why, I suppose: well, cease to wonder. It
had to be a feast day (as the saying goes)[2] when someone as learned and
distinguished as you deigned to write to a quite undistinguished person
like me. At the same time I was deeply vexed because you have come to 5
suspect me of something, I know not what, although up to this point I have
preserved an unblemished innocence in all my actions.

Janus Cornarius is certainly an erudite man,[3] but utterly godless – he
published a learned but most impious speech, which he entitled 'The Crucified Bachelor.'[4] He is the only person in Basel who could have made such a 10
damaging remark about me, for I am sure there is no one else there whom
I have ever known by sight. I spent several years in Louvain, which is like

* * * * *

2246
1 See Ep 2222 n16. The letter is not extant.
2 Cf *Adagia* I ii 69.
3 On Cornarius, see Ep 2204 introduction.
4 Unidentified

an open theatre. There I took him into my house when he was a needy stranger. I remember that an immediate antipathy arose between him and my wife, who was terrified by the very sight of the man – she was like a 15 young fawn who has seen an elephant.[5] Moreover my wife, the most even-tempered of women, quarrelled with Cornarius because he never spoke of God with proper reverence, and when a sum of money was paid out on his behalf, he was unwilling to repay it in full. This perhaps explains his deep animosity towards me and mine, although outwardly he has always main- 20 tained the same demeanour towards me. Had I earlier detected in the man such an uncouth and godless nature, I would never have wished even to set eyes on such an ugly and detestable creature. Need I say more? I am not conscious in my own mind of having done any shameful act – unless perhaps he wants to accuse me of ignorance: that I readily acknowledge. 25

It was my intention to write at length on this subject to you, but I have changed my mind. For if by these few words I am unable to clear myself of suspicion, and if you will not accept the independent verdict on my character of such good and learned men as Goclenius, Rescius, Campen, the count of Neuenahr, and Heresbach,[6] I feel it would be a waste of time to go on at 30 length. But let this be! The unalterable affection that I feel for you I shall retain to my last breath.

The gift that the prince is sending you should not be judged by its value but by the good will that this generous man shows towards you, someone whom he greatly admires; he will continue to reveal himself to you more 35 liberally in the future.[7] If you wish, we shall endow Quirinus with a re-spectable living; you need only leave the matter in my hands. The prince is about to write to you through his assistant and will include an elegant little

* * * * *

5 For 'young fawn,' Riquinus writes *hinnulus*, the literal translation of which into English is the archaic word 'hinny' (the offspring of a male horse and a female donkey, ie the obverse of a mule). The image is that of a small, timid creature confronted with a large, aggressive one. 'Fawn' conveys the meaning better than either 'hinny' or 'mule.' Cf *Adagia* I iii 49, where CWE, on the authority of the parallel Greek adage, translates *Hinnulus leonem* as 'A fawn against a lion.'

6 Conradus Goclenius (Epp 1209, 1994A), Rutgerus Rescius (Ep 546), and Jan van Campen (Ep 1257 n12) were, respectively, the professors of Latin, Greek, and Hebrew at the Collegium Trilingue in Louvain; Hermann von Neuenahr (Epp 442, 1926) was provost and archdeacon of the Cologne cathedral chapter and chancellor of the University of Cologne; Konrad Heresbach (Ep 1316) was tutor to young William V of Cleves and an influential member of the ducal court.

7 The gift was from the young duke, William V; see Ep 2234:17–20.

gift.[8] Your recommendations, if I am not mistaken, would have been very
helpful with the people of Brabant if I had decided to make myself avail-   40
able.[9] I am sending a copy of our *Iudicium* on the new sweating sickness.[10]
It was written amid the noisy distractions of the court, so don't subject it to
a rigorous examination!

Farewell. But I ask you this one favour in the name of Heaven, that you
never suspect anything about your friend Riquinus other than that his life   45
and character are blameless and that he is as devoted a friend of Erasmus
as anyone could be. I hope that you in turn will not refuse to testify to your
feelings in your writing, when the occasion offers. The provost has now left
here.[11] He had waited eagerly for Quirinus. Farewell again, glory of the
world.   50

In haste, on the very first day of January, 1530
Simon Riquinus, your most devoted friend
To the most celebrated Master Erasmus of Rotterdam, theologian. In
Freiburg

2247 / From Jan Horák   Leipzig, 6 January 1530

This letter was first published as Ep 120 in Förstemann / Günther. The autograph, with address-sheet missing and the right margin damaged at the bottom
(see line 56), was in the Burscher Collection at Leipzig (Ep 1254 introduction).

Jan Horák (Johannes Hasenberg) was born near Hasenburk (Bohemia) in
the district of Litoměřice (north and west of Prague). He studied at Leipzig,
where he took his MA in 1523. At some point he attracted the favourable at-

* * * * *

8 The reference is to reigning duke, John III; the letter is not extant and there
  is no record of the gift. The 'assistant' was perhaps the chancellor, Johann
  Gogreve (Ep 2298 n5), or Johann von Vlatten (Epp 1390, 1948), who was (or
  would shortly become) the vice-chancellor.
9 There is no way of knowing what Riquinus is referring to here. Perhaps he
  considered some position in Louvain or elsewhere in Brabant before deciding
  to accept the call to the court of Jülich-Cleves.
10 *De novo hactenusque Germaniae inaudito morbo sudatoria febri, quem vulgo sudorem
  Britannicum vocant ... iudicium doctissimum* (Cologne: J. Soter, October 1529).
  The work consists of two letters: one from Hermann von Neuenahr to Riquinus, dated 7 September at Cologne; and one from Riquinus to Neuenahr, dated
  10 September at Benrath.
11 Ie Neuenahr; see n6 above. Allen took this reference as a sign that Riquinus
  was writing from Cologne, but it seems more likely that Neuenahr had now
  returned to Cologne from a visit to the ducal court in Jülich-Cleves.

tention of Duke George of Saxony, who in 1525 imposed him on an unwilling faculty of arts as its dean. By 1533 he was vice-chancellor of the university. In 1534 he returned to Litoměřice, where he founded a school for the children of the nobility. In April 1539 he assumed responsibility for the education of the children of King Ferdinand and spent the rest of his life in Ferdinand's service. In 1545 Ferdinand sent him to the Council of Trent, and in 1546–7 he accompanied the king on his invasion of Saxony during the war against the League of Schmalkalden. He died early in 1551 while attending the imperial diet in Augsburg.

During his Leipzig years Horák joined with others, particularly Johannes Cochlaeus (Ep 1928), in the production of abusive satires against Luther. Horák's were devoted principally to lampooning Luther's marriage to Katharina von Bora. In Ep 2143 Erasmus took polite exception to the violence of one of Horák's early efforts. Here, in lines 43–7, Horák acknowledges Erasmus' criticism in the painfully obsequious and affectedly elegant style that marks the entire letter.

With cordial greetings and the assurance of my readiness to serve you. Dear Erasmus, most eloquent among eminent scholars, although perhaps I am unknown to your Excellency, either by appearance or by name, I feel constrained to write to you, first, by reason of your virtue, which is lauded in sundry ways throughout the Christian world, and your astonishing and widely recognized erudition; second, by command of the illustrious Doctor Cochlaeus, a great friend of mine, who has succeeded to the position of my former patron Emser;[1] and finally, because of a gift sent by the erudite Doctor Conradus Wimpina.[2] Tell me, my dear Erasmus, is there anyone who would not be prodded and driven to write a letter by such a heavy battering on many fronts? But what influenced me most

5

10

* * * * *

2247
1 Ep 1928 n4
2 For the gift, see lines 25–37 below. Conradus Coci de Wimpina (d June 1531), who was born Konrad Koch at Buchen in the Odenwald, called himself de Wimpina after the town of Wimpfen on the Neckar, where his family had originated and where he later held a canonry. He studied at Leipzig (MA in 1484, doctorate in theology in 1503), and then in 1506 was appointed professor of theology at the newly founded University of Frankfurt an der Oder. He was an early and persistent defender of the traditional church against Luther and died a year after having voiced his opposition to Luther and his followers one last time at the Diet of Augsburg in 1530.

of all was your most civilized devotion to the Muses and (if I may say so without flattery) your heroic and Platonic virtues,[3] which could inspire even an insensate log to love them ungrudgingly. How, then, could they not have some effect on me, a poor creature from Bohemia, who am as 15 devoted and respectful an admirer of Erasmus as anyone could be? So, most honoured sir, for all that I am worth, I beseech and implore you of your kindness to think of me with the usual warmth of your generosity (for I believe you are acquainted with few other Bohemians)[4] if, perchance, by any service, or attention, or faithful act, or through mutual 20 friends, either here or in my native Bohemia, I might do something to find favour in your kindly heart. For such are my feelings towards your generous person that, even if I were dead, I would most eagerly try to serve you.

But with regard to the gift that the most learned Wimpina has sent you, 25 the situation is as follows. A few days ago he gave me instructions from Frankfurt an der Oder to send you as a gift a copy of his magnificent work either through the accomplished physician Auerbach,[5] or if not, through Hieronymus Walther.[6] Since there was no possibility that the book could be sent at present, I arranged with Walther for it to be taken to the next fair at 30 Frankfurt am Main. So it will be delivered to the Welsers' firm by Hieronymus Walther, a great admirer of your Excellency. You should claim the book from the Welsers' firm at an appropriate time. You will see, excellent and mighty Erasmus, what a great and distinguished work this is, full of godly and serious learning, fortified against heretics with the sharp edge of argument and Scripture, and heavily armed against the ludicrous absurdities 35 of Luther.[7] I do believe, dear Erasmus, that ten Anticyras full of hellebore

* * * * *

3 The heroic virtues are courage, fortitude, and so forth. By Platonic virtues Horák presumably means spiritual qualities like contemplation and the love of truth.
4 Other Bohemian friends were the now deceased Jan Šlechta (Ep 950) and Sigismundus Gelenius (Ep 1702 n1).
5 Ie Heinrich Stromer (Ep 1326)
6 Walther (documented 1508–37) was the agent in Leipzig for the Welser banking firm of Augsburg (Ep 2153 introduction). He was a member of the Leipzig city council from 1514 to 1536. A staunch Catholic, he enjoyed the favour of Duke George of Saxony and was a close friend of both Horák and Cochlaeus. Cf lines 49–50 below, where Horák refers to Walther as 'my patron.'
7 Judging by this description, the work in question was almost certainly *Sectarum errorum, hallutinationum … librorum partes tres* (Frankfurt an der Oder: n p 1528).

would scarcely be enough to cure that person.[8] So kind sir, greatest of all the Germans, I beg you by the sacred Muses to be pleased to accept this work in good part and to send us your truly Apollonian judgment on it,[9] 40 for Doctor Conradus Wimpina is very anxious to have this.

I was about to finish this letter when the following thought suddenly occurred to me. In the *Opus epistolarum*, in your last letter to Cochlaeus, kind and courteous though you are, you made a scarcely flattering mention of me.[10] I confess that, contrary to my natural moderation, I wrote some 45 strong words against a libellous publication of our evangelicals to defend my reputation;[11] the result may perhaps have come close to insolence. But whatever I may be, dear Erasmus, whom I love with all my heart, I commend myself to your kind and gentle nature along with Hieronymus Walther,[12] my patron and as staunch a defender of the Catholic faith here as you will find. 50 May you flourish, distinguished and gentle sir, to be a perpetual beacon and ornament to the church and to all Christians.

Leipzig, on the feast of the Magi 1530

Master Johannes Hasenberg Montanus,[13] canon of Prague and member of the Prince's College in Leipzig at ...[14] 55

* * * * *

8 The Greek town Anticyra was famous for its hellebore, a plant reputed to cure madness; see *Adagia* I viii 52.

9 Apollo was the god of prophecy and a patron of poetry and music. An 'Apollonian judgment' would be clear, reasonable, and well ordered. There is no record of Erasmus' reaction to the work.

10 Ep 2143:5–15

11 Horák's first foray against Luther had been the *Epistola Martino Ludero et suae parum legitimae uxori Catharinae a Bhor* ..., published in both Latin and German ([Leipzig]: [Valentin Schumann], c 10 August 1528). Luther responded with *New Zeittung von Leyptzig*, published at Wittenberg in late August but with no indication of author or publisher. Horák's reply to this, *Ad Luderanorum famosum libellum – Responsio* ([Leipzig]: n p, 30 September [1528]), is the work that elicited Erasmus' disapproval; cf Ep 2143 n2. Horák continued his attacks with a letter, dated 14 April 1529, that was included in Cochlaeus' *Septiceps Lutherus* (Ep 2120 n31) and a satirical play, *Ludus ludentem Luderum ludens* (Leipzig: [Michael Blum]) that has a dedicatory letter to Cochlaeus dated 1 May 1530.

12 See n6 above.

13 In Czech *horák* means 'mountaineer,' which in Latin is *montanus*.

14 The *Collegium principis* was one of the two masters' colleges (*Magisterkollegien*) founded in 1409 by the margrave of Meissen (before Meissen was absorbed into Saxony in 1423) as residences for those with master's degrees or higher who were members of the university.

2248 / From Bonifacius Amerbach   Basel, 9 January 1530

There are two hastily written rough drafts of this letter (= AK Ep 1405) in the Öffentliche Bibliothek of the University of Basel: MSS C VIa 54 40 and 73 173. Allen, who was the first to publish the letter, used as the basis for his text the draft that he judged to be that of the the letter actually sent (54 40) but recorded some of the variants in his apparatus.

I hope you won't think me a traitor, Erasmus, my distinguished friend, for not visiting you at Christmastime.[1] The reason was some difficulty with the countryfolk who collect firewood; this came to a head unexpectedly on 2 January, just when I was about to set out. Otherwise, neither bad weather nor the inconvenience of the journey would have kept me at home and prevented 5 me from going to pay my respects to you, best of masters. However, I bear this delay all the more lightly because I understand from our friend Frans van der Dilft that you are in good health.[2] I wish with all my heart that this may continue for a long time – indeed forever.

As for the situation in our city, I hardly know what I should say to 10 you. To make war on the images,[3] and then wreak havoc also on the sacristy, to put the churches' possessions up for auction for a paltry price,[4] to compel people to listen to sermons by imposing fines (and substantial fines at that),[5]

* * * * *

2248
1 See Ep 2223 n7.
2 Having returned to Freiburg from his journey to Besançon to fetch wine for Erasmus (Ep 2222 n15), Dilft was now preparing to set out for Spain; see Epp 2251–3.
3 See Ep 2097 n1.
4 The sale took place in December 1529; see Burckhardt Ep 51 n3. In the variant draft of this letter (Allen VIII 317) Amerbach refers to the sale of 'woollens and silks,' presumably church vestments, and imagines the citizens of Basel wearing these gorgeous materials 'as a mark of Christian humility.'
5 The *Reformationsordnung* of 1 April 1529 required regular attendance at Sunday sermons and imposed a fine of 'ein pfund pfennig' on those who absented themselves without good reason. See *Aktensammlung zur Geschichte der Basler Reformation in den Jahren 1519 bis Anfang 1534* ed Paul Roth 3 (Basel 1937) 403:20–9. One pfund pfennig was worth approximately 42 or 43 kreutzers (60 kreutzers = 1 florin or gulden). As Bonifacius indicates, that was a substantial fine. The value of the kreuzer, a silver coin that circulated widely in southern Germany, Switzerland, Austria, and Tyrol, was fixed by the imperial mint ordinance of 1551 at 4d, with 60 kreuzer to the imperial florin (*Von Aktie bis Zoll: Ein historisches Lexikon des Geldes* ed Michael North sv 'Kreuzer'). Forty-

and to introduce other measures of the same sort – if this is what is meant by
'the fruits of the gospel,' then we really are what we want to be called, 'true   15
evangelicals.' We narrowly escaped being forced to be present at Oecolampadius' table as well. This good man is so hospitable that he is hustling even
the unwilling to attend.[6] Under the pope they called this tyranny; now that
they are in control, they call it 'evangelical.' I often think, dear Erasmus, of
the kindly (or should I say, the fatherly) warning you used to give me: that   20
in your heart you could foresee nothing that was good.

With regard to my own affairs, I took the initiative from the start
by presenting to the university authorities the conditions under which I
could be retained here.[7] At that time they agreed to everything, adding
the hope that if I asked for more, I would get a sympathetic hearing. Now   25
I have learned from experience what Ovid means when he writes somewhere, 'Anyone can be rich in promises.'[8] For not only are their promises

* * * * *

three kreuzer were equivalent to about 30d groot Flemish, about three days'
wages for an Antwerp master mason or carpenter in 1526–30 at 9.05d per day
(CWE 12 691 Table 13).

6 By 'Oecolampadius' table' (an ironic allusion to 'the Lord's table') is meant the
new evangelical celebration of the Lord's Supper. Participation was not mandated by the *Reformationsordnung*. Soon, however, the pastors, supported by
the city council, began to argue that those who abstained from taking communion were not doing their duty as Christians or as good citizens; cf Epp
2281:9–10, 2312:6–11, 2321:43–52. On 18 June 1530 those members of the city
council who had not participated in the reformed Eucharist were forbidden
to stand for re-election, and by the end of the month a systematic inquiry was
under way into the conduct of ordinary citizens who had not taken part. An
edict of 23 April 1531 imposed on recalcitrant non-communicants the penalty
of excommunication. Bonifacius' refusal to participate in the evangelical ceremony persisted until 1534 and came close to causing his excommunication,
which would have entailed the loss of his professorship and his expulsion
from the city. This unhappy outcome was avoided, in part because the municipal authorities were eager to retain Bonifacius' services, and also in part
because he placated the authorities by adopting a view of the Real Presence
in the sacrament virtually identical with that formulated by Martin Bucer in
1534 in his (ultimately successful) attempt to reach an accommodation with
Luther and Melanchthon. For details, see Burckhardt 78–103, and *Das Buch der
Basler Reformation* ed Ernst Staehelin (Basel 1929) 236–8.

7 The conditions, which included a substantial raise in pay and exemption from
participation in evangelical worship, were set out in a letter submitted to the
Basel city council at the beginning of June 1529; see AK Ep 1356, and cf Ep
2180 n5.

8 *Ars amatoria* 1.444

not kept, but even the exemptions that were granted to professors many
generations back are being taken away.[9] But more of this when we meet.
Farewell Erasmus, my distinguished friend and incomparable master.   30
  Basel, 9 January [15]30

2249 / To Giambattista Egnazio   [Freiburg, c January] 1530

This letter was first published in the *Epistolae floridae*. Allen's conjectural month-
date is strongly supported by the reference in lines 22–3 to the expected arrival of the emperor in Germany, which parallels a similar reference in the
more securely dated Ep 2250 (see n7), and the reference in line 30 to the 'villainy of monks' in Brabant, which has its counterpart in three clearly dated
letters of January–February 1530 (see n8).

For Egnazio, the Venetian humanist whom Erasmus had known and admired
for many years, see Ep 2105 introduction.

ERASMUS OF ROTTERDAM TO BATTISTA EGNAZIO, GREETING
I have learned from a letter of that distinguished young man Uutenhove that
you hold the dignified position of professor of humane letters at Venice.[1] It is
great news that this field of study is flourishing everywhere, but I fear that,
by the actions of a few, learning will be ruined by conflicts no less bitter than   5
those that have harmed religion. There is much gnashing of teeth because
my *Ciceronianus* is critical of those who ape Cicero ineptly and urges them
towards a genuine imitation of the master.[2] Some Frenchmen are lashing out
against me in malicious little poems because I named Budé and Bade on the
same page;[3] they are as angry as if I had peed on his face, though I have   10
always given Budé's reputation my warm and constant support, precisely
because of his contribution to learning, which he has advanced so fruitfully
and now adorns magnificently. As far as I am concerned, I owe him nothing
except to reciprocate our friendship. Think of the many passages throughout

* * * * *

9 The traditional exemptions were from menial tasks like guard duty and militia
  service. Bonifacius had stipulated that these were to apply to him; see AK Ep
  1356:8–14.

2249
1 Karel Uutenhove's letter, which is not extant, is also mentioned in Ep 2209:1.
2 See Ep 1948.
3 For the uproar over the joke about Budé and Bade in the *Ciceronianus*, see
  Ep 2021 introduction. For the malicious verses (by Janus Lascaris and Jacques
  Toussain) see Epp 2027:25–8, 2077:10–16, 2119, 2223:6–9.

my works where I mention him in the most affectionate terms![4] And even   15
in the *Ciceronianus* itself, though the mention is brief, what a warm tribute
I pay him![5]

I left Basel and moved to Freiburg, for I was afraid that after they had
plundered the churches, they would arrive at my house, and when they had
vented their rage on the statues of the saints, they would jump on real living   20
people.[6]

I fear that the arrival of the emperor will cause a bloody revolution in
Germany.[7] Several cities are preparing for the worst. I know that the emperor's power is great. But the majority everywhere are committed to the
new sects, as are almost all the peasants, who have not forgotten their ear-   25
lier defeat. Once the signal is given, those who are now quiet will perhaps
join in. We are all seeking revenge: no one even dreams of changing his
life. I think that there would be more chance of success if the pope placed
his hopes in the protection of Christ rather than in a bevy of cardinals, in
the weapons of princes, and in the villainy of monks, whose behaviour pro-   30
vided the seedbed for our present troubles. These men are now tyranniz-
ing over Brabant, and from time to time they burn their sacrificial victims.[8]

* * * * *

4 Particularly in the Annotations to the *Novum instrumentum* of 1516, but in a
few other places as well; see Ep 2046:104–6 with n14. There is, however, little
evidence of 'affection' in any of Erasmus' letters to Budé.
5 For Erasmus' revision of the passage at which Budé and his admirers took
offence, see CWE 28 587 n676.
6 See Ep 2097 n1.
7 Cf Ep 2250:31–5. Charles was still in Italy, but his plans to return to Germany
(Ep 2240 n8) were known, and his summons to the German estates to attend a
diet in Augsburg would be dated 21 January 1530. Meanwhile, ever since the
Diet of Speyer in the spring of 1529, the Protestant cities and principalities
had been preparing to defend themselves against a possible attack on them
by the emperor and the Catholic princes; see Ep 2219 n10.
8 Cf Epp 2256:7–8, 35–6, 69–71; 2263:111; 2268:4–6. The reference to the burning
of 'sacrificial victims' appears to be Erasmus' reaction to the news that in the
Netherlands, on 14 October 1529, Charles v had issued a new decree against
heresy. The decree attempted to remove from the municipal and provincial officials in charge of prosecuting heretics the discretion to determine the severity
of punishment. The death penalty was mandated for all who had not brought
their Lutheran books to be burned or had otherwise violated previous edicts.
Relapsed heretics were to be burned at the stake. Otherwise, men were to
be beheaded and women buried alive. Death and forfeiture of goods were
also prescribed for those who harboured or concealed a heretic. One heretic,
already condemned and imprisoned, was immediately brought out and exe-
cuted at The Hague. Otherwise, the reluctance of officials to impose the ulti-

Here many are worried about what the Turk will do next,[9] for there is no doubt that he fears the steadily increasing power of the two brothers.[10]

There is peace nowhere, no road is safe; people are suffering every-   35 where from the high cost of living, and from poverty, hunger, and plague; the whole world is torn apart by sects. To this Lerna of troubles[11] has now been added the deadly sweating sickness,[12] which carries off many of its victims within eight hours and to those who escape it often returns after a brief interval, not just once, but twice, three times, four times until it turns   40 into dropsy or the plague or some other kind of illness and finally snuffs out the patient, who has suffered the most painful torment. Yet, unlike the Phrygians, we do not become better after so many blows.[13]

The man who, I expect, will deliver this letter is Johann Herwagen.[14] He married Johann Froben's widow and has succeeded him in the task of   45 restoring good authors. He is reliable and not without learning. If you can assist him in any way without inconveniencing yourself, I have no doubt that, with your usual courtesy, you will gladly do what you can for the cause of learning.[15]

Farewell. 1530   50

2250 / To Juan Maldonado   Freiburg, 13 January [1530]

> This is the first of six letters (2250–2, 2253–5), all first published in the *Epistolae floridae*, that were carried to Spain by Frans van der Dilft (see Ep 2255:3–5). In the *Epistolae floridae*, two of the letters (2251–2) have the year-date 1530, while three (2250, 2254–5) have 1531. On several grounds, however, Allen firmly placed all six of the letters in 1530: five of them (all but the present letter) name

* * * * *

mate penalty continued. See James D. Tracy *Holland under Habsburg Rule, 1506–1566: The Formation of a Body Politic* (Berkeley 1990) 159–60. 'Villainous monks' may well have approved of this harsh policy but, contrary to what Erasmus indicates, they were not its authors or its enforcers.

9 See Ep 2211 n9.
10 Ie Emperor Charles and King Ferdinand. On their 'steadily increasing power' see Ep 2211 n12.
11 *Adagia* I iii 27. The swamps of Lerna near Argos were home to the hydra, the many-headed serpent that grew two heads to replace every one that was cut off. Hercules eventually killed it with the aid of his nephew, Iolaus, who cauterized the neck-stumps as soon as Hercules had cut off the heads.
12 See Ep 2209:110–89 with n31.
13 *Adagia* I viii 36; cf Ep 2209:194–9, 2285:14–18.
14 Ep 2231 n5.
15 Herwagen had gone off to Venice in search of manuscripts. He returned to Basel between 23 March (Ep 2288:2–3) and 31 March (Ep 2302:28–9).

Dilft as the bearer; this letter and Ep 2253 both mention Erasmus' move to Freiburg in April 1529 as something recent; and Ep 2253 mentions that the Froben
edition of Chrysostom (Ep 2359) is expected to be published in the autumn.

On Juan Maldonado, humanist scholar and vicar-general at Burgos, see Epp
1742 and 1805.

ERASMUS OF ROTTERDAM TO MALDONADO, GREETING

I received your letter, dearest Maldonado; in fact I received two letters,[1] both
with the same text except that you had added a postscript to the later one.
Let me reply to it very briefly. Some time ago I responded to that very long
letter of yours,[2] in which, acting as a sort of spokesman for your friends,   5
you described one or two scenes from the painful melodrama created by
the monks,[3] with an even longer letter of my own.[4] As soon as I discovered
that my letter had not reached you, I sent you a second copy,[5] and I would
not regard it as an imposition to send a third, but moving house has thrown
all my effects into such a state of confusion that a lot of things have van-   10
ished[6] (you know I left Basel at considerable personal expense, but, thank
God! without harming my health).[7] What I wrote in those letters is now
such stale news that it would not be worthwhile starting a thorough hunt
for them. I wonder what went wrong. This much is absolutely certain, that I
sent the letter twice. The last thing I would suspect is that the problem was   15
caused by Valdés' carelessness,[8] for I can imagine no one more honourable
or friendly than that young man. I have no doubt that those mountebanks in
your country are continuing to act out the remaining scenes of their melodrama. But I am so fed up with these miserable tussles that I do not want
to know even about those that affect me personally. Let the Lord do with   20
me whatever seems good to him, provided, as the saying goes, we keep the
tiller steady.[9]

When you congratulate me on my many splendid achievements and
my special gifts, I wish, my dear Maldonado, that this said as much about

* * * * *

2250
1 Neither is extant.
2 Ep 1742
3 See Ep 1791 introduction.
4 Ep 1805
5 Cf Epp 1908 n9, 1971:1–8.
6 Cf Epp 2143:5, 2253:4.
7 See Ep 2209 n12.
8 Alfonso de Valdés (Ep 1807); see Ep 1805 introduction.
9 *Adagia* III i 28; according to Erasmus the adage means that no one can be
  blamed for the outcome of an action if he has done what is required of him.

my merits as about your generosity and eloquence. The deadly conflicts that   25
now divide the world, these grim disasters that seem to have no end or limit,
the last always followed by something worse, a degree of wickedness in the
world that has not been seen before, these things have almost turned me
against all learning, not just against this kind of gladiatorial contest.[10] I have
already retired from the arena.[11] I hand on the torch to younger men like   30
you. There are many things here that threaten future trouble. In preparation
for the arrival of the emperor those who owe allegiance to the new sects are
so busy strengthening their defences that if I cared for nothing but my own
safety, I would hardly know on which side I would rather be. I pray that
the Lord will bring all to a happy conclusion. Unless he takes a part in the   35
drama, I fear it will have a bloody ending. Farewell, and continue to love
me as you do.

Freiburg im Breisgau, 13 January 1531[12]

2251 / To [Juan de] Valdés   Freiburg, 13 January 1530

This letter was first published in the *Epistolae floridae*. There is nothing in the
salutations of this letter or Ep 2252 to distinguish between the brothers Valdés.
But the brother whom Erasmus hoped to see in Germany in the spring (lines
4–5) can only have been Alfonso, the emperor's Latin secretary. The recipient
of this letter must therefore be Juan (Ep 1961).

ERASMUS OF ROTTERDAM TO VALDÉS, GREETING
There is nothing that I do not owe to your brother, my dearest Valdés, for he
knows no limit in his love for me and in the way he defends and supports
me. In his absence it is only right that you take the place of your brother,
whom I hope to see here next spring.[1] I readily forgive you for not respond-   5
ing to my letter,[2] provided you respond in reciprocating my love, as I am

* * * * *

10 Erasmus was fond of describing the conflicts with his critics as gladiatorial
   combat; see Epp 1934 n1, 1943 n4.
11 Literally 'I have already presented myself with the wooden sword,' a reference to the practice of presenting a gladiator on his retirement with a wooden
   sword; see *Adagia* I ix 24 and cf Ep 2143 n10.
12 On the year-date of the letter, see the introduction above.

2251
 1 Alfonso was in Italy in the entourage of Emperor Charles and would accompany him to Germany in the spring; see Ep 2109 nn4, 15.
 2 Ep 1961

sure you do, unless I am totally mistaken. I shall not bother you with a
longer letter; you will find out the rest of our news from Frans van der
Dilft,[3] who, having once fallen in love with Spain, cannot leave it. Farewell.

Freiburg im Breisgau, 13 January 1530   10

2252 / To [Alfonso de] Valdés   Freiburg, 13 January 1530

> This letter was first published in the *Epistolae floridae*. As was the case with Ep
> 2251, Erasmus does not indicate which of the brothers Valdés is the intended
> addressee. But since Ep 2251 has to be the letter to Juan, this letter can only
> be the one intended for his brother Alfonso (Ep 1807).

ERASMUS OF ROTTERDAM TO VALDÉS, GREETING
I have not yet been able to discover, my dear friend, whether you received
my last letter.[1] I hear complaints from several people about letters being
intercepted or delivered irresponsibly. I had written to you at considerable
length. I had also sent a bundle of letters to the Right Reverend bishop of   5
Burgos when he was on a diplomatic mission to England;[2] I asked him to see
that they were delivered to Spain, and he replied that he would look after it.

    There is no need for me to write now at length since I have obtained
Frans van der Dilft as courier;[3] you will be able to find out from him, better
than from me, everything that is going on here. He is articulate, a man of   10
proven honesty, one of my closest friends, and a member of my household
– and he is not unknown to you. He never ceases praising you in my presence for the courtesy and kindness you showed him. From him I fished out
all about you and your brothers – your health, your fortunes, your mind
and character. He gave me such a detailed picture that I know all of you as   15
well as if I had spent a year in your company. In short, even though you
have always been very dear to me, he has made you dearer still; moreover,
any service you did for him I consider as a service to myself. So although
his first visit to Spain did not turn out altogether happily for him, it was
very fortunate for me. But if the old saying can be trusted, 'Better luck next   20

* * * * *

3 See Ep 2222 n15.

2252
1 A recent exchange of letters between Valdés and Erasmus has not survived;
  for traces of it see Ep 2198 introduction.
2 See Ep 2163:5 with n2.
3 Ep 2222 n15

time!'[4] To have van der Dilft with you will add considerably to my blessings, for I could confidently trust anything to him; in fact without being asked he will look out for anything that seems to further my interests or reputation. So just as I have wormed out of him everything I wanted to know about affairs in Spain, it will now be your turn to dig out of him whatever you want   25
to hear about the situation here. Farewell.

13 January 1530, Freiburg im Breisgau

2253 / To Juan de Vergara   [Freiburg, c 13 January 1530]

This letter was first published in the *Epistolae floridae*. For Allen's assignment of the approximate date, see Ep 2050 introduction. On Vergara, who was secretary to Alonso de Fonseca, archbishop of Toledo, see Epp 1277, 1814.

ERASMUS OF ROTTERDAM TO JUAN DE VERGARA, THEOLOGIAN,
GREETING

I had decided to send four sets of the works of Augustine to your part of the world,[1] but the move threw all my affairs into confusion, and no one came along who was willing to undertake the job of transporting such a trouble-   5
some burden. Moreover, I believe these volumes have been on sale in your country for some time, and it would be foolish to ask for copies to be purchased there at my expense for presentation to such friends as you. I was well aware how much I owed to the kindness of that most kindly prelate,[2] or more accurately, to the devotion he feels for me. His gift,[3] however, was   10
particularly gratifying because it was a pledge and indication of his feelings towards me. I apportioned the money scrupulously among those who had helped me in collation and writing so that there was not a single ducat left over for me – in fact I added something from my own money. As a result several people, not just Erasmus, have reason to be grateful for the arch-   15
bishop's generosity.[4] If I find that my efforts meet with his approval, that will be the real triumph.

* * * * *

4 *Adagia* I iii 38

2253
1 The ten-volume Froben Augustine of 1529 (Ep 2157)
2 Alonso de Fonseca, archbishop of Toledo (Ep 1748), to whom the edition of Augustine was dedicated
3 See Ep 2208 n11.
4 See Ep 2126 n58.

Chrysostom is now well in hand and will appear next autumn in an equally splendid format.[5] It will contain some new pieces, translated partly by me and partly by others. There are, however, some spurious works among them, including, in my opinion, the Commentary on the Epistle to the Hebrews and those on the Second Epistle to the Corinthians and the Acts of the Apostles;[6] it seems that a precedent for the desecration of sacred texts has come down to us from the Greeks.

The cardinal of York has so seriously offended the king that he has been stripped of his property and all his offices and is being held, not in prison, but in one of the king's palaces with no more than thirty people, acting either as servants or as guards, in attendance. Countless charges are being levelled against him, so that it is thought he cannot escape the death penalty. Such is the play of Fortune![7] He was elevated from the schoolroom to a position of royal power, for he was more truly king than the king himself. He was feared by all, loved by few (perhaps by no one). A few days before he was arrested, he had Richard Pace thrown into prison[8] and was threatening even my friend the archbishop of Canterbury.[9] 'The spirit is exalted before a fall,' says Solomon.[10] The archbishop of Canterbury was called, or rather recalled, to the chancellorship, the highest office in England. But he excused himself on grounds of age, feeling already unequal to so great a burden.[11] The office was given, therefore, to Thomas More amid general applause;[12] his elevation gave no less pleasure to all good men than did the fall of the cardinal. I learned all this from my servant, who has recently returned from England.[13]

With regard to my own situation and the general situation in Germany, since it is a long story, it is better that you hear it from the lips of Frans van

* * * * *

5 See Ep 2359.
6 Cf Epp 2253A:33–7, 2261:54–6, 2359. Modern scholarship affirms the attribution of the works in question to Chrysostom.
7 See Ep 2237:22–3 with n2.
8 In the summer of 1528 Erasmus reported rumours that Richard Pace (Ep 1955) had been imprisoned for having written something scurrilous about Cardinal Wolsey; see Epp 2031:10–18, 2033:66–73. In reality, however, Pace was in custodial confinement because of the illness from which he never fully recovered. See LP 4 no 4927 (14 November 1528), and cf Ep 2287.
9 It is not known what basis Erasmus had for thinking this.
10 Prov 16:18
11 This rumour appears to be confirmed by no other source. Warham had been lord chancellor from 1504 to 1515.
12 See Ep 2228.
13 Quirinus Talesius; see Ep 2222 n16.

Thomas More
Hans Holbein the Younger
By permission of the Honourable Society of Lincoln's Inn

der Dilft,[14] for none of my affairs is a secret to him. He lived with me for
several months – I only wish I could have enjoyed his company longer. But   45
he is smitten with a strange longing for his beloved Spain, although he has
an honourable station in his own country and was born to a wealthy family.
But there is something of Ulysses in him,[15] and with his love of freedom he
dreads the matrimonial halter. I have seen much to convince me that he is a
young man of considerable ability, very able in the management of affairs,   50
lacking neither in eloquence nor common sense, utterly trustworthy, and
very affectionate towards his friends. I would not wish, dear Vergara, to put
pressure on you with my commendation, but if you can further his interests
without inconvenience to your own, you will put me further in your debt by
your kind offices and, if I am not totally mistaken, your assistance will not   55
be misplaced. In this I am acting partly in my own interest, for I shall have
a second self in Spain, who will look out for me as attentively as I would
myself. He will fit in well to a place in the empress's court,[16] for that is his
ambition. His handwriting is neat, and when he puts his mind to it he has
a good literary style, so much so that I could not do better myself. If some   60
people had favoured his suit as I wished, he would not have left Spain. But
what a dreadfully brazen person I am! Although I owe everything to you
and am giving nothing in return, here I am demanding your help just as if
you were in my debt.

If I had not been lucky enough to find such a courier as this, I would   65
have written to you about various matters, but my friend Dilft will be as
good as several letters. He never stops telling me how much he owes to
you and to your brothers.[17] He has painted such a complete picture of your
patron that I admire and love him more than ever.

There has been a persistent rumour here that the archbishop of Toledo   70
has met his end.[18] When the news came and appeared to be convincing, I felt
a sharp pang of sorrow in my heart. The Augustine was not then complete, so
it would have been possible to dedicate this onerous undertaking to someone
else. Nevertheless I never wavered in my intention to dedicate to his memory the work that I had destined for him when he was alive. In a letter from   75

* * * * *

14 The bearer of the letter; see Ep 2250 introduction.
15 Ulysses symbolizes the wanderer, eager to learn of men and places; see Homer
   Odyssey 1.3 and cf Ep 1972:2–3.
16 See Ep 2208 n7.
17 Francisco de Vergara (Ep 1876) and Bernardino Tovar (Ep 2004 n11).
18 Cf Epp 2208:13–16, 2253A:1–8.

Valdés,[19] however, I received the news that wiped away all my grief. In the expanded edition of my letters[20] you will find your name several times and the names of your brothers and of the archbishop. I hope he will be happy with this – I have no doubts as to how you and your brothers will feel.

2253A / To [Alonso de Fonseca]   Freiburg, 13 January 1530

This letter was first published by Giovanni Maria Bertini in *Convivium: Rivista di lettere, filosofia et storia* 9 (1937) 44–52, on the basis of a copy supplied to him by the Spanish scholars Miguel Batllori and Justo Bona. The copy had been made from the original manuscript that at the time was preserved in the Cistercian Abbey of Veruela, near Zaragoza. The Spanish Civil War, and then the Second World War, made the original manuscript inaccessible to Bertini. The current location of the manuscript, if it has survived, is unknown. Bertini drew his edition of the letter to the attention of Helen Mary Allen, the widow of P.S. Allen, and H.W. Garrod, who together had assumed responsibility for completing Allen's edition of the correspondence. With Bertini's permission, they printed the letter as Ep 2253a in Allen XI xxvii–xxix.

In the copy, the letter is addressed in Spanish to Ferdinand of Aragon (grandson of King Ferdinand the Catholic), a monk in the Cistercian monastery at Nuévalos who in 1531 would become abbot of Veruela and then in 1539 archbishop of Zaragoza. But it was not to him that Erasmus wrote the letter. There is no evidence that Erasmus ever knew Ferdinand, and in any case, he would never have addressed as prelate (*praesul*) someone who in 1530 was a mere Cistercian monk. As the opening lines of the letter make clear, it was addressed to Alonso de Fonseca, archbishop of Toledo. The date and the contents, moreover, coincide so closely with those of Epp 2250–5 as to preclude doubt that this was one of the letters in the packet carried to Spain by Frans van der Dilft. The address on the copy, therefore, indicates only that at some point the letter was forwarded by Fonseca to Ferdinand of Aragon at Veruela.

Cordial greetings. Most reverend prelate, there was a remarkably persistent rumour here that the archbishop of Toledo had died,[1] submitting to the laws

* * * * *

19 Not extant. It was presumably one of the packet of letters from Spain mentioned in Ep 2241:28.
20 The *Opus epistolarum*; see Ep 2203.

2253A
1 Cf Epp 2208:13–16, 2253:70–6.

of God and of nature; the story was gathering strength here and had nearly
knocked the life out of us. I grieved more for my own loss and for that of
many others who are supported by your kindness, honoured by your high 5
position, and delighted by your success, but I grieved much more because
the empress's court had lost such an eminent leader,[2] Spain such an ornament, and the church so great a prelate. I felt this sorrow in common with
all good men. Meanwhile St Augustine was rapidly nearing the finishing
post; all that remained was my preface. Friends were asking to whom the 10
work should be dedicated now that we had reason to believe that you had
departed from this earth. But I did not hesitate. 'However much others may
regard him as dead,' I said, 'as far as I am concerned, he is still alive. Let the
work that was intended to honour him when he was alive on earth honour
his memory now that he is enjoying a more blessed life in heaven. With this 15
small courtesy I, his devoted protégé, shall pay my last respects to a most
generous patron.' I think that the *Augustine* had reached Spain before letters
arrived from friends that revived our fainting spirits. The first of my correspondents was our friend Valdés, who wrote from Italy to say that not so
long ago he had received a personal letter written in your own hand.[3] I tell 20
you this, most illustrious prelate, so that you will not wonder why I have
not sent you copies of the work. I had decided to send five sets, one to you,
a second to Juan de Vergara,[4] a third to the archbishop of Seville,[5] a fourth
to Valdés, and the fifth to the chancellor Mercurino.[6] Shortly afterwards I
heard of the emperor's departure and of your death.[7] I was no longer res- 25
ident in Basel, and there was no one available here on whose help I could
rely, so as a consequence none of the volumes was dispatched. I know that,
with your characteristic kindness, you will say that an apology from me is
quite unnecessary. I thank you for the gift you sent, as do all those with
whom I shared your generosity – shared so widely, in fact, that (so help 30
me!) I did not leave a cent for myself, and even contributed something of
my own.[8] If I hear that the result is good enough to earn your vote of approval, I shall not regret the hard work that was put into it. Chrysostom,
that most eloquent of preachers, is now in hand; a complete text will see the

* * * * *

2 See Ep 2208:15–16.
3 See Ep 2253 n19.
4 Ep 2253
5 Alonso Manrique de Lara (Ep 1846)
6 Gattinara (Ep 1150)
7 The emperor departed from Spain for Italy on 27 July 1529; see Ep 2208 n12.
8 Cf Ep 2253:10–16.

light of day in a comparably splendid edition, in fact it is not just a complete   35
text, but has several pieces added to it, some translated by me and some by
other scholars.[9]

There is a fierce uproar in Brabant ...[10] Here the expectation of the
emperor's arrival affects people in different ways. Some think of nothing
but revenge and the restoration of former control. Others are strengthening   40
their position with alliances,[11] just as I, if I did not regard the saving of my
soul as more important than the saving of my body, would prefer to be in
the camp of those from whom I fled of my own free will; and I do not regret
that I left, though the move caused me considerable trepidation, some danger, and heavy expense; it did, however, no damage to my health.[12] Not all   45
of the troublesome peasants have yet been quelled, nor are the priests trying to lessen their unpopularity among the laity by changing their lives; the
monks, in fact, are making things worse. Meanwhile the Turks are coming
closer; they have suspected for some time that the power of the emperor and
of Ferdinand is growing every day, and they have been stung by the recent   50
defeat of their forces.[13] At the same time the count Palatine with the help of
the landgrave of Hessen is making warlike moves against the archbishop of
Mainz.[14] This stands in the way of my returning to Brabant; for some time
I have been contemplating going there, hoping to find a safe haven from

* * * * *

9 Erasmus appears to be making the illogical claim that he has made additions to
   something already complete. What he no doubt means to say is that his Latin
   edition of Chrysostom will include all the extant works that have already been
   published in Latin, with the addition of works not previously translated from
   the Greek. See Allen Ep 2359:52–64.
10 The gap in the manuscript precludes certainty about what Erasmus is referring to here: probably the 'villainy of monks' in Brabant (see Ep 2249:30–2
   with n8), but possibly his controversy with Frans Titelmans (see Ep 2206), or
   both.
11 Emperor Charles was expected back in Germany in the spring of 1530, with the
   settlement of the religious divisions there at the top of his agenda. While hard-
   line defenders of the traditional church wanted harsh action against heresy, the
   Protestant estates were busy forging an alliance to defend themselves against
   any such action. See Ep 2219 n10.
12 See Ep 2209 n12.
13 See Ep 2211 nn9, 12.
14 Cf Ep 2256:18–19. The electorates of Mainz and the Palatinate had a long history of border disputes. The details of the dispute in question are not known,
   but we do know that in February 1530 the landgrave of Hessen attempted to
   mediate a friendly settlement by summoning a conference to be held at Darmstadt on 14 March. See *Politisches Archiv des Landgrafen Philipp des Grossmütigen
   von Hessen: Inventar der Bestände* ed Friedrich Küch 1 (Marburg 1904; repr Osna-
   brück 1965) 163 no 250.

the present storms.[15] But the situation among the nations everywhere has   55
become so inflamed that many people fear where these worldwide conflicts
are taking us.

On top of all these misfortunes we have the sweating sickness,[16] a
dreadful disease that is highly contagious; it quickly snuffs out those whom
it has seized, and if someone recovers, the disease returns again and again,   60
often transforming itself into one type of illness or another until it buries its
tormented victim. I think the Egyptians were punished with fewer and gentler plagues, and yet no one seems to me to recognize the hand of the Lord
and change his life for the better. Here, as the saying goes, I am caught between the altar and the knife,[17] and can only wait upon the pleasure of the   65
Lord. You will learn from Frans van der Dilft,[18] whom I wish to commend
to your Lordship's friendship, the long involved tale of the cardinal of England;[19] he will also inform you about my present state and give you all the
rest of my news. He is a young man who holds by birth a most honoured
position among his own people. He has very great ability, exceptional learn-   70
ing, and good sense beyond his years. All of these qualities I have observed
myself, for he shared my household. If your Lordship judges him worthy
of your favour, you will of course make him happy and you will put me
under an even greater obligation, though I have long been deeply in your
debt. Any favour you bestow on him I shall consider as done to me. What he   75
is aiming for you will learn more fully from Juan de Vergara, for I have explained the whole business to him.[20] May the Lord Jesus long preserve you
for us, Most Reverend Archbishop. If there is any task it may please you to
impose upon me, I shall regain my youth and do as you wish.

Freiburg im Breisgau, 13 January in the year of our Lord 1530   80
Your Lordship's obedient servant
Erasmus of Rotterdam. I signed this in my own hand.

2254 / To Francisco de Vergara   Freiburg, 13 January [1530]

This letter was first published in the *Epistolae floridae*, where the year-date (line
24 below) is incorrect; see Ep 2250 introduction. Francisco de Vergara (Ep

* * * * *

15 See Ep 2222 n9.
16 See Ep 2209 n31.
17 Literally 'between the shrine and the stone' (*Adagia* i i 15); cf *Adagia* i i 16
   'Between the shrine and the anvil.'
18 See Ep 2222 n15.
19 See Ep 2253:25–34.
20 See Ep 2253:42–64.

1876), the brother of Juan de Vergara (Ep 2133), was professor of Greek at Alcalá and, like his brother, an ardent Erasmian.

ERASMUS OF ROTTERDAM TO FRANCISCO VERGARA, GREETING
My dear Vergara, I appreciated the very courteous reception you gave to my friend Dilft, the bearer of this letter,[1] although he was unknown to you and a stranger, and I admired that warm heart of yours, of which I had experience myself in the past; but there has been a special pleasure in recalling the   5
memory of it on this occasion. A fine mind and spirit like yours deserved to be accommodated in the most favoured of dwellings, but such is the life of man that nothing is happy for long or blessed in every aspect.[2] We are told that men who are distinguished by outstanding qualities of mind have generally suffered from ill health.[3] But after the clouds will come the calm,   10
and if it does not, much of the affliction disappears if you are blessed with a brave and contented mind. I hope, however, that better news of you will reach us soon.

     A new plague, which was formerly peculiar to Britain alone, has suddenly spread over the whole world.[4] Since the disease, when it first appeared,   15
was sudden and frightful, killing its victim within twenty-four hours, often in less, it struck such terror into everyone that in many cases fear and imagination helped on the disease. It has affected a large number of people, but it kills fewer than that other epidemic which the world knows all too well.[5] Later hardly anyone died unless through the ignorance of physicians or ne-   20
glect of the sick. If this plague has not reached Spain, that is something for genuine congratulations. May the Lord bring you back to us safe and well, dearest Vergara.
     Freiburg im Breisgau, 13 January 1531[6]

2255 / To Giovanni and Bernardo Boerio   Freiburg, 13 January [1530]

     This letter was first published in the *Epistolae floridae*, where the year-date (line 20 below) is incorrect; see Ep 2250 introduction. Learning that Frans

* * * * *

2254
1 See Ep 2222 n15.
2 Horace *Odes* 2.16.28
3 For Vergara's bout of ill health, see Epp 2004:52–5, 2125:2–3, 24–5.
4 See Ep 2209:106–84 with n31.
5 Ie the long-familiar bubonic plague; see Epp 2009:74–5, 2219:5–6, 2225:4–5.
6 The correct year-date is 1530; see introduction above.

van der Dilft was planning to embark at Genoa on his journey to Spain,
Erasmus decided to take the opportunity to write to his former pupils, Giovanni and Bernardo Boerio, whom he knew to be living in their native city
of Genoa. Giovanni and Bernardo were the sons of Giovanni Battista Boerio
(Ep 267), physician to Henry VII and later to Henry VIII. The father had hired
Erasmus to accompany the boys to Italy in 1506 (Ep 194:33n). On 15 March
1530 Bernardo replied to this letter with one that is not extant; see Allen Ep
2481:34.

ERASMUS OF ROTTERDAM TO GIOVANNI AND BERNARDO BOERIO,
GREETING

Frans van der Dilft, the bearer of this letter,[1] is a young man endowed with
many talents, who enjoys an honourable station in his own country, and
who has won my deep affection on many counts. When he decided to sail 5
to Spain from your city, I thought I should not make the mistake of letting
such a good opportunity slip by. So among his various commissions I told
him to visit you and convey to you my best wishes. If you have any curiosity
about Erasmus' doings, you will be able learn everything from him, for, as
a member of my household, he has enjoyed a close friendship with me for 10
some time.

    A tiny cloud descended on the friendship that existed between me and
your father of blessed memory.[2] But friendship, as you know, was never
broken on my side. So there is hope that Erasmus has not completely faded
from your memory. He was once a brave fellow when he used to struggle 15
against the Beetle,[3] now in old age he has become a gladiator, since he must
fight constantly against a host of monsters.[4] It will make me very happy if
I find that you are both safe and well and energetically sweating over the
studies that you began so felicitously long ago. Farewell.

    Freiburg im Breisgau, 13 January 1531[5]   20

            * * * * *

2255
1 See Ep 2222 n15.
2 See Epp 289:6–9 and 292:22–36, which record Erasmus' anger at Giovanni Battista but do not make clear what the nature of the misunderstanding
  was.
3 The more ample reference to the 'Beetle' in Allen Ep 2481:32–42 makes clear
  that Erasmus is talking about the boys' tutor, Clyfton (Ep 194:36n), of whom
  he had formed a poor opinion during their journey to Italy in 1506; see Ep
  1341A:98–113.
4 See Ep 2250 n10.
5 The correct year-date is 1530; see introduction above.

2256 / To Bonifacius Amerbach   Freiburg, 16 January [1530]

This letter (= AK Ep 1407), which was first published in the *Epistolae familiares*, is Erasmus' reply to Ep 2248. Bonifacius' reply is Ep 2267.

Cordial greetings. I am afraid, dear Bonifacius, that the events you describe,[1] tragic though they may be, are but the prelude to a more serious tragedy. The threat of similar upheavals can be observed on all sides, so I do not know what advice to give you. Is there anything the pope will not be able to induce the emperor to do now that he has kissed his most 5 holy feet?[2] It is not hard to guess how jubilant that Most Holy Person must be and his own people too.[3] In Brabant those barefoot tyrants are clearly in control,[4] while the people fret in secret. In England things are in the greatest confusion, not only on account of the dismissal of the cardinal,[5] but also because of the quarrel between the king and the queen.[6] Cardi- 10 nal Campeggi has left England, having given no other response than 'It is a great matter: I believe it needs further discussion,' although he had been summoned precisely to resolve the issue.[7] But so that it would not be said that he had accomplished nothing, he had carried off a large quantity of gold to Calais. However, the loot was intercepted, doubtless with 15 the connivance of the king.[8] But you will hear all about this Iliad from Dilft.[9]

The count Palatine, with the encouragement of the landgrave of Hessen, is taking action against the cardinal of Mainz.[10] Here we are also afraid

* * * * *

2256
1 In Ep 2248
2 See Ep 2240 n8.
3 The 'jubilation' of Clement VII would have been caused by the agreement of the emperor to undertake the restoration of the rule of the pope's Medici kinsmen in Florence (a task that would not be completed until August 1530); cf Ep 2211 n14.
4 See Ep 2249:31–2 with n8.
5 See Ep 2240 n4.
6 Ie King Henry's pursuit of a divorce from Queen Catherine
7 See Ep 2215 n17. Having failed in his mission, Lorenzo Campeggi left England, crossing the channel on 26 October 1529 (LP 4 no 6050).
8 There is no independent confirmation of this rumour, which would have reminded Erasmus of his own 'English disaster'; see Ep 119:9n.
9 Dilft (Ep 2222 n15) was to pass through Basel on his journey from Freiburg to Spain. On the use of 'Iliad' here, see *Adagia* I iii 26.
10 See Ep 2253A:51–3 with n14.

of the anger of the Turk.[11] Meanwhile the emperor takes to kissing and is   20
revelling in Italian pomp – involving himself in considerable expense.[12] The
red cross has been raised again in Brabant for defence against the Turk; the
monks paint vivid pictures of Turkish savagery and shout at the top of their
voices, but no one gives a penny.[13] We live here between the altar and the
sacrificial knife,[14] committing everything to God; not only is our little town   25
poorly defended but it is beset on every side by enemies,[15] of whom there
are not a few inside. It is up to you to decide for yourself if it would be
expedient to move now.[16] I think that the course you have adopted on the
advice of your father-in-law will not turn out badly.[17] Many people found
it strange that you continue to reside there in the present state of things.   30
Certainly I was surprised that the small salary and the promises of those
dreadful people had so much weight with you.[18] The owner of the house
here has taken a husband, who does not want either to sell or to rent. It is
said that he will move here soon. That will mean that I will have to move.[19]

* * * * *

11 See Ep 2211 n9.
12 See n2 above.
13 Ie the red cross surmounted by a papal crown that was displayed by indulgence pedlars. Threatened by the Turkish advance into Hungary and Austria
   in the summer and autumn of 1529, King Ferdinand appealed to Rome for
   help. At their meeting in Bologna in October 1529, Emperor Charles and Pope
   Clement agreed that Charles could raise funds for the 'crusade' in Hungary
   by the sale of indulgences in the Low Countries. The sale commenced in December 1529, and another was proclaimed at the end of March 1530. See Rémy
   200–4, and cf Ep 2285:83–5.
14 See Ep 2253A n17.
15 This appears to be a reiteration of Erasmus' fear in 1529 that a conflict between
   the Catholic and evangelical cantons in Switzerland might spill over into the
   adjacent areas of South Germany (including the Breisgau), where both sides
   had allies; see Ep 2173:31–5 with n10. For rumours at this time of plans by
   Charles v and King Ferdinand to make war on the evangelical Swiss cantons
   and South German free cities, see Ep 2267 n5.
16 Both Erasmus and Udalricus Zasius (Ep 2209 n8), had urged Bonifacius to
   move to Freiburg; see AK Ep 1399:82–4.
17 The father-in-law was Leonhard Fuchs, mayor of Neuenburg am Rhein; cf Ep
   2130:6–11. It is not known what course he advised. He had earlier advised
   Bonifacius to move to Freiburg; see Ep 2179 n2.
18 For the terms of employment at the university that Bonifacius had demanded
   as the price of his remaining in Basel, see Ep 2248 nn7 and 9.
19 The house 'zum Walfisch' in the Franziskanergasse was the property of Ursula
   Adler, the widow of its builder Jacob Villinger; see Ep 2112 n4. Her new husband was Johann Löble, an official in Ferdinand of Austria's treasury. Erasmus
   did not actually move until September 1531.

I prefer to hear about the crisis in the tragic drama of Brabant rather than   35
witness it with my own eyes.[20] From time to time I think of Padua, but they
say that no road in Italy is safe because of the peasants who lie in wait for
soldiers sent away from Venice.[21]

I would like you to reflect on that business of the king of England, not
that I wish to involve myself in it, something that cardinal Campeggi did not   40
dare to do.[22] It is likely there will be terrible bloodshed in England unless an
unchallenged heir can be found. On the other hand, it is hard that the queen
should be repudiated, when she has been married for so many years and
suffered a number of miscarriages and finally produced a most charming
daughter.[23] And yet people say, presumably citing medical opinion, that she   45
has no hope of offspring.

The fact that the king married his brother's widow is not inconsistent
with divine law, and a letter from the pope was acquired beforehand.[24] But
the king has testified before the people that he has never slept with her as
a husband.[25] That is true, for while he was still under his guardians, he   50
was violently opposed to marrying her.[26] But when his guardians were raising various fears, even that he would be removed from the throne and,
on being removed, put to death, as the custom is there, he married her, at

* * * * *

20 Ie the 'tyranny' of the monks in Brabant (lines 7–8 above) was another reason
for Erasmus' reluctance to return there; cf Ep 2222 n9.
21 Cf Ep 2209:29–31.
22 As the papal legate sent to England to deal with the matter of the royal divorce (Ep 2215 n17), Campeggi was certainly 'involved.' The meaning here is
doubtless that, given the exigencies of papal politics, Campeggi had not dared
to deliver a clear decision for or against Henry's petition. See n7 above.
23 Princess Mary, born on 18 February 1516; see Ep 389:64n.
24 On 26 December 1503, Pope Julius II issued a bull that set aside the canonical
obstacles to Henry's marriage to Catherine of Aragon, the widow of his brother
Arthur. The marriage took place in 1509. In order to achieve the annulment of
his marriage to Catherine, Henry had to prove, one way or another, that the
dispensation should never have been granted. For a reliable guide to the bewil-
deringly complex issues of theology, law, and diplomacy that were involved in
Henry's struggle to divorce Queen Catherine, see Scarisbrick chapters 7 and 8.
25 If Henry ever said any such thing, it must have been long before the divorce
controversy, in which his case for the annulment of his marriage to Catherine
rested on the assumption that he had consummated a marriage that was contrary to the Levitical ban on marriage to the widow of one's brother and that
the failure to produce a male heir was the appropriate divine punishment.
26 *Calendar of Letters, Despatches, and State papers, relating to the Negotiations Between
England and Spain . . . 1485–1603* ed G.A. Bergenroth et al 26 vols (London 1852–
99) I 435 (27 June 1505).

Catherine of Aragon
Artist unknown
National Portrait Gallery, London

the same time making it very clear that it was not a genuine marriage. If
he had not touched her and had overcome his fears and declared his mind   55
early on, the case would be similar to that of Louis XII, king of France.[27]
Some advise that their daughter should marry some high-born person and
that a son of this marriage should succeed to the throne. But besides the
fact that there is no certainty that this would prevent sedition, there is the
further obstacle that the king has publicly stated that he never had congress   60
with her with the intent of a husband. This admission makes the daughter
illegitimate. Only one possibility remains, that the marriage, even if it was a
genuine marriage, might be dissolved in consideration of the public peace.

If you are preparing to move, it is my opinion that the sooner you do
it, the safer it will be. Farewell, my incomparable friend.   65

Freiburg, 16 January

My best wishes to your wife and your brother

Your friend, Erasmus of Rotterdam

I am sending a little book on the sweating sickness.[28] In Brabant they
set several people on fire from time to time, to eliminate heresies and clean   70
the air; for they think that this sort of fumigation purifies the atmosphere.[29]

To Master Bonifacius Amerbach, the most learned doctor of laws. In
Basel

2257 / To Nicolaus Episcopius   Freiburg, 17 January 1530

> This letter was first published by Johannes Isacius Pontanus in *Iusti Lipsi Epi-*
> *stolarum ... Decades XIIX* (Harderwijk: apud viduam Tomae Henrici 1621). The
> manuscript that Pontanus used seems to have disappeared. For Episcopius,
> see Ep 2233A n4.

I shall be quite content that you have taken over my house,[1] provided you

* * * * *

27 In 1498 Alexander VI gave Louis a dispensation from his marriage to Jeanne
   of France so that he could marry Anne of Brittany in 1499.
28 Possibly the *Iudicium* of Neuenahr and Riquinus (Ep 2246 n10), or perhaps *Su-*
   doris Anglici exitialis pestiferique morbi ratio, praeservatio et cura, written at the
   behest of the bishop of Strasbourg by two physicians in Metz, Joannes Nide-
   pontanus and Laurentius Frisius (Strasbourg: Johannes Knoblauch 1529).
29 See Ep 2249 n8.

2257
1 After their marriage in the summer of 1529, Episcopius and his bride, Justina
  Froben, moved into the house 'zur alten Treu,' which Erasmus had rented from

also take over my work, so that people will think that Erasmus has not moved, but has been rejuvenated in the guise of Episcopius. The young man who bears this letter wishes to be commended to you.[2] He has a terrible master, however grand his rhetoric. I hope, my dear friend, that you and   5
all your nearest and dearest are in the best of health.

Freiburg, 17 January 1530[3]

You will recognize your friend Erasmus.

2258 / From Levinus Ammonius   St Maartensbos, 17 January 1530

This letter was first published by Allen from the autograph in the Bibliothèque municipale at Besançon (MS 599 page 257). On Ammonius, see Epp 1463, 2016. This letter is unusual among the letters of Ammonius to Erasmus in that it contains no passage in which he switches from his fluent Latin into his excellent Greek.

LEVINUS AMMONIUS TO MASTER ERASMUS OF ROTTERDAM,
GREETING AND PEACE

I received two letters from you, dear Erasmus, beloved in Christ: one, written on the Nativity of the Blessed Virgin,[1] Mother of God, arrived around St Luke's day[2] along with the letters of Basil,[3] revised and corrected in many   5
places; the other, sent on St Martin's day,[4] reached me finally on 6 January.[5] But what concerned me particularly was that it arrived naked, for the Greek text of Chrysostom on the Epistle to the Romans, which you said you were sending at the same time, may have been intercepted on the way – at all

* * * * *

Johann (and then Hieronymus) Froben from 1522 until his move to Freiburg; see Epp 1316 n10, 2202:56–9.

2 Probably Frans van der Dilft, who also delivered Ep 2256; see Ep 2256 n9.

3 The year-date in the Pontanus text is 'M.D.C. XXX' (1630), which Allen has corrected thus: 'M.D.[C]XXX.'

2258

1 8 September

2 18 October

3 As lines 98–9 show, Erasmus had sent the manuscript with a request that Levinus make him a copy of it; cf Ep 2214 n5.

4 11 November

5 Neither letter is extant. The first, delivered by Quirinus Talesius to Erasmus Schets for forwarding to Ammonius (Ep 2222 n16), was probably in answer to Ep 2197. The second was no doubt carried by Nicolaus Episcopius (Ep 2235 n4).

events it was not delivered.[6] Believe me, I am more sorry than I can say that 10
I have been deprived of an opportunity either to comply with your wishes
(and nothing would give me greater pleasure than that), or to confess honestly that I am not up to the task. I can do neither of these things properly
since I have not yet seen the book. My friend Edingen,[7] who is very devoted
to you, keeps pestering Erasmus Schets with letters of complaint, request- 15
ing that the work be delivered in good faith, but up to the present nothing has happened.[8] In the meantime let me thank you as warmly as I can,
partly for your two letters, which I treasure as highly as anything I possess,
partly for the volume of edited letters that you sent me,[9] and partly also for
the text of Chrysostom, even though it has not arrived (and that is certainly 20
not your fault). I have not yet abandoned all hope that it will eventually arrive, but I fear it may come too late. You know there is a little more than
three months between now and May, the date by which I must complete
either all of the assignment, or at least half of it, if I am to comply with your
wishes. 25

Let me tell you frankly, dear Erasmus, what the situation is. I am not
competent enough in the two languages to command the rich vocabulary
needed for translation, especially given such a short deadline. Only once
before have I tested these waters,[10] and that was when I had nothing else

* * * * *

6 Erasmus had sent it to Louvain in the hope that Conradus Goclenius would
translate it himself or persuade Frans van Cranevelt or Levinus to do so; see
Ep 2352:329–33. If the task fell to Levinus, the manuscript was to be sent to
Ghent (Ep 2270:16–18, 2286:2–7). Erasmus had stipulated that the translation
should be done by May (see lines 21–5 below). The manuscript was kept at
Louvain (cf Ep 2291:15–17), only to be returned untranslated after six months
because of the difficulty of the script. As a result, the homilies on Romans do
not appear in the Latin Chrysostom of 1530 (Ep 2359). In the end, the translation was done by Germain de Brie and the work published separately by the
Froben press in March 1533.
7 Omaar van Edingen of Ghent (Ep 2060)
8 See Ep 2270:20–3.
9 The reference is probably to the *Opus epistolarum* (see Ep 2203), which on its
title-page is described as *diligenter recognitum* (diligently revised or edited).
Erasmus had sent a copy of the volume to Willibald Pirckheimer at just about
the same time that he sent the manuscript of the Basil letters to Levinus; see
Ep 2214:1–2 and n5. It is also possible, however, that Ammonius is referring
to the Basil manuscript (lines 5–6, 98–9), which he describes as 'revised and
corrected in many places.'
10 Literally 'tested the ice'; for a similar image see *Adagia* III v 95: *Scindere glaciem*
'To break the ice.'

to do, and this was such a wonderful success that I failed even to satisfy   30
myself. However, the little homily of Chrysostom *De fato et providentia Dei*
was handed to the printer despite my strong objections.[11] I did not have
publication in mind when I translated the work;[12] my purpose was partly
to try myself out and partly to give my patron[13] some vague indication,
like a glimpse through a trellis,[14] that my devoted study of Greek had not   35
been entirely wasted. How could I feel confident when the fact is that I have
never had the advantage of a teacher? Certainly, twelve years earlier, so far
was I from possessing any Greek books or, if I had possessed them, being
able to read them, let alone understand them, I did not even know all the
letters of the Greek alphabet, although I had already spent several years in   40
the religious life.[15] You may be surprised at this, but I swear, as God is my
witness, that what I am telling you is true. There was no one in the world to
help me beyond providing me with 'silent teachers' (as the phrase goes),[16]
and from these I absorbed all that I know. Nonetheless, I do not regret the
hard work I put into it, for as a result I am confident that I know what is   45
needed, if not to translate (a task I am happy to leave to others), at least to
understand a text and make judgments. Anyone who examines this situation
more closely will easily imagine how hard it was for me to enter upon that
road, for I had only a shadowy idea how to begin.

I would not wish you to think, excellent Erasmus, that I said this to   50
make myself out a prodigy (for I have nothing to justify such a claim); rather
I want you to measure my strengths by the length of my step, not yours.[17] If
I decided to attempt a translation, I am afraid I would suffer the fate of the
man in the Gospel who wanted to build a tower without first counting the
cost to see if he had the means to finish it.[18] But even supposing I could do   55
it easily, there is something else that deters me from any such attempt – the
fear that the work would be published under my name. I have set myself

* * * * *

11 Allen cites letters of Levinus in the Bibliothèque municipale at Besançon show-
    ing that the printing was done (by M. Hillen at Antwerp) at the behest of Le-
    vinus' patron, Frans van Massemen (Ep 2197 n19).
12 Erasmus did not use Levinus' translation for his Latin Chrysostom (Ep 2359)
    but reprinted that of Oecolampadius instead.
13 See n11 above.
14 *Adagia* iii i 48
15 He made his profession in the Carthusian monastery at St Maartensbos on 18
    August 1506.
16 See *Adagia* i ii 18, where books are called 'silent teachers.'
17 *Adagia* i vi 89
18 Luke 14:28

this firm rule, that I would do anything rather than act a part on the public
stage before the judgment of the world, for everyone can see how many
have come to grief from this same ambition. I care nothing for an undying   60
name: I shall be happy enough if I find favour with Christ alone. If in the
future he decides that I can be of use to his people, he will not need a pretext
for pushing me into the light, however much I hide. Let him do what he
wishes for his glory and his alone. Meanwhile I shall not be unhappy in my
seclusion, enjoying close and friendly conversations with my poor friends,   65
writing provocative letters, and replying when provoked. Conscious of my
inadequacy, I shall never thrust myself into the throng, nor scheme to be
pushed from this happy hiding-place into the turmoil of a worldly life.

If these scourges (or should I say, these scoundrels?)[19] would permit
you, no one, excellent Erasmus, would translate better than you, nor would   70
anyone be likely to publish a more successful version than you, for you are
beyond the reach of malicious criticism. But I am a newcomer, or rather a
nobody,[20] hardly known beyond the threshold of our house; and as Euclio
says in the play, there is great risk when asses aspire to associate with oxen
who have long borne the yoke[21] – and I have lived among asses until now   75
and am no better myself. Yet if at any time I can be of use to Christendom,
I shall not fail, provided I am not betrayed by my own rashness and come
to grief, like the shrew-mouse, by disclosing my own identity.[22]

Then, when you say in your letter that perhaps you will take on the rest
of the translation yourself, would anyone, even a great scholar, not be fright- 80
ened off by that? For who at the present time could match you in eloquence
and richness of vocabulary? So will you really allow the brilliant flow of
your language to be muddied by my lifeless mumbling? Will you suffer my
inarticulate babbling to spoil that honeyed eloquence of yours, which you
have gained by study and strengthened by long practice? If you listen to   85
me, excellent Erasmus, you will do no such thing, for nothing would produce an uglier effect than a mishmash of that kind. So, my dear Erasmus,
if I can oblige you in some other matter – by copying whatever you wish
in Latin or Greek, or doing something else that does not exceed my meagre

* * * * *

19 Here the Latin text puns on *mastiges* (whip or scourge) and *mastigia* (a scoundrel, someone who deserves to be whipped).
20 Here there is a play on *novus homo* (the first person in a family to achieve high
political office) and *nullus homo* (a nobody).
21 Euclio is a character in Plautus' play *Aulularia* who expands on the dangers
that arise when a poor man marries into a rich family, thus 'rising from ass
to ox'; see *Adagia* I vii 30.
22 The line is modelled on Terence's *Eunuchus* 1024; see *Adagia* I iii 65.

talents – believe me there is nothing I would agree to more willingly or   90
more eagerly. So you need not worry about doing something to oblige me,
a concern I seem to detect in your earlier letter, since I readily admit that I
owe you a great deal more than I am ever likely to repay.

I think this is enough by way of reply to your two letters, perhaps
too much. Your man Quirinus,[23] who, you said, was going to visit me, has   95
not arrived, nor perhaps was there any reason why he should wear himself
out for my sake. You know my circumstances and you are also aware of the
scorn with which most people treat humane letters and humane learning. I
have not yet begun to copy the letters of Basil.[24] Shortly after I sent off that
letter to you,[25] I was tossed headlong into a busy life by authority of the   100
fathers, who appointed me sacristan, or keeper of the sacred furnishings;
what I do there is always too much. However, for your sake and in the cause
of the Christian faith, I shall gladly steal some time from sleep, although
my weak eyesight hardly permits me to work by lamplight. I have badly
weakened my eyes by almost continuous study, and there is no remedy at   105
hand that could restore them. I wanted to discuss other matters with you,
but embarrassment prevents me, for I know you are busy enough without
all this. So I shall stop here. May Christ keep you safe, my beloved Erasmus.

From St Maartensbos, on the Nativity of St Anthony 1530

2259 / From Bonifacius Amerbach   [Basel, ? January 1530]

For the reasons stated by Alfred Hartmann in his introduction to AK Ep 1783,
this letter has been redated to 'mid-October 1533' and will appear as Ep 2873A
in CWE 20.

2259A / To Cornelis Croock   Freiburg, 23 January [1530]

This letter was first printed on folio A1 verso of the long-lost first edition of
Cornelis Croock's *Propaedeumatum grammaticae institutionis libelli duo* (Amsterdam: Doen Pietersz 1532). It was omitted from later editions of the work and
thus remained unknown for centuries. Not until a copy of the first edition
showed up in the private collection of Johan Devroe, antiquarian bookseller
of Haasrode, Belgium, was the letter rediscovered. It was published by Marcus
de Schepper, together with an English translation by Charles Fantazzi, in the
journal *Humanistica Lovaniensia* 39 (1990) 85–92. Fantazzi's translation, slightly

* * * * *

23 See Ep 2222 n16.
24 See lines 5–6 above.
25 Ep 2197; cf n5 above.

emended by Fantazzi himself, is used here. This letter and the answer to it,
Ep 2354, constitute the entire surviving correspondence between Croock and
Erasmus.

Cornelis Croock (Cornelius Crocus) of Amsterdam, c 1500–1550, matriculated at Louvain in 1527, where he studied with Alaard of Amsterdam (Ep
433) and Adrianus Cornelii Barlandus (Ep 492). By 1522 he was Latin teacher
in his hometown. From 1531 to 1537, and again from 1544 to 1549, he was rector of one of the two Latin schools at Amsterdam. In 1549, having decided to
join the Society of Jesus, he travelled to Rome for that purpose. In Rome he
fell ill and died at the end of 1550, shortly after having achieved his goal.

Croock's first literary publication was a *Farrago sordidorum verborum*, which
was appended to the unauthorized first edition (by Alaard of Amsterdam) of
Erasmus' *Paraphrasis in Elegantias Vallae* (Ep 2260 n18). Erasmus was greatly
displeased by this publication (see Epp 2260:70–134, 2412, 2416) but, as the
friendly tone of this letter shows, he did not hold Croock responsible for it or
disparage the quality of his *Farrago*. For Croock's account of the unauthorized
publication of both works, see Ep 2354:37–48.

TO THE LEARNED YOUNG MAN CORNELIS CROOCK OF
AMSTERDAM

Cordial greetings. Both to you personally and to our country of Holland
publicly I give my congratulations, dearest Croock: to you because you continue to enhance and enrich your mind with true and lasting blessings, to   5
your country because with each passing day it gains more and more lustre
in the field of polite letters, and it strives to make acceptable offerings to
the Muses and philology instead of Comus and Bacchus.[1] For the friendly
sentiments you bear towards me I willingly admit my debt, but certainly
in mutual affection I shall not yield to you, though I be inferior in all else.   10
If you are desirous of knowing what is going on here, you will hear many
Iliads from my servant Nicolaas Kan.[2] Take care that you keep yourself in
excellent health and that in your splendid literary career you successfully
finish what you have begun.

* * * * *

2259A
1 Comus was the god of festivity, merrymaking, and naughty revels. His father,
  Bacchus, was the god of wine, inspired madness, and ecstasy.
2 Kan (Ep 1832) had just left Erasmus' service to return to his native Amsterdam
  and settle down as a parish priest. He took his time getting there (Ep 2356:1–
  11), arriving sometime before 1 March (Ep 2352:1–2). On 'Iliads' see *Adagia* I
  iii 26.

Given at Freiburg, 23 January   15
Erasmus of Rotterdam, in my own hand

2260 / To Pieter Gillis   Freiburg, 28 January 1530

This letter is Erasmus' answer to a letter from Gillis that is no longer extant. It
was appended to Erasmus' translation of Xenophon's *Hieron* (Ep 2273) and then
never included in any edition of the letters until Allen's. In Allen's words, the
letter is 'a singular medley.' Beginning with expressions of regret and condolence for the death of Gillis' two wives and his friend Clava, it passes abruptly
(line 70) to a complaint about the unauthorized publication of Erasmus' early
paraphrase on Valla's *Elegantiae*. From there it turns with equal abruptness
(line 135) to a complaint about the publication at Antwerp of Erasmus' first
reply to Frans Titelmans. This leads (line 169) to yet another reply to Titelmans' *Collationes quinque super epistolam ad Romanos* (see Ep 2206 introduction),
which constitutes more than half the letter. Finally (line 339), Erasmus reports
at length on his health before returning (line 359) to the verses of condolence
with which the letter had begun.

   Gillis (Ep 184) was one of Erasmus' oldest and closest friends. Ep 2089 is the
last surviving letter from him to Erasmus; this is the last of Erasmus' surviving
letters to him.

DESIDERIUS ERASMUS OF ROTTERDAM TO PIETER GILLIS,
CLERK OF THE CITY COUNCIL OF ANTWERP, GREETING
Heaven has decided, my dearest Pieter, that I should perform this office for
you at a time of mourning[1] – I only wish it could have been on a happier
subject. If the result is not too successful, I know that with your kind heart   5
you will give me credit for my good will and my readiness to do what I
could. For some time now I have had little practice in writing verse; so I
fear you will judge that what I am sending you is not really poetry.[2] Otherwise, I would most willingly have complied with your wishes and done
justice to the memory of your former wife Cornelia,[3] who was a woman of   10
such integrity that even in those distant ages when Astraea still lived on the

* * * * *

2260
1 Ie the office of writing memorial verses
2 The verses were printed on folio F[3] of the *Hieron* and never reprinted by Erasmus. They are found, in both Latin and English, in CWE 85 162–7 nos 83–6.
3 Cornelia Sandrien, d 1526; see Ep 1740 n2. Erasmus' two epitaphs for her are
  in CWE 85 162–5 nos 83–4.

earth,[4] she might have been hailed as a model of piety, faithfulness, and chastity.

It was remarkable how she hung upon your every expression and attended to your every wish. She was merry or melancholy according to the mood she observed in you. If you fell ill, she became even sicker than you, and would have died if anything more serious had happened to you. Even as a young girl, she took no pleasure in dancing, nor was she interested in parties at which her husband was not present, or in visits to other people's houses, or shows, or chatting with neighbouring women. She devoted all her energies, all her spare time and her working hours, all her compassion to attending to her family and bringing up the children. As for myself, she counted me a friend simply because she noticed that you and I were so like-minded. Given that almost all your time was devoted to public business, you needed a chatelaine like her, and your young children required someone like her to attend to them. She deserved a longer life so that she could enjoy her beloved husband and her precious children. But Death is never readier to dissolve a union than when there is a very close and loving bond. You took a second wife,[5] more for the care of your children than for your own pleasure. She too was soon taken from you by cruel destiny. As a result, my dear Pieter, although you are far from the threshold of old age,[6] you are even now beset by the misfortunes of the old, twice widowed, twice plunged into mourning by the death of a wife. Fortunately, you have not experienced so far the grief of losing a child.

I do not propose now to offer you a formal consolation, for I know that your mind has long been fortified by the teachings of philosophy against all the vicissitudes that beset the life of man. But I feel a fluttering palpitation in the heart when I learn from your letter that you have been repeatedly attacked by the sweating sickness;[7] even now I cannot help being anxious when I reflect that a great part of your day must be spent in the business of the city. Those who stay at home are at less risk, especially if they use an open fire.

* * * * *

4 Astraea, goddess of justice, was the last of the gods to leave the earth at the end of the Golden Age; see Ovid *Metamorphoses* 1.150.

5 Maria Denys, a widow, who died following the birth of her first child in the winter of 1529–30. See Erasmus' epitaph for her in CWE 85 164–5 no 85.

6 Born c 1486, Gillis was now a little over 43 years of age. He would die in 1533.

7 See Ep 2209:110–68 with n31.

Pieter Gillis
Quentin Metsys
Private collection, England

They tell me that Antonius Clava of Ghent too has departed this life.[8] What a remarkable man he was! His old age showed little evidence of his 45 years – he remained affable, merry, generous, and witty. He was fair-minded and judicious, a friendly patron, a great lover of books. All his books had gold on the outside and were decorated on the inside with gold lettering. You would have said they looked more like treasure chests than books. His wife was sterile, so he loved his books as though they were his children.[9] 50 What a generous supporter he was of men of letters! When he was already advanced in years, he learned Greek so well that even in the minutiae of grammar he was more adept than I am myself.[10]

But this is the old and universal sorrow that all mortal men must face. In these times, however, such is the state of human affairs that everything 55 seems to threaten some great and deadly catastrophe. How long now have we witnessed wars and famine and pestilence? The French pox, a more terrible plague than leprosy, we turn into a joke.[11] We have irreconcilable disagreements over dogma, while the Turk is breathing down our necks.[12] And as if this were not trouble enough, this deadly sweating sickness has broken 60 out and suddenly spread over the whole world.[13] By all these troubles God is warning us that we should turn to him with all our hearts and flee for refuge to the shelter of the ark. But we see the same thing happening now as happened according to the testimony of the Lord in the time of Noah.[14] We eat, we drink, we marry, we buy and sell, we build houses, we take 65 part in public festivals, all without a care as though everything were tranquil and no danger threatened. I greatly fear we shall be overtaken by some unexpected disaster. But those who abide in Christ Jesus have no cause to fear.

There emerged into the light of day, first, I am told, at Cologne and 70 shortly afterwards in Paris, a little book with, if you please, the title *A Paraphrase by Erasmus on the Elegantiae of Lorenzo Valla*.[15] I wonder what people

* * * * *

8 Clava (Ep 175:13n) had died on 31 May 1529; see Ep 2197:68–70. Erasmus' epitaph for him is in CWE 85 165–7 no 86. In it Erasmus says that Clava was past 70 when he died.
9 The sentence puns on *libri* 'books' and *liberi* 'children.'
10 Ep 530:40–2, 841:1, 1306:73–6
11 See Ep 2209:84–5 with n40.
12 See Epp 2211 n9, 2285.
13 See n7 above.
14 Matt 24:37–8
15 The Cologne edition (Johann Gymnich 1529) bore the title *Paraphrasis luculenta: iuxta ac brevis in Elegantiarum libros Lau. Vallae ... scripta quondam Lutetiae*

of this sort are like, what they are thinking when they arrogate to themselves such authority over the writings of others, even when the author is still alive. Long ago when I was barely twenty years old,[16] a schoolmaster 75
who had recently gathered a number of students around him asked me to suggest an author who would be particularly helpful to children in learning Latin.[17] I recommended Lorenzo's *Elegantiae*. He replied that Valla was too detailed and was therefore hardly suitable for teaching to children, and that he did not have the leisure to select the main points from it. This is what he 80
said, but the fact is that he was never going to understand Lorenzo, however much time he could spare to read and reread him. My good nature was overcome by his prayers and coaxing. I made a cursory reading of the text and noted down anything that seemed appropriate for a schoolmaster at such a level. Far from having any thought of publication, I did not even 85
keep a copy by me and have never sought to have him return it. This is the work that they are publishing while I am still alive and without giving me notice, and they attach to it a title of their own choosing.

The person who provided the preface for Cornelis Croock's book thinks that I wrote the work in Paris,[18] although I copied it out in Hol- 90

* * * * *

a *D. Erasmo Rot.* The Paris edition (Robert Étienne, 1 November 1529) was entitled *Paraphrasis luculenta, iuxta ac brevis in Elegantiarum libros L. Vallae.*

16 The paraphrase dates from 1489 or a bit earlier, when Erasmus was still a monk at Steyn; see Epp 23:108n. How old he was at the time depends on which of the dates of his birth one accepts: 1466, 1467, or 1469. Cf lines 89–91 below, where Erasmus dates the writing of the paraphrase at seven years before his arrival in Paris.

17 The schoolmaster has never been identified with certainty; see ASD I-4 192–3 n7.

18 The Cologne edition of the *Paraphrase* was published together with the *Farrago sordidorum verborum* (Farrago of Inelegant Expressions) of Cornelis Croock (Epp 2259A, 2354). The *Farrago*, which comes after the *Paraphrase* in the volume, is preceded by a letter of Cornelis Gerard (Ep 17) to Jan Arentszoon Beren (Ep 1668 n4). This led Allen to the mistaken identification of Gerard as the author of the preface in question. But there is no mention of the supposed Parisian origins of the *Paraphrase* in Gerard's letter. As Allen himself points out, it was Alaard of Amsterdam (Ep 433) who, in the letter to Croock (1 February 1522) that precedes the *Paraphrase* in the volume, described it as 'scripta quondam Lutetiae a D. Erasmo Rot.,' a phrase reproduced verbatim on the title page of the Cologne edition (see n15 above). In the same letter Alaard describes how, no later than 1510, he had purchased the manuscript of the *Paraphrase* from Willem Hermans (Ep 33), Erasmus' friend and fellow monk at Steyn. It was in fact Alaard who went to Cologne to arrange for the publication of Erasmus' work along with the *Farrago* of Croock. See ASD I-4 194–6.

land seven years before I set eyes on Paris.[19] What I wrote in Paris is a huge
volume; it too was not intended for general circulation. A certain English-
man had contrived to become my pupil.[20] When I discovered that he was
more of a blockhead than a human being and that he had a poor mind and
a poor memory, and when I realized that my words made absolutely no im-   95
pression on him, I began for his benefit to write down a fuller version and,
as it were, to embroider what Lorenzo teaches. When I saw that he was delighted with this and was exhibiting some signs of progress, I completed
what I had begun. I gave him one copy written in my own hand, but only
after he had sworn not to give it to anyone. I hear that he too did not keep   100
his word; at least he refrained from publication.

I return to the other version.[21] Would it not seem shockingly unfair if
someone printed a work that a writer has tossed off in his youth perhaps to
please a friend or simply as an intellectual exercise, especially if the author
were alive and in his right mind and was not aware of what was happen-   105
ing or, if he was aware, disapproved? But what is more shocking still is that
they made additions. They reorganized the work in alphabetical order, thus
spoiling the whole point and impairing the book's usefulness, because the
proper meaning of words becomes clear by their juxtaposition, as when distinctions are made, either in meaning or usage, in such words as *quamvis,*   110
quamquam, etsi, tametsi, licet,[22] similarly, *quisquis, quisque, quivis, quilibet, qui-
cunque;*[23] *dudum, iamdudum, olim, iam olim, nuper, quondam, pridem, iampridem,
heri, cras, nudiustertius, perhendie, pridie, postridie.*[24] If these words, which are
related to one another, are separated by being placed in alphabetical order,
is not part of the value of the work lost and the whole point of the argument   115
ruined? So I find these people lacking not just in good faith and decency,
but also in judgment and good sense. If they could not prevent themselves
from publishing the work, at least they should have given me notice. With
four days to work on it, I could have refashioned the work (whatever its

* * * * *

19 Erasmus arrived in Paris c September 1495.
20 Perhaps Robert Fisher; see Ep 62.
21 Ie to the earlier, shorter version of the *Paraphrase,* written in Holland and now
   just published at Cologne and Paris.
22 These five words, which introduce concessive clauses ('although'), have
   slightly different nuances and are used in different constructions.
23 Words from a similar root that differ in meaning: *quisquis* 'whoever,' *quisque*
   'each' etc
24 This is a list of adverbs expressing time; the last two, for example, mean 'on
   the preceding day' (*pridie*) and 'on the following day' (*postridie*). *Perhendie* =
   perendie 'day after tomorrow.'

merits); it could then have been read with profit to the young and without 120
disgracing my name.[25]

Can you imagine anything more sinister than people who act like this?
Not only do they contribute nothing themselves to the general advancement
of learning, but by ruining other people's work they damage the reputation
of those who use their industry to produce something useful. I have become 125
hardened to greater insults than this, so I can easily swallow this one. Nevertheless the sheer audacity of such people deserves harsh punishment. If
they are friends, I must question their judgment, for they are committing
an unfriendly act. If they are enemies, their injury is all the more shameless since it is done in the guise of friendship. If they are neither friends 130
nor enemies but are acting to amuse themselves, let them have their fun,
but without hurting someone else; let them entertain themselves without
causing pain to others. The same thing happened some time ago with the
Colloquies.[26]

I could wish my little book had not been published there,[27] for not only 135
do I find that it has been as shabbily produced as it is inaccurate, but I hear
that what I rather feared has happened – the grasshopper has been taken
by the wing.[28] Since I thought that this matter had better be looked into by
friends living there,[29] I referred the question to their judgment and asked
for an opinion on whether the work should be published or suppressed. 140
If I had made up my mind to publish it, I could have done so here more
rapidly and conveniently and with greater accuracy. I had some hope that the
young man[30] would take a hint from the courteous nature of my *Responsio*
and change his manner of writing, especially since I had even concealed his
name.[31] I am myself naturally sympathetic to all who are trying, whatever 145
the quality of their efforts, to advance the cause of letters. But in this case I

* * * * *

25 The first authorized version of the work would appear in March 1531 (Ep
   2416)..
26 See Epp 130:108–9n, 909.
27 Literally 'there where you are,' ie in Antwerp. This marks the abrupt switch
   to Erasmus' quarrel with Frans Titelmans. The 'little book' (*libellum*) is Erasmus' *Opus recens* (or, as he refers to it in line 143, his *Responsio*), published at
   Antwerp; see Ep 2206 introduction.
28 *Adagia* I ix 28; the adage refers to an action that exacerbates the problem, makes
   an antagonist more quarrelsome.
29 Ie in Antwerp
30 Titelmans
31 In the work Erasmus refers to Titelmans as *gerontodidascalus* 'teacher of old
   men'; see Ep 2206 n1.

seem to detect an incurable malady, so I have made up my mind to abandon
him to his own affliction. I find to my sorrow that this kind of person sinks
gradually to the level of the world. Their savagery, it appears, comes from
the hope of victory. I only wish this plague could somehow be quelled –   150
provided the victory falls to Christ. But from what can be observed so far,
I am dreadfully afraid that Christ's business will fare no better, and as for
the factions among men, we are likely to have what is called a Cadmean
victory.[32] But the present tragedy has long ago gone beyond human control;
it requires a deus ex machina. All we can do now is to put ourselves gladly   155
in the hands of God, as in fact we are.

I know, my dear Pieter, that you are too busy to have time to read
through such a load of rubbish. Indeed I would be loath to wish such
a fate on an enemy, much less on you. But I want to show you a speci-
men (it is quite short) from which you can guess how much time and pa-   160
per the fellow wastes. At Romans chapter 8 the Old Translator had rendered the Greek φρόνημα by *quid desideret spiritus* 'what the Spirit desires.'[33]
I do not challenge this, but I suggest a more apt expression, *sensus* or *af-*
fectus spiritus 'the "sentiments" or "feelings" of the spirit.'[34] Valla also had
made a similar comment.[35] Jacques Lefèvre prefers *prudentia* 'good sense,'   165
a word that is not suited to this passage.[36] Our young opponent, however,
has not a word of criticism for Lefèvre; his quarrel is only with me for
preferring *sensus* and *affectus* to *desiderium* 'desire.' Here, finding an open
field to display his eloquence, he says,[37] 'the words *sensus* and *affectus* are
too coarse to be applied to the spirit, which has no part in the passions   170
of the body. So *sensus* and *affectus* will be appropriate[38] to the flesh –

* * * * *

32 A Cadmean victory is one where both sides suffer disastrous losses; see *Adagia*
   II viii 34.
33 Romans 8:27. The 'Old Translator,' also known simply as 'the Translator' (see
   lines 216–17 below) was the translator of the Vulgate New Testament, whom
   Erasmus always distinguished carefully from St Jerome, the acknowledged
   translator of the Old Testament; see Ep 2172 nn2 and 5.
34 In the Annotations for the *Novum instrumentum* of 1516 and in all later editions.
   Both *sensus* and *affectus* can refer to mental as well as emotional states, so the
   meaning ranges from 'thought,' 'idea,' to 'feelings' and 'emotions.'
35 *Adnotationes in latinam Novi Testamenti interpretationem*, edited by Erasmus and
   published by Josse Bade at Paris in 1505 (see Ep 182), folio 27 verso: 'the *sensus*
   of the spirit.'
36 *Commentarii in Epistolas Pauli* (Paris: Robert Étienne 1512) folios 6, 87 verso.
37 Titelmans *Collationes* (see Ep 2206 introduction) folio 177
38 Here Titelmans' text actually says 'let *sensus* and *affectus* be appropriate . . .'

coarse, physical words for the coarse and lowest part of ourselves.' End of quotation.

Now observe the authoritative tone with which he presents this absurd trifle. He had heard perhaps that the stricter Stoics condemned the πάθη 'pas-   175
sions,' which some translate as *affectus* 'feelings' or *perturbationes* 'perturba-
tions.' But it does not immediately follow that 'perturbations of the mind'
is the only meaning of *affectus*, since Latin writers, in trying as best they
can to convey the thought of the Stoics, have translated πάθη 'passions' by
affectus 'feelings,' *motus* 'emotions,' *perturbationes* 'perturbations,' *cupiditates*   180
'desires,' and *morbi* 'afflictions.' Moreover, this paradox of the Stoics was
rejected long ago not just by Christians,[39] but also by other philosophers,
and even by the later Stoics themselves. Nowadays anyone who chose to
stand stubbornly by the Stoic doctrine of ἀπάθεια would even be considered a heretic.[40] For joy, grief, hope, fear, love, hate, benevolence, pity are   185
unquestionably 'feelings,' and yet throughout the sacred writings they are
used of men living not just according to the flesh but according to the spirit,
they are used also of Christ, indeed they are used even of the divine nature.
Does not David say in the Spirit 'I hate them with a perfect hatred?'[41] How
often Paul is tortured by grief, filled with joy, and torn apart by fear? And   190
does not the Virgin Mother have maternal feelings towards her son, and the
son likewise towards his mother? Do we not read in the Gospel that the Lord
exulted in spirit, shouted in anger, wept, was indignant and moved to pity?
And the word *affectus* encompasses all these emotions – unless my critic accepts the species while rejecting the genus, in despite of logic! And are not   195
joy and love attributed to the angels although they are incorporeal? And
does Paul not mention joy among the fruits of the Spirit,[42] while including
things of a very different nature among the works of the flesh? But in Paul
the flesh and the spirit are in conflict one with the other, fighting an irreconcilable battle. Yet in Galatians chapter 5 he applies to the flesh and the spirit   200
the same verb, 'to lust,'[43] which undeniably pertains to feeling [*affectus*].

* * * * *

39 The 'Stoic paradoxes' were concepts that were believed to be true despite their
superficial improbability. The 'paradox' here is that all the passions are to be
condemned; see the following note.
40 The literal meaning of ἀπάθεια is 'absence of feeling or passion.' Erasmus here
expresses the common (but doubtful) view that the early Stoics advocated
complete indifference to all feeling. The later Stoics appear to have abandoned
the word altogether, see Aulus Gellius 12.5 fr 111.
41 Ps 139 (138 Vulgate):22
42 Gal 5:22–3
43 Gal 5:17

I am not unaware that 'feelings' used of Christ is one thing, used of us is something else; yet it would be wrong to deny that Christ experienced genuine human feelings. No one would be so stupid as to imagine that in God there is anger, fury, hatred, love, joy, grief, pity, regret, yet everywhere   205
in Holy Writ these words are applied to him in a pious sense. Here too my critic will exclaim, 'the words "fury" and "regret" are too coarse to be appropriate to the divine nature.' But he ought to know that, just as in a human being there are two kinds of will, one good, one bad, so there are two kinds of feelings, good and bad, spiritual and carnal. Perhaps he thinks that   210
sensus belongs only to the body, like seeing and hearing, or that it means 'carnal desire,' whence the common, but barbarous, use of the word *sensualitas* 'sensuality.'[44] He fails to notice that the word *sensus* is frequently attributed in sacred literature to the divine nature, as in this very epistle, chapter 11: 'Who has known the understanding [*sensus*] of the Lord, or who   215
has been his counsellor?'[45] What Jerome translates in Isaiah as *spiritus*,[46] the Translator,[47] whom this man has undertaken to defend, translates as *sensus*, which must be blasphemy if what this young man says is true. For anyone who attributes flesh or anything carnal to the divine nature is as much a blasphemer as if he attributed to him change or a beginning and an end.   220

Yet this was not enough for our young friend. This amazing scholar adds:[48] 'Nor does it seem quite proper that I should compare the desire of the Spirit to come to our aid with the carnal *sensus* of that sly and good-for-nothing slave in Terence.[49] For the spiritual should be compared to the spiritual with words appropriate to the situation, and the carnal compared   225
to the carnal. If we have a pious attitude towards God, we shall speak in one way about the divine and holy Spirit and in another about the spirit of a sly and impudent human being.' So our critic. What, I wonder, is the point of this remark? Is he warning me against thinking that the Holy Spirit has the same *sensus* as Syrus had in Terence (though in the play Syrus is   230
speaking of the *sensus* of the old man Demea, not about his own)? Even a blockhead would not need to be reminded of this. Or is he concerned that

* * * * *

44 Erasmus considers the word barbarous because it is not found in classical authors, though it does appear in Tertullian.
45 Rom 11:34, where the Vulgate has *sensum*; all English translations have 'mind.'
46 The Pauline verse is based on Isa 40:13; see Jerome *Commentarii in Isaiam* 12 (on 40:13).
47 See n33 above.
48 Titelmans *Collationes* 177
49 Terence *Adelphi* 533

we use the same words when speaking about God or the saints as we use of men, whatever their character? If this is wicked, then all orthodox writers, along with Holy Writ itself, are guilty of impiety: 'Christ thirsts for the sal-   235 vation of men, the devil thirsts for the destruction of their souls.' We shall be compelled to say absolutely nothing about God, for no human words fit him precisely. Weak humanity, in talking about God, must lisp as best it can. Because a wily and petulant character in Terence loves a Bacchis or a Thais,[50] is it wrong, then, to say 'God the Father loves God the Son'? And   240 because Hadrian loved Antinous,[51] is it impiety to say 'God so loved the world'?[52] And because the traitor Judas said, 'Hail, Master,'[53] may the other disciples not greet the Master in the same words?

Does he think that when Christians discuss purity of diction it is wrong to look for linguistic norms in pagan authors? From where, then, do Cyprian,   245 Jerome, and Augustine get them? Can you imagine anything sillier than this? What does he mean when he says, 'Let us compare'? If someone shows from the evidence of Terence that *sensus* is used not only for the external senses but also for the mind or for a man's particular temperament, is he compar- ing the *sensus* of a comic character with that of God? When we attribute   250 fury to God,[54] or when we say that he kills and brings to life,[55] or when in the Scriptures he swears an oath,[56] do we not use the same terms of him as we use for a homicidal maniac or a pander? Why, then, should some man's cunning and effrontery stop us from using in a pious sense some particular word about God or the saints? In any case, he has failed to notice that this   255 word *sensus*, on which he has so many impudent and stupid things to say, is employed very frequently in a good sense by the Translator (on whose be- half he professes to be taking up the sword) and what is more, is used often for the mind itself and for the spirit rather than the flesh: in Luke 24, *tunc aperuit illis sensum* 'then he opened to them their understanding,' the Greek   260 is νοῦν 'mind';[57] in Romans 11, *Quis cognovit sensum Domini* 'Who has known the understanding of the Lord?'[58] the Greek is νοῦν 'mind'; a little later, in

* * * * *

50 Typical courtesans in the comedies of Terence, Bacchis in the *Adelphi* and Thais in the *Eunuchus*
51 Antinous was a beautiful young man beloved of the emperor Hadrian.
52 John 3:16
53 Matt 26:49
54 Exod 22:24; 32:10–11 and frequently elsewhere in the Old Testament
55 Deut 32:39; Tob 13:2; Wisd of Sol 16:13
56 Ps 110 (109 Vulgate):4; cf Heb 7:21.
57 Luke 24:45
58 Rom 11:34

chapter 12, *renovamini in novitate sensus vestri* 'you are renewed in the new-
ness of your understanding,'[59] for *sensus* Paul wrote νοός 'mind'; again in
1 Corinthians 1, *in eodem sensu* 'in the same understanding,'[60] the Greek is   265
νοΐ 'mind'; in 2 Corinthians 11, *ne corrumpantur sensus vestri* 'lest your understandings be corrupted,'[61] Paul has νοήματα, that is, 'understandings' or
'thoughts'; in Philippians 4, *Pax Dei quae exuperat omnem sensum* 'the peace
of God which passes all understanding,'[62] the Greek is νοῦν 'mind'; likewise
in the First Epistle of John chapter 5, *Filius Dei venit, et dedit nobis sensum,*   270
'the son of God has come and has given us understanding,'[63] [the Greek
is] διάνοιαν, meaning 'mind.' Similar translations are to be found in several
other passages, both in the Old and the New Testaments. If *sensus* is a word
to be reserved for the sly and the impudent, then my critic had more reason to be angry with the Translator, who, when he had a spiritual word in   275
the canon of Scripture, gave it a carnal meaning [*sensus*].

Then if *sensus* ought to be applied to the flesh, why does Paul, as a
reproach, call the Galatians *insensati*, Greek ἀνόητι 'foolish'?[64] And if *affectio*
'affection' smacks of the flesh, why does the same Paul blame the Romans
for being ἄστοργοι, which means 'without affection' [*affectio*]?[65] Moreover,   280
when he says in 1 Corinthians chapter 14 that he prefers to utter five words
with his own understanding [*sensus*] than ten thousand in the spirit,[66] surely
he was not speaking in the offensive language of the flesh? Is the fellow not
ashamed to talk such ignorant rubbish in so supercilious a manner?

You may now wonder whether the man who wrote these things was   285
in his right mind. He rejects the word *affectus* 'feeling' and then a little later
writes 'It is a pious attitude [*affectio*] towards God that teaches us to speak.'
But there is no difference between *affectio* and *affectus*, except that Cicero
liked the former and Quintilian the latter. If there is any difference, *affectio*
is a coarser word than *affectus*. For *affectio*, apart from seeming to represent a   290
temporary emotional state of the mind, is more related to the physical than
affectus, for distress of body, such as hunger or thirst, is called an *affectio*.
Finally if the word *affectus* is not appropriate for the Holy Spirit, neither is

* * * * *

59 Rom 12:2
60 1 Cor 1:10
61 2 Cor 11:3
62 Phil 4:7
63 1 John 5:20
64 Gal 3:1
65 Rom 1:31
66 1 Cor 14:19, 'in the spirit' is Erasmus' gloss, based on verses 14–15, on Paul's
'speak ... in a tongue.'

desiderium 'desire,' since desire is a cruder emotion than charity. For charity enjoys what it has, while anyone who experiences desire is tormented   295
by the absence of the thing desired. 'But it is not strictly correct,' he writes,
'to say that the spirit desires because it engenders a desire in us, just as it
is said to intercede for us with unspeakable groanings.'[67] But suppose we
concede that the word *spiritus* here is used not of the spirit of man but of
God, surely, by the same token, *affectus* or *sensus* must be attributed to the 300
spirit? Is not exulting in the spirit one kind of *affectus*, penitence another,
feeling happy for a neighbour on account of his good fortune another, feeling sorry for his misfortunes yet another; and all these emotions are produced in us by the Spirit of God. Φρήν, φρονεῖν, φρόνημα, and φροντίς are
related words,[68] the first of which is sometimes translated by *mens* 'mind,' 305
sometimes by *sensus* 'understanding': in 1 Corinthians 14, 'Do not become
children in understanding [*sensibus*],' [the Greek is] φρεσί, from which come
the words *phrenesis* and ἀφραίνει.[69] The second [φρονεῖν] sometimes means
'to be minded,' sometimes 'to be wise'; occasionally it has the meaning 'to
care for,' for φροντίς means 'care.' Likewise φρόνημα means now 'under-   310
standing,' now 'feeling,' now 'care' and can take on any of these meanings
rather than 'desire.' Yet our friend declares that he prefers the word 'desire'
– and with a certain conceited self-confidence, as though his preferring it
makes it at once more correct.

Finally, he concludes his comment as follows, 'However, if you are   315
more satisfied with your own ideas, we have no desire to attack them.'[70]
What is this I hear? That he has no desire to attack what he has maintained
at such great length to be blasphemous? Is it not blasphemous to apply to
God terms that belong to the flesh and to impudent men, and to compare
the feelings [*sensus*] of the eternal deity with those of such men? If what   320
he maintains is true, how can he not attack something that he sees as impious? But if he believes his view to be frivolous, why has he not applied the

* * * * *

67 Titelmans on Rom 8:26–7. This is not a direct quotation, but a very free paraphrase of the passage in the *Collationes* that falls between the two already cited
   in nn37 and 48.
68 Φρόνημα is the word used in the Greek text of Rom 8:27; Erasmus translated
   it by the disputed *sensus*, and the Vulgate by the verb *desidero* 'desire.'
69 Here Erasmus argues for 'understanding' as an appropriate meaning for *sensus* by pointing out that in 1 Cor 14:20 the Vulgate itself translates as *sensus* a Greek word (φρεσί) that clearly means 'mind' or 'understanding,' as
   is illustrated by its cognates *phrenesis* 'disease of the mind' and ἀφραίνει 'be
   mindless.'
70 *Collationes* folio 177

sponge?[71] Or why has he filled a whole page with such silly nonsense and wasted the reader's time? Or has he such authority that a thing takes on the character of piety or impiety by the simple fact that it appeals, or does not appeal, to his mind? 325

Most of his comments are of this kind, yet he considers himself an admirable writer. If I attempted to examine in detail such a load of long-winded piffle, there would be no end to it – and what would be the point? And this is the man who is slaying Goliath, restoring the authority of the great men of the past, and defending the teachings of the church! So let him take pleasure in his own pen. From now on it will not be my doing if he becomes more learned or more ignorant, except that it is a mark of Christian charity to wish him a better frame of mind, and it troubles me that the studies of young men should be disturbed by brawling of this kind. 335

If you are interested in hearing how things are with us, unless we are deceived by all the signs we see, we are expecting here a bloody tragedy, unless some divine power, more powerful than the designs of men, suddenly brings order into the tangled plot.[72] I do not have much to complain about on the score of old age.[73] With regard to my literary work, many young men have not accomplished much more. However, for two years now I have been nursing in my bladder a creature of stone that grows bigger every day and causes me constant pain, though it is still bearable.[74] But when it increases to a point where it prevents the urine from passing, that means death – and a death that is as painful as it is certain. I only wish that this death came once only! I must die a thousand times unless a surgeon frees me from the torment. What a malady this is when to hasten death seems a great blessing and one envies a stroke or the plague! The ancient experts were right when they gave this illness the foremost place among all those that torment the human body. I suspect that the problem arose from the wine that I drank from time to time and which had been hung up through the thoughtlessness of the kind of servants that generally fall to the lot of scholars.[75] The bitumen from this, added to undigested matter, caused the accretions that 330

340

345

350

* * * * *

71 *Adagia* I v 58
72 For 'tangled' Erasmus uses the Greek word ἐπίτασις, a technical term for the point in a drama where the plot thickens.
73 Cf Epp 2263:124–8, 2275:24–37.
74 See Epp 1989 n4, 2263:124–6, 2271:3–4, 2277:12–13, 2278:10–12, 2290:54–5. But see also Ep 2275:32–33.
75 Cf Ep 1759:23–4. The meaning is that the wine had been 'hung up' but not left long enough for the impurities to settle to the bottom before being served.

generally collect in the kidneys to solidify in the bladder. No hope is to be
found in doctors, nor have I any intention of resorting to a surgeon unless   355
death should begin to be preferable to life. But we belong to the Lord, dear
Pieter; we must commit ourselves totally to him, for he knows what is best
for us.

But what am I doing? I ought to have been your comforter and I am
burdening you with my grumbles. Now read the epitaphs, and my very best   360
wishes to you and to all who are dearest to you.

Freiburg im Breisgau, 28 January in the year of our Lord 1530

2261 / To Haio Herman   Freiburg, 31 January 1530

This letter was first published in the *Epistolae floridae*.

On Haio Herman (Hermannus Phrysius) and his relations with Erasmus,
see Epp 903:14n, 1131, 1479, 1978, and 2056. Since 1525, following the acquisi-
tion of a doctorate in both laws in Italy, Haio had been pursuing a career in
public administration in his native Friesland. In July 1528, he was appointed
a member of the council of Friesland at Leeuwarden. This letter, Erasmus' response to a letter now lost, is the last in his surviving correspondence with
Haio.

Like Ep 2262, this letter was carried by Haio Cammingha (n1), and doubtless
suffered the same delay in delivery (ie until 1532).

TO HAIO HERMAN OF FRIESLAND, DOCTOR OF LAWS, COUNCILLOR,
FROM ERASMUS OF ROTTERDAM, GREETING
You ask for a long letter, my dear Haio; but Haio Cammingha has relieved
me of this burden, for all my interests and affairs, public as well as private, indeed even my very thoughts and intentions are known to him as in-   5
timately as to myself.[1] We lived together in such harmony that I cannot say
whether he was sorrier to leave than I was to see him go. Certainly it has
been a long time since I lived as happily with anyone as with him, such is
his courtesy, his loyalty, and his integrity. He brought me the warmth and

* * * * *

2261
1 Like Haio Herman, Haio Cammingha (Ep 2073) was from Friesland. By February 1529, after a brief period of study at Dôle, he had become a paying guest
in Erasmus' household, remaining until the end of January 1530. He departed
owing Erasmus money and promising to return in the spring. But he did not
return, and he earned Erasmus' enduring wrath by taking nearly two years
to settle his debt.

encouragement of his companionship and looked after me so well that amid   10
the problems of my health, the burden of my work, and the present turbulent state of affairs, he was a very great consolation to me. But when I realized that to see his family again was something that mattered greatly to him
(you know the old saying about 'the eye of the Lord'),[2] far from holding the
young man back, I almost pushed him out when he himself seemed inclined   15
to linger. But for both of us the prospect of his return will ease the sense of
loss. So you will be able to ferret out from him anything you wish to know
about private or public matters here. I only wish the news were happier.

In the public square at Bologna the emperor kissed the feet of his Holiness three times, and it was there too, and not at Rome, that he received   20
the imperial crown – I have no doubt that, given the religious sensibilities of
this most excellent prince, the event was accompanied with all the customary
ceremonies.[3] Pressure has been put on the Florentines, backed up by a serious threat of arms, to make them submit to the pope, but all to no purpose,
for they were determined to suffer any extreme rather than acknowledge   25
him as prince. To the emperor, however, they offered everything he wanted,
putting themselves under his protection on terms that are most favourable
to him.[4] A truce was agreed with the Venetians until time allows an opportunity to settle the remaining issues.[5] They write that the emperor will be
in Oenipons, commonly known as Innsbruck, where a discussion will take   30
place on the Turkish situation.[6] From there he will travel to Augsburg to resolve the problem of the dissident sects – if possible without bloodshed.[7] But
cities that have taken extreme positions seem to be preparing themselves for

* * * * *

2 The 'old saying' has not been identified. Allen's tentative suggestion of Zech
  4:10 ('for they are the eyes of the Lord, which run to and fro through the
  whole earth') does not seem apt. Perhaps this is a more general reference to
  the many biblical injunctions to do what is right 'in the eyes of the Lord.' See
  for example Ps 33 (32 Vulgate):18, Prov 15:3, 1 Peter 3:12.
3 See Ep 2240 n8.
4 See Ep 2211 n14.
5 An apparent reference to the negotiations that led to the conclusion in December 1529 of a treaty of peace whose signatories included the emperor, the
  pope, Venice, and other North Italian states; see Pastor 9 87–8.
6 On Charles' slow progress from Italy into Germany, cf Epp 2294 n7, 2308 n15.
7 On 21 January 1530 Charles had summoned the German estates to attend an
  imperial diet at Augsburg, where the principal item on the agenda was to be
  the religious divisions in the Empire. The diet (20 June–19 November) would
  be the scene of the first of many unsuccessful attempts in the 1530s and '40s
  to restore ecclesiastical unity by means of negotiation.

the worst. Lately Zürich, Bern, and Strasbourg have made a treaty,[8] which
has been celebrated in a poem by Gerard of Nijmegen.[9] They say that King   35
Ferdinand has lost Vienna.[10] A great part of Austria has been sadly devastated. However, the king is said to have recovered Buda, although that is of
little significance for the recovery of his kingdom, since he could easily be
driven from such a poorly fortified place.[11] That whole domain is generally
under the control of the bishops, several of whom have returned to Ferdi-   40
nand.[12] What the Romanizers are up to is more a matter of guesswork than
real knowledge.[13] But it is not safe to put everything down on paper.

   Our studies are suffering a deep chill, for who would want to publish anything these days for such an ungrateful generation where the critics
rage at everything? I produced a book 'On early liberal education for chil-   45
dren,'[14] which I believe you have already read. Now I have nothing new
to offer except a homily on Psalm 22.[15] I published *The Christian Widow* in
Basel.[16] Several people are pressing me for a treatise on preaching, and I
had begun it, but my interest in the project soon cooled.[17] I have worked

* * * * *

8 The reference is to the Christian Federation (*das Christliche Burgrecht*), formed
   in January 1529. Basel joined in March 1529, but Strasbourg not until 5 January
   1530. See Ep 2173 n10.
9 Gerard Geldenhouwer (Ep 2219 n4). For the poem, see *Collectanea van Gerardus
   Geldenhauer Noviomagus, gevolgd door den herdruk van eenige zijner werken* ed. J.
   Prinsen (Amsterdam 1901) 92.
10 As recently as 2 November 1529, Erasmus had heard nothing about the siege
   of Vienna by the Turks in September–October; see Ep 2230 n7. At this point
   he still does not know that the Turks had raised the siege on 15–16 October
   and withdrawn deep into Hungary.
11 The Turks had in fact taken Buda in September 1529, and it was from there
   that they advanced on Vienna. In the wake of the Turkish withdrawal from
   Vienna, Ferdinand managed to reoccupy some of western Hungary, but he
   did not make it as far as Buda. In December 1530, he concluded a one-year
   truce with John Zápolyai, his rival for the crown of Hungary. The truce was
   renewed the following year, but a final settlement did not come until 1538; cf
   Ep 2177 n3.
12 Ie rather than submit to the rule of John Zápolyai
13 'Romanizers' (*Romanenses*) is a pejorative term that Erasmus sometimes used
   to describe the conservative theologians and their allies who treated all efforts
   at reform as evidence of heretical intent. See Ep 1719 n3, and cf Ep 2263:27.
14 See Ep 2189.
15 See Ep 2266.
16 See Ep 2100.
17 See Ep 2225:22–4 with n10.

hard enough for people who don't show the least gratitude. Perhaps I shall 50
complete the paraphrase on the Apophthegms of Plutarch to correct errors in translation, explain obscurities, point out the subtlety of the language (which not everyone appreciates), and demonstrate the value of the
work.[18] Here at least they will not discover heresies. The complete Chrysostom is now being printed in the same splendid format as the Augus- 55
tine.[19] To this edition I added certain works that I had not previously translated, but on discovering that they were spurious, I did not complete the
task.[20]

Budé has issued an exceptionally learned work on the Greek language.[21] In my opinion he shows more diligence in amassing material than 60
acuity in organizing it. I hear from my correspondents that Bade is printing
a collection of Budé's letters,[22] among which, if the story is true, there is one
in which he collects several passages from my letters to demonstrate that I
am biased against the French, although (God love me!) I have favoured no
nation more.[23] There is one passage in the *Colloquies* where someone says 65
'the French love whatever is cheap'; somewhere else another speaker says,
'What? Is a Frenchman daring to do battle with the eagle?'[24] There is a third
example in my Argument to the Epistle to the Galatians, where I cite Jerome
and Hilary, who considered dull-wittedness an attribute of the French.[25]
What marvellous logic we have here, designed to demonstrate to us the 70
power of eloquence! But unless I totally misunderstand the mind of Budé, I
think all this is nothing but windy rhetoric.

The king has established in Paris a College of the Three Tongues under the presidency of Budé, offering princely salaries. I was once invited

* * * * *

18 The book was published by Froben in March 1531, with a dedicatory letter to
Duke William v of Cleves dated 26 February (Ep 2431). See CWE 37 3–18.
19 The five-volume Froben edition of Chrysostom was published with a dedicatory letter to Christoph von Stadion (Ep 2359) that is dated 5 August 1530. For
the Augustine, see Ep 2157.
20 See Ep 2253:18–24.
21 *Commentarii linguae graecae* (Paris: Josse Bade, September 1529); cf Epp 1794 n2,
1812 n1, 2077:66–8.
22 *G. Budaei Epistolarum latinarum lib v ... [Epistolarum] graecarum lib i ...* [edited
and annotated by Jacques Toussain] (Paris: Josse Bade, February 1531). Cf Ep
2291:55–7.
23 Cf Ep 2291:61–4. The rumour was false.
24 CWE 39 148:2; ibidem 18:37–8. In neither case does Erasmus quote the colloquy
verbatim.
25 See CWE 42 94 with nn1 and 2. For Budé's lively resentment of these jibes
against the French, see Ep 1812:44–77.

to take this post, but declined.[26] Your friend Alberto,[27] with the help of the   75
Spaniard Sepúlvela,[28] who lives with him, is preparing a vigorous response
to my apologia, though nothing has appeared so far.[29] At Louvain there has
emerged a certain Titelmans (or should we rather call him 'Kakelmans'?),[30]
a self-confident and reckless young man with a certain penchant for effrontery.[31] Every single month he produces the proverbial bad egg of a bad   80
crow[32] to the applause of his Seraphic brethren.[33] He is laughed at by the
learned, but is nonetheless well pleased with himself.

   You will learn the rest of my news from Cammingha. A few days ago
I sent you a letter by Nicolaas Kan.[34] I am very happy to hear of your good
health and of your success in the task you have undertaken.[35] Please remem-   85
ber to give my greetings to your most distinguished colleagues, Everardus
Nicolai[36] and Maerten van Naerden.[37]

   Freiburg, 31 January 1530

        * * * * *

26 The invitation came in 1517; see Ep 522 introduction. Not until March 1530,
   however, did the much-discussed project of a royal trilingual college finally
   reach fruition with the establishment of the *lecteurs royaux* (regius professors)
   at the University of Paris. Budé had for many years actively promoted the
   establishment of the regius professorships, but they did not yet constitute an
   autonomous college and he never functioned as their president.
27 On Haio's supposed friendship with Alberto Pio (Ep 2080), cf Ep 2108:16 with n8.
28 Juan Ginés de Sepúlveda (Ep 2198 introduction), whom Erasmus invariably
   calls 'Sepúlvela'; cf Epp 2328:46, 2329:97.
29 Pio's *Tres et viginti libri in locos lucubrationum Erasmi*, written in response to
   Erasmus' *Responsio ad epistolam Alberti Pii* of March 1529 (CWE 84 1–103) was
   published at Paris by Josse Bade in March 1531.
30 Erasmus writes Κακelmans. Κακ-, the root of the Greek word for 'bad' or 'evil,'
   also calls to mind (doubtless not coincidentally) the word *kak* 'shit' in Dutch,
   kacke in German, and *cacare* 'to shit' in Latin.
31 See Epp 2206 introduction and n1, 2245, 2260:135–335, 2263:112–23, 2275,
   2277:8–9, 2299:114–17, 2300:29–43, 2312A:280–3.
32 *Adagia* I ix 25
33 The Observant Franciscans
34 The letter is not extant. For Kan, who had now left Erasmus' service, see Epp
   1832, 2343:24–5, 2348:21–2, 2349:10, 2352:1–9, 2356:1–11.
35 As a member of the council of Friesland at Leeuwarden
36 Everardus Nicolai (1497/8–1561), the second son of Nicolaas Everaerts (Ep
   1092), was appointed to the council of Friesland in 1526. In 1533 he joined the
   grand council at Mechelen but returned to Leeuwarden in 1541 as president
   of the council of Friesland. In 1557 he returned to Mechelen as president of
   the grand council.
37 Allen could not identify this person because Erasmus, evidently misreading
   Haio's 'Nardenus,' calls him 'Hardenus' in the letter. Maerten van Naerden

2262 / To Gerard van Herema   Freiburg, 31 January 1530

Gerard (or Gerold) van Herema, one of the wealthiest lords of Friesland
(documented 1515–30), had been appointed to the council of Friesland in
1515.

Like Ep 2261, this letter was entrusted to Haio Cammingha, who was supposedly on his way to Friesland. But after reaching Louvain (Ep 2352:305–6),
Cammingha turned south to Italy and did not deliver the letter until 1532,
several months after Erasmus had already published it in the *Epistolae floridae*.
Herema's gratitude for the letter was expressed in March 1532 in a letter from
his son-in-law, Hector van Hoxwier (Allen Ep 2624:92–102).

ERASMUS OF ROTTERDAM TO GERARD VAN HEREMA, GREETING
If I look up to you as a person of outstanding virtue and a great lover of
learning, this is only natural; for anyone who loves these fine qualities must
love all in whom they are seen to be conspicuous. That I reciprocate the
affection that I hear you have for me is simply a grateful response to your   5
kindness. But to write to a man who is distinguished by the long line of his
ancestors will perhaps look like presumption. If, however, you are willing to
accept the two earlier reasons, then I leave whatever fault remains for Haio
Cammingha to excuse. For by speaking so frequently of your exceptional
kindness and the uncommon warmth of your affection for me, he is the real   10
cause of this boldness of mine. I am so fond of my dear Haio, not just on
account of the integrity of his mind and character but also for his incredible
devotion to me, that I can deny nothing to so dear a friend, nor ought I to
do so to one to whom I owe so much.

His stay here was a great solace to me,[1] but he was snatched away by   15
the demands of business, something that neither of us wanted. He conducted
himself with such good sense and such affability that his loss was felt not
just by me but by all decent people. So if my audacity in writing to you turns

* * * * *

(d 1567) obtained a licentiate in both laws at Orléans before entering on a career
in public administration in his native Netherlands. In 1526 he was appointed
to the council of Friesland along with Everardus Nicolai, becoming its vice-
president in 1527. He went on to become president of the council of Utrecht
(1538) and president of the court of justice in Groningen (from August 1541).

2262
1 See Ep 2261 n1.

out well, I shall thank him for pushing me to it and congratulate myself on
taking his advice. My best wishes to you, distinguished sir, and to all your   20
nearest and dearest.

Freiburg, 31 January 1530

2263 / To Cuthbert Tunstall   Freiburg, 31 January 1530

Sent via Erasmus Schets (see Ep 2268:3), this is Erasmus' spirited response
to the friendly but tough criticisms of him in Ep 2226. The letter was first
published in the *Epistolae floridae*.

ERASMUS OF ROTTERDAM TO CUTHBERT TUNSTALL, GREETING
It is wonderful how that old friend of mine[1] keeps to his old ways through
everything, heaping kindness upon kindness and promoting the interests
and reputation of his friend with the most affectionate and honest advice
and counsel.   5
     As far as one can guess from the way things have begun, the long war
of words and pamphlets will soon be waged with halberds and cannons.[2]
If I did not value the salvation of my soul above security of life and property, I would prefer to settle in the camp of those from whom I fled. But
perish the thought that I should desert the unity of the church for the little   10
life that is left me,[3] an old man, nursing a stone in his bladder, which means
certain death![4] Whatever the ministers of the church decide about my writings is their affair. If the church were ruled today by men like Augustine,
there would be a happy rapport between them and me. But I fear that if
Augustine were to write now what he wrote then or what the present times   15
demand, he would not get a much better reception than Erasmus.[5] There is
that fine statement in your letter, that fire is not extinguished by fire, but
when one is falsely accused of impiety, it is impious to put up with it. What
did Augustine do? I could collect hundreds of passages from him – and not
many fewer from St Paul – that would now be charged with heresy. They   20

* * * * *

2263
1 Tunstall
2 See Ep 2219 n10.
3 On the importance to Erasmus of remaining within the 'unity (or consensus
  or fellowship) of the church' see Ep 2082 n78 and cf Ep 2204 n4.
4 See Ep 2260:341–58, and cf lines 124–8 below.
5 Cf Ep 2264:5–7.

will take me for a sheep,[6] but meanwhile even a poor sheep may lament
that certain people have destroyed the power of the gospel by human cleverness. Many do not understand what this is, many misuse these words.[7] If
scholastic theologians and monks think that by these means they can defend
the peace of the church, they are badly mistaken. We must flee to Christ   25
for refuge. It is here, in this context, that 'fire is not extinguished by fire.'
The present conflagration arose from the tyranny of Romanizers[8] and evil
monks. In an effort to extinguish the flames, these people are pouring oil
on the fire. We see the results and our hearts are sore. But Christ is the director of this drama, and we leave its ending to him. I know that here I am   30
stuck between the altar and the knife,[9] and I do not see where I can go to
be safe. All that remains is for me to commend myself to God.

I congratulate Thomas More but without much enthusiasm – though
I do not feel sorry for him either.[10] But I am genuinely happy for your
beloved Britain, and somewhat also for myself.   35

I had translated three homilies on Acts by Chrysostom.[11] Now I have
repented of the trouble I took, for I saw nothing of Chrysostom there. On
your urging I took up the manuscript again, but I have never read anything so foolish. I could write better in a drunken stupor. It contains silly
and pointless ideas, which the author cannot explain satisfactorily. From   40
the Commentaries on the Second Epistle to the Corinthians I translated six
homilies.[12] I recognize the same culprit speaking there. So I do not intend
to waste my valuable time on such things. Chrysostom breathes a different
spirit. I have arranged with several scholars to translate some of the pieces
already translated by Oecolampadius. Brie has translated the *Babylas* and is   45
now working on the *Monk*.[13] But all of them, I find, are slow workers. The

* * * * *

6 For sheep as symbols of stupidity see *Adagia* III i 95.
7 Erasmus' language here is vague. Presumably 'this' is the 'power of the gospel,'
  the language of which many misunderstand and misuse.
8 On this word and its meaning, see Ep 2261 n13.
9 See Ep 2253A n17.
10 See Ep 2228 n1.
11 See Ep 1801.
12 Volume 1 of the Froben Chrysostom (Ep 2359) includes Erasmus' translations of
  seven. In Epp 2291:12–13 and 2283:183 he again gets the number wrong at ten.
13 On Brie's translation of *De Babyla martyre*, see Ep 1856 introduction. Brie was
  so slow in producing his translation of the *Comparatio regis et monachi* that
  Froben had to use the translation by Oecolampadius. See Epp 2291:5–6 and
  2340:23–5. Brie's translation eventually appeared in the edition of Chrysostom
  published by Chevallon at Paris in 1536.

plan is that the works already translated by Oecolampadius should be corrected partly by Oecolampadius himself and partly by other scholars. His
comments and marginal notes will be suppressed; even his name will not
appear. He himself, as he says, has compared his work with the Greek. I did 50
the same in my pieces. As for accuracy in rendering the Greek, there are
more faults in Anianus,[14] Aretino,[15] and the rest than in Oecolampadius,
whose errors arise more from haste than ignorance.[16] We have Francesco
Aretino's version of First Corinthians as far as chapter 30. I examined a
sample to see how well he had handled the job, and there right at the very 55
start we have – τὸν τῦφον κατέβαλε καὶ χαμαὶ ἔρριψε πᾶσαν αὐτῶν οἴησιν 'he
overthrew their pride and cast all their arrogance to the ground,' where he
translates οἴησιν as 'opinion' instead of 'arrogance.' A little later we have
οὐδὲν γὰρ ἡμεῖς κατωρθώσαμεν ἀλλὰ διὰ τοῦ θελήματος τοῦ Θεοῦ τὴν σωτηρίαν
εὑρόμεθα καὶ ἐπειδὴ αὐτῷ ἔδοξεν ἐκλήθημεν 'for we succeeded in nothing, but 60
by the will of God, we have found salvation, and when it seemed good to
him, we were called,' where he translated 'we shall do nothing rightly and
we shall find salvation,' making no distinction between the aorist and the
future, even in spite of the warning provided by the verbs in the past tense
that follow directly. You may judge the rest from this. 65

Anianus began his commentary on Matthew no more auspiciously. For
right at the third line, for δεύτερον πλοῦν, that is, 'the second-best course,' he
wrote 'second riches,' imagining that πλοῦν was a shortened form.[17] There
are so many errors of this sort that it was almost easier to make a fresh
translation than correct the existing one. 70

I translated the fragment of Origen in good faith.[18] Even if it had contained something erroneous, there was no danger since no one reads him
today as a dogmatist, the man's errors having been pointed out long since.
The old authorities talked about the Eucharist with proper reverence before
the subject became a matter of debate. Perhaps even now the church has not 75
clearly defined how the body is present in the Eucharist beneath the accidents or beneath the actual bread. Moreover it is agreed that in the time

* * * * *

14 On Anianus, a contemporary and translator of Chrysostom, see Ep 1558 n22.
15 See Ep 2226 n19.
16 On Oecolampadius' shortcomings as a translator of Chrysostom, see Ep 2226:
70–5 with n18.
17 Ie a shortened form of πλοῦτον, the accusative case of πλοῦτος ('wealth'). This
passage from Chrysostom and Anianus' mistranslation of it are also discussed
in Adagia III iv 71.
18 See Ep 1844.

of the apostles there was a divine service[19] that the laity conducted among
themselves involving prayer and a blessing; and it is likely that they called
the bread at that service 'the body of the Lord' just as frequently in Sacred   80
Scripture the same word is used of the sign and the thing signified. It is possible that in this work Origen is speaking of such a service.[20] Nowhere in
the canonical Scriptures will you find a passage where the apostles certainly
consecrated the body of the Lord, as it is now consecrated on the altar, with
the single exception of a passage in the First Epistle to the Corinthians chap-   85
ter 11,[21] and yet in chapter 10, where Paul's discussion begins, it does not
seem that we are dealing with consecration by a priest. Furthermore, even
supposing we admit that Origen was speaking here of a real consecration,
there is nothing absurd in his account; for what is material there, that is,
the bread or the accidents, withdraws into the background, nor is there any   90
value in consuming it if faith is lacking. Also it is not wrong to speak of the
real body there as an image and symbol, for beneath the symbols there lies
the invisible body, and this real body which is consumed is itself a symbol
of the unity of the body with the head and of the members one with another.
    As for your suggestion that I should make clear my views on this sub-   95
ject so that suspicion will not cling to me, why should I, rather than someone
else, do this, for I have never thought, or spoken, or written anything inconsistent with Catholic truth. In fact I have already done what you suggest
in my letter to the assembly at Baden, which was published two years ago,[22]
and in a brief treatise issued shortly thereafter, which is now available in   100
a German translation.[23] What am I to do with people who do not read my
work? In your case I understand that the pressure of business does not leave
you time.
    I replied to the bishop of Lincoln on the subject of the *Colloquies*.[24] Any-
one who says that I am mocking Christian fasting, holy vows, ecclesiastical   105
ceremonies, the prescribed fasts of the church, invocation of the saints, and
pilgrimages for the sake of religion, is, to put the matter simply and briefly,
an absolute liar. I do make fun of the superstition that certain people attach
to these observances, and that is something that deserves to be mocked. If
you had time to read what I wrote in reply to the Spaniards and to Béda, you   110

* * * * *

19 For 'service' Erasmus uses the word *synaxis*, ie a gathering for religious worship, especially for celebrating the Eucharist.
20 Cf Ep 2226:39–55.
21 1 Cor 11:23–7
22 See Ep 1708.
23 *Detectio praestigiarum* (1526); for the German translation see Ep 1708 n2.
24 See Epp 1704:24–46, 2037:16–42.

would see that these people have nothing on which to base their slanders.[25] Something else is urging them on. In Brabant the monks are in control,[26] especially the Observants.[27] They have worked on a young member of their order, a shameless fellow, inexhaustibly long-winded, unrestrained in his impudence, who was born to spit on Erasmus and will stop at nothing to   115 gain notoriety.[28] Scholars laugh at him, but in spite of this he is well pleased with himself. It does not surprise me that a young man should be insanely eager for fame. But I am surprised at his older colleagues, on whose authority he relies when he engages in such outrageous behaviour. If they do not realize how much hostility and shame this young man's rash and preco-   120 cious activity is likely to bring on their order, I think they are sadly lacking in judgment; if, as I believe, they support and secretly provoke him,[29] then I find them lacking in seriousness.

I have become hardened to such attacks. If I could get rid of the stone that I have been harbouring in my bladder now for two years,[30] I would eas-   125 ily despise the rest.[31] The discomfort is constant, but still tolerable. I do not fear death, but I would wish for a gentler end. Many recommend surgery, but I shall summon the surgeon only when I am tired of life. Here there are high hopes that the emperor's authority will curb the recklessness of the sects, which no one can put up with any longer.[32] I hope that this will come   130 about without a painful loss of human blood, and that the victory will not fall to the benefit of the pope and the monks, but of religion and of Christ. We are all working for revenge, no one for a purer life.

Farewell, my great patron. My good wishes to the lord chancellor and my thanks for his gift.[33]   135

Freiburg, 31 January 1530

* * * * *

25 For the Spaniards see Epp 1869, 1967; for Béda see Epp 1664, 2110 n8, 2213 n8.
26 See Ep 2249 n8.
27 See Ep 2275.
28 Frans Titelmans; see Ep 2261 n31.
29 Literally 'pour cold water on him.' The Latin adage has the opposite meaning to that of its literal translation; it means 'to provoke secretly,' possibly from the practice of pouring cold water over racehorses to make them run faster. See *Adagia* I x 51.
30 See Ep 2260 n74.
31 Ie old age; see Ep 2260 n73.
32 Charles v was currently en route to Germany with the intention of resolving the religious conflicts there; see Ep 2261 nn6 and 7.
33 The chancellor was Thomas More (Ep 2228:1–3). The gift may have been the four rings that are listed in the inventory of April 1534; see Major 38.

2264 / To a Theologian   [Freiburg, January 1530]

This letter was first published in the *Epistolae floridae*. Allen assigned the approximate date on the basis of the return of Erasmus' servant-messenger, Quirinus Talesius (line 1), in January 1530: see Ep 2222 n16. In the letter, Erasmus
responds with studied politeness to reported charges of heresy (lines 2–3). He
may have received a conciliatory reply; see Ep 2277:11–12).

As to the identity of the theologian who made the charges, Allen speculated plausibly that it could well have been the Dominican Eustachius van der
Rivieren, a member of the faculty of theology at Louvain who had published
books against Luther and who would, on 12 July 1530, deliver before an audience that included a number of Erasmus' friends a speech fiercely denouncing 'languages' (see Ep 2353:15–21). In 1531, moreover, Rivieren would publish his *Apologia pro pietate in Erasmi Roterodami Enchiridion canonem quintum*
(Antwerp: W. Vorsterman), a denunciation of Erasmus' 'heresies,' the preface
to which was incongruously filled with praise of Erasmus' learning. Erasmus
deemed the work too childish to merit a reply.

ERASMUS OF ROTTERDAM TO A CERTAIN THEOLOGIAN, GREETING
Most accomplished theologian, on his return my servant Quirinus reported
that you once said at a dinner party that there were things in my works that
could by no means escape the charge of heresy. It is possible that he did not
quite understand what you meant; it is also possible that, unknowingly, I   5
admitted some such error into my writings, for errors of this sort can be
found in the works of Jerome, Ambrose, and Augustine.[1] But my position
is this: I believe that there is nothing in my writings that could properly
be called heretical, provided the reader is not bent on quarrelling and finding fault. I am not now talking about the sort of slip that often creeps into   10
the work of ordinary mortals. You will do me a very great favour, therefore, if you point out any serious errors. As soon as something is pointed
out, it will immediately be expunged. I hate heresy as much as anyone.
I am told that you are a courteous and fair-minded man and totally unlike Béda, who seems to me to mistake ranting for true criticism.[2] I pray   15
he may come to a better frame of mind. You may perhaps see which of
us is the more effective in weakening the power of the sects from the fact
that the sects hate no one more bitterly than me and fling their stinging

* * * * *

2264
1 Cf Ep 2263:14–20.
2 See Ep 2213 n8.

insults at no one more frequently than at me, while no one is angry with
Béda.   20

Moreover, Erasmus dares to take a stand in Germany, not without
grave risk to life and fortune. Nor is it only slander that I must face, but
also criminal charges and secret conspiracies. These people note down from
my books anything that might turn cities, people, and princes against me.
They publish hateful things about me anonymously and suborn others to   25
raise suspicion against me. Some of the worst and most cunning villains lurk
under the banner of the gospel. I did not leave Basel as long as there was
hope that better counsels would prevail. If certain theologians were aware
of this, they would judge me worthy at least of some support. May the Lord
prosper you in all things.   30

Send a letter back with the courier, if it is not inconvenient. His name
is Ottmar Nachtgall and he is the foremost preacher in this city, a man who
is no stranger to languages and the Muses.[3] He shares this much with me,
that he is a refugee from Augsburg as I am from Basel, for neither of us
wanted to witness what it would pain us to see.   35

2265 / From Theodoricus Cortehoevius   Antwerp, 1 February 1530

Nothing is known of Theodoricus Cortehoevius (presumably from Korten-
hoef, west of Hilversum) except that he published two books, one of which
was *Adagiorum aureum flumen* (Antwerp: M. de Keyser for G. van der Haeghen,
16 February 1530), a selection of Erasmus' adages for which this letter was the
dedicatory epistle.

THEODORICUS CORTEHOEVIUS TO THE EXCELLENT
MASTER ERASMUS OF ROTTERDAM, LEARNED SCHOLAR
IN THE THREE TONGUES, GREETING
Let me explain to you in a few words, dear Desiderius, my distinguished
friend, by what right and with what audacity I have presumed to emerge   5
from my little corner into the light of day. In this truly golden age of the renaissance of learning, in which not only are the three famous languages being taught but everyone to the extent of his ability is advancing the cause of
liberal studies, one man translating from Greek what had previously been
unfamiliar to Latin ears, another revising and perfecting works that were ig- 10
norantly or badly translated, yet another collating old manuscripts to restore

* * * * *

3 See Ep 2166 n3.

Latin authors that have been corrupted by the ravages of time, or making
sense out of obscure passages – in this age, although I am a man of modest abilities and little learning, I do not want to be a total parasite, so I have
thought it worthwhile to employ my energies in helping many young stu-   15
dents to make progress, especially those from among the poor. They cannot
afford to purchase so large a volume as the *Chiliads*;[1] they would be embarrassed by the high cost, and as a result would be deprived of part of
the fruit of their studies. I call Almighty God to witness that no thought
of gain has ever crossed my mind; my only aim is to do all I can to pro-   20
mote the interests of others. It is enough for me to remember those words
of Socrates, that we know nothing at all.[2] All I want is to assist others with
their education as best I can.

There is nothing of my own here, nor am I seeking renown for my-
self. The results of my labours will make clear what my contribution is. In   25
fact, more than anything else, it was your modesty and good sense that inspired me to take up this task enthusiastically and to pursue it diligently
to the end, for I have no doubt that I shall be criticized by some censorious and half-educated people who are forever finding fault with all honourable studies. They will accuse me of attempting to wrench his club from   30
the hand of Hercules, just as in the past critics with the severity of a Zoilus
used to attack Virgil for stealing many of his lines from Homer and using them as his own;[3] to this Virgil replied that it was indeed a magnificent achievement to steal Jove's thunder or wrench his club from the
hand of Hercules.[4] We are all disciples of the generations that preceded   35
us; we swing our scythe into someone else's harvest. Our beloved Terence
says:

> Nothing is said now that has not been said before.
> So you should try to understand and forgive the moderns
> If they do what the ancients did repeatedly.[5]   40

* * * * *

2265
1 Ie the *Adagia*; see Ep 2210 n7.
2 Plato *Apology* 21A–23B
3 Zoilus was a Greek philosopher (fourth century BC) who is remembered prin-
    cipally for his biting criticisms of Homer. His name became proverbial for the
    severe critic; see *Adagia* II v 8.
4 The story is told by Asconius Pedianus, cited in Suetonius *Vita Vergili* 46.
5 Terence *Eunuchus* 41–3

Certainly, as Pindar says, something that has been nobly done should not be buried in silence in the earth.[6]

I am not here claiming praise for myself that was earned by another's industry, nor, in my writing, am I attributing to myself an honour that was won by someone else's labour;[7] rather I am contributing to the reputation of the author himself. Like you I care nothing for praise, especially praise that comes from people whom I regard as lacking intelligence, learning, and eloquence. Someone may be offended by this, but I take no offence myself, for I am completely unaffected by the censure of others; on the contrary I congratulate myself that I am free from those faults to which I see that so many are a prey. True learning has no worse enemy than the ignorant fool, whose envious or captious nature finds nothing at all to its liking.[8] The same may be said of those who are now cock of the walk,[9] for there is nothing more arrogant than inexperience. Can you think of anything more shameless and stubborn than ignorance? It is a mark of the modesty and integrity of the truly learned man that he sees everything in the best, not the worst, light. Barbarians and empty boasters are like Niceas and Demosthenes in the story, who complained about the glory that was snatched from them by Cleon, a tanner turned general, who kneaded the cake they had already prepared.[10]

But since it is impossible to satisfy Momus,[11] who looks at everything with a searching eye, you are the only person whom I wish to please, for you are my special patron, and you, more than anyone else, seem to me worthy of respect. For the exceptional felicity of your godlike mind always had, and still has, few equals. You possess great erudition and a wide knowledge of the best disciplines; you are endowed with a perceptive intelligence, and commended by the modesty of your life; so your support will defend this book from cantankerous critics, who are so stubborn that not even Vertumnus himself could change their minds;[12] in fact the book is really yours, not

* * * * *

6 Pindar *Nemean Odes* 9.6–7
7 Terence *Eunuchus* 400
8 Something has gone wrong here with the grammar of the sentence, but the general sense is clear enough.
9 Literally 'those who now display the comb [of a cock]'; *Adagia* i viii 69
10 For the story about Cleon and the adage about kneading a cake already kneaded by someone else see *Adagia* ii x 1.
11 Momus is the traditional Greek prototype of the carping critic who can never be satisfied; see *Adagia* i v 74.
12 Vertumnus was an Etruscan god who was taken over by the Romans and seen as the deity who presided over change; see *Adagia* ii ii 74.

mine. Your judgment in particular weighs heavily with me, as does that of
certain learned men who are not likely to attack me for my presumption,   70
but will lend their support to my labours.

There is no need now for me to sing your virtues to the music of the
long pipes[13] or praise your learning and your high moral character, for these
are respected not just in Germany but are admired and revered by all Christendom. True virtue can never be hidden. When I consider to whom this dis-   75
tinguished literary production should be dedicated, you alone can rightly
claim that distinction for yourself, as all will agree. We are all your young
pupils and we follow at a distance after you and the venerable fathers of the
past, drinking in your fine words like children sucking milk at the breast.
So, like you, I earnestly request that no one be put off because this work   80
has already appeared so often. For according to Plato, 'what is beautiful can
be repeated twice or thrice.'[14] One should never tire of noble things. One
thing constantly inspires another, adding effort to effort. I beg you with
your warm heart and sense of honour to accept the affection that I feel for
your modest self. My wish is that you have a long and happy life in Christ   85
and good health.

Antwerp, 1 February 1530

2266 / To Thomas Boleyn   [Freiburg, February 1530]

This is the preface to *In psalmum 22 enarratio triplex* (Basel: Froben 1530), which
Boleyn had requested of Erasmus in November 1529 (Ep 2232). The work was
well in hand by the end of January (Ep 2261:46–7). Allen assigned the conjectural
date on the ground that the book was doubtless intended for the March book
fair at Frankfurt. A gift copy sent before May is acknowledged in Ep 2314:39.

Thomas Boleyn (c 1477–1539) was a courtier who had risen to prominence
in the service of both Henry VII and Henry VIII. The latter entrusted him
with many important diplomatic missions. In 1527 Boleyn was created Viscount Rochford; in 1529 he was made earl of Wiltshire and Ormond; and in
January 1530 he became keeper of the privy seal. Much of the royal favour
shown to Boleyn in recent years was the result of Henry VIII's infatuation with
his daughter Anne, the designated replacement for Queen Catherine. Erasmus
suspected that this was the motive behind the request for the commentary:
in 1526 he had obliged Catherine with the *Institutio christiani matrimonii* (Ep
1727), and now the other side in the battle over the royal divorce wanted the

* * * * *

13 'To play on the long pipes,' ie to engage in pointless effort; see *Adagia* I v 97.
14 Quoted in Greek from Plato *Gorgias* 489E; cf *Adagia* I ii 49.

honour of a work from Erasmus' pen. After much hesitation, Erasmus decided that he could yield to the request because there was nothing in the psalm that compelled him to discuss the subject of marriage. See Ep 2312A:134–54.

A translation of the letter by Emily Kearns has already been published in CWE 64 124. The notes for this new translation incorporate some of those that Dr Kearns prepared for hers.

TO THE RIGHT HONOURABLE THOMAS, VISCOUNT ROCHFORD, FROM DESIDERIUS ERASMUS OF ROTTERDAM, GREETING

Honoured sir, you have given us long since ample evidence of the excellence of your mind when you seemed not content with all the adornments that came to you from your lineage, from the busts of your ancestors, from 5 gold rings and gold chains, adornments that you had gained the right to wear from the nobility of your ancient line and a character that did honour to your ancestry, but you wanted also to adorn your mind with a more precious chain, whose links are formed by the noble lessons of philosophy. But now I have even greater reason to congratulate you on your happy fortune, 10 for I see you, a man of influence, a layman and a courtier, taking to your heart the sacred word and craving to possess that noble pearl.[1] So it was with increased pleasure that I acceded to your most pious request. I have written a threefold commentary on the psalm you chose. How well I succeeded is for you to judge. In any case I myself have derived no small profit 15 from this little effort, for the work brought my mind considerable pleasure and consolation. If it brings the same pleasure to your mind too, I shall be delighted to have obeyed your request. But if there are things in it that displease you, please do not hesitate to point them out. Let me thank you for the opportunity you have given me to expand my knowledge. 20

St Jerome wrote on this psalm, but briefly, as is his way;[2] Arnobius is even briefer.[3] St Augustine did not write a commentary; he added only the briefest of notes, the sort of thing, I believe, which preachers do as an aide-memoire in preparing to speak to the people;[4] I wonder if by some chance a commentary has disappeared. Cassiodorus was not 25 available to me, but he does not usually have much that is important to

* * * * *

2266
1 Matt 13:45–6
2 The commentary attributed to Jerome is part of the Pseudo-Jerome *Breviarum in psalmos.*
3 Arnobius the Younger *Commentarium in psalmum* 22 PL 53 354–5
4 *Enarratio in psalmum* 22 PL 36 182

say.[5] So for the most part I was left, as the saying goes, to fend for myself.[6] If, however, anything here has turned out well, the credit belongs wholly to Christ and to him alone.

2267 / From Bonifacius Amerbach   [Basel] 2 February 1530

This letter (= AK Ep 1409), Bonifacius' reply to Ep 2256, was first published in Burckhardt (Ep 56). Writing it cost Bonifacius much trouble and effort. Allen found four rough drafts in the Öffentliche Bibliothek of the University of Basel and based his text on the longest of them (MS C VI a 54 58), which Boni- facius himself had extensively corrected, scratching out and rewriting whole passages between the lines. He cited his legal authorities in the margins.

Greetings. Things have now come to such a pass, illustrious Erasmus, that I would be happy to be counted at least in the second rank of men, by which I mean that, although I cannot decide what is best in my own interests, I am ready to listen to good advice from others. I realize that my feelings for my native Basel are like those of a husband for a quarrelsome and rather diffi-   5 cult wife. Willy-nilly, I am forced to say 'I cannot live with you or without you'![1]

There are several reasons for staying here. First of all 'the smoke rising from my native land.'[2] Then there are the returns coming in each year from my property in Basel. I am beginning to doubt if they would be paid in   10 my absence, and I am not encouraged by what happened to the monks and priests,[3] who, I hear, have gained little even from documents sealed with the stamp of the magistrate. Finally, whatever one may think of the terms of my appointment (which are better than those of any professor at Freiburg with the exception of Zasius),[4] they are not to be despised by a man like me,   15

* * * * *

5 For Cassiodorus' *Expositio in psalmum* 22 see PL 70 167–71.
6 Literally 'to do it by my own Mars,' ie 'to do it by my own prowess'; see *Adagia* I vi 19.

2267
1 Martial 12.47.2, cited in *Adagia* II ix 92
2 See Homer *Odyssey* 1.58–9 (cf 9.34–5), where Odysseus longs for home and 'the smoke rising . . .'
3 Ie those who, like the members of the cathedral chapter, left the city rather than submit to the new evangelical church order; see Ep 2097 n1.
4 On the terms of Bonifacius' appointment, cf Ep 2248 nn7 and 9. Zasius (Ep 2209 n8) earned a salary of one hundred gulden. See Roderich von Stintzing

who does not possess a very splendid fortune and is encumbered with a
family at a time when the cost of living is so high. Nor is it very clear where
I should move to, since on account of the perpetual lethargy of the princes
the present evils spread from day to day like a contagion, threatening every
neighbouring city and indeed the whole region. If that happens (and I hope   20
that I am a false prophet), how much better it would be to have fled from the
danger once and for all by moving further away than to incur great expense
only to end up in a similar or worse situation. But the truth is that to move
a considerable distance is precluded by my wife and family. Otherwise, if
I were free, I would have packed my bags long ago and considered either   25
France or Italy.

On the other hand, there are just as many reasons for anxiety if I plan
to stay here. I foresee that half my fortune will disappear if the emperor ex-
acts reparations from us.[5] I foresee evangelical rule degenerating into sheer,
unadulterated tyranny. I foresee many other things that I do not wish to   30
mention. But if I were permitted to absent myself from the new liturgy, I
would call to mind that line of Homer

all that happened in thy house, both good and bad[6]

and imagine I was living in Constantinople under the Turk. I would trust
that Christ would not demand of me anything more painful, even if I did   35
not hear mass every day. If long ago it was possible for Christians to live

* * * * *

*Ulrich Zasius: Ein Beitrag zur Geschichte der Rechtswissenschaft im Zeitalter der
Reformation* (Basel 1857; repr Darmstadt 1961) 43–4.

5 The Latin here is *si clarigationibus suis Caesar nos devoveat*. This appears to be
related to reports at this time that Charles v and Ferdinand of Austria were
planning to attack and subjugate the evangelical cantons of Switzerland and
their allies among the South German imperial cities because of their adher-
ence to the Reformation; see *Amtliche Sammlung der älteren Eidgenössische Abschiede* 4/1b: *Die Eidgenössischen Abschiede aus dem Zeitraume von 1529 bis 1532*
ed Johannes Strickler (Zürich 1876) 503–4, 506–7. A *clarigatio* was a solemn demand for redress or satisfaction, failure to comply with which would result
in a declaration of war. So it seems that Bonifacius was worried that Basel
and the other evangelical cantons might either be compelled to pay tribute to
avoid war with the emperor or else have to pay heavy reparations in the event
of defeat at his hands.

6 *Odyssey* 4.392 (cited in Greek), where Odysseus is assured that he will be told
all that is happening in his home. The meaning seems to be that Bonifacius
needs to know everything, good and bad, about the religious situation in Basel
in order to determine whether he can continue to live here.

under the pagans, it should also be possible today to live under these people, who proudly claim the name of the gospel.

These and similar arguments pull me cruelly now in one direction and now the other, and I cannot decide what choice to make, unless you guide   40
me by your counsel. I beg you most earnestly to do this, though I do not mean to be a nuisance. Perhaps, my dear Erasmus, I am taking too great a liberty, but you will forgive me because of my love for you. I rely on this, or rather it is because of this that I do not blush to pour into your lap all the worries of my heart, for you are the best of mentors.   45

You want me to consider that matter of the king of England, presumably because people give me the title of jurist. Of course there is no one who knows better than you what ought to be done, for with your exceptional knowledge and wisdom, you are as good as a score of other men.[7] But I fear that failure to comply with your request would be a sin, so let me tell you   50
in a few words what I think. You are aware of the usual distinction made by experts in canon law between a consummated and an unconsummated marriage, whereby the pope has authority to dissolve the marriage in one case and not in the other.[8] The reasons given for this distinction do not satisfy me; for I consider them somewhat strained, especially since I have learned   55
from Ulpian that it is not intercourse but consent that constitutes marriage.[9] I would set out the reasons for my doubts if I did not see from that masterly discussion of the subject in your defence against Lee that you share my opinion.[10] That common distinction, however, was not accepted even by all legal scholars, as is shown by Peter of Ancharano,[11] who, when about   60
a century ago he was consulted by the king of England about marriage to the wife of one's uncle,[12] replied that in all matters, except where articles

* * * * *

7 'As good as ... other men' is cited in Greek from Homer *Iliad* 11:514.
8 In the margin (see introduction above) Bonifacius cites *Decretals* 3.32.7.
9 Bonifacius cites *Digest* 23.1.4. The AK editors correct this to *Digest* 50.17.30. The writings of Roman jurist Ulpian (d AD 228) supplied one-third of the total content of the *Digest* (also known as the *Pandects*).
10 *Responsio ad annotationes Lei*; see CWE 72 386–9, and cf n22 below.
11 The canonist Petrus de Ancharano / Pietro d' Ancharano (c 1330–1416) taught at Bologna and at Ferrara.
12 No king of England in Ancharano's lifetime applied for such a dispensation for himself. But in 1410, Thomas, duke of Clarence (1388–1421), son of Henry IV, received a papal dispensation to marry the widow of his father's half-brother, John Beaufort (d 1410). The king may have asked for the dispensation on his son's behalf.

of faith are concerned, the pope has authority to 'dispense' (I use his own word).[13] What is more, Marianus Socinus gives it as his opinion that the pope, as president of the penitential court,[14] could dissolve a marriage even 65 after a lengthy cohabitation if the young man claimed that he had entered into it with no intention of binding himself, driven only by uncontrollable passion.[15]

I could bring forward many opinions of that kind, but you have not the leisure to listen to such things nor I to write them down. Not to beat 70 about the bush, as long as there is nothing the papalists will refuse their master, the pope,[16] will there be any limit to his powers? This is especially true, now that the teaching of Ancharano has been taken as an oracle[17] by Felino, Decio,[18] and several recent authorities, and considered worthy to

* * * * *

13 Bonifacius cites Ancharano's Consilia [sive juris responsa] no 373. There had been several incunable editions of the work, including the one cited in Burckhardt 239 n2 (Pavia: Franciscus Gyrardengus 1496).

14 Ie the Apostolic Penitentiary, the curial tribunal authorized to grant dispensations in cases reserved to the pope

15 Marianus Socinus / Mariano Sozzini (1401–67) was a canonist who taught at Padua, Bologna, and Siena. According to Burckhardt 240 n1, Bonifacius' citation here was to Socinus' Responsa non delphica sed coelestia (Venice 1502) I 53–4.

16 Here Bonifacius notes in the margin several passages from Johannes Andreae / Giovanni d'Andrea (c 1270/5–1348), the renowned canonist who taught at Padua, Pisa, and Bologna: '[Novella] in Decretales 3.528 etc.' Andreae's Novella super cinque libris Decretalium had been published at Venice (Johannes and Gregor de Gregoriis) in 1489.

17 Literally 'as coming from the tripod,' ie as true as though it came straight from the oracle of Apollo at Delphi, where a great tripod stood at the entrance to the cave; see Adagia I vii 90.

18 Felinus Sandeius / Felino Sandeis (1444–1503), an eminent canon lawyer, taught at both Padua and Pisa before joining the rota in Rome in 1484. He later became bishop of Penna (1495) and Lucca (1501). From 1476 Philipus Decius / Filippo Decio of Milan (1454–1535), caught in the storms engendered by the French invasion of Italy and struggles between Louis XII and Pope Julius II, had a brilliant but stormy career as professor of civil and canon law at Pisa, Padua, Pavia, and Valence, and then again at Pavia and Pisa. For Sandeis, Bonifacius cites 'super Decret. 1.2.7,' which is doubtless a reference to the Commentaria eruditissima in quinque libros Decretalium, an edition of which had been published by Sebastian Gryphius at Lyon in 1529. For Decius he cites 'Consil. 112, 133,' which would be a reference to the Consilia elegantissima, an edition of which had been published by Vincent de Portonariis at Lyon in 1512.

receive the stamp of approval.[19] If I were asked my opinion in cases such as   75
these, I would appeal to the canon given by Christ: 'Whom God has joined
together, let not man put asunder.'[20] Unless I am mistaken, we are not to use
this as a Lesbian rule to be bent according to our will,[21] but as a standard
by which to test and measure all our actions. So I would reply that after
a couple are duly joined in marriage, all power is removed from the pope   80
unless some great and just cause calls for a divorce as a matter of right. No
one has written more definitively on this subject than you.[22]

In the case before us the king is thinking of divorce in the interests of
public peace. I am afraid, my dear Erasmus, that this is not a good reason
for divorce. Not to mention other possibilities – weariness perhaps of his   85
former wife, for

> Nature loves the fascination of another's complexion
> And ever seeks a stranger for an amorous intrigue
> (Epigram 2, Nicearchus *Sympotica*)[23]

the case is highly doubtful and has no solid arguments to fall back on. What   90
if his fiancée should turn out to be sterile? What if she will not produce a
male heir? Or, if she does produce an heir, will those who see themselves
next in line abandon hope on that account? As for the statement in which
he admitted never having treated his wife with true marital affection,[24] I
don't know what to say. While it has not helped his case, it has cast a heavy   95
shadow over his wife's chastity and especially over the parentage of his
daughter.[25] Quite apart from the fact that in law we have this widely held

* * * * *

19 Literally 'the mark of a whiter stone.' Not found in the *Adagia*, but a common
    expression in Latin authors; see eg Persius 2.1, Pliny *Epistles* 1.2.5, Martial
    9.53.5. The sense here may be derived from the practice in criminal trials of
    using a white pebble for acquittal and black for condemnation.
20 Matt 19:6
21 To act 'by the Lesbian rule' is to do things the wrong way around, eg by ad-
    justing law to conduct instead of correcting conduct by law. See *Adagia* I v 93.
22 In the margin Bonifacius cites not only the treatise against Lee (see n10 above)
    but also Erasmus' annotation on 1 Cor 7:39. First inserted in 1519 and much
    expanded in later editions, the annotation was in fact a substantial essay on
    divorce; see LB VI 692D–703C, and cf John B. Payne *Erasmus: His Theology of the
    Sacraments* (Richmond Va, 1970) 121–5.
23 Cited in Greek from an epigram of Nicarchus *Anthologia Palatina* 11.7.3–4.
    'Nicearchus' in the reference is Bonifacius' own misspelling.
24 Cf Ep 2256:48–50 with n25.
25 Princess Mary, the future queen

axiom that an intention held only in the mind has no force,[26] will anyone
say that there was no marital intent towards a woman with whom he had
gone through all the solemn rites of marriage in a public ceremony and   100
with whom he had lived without distaste for so many years? Suppose that
at the beginning, when he was a minor, he had been motivated by fear;
suppose he had been tricked by the wiles of his guardians; surely when he
became his own man and took control of his own affairs, if at that point he
had not recognized her as his legitimate wife, he ought, as the lawyers say,   105
to have issued a writ for divorce and return of dowry. How his wife and
above all his daughter can recover completely after this admission, I leave
to your wise judgment to consider. To confess that the remark just slipped
out inadvertently is unworthy of a king, if we are to believe that these gods
in human form surpass other men not just in power but in wisdom also.   110
That the remark had its origin in his heart, not on his lips, seems clear from
the fact that it was designed precisely to put his plans in a favourable light
before the people.

     After it became clear that everything hinged on finding a son to suc-
ceed to the realm, there was still a way of producing sons that was adopted   115
long ago by the Greeks and later also by the Romans, namely by adoption.
What if, to lessen the possibility of trouble, he gained the consent of the
lords and the people and adopted a son-in-law or a child of his daughter's
or someone from outside to take the place of a son of his own? Perhaps the
open consent of the lords of the realm and the people would discourage any-   120
one inclined to cause trouble. You are aware that the practice of obtaining a
successor by adoption was frequently used by Roman emperors. Thus Oc-
tavian adopted Tiberius, Hadrian adopted Antoninus Pius; again when Antoninus Pius had no male offspring, he adopted Commodus, not to mention
a countless number of other examples. This tactic might even prove benefi-   125
cial to the realm, because there is generally a great difference between a son
we have produced and one we have chosen, for we must accept whatever
nature brings us; but adopted sons are matched to the needs and wishes of
the realm.

     But if the king were willing to divorce his wife and leave her in abso-   130
lute control of her own affairs, I have no doubt the pope would be generous, if he were not afraid of the power of the emperor.[27] However the matter turns out, the king ought to pay handsomely for the confession he made

                    * * * * *

26 Bonifacius cites *Codex Justinianus* 4.6.7, a passage that appears to have nothing
    whatever to do with the axiom in question.
27 See Ep 2211 n12.

at a crowded assembly, which cast an almost indelible stain on his daughter's reputation, an action that is inconsistent with the love a father owes his 135
children.

But to tell you this is sending owls to Athens.[28] If I were a follower of
Luther, I would add to what I have said that he could retain his former wife
and take a new wife as well. For while polygamy was very common among
the patriarchs of the Old Testament, Luther teaches in his commentary on 140
Genesis that there is no statement prohibiting it in the New.[29] This is my
attempt to comply with your request; please accept it with a good grace. The
rest when we meet.

2 February 1530

2268 / To Erasmus Schets   Freiburg, 2 February [1530]

Allen was shown the autograph of this letter in Rome in March 1909 by Cava-
liere Luigi Azzolini, in whose collection it then was. The letter was first published by G. J. Hoogewerff *Bescheiden in Italië omtrent nederlandsche kunstenaars
en geleerden* III: *Rome. Overige bibliotheken* (The Hague 1917) 200. The current
location of the manuscript is not known.

Because Erasmus writes from Freiburg, the year-date 1529 (see line 7 below)
has to be understood as 1530. As Allen notes, there are four other letters from
this period (Epp 2274, 2277, 2292, 2295), all of them original manuscripts, in
which Erasmus follows the practice of Freiburg by taking Easter (17 April in
1530) as the beginning of the new year.

Cordial greetings. I am swamping you with letters, my dearest Schets. Will
you please have these sent on as quickly as possible, one to Luis de Castro,
and the other through him to Bishop Tunstall.[1] My very best wishes, dearest
Schets, to you and all your family. I am sorry that in your country the

* * * * *

28 'Owls to Athens' is the equivalent of 'coals to Newcastle'; see *Adagia* I ii 11.
29 *Declamationes in Genesin* (1527) on chapter 16; see WA 24 303–5. Here Bonifacius notes in the margin that 'not all of [Luther's] disciples support him in
   this, as is seen in what Jo[hannes] Brenz has recently published in German on
   marriage.' The reference is to Brenz's *Wie in Eesachen – nach Götlichem billichen
   rechten Christlich zu handeln sey* (1529); see Johannes Brenz *Frühschriften Teil 2*
   ed Martin Brecht et al (Tübingen 1974) 277–80.

2268
1 The letter to Tunstall is Ep 2263; that to Castro is not extant.

monks are continuing to exercise their tyranny over honest, simple people   5
who deserve the best pastors.[2]

The day of the Purification 1529. Freiburg

Your friend, Erasmus

To the honourable Master Erasmus Schets, merchant. In Antwerp

2269 / From Johann Koler   Augsburg, 3 February 1530

The autograph of this letter, first published as Ep 80 in Enthoven, is in the
Rehdiger Collection of the University Library at Wrocław (MS Rehd 254.51).
On Johann Koler, canon of St Moritz in Augsburg, whose friendship facili-
tated Erasmus' contacts with Anton Fugger, Christoph von Stadion, and other
influential people in Augsburg, see Ep 2195 introduction. Erasmus' answer is
Ep 2308.

Cordial greetings. On 29 January, when by the mercy of God I had returned home safe and sound from Italy,[1] my very good friend, Master
Wolfgang Rem, eminent counsel and one of the three members of the tribunal of the Swabian League,[2] handed me a most delightful letter from
you.[3] You had written it in the expectation that it would reach me as I was   5
setting out for Italy or be delivered there when I had settled in. But this

* * * * *

2 See Ep 2249:31–2 with n8.

2269
1 See lines 38–46 below.
2 Founded in 1488, the Swabian League was an alliance of princes, prelates, imperial cities, and imperial knights that had as its purpose the maintenance of
   order and the status quo in the 'Swabian Circle' (*Schwäbischer Reichskreis*), one
   of the regional administrative districts of the Holy Roman Empire. Remembered primarily for its role in the suppression of the Peasants' Revolt in 1525,
   it had a long list of more positive achievements to its credit. By 1530, however,
   it had already lost much of its effectiveness, largely because of internal ten-
   sions between those members that had adhered to the Reformation and those
   that had not. It was formally dissolved in 1534. Highly organized and pro-
   fessionally staffed, the League had as one of its organs a three-member judi-
   cial tribunal that from 1512 was located in Augsburg. Wolfgang Rem of Ulm
   (d after March 1532), doctor of civil and canon law and a former assessor at
   the Reichskammergericht (Imperial Supreme Court), had recently settled in
   Augsburg and become a member of the league tribunal.
3 Not extant

plan failed on both counts, and it was not until I eventually returned home
that it was delivered. On account of Master Anton Fugger's absence the letter arrived too late,[4] and since my friends had already received word of my
return, they chose to hold it until I came back rather than entrust it to the   10
vagaries of fortune. As a result it was not delivered during my stay in Italy.
This, however, did not affect the mission you wanted me to carry out, for
your urgent request to be commended to my friends at the imperial court
I carried out on my own without being asked.[5] I have always been most
careful to commend my dear Erasmus, if not specifically to those whom you   15
named in your request, at any rate to all men of standing with whom I
was on familiar terms. Indeed, whenever there was a pressing need, I have
always defended your dignity and reputation against those who were ill disposed towards you, and I have done so vigorously and enthusiastically as
an obligation imposed by our mutual friendship. In fact very few dared to   20
open their mouths in my presence.

To turn now to your most courteous letter: you congratulate me par-
Your friend Zúñiga spoke in a most amicable way about you, which
pleased me greatly.[6] I am very happy to have got to know him even at this
point. I no longer wonder at his temerity. After I was informed of the illness
from which he suffers and could observe it at first hand, I immediately came   25
to the conclusion that the man should be pardoned, and I still think the
same way. It was a special joy and delight to me to form a close friendship
with Johannes Dantiscus, ambassador of his most serene Majesty, the king
of Poland.[7] He is such a courteous man that I have scarcely ever seen his
equal. He is a great supporter of yours; he never says or thinks anything   30
about you that is not splendidly complimentary, and for this reason he will
always be most dear to me. I regret that I got to know him so late, being
obliged to leave much sooner than I would have wished. But no distance
can ever separate him from me, for his great virtue and generous nature
have bound him closely to me.   35

To turn now to your most courteous letter: you congratulate me particularly on obtaining the Reverend Father Christoph, bishop of Augsburg,

* * * * *

4 On Anton Fugger, see Ep 2145. Erasmus' letter had presumably been delivered
   to him for transmittal to Koler.
5 Charles v and the imperial court were in Italy from mid-August 1529 until
   late March 1530.
6 On Erasmus' old adversary, Diego López Zúñiga, see Ep 1260 n36. For Erasmus' belated response to one of Zúñiga's attacks on him, see Ep 2172. Zúñiga
   was a member of the party of Cardinal Francisco de Quiñones that met Charles
   v when he landed at Genoa on 7 August 1529.
7 See Ep 2163 n34.

as a guide on my journey. I see, my dear Erasmus, that you are the victim
of a misunderstanding. When I wrote that I was setting out for Italy in the
company of my reverend bishop, I did not mean the Reverend Father Chris-   40
toph of Augsburg,[8] but Paul, bishop of Chur.[9] I rightly call him 'my bishop'
because I hold the position of provost of the church there, and it was principally on that account that I went to Italy. I recognize both bishops as mine,
one by reason of rank, the other as bishop of the diocese. I tell you this so
that you do not mistakenly imagine that I set off for Italy in the company of   45
the reverend bishop of Augsburg.

In expressing, distinguished sir, how delighted you are that the emperor Charles has turned all his thoughts to peace, you act as I would expect,
given your godly character and your long held principles; for what could be
more welcome, more useful, more desirable, or more beneficial to mankind   50
than peace? In this matter the emperor has shown a spirit that (to say no
more) is worthy of an emperor; for putting aside every other consideration,
forgetting the injuries and losses on all sides, he has thought nothing more
important than the settling of these long internal conflicts, the ending of
quarrels, and the making of reciprocal treaties among the Christian princes,   55
nor has he had any other aim than to pacify the Christian world and thus restore peace and tranquillity to his empire.[10] I feel confident that after he has
settled matters in Italy, he will proceed to resolve the conflicts in Germany
also. I have seen how strongly the truly Catholic heart of the pope supports
these godly enterprises of the emperor, and if I have drawn the right con-   60
clusion from a good deal of evidence, especially from a conversation I had
with the emperor when I described the wretched devastation of the church
at Chur,[11] I have come to realize how staunch has been his support of true

* * * * *

8 Christoph von Stadion; see Ep 2029.
9 Paul Ziegler of Nördlingen (d 1541), since 1517 prince-bishop of Chur in
   Grisons, where he was disliked and distrusted as a foreigner and an ally
   of the Hapsburgs. Locked in bitter conflict with the estates of Grisons, who
   wanted to eliminate his role in the secular government of the region, severely
   curtail his jurisdiction and his revenues as bishop, and foster the spread of
   the Reformation, he moved in 1524 from Chur to his castle in Glorenza, Alto
   Adige, where he remained for the rest of his life. See also n11 below.
10 For 'empire' Koler uses *imperium*, uncapitalized. It seems that he is not referring to the Holy Roman Empire, which would be shortened to *Imperium*,
   but rather to Charles' dynastic 'empire,' ie the conglomeration of all the lands
   in central, western, and southern Europe that Charles had inherited from his
   Austrian, Netherlandish (Burgundian), and Spanish forebears.
11 This could be a reference to the assault by an armed mob on the episcopal
   residence at Chur in June 1525. More likely it is a general reference to the

religion, how bitterly he has detested the spilling of Christian blood, how great is his thirst for peace and tranquillity, and how troubled he has been 65 by the unconscionable manoeuvring of the heretics; so much so that I believe he is prepared to suffer and endure absolutely anything, even a loss of his own prerogatives, if only peace might return to the world, harmony to Germany, and unity to the faith. So, my dear Erasmus, there is no reason to despair. 70

Please God, those with whom the emperor lately entered into a treaty will keep the peace with an honesty that matches the reverent, godly, and truly Christian spirit with which the emperor signed it.[12] I do not doubt that the golden age of which you write will return. But it is no secret whose fault it is that treaties signed in the past have come to nothing, nor has 75 there been any hiding the fact that these people have so far succeeded. So I greatly fear that some evil spirit will drive these same people to undermine the measures taken by the emperor and thwart his godly plans and noble intentions lest true godliness reign supreme. We pray Almighty God that he will be pleased to bring great blessings to his people. But if things turn 80 out differently because of our evil ways, we shall endure whatever comes with a patient mind, knowing that it is on account of our sins that adversity will be our destiny.

I am sending herewith a letter from a friend of yours that was entrusted to me by a teacher from the school in Padua.[13] If you wish to reply 85 to him, send your letter to me; I shall see that it is duly delivered.

Finally, Master Anton Fugger has asked me to send you his best wishes. At present, because of both the courier's haste and the pressure of business he is not free to write to you. You will receive a letter from him with the next courier.[14] Farewell, Erasmus, my illustrious and beloved friend, and 90 continue to reciprocate my love as you are doing.

Augsburg, 3 February 1530

* * * * *

concerted assault on the secular and ecclesiastical prerogatives of the prince-bishop in the period 1524–9, with individual communities left free to implement the Reformation or not, as they chose. In Chur itself, mass was forbidden in 1527 and images were removed from the churches in 1528. See Friedrich Pliet *Bündnergeschichte* (Chur 1945) 119–41.

12 Treaty of Barcelona with Clement VII (Ep 2211 n14), and the the Peace of Cambrai with Francis I (Ep 2207 n5)

13 Possibly Ep 2144, from Bembo, to which Erasmus would respond with Ep 2290

14 Perhaps the letter in response to Erasmus' 'lengthy and delightful letter'; see Ep 2307:1–2.

Please give my greetings to our friend Nachtgall.[15] The distinguished
Master Wolfgang Rem also asks me to send you his best wishes and professes his total devotion and his willingness to serve you.   95

To the most learned and distinguished doctor of sacred theology, Master Erasmus of Rotterdam, his very special friend. In Freiburg

2270 / From Erasmus Schets   Antwerp, 4 February 1530

This letter was first published by Allen from the autograph in the Öffentliche
Bibliothek of the University of Basel (MS Scheti epistolae 21). On Schets, see
Ep 2243 introduction.

Cordial greetings. I wrote you in the month of December, my good friend
Erasmus – your man Quirinus carried the letter.[1] Because I had money belonging to you, I followed the instructions you had given me,[2] and he received the money in Philippus florins and a few crowns.[3] He had asked for
gold florins, but because these are rare here, I could not oblige. However,   5
the currency I gave him could be changed at the Frankfurt fair and taken in

* * * * *

15 Ottmar Nachtgall, the downstairs neighbour in Freiburg with whom Erasmus
   would soon have trouble; see Epp 2166 n3, 2308 n19.

2270
1 Ep 2243. Quirinus was on his way back from England; cf n7 below.
2 Via Quirinus; see Ep 2243:14–17.
3 The gold *Philippus* or florin of St Philip was struck in the Burgundian-Hapsburg
  Low Countries from May 1496 (initially by Archduke Philip the Fair) to just
  before February 1521 (the last, at 15 carats 11 grains, 2.193g fine gold), when its
  official value was 50d groot Flemish. It was then replaced by the Carolus florin
  (at 14 carats, with 1.700g fine gold), in honour of Emperor Charles v, with an
  official value of 40d groot Flemish (CWE 1 318; CWE 8 349–50 Tables A–B). Given
  its gold content, the market value of the Philippus florin, which continued to
  circulate, should have been 54d groot in 1530, but the mint ordinance of 1521
  had stipulated that previous issues of Hapsburg gold coins were to retain their
  former value and thus be undervalued thereafter (CWE 8 348). A letter from
  Conradus Goclenius to Erasmus dated 14 July 1530 states that the current value
  of the gold Philippus, which had been worth 26 stuivers (52d) in 1522, was
  25 stuivers (50d); see Ep 2352:47–9. The crowns mentioned here were presumably English double-rose gold crowns, officially worth 5s 0d or 60d sterling,
  the equivalent of 10 days' wages for a Cambridge master mason (CWE 14 467
  Table 2). The gold florins were Rhenish florins (florins of the Four Electors),
  then worth 56d groot Flemish in the Hapsburg Netherlands. See Ep 2222 n4;
  CWE 8 349–50 Tables A–B; CWE 12 650 Table 3D; CWE 14 476 Table 3.

gold florins. Quirinus was not pleased at this. I do not know how he made the exchange, for he divulged nothing of that to me.

Luis de Castro, who on Quirinus' recommendation has become better known than previously to your English friends, will devote whatever time 10 or travel is necessary to extract from them (courteously of course) whatever pension they are pleased to offer you.[4] When these have come into my hands, I shall arrange with the Fuggers that whatever I receive be remitted to you, for I see from your letter how warmly Anton Fugger has embraced you and that he will not fail to serve your interests more warmly still.[5] 15

I am being badgered, and almost abused, by Ammonius and Omaar van Edingen for having received a Greek text of Chrysostom on Paul's Epistle to the Romans, which I was supposed to send on in your name.[6] Your man Quirinus, before going to England,[7] handed me a Greek text of the letters of Basil the Great to be delivered to Ammonius.[8] This was delivered 20 into Omaar's hands with the good faith with which it was given to me and sent on to Ammonius. Apart from this I have not received the merest scrap on your behalf either from Quirinus or anyone else. I am afraid, indeed I am almost sure, that these good people are beginning to suspect that I did receive something and am denying it. This distresses me greatly. Will you 25 please find out from Quirinus what is up. If perchance the book was delivered to some other address, it should be demanded from those who received it, not from me. By explaining what the situation is and by your writing to these men, I could be freed from suspicion. This action on your part will be most welcome to me. 30

Farewell.

From Antwerp, 4 February 1530

Your friend, Erasmus Schets

† To the erudite and incomparable Master Erasmus of Rotterdam, his best friend. In Freiburg 35

2271 / To Bonifacius Amerbach   [Freiburg, February 1530]

This letter (= AK 1410) was first published in the *Epistolae familiares*. The autograph is in the Öffentliche Bibliothek of the University of Basel (MS AN III

* * * * *

4 See Ep 2115:48–58. Castro (Ep 1931 n3) was Schets' agent in London responsible for the collection and remittance of Erasmus' English revenues.
5 See Epp 2159:17–19, 2193:23–8.
6 See Ep 2258:7–17.
7 For the trip to England, see Ep 2222 n16.
8 See Ep 2214 n5.

15 81). Allen assigned the date on the basis of his conjecture that this is Erasmus' answer to Bonifacius' comments in Ep 2267 concerning the royal divorce in England.

Greetings. All we can do now is to pray to Heaven to bring everything to a happy conclusion. I am sorry that the king is entangled in such a labyrinth. If only I could conjure this stone out of my bladder, I would bear everything else bravely.[1] Best wishes to you and all your family.

Your friend Erasmus   5

To Doctor Bonifacius Amerbach

2272 / From Jacopo Sadoleto   Carpentras, 12 February 1530

This letter was first published in the *Epistolae floridae*. The manuscript, in a secretary's hand except for the heading, which is autograph, is in the Rehdiger Collection of the University Library at Wrocław (MS Rehd 254.131). The year-date is confirmed by the connection with Epp 2059, 2074, and 2312A. The letter reached Erasmus on 30 March; see Ep 2299 n26. His reply is Ep 2312A.

JACOPO SADOLETO, BISHOP OF CARPENTRAS

It is a year or more since I received two letters from you with the same text.[1] The letter that was written later was delivered first; it contained the most friendly good wishes along with congratulations on my escape and on my timely retreat to my church. I remember that I duly replied to it at that time,   5 as our close friendship obliged me to do.[2] The other copy arrived later along with Psalm 85 and the commentary that you wrote on it.[3] I read the commentary with enormous delight; I recognized in it yet again the remarkable power and scope of your intellect.

What prevented me at that point from acknowledging this second let-   10 ter was the pressure of my work and a similar commitment that I had made a little earlier to produce a commentary on Psalm 93.[4] But I completely lack the facility, intelligence, and learning that you possess, which would have

* * * * *

2271

1 See Ep 2260 n74.

2272

1 Ep 2059; cf Ep 2074:3–5.

2 Ep 2074

3 See Ep 2017.

4 *In Psalmum 93 interpretatio* (Lyon: Gryphius 1530)

allowed me to free myself rapidly from the meticulous effort that the work
demanded. I have been held up, as you can see, until today. However, when   15
I finally finished it, there was nothing I wanted more than to send you immediately what my burning of the midnight oil had produced – evidently a
gift of bronze in return for gold.[5] My hope is that if you approve it, I shall
have the singular pleasure of a favourable judgment from a most learned
scholar and a generous friend, and if you do not approve it, your advice and   20
your learning will help me to do better in the future. Which of these two
I would prefer and which would be more useful to me, I cannot quite decide. Approval would perhaps be sweeter, coming from a loyal and learned
friend, but criticism would certainly be more useful. So if you find something amiss – and there will, I am sure, be much to bother so acute a critic   25
as yourself – please, please, I beg you, do not hesitate to be honest and
frank with me and to demonstrate, without holding back, the good faith
that friendship demands, for I do not doubt that you regard this as a most
sacred obligation. So be assured that your judgment, either for or against,
will be gratefully received by me and eagerly awaited.[6]   30

   With regard to your Psalm and the many distinguished pieces in this
genre that you have produced and are continuing to produce every day, I
always admire not just your intellect, your command of language, and your
facility, but your courage and persistence, for despite the many antagonists
who try to disparage your success you are not deterred from the course you   35
have embarked on; instead you work all the harder every day to advance
the cause of good letters and sound morals. In this enterprise your erudition
and your noble ambition deserve the very highest commendation.

   I have only one wish – for why should I not perform for you the same
friendly office that I seek from you? As I say, I have only one wish – and it   40
is something I would strongly urge on you – that you back away from all
controversies and in your writing glide over certain subjects, which, though
they may not be inconsistent with true piety, are nevertheless contrary to
the deeply held opinions of the people and the cherished views of certain
men or even of certain orders.[7] I think it would be more dignified not to   45
confront these people. For what is driving you, a man who excels in every

* * * * *

5 'Bronze for gold' is proverbial for an unequal exchange. There is no separate
   entry for it in the *Adagia*, but there is an ample discussion of it in i ii 1: *Diomedis
   et Glauci permutatio* 'Exchange between Diomede and Glaucus.' The phrase is
   also biblical; see Isa 60:17.
6 For Erasmus' response to this request, see Ep 2312A:17–90.
7 Cf Epp 2120:14–22, 2124:7–11, 2226:13–20.

NALIS · IACOBVS · SADOLET · CARDIE

Docte deum interpres, non solum oracula Christi
Sed dictata sacro Verba Helicone canis.

Jacopo Sadoleto
Unidentified artist
Bibliotheca chalcographica, 1669

branch of learning, to engage in fractious argument and dispute with men who are by far your inferiors, especially when sacred literature offers such a wide field that opens out in all directions? Here you could work to your heart's content and deploy the great riches of your mind, which all men 50 admire, instead of raising issues that provoke a quarrel.

Everything I write, I write with the best of intentions and in a most friendly spirit and from an ardent wish that your great abilities will not be spurned by the people on account of, I will not say some fault of yours, but even from suspicion of a fault. But you understand these things better. Let 55 us do what we can, dear Erasmus, each according to his ability, to support the Christian faith, which is now in danger of collapse, for, as you yourself are aware, it is under attack not only from the rampant evils of our time and a host of wicked men, but also from its enemies at home and abroad, and all the engines of war and godlessness. It is now likely to collapse unless God, 60 who alone is all-powerful, looks favourably upon it and upholds it. If we do what we can to pay our debt to God, our Lord and Master, we shall find a blessed life ourselves, and our labour will not be without value or profit to others. I know that you do not need to be treated to a lecture – all the more reason why we must be more careful not to desert our post. 65

But enough of this. Please look after yourself and give us your love. Know that we are deeply concerned for your peace and reputation. We send you, dear Erasmus, our very best wishes. Please give our cordial greetings to Amerbach; I wish he would write more often.[8]

Carpentras, 12 February 1530 70

2273 / To Anton Fugger   Freiburg, 13 February 1530

This is the preface to Erasmus' translation of Xenophon's *Hieron,* a dialogue on tyranny (Basel: Froben 1530). The dedication to Fugger is doubtless Erasmus' response to the famed banker's gift to him of a valuable gold cup (Ep 2192:58– 60). Ep 2260 was also printed in the volume. The presentation copy was delivered to the delighted Fugger in Augsburg on 7 April; see Ep 2307:1–5. For Fugger, see Ep 2145.

DESIDERIUS ERASMUS OF ROTTERDAM TO THE MOST ILLUSTRIOUS MASTER ANTON FUGGER, GREETING
It is not without reason, my very good friend, that in your letter to me you

* * * * *

8 Bonifacius responded to this request on 15 May; see Ep 2312A introduction.

raise again the old lament about Ate,[1] for in no age has she ever been so true
to her name as in the present or spread her influence so widely through the   5
minds of all. It is to her that we rightly credit, besides innumerable disasters,
this unhappy fact that we, whose hearts are joined so closely in friendship,
are separated in our daily lives.

I think I have found a remedy to console us for this misfortune. For during the past few days, when I was searching for something through piles of   10
my papers, there came to hand, unexpectedly and, I believe, providentially, a
translation of Xenophon's *Tyrant* that I had attempted some years ago. Among
several reasons why I never finished it was the impression that the manuscript was badly corrupted. To this task I have now returned with renewed
energy and have finished the work[2] without stopping to catch my breath.   15

The ancients recognized no distinction between a 'king' and a 'tyrant';
later, however, the word 'tyrant' and the word 'king' came to be abominated
by everyone, at least in those states where democracy was well established.
Otherwise the fact that Simonides habitually calls Hieron a 'tyrant' would
be no more discourteous than if someone who was on familiar and friendly   20
terms with a pirate commonly addressed him as 'pirate.'[3] I admit that the
subject of this book does not entirely fit the present state of affairs, since now
vast regions, not just single city-states as in Hieron's time, live harmoniously
under very powerful monarchs. Nevertheless there are many lessons here
that our present-day princes could profitably learn. Whenever you take up   25
this little book, which is dedicated to you, my dearest Anton, imagine you
are having a conversation with your friend Erasmus.

Give my cordial greetings to the honourable Johann Koler; there is no
one among my friends who is more warm-hearted than he, nor do I have a

* * * * *

2273
1 The letter is not extant. 'Ate,' Greek for 'blindness' or 'ruin,' is also the name
  of the goddess who brings disaster.
2 Literally 'have come to the end of the scroll'; see *Adagia* I ii 32.
3 'Tyranny' was the name for the form of monarchy set up by usurpers in many
  Greek states from the seventh century BC onwards. The tyrant's rule might
  be benevolent or malevolent, but many were known for their public works
  and their patronage of writers and artists. 'Tyranny' acquired its pejorative
  meaning largely through the influence of Plato and Aristotle, who described
  it as the worst possible form of government. Hieron, tyrant of Sicily (478–
  466 BC), was a military dictator who sought glory by, among other things, his
  patronage of Greek festivals and their poets. Simonides (d 468 BC), a Greek
  lyric poet little of whose work survives intact, spent the last years of his life
  in Sicily.

more resolute defender. Believe me, his letter,[4] which breathes throughout a   30
spirit of true affection, gave me as much pleasure and comfort as anything
that has come my way. Farewell.

Freiburg im Breisgau, 13 February AD 1530

2274 / To Andreas and Christoph von Könneritz

Freiburg, 18 February [1530]

This is the letter prefixed to the dialogue *Bermannus sive de re metallica* by
Georgius Agricola (Basel: Froben 1530). Erasmus had recommended the book
to Froben for publication at the request of Petrus Plateanus (see Ep 2216), who
had composed for the work a preface addressed to Heinrich von Könneritz,
superintendent of mines at Jáchymov (Joachimsthal) in the Erz mountains of
Bohemia. Erasmus' letter is addressed to two of Könneritz's sons, Andreas
(d 1552) and Christoph (d 1557).

After brief periods of study at Leipzig and Wittenberg, Andreas studied
at Bologna (1523–8) where he met Agricola. In December 1528, Andreas and
his brother Christoph matriculated at Freiburg, the former becoming a student of Udalricus Zasius. After Erasmus' arrival in Freiburg in April 1529, the
two brothers lived for a time in his house. Andreas subsequently acquired a
doctorate in both laws at Leipzig (1531) and spent a decade at the Reichskammergericht (Imperial Supreme Court) in Speyer before entering the service
of King Ferdinand in 1541. Settling in Freiburg, where he bought property,
Andreas became (1551) Ferdinand's governor (*Landvogt*) in the district of the
Ortenau (on the right bank of the Rhine, opposite Strasbourg). Meanwhile,
Christoph had continued his studies at Ingolstadt and Bologna before, like
his brother, entering the service of King Ferdinand in 1542. After service as a
councillor in the government of Lower Austria, he advanced to the position
of superintendent of mines in Hungary and Bohemia.

Erasmus put the year-date at 1529 (see line 29 below) but that has to be
interpreted as 1530; see Ep 2268 introduction.

DESIDERIUS ERASMUS OF ROTTERDAM TO THE MOST HONOURABLE
BROTHERS ANDREAS AND CHRISTOPH VON KÖNNERITZ,
GREETING

My most distinguished young friends, I have read through, almost without pausing to draw breath, but always attentively, Georgius' dialogue *On*   5

* * * * *

4 Ep 2269

Metallurgy, and I cannot really say whether I got more pleasure or more profit from it. The novelty of the subject delighted me, the urbane humour that is scattered throughout the work put me in a cheerful mood, and I was not displeased by the simplicity of the style, which had something Attic about it.[1] But what particularly captured my interest was the graphic way 10 in which everything was brought so vividly before my eyes. I seemed not to be reading, but actually seeing those valleys and hills and mines and machines. All those veins of silver and gold almost made me want to possess things of that kind! I only wish we were carried up to heaven with the same enthusiasm with which we burrow into the earth. Not that I disapprove of 15 this activity, for everything that the earth produces it produces for us; it is rather that these veins of metal, however abundant they may be, cannot create such happiness that many do not regret the labour and expense devoted to them – only the vein of Scripture truly enriches a man. Our Georgius has made a splendid beginning, but we do not expect anything mediocre from 20 a man of his ability.

I see that a number of young men are ready to revive the art of medicine.[2] Among these are Simon Riquinus, who besides uncommon erudition has great powers of intellect and character, and Joachim Martens of Ghent, whose abilities seem to promise something precise and vigorous.[3] 25 And this first exercise of Georgius' is no less promising. So I am not sorry to have been given this task, and I have no doubt that Hieronymus Froben will be glad to print the work as a favour both to you and to learning. Farewell.

Freiburg, 18 February 1529[4]

2275 / To the Franciscans   [Freiburg, February 1530]

This is an apologia in the form of a letter: *Epistola ad quosdam impudentissimos gracculos* (Letter to Certain Highly Impudent Jackdaws). (On the proverbial meaning of 'jackdaws' as stupid, ignorant people who brazenly attack men of real learning, see *Adagia* I iv 37, I vii 22, III iii 97.) The writing of the *Epistola* was provoked by the publication of Luis de Carvajal's *Dulcoratio*

* * * * *

2274
1 In Greek and Roman rhetoric the simple, direct style was known as 'Attic.'
2 Erasmus is referring to pages 65–7 of the *Bermannus,* where Agricola argues the need for new work on medicine and praises the efforts of John Clement (Ep 388:185n) and Pierre Brissot (Ep 1407 n30).
3 For Riquinus see Ep 2246; for Martens see Ep 2049.
4 The correct year-date is 1530; see introduction above.

amarulentiarum Erasmicae responsionis (Paris: S. de Colines 1530); see Ep 2110
n10. But Carvajal was not the only 'jackdaw' at whom Erasmus took aim; the
other was Frans Titelmans; see Ep 2206 introduction. Neither man is named
in the letter, but both were Franciscans of the Observance, and they are un-
mistakably the 'certain friars without observance' named in the greeting. At
the same time, however, Erasmus also had in mind the Franciscan Observants
who had been prominent in the effort of the religious orders in Spain to con-
vict him of heresy in 1527; see Ep 2094 introduction and n1. Erasmus would
have more to say in response to his Franciscan detractors in Epp 2299 and
2300, both of them published in the *Epistolae floridae* in 1531.

The *Epistola* was published as a pamphlet, without indication of place or
date, by Johann Faber Emmaeus at Freiburg. Allen assigned his conjectural
date on the basis of evidence that Carvajal's *Dulcoratio* had reached Erasmus 'in
the latter part of February' and that Erasmus had hastily dashed off the *Epistola*
so that it would be ready for the spring fair at Frankfurt. For the details, see
Allen's introduction. The work was included in the 1540 Basel edition of the
Opera omnia (IX 1432), but among the *apologiae* rather than the letters. LB (X
1745–6) followed the same procedure.

The *Epistola* is remarkable for the vigour of Erasmus' defence of his achievements as a scholar and for the vehemence of the abuse that he heaps on the
heads of his unnamed antagonists. He sent a copy of the pamphlet to Louvain intended for Franciscan friends there, but Conradus Goclenius discreetly
abstained from delivering it; see Ep 2352:311–14.

DESIDERIUS ERASMUS OF ROTTERDAM WISHES A BETTER FRAME OF
MIND TO CERTAIN FRIARS WITHOUT OBSERVANCE
Dear brothers and fathers,[1] I realize what you are up to: you are suborning
several brazen and ignorant young men to band together and destroy Erasmus. They have no shame, no brains, there is nothing that can be taken from   5
them, they cannot be apprehended, they are worse than octopuses, moving,
as they do, from place to place;[2] a whole army hides under a single warrior's
shield.

Salamanca has one of them, whose name I used to think was made
up. I had never heard it and could not persuade myself that such   10
rudeness lay hidden in that community. His additional name sounded

* * * * *

2275
1 The Latin is *fratres patres*, literally 'brothers fathers.' Cf Ep 2299:141, where it
  is *fratres ac patres*.
2 *Adagia* II iii 91

Jewish.[3] It is not just in Spain that there are Jews who conceal their identity: in many other countries they live disguised as Christians. But this fellow was unwilling to forego his triumph and thought that the glory should be claimed for his order.

Brabant has another of the same kidney, a man of the most pretentious loquacity.[4] Flaunted modesty is nothing but hypocrisy. (Please realize that these strictures are directed against the wicked – I do not wish to cast a slur on good men.) By this document I give you warning, reverend brothers: suborn, invent, deceive, despise the laws of the emperor and the bishops,[5] publish furtive little pamphlets, from now on I shall not bother to read the rubbish that comes from you or answer it. God himself will find the impious hypocrites. It is to him, whose judgments are just, that I entrust retribution.

How decrepit do I appear in their eyes?[6] Budé is only two years younger than I, Béda perhaps four or five, Latomus three.[7] Up to the present time I have been constantly engaged in grinding labour, which has the most deleterious effect on health and aging. Old man though I am, I can do the work of four vigorous young men. My eyes, thank God, are not failing – many people wonder that I have not gone completely blind long ago. So far I have never used spectacles either in daylight or in

* * * * *

3 This initial suspicion that 'Ludovicus Carvaialus Minorita' was the pseudonym for someone who was neither a Franciscan nor a Christian but a Jew was expressed in the *Responsio ad cuiusdam febricitantis libellum*; see LB X 679E, 1683A, 1684C. For Erasmus' continued confusion over the true identity of Carvajal, see Epp 2110:24–31; 2126:60–2, 103–8; 2198:15–17. 'Carvajal' was in fact a fairly common Sephardic Jewish name, but Erasmus' Carvajal came from a noble Christian family of Andalusia.

4 Clearly Titelmans; see Ep 2261:77–82.

5 For Erasmus' charge that both Carvajal and Titelmans had published works in defiance of decrees of the emperor, local bishops, and other authorities, see Epp 2299:123–7, 2300:24–8 and 52–73, 2301:2–16, 2312A:273–7.

6 In the *Dulcoratio* Carvajal had called Erasmus 'a septuagenarian with one foot in Charon's boat' and had made several other references to his supposed physical and mental decrepitude. See Rummel II 103 with n69. Erasmus' indignant assertion here of his physical and mental vigour is in marked contrast to his customary complaints of age and ailments. For the return of such complaints see Ep 2321:18–20.

7 Guillaume Budé was born on 26 January 1468. Noël Béda's birth date is uncertain (c 1470), as is that of Jacobus Latomus (c 1475). As is usual with Erasmus' references to his age, the year of his birth cannot be determined with any certainty from the information provided. But by no calculation was he yet 70. Even if one accepts 28 October 1466 as the date of his birth – and none earlier has ever been suggested – then in February 1530 he was 63.

lamplight.[8] I have never used a walking stick; I walk quickly with a firm step. My hands are steadier than a young man's. Every day the stone becomes less painful,[9] and if I were to reduce my intellectual labours, I might, by the mercy of God, live another fourteen years with my senses intact. But the span of my life is in the hands of God. Those who live with me notice   35
no great loss of intellect or memory. So what is all this about a shrivelled death's-head, apt at any moment to fall apart!

What a dead weight these scurrilous clowns are, not just on me but on the whole world! What do they hope to gain from such silly and long-winded drivel? The learned will not read it; godly men will loath it. As   40
yet, I have been unable to find anyone willing to read this gibberish for me. Yet with such stuff they expect to destroy a feeble old man. They could accomplish this more easily with a dagger, for when the aim is murder, it does not matter what weapon is used. Yet this feeble old man has given you Jerome and Cyprian and Augustine and is now giving you Chrysostom,[10]   45
from whose works and from those of Athanasius he has also made many translations.[11] By the use of Greek authors he has thrown light on many passages in the New Testament. Let them read the list and they will see how much this feeble old man has done both for the cause of learning and for godliness.   50

They hamper the work of others with their croaking and squawking, while contributing nothing themselves beyond a crude and ignorant gabble. Do they think the world is occupied only by swine and donkeys? On one occasion the emperor gave them authority to make a legal case against me and appointed eminent judges; that was the moment for them to demonstrate   55
their wisdom.[12] By the sort of books they write they expose themselves to the derision of all good and learned men, while I still have strength to look down on them and mock, even if three thousand were to rise up against me. Learned men and later generations will still hear the song of the swans when jackdaws will be silent.[13] If they wish to destroy this old man, they   60

* * * * *

8 Cf Ep 2046:420–1 with n61.
9 Erasmus appears to have been going through a period of relative freedom from his attacks of the stone. From January through early March he mentions it as but a slight problem (Epp 2260:341–3, 2263:124–6, 2271:3–4, 2277:12–13), but by late March it is once again severe (Epp 2290:54–5, 2295:32–3).
10 For these editions, see Epp 396, 1465 (Jerome), 1000 (Cyprian), 2157 (Augustine), 2359 (Chrysostom).
11 For the Latin translations of Chrysostom and Athanasius, see Ep 1790.
12 At Valladolid in 1527; see Ep 1791 introduction.
13 *Adagia* III iii 97

will need their daggers. Unless they learn to write in a different manner, they will get nothing from the best judges but disgust and mockery. I appeal to you, pious friars, control these donkeys, and to you, pious laymen, when you see such madness, give nothing to these communities unless they drive from their midst these babbling idiots; perhaps in this way they will   65 get the warning and come to their senses, for their ears are attached not to their heads but to their bellies.[14] Let them put their stupid 'sweeteners' on their own pap and expect nothing from me.[15] But let them understand where malice leads in the end!

Let me say once more that these words are not directed against the   70 godly.[16] I know there are very many men in that society who detest this scurrilous behaviour.[17] When I say these things, these people break in with a threat of papal excommunication for injury to the Order of Minorites.[18] If this excommunication means anything, it applies in fullest force to those who by their stupid writings make their order an object of hatred to all   75 good and learned men. I have warned them often enough; every day they grow worse; soon they will be ignored. I only wish that had happened at the start! I do not relish croaking back at frogs.[19] Let them boldly turn their backs on every law, both human and divine, and say, 'One must obey God rather than men.'[20] This was rightly said by the apostles, and it is   80 not completely incongruous when these wretches say it. But they and the apostles do not have the same God. In the minds of the apostles God was the creator of heaven and earth; for these men their belly is their God.[21] Farewell.

2276 / From Andrea Alciati   Bourges, 1 March 1530

The manuscript of this letter, written and signed by a secretary, was a late addition to the Deventer Letter-book (Deventer MS 91 folio 237); cf Allen I 603. First published in LB III/2 1745–6 *Appendix epistolarum* no 356, this is Alciati's

* * * * *

14 Cf *Adagia* II viii 84. On Erasmus' habit of describing monks, particularly members of the mendicant orders, as devoted to their own bellies, frequently referring to them as 'potbellies,' see Ep 1980 n1.
15 The Latin for 'sweeteners' is *dulcorationes*, an allusion to Carvajal's *Dulcoratio*.
16 Cf lines 17–18 above and Epp 1033:138–40 and 297–8, 1469:77–8.
17 See Ep 2300:133–42.
18 See Ep 2300 n47.
19 Cf *Adagia* III i 76.
20 Acts 5:29
21 Phil 3:19; cf Ep 1980 n1.

reply to Erasmus' letter of 2 September 1529, which was delivered at Bourges in January 1530; see Ep 2213 n10. Erasmus' reply is Ep 2329.

Erasmus, my excellent friend, for several years now I have been tossed up and down on the waves of fortune and, as you put it in your letter, constantly driven from one place to another – with considerable loss to myself.[1] But I have taken your advice and I bear these misfortunes most philosophically in the belief that suffering is the common lot of all men (for, as Plau- 5 tus says, 'the Gods use us mortals as footballs'),[2] or perhaps because all my fellow citizens were (to use a common expression) in the same boat.[3] Like the daemons in Empedocles, they are tossed from the sky to the bottom of the sea, then move rapidly to the earth, then back to the sky, from which they are rolled back once more,[4] impelled, it would seem, by some 10 blunt instrument.[5] But up to the present I have borne these misfortunes with equanimity. Indeed thus far things have worked out so well for me that I reckon I have gained considerable profit and distinction. I realize that for all this I must give thanks to Almighty God, who, by encompassing me in these disasters, has made me better off. I had a good income, and was gen- 15 erously provided with money and with all the other blessings of fortune, which, as you know, Plutus confers particularly on lawyers.[6] Everything has now been diminished, destroyed, lost during the recent storms of war. I did not follow the example of Diagoras of Milos, who became an atheist when he suffered a loss that was perhaps less serious than mine.[7] On the con- 20 trary I looked on the bright side and learned from experience that all these things are fleeting and almost of no importance on this pilgrimage that is our human destiny.

* * * * *

2276
1 After four years as professor of law at Avignon (1518–22), Alciati had returned to his native Milan just in time for one of the worst phases of the Italian wars (1522–7). His home was twice occupied by foreign troops, first French (1523) and then Spanish (1526). He returned to Avignon in 1527 but in the spring of 1529, at the invitation of Francis I, he departed for Bourges, where he spent the next four years. Cf Ep 2209 n19.
2 Plautus *Captivi* 22
3 *Adagia* II i 10
4 The reference is to fragment 115 of the *Purifications*, where the Greek philosopher Empedocles (fifth century BC) describes the fate of lost souls (daemons) doomed to return to earth and revisit all the elements of the world.
5 Literally a 'pestle.' See *Adagia* III vi 21: *Pestillo retusius* 'As blunt as a pestle.'
6 Plutus, whose name means 'wealth,' was the Greek god of wealth.
7 See *Adagia* III iv 72.

So I have changed my opinion about settling in my homeland and
gone back to France to take up a teaching post,[8] like Dionysius in Corinth.[9]   25
I found, as I hoped, that all recollection of my name had not faded from
the hearts of serious scholars. My decision has turned out so well that it
has erased almost all memory of past misfortunes. I now believe that I have
gained considerably, for at the modest loss of my previous assets I have won
the distinction of lecturing in a crowded theatre to many young men who   30
will one day add lustre to my name and to this branch of study. Among
the most distinguished are Viglius and Sucket,[10] whom you recommended
to me in a recent letter,[11] and who are already beginning to show signs of
progress and maturity. Certainly Karel has recently given a good account
of himself when I thrust him into the arena and co-opted him to the teach-   35
ing staff. The manner in which he carries out his responsibilities wins him
the highest praise and attracts a crowd of students. He has clearly eclipsed
certain fellow initiates, devotees of the barbarians,[12] whom I greatly wished
to see taken down a peg. In this he has proved himself so valuable to me
that I would not part with him in exchange for the most precious gifts.[13] I   40
write this so that you may understand how unnecessary your commendation was, for I myself am much in the debt of these young men, and they
have gained what they willingly credit to my account. Wine of such quality
needs no ivy.[14] If you really want to know how much Alciati values your
letters, you will send him less meritorious students. They will have cause to   45
thank you profoundly when they have been accepted as though they fully
deserved their place.

* * * * *

8 See n1 above.
9 Dionysius II, tyrant of Syracuse (377–357 BC), was forced into exile in Corinth,
   where he is said to have become a paid teacher of letters and music to boys.
   The phrase 'Dionysius in Corinth' became proverbial for someone reduced
   from the highest rank to humble status; see *Adagia* I i 83.
10 On Viglius Zuichemus see Ep 2210; on Karel Sucket see Ep 2191.
11 See Ep 2213:23–4.
12 'Fellow-initiates' and 'devotees of the barbarians' are literal translations of two
   Greek words. The 'fellow-initiates' whom Karel outclassed were perhaps 'devoted to the barbarians' in that they were the disciples of professors who were
   hostile to humanist scholarship.
13 Alciati uses the Greek words ἐπαύλια δῶρα, which originally meant 'gifts given
   to a bride the day after her marriage.' The phrase became proverbial for magnificent gifts generally; see *Adagia* IV ii 81.
14 In other words, true excellence needs no advertisement; see *Adagia* II vi 20.
   The proverb is derived from the practice of hanging a branch of ivy (sacred
   to Bacchus) over a wineshop as an advertisement.

Because of our friend Amerbach's kindly feelings towards me I cannot but reciprocate his affection. But you yourself, Erasmus, are the tight chain that bound him so closely to me, because, I have no doubt, he was our 50 Hermes and the originator of the affection that you feel for me.[15] So great a favour as this I am in no position to repay. Farewell.

Bourges, 1 March 1530

Andrea Alciati, your most devoted servant

To the outstanding theologian, Master Erasmus of Rotterdam, his ex- 55 cellent friend. In Freiburg im Breisgau

Andrea Alciati from Bourges

2277 / To Johann von Botzheim   Freiburg, 3 March [1530]

This letter was first published by Allen, using the autograph, formerly in the Grandducal Library at Darmstadt and now in the Universitäts- und Landes-bibliothek Darmstadt (Br / Erasmus 1).

On the interpretation of the assigned year-date 1529 (see line 14 below) as 1530 see Ep 2268 introduction. The events mentioned in the letter are additional confirmation of the date. For Botzheim, see Epp 1285, 2205.

Cordial greetings. Was I not a true prophet when I said you would deceive me?[1] The bishop of Augsburg came here, but without revealing who he was.[2] He told me he had come for no other reason than to see Erasmus. I have never seen a better combination of learning and courtesy than in that man. He presented two magnificent cups, in which there 5 were two hundred florins.[3] The cup that the duke of Jülich sent is on its

* * * * *

15 Hermes was the messenger and intermediary of the gods. The friendship between Erasmus and Alciati had its origin in their common friendship with Bonifacius Amerbach, who studied with Alciati in Avignon (1520–3). Bonifacius soon became and remained the principal channel of communication between Alciati and Erasmus.

2277
1 There is nothing in the surviving correspondence to indicate what this deception might have been.
2 Christoph von Stadion (Ep 2029); for this visit, see Epp 2299:50–6, 2308:21–6.
3 The cups, which bore the arms of Bishop Christoph, are listed as *poculum du-plex* among the *aurea* (gold items) in the inventory of 1534; see Sieber 5, Major 41. If Erasmus refers to the Carolus florin, valued at 42d *groot* Flemish, this was equivalent to almost 4.5 years' money wages of an Antwerp master artisan in 1526–30; if he means the Rhenish florin (*Rijnsgulden*), which circulated

way,[4] also another sent by Johann Rinck.[5] Gifts like these from such men give me comfort, something to set against the attacks of that drivelling madman.[6]

In England all my friendships are intact. The cardinal has been over-   10
thrown. More is now lord chancellor of England.[7] The theologians at Louvain are becoming more restrained in their attitude towards me.[8] If I could get rid of the stone, all the rest I could surmount easily.[9]

Farewell. The morrow of Ash Wednesday, Freiburg 1529[10]

Your friend Erasmus   15

To the erudite Johann von Botzheim, doctor of laws. In Überlingen

2278 / From Jan van Fevijn   Bruges, 6 March [1530]

The autograph of this letter, which was first published as Ep 71 in Enthoven, is in the Rehdiger Collection of the University Library at Wrocław (MS Rehd 254.64). Allen found on the manuscript the year-date 1529 (line 29) but concluded that it had probably been added later and was not accurate. Given that Erasmus writes from Freiburg and that the edition of Augustine is finished, Allen concluded that the year-date could not be earlier than 1530 and saw in the reference to the English sweat in line 14 evidence for the probability of that date. Fevijn's accounts of the events of the early to mid-1520s suggest that he had not written to Erasmus for a long time.

On Jan de Fevijn, canon and scholaster of the chapter of St Donatian's at Bruges, see Ep 1012, which is the only other surviving letter in their correspondence. In the decade or more between the two letters, however, they had on several occasions sent greetings via others (Epp 1145, 1303, 1317, 1665, 1792).

* * * * *

widely in southern Germany and was valued at 59d *groot* Flemish, just over six years' worth in the same period (CWE 12 649–50, 691 Tables 3C–D, 13).

4 See Ep 2234 n4.

5 For Rinck, see Ep 2285. The cup, which bore Rinck's arms, is listed as *poculum duplex* among the *semiaureata* (gold-decorated items) in the inventory of 1534; see Sieber 7, Major 42, and cf Ep 2353A:2–7.

6 Presumably Frans Titelmans, about whom Erasmus had complained at length to Botzheim in Epp 2205:232–60 and 2206.

7 On the fall of Thomas Cardinal Wolsey and his replacement as lord chancellor by Thomas More, see Ep 2237 n2.

8 Cf Ep 2033:33 with n12, 2264, 2299:112, 2310:25–6 with n8.

9 See Ep 2260 n74.

10 The correct year-date is 1530; see introduction above.

Cordial greetings. Although I am being kept exceedingly busy at present, particularly in entertaining friends (Laurinus among others),[1] our dear Lieven, who is with me now,[2] has extorted a promise from me to write at least a word of greeting and let you know how things stand with me and my friends. So here goes. If you are well, that gives me reason to rejoice, and I pray this happy state will continue. We have seen what benefit your advancing years have brought to Christendom – and to yourself too: you have vigorously defended many of your writings from the calumnious attacks of your rivals; you have finished off Luther, who was such a fierce and savage foe, and now you have finally completed your Augustine. I only hope that Christ our Lord and Master will some day rid you of the stone and, for our sakes, keep you in good health for a long time to come.[3]

As for myself, I am as well as may be expected; in recent months I fell victim to the dreadful sweating sickness; but, thank God, I have recovered.[4] Laurinus too is well. It is to his kindness that I owe my promotion to the position of scholaster of our school.[5] Dear old Karel, Robert, and my beloved sister, all of whom, as you know, were keen supporters of yours, have been taken from us.[6] Some evil genius lashed out so furiously against our family that within a few days it robbed us of four of our relatives. So I have moved from the Prinsenhof, which is now empty, to a place not far from Laurinus' house; it is not so distinguished a location as the Prinsenhof, but it is suitable

* * * * *

2278
1 Marcus Laurinus, canon of St Donatian's (Ep 1342)
2 Lieven Algoet (Ep 1091), who evidently carried this letter. He reached Freiburg in late March, whereupon Erasmus immediately sent him on an errand to Augsburg, where Emperor Charles v and his court were expected to arrive for the coming imperial diet; see Ep 2294:15–17. Arriving in Augsburg in early April (Ep 2307:1–4), Lieven went from there to Trent, where he found the imperial court. Attaching himself to Cornelis de Schepper in the hopes of finding employment (Ep 2336:48–52), Lieven returned to Augsburg with the court and later published his own account of the diet. In 1532, after much effort and with strong support from Erasmus, he was appointed personal secretary to Nicolaus Olahus (Ep 2339), the chief minister of Mary of Austria, regent of the Netherlands.
3 See Ep 2260 n74.
4 See Ep 2209 n31.
5 He was probably in office by 1523, or perhaps even earlier; see *Literae virorum eruditorum ad Franciscum Craneveldium, 1522–1528* ed Henry de Vocht (Louvain 1928) xciv.
6 For Karel van Hedenbault (d 1527), Fevijn's cousin, see Ep 1012 n1. For Robert Hellin (d 1527), who was married to Fevijn's sister Eleanor (d 1526), see Ep 1012 n3.

for my studies and convenient for friends.[7] So if ever you think of flying this way (and you should fly as rapidly as you can from the turbulence of Germany), you will find a warm welcome here from Laurinus and me. He, being now alone and free to do as he wishes,[8] has assumed the role of head 25 of his family. I look after my little household, such as it is. However, I would be glad to be of service to any of my friends, and of course most of all to the prince of letters. Do look after yourself.

Bruges, 6 March

Your affectionate friend, Jan van Fevijn, doctor of canon and civil laws, 30 scholaster and canon of St Donatian's

To the eminent doctor of theology, Desiderius Erasmus of Rotterdam, his most respected mentor. In Freiburg

2279 / To Bonifacius Amerbach [Freiburg, March 1530]

This letter (= AK Ep 1414) was first published in the *Epistolae familiares*. The autograph is in the Öffentliche Bibliothek of the University of Basel (AN III 15 82).

Like the two letters that follow it in immediate sequence (2280–1), this one is undated. Allen reasoned that the letter was probably written before the composition of Erasmus' *De bello Turcico* (lines 1–2) but after Bonifacius' visit to Erasmus at Freiburg (Ep 2280:9), which was supposed to have taken place in early January (Ep 2248:1–6) but had still not happened on 16 January (Ep 2256). The reference in Ep 2281 to renewed pressure from Oecolampadius to participate in the reformed celebration of the Lord's Supper suggests that this trio of letters was written at some point between Epp 2248 and 2312.

Cordial greetings. Will you send as soon as possible Luther's pamphlet on the war against the Turks.[1] Jan Łaski excuses himself for his silence on the

* * * * *

7 The Prinsenhof was an old residence of the dukes of Flanders at Bruges, most recently occupied by Karel van Hedenbault. Erasmus wrote Ep 1012 to Fevijn after a particularly enjoyable visit to him at the Prinsenhof.
8 It appears that Laurinus had been deprived of the company of his two widowed sisters-in-law; see Epp 1342:1123, 1438:73, 1848:37 (where they are identified as Laurinus' sisters). One of them, Elisabeth Donche, had by 1529 married the diplomat Cornelis de Schepper; see de Vocht (n5 above) xcvii.

2279
1 By the autumn of 1529 Luther had published two treatises on this topic: *Vom kriege widder die Türcken* (On War Against the Turks) April 1529, WA 30/2 81–148 / LW 46 155–205, and *Eine Heerpredigt widder den Türcken* (A Field Sermon Against the Turks) WA 30/2 149–97; cf Ep 2338 n16. The language

ground that he did not wish to compromise me,[2] for he has got involved in
that business of his brother's, who has joined forces with the Turk against
Ferdinand.[3] Justus, the king's secretary, wrote to say that Jan has been ap-   5
pointed a bishop in Hungary and that he has already set out there, though
he does not know where he resides.[4] I am sorry at what has happened to
the man. I tell you this so that Beatus will learn of it from you,[5] though I
think it better that the news go no further.

Farewell. Midnight.   10

Give my sincerest good wishes to Basilius and your wife.[6]

You will recognize your friend's handwriting.

To Master Bonifacius Amerbach. In Basel

2280 / From Bonifacius Amerbach   [Basel, March 1530]

This letter (= AK Ep 1415), Bonifacius' reply to Ep 2279, was first published

* * * * *

here suggests that Erasmus was asking for the first of the two treatises,
which he had probably learned about by reading Johannes Cochlaeus' satirical attack on it (see Ep 2285 n35). Erasmus was doubtless at work on his
own *De bello Turcico* (Ep 2285), dated 17 March 1530. It seems doubtful
that the copy of Luther's work arrived in time to be used in the composition of Erasmus' treatise; see CWE 64 203. Moreover, his later references to it leave the impression that Erasmus knew of Luther's treatise only
via the parody of it published by Johannes Cochlaeus; see Ep 2338 nn14
and 17.

2 This letter is not extant.

3 In the Hungarian conflict that erupted in 1526 between Ferdinand of Austria
  and John Zápolyai, Hieronim Łaski (Epp 1242 n5, 1341A n310), brother of Jan
  (II) Łaski (Ep 1593 n18), had sided with Zápolyai and become his chief envoy.
  In 1530 he was rewarded with the title of *voivode* of Transylvania and large estates in Slovakia. Only later, and after much trouble (1531–6), did he reconcile
  with King Ferdinand and enter his service.

4 The letter from Justus Lodovicus Decius, secretary to the king of Poland (Ep
  1341A n210), is not extant. In 1529 Jan (II) Łaski had gone to Hungary as an
  aide to his brother, entered the diplomatic service of John Zápolyai, and was
  appointed bishop of Veszprém (a see located in territory occupied by the Turks).

5 Ep 2281:7–9 indicates that Beatus Rhenanus was expecting a letter and a gift
  from Jan, probably in acknowledgement of the dedication to him of the volume
  of notes on the younger Pliny, published under the title *In C. Plinium* (Basel:
  Froben, March 1526). In a letter of 20 February 1528, Łaski apologized to Beatus for not yet having sent a promised gift; see *Lasciana, nebst den ältesten evan-
  gelischen synodalprotokollen Polens, 1555–1561* ed Hermann Dalton (Berlin 1898;
  repr Nieuwkoop 1973) 114–15 (no 17).

6 See Ep 2223 n8.

by Allen from the autograph rough draft in the Öffentliche Bibliothek of the University of Basel (MS C VI a 54 31). Erasmus reply is Ep 2281.

Greetings. I am sending you Luther's book on the war against the Turks. I was lucky enough, through my father-in-law,[1] to find a courier who was going to Neuenburg; no one else was available. It will be brought to you on the very first delivery – you see how thoughtful my father-in-law is.

The passage from the Council of Nicaea that Valla refers to in his *Apolo-* 5
gia is in Gratian's *Decreta*, distinctio 15, in the chapter 'Canons of ecumenical councils.'[2] I mention this because, when asked for the reference recently, I was unable to give it immediately.

I would thank you for the hospitality you extended to me recently, were it not that, by your countless services and benefactions, you have left 10 me nothing to say except what Furnius once said to Augustus: 'The only injury I have ever suffered at your hands is that you have made me live and die an ungrateful wretch.'[3] But I thank you just as much as if I were in a position to reciprocate and square the account. The courier is in a hurry, so I cannot write more. 15

Basilius and my wife[4] wish to be commended to you most sincerely. That business of Łaski's will not be spread about by me. I don't know what I know. Farewell.

* * * * *

2280
1 Leonhard Fuchs, mayor of Neuenburg am Rhein, halfway between Basel and Freiburg
2 *Decretum* pars 1 D 15 c 1. Erasmus was interested in this passage from Gratian, which Lorenzo Valla, in his *Apologia ad Eugenium* IV and *Antidoti in Pogium*, had used in a way that seemed to Erasmus to support his view of the authorship of the Apostles' Creed. Although Erasmus deemed the Creed to be an authoritative statement of apostolic doctrine, he was skeptical of the traditional view that it had been set down in writing by the apostles themselves, and was inclined to date it from the time of the First Council of Nicaea (325). This had caused him to be furiously denounced by Noël Béda and the Paris theologians, the Spanish monks, and Alberto Pio; see CWE 45 19 with n70. Now, it appears, Erasmus was preparing to return to the subject, which he would do in 1531 in his *Apologia adversus rhapsodias Alberti Pii*. There he would mistakenly argue that Valla, citing Gratian, had convincingly attributed the authorship of the Apostles' Creed to the Council of Nicaea. Valla had in fact only argued that the Council had affirmed the apostolic authority of the Creed. See CWE 84 268 with nn956–60. For an informative essay on the subject of Erasmus and the Apostles' Creed, see CWE 39 432–4 (the colloquy *Inquisitio de fide* n16).
3 Seneca *De beneficiis* 2.25
4 See Ep 2223 n8.

2281 / To Bonifacius Amerbach   [Freiburg, March 1530]

This letter (= AK Ep 1416), Erasmus' reply to Ep 2280, was first published in
the *Epistolae familiares*. The autograph is in the Öffentliche Bibliothek of the
University of Basel (MS AN III 15 37).

AUGUSTUS TO FURNIUS,[1] GREETING

Will you never give over your rhetorical exaggerations! So 'you will live
and die an ungrateful wretch' is it? But you have weighed me down with so
many services that no donkey could bear a heavier load. Far from demanding any thanks for the hospitality I offered, I would be ready to pay a high   5
price if I could have such a guest for several months.

Many thanks for giving me the reference. I would like Beatus to know
about Łaski so that he doesn't wonder why Łaski fails to write or send anything. I hear that you people are being invited again to Oecolampadius'
table.[2] There's evangelical hospitality for you!   10

Please get a servant to deliver the enclosed page to Hieronymus Froben
as soon as possible. If you could perform the task I am asking of him before
he can, you will make me very grateful.

My best wishes to you and to all who are dear to you.

To the right honourable Master Bonifacius Amerbach. In Basel   15

2282 / To Henry of Burgundy   Freiburg, March 1530

This letter consists of the opening and concluding passages of the little treatise *De civilitate morum puerilium* (Basel: Froben, March 1530). In the first edition, which was prepared in haste for the spring book fair, Erasmus did not
yet know the name of the boy to whom he was dedicating the work, and he
gave the wrong name (Jacobus Ceratinus instead of Jan van der Cruyce) for
the boy's current teacher (see lines 12–13). For the second Froben edition of
August 1530, Erasmus made the needed corrections. This was the version included in LB and followed by Allen. An annotated translation of the complete
work by Brian McGregor has already been published in CWE 25–26 270–89
(text), 562–7 (notes). Although it contains much from McGregor's version, this
is a new translation, and the annotation has been completely redone.

    De civilitate enjoyed a huge success, with at least twelve printings in 1530
alone. It was soon translated into all the major European languages and long

* * * * *

2281
1 See Ep 2280:10–13.
2 See Ep 2248 n6.

retained its influence as a textbook for boys on the rules of civility; see Allen's introduction and CWE 25 272.

Henry of Burgundy (1519–after March 1530) was the youngest son of Adolph of Burgundy, lord of Veere (Ep 93). He was tutored at home for a time by Jacobus Ceratinus (Ep 2209:79–83), and then appears to have gone off to study at Louvain. His disappearance from the historical record at this point seems to indicate that he died young.

DESIDERIUS ERASMUS OF ROTTERDAM TO THE MOST NOBLE
HENRY OF BURGUNDY, YOUTH OF OUTSTANDING PROMISE
AND SON OF ADOLPH, PRINCE OF VEERE, GREETING
If the thrice-mighty Paul was not averse to becoming all things to all men so that he might benefit all,[1] how much less should I hesitate from time to time   5
to assume the mantle of youth out of a desire to help the young! And so, just as formerly, when I was instructing young people in the correct use of language, I adapted myself to the early adolescence of your brother, Maximilian of Burgundy,[2] so now, my dearest Henry, I adapt myself to your boyhood years so that I may lay down some rules for the behaviour of boys. It is not   10
that you are in any great need of these rules, having been brought up from infancy in court, and then having obtained in Jan van der Cruyce an outstanding teacher of the very young;[3] nor are all the suggestions I shall make apposite to you, for you were born of a line of princes, and destined to rule. My aim is rather to make all boys more willing to learn these rules when   15
they see they are dedicated to a boy of such momentous destiny and such outstanding promise. For it will be a considerable spur to all the young to see that children of illustrious descent are dedicated to learning right from their earliest year, and are competing in the same race as themselves.

Whatever the merits of this work, dearest Henry, it is my wish that it be   20
made available, through you, to the whole community of boys, so that by this collective offering you may win the hearts of your comrades and commend to them the pursuit of morals and good letters. May Jesus in his mercy be pleased to preserve your splendid qualities and carry you always from strength to strength.   25
Freiburg im Breisgau, March 1530

* * * * *

2282
1 See 1 Cor 9:22. On 'thrice-mighty' (*ter maximus*) cf Ep 2230 n6.
2 Erasmus had dedicated *De recta pronuntiatione* to Henry's older brother Maximilian (II) of Burgundy; see Ep 1949.
3 See Ep 1932.

2283 / To Hector Boece   Freiburg, 15 March 1530

This letter is Erasmus' reply to Ep 1996, which took nearly two years to reach
him (lines 3–6). Erasmus included the letter at the end of *De bello Turcico* (Ep
2285), and it was the printed volume rather than a handwritten letter that
he sent to Boece (lines 7–9). Appended to the letter was an up-to-date list
of Erasmus' writings. An earlier list, compiled in 1524, had been included in
the second edition of the *Catalogus lucubrationum* (Ep 1341A:1500–1639; cf CWE
24 694–7). The present translation of the list for Boece is taken, with minor
revisions, from CWE 24 697–702. The numbers in square brackets, supplied by
Allen, refer to the letters in which information about the history of the work
in question can be found. Where Allen added line numbers to his references,
the corresponding numbers in CWE have been supplied.

DESIDERIUS ERASMUS OF ROTTERDAM TO THE MOST LEARNED
HECTOR BOECE OF DUNDEE, GREETING
Your letter, most honourable Boece, sent from Aberdeen on 26 May in the
year of our salvation 1528, reached me in Freiburg, a city in the Breisgau
under the rule of King Ferdinand and with a not undistinguished university. 5
I received it around 13 February in the year of our Lord 1530. I tell you this
so that you won't ask why I am so late in replying. This circumstance also
explains my decision to send this letter in printed form rather than in a copy
made by a secretary, for I thought it would reach you sooner that way. Here
then in a few words is my response to your letter.   10
    I greatly enjoyed your company, most learned Hector, when, thirty-two
years ago in Paris,[1] we were fellow runners on the racetrack of letters, although with your exceptional intellectual gifts you were many strides ahead
of me. So I was naturally delighted to have that happy memory revived by
your letter after so long an interval. To the lavish praise which, with your 15
characteristic generosity, you heaped upon me in handfuls (as the saying
goes),[2] I can only reply that your eloquent and affectionate remarks about
Erasmus, if not a lie (for lying has always been completely alien to your character), are at least some distance from the truth. For the moment, however,
I am happy to accept this flourish of praise, for it is my earnest wish that   20
my writings will have some value to those who seek to attain knowledge

* * * * *

2283
1 Actually, thirty-four years ago; thirty-two years, the figure given by Boece in
  Ep 1996, was accurate in 1528.
2 *Adagia* II i 16

and true piety. I shall attach to this letter a catalogue of my writings, as you request.[3]

I also found no small cause for delight in the knowledge that the king- 25
dom of Scotland, among many other distinctions, is daily becoming more
and more cultivated through its interest in the liberal arts. It is on this account that I always loved King James, for it was his ambition not so much
to extend his kingdom as to enhance it. If only his fortune had matched his
sterling virtues, he would have to be counted among the happiest of monarchs.[4] I have no doubt that his son has not just succeeded to his father's 30
throne, but is also following in his father's footsteps.[5] When at Siena I was
tutor to King James' son Alexander, archbishop of St Andrews,[6] his brother
was present also; he was then scarcely ten years old, a boy of remarkable
ability, who already showed signs of exceptional promise. I would like to
know what became of him: did he share the fate of his father and his brother, 35
or is he still alive?[7]

* * * * *

3 No such request is found in Ep 1996. Erasmus himself is the only known
   source for the assertion that Boece had requested the catalogue of him.
4 James IV (1473–1513), who had fostered literature and education and refused
   to execute heretics, perished at Flodden after invading England in alliance
   with Louis XII of France. Erasmus lamented the invasion in the *Institutio principis christiani* (CWE 27 278) and mourned James' death here, in *Adagia* II iv 99
   CWE 33 240–1, and in Ep 2886.
5 James V (1512–42), only a year old at the time of his succession, eventually
   renewed the old hostility to England in alliance with France. His forces suffered a humiliating defeat at the hands of the English shortly before his own
   death from illness. His only legitimate child was Mary Stuart, the daughter of
   his second wife, Mary of Guise.
6 Alexander Stewart (Ep 604:4n), illegitimate son of James IV, spent the early
   months of 1509 with Erasmus at Siena. His parting gift to Erasmus was a
   ring with an image that Erasmus took to be that of the god Terminus and
   later adapted for use in his personal seal; see Ep 2018. In 1513 Alexander,
   seemingly destined for a brilliant political career in Scotland, perished with
   his father at the battle of Flodden. Erasmus, who had greatly admired the boy's
   intelligence, character, and piety and had high hopes of him as a patron of
   learning, mourned his death and remembered wistfully their time together in
   Italy; see *Adagia* II v 1 CWE 33 241–2.
7 James Stewart, earl of Moray (c 1499–1544/5), another illegitimate son of James
   IV, accompanied his older half-brother Alexander (see preceding note) to Italy
   and was also tutored by Erasmus at Siena in 1509. Although he did not make
   the same impression on Erasmus as did Alexander, Erasmus had clearly not
   forgotten him. After his return to Scotland James pursued a military career
   and was known for his staunch support for the church of Rome as well as for
   his hostility to England.

I am very grateful for the favour and kindness shown me by your distinguished university. I only wish there was something I could do to add to its success and reputation. There is one thing that I can certainly do: pray that, through you and men like you, the Lord will prosper and enrich it in   40
every branch of learning and in the blessings of true piety.

From the famous University of Freiburg, 15 March AD 1530

LIST OF
ALL THE WORKS OF ERASMUS OF ROTTERDAM

SERIES OF BOOKS THAT CONCERN LITERATURE AND EDUCATION[8]   45
De copia, two books [260]
Ratio conscribendi epistolas [71, 117, 1284]
Ratio studiorum, addressed to Pierre Vitré [56, 66]
De pueris statim ac liberaliter instituendis 1529 [2189]
De recte pronunciando [1949]   50
Ciceronianus [1948]
De civilibus puerorum moribus [2282]
Theodorus' *Grammar*, two books, in my version [428, 771]
Syntaxis[9] [341]
All my translations from Lucian; the titles are: 55
   Saturnalia[10] [261, 293]
   Epistolae Saturnales
   Chronosolon, that is, *Leges Saturnales*
   De luctu
   Icaromenippus   60
   Toxaris [187]
   Pseudomantis [199]

* * * * *

8 As in 1524, Erasmus here divides his works into *ordines* (series or categories). The ten *ordines* of 1524 have here been reduced to nine, though they are not yet quite the nine that would be used, starting in 1538–40, in all editions of Erasmus' complete works. (Cf Ep 1341A n357, where it is erroneously stated that the ten-volume scheme of 1524 was the basis of the Basel and Leiden editions of the *opera*). The first five *ordines*, as well as the eighth and ninth, are the same in 1524 and in the current list. The modifications introduced with the Basel edition are indicated in the notes that follow.
9 This work usually bears the title *De octo orationis partium constructione*.
10 *Saturnalia* is the name given to a work in three short parts, the second and third of which are listed separately by Erasmus as the *Chronosolon* and *Epistolae Saturnales*.

Somnium sive gallus [193]
Timon [192]
Abdicatus   65
Tyrannicida
De mercede conductis in aulis potentum [197]
Sundry dialogues [205]
    Cnemon and Damippus
    Zenophantes and Callidemides   70
    Menippus and Tantalus
    Menippus and Mercury
    Menippus and Amphilochus
    and Trophonius
    Charon and Menippus   75
    Crates Diogenes
    Nireus and Thersites
    Diogenes and Mausolus
    Simylus and Polystratus
    Venus and Cupid   80
    Mars and Mercury
    Mercury and Maia
    Venus and Cupid
    Doris and Galatea
    Diogenes and Alexander   85
    Menippus and Chiron
    Menippus and Cerberus
Hercules Gallicus
Eunuchus
De sacrificiis   90
Lapithae [550]
De astrologia [267]
I should not wish the prefaces to these, which make clear to whom
    each is dedicated, to be omitted.
A short declamation rendered from the Greek of Libanius, with several   95
    themes[11] also translated [177]
A declamation against a tyrannicide, in answer to Lucian's [191]
Laus medicinae [799]
Encomium matrimonii 1529 [604:10 / CWE 604:12]

* * * * *

11 Erasmus' word is thematium, a term taken from Greek for a 'theme' for rhetorical treatment.

Similia,[12] one book [312]   100
Colloquia, one book, but frequently enlarged; latest edition 1529 [130:92 /
    CWE 130:108–9, 909, 1041, 1262, 1476]
Hecuba and *Iphigenia* of Euripides translated [188, 198, 208]
Miscellaneous poems on other than religious subjects; these I have assigned
    to their appropriate sections.   105
Commentarius in Nucem Ovidii [1402]
Prooemia Galeni translated, addressed to the physician Antoninus [1698]

SECOND SERIES
Opus adagiorum, often revised and enlarged, most recently in 1528 [126, 211,
    269, 1204, 1659, 2022–3]   110

THIRD SERIES
A volume of letters, enlarged by more than a third, 1529 [2203]

FOURTH SERIES, ON MORAL QUESTIONS
Translations from Plutarch:
    De discrimine adulatoris et amici, addressed to the king of England [272,   115
        657]
    Quomodo possit utilitas capi ex inimico [284, 297, 658]
    De tuenda bona valetudine [268]
    Principi maxime philosophandum
    An graviores sint animi morbi quam corporis   120
    De cupiditate divitiarum
    Num recte dictum sit ab Epicuro λάθε βιώσας
    De inutili verecundia [1663]
    Moriae encomium [222]
    Panegyricus, a speech congratulating Philip, father of the emperor   125
        Charles, on his return from Spain [179, 180]
    Institutio principis christiani, addressed to the emperor Charles [393,
        853]
    Isocratis de regno,[13] to the same [393]

* * * * *

12 Better known as the *Parabolae*
13 Ie Erasmus' translation of Isocrates' *Praecepta de regno administrando ad Nico-
    clem*, also addressed to Emperor Charles and published with the *Institutio prin-
    cipis christiani*. Allen's misleading reference to Ep 677 has been corrected to
    Ep 393.

Consolatio de morte filii[14] 130
Querimonia pacis [603]
Carmen de senectute, to the physician Cop
Lingua [1593]
Cato, and other things [298, 676, 1725]
Officia of Cicero, edited not without success, 1528 [152, 1013, 1994A] 135
Opera Senecae oratoris, diligently edited, 1528 [2091]
Xenophantis Tyrannus, translated, 1530 [2273]

FIFTH SERIES, WORKS OF RELIGIOUS INSTRUCTION
Enchiridion militis christiani [164, 858]
De contemptu mundi [1194] 140
Methodus verae theologiae [745, 1365]
Paraclesis [1253:22 / CWE 1253:24–5]
Exomologesis, enlarged 1529 [1426]
Commentarii in Psalmos primum et secundum [327, 1304]
De matrimonio christiano, addressed to the renowned queen of England, 145
    Catherine [1727]
Vidua christiana, addressed to Mary, sometime queen of Hungary and sister
    of the emperor Charles [2100]
Paraphrasis in Psalmum tertium [1427]
Concio in Psalmum quartum [1535] 150
Concio in Psalmum octuagesimum quintum [2017]
Concio in Psalmum vigesimum secundum [2266]
Paraphrasis in Precationem Dominicam [1393]
Commentarii in duos hymnos Prudentii [1404]
Concio de puero Iesu [175] ·155
Libellus concionalis de misericordia Domini, addressed to Christoph, sometime
    bishop of Basel [1474]
Comparatio virginis et martyris, addressed to the Maccabeitic nuns of Cologne
    [1346, 1475]
Expostulatio Iesu, in verse 160
Casa natalitia, in verse [47]
Michaelis archangeli encomium, in verse
Virginis matris paean [93:101 / CWE 93:112–13]
Ad eandem obsecratio [93:101 / CWE 93:112–13]

* * * * *

14 More commonly known as the *Declamatio de morte*; see Ep 1341A:669–71.

Precatio ad Iesum servatorem   165
Liturgia virginis Lauretanae cum concione [1391, 1573]
Consolatio, addressed to the nuns of St Clare, in England [1925]
De bello Turcico, 1530 [2285]

SIXTH SERIES[15]
Novum Testamentum cum annotationibus, fourth edition revised and enlarged   170
    1527 [1571:19 / CWE 1571:20, 1789]
Paraphrasis in Novum Testamentum, 1524 [1255, 1400, 1381, 1333, 1414]

SEVENTH SERIES[16]
Translations from Chrysostom:
    Adversus Iudaeos, five homilies [1800]   175
    De Lazaro et divite, four homilies
    De visione Esaiae, five homilies
    De Philogonio martyre, one homily
    In Epistolam ad Philippenses, two homilies [1734]
    De orando Deum, two homilies [1563]   180
    In Acta apostolorum, four homilies [1801]
    Commentarium in totam Epistolam ad Galatas [1841]
    In secundam ad Corinthios, ten homilies
Translations from Athanasius
    Epistolae de Spiritu sancto duae [1790]   185
    Epistola contra Eusebium de Niceno synodo
    Apologeticus adversus eos qui calumniabantur quod in persequutione
      fugisset
    De passione Domini, one homily
    De eo quod scriptum est, 'Euntes in castellum quod contra vos est' etc   190
    De virginum instituto
    De peccato in Spiritum sanctum
    De Spiritu sancto liber illi inscriptus
Translated from Origen
    Fragmentum in Matthaeum [1844]   195
Translated from Basil
    Principium Esaiae [229]

* * * * *

15 In 1524 the New Testament Paraphrases had been treated separately as *ordo*
    VII, and that separation into *ordines* VI and VII would be restored in 1540.
16 *Ordo* VIII in 1540

EIGHTH SERIES, CONTAINING THE DEFENCES[17]

Ad Iacobum Fabrum Stapulensem de Eloim [597:37–45]

Ad Eduardum Leum, two books [1037, 1100]   200

Ad Iacobum Latomum de Linguis, one book [934:3 / CWE 934:3–4]

Adversus Nicolaum Ecmondanum de loco Pauli, 'Omnes quidem resurgemus,' etc [1126:129 / CWE 1126:138–9]

Adversus quorundam clamores quod verteram, 'In principio erat sermo,' one book [1072]   205

Ad Iohannem Briardum Atensem, quondam Lovaniensis Academiae cancellarium, pro Encomio matrimonii, one book [670]

Ad taxationes Stunicae in Novum Testamentum [1428]

Adversus libellum Blasphemiarum eiusdem [Allen IV 622, Appendix 15]

Appendix adversus eiusdem Πρόδρομον   210

Ad Sanctium Caranzam theologum de tribus locis ab illo notatis [1277:22 / CWE 1277:25–7]

De delectu ciborum,[18] addressed to Christoph, bishop of Basel [1274:14 / CWE 1274:15]

Ad Martinum Dorpium theologum Epistola, which hitherto has been appended   215
to the *Moria* [337]

Spongia adversus Ulrichum Huttenum [1378, 1389]

Liber antibarbarorum, one book, for the second and third perished through the dishonesty of certain men [30:16 / CWE 30:17, 1110]

Adversus Petrum Sutorem Cartusianum, one book [1591]   220

De libero arbitrio diatribe sive collatio, one book [1419]

Adversus Martini Lutheri Servum arbitrium Hyperaspistes, two books [1667, 1853]

Adversus Natalem Beddam theologum Parisiensem Elenchus, Divinationes et Supputationes [1664]   225

Ad epistolam Alberti Pii Carporum principis, one book [1634]

Adversus calumnias monachorum Hispaniensium, 1529 [1877, 1879, 1967]

Ad quendam Franciscanum qui notarat aliquot loca in annotationes meas ad Romanos, one book [1823]

Contra Pseudevangelicos Epistola una, 1530 [2219:11 / CWE 2219:10–14, 2238]   230

NINTH SERIES[19]

Totus Hieronymus cum scholiis, edited anew, 1526 [1465, 1451, 1453, 1504]

* * * * *

17 *Ordo* IX in 1540
18 More commonly known as *De esu carnium*
19 Omitted in 1540, but with dedicatory letters assigned to *ordo* III

Cyprianus, often revised; added to it in the last edition 1529 was *Liber de duplici martyrio*, hitherto unpublished, 1529 [1000]

Hilarius, edited with great effort, 1523 [1334]   235

Irenaeus, revised anew from the oldest manuscripts 1528 [1738, 2007]

Ambrosius, in part edited by me 1527 [1855]

I edited two new short works of Ambrose, *Apologia David* and *Interpellatio David*, 1529 [2190, 2076]

Lactantius de opificio Dei, edited with scholia [2103]   240

Opera omnia divi Augustini, edited with infinite toil 1529 [2157]

Algerus de Eucharistia, edited [2284]

2284 / To Balthasar Merklin   Freiburg, 15 March 1530

This is the preface to Erasmus' edition of the treatise *De veritate corporis et sanguinis Dominici in Eucharistia* (Freiburg: Johann Faber Emmeus 1530) by the twelfth-century scholar Alger of Liège, also known as Alger of Cluny or Algerus Magister (d c 1131). Alger's work is a classic summary of the theological arguments in support of the doctrine of the Real Presence against Berengar of Tours, whose arguments against it were revived and developed by Zwingli and his allies (see n4) in the 1520s. In so doing, they were given to claiming that they had been inspired by Erasmus (see Ep 2204 n4). Erasmus' publication of Alger's treatise, with this approving letter as its preface, was clearly designed to indicate his firm support for the consensus of the church on the subject of the Real Presence and to distance himself from the 'foolish error' of former disciples who had come to deny it. It is interesting that, despite pursuing a line of argument much different from that of Martin Luther, Erasmus comes to essentially the same conclusion, namely, that while the presence of the body and blood in the bread and wine of the sacrament is real, the mode of that presence is a mystery that eludes rational explanation (by, for example, the doctrine of transubstantiation) and can be apprehended only by faith (see lines 107–9).

On Balthasar Merklin, imperial diplomat, bishop of Hildesheim and, since March 1529, bishop of Constance, see Epp 1382 n8 and Ep 2123 introduction.

TO THE RIGHT REVEREND FATHER IN CHRIST BALTHASAR,
LORD BISHOP OF HILDESHEIM, HIS MOST RESPECTED PATRON,
FROM ERASMUS OF ROTTERDAM, GREETING

I am aware, distinguished prelate, that it is hardly polite to interrupt one who is beset by such a flood of business, but with your deep and pious con-   5 cern for the welfare of the church I think you will not object to being interrupted on a matter that is of the first importance for the peace and reputation

Balthasar Merklin
Eltztaler Heimatmuseum, Waldkirch

of the church. For the church knows no moment more sublime than when, by sharing the body and blood of the Lord according to both its nature and its substance, it becomes one with Christ and in some way is transformed into God. Nothing can more effectively create a perfect and indissoluble harmony in the church than this, for by eating the same body and drinking the same blood, it is made one body by the same spirit and is joined, a living church, to Christ its living head. And yet we see that, through the wiles of Satan, what was given to bring all men together caused much dissension in the past and has lately been the source of conflict once more. Some deny that there is anything in the Eucharist except symbols of the body and blood of the Lord; others profess that Christ is truly present but beneath the substance of bread and wine; then again there were those who held that, through the words of consecration, the substance of the bread and wine perished and the body and blood of the Lord took their place; others suppose that Christ is impanated and invinated – as though to have been incarnated once is not enough. Then there appeared upon the scene the appropriately named Stercoranists,[1] and Greece gave us the Fermentarians.[2] Later a controversy broke out over receiving communion in both kinds. In this matter papal authority has varied: Gelasius decreed that those who wished to take communion only in one kind should be banned from both.[3] Some have argued that nothing performed by an ungodly priest is effective, and that the true body is not received by wicked men. The errors of all these people, however, have had this beneficial effect, that the church has gradually become better informed and more secure in its understanding of this great mystery. Paradoxically, it owes more to no one than to Berengar – or rather not to Berengar, but to the wisdom of Christ, who turns the wickedness of men to the good of his bride. Just think of the kind of men and the kind of writing that was inspired by Berengar's foolish error.[4]

* * * * *

2284
1 'Stercoranists' (from *stercus* 'dung') was a name applied to those who asserted that the body and blood of Christ were digested and excreted by those who received them in the sacrament. Though written of as a sect, there is no evidence that any such sect ever existed.
2 *Fermentarii* (from *fermentum* 'yeast') an appellation applied by Latin Christians to the Greeks, who used leavened bread in the Eucharist
3 Pope Gelasius II (d 1119). For the decree see Gratian's *Decretum* pars 3 D 22 c 12.
4 Berengar of Tours (c 999–1088), French monk and theologian noted for his quick intelligence and singular opinions, particularly those on the Eucharist. In the period 1050–78 he was repeatedly condemned by church councils for

Recently there appeared a work by Guitmund, a Benedictine monk, who became bishop of Aversa.[5] Now here is Alger, a scholasticus, later a monk of the same order. Guitmund is more vehement and more heated and has more rhetorical fire; Alger is gentler and more devout. Both are well grounded in logic and in the other branches of philosophy, though they 40 do not parade their knowledge. Both have carefully studied the canonical scriptures and the old Doctors of the church, Cyprian, Hilary, Ambrose, Jerome, Augustine, Basil, and Chrysostom, whose writings still best reflect the apostolic spirit. Both have as much eloquence as one may legitimately ask of a theologian. Certainly you would nowhere find them wanting in 45 clarity of expression or incisiveness of argument. They build a case on sound reasoning, not like certain people today who fill the greater part of a volume with controversy and invective or treat an issue with sophistical quibbles. And yet it appears that these men and others like them flourished before the time of Bonaventure, Thomas, Scotus, Albertus Magnus, and even before 50 Peter Lombard.[6] As for more recent philosophers, the greater their pride in the philosophy of Aristotle, the more arid the style in which they write, presumably in imitation of their hero. It is true that Aristotle dispensed with emotional effects and stylistic ornaments, but he did so in such a way as to produce a high degree of elegance, an accomplishment that is beyond the 55

* * * * *

denying that, when consecrated, the substance of the bread and wine of the Eucharist is transformed into the real body and blood of Christ, the same body that was born of Mary and crucified. While not explicitly denying that there is a Real Presence of some sort, Berengar argued that it is an intellectual and spiritual presence that does not alter the substance of the bread and wine. His arguments, eg that the ascended body of Christ is spatially confined in heaven and thus cannot be present elsewhere, anticipated those of Huldrych Zwingli and other 'sacramentarians' of the sixteenth century. The issues he raised, and the influence he seemed to have, forced prelates and theologians of the medieval church to clarify the church's thinking on the subject of the Real Presence, a process that culminated in the formal promulgation of the doctrine of transubstantiation at the Fourth Lateran council in 1215.

5 Guitmund (d c 1094), a Norman who in 1088 was appointed bishop of Aversa (near Naples). In the mid-1070s he wrote a treatise against the heresy of Berengar entitled *De corporis et sanguinis Jesu Christi veritate in Eucharistia*. The first printed edition, edited by Augustinus Marius (Ep 2321), was published by Johann Faber Emmaeus at Freiburg in 1530. The title-page stated that the work was 'now at last published because of the widespread attacks by those who are undermining the sacraments.'

6 Bonaventure, the youngest of this group, died in 1274; Lombard, the oldest, in 1160.

powers of these people. But it seems to me only fitting that, in explaining the mysteries of faith, we should seek by one means or another to achieve a certain dignity of language and that one's feelings should not be hidden. For in this way not only will the reader understand what he is being taught by his teacher, but come to love what his teacher loves. We have in the gospel: 60 'This is my body which is given for you,'[7] and from Paul 'I have received from the Lord that which also I delivered unto you' etc and 'Whosoever shall eat and drink unworthily shall be guilty of the body and blood of the Lord.'[8] This is the solid ground on which we stand.

Some of the ancient Doctors of the church, in speaking of this sacra- 65 ment, seem at times rather obscure; at other times they appear to differ from, not to say contradict, one another. Their obscurity is perhaps to be attributed to the inexpressible profundity of this mystery, or possibly to caution, for they frequently spoke before a mixed audience of Jews, pagans, and Christians and were unwilling to give that which is holy to dogs.[9] The divergence 70 of opinion arises because sometimes the word 'symbol' is used of the sacramental elements, sometimes it is the actual partaking of them that is called a 'symbol'; finally the body is sometimes called a symbol of itself or of something else. Moreover, since under these signs lies, by synecdoche,[10] the body of the Lord, anything that applies to the appearances is also attributed to 75 the body, such as the capacity to be broken or crushed. Then, since the consecrated body is identical in substance to the body that hung on the cross, but not in quality, for it is now the glorified and spiritual body, inattentive readers may imagine that the ancients contradict themselves when they say that the body is the same and not the same, although in fact there is no con- 80 tradiction. Finally, the body of Christ is sometimes called 'natural' because it was born from the Virgin, at other times it is called 'mystical,' as being the church. This prompts the careless reader to say that the Fathers seem inconsistent.

So since we have such clear testimony from Christ and Paul, and since 85 these men[11] have demonstrated in the clearest possible fashion that the ancient Fathers, to whom the church rightly assigns such authority, have been in agreement that the real substance of the Lord's body and blood is present

* * * * *

7 Luke 22:19
8 1 Cor 11:23–6, 27
9 Matt 7:6; cf *Adagia* III v 14.
10 A synecdoche is a figure of speech in which a part is made to represent the whole, or vice-versa, eg 'all hands on deck,' or 'Canada won ten gold medals.'
11 Alger and Guitmund

in the Eucharist, and when to all this we add the constant approval of syn-
ods and the general agreement of Christian people, let us too be of one mind   90
about this heavenly mystery and let us partake of the Lord's bread and of
the chalice with our darkened understanding until in a different light we eat
and drink in God's kingdom. Would that those who have followed Berengar when he was in error would also follow him when he repented,[12] and
that their error too would turn out to the advantage of the church!   95

There are innumerable questions surrounding this sacrament: how
transubstantiation takes place; how the accidents remain when separated
from the underlying matter; how they retain colour, smell, taste, and the
power possessed by bread and wine before they were consecrated to satisfy, intoxicate, and nourish; at what moment they become the body and   100
blood of the Lord; when the substance of the body and blood ceases to exist and whether, when the appearances are destroyed, a change in substance
comes about; how the same body can exist in countless places; how the full
body of a man can exist in a tiny piece of bread; and many other questions that are appropriate subjects for sober discussion among people with   105
trained minds.

It is generally sufficient to believe that after the consecration the real
body and blood are present and that they cannot be divided or injured or
suffer any indignity, whatever happens to the appearances. For if the body
of the Lord were defiled when thrown into the mud, or into a privy, or into   110
a man's stomach, it would suffer no worse defilement than when taken by
a man with the stain of his sins upon him. Christian practice demands that
one handle the elements with all due reverence. Nevertheless, just as God
by his nature is no less present in a privy than in heaven, and cannot be
harmed or defiled, so neither can the glorified body of the Lord. In brief,   115
when faced with all the thorny issues invented by the human mind, our first
thought should be of the immeasurable power of God, to whom nothing is
impossible and nothing is difficult, and then of the incalculable riches of the
glorified body, especially that of our Lord Jesus. It is left to us to celebrate
in a fitting manner a truth that has been amply proven and to show in our   120
lives that we believe what we believe. For who could find fitting words to
say what purity of heart, what reverence, what awe this mystery demands.

* * * * *

12 Berengar twice (in 1055 at Tours, and in 1078 in Rome) retracted his opinions
   and signed a statement of the orthodox view of the Real Presence, only to
   renew his attack on that view. In 1080, at a council in Bordeaux, he signed a
   final retraction and then spent the rest of his life in solitude and in union with
   the church.

Who would believe in the sincerity of those who, while this mystery is taking place, walk around the church chatting or,[13] as happens habitually in some places, stand in the square in front of the church doors passing   125 the time in idle chatter. In the past this was the place for penitents and catechumens. Some, immediately after the elevation of the mysteries, rush off to a tavern and leave the church empty. What kind of behaviour is that? When a comedy is being performed, you stay in your place until you hear the words *Valete atque plaudite*; can you not wait, then, for the conclusion of   130 this great heavenly mystery?[14] The angelic spirits stand around that table in adoration, and he is present on whom the whole angelic host delights to gaze: do you, as if some farce were being acted, show your disgust and boredom, or natter, or start drinking?

I see that a practice has now been widely accepted that it would not   135 be right perhaps to call unchristian, since it seems to spring from a pious, though human, impulse; nevertheless it has been introduced contrary to the ancient practice of the church and with little regard for propriety. While the mystery of the consecration is taking place, the choir sings a canticle to the Virgin mother with a lengthy prayer. Is it fitting, when the Son himself is   140 present, to call upon the mother? But if we want to preserve the ancient custom of the church, we should remember that at this point no sound was heard throughout the church, and that the people prostrated themselves upon the ground and gave thanks to God with silent hearts for sending his Son to die for the salvation of the human race. It is to this that the priest exhorts   145 the people when he turns to them and says 'Lift up your hearts! Let us give thanks unto the Lord our God!' For nothing is more appropriate to these ineffable mysteries than silence, nor is there any better way in which we can celebrate the amazing love for us of the Lord Jesus than by this most eloquent silence, when the noisy din of human voices is stilled, the body is low-   150 ered in submission, and the mind, raised in adoration, speaks to God alone.

If the people are to venerate this mystery properly, it is of no small importance how priests live their lives. Once in its great days the church

* * * * *

13 Allen notes that at this point in his copy of the Alger volume, a sixteenth-century hand has written in the margin in German: 'At Freiburg, in the new choir.' For further description by Erasmus of unseemly behaviour at mass, see *De sarcienda ecclesiae concordia* (1533) CWE 65 207, 209.

14 The phrase *Valete et plaudite* 'Farewell and give us your applause,' or some variation of it, is commonly addressed to the audience at the end of the Roman comedies of Plautus and Terence. At the conclusion of mass, the priest says to the people: *Ite, missa est* 'Go, you are dismissed.'

recognized only one sacrament, which no one but a bishop performed. Later
a host of priests was called in, at first for religious reasons, later for finan-   155
cial gain. Things then reached the point where many learn to celebrate mass
in the same spirit as an ordinary person learns a trade, like that of the shoe-
maker, the cement worker, or the clothier. To them the mass is nothing more
than a way of earning money. It is right of course that those who serve at
the altar should live by the altar.[15] Yet this mystery must be kept clear of   160
any appearance of hucksterism. The ministers of this sacred office should
live up to the dignity of their calling not just in gestures and vestments and
speech but in the whole tenor of their lives. Sobriety, chastity, purity, contempt for vulgar pleasures, love of Holy Scripture, these are the things that
most become a priest.   165

How inappropriate it is for a priest, immediately after celebrating such
a mystery, to devote the rest of the day to drinking, irreligious chatter, cards
or dice, hunting, or aimless rambles, and to spend little or none of his time
in reading the Holy Scriptures and in the contemplation of heavenly things!
Priests should recognize the lofty nature of their profession. When they   170
stand at the altar, they have angels attending them. Some priests, on leaving the sanctuary, are not ashamed to associate with the lowest dregs of
society – not to use a harsher term. Let those who hold an office that sur-
passes in dignity the office of the angels behave in such a way as to give
heretics no pretext for thinking blasphemous thoughts about such an ineffa-   175
ble mystery. Rather let their way of life do honour to their ministry so that
the Lord in turn will honour them both among men and before his heavenly
Father.

But why am I saying this? Alger and Guitmund will make this case
more effectively; I confess that I have read them myself with great profit. I   180
have never at any time doubted the Real Presence of the Lord's body, but
somehow, by my reading of these works, my opinions have been greatly
strengthened and my reverence increased.[16] Whatever the merits of my
work, I have wanted to dedicate it to you, most honoured prelate, so that
there would be something to bear witness that your humble servant Eras-   185
mus is mindful of his excellent patron and in turn to remind you of me.
May the Lord prosper your most holy endeavours for his glory and the
advancement of the Christian faith.

Freiburg im Breisgau, 15 March AD 1530

* * * * *

15 1 Cor 9:13
16 Cf Ep 2175:24–9 with n9.

2285 / To Johann Rinck   Freiburg, 17 March 1530

This letter consists of the opening and closing passages, with one other, of the *Ultissima consultatio de bello Turcis inferendo, et obiter enarratus psalmus 28*, more commonly known as *De bello Turcico* (Basel: Froben 1530). An annotated translation of the entire treatise by Michael Heath is found in CWE 64 201–66. This translation of the partial text published by Allen is entirely new. The notes, too, have been redone, though not without the inclusion of a considerable amount of material from Dr Heath's notes.

The treatise was written in response to a letter now lost in which Johann Rinck of Cologne asked Erasmus to address the question of war against the Turks, a topic that had become (and would long remain) a central preoccupation of the politics of the Holy Roman Empire. Rinck (d 1566), whose life is not well documented, was a member of the faculty of law at Cologne as well as a member of the Cologne city council. Accompanying his letter to Erasmus was a handsome gift (Ep 2277 n5). Whether this initiative marked the origin of Rinck's contact with Erasmus is not clear, but it is clear that the relationship quickly developed into a lasting friendship. One of Rinck's letters to Erasmus (Ep 3004), and three more of Erasmus' to him (Epp 2353A, 2534, 2618) survive. The last of these is the dedicatory letter to the *Precatio pro pace ecclesiae* (first printed in 1532; see CWE 69 111).

DESIDERIUS ERASMUS OF ROTTERDAM TO THE HONOURABLE
MASTER JOHANN RINCK, EMINENT JURIST, GREETING
Respected sir, realizing that I could never match the scholarship, elegance, and kindliness of your letter,[1] I have decided to surpass you in the abundance, or rather the flood, of my words by as much as you surpassed me in   5
all other respects.

We all understand what kind of web the monarchs are weaving. Most of them are engrossed in collecting the sinews of war,[2] some in mustering their generals and armaments; but I see hardly anyone reflecting how to change life for the better, which is the most vital of their responsibilities and   10
is something that concerns all men equally. Nor can I explain to myself the reason for the dreadful numbness that has gripped the hearts of Christian people.

* * * * *

2285
1 Not extant
2 Ie raising money; see Cicero *Philippica* 5.2.5: 'money, the sinews of war.'

God is sending us a warning by afflicting us with more plagues than
the Egyptians suffered and harsher plagues than those mentioned in the   15
Revelation of John;[3] yet we are more stubborn than the Phrygians, for all
this severity, intended by the Lord to encourage us to bear better fruit, does
not change us for the better.[4] On the contrary, like wretched slaves hardened
against the lash, we take advantage of God's indulgence to persist in our
wickedness, and in face of the divine compassion that sends these passing   20
ills to help us to amend our lives, we become more intransigent still. We are
now so inured to wars, banditry, riots, party strife, looting, plagues, famine,
and shortages of all kinds that we no longer think of them as misfortunes.

But God has acted like a responsible physician, repeatedly trying some
new treatment. He sent among us an unprecedented and incurable form of   25
leprosy, commonly known as the French pox, though why it is so named, I
do not know, since it is to be found in every country.[5] It is a truly dreadful
scourge upon the human race. But far from this horrible disease teaching us
chastity and sobriety, we have openly turned it into a subject of laughter. We
seem to have reached the point where among our courtiers, who suppose   30
themselves to be such fine and witty fellows, anyone not infected with the
disease is thought to be a boorish peasant. How else can I describe this than
as farting in God's face, or showing him the middle finger, as they say,[6]
when he is trying to correct us?

Then there followed an intractable dispute over religion, which was   35
certainly no simple affair. There can be no doubt that the very men whose
good sense should have tempered the people's folly were in no small measure responsible for giving the dispute a footing. The critics set no example
of improvement in their lives, and those who are criticized give no thought
to mending their ways. We are not far short of turning even this latest ap-   40
palling disaster for Christendom into a joke or a subject for amusement.

Of all the punishments that God threatens in Leviticus 26 and Deuteronomy 28 against those who break his commandments, is there a single one
that has not been visited upon us? For how many years now have we witnessed all the horrors of war? 'What land is not stained with our blood'?[7]   45

* * * * *

3 Rev 16. For the plagues on Egypt, see Exodus 8–13.
4 *Adagia* I viii 36; cf Epp 2209:194–9, 2249:42–3.
5 Ie syphilis; cf Ep 2209:184–5 with n40.
6 Both of these vulgar expressions have a classical pedigree and are found in
   the *Adagia*: I vii 76: *Oppedere* and II iv 68: *Medium digitum ostendere*.
7 Horace *Odes* 2.1.36

How often have we felt the Turkish sword avenging our transgressions
against the covenant made with God? What kind of plague have we not suffered, in town and country alike, so that flight has meant merely exchang-
ing one danger for another? How often have we seen our daily bread cut
short? How many throughout Europe have eaten their ration of bread and   50
not been satisfied?[8] Recently, in Italy, that most fertile of regions, how many
have perished of hunger?[9] It may be that so far no one has eaten the flesh of
his sons or daughters;[10] but is it not true that we all live by devouring one
another? The nobles engage in plunder, the farmer sells his produce at four
times its value, merchants impose huge increases in their prices, and work-   55
men charge as much as they please for their services. Each man cheats his
neighbour by some form of fraud or trickery. We see magnificent churches
ruined, images thrown down, priests expelled.[11] Did he not, a few years
ago, send wild beasts among us to destroy everything in the fields[12] when
bands of peasants ran amok, recognizing no restraint?[13] Nor have we es-   60
caped the curse mentioned in Deuteronomy: Men marry wives and others
sleep with them.[14]

Here perhaps someone will think that I have taken on the task of opposing the Turkish war. On the contrary, my point is rather that we should
make war against them successfully and win truly splendid triumphs for   65
Christ. For merely to clamour for war against the Turks, calling them inhu-
man monsters, enemies of the church, and a race tainted with every kind
of crime and villainy, is simply to betray an untrained multitude to the
enemy. We have been hearing from close at hand of the recurrent disasters in Hungary, most recently of the tragic death of Louis and the sad   70
fate of Queen Mary;[15] and now, besides the occupation of the kingdom

* * * * *

8 Lev 26:26
9 Cf Epp 2109:8–9, 2115:66–8.
10 Lev 26:29 and Deut 28:53
11 This had happened in many places, but Erasmus had personally experienced
   the tumults and the iconoclasm that accompanied the victory of the Reformation in Basel in the winter of 1528–9; see Ep 2097 n1.
12 Lev 26:22
13 In the Peasants' Revolt of 1524–5
14 Deut 28:30
15 Louis II of Hungary perished at the battle of Mohács in August 1526, and
   his young bride Mary of Austria had to take refuge in Moravia under the
   protection of her brothers, Charles v and Ferdinand. See Ep 2100 introduction.

of Hungary, we learn of the merciless devastation of Austria.[16] During all
these events I have more than once been astonished at the nonchalance of
other Christian lands, and especially of Germany herself, as if these events
are no concern of ours. We become tightfisted, and spend on pleasures   75
and silly trifles what we are reluctant to spend on the defence of Christendom. I am well aware of the excuses that some apologists for this attitude put forward. This charade, they say, has been played too often by
the various popes, and the outcome has always been a farce.[17] Either nothing at all was accomplished, or the situation took a turn for the worse.   80
The money collected stuck fast in the hands of popes, cardinals, monks,
princes, and dukes; the common soldiers, instead of receiving their pay,
are given a licence to plunder. We have heard so often of a new crusade, of recovering the Holy Land; we have seen the red cross embla-
zoned with the triple crown, and of course the red chest;[18] we have lis-   85
tened to holy sermons promising the earth; we have been told of valiant
deeds and boundless hopes – but the only thing that has triumphed has
been money. How can we, who have been misled thirty times over, believe
any more promises, however splendid? We have been cheated to our face so
often, and, as the proverb says, it is shameful to stumble twice on the same   90
stone.[19]

It was this same experience that almost turned men against indulgences altogether.[20] We came to realize, they say, that these were nothing
but a commercial transaction. From time to time the pretext was changed:
now it was a campaign against the Turks, then the pope was being hard   95
pressed in war,[21] or there was a jubilee,[22] which turned into a double jubilee

* * * * *

16 See Ep 2211 n9.
17 Erasmus is here reflecting on the history of the efforts of fifteenth- and
   sixteenth-century popes to renew the crusading spirit of earlier centuries and
   unite the powers of Christian Europe in a war against the Turks.
18 See Ep 2256:21–4.
19 *Adagia* I v 8; the meaning is essentially the same as 'once bitten, twice wary.'
20 Erasmus was a consistent critic of the abuses connected with the sale of indulgences; see Ep 2205:80–8 and *Moriae encomium* CWE 27 114.
21 Fifteenth- and sixteenth-century popes were often 'hard pressed in war,' either
   in defence of the papal states against Italian rivals or as unhappy participants
   in the Italian wars between the Hapsburgs and the Valois. It is not clear whether
   Erasmus has a specific incident in mind here.
22 A holy year during which special indulgences are granted to people who make
   a pilgrimage to Rome and meet certain other conditions. Originally occurring
   every 100 years, they had by 1400 come to be held every twenty-five years.

to bring in twice the profit, and in the pontificate of Alexander there was
even a triple jubilee,[23] perhaps because he was disappointed with sales.
Then again we were offered a more than plenary indulgence, and Purgatory was in danger of losing all its inmates.[24] On another occasion it was   100
the building of St Peter's in the Vatican.[25] Then St James of Compostela was
starving,[26] the Holy Spirit, the giver of all things, was begging for aid,[27]
or the monks on Mount Sinai needed help.[28] Finally, those owing restitu-
tion were offered most generous indulgences and were pardoned for the
theft of property, even property looted from a church.[29] In short, there was   105
no end or limit to these pardons. The princes diverted part of the money
to obtain a brief from the pope; deans and officials took a share, as did
commissaries and confessors. Some were given money to make them talk,
others to buy their silence. By no means the smallest amount disappeared
into the pockets of agents and hawkers of papal briefs, criminals as these   110
people generally are. So, say these critics, the dull-witted people of Germany and the even duller people of France allowed these tricks to be played
quite openly and over and over again, although they understood what was
going on.

When the sea flooded the western part of Flanders, and the whole   115
region presented a pitiful sight, the most liberal indulgences were soon
ready. The cause, and to a certain extent the influence of the late Pope
Adrian, touched everyone deeply. Enough money was collected to help
those in distress, and legates were sent to inspect the area and to report on the necessary repairs and how they could be carried out. The   120

* * * * *

23 Under Pope Alexander VI, in 1500; see Ep 1211:173–5.
24 The first authentic application of indulgences to the souls in Purgatory was
   the bull *Salvator noster* of Sixtus IV (1476).
25 The rebuilding of St Peter's basilica began under Pope Julius II in 1506. Martin
   Luther's *Ninety-Five Theses on the Power and Efficacy of Indulgences* (1517) were
   occasioned by the sale of indulgences, authorized by Pope Leo X, to finance
   the same project.
26 Santiago de Compostela in Spain was, next to Rome, the most popular goal of
   pilgrims in search of indulgences; see also the colloquy *Peregrinatio religionis
   ergo* 'A Pilgrimage for Religion's Sake' CWE 40 651 n5, and cf Epp 1202:247–50,
   1697:70–2.
27 Ie the Order of the Hospitallers of the Holy Spirit, whose mission of caring
   for the sick and the poor was supported by the sale of indulgences
28 See Epp 594:7–11, 1132:25–35.
29 Cf the colloquy *Militaria* 'Military Affairs,' where Erasmus satirizes the frivolous ease with which soldiers were granted absolution for their looting and
   plundering; CWE 39 56–60, with nn12, 15, 24, 26.

disaster was portrayed in paintings. I need not say where that money disappeared to, but certainly none of it was directed to the use for which it was
collected.[30]

These and other objections are raised whenever men are urged to assist their rulers against the cruelty of the Turks. I only wish I could clearly   125
show that all these claims are without foundation. In the past this enterprise
has been vigorously advocated by many popes and, surprisingly, even by
Bernard himself, a monk and a saint.[31] Bessarion and Pius II both did their
utmost for this cause.[32] The idea has generated several orders of crusaders,
for whom plentiful provision has been made and new honours approved.[33]   130
What has come of it all is clear from the record. Leo x was particularly pre-
occupied with the enterprise and sent cardinals as legates to every province
of Christendom, the most learned of his cardinals at that. But everywhere
people listened to the envoys without much interest,[34] although Luther had
not yet written against papal indulgences and had not yet produced his   135

* * * * *

30 In September 1515 Charles v secured from Leo x a bull, valid for three years,
granting plenary indulgence to all those who contributed to the restoration of
the dikes along the shore of the North Sea in Flanders, Zeeland, and Friesland.
One third of all the money collected was to go to the pope for the building of
St Peter's basilica. The preaching of the indulgence was entrusted to Adriaan
of Utrecht, the future pope Adrian VI, but he was unable to discharge this
duty because of his departure for Spain in October 1515 to prepare the way
for Charles' succession in Aragon and Castile (1516). Leo x and Charles v
received their shares of the money collected; whether Charles' share was used
for the announced purpose is not clear. See Rémy 183–92.
31 In the years 1146–7 St Bernard of Clairvaux preached a series of sermons that
was crucial to the successful launching of the the Second Crusade (1146–9).
Erasmus finds this surprising because Bernard, his admiration for the Knights
Templar notwithstanding, had expressed great hostility to war and soldiering
and was given to punning on the words *militia* 'military service' and *malitia*
'roguery, vice.' See CWE 64 234 with n133.
32 Cardinal Bessarion (Ep 554:79n) and Enea Silvio (Aeneas Sylvius) Piccolomini,
who became Pope Pius II (reigned 1458–64), were the two most active cam-
paigners for a renewed crusade against the Turks following the fall of Constantinople in 1453.
33 The best known of the long list of local, national, and international crusading
orders are the Knights Templar, founded c 1119 and dissolved in 1314 (cf n31
above), and the Knights Hospitaller of St John, expelled from Rhodes in 1522
when it fell to the Turks and re-established on Malta by Charles v in 1530.
34 For Leo x's persistent but unsuccessful efforts, in the early years of his reign,
to get the monarchs of Christian Europe to unite in a crusade against the
Turks, see Pastor 7 chapter 5.

thesis that to fight the Turks is simply to resist the will of God, who is using them to punish us.[35]

I thought it worth while, distinguished sir, to send you these thoughts, arising out of my studies, though humane letters and the subject of war do not make a good match; my aim is to spur you to produce something better for   140
us, based on the wisdom of the law, in which you have won such high esteem. I beg you urgently to do so. You will thereby uphold the name of the Rinck family, whose chief merit, it is agreed by all, is that it has always devoted itself to serving the state to the best of its ability and continues to do so. May the Lord Jesus preserve you and those dearest to you, my   145
incomparable friend.

Freiburg im Breisgau, 17 March AD 1530

2286 / To Erasmus Schets   Freiburg, 19 March 1530

This letter, Erasmus' answer to Ep 2270, was first published by Allen on the basis of the autograph in the British Museum (MS Add 38512, folio 42).

Greetings. I am sorry for the trouble caused you by an error. Let me tell you what happened. I entrusted certain people with a volume of Chrysostom

* * * * *

35 In his *Explanations of the Ninety-Five Theses*, published in August 1518, Luther attempted to explain the assertion (in thesis number five) that the pope has authority to remove only those penalties imposed by himself or canon law and not those imposed by God. Among the punishments sent by God and thus beyond the power of the pope to remit are 'plagues, wars, insurrections, earthquakes, fires, murders, thefts, as well as the Turks, Tartars, and other infidels.' Thus for the pope to call for war against the Turks is to 'oppose God,' in whose hands the Turk is a lash for the punishment of human iniquities. See LW 31 91. This was widely misunderstood to mean that Luther thought it was sinful to take up arms against the Turks under any circumstances, and for this he was harshly condemned by the papacy (1520) and the Paris theologians (1521), among others; see CWE 64 205–6. Against this background, Luther's treatise *On War Against the Turks* (Ep 2279 n1), published just weeks before the Turkish advance of May–October 1529, seemed to mark a sudden change of heart. For in it he argued that, as temporal sovereign, Emperor Charles had the divinely imposed obligation to defend his subjects against wrongful invasion by the Turks. Erasmus subsequently described the work as a 'palinode,' ie a retraction; see Ep 2338 n14.

in Greek[1] on the understanding that if they could not find someone in Louvain willing to undertake the burden of translating it, they should sent it
on to Ghent. If they did find translators, they should either hold on to the   5
letters[2] or attach a page explaining why the volume was not included. This
they forgot to do.

The money arrived safely with Quirinus. The parcel, however, has not
yet come, and I fear it has gone astray.[3] I shall make use of the Fuggers
when there is need. Meanwhile continue to collect what is owed. Marcus   10
Laurinus is holding six months' pension, that is, sixty-five florins.[4] A certain Frisian owes me a goodly sum, which I asked him to remit to you.[5] I
hope that you, your wife and children, and your friends are in the best of
health.

Freiburg im Breisgau, 19 March AD 1530   15
Yours truly, Erasmus of Rotterdam
To the most honourable Master Erasmus Schets. In Antwerp

2287 / To Richard Pace   Freiburg, 22 March 1530

First published in the *Epistolae floridae*, this is Erasmus' reply to a letter now lost.

ERASMUS OF ROTTERDAM TO RICHARD PACE, GREETING
I jumped for joy, my dearest Pace, when I saw that familiar handwriting
and learned that after such terrible disasters and the appalling shipwreck of
your fortunes you had swum safely ashore and had even been restored to
your former dignity.[1] This was more welcome news to me than if someone   5
had sent me 600 angelets.[2] I see that the deity who delivers the innocent and

* * * * *

2286
1 See Ep 2258:7–10.
2 Of 11 November to Levinus Ammonius (Ep 2258:6), and probably another to
   Omaar van Edingen (cf Ep 2270:16–18).
3 There is no mention of any parcel in Epp 2243, 2270.
4 The Courtrai pension (Ep 751 introduction). On the half-yearly payment of 65
   Rhenish florins, see Ep 1094 n3.
5 Haio Cammingha; see Ep 2073 and cf Epp 2325:1–6, 2356:46–8, 2364.

2287
1 See Ep 1955.
2 Half angel-noble gold coins, then worth 45d each, and thus £112 10s 0d sterling,
   equivalent in value to 4,500 days' wages (21.43 years' money-wage income,

brings down the arrogant is not asleep.[3] I myself, although overwhelmed by unspeakable woes on account of the fury of the Pseudo-Evangelicals,[4] have, in a manner of speaking, been brought back to life because of you. If only I could see you and enjoy your sweet company before I die! I trust that, after 10 these deadly tempests, the sea from now on will be smooth and calm for you.

There is no need to worry about the letter that was returned to me;[5] there was nothing in it beyond the usual courtesies and good wishes. My man Quirinus tells me that it is among the letters recently published.[6] I 15 wish Robert Field every success, as I would even if he despised my work, since he is a dear friend of yours.[7] Although More deserves the high office he has received and is equal to it, I do not congratulate him so much as I congratulate the English realm and the king also.[8] I know of no man there who can equal him for the quality of his intellect and the incorrupt- 20 ibility of his character. May your life be pleasant, dear Pace, especially in the company of my patrons, and may you live in trusted harmony with your friends.

Freiburg im Breisgau, 22 March 1530

2288 / To Karel Uutenhove   Freiburg, 23 March 1530

This letter was first published in the *Epistolae floridae*. On Karel Uutenhove, see Ep 2209.

* * * * *

with an average of 210 days' employment per year), and thus a very large sum of money. Cf Ep 2237 n1.
3 Cf Pss 147 (146 Vulgate):6, 121 (120 Vulgate):4. Erasmus still believes the rumours that Pace had been imprisoned by the now-fallen Cardinal Wolsey; see Ep 2253:32–3 with n8.
4 This is the first recorded use of the word *pseudevangelicos*, which appears to have been Erasmus' invention; see CWE 78 xix with n60. It does not appear in the original title of the apologia that came to be known as the *Epistola contra pseudevangelicos*. See Ep 2219 n4.
5 Presumably Ep 1955, which Quirinus Talesius (Ep 1966) had apparently been unable to deliver, perhaps because of Pace's misfortunes; see Epp 1955 introduction, 2033:66–73.
6 In the *Opus epistolarum*
7 Robert Field (*Robertus Feldus*) is doubtless Robert Wakefield (Ep 1311 n14), with whom Pace had studied Hebrew.
8 On Sir Thomas More's appointment as lord chancellor, see Ep 2228:1–3.

ERASMUS OF ROTTERDAM TO KAREL UUTENHOVE, GREETING

I believe our friend Herwagen has been with you and has delivered my letter; for he has not yet returned here.[1]

I received two letters from you.[2] The later of the two was sent to me from Augsburg by Johann Koler, provost of Chur.[3] He says it was given 5 him by a certain scholaster. When it reached me, it was not just unsealed but torn. I missed in it, dear Karel, your usual caution and good sense. You know that today nothing can safely be put in a letter. You were remarkably free in what you wrote about one who has failed to meet the expectations of many people,[4] but even freer still when you spoke of one whom all assert 10 with one voice to be a tyrant.[5] I am delighted by your frankness, but in these times a scorpion sleeps under every stone.[6]

I thought your last letter was rather carelessly written; at no point did it come up to the standard of elegance I expected from Karel after living in Padua for so many years. You must make every effort, my dearest Uuten- 15 hove, to outdo even what your friends expect of you. This you could eas-ily accomplish if you matched your natural abilities with an equal indus-try. I hope you do not really need to be prodded in this way. But the spe-cial feeling that I have for you, which makes me more concerned for your glory than my own, has persuaded me to apply the spur to a running horse.[7] 20 Farewell.

Your friend Edingen has written to me most affectionately;[8] Ammo-nius writes more frequently.[9] I do not think there is anyone alive who has a more saintly character or a saner mind than he. Polyphemus is in Bohemia, drinking valiantly.[10] He writes to me often, but I never reply. You will learn 25

* * * * *

2288
1 Johann Herwagen (Ep 2231 n5) was on a trip to Italy and had not yet returned to Basel; see Ep 2249 n15. The letter mentioned is not extant.
2 Neither is extant.
3 Ep 2269 introduction
4 Possibly Charles v
5 Possibly Henry VIII. The words 'to be a tyrant' are written in Greek, presum-ably to muffle the harshness of the judgment.
6 *Adagia* I iv 34
7 *Adagia* I ii 47
8 The only extant letter from Edingen is Ep 2060.
9 Erasmus had doubtless now received Ep 2258 as well as Ep 2107.
10 See Ep 2130.

the rest of our news from Marcus,[11] who, I believe, will carry this letter. Farewell again.

Freiburg im Breisgau, 23 March AD 1530

2289 / From Bonifacius Amerbach   [Basel], 24 March 1530

The autograph of this letter (= AK Ep 1420) is in the Öffentliche Bibliothek of the University of Basel (MS C VIa 54 28). Bonifacius' answer is Ep 2294.

Greetings. Today my brother[1] dropped into the bookshop in the market square, where your letter to Neocomus, still wet from the press, was on sale.[2] When I had sampled the notes that had lately been added to the letter, I thought I owed it to the respect I feel for you to send the work to you at once, for that good-for-nothing has done everything in his power to destroy 5 the reputation of your name. The Frankfurt fair is imminent, and books of that sort are generally taken there; so it is up to you, in your wisdom, to consider if you should let the matter drop or send a letter as a counter-balance to the fellow's shameless behaviour.[3] Farewell, Erasmus, my most distinguished friend   10

In haste. On the vigil of the Annunciation of the Blessed Virgin 1530

Yours sincerely, Bonifacius Amerbach

2290 / To Pietro Bembo   Freiburg, 25 March 1530

This is Erasmus' reply to Ep 2144, which had taken a long time to reach him, arriving possibly as late as February 1530; see Ep 2269:84–5 with n13. The letter was first published in the *Epistolae floridae*. Allen used as the basis of

* * * * *

11 Unidentified

2289
1 Basilius, Bonifacius' older brother
2 Ie the unauthorized edition of the *Epistola contra pseudevangelicos* with anno-tations (*scholiis illustrata*) by Gerard Geldenhouwer, whom Erasmus had ad-dressed in the *Epistola* as 'Vulturius Neocomus'; see Ep 2238 introduction and n1. The volume had just been published with no indication of place, date, or printer. The place was Strasbourg, the time was March 1530, and the printer was Christian Egenolff; see Ep 2293 n2.
3 On 28 March Erasmus dispatched a letter of complaint to the magistrates of Strasbourg (Ep 2293) that seems to have caused serious trouble for the printer (Ep 2321:27–9).

CONTRA

QVOSDAM, QVI SE FALSO IAC-
tant Euangelicos, Epistola Def· Erasmi Roterodami, iam recens edita, & Scholijs
illustrata.

HORATIVS.

Mordear opprobrijs falsis, mutemq; colores?
Falsus honor iuuat, & mendax infamia terret,
Quem, nisi mendosum, & mendacem?

Title-page of Gerard Geldenhouwer's
unauthorized edition of Erasmus'
Epistola contra pseudevangelicos

!RASMVS ROTERODAMVS, GER⸗
ardo Nouiomago. S.

Doleo literas tuas nobis sero redditas . Iam e⸗
nim excuditur epistola, qua inuidiam per il⸗
los libellos mihi conflatam depello, quanquàm abs⸗
stinens tuo nomine, quod immutaui. Miror per quos
hic ludus ludatur . Bene uale . Friburgi tercio die
Decembris . Anno . 1 5 2 9 .

Quae lunulis inclusa, Lector, uideris, hoc pac⸗
to, ( ) . Scholia sunt à Gerardo Nouioma⸗
go in Euangelicae ueritatis gloriam addita .

ERASMVS

Verso of the title-page of Geldenhouwer's unauthorized
edition of Erasmus' *Epistola contra pseudevangelicos,*
where Ep 2238 was first printed

his text the original manuscript in the Vatican (MS Barb Lat 2158 folio cv). On
Bembo, see Ep 2106 introduction.

ERASMUS OF ROTTERDAM TO PIETRO BEMBO, GREETING
I would have reckoned that my audacity had paid off handsomely for me,
dear Bembo, my brilliant and incomparable friend, if that really Dutch letter
of mine,[1] and a carelessly written letter at that, had met a fair and courteous
reception from so great a man as you, accomplished, as you are, in every   5
branch of learning. But with that almost unbelievable generosity of yours,
you sent me a jewel in return for a glass bauble, for everything in your reply
was lovelier and more precious than pearls and emeralds. How sparkling is
the brilliance of your mind! What pleasing diction, what good sense, what
precision of language, what harmony of structure! When I read your words,   10
I became dreadfully dissatisfied with myself! I felt ashamed. But better not
to say anything more in case my carefully considered judgment is put down
to affection, and words that come from the innermost recesses of the heart
are thought to have been designed to please the ear, for this sort of thing
happens often enough.   15
   I turn to your letter. I was very confident that Karel Uutenhove would
do justice to the distinguished line of his ancestors and especially to his father, as learned and upright a man as Flanders has produced for many a
year, and, more to the point, I was sure that Karel would be true to himself.
For over a period of several months he had given me ample evidence of un-   20
common ability. Now that he has proved himself in the judgment of so great
a man, he will be more loved and cherished not just by me but by all his
friends. It is better to have won the approval of a single Roscius than the applause of everyone else in the theatre.[2] I think he realizes how much the expectations of his friends have been raised first by Italy, then by the celebrity 25
of the city of Padua (which could rightly be called the 'Italy of Italy,' just
as some people called Attica the 'Greece of Greece'), and finally by having
Pietro Bembo, the outstanding glory of the age, as his teacher and friend.
   Jacopo Sadoleto indicated that you were forced to return to Padua because of some problem with your health.[3] If this was an excuse, I praise your 30

* * * * *

2290
1 Ep 2106. On the proverbial dullness and lack of sophistication of the Dutch,
  see *Adagia* IV vi 35.
2 Quintus Roscius Gallus (c 126–63 BC), the famous Roman actor whose name
  (Roscius) came to be synonymous with 'outstanding actor.'
3 See Ep 2074:36–41.

tact. If not, I am glad you have recovered from the upset, since your letter contained no word of complaint. I hope you will find in Padua a quiet and delightful haven in which to pursue your sublime studies.

I have received nothing from Sadoleto since his last letter, in which he made mention of you.[4] My change of residence explains why I now re- 35 ceive fewer letters from my friends. They had heard I had moved but were uncertain where I had moved to. Moreover, this town, being further from the Rhine, is more off the beaten track, and so is less well known and less populated than Basel. It does possess a university, which is well established, though it does not attract a large enrolment, being distinguished by the qual- 40 ity rather than the number of its students. Among professors of law Zasius stands in the first rank,[5] a man greatly advanced in years but with a lively mind and unflagging eloquence. I have seen nothing in Germany so far to touch him for integrity and friendliness. Nor is there anyone on the horizon who seems so promising a successor that we would not regret the loss 45 of Zasius – though there are several by no means despicable possibilities. Theology here is limper than I would wish, but, I hope, will soon flourish again. The study of languages thrives up to a point. Henricus Glareanus is fairly successful at keeping the liberal disciplines alive.[6]

I wish, most honoured Bembo, that I were the sort of man who at this 50 point in his life could take comfort in the practice of virtue and in the contemplation of his character (which you are pleased to describe as 'excellent'); at least I would like to be permitted to grow old in the peaceful study of sacred literature. But although, as you rightly say, I am in my declining years and must fight a daily battle with that grim torturer, the stone,[7] I am nev- 55 ertheless compelled from time to time to go down into the arena with net and sword and act the part of a Thracian gladiator;[8] or what is worse, fight against wild beasts of every kind.[9] Up to now the crisis has brought us nothing worse than panic; this happened first during the mad uprising of the peasants,[10] when Basel came within an ace of being taken, and later at the 60 height of the iconoclasm, when an armed mob spent several nights in the

* * * * *

4 Ep 2272 did not arrive until 30 March; see Ep 2299:57–8.
5 See Ep 2209 n8.
6 In February 1529 Glareanus (Ep 440) moved from Basel to Freiburg, where he received a lectureship in poetry.
7 See Ep 2275 n9.
8 The Latin is *mirmillo*, a heavily armed gladiator who did not carry a net, though his usual opponent, the *retiarius*, did.
9 On Erasmus' use of the image of himself as engaged in gladiatorial combat with his opponents, see Ep 2250 n9.
10 In 1524–5

market square with their cannons drawn up in rows. But on that occasion the
damage was confined to wooden saints and saints of stone. Terror gripped
everyone who had anything they did not want to see destroyed.[11] We owe it
to the goodness of God that so far, amid all these disturbances, when people   65
on one side or the other have been so ready to rush to arms, not a drop of
blood has been shed.[12] The scene is now changing, I see strange and ominous events, but what the end of the story will be I do not know. Provided
we can avoid war in Germany, perhaps 'God, by a kindly change of fate,
will restore our fortunes to their former state' – you see that I am happy to   70
adopt the words of Horace.[13]

Whatever assistance you have given Uutenhove, I shall mark down in
my ledger as a debt to be paid. In exchange I give you the right to call
upon Erasmus on any occasion when you feel like testing how far I am
ready to go for Bembo. I most willingly accept your generous offer to share   75
all good things in accordance with the laws of friendship. I promise the
corresponding right over what is mine, if I have anything worth offering
except my good will. That at least I shall assuredly provide and anything
besides that my poor talents are capable of. Farewell.

Freiburg im Breisgau, 25 March AD 1530   80
Erasmus of Rotterdam. I signed in my own hand.

I used the services of an amanuensis so as not to torture you with my
cacography.

To the most honourable Pietro Bembo. In Padua

2291 / To Germain de Brie   Freiburg, 27 March 1530

This letter was first published in the *Epistolae floridae*. Germain de Brie (Ep
2021 introduction), was Erasmus' best friend and supporter among the French
humanists. In the uproar following the publication of the *Ciceronianus*, Brie
had done his best to reconcile Erasmus with his French critics; see Epp 2021,
2046. Brie was also a formidable Greek scholar with a special interest in St
John Chrysostom, a number of whose works he had translated into Latin; see
Ep 2082 n48. Brie's reply to this letter is Ep 2340.

ERASMUS OF ROTTERDAM TO GERMAIN DE BRIE, GREETING
You yourself are the reason for my silence, for you wrote that you were

* * * * *

11 See Ep 2097 n1.
12 On the bloodless First Kappel War, see Ep 2173 n10.
13 Horace *Epodes* 13.7–8

about to go off for a protracted stay.[1] I had written to certain friends of mine, but as I understand it, it was only after four months that the printer returned the letters.[2] Your *Monk* arrived too late, after another version had already been printed.[3] I see that I may expect nothing at all from you, at least as far as this project is concerned, except figwood support or (should I say?) an alliance with Rhesus.[4] The whole work will come out at the next autumn fair.[5] Printing is going forward on several presses. From the commentaries on Acts I translated three homilies and have added a fourth.[6] But I shall go no further, since I am sure the work is spurious. The commentaries on the Second Epistle to the Corinthians are similar. I have translated ten homilies from this,[7] someone else has undertaken to do the rest.[8] The commentaries on the First Epistle to the Corinthians were translated by Francesco Aretino as far as number 30, but badly.[9] Another scholar completed the rest.[10] Unless I am mistaken, scholars at Louvain are translating the commentaries on the Epistle to the Romans.[11] If you have anything apart from these that has not been printed, it should be sent promptly. I do indeed have a Greek text of the commentaries on Acts, but it is very heavy.[12] If you can obtain one where you are, work on a translation. But see that I am told as soon as possible in case this assignment is inadvertently entrusted to two different persons.

I do not remember very well what I wrote about the cardinal,[13] unless perhaps I mentioned the disgruntlement of the Froben people, who have so

* * * * *

2291
1 The letter is not extant.
2 Nothing survives of this packet of letters to friends in Paris.
3 See Ep 2263 n13.
4 Figwood was notoriously breakable and thus virtually useless, which led to the term being applied to anybody or anything weak and worthless; see *Adagia* I vii 85. Rhesus, king of Thrace, was an ally of the Trojans. Learning of his arrival before Troy, Odysseus and Diomedes stole into his camp, killed him and carried off his splendid horses. There had been a prophecy that, had those horses eaten or drunk at Troy, the city would not have fallen. So an alliance with Rhesus is one that proves worthless. See *Iliad* 10, *Aeneid* 1.469–73. One suspects that these references were intended to be humorous.
5 Ie the Froben edition of Chrysostom in Latin; see Ep 2359.
6 See Epp 1801, 2263:36–40.
7 In fact only seven; see Ep 2263:40–2 with n12.
8 Oecolampadius; see Allen Ep 2379:46n.
9 See Ep 2226 n19. Aretino in fact stopped at homily number 29.
10 Simon Grynaeus (Ep 1657); see Allen Ep 2359:57–8.
11 See Ep 2258 n6.
12 This manuscript has not been identified.
13 Antoine Duprat, chancellor of France (Ep 2038 n15)

often negotiated in vain over a royal privilege for the *Augustine*.[14] I myself
was asked to write on this matter and sent a letter to the cardinal-chancellor, 25
and that too was unsuccessful.[15] If there was something else, I do not remember. I certainly sent a brief note to Toussain,[16] but I suspect it was suppressed by Berquin, something that he liked to do from time to time. For example, I had written also to Alberto Pio, and Berquin admitted that he was
responsible for the fact that the letter was not delivered, since he judged it 30
unhelpful.[17] Berquin had written to me that the poem was the work of Lascaris, and only the final couplet was Toussain's.[18] Later a person whose word
carries considerable weight sent me a letter that gave it as an established fact
that the whole poem was Toussain's.[19]

However, this whole business did not trouble me greatly. What de- 35
pressed me more was that people are searching for material to foment this
kind of dissension, which is bound to do serious damage to humane letters.
In his public lectures this same Toussain repeatedly criticized my interpretation of *peripsema*[20] (the same passage was criticized by Budé in a printed
volume,[21] with what success I do not propose to discuss at present). In deal- 40
ing with this problem, Toussain certainly distorted an erroneous reading in
Suidas, in which we have κατέχον τῶν κακῶν, when it should be κατεχόντων
κακῶν 'evils pressing.'[22] The same Toussain criticized what I wrote about the
helmet of Orcus, but that was corrected long ago in the last edition of the

* * * * *

14 See Epp 2053:16–20, 2075.
15 The letter is not extant.
16 Ep 2119
17 The only known letter of Erasmus to Pio after the latter's arrival in Paris is
 Ep 2080, which does not seem to be the sort of 'unhelpful' letter, delivery of
 which Berquin would have wanted to interdict. In the absence of the letter that
 included Berquin's confession of responsibility for non-delivery, we cannot
 know for sure what Erasmus is referring to.
18 Presumably in the lost portion of Ep 2066; cf Ep 2077:10–15.
19 Allen speculated that the person in question might have been Philippus Montanus (Ep 2065), whose correspondence with Erasmus (all of it but Ep 2065
 lost) is known to have included a detailed account of the execution of Berquin
 in 1529.
20 The reference is to the annotation on 1 Cor 4:13, where Erasmus discusses the
 meaning of the rare Greek word περίψημα 'offscouring.' Cf Ep 2239 n16.
21 In his *Altera aeditio annotationum in Pandectas* (Paris: Josse Bade, 1526) folio 28
 verso.
22 Without knowing what Toussain said, we can only guess what was the point
 of Erasmus' criticism. It appears that Toussain cited the definition of the word
 περίψημα in Suidas and tried, unsuccessfully, to wrestle meaning out of a bad
 text.

Adages.[23] As for his objections to a translation of mine from Euripides, χὠ   45
κείνων κρατῶν νόμος, it is agreed that the wording of the text is ambiguous.[24]
I know that I hesitated for some time over the passage when I translated it.
Nor am I much more impressed by his criticism of a line from the *Iphigenia*,
εἴη δέ μοι μετρία etc.[25] If he criticizes when a problem comes up and if his
criticisms are justified, then he acts as a good teacher should; yet even if he   50
goes out of his way to criticize and does so in a contumacious manner, provided that what he says is correct, my delight in the benefit this will bring
his listeners outweighs the pain I suffer from the damage to my reputation.

You could not imagine the horrors to be found in the translation of
Plutarch's *Lives* made by the Italians! Trebizond discovered many errors in   55
the translations of Theodorus Gaza, who was unquestionably a superlative
scholar.[26] When these were pointed out to him, he corrected them. That story
was told me at Rome by Gaza's secretary.[27] So far be it from me to imagine
that I never made a mistake! Why, even in Budé's translations I can find
several glaring errors.   60

I am informed by certain people that Budé's letters are being printed
in Paris, in which I am pilloried as a hater of the French nation, though
(Christ love me!) there is no other nation towards which I have more positive feelings.[28] They also point out that in his *Notes on the Greek Language*
there are several veiled attacks.[29] But I reject all these suspicions as equally   65
unworthy of Budé and of me. Those who sow such rumours do a disser-
vice no less to Budé than to the cause of learning.[30] There may be some who

* * * * *

23 In the original version of *Adagia* II x 74 Erasmus had mistranslated a line in
    Homer (*Iliad* 5.844–5). The correction was not made until the edition of 1536;
    see CWE 34 368 n5 under 74.
24 The passage in question is *Hecuba* 799–800, which reads: '[the gods are strong]
    and so is the law that controls them.' The ambiguity lies in the Greek *nomos*,
    which can mean state law, legal convention, some high principle of right, etc.
    The difficulties of the passage were already discussed in the ancient scholia to
    the play.
25 Euripides *Iphigenia in Aulis* 556. The completed phrase reads: 'May the delights
    of love be tempered for me.' The text does not appear to be problematical, and
    we do not know what fault Toussain found with Erasmus' rendering of the line.
26 Gaza (Ep 234:12n) published no translation of Plutarch, so Erasmus' point is
    that George of Trebizond (Ep 36:3n) found errors in Gaza's other translations.
27 Unidentified. Gaza had been dead for forty years by the time Erasmus went
    to Rome in 1509.
28 See Ep 2261:61–5.
29 See Epp 2052:7–9, 2077:68–9.
30 In Ep 2340:82–97, Brie will attempt to reassure Erasmus on this point.

would like to see Budé lock horns with Erasmus. But that will never happen
if I have anything to do with it – or rather I shall do everything to see that it
does not happen. However, although Budé is beyond any suspicion of envy,   70
he will not escape some loss of reputation for candour. And although the
whole scholarly world applauds him – and they have every reason to applaud – there are still several who are well disposed to Erasmus also. But in
scholarship what I want to see is harmony and generosity. If some people
have time to take up the sword in pursuit of glory, they are welcome to   75
the victor's palm for all I care. I would prefer to use my eloquence for the
benefit of others. Farewell.

Freiburg im Breisgau, 27 March 1530

2292 / To Alfonso de Valdés   Freiburg, 27 March [1530]

The autograph of this letter is in the Real Academia de la Historia at Madrid
(MS Est 18, gr I 5, folio 19). It was first printed in Fermín Caballero, *Alonso y
Juan de Valdés* (Madrid 1875; repr Cuenca 1995) 430. Given Erasmus' residence
in Freiburg and the references in the text to contemporary events, the date
1529 in line 5 has to be corrected to 1530; see Ep 2268 introduction. Lieven
Algoet delivered the letter to Valdés at the imperial court; see Ep 2294:15–16.
For Valdés, see Ep 2252.

Cordial greetings. That you do not write I interpret to mean that you will be
here soon. I only hope you will find Erasmus well and be well yourself. Here
I am totally immersed in my *Consultations*.[1] The emperor's arrival affects us
in different ways.[2] Farewell, my dearest Valdés.

Freiburg im Breisgau, 27 March 1529   5
You recognize your Erasmus' hand.
To the most honourable Alfonso Valdés, secretary to his imperial
Majesty

2293 / To the Magistrates of Strasbourg   Freiburg, 28 March 1530

The autograph rough draft of this letter is in the Royal Library at Copenhagen
(MS GKS 95 Fol, folio 234). Erasmus wrote it in response to the news received
from Bonifacius Amerbach in Ep 2289.

* * * * *

2292
1 Ie *De bello Turcico*; see Ep 2285.
2 See Epp 2249:20–21, 2250:31–4.

TO THE MAGISTRATES OF STRASBOURG

Right worshipful and most noble lords, Gerard of Nijmegen has published
a letter of mine accompanied by notes of his own,[1] that is, accompanied by
a womanish tirade, which, far from helping the cause he claims to defend,
encumbers it with a load of infamy; and he did so in contravention of your   5
city's just and admirable edict, since neither the name of the printer nor
place of publication was added. The work was carried out, I imagine, by the
same workman who quite some time ago showed contempt for your edict by
bringing out, once, twice, three times, a libellous attack by Otto Brunsfeld.[2]
This workman is still lying low, wrapped in a cloud of his own smoke, but   10
Cacus will soon be dragged from his cave.[3] My letter contained nothing that
was harmful either to the cause of the gospel or to your city, for I do not
speak of all Evangelicals, only of those who by the evil of their lives injure
the work of the gospel. There are such people everywhere, and you, I think,
are aware of this and are pained by it. At the same time I advise the other   15
side to amend their lives and thus remove any cause of offence, so that God
may be reconciled to us and he may bring us again the blessings of peace.

This is the sum and substance of my letter. Anyone who reflects on the
situation that looms over us will pray, if he is wise, that our present conflicts may be settled without a torrent of blood, a result that I have always   20
tried, and will continue to try, to bring about. But nothing save greater tur-

* * * * *

2293
1 Ie Gerard Geldenhouwer's annotated edition of Erasmus' *Epistola contra pseude-*
   vangelicos; see Ep 2289 n2.
2 Erasmus means Otto Brunfels (Ep 1405). The printer ('workman') whom Erasmus has in mind was Johann Schott, who in 1524 had published Brunfels' *Re-*
   sponsio to Erasmus' *Spongia* against Ulrich von Hutten. Erasmus had written
   letters of complaint about Schott and Brunfels to the magistrates of Strasbourg,
   who summoned both men to explain themselves. See Epp 1405 introduction,
   1429, 1477. The real culprit, however, was not Schott but Christian Egenolff
   (1502–55), who had been publishing books at Strasbourg since 1528. By the
   end of 1530, he had moved to Frankfurt, where he became a prolific publisher of books in both German and Latin and was particularly well known
   for herbals and other lavishly illustrated books on scientific and medical subjects. For his edition of the *Epistola contra pseudevangelicos* with Geldenhouwer's
   annotations, see [Carsten Jäcker] *Christian Egenolff, 1502–1555: Ein Frankfurter*
   Meister des frühen Buchdrucks aus Hadamar (Limburg 2002) 50; and for the little
   that is known of his years in Strasbourg, see ibidem 29–31.
3 Cacus, a murderous, fire-breathing giant who terrified his neighbours, was
   killed by Hercules and dragged from his cave. Virgil tells the story in *Aeneid*
   8.190–279.

moil will come from the sort of books that Nijmegen has been writing up
to now. Let the clever and the learned continue to write, though we have
more than enough pamphlets already. I do not count the injury done to me
important. But if in your mercy you constantly turn a blind eye to the law-   25
less behaviour of these wretched people, they will be encouraged in the end
to show contempt for all your regulations. The printer is not known? But
the author will be able to reveal who printed this trash if there was a legal
arrangement. May the Lord prosper your city.

Freiburg im Breisgau, 28 March 1530   30

2294 / To Bonifacius Amerbach   [Freiburg, c 28 March 1530]

This letter (= AK Ep 1421), first published in the *Epistola familiares*, is Erasmus'
reply to Ep 2289. The autograph is in the Öffentliche Bibliothek of the University of Basel (MS AN III 15 23). It is clearly contemporary with Ep 2293 and, like
it, comments on the latest developments in Erasmus' controversy with Gerard
Geldenhouwer.

Greetings. It is not my intention to reply to such a stupid tirade.[1] Either I
am no judge, or the man is simply mad. He has joined forces with Eppendorf and dropped some private information into his ear. At one time, you
know, he was a jolly companion of mine.[2] Eppendorf too is threatening to
publish a horrific book.[3] But this worthless trash[4] was issued secretly con-   5
trary to an edict of the Strasbourg council, since it reveals neither the name
of the printer nor the place of publication. They have omitted the place,
date, and year in which the letter was written so that the reader will think
it was printed here. These are old familiar Eppendorfian tricks. He played
the same game with Otto's pamphlet.[5] One day God will catch up with this   10
abominable wretch.

* * * * *

2294
1 See Ep 2293 n1.
2 Erasmus' surviving correspondence with Geldenhouwer commences in 1516
   (Ep 487), but their acquaintance had doubtless begun much earlier. Their relations remained friendly for quite some time but appear to have turned sour
   at some point before the outbreak of the current quarrel; cf Ep 2219 n5.
3 This may have been true, but it was Erasmus who would renew the quarrel
   with Eppendorf (Ep 1934 introduction) with the publication of the *Admonitio
   adversus mendacium* towards the end of the year.
4 The 'worthless trash' is the 'stupid tirade' mentioned above.
5 See Ep 2293 n2.

I have been seized by some sort of malady as a result of the dryness of the air. I can find no remedy to relieve my bowels.[6] Farewell, my dear Bonifacius.

If there is anything you want taken to the imperial court,[7] my man   15
Lieven is making a rapid journey there, without, I fear, much hope of success.[8] Perhaps there is a pamphlet of Thraso's lurking somewhere else.[9] Do sniff around. I shall write about Budé at another time.[10] Farewell again.

To the most accomplished Bonifacius Amerbach. In Basel

2295 / To William Blount, Lord Mountjoy   Freiburg, 28 March [1530]

This letter was first published in *Illustrium et clarorum virorum Epistolae selectiores* ed Daniel Hensius (Leiden 1617) 300. Allen took as the basis of his text the original manuscript, in a secretary's hand but with the final paragraph and address added by Erasmus, which in 1923 was in the private collection of Baroness James de Rothschild at Paris. Efforts to establish the current location of the manuscript have been fruitless. The interpretation of the year-date 1529 (see line 47 below) as 1530 is confirmed by the events mentioned, particularly Erasmus' move to Freiburg; see also Ep 2268 introduction. On Mountjoy, see Ep 2215.

Cordial greetings, my most honoured Maecenas.[1] If you look at individual letters, I must be classed as a laconic writer. But if you consider the whole correspondence that I am obliged to send to every quarter of the world, I

* * * * *

6 Cf Epp 2295:1, 46. This is the first hint of the illness that would take a turn for the worse in April; see Ep 2320 n1.

7 The imperial court had left Bologna on 22 March and was now moving slowly into Germany. On 4 May it would reach Innsbruck, and on 15 June, Augsburg, whither Charles v had summoned a meeting of the imperial diet.

8 Algoet was seeking employment; see Ep 2278 n2. He was also doubtless carrying with him Ep 2292, the presentation copy of Xenophon for Anton Fugger (Ep 2307:1–5), and three books for Cornelis de Schepper (Ep 2336:41–3). He may also have carried Epp 2299–2301 for forwarding to Spain. He arrived in Augsburg on 7 April (Epp 2307, 2308:20–1) but, finding that the imperial court had not yet arrived, went off to Trent to meet it; see Epp 2327:5, 2336 n6.

9 Thraso was Erasmus' customary nickname for Heinrich Eppendorf; see Ep 2216 n9.

10 Perhaps, as Allen suggests, to explain to Bonifacius his feelings about Budé, which he had already explained to Germain de Brie in Ep 2291; cf Ep 2302:1–5.

2295
1 Ie generous patron; see Ep 2215 n1.

am the complete Asianist.[2] I live here in tolerable conditions, except that everything is incredibly expensive.[3] I only wish we could avoid war, but I fear this may not be possible, considering how this tragedy is unfolding thus far.[4] But our fate is wholly in the hand of God. Would that our destiny might match in everything our best desires, just as God in his goodness responds generously to mine!

I had a superlative patron at the court of King Ferdinand in Bernhard, bishop of Trent. I hear that he has withdrawn from the palace, offended, I imagine, by the current preparations for war.[5] God only knows what the end of this will be. I cannot imagine on what plans the emperor is acting. Some people think that, with Hungary lost, Austria miserably devastated, and the Turk again on our doorstep, the emperor is remaining in Italy too long.[6] Several wonder what kind of peace there will be between the emperor and the Frenchman, when two sons are still being held in Spain.[7] King Ferdinand has an indomitable spirit, but as a new prince he lacks the sinews of war.[8] If the emperor attacks the Lutherans,[9] it will be all over with us here.

* * * * *

2 In ancient rhetoric the Asianists were the advocates of a copious, elaborate, and ornamental style in preference to the plain, unadorned style of the Atticists. Erasmus is complaining of the great volume of the correspondence that he is obliged to maintain.

3 See Ep 2215 n10.

4 Erasmus was worried not only by the possibility of a civil war in Switzerland between the advocates and opponents of the Reformation, which could easily spill over into the neighbouring Breisgau (see Ep 2256 n15), but also by the already perceptible drift towards armed conflict between the Catholic and Protestant estates in Germany (see Ep 2219 n10).

5 Two days later, Erasmus received from Bernhard von Cles (Epp 1357, 2207) a letter reiterating his invitation to Erasmus to come live with him. Erasmus' inclination to accept the invitation indicates that the rumour reported here was false. See Ep 2299:33–9.

6 The emperor had just left Italy and was on his way to Germany; see Ep 2294 n7.

7 One of the provisions of the Peace of Cambrai (Ep 2207 n5) between Charles v and Francis i was the release, in return for the payment of a ransom, of Francis' two sons, who had been held captive in Spain as guarantee of Francis' observance of the Treaty of Madrid (1526). The stipulated date of release was 1 March 1530, but a variety of delays postponed the actual release to 1 July. See Knecht 222–3.

8 Ie money; cf Ep 2285 n2. Ferdinand was a 'new prince' in the sense that he had only recently been elected king of Bohemia (December 1526) and Hungary (early 1527). His coronation in Bohemia was on 24 February 1527, that in Hungary on 28 October.

9 The attack, long feared, would not come until 1546.

What your excellent and pious king has done as intermediary between   20
the emperor and the Frenchman,[10] Sigismund, king of Poland, has tried hard
to do for Ferdinand and John, his rival for the kingdom.[11] But the Fates are
stronger than the counsels of men.

It was a very great pleasure to me to know that the courtesy I showed
your Charles was not unwelcome to you.[12] I pray that the Lord Jesus will   25
be pleased to preserve his natural gifts and raise them to greater and nobler
heights.

I do not know what food Fortune will offer me when I am hungry. Certainly Pierre Barbier, whom I loved fondly and celebrated in my letters,[13]
has treated me with unheard of perfidy and robbed me of my Courtrai pen-   30
sion.[14] I hear that the archbishop of Canterbury is failing;[15] if anything happens to him, I shall have nothing to expect by way of a pension.[16] I would
have courage enough, if I could shake off this murderous stone.[17] A Budéist
faction is developing in France, however, which is engaged in a stupid skir-
mish with me. They do not know themselves why they are angry with me.[18]   35

I do not congratulate Thomas More,[19] nor for that matter do I find much
reason to congratulate the cause of learning. My congratulations go to your
realm, which could not have found a more upright or a better judge.

You console me over the ruckus caused by my critics. But you scarcely
know a tenth part of all the devious and diabolical schemes that are con-   40
trived against me by evil people hiding under the name of the gospel.[20]

* * * * *

10 On the blatantly self-serving and duplicitous efforts of Henry VIII to bring
    about peace between Charles V and Francis I in 1529, see Epp 1993 n2, 2207
    n5.
11 The efforts of King Sigismund I to mediate peace between Ferdinand of Aus-
    tria and his rival for the kingship of Hungary, John Zápolyai, were rewarded
    with the conclusion of a one-year truce in December 1530. In May 1531, the
    truce was extended for another year. Cf Ep 2261 n11.
12 The favour was a preface to the new edition of the *Adagia* published in 1528;
    see Ep 2023.
13 See Epp 695, 795, 1216, 1225, 1235, 1294, 1302, 1358, 1470, 1605, 1621.
14 On the Courtrai pension, see Ep 436:6n. For Barbier's alleged perfidy, see Epp
    2332:57–60, 2356:17–18, and cf Ep 2015 n4.
15 Cf Ep 2253:35–8.
16 Ie the pension awarded to him by Archbishop Warham in 1512; see Ep 255.
17 See Ep 2275 n9.
18 For recent evidence of continued ill feeling, see Ep 2291:61–73.
19 He had succeeded Wolsey as lord chancellor on 25 October 1559; see Ep 2228.
20 An allusion to the controversy with Gerard Geldenhouwer and the other 'false
    evangelicals' of Strasbourg; see Epp 2219 nn4–5, 2338:56–7.

I shall write to your son and his teacher (on both of whom I congratulate you) if my health permits,[21] for because of my voluminous correspondence,[22] I have become deeply anxious about my health, and I cannot guess
the cause unless it is dryness affecting my inner organs.[23] Forgive me, my   45
sweet Maecenas, I did not have time to reread this.

Freiburg, 28 March 1529[24]

You will recognize the hand of your old protégé.

To the most distinguished baron of England, William Mountjoy. In the
kingdom of England   50

2296 / To Franciscus Cassander   Freiburg, 28 March 1530

> First published in the *Epistolae floridae*, this is the first of two letters from Eras-
> mus to Cassander (the other is Ep 2442). The letter to which it responds is
> not extant. Nothing is known of Cassander except that he was from Colmars
> (Département des Alpes-de-Haute-Provence), had an interest in the Fathers of
> the church, and was in some way connected to Jean-Baptiste de Laigue, bishop
> of Senez, and his brother, Antoine d'Oraison.

ERASMUS OF ROTTERDAM TO CASSANDER OF COLMARS, GREETING
I was amused, gentle sir, at the argument you and your friends are engaged
in. My health compels me to be brief,[1] so I shall explain in a few words
what the problem is in Augustine letter 59.[2] There is no doubt that the letter
is genuine; and there was no need to prove that Augustine was not entirely   5
ignorant of Greek. He makes this clear in the *Categories*, the *Psalms*, and
many other of his works, and he writes to Jerome that he has compared
emendations of his with the Greek manuscripts.[3] Moreover, in a polemic

* * * * *

21 The letter to Charles Blount, if written, is not extant, but the letter of Blount
   to Erasmus mentioned in Allen Ep 2367:5 may have been the answer to such
   a letter. Erasmus addressed a letter to the teacher, Petrus Vulcanius, on 18
   March 1531 (Ep 2460).
22 Cf lines 2–3 above.
23 Cf Ep 2294:12–14.
24 The correct year-date is 1530; see introduction above.

2296
1 Cf Ep 2294:12–14.
2 Ep 149 in modern editions. In it Augustine several times cites Greek manuscripts in elucidating passages of Scripture.
3 Ep 71.4

against the Pelagians he translates a passage from Chrysostom with some
felicity.[4] 'How could he have done this,' you will say, 'if lacking a solid   10
foundation in languages'?[5] In the latest edition I find, 'not well equipped
with a solid foundation in languages, even if he was not entirely ignorant of
Greek; but he was inadequately trained to be capable of reading the Greek
interpreters easily.'[6]

Perhaps the reading cited by the celebrated Viscount of Cadenet[7] was   15
that of the first edition.[8] The sense, however, is the same, but I made my
meaning clearer because of carping from my critics. For in the preceding
passage I had cited Greek authors and other writers who had a fine command of the language and had drawn most of their material from Greek
commentaries. Augustine did not do this except in extreme old age when,   20
in his battle with the Pelagians, he was forced to gather support from every
quarter. As a result, in the writings of his early years he often makes mistakes, led astray by his Latin texts, as I point out in several places. And in
the latest edition, in the passage where Peter denied the Lord, I restored the
true reading from Cyril.[9] Even when he was already advanced in years, Au-   25
gustine argues for free will from the fact that one often reads in the gospel
phrases such as, 'Do not judge,' 'Do not swear,' 'Do not be angry,' etc although the word *nolite* 'be unwilling' originates with the Translator, not the
evangelist or apostle.[10] It is clear, then, that however much Greek Augustine

* * * * *

4 *Contra Iulianum* 1.6.21–8
5 The phrase 'lacking a solid foundation in languages' is a direct quotation from
  Erasmus' annotation on John 21:22 in the first edition of 1516.
6 The latest edition of the Annotations was that of 1527, but the words here cited
  had already in 1519 been substituted for those of the preceding edition.
7 See n13 below.
8 Of the New Testament, 1516. See n5 above.
9 Erasmus here refers to a problem of interpretation that Augustine had not been
  able to resolve. The Gospels of Matthew, Mark, and Luke are in agreement that
  Peter's three denials took place when Jesus was being tried before Caiaphas.
  John 18:13–14, on the other hand, implies that the trial took place before Annas. At the very end of the Annotations of 1527, Erasmus inserted a note on
  the passage in John in which he took over from Cyril's commentary a reading
  that allowed for a second trial before Caiaphas following that before Annas,
  thus bringing John into closer harmony with the other three evangelists.
10 Erasmus is here making a point that cannot be expressed in idiomatic English.
   In making the case for freedom of the will, Augustine (*De gratia et libero arbitrio*
   chapter 2) pointed out that the New Testament is full of negative commands,
   which in Latin are expressed by *noli* / *nolite* and an infinitive (literally 'be
   unwilling [to do something]'). But no such idiom implying the involvement
   of the will is found in the original Greek, which means that the commands in
   question do not support Augustine's argument.

may have known, he rarely turns to the Greek commentaries in his exposi-   30
tion of Scripture. So it is reasonable to say that one who possesses the tools
of war but does not use them in battle is lacking in arms for the conflict.
As a boy Augustine had learned a little grammar[11] – you must remember
that in those days both languages were taught side by side. But as a youth
he came to hate Greek and avoided reading Greek authors, something for   35
which, as an old man, he expresses regret in the *Confessions*.[12]

I would like to continue chatting with you for a very long time, but
this is as much as my health permits. All that remains is to ask you to give
my thanks to my lord Baptiste, bishop of Senez, and to the illustrious Antoine d'Oraison, viscount of Cadenet, and to convey to them my respectful   40
and cordial greetings.[13] In future I shall count Cassander among my good
friends. Farewell.

Freiburg im Breisgau, 28 March AD 1530

2297 / From Diego Gracián de Alderete   Madrid, 28 March [1530]

The manuscript of this letter is in on folio 28 verso of the volume of Gracián's
letters in the Casa de Alba at Madrid (see Ep 1913 introduction). It was first
published by Don Antonio Paz y Mélia in *Revista de Archivos* 5 (1901) 126.

TO DESIDERIUS ERASMUS OF ROTTERDAM

Since our dear Valdés left for Italy,[1] we have received no letter from you,
most learned Erasmus, though we have gathered from a letter sent to the
archbishop of Toledo that you are in excellent health.[2] Don Juan Manuel,[3]
whose secretary I once was, asks frequently what news I have of you. I have   5
the same question from the archdeacon of Alcor,[4] Doctor Coronel,[5] and all

* * * * *

11 'Grammar' here means the study of literary texts as well as the study of
   language.
12 1.13–14
13 Jean-Baptiste de Laigue (documented 1509–46) was bishop of Senez (Départe-
   ment des Alpes-de-Haute-Provence) and abbot of St Eusèbe at Apt (Départe-
   ment de Vaucluse). His older brother was Antoine Honorat, sieur d'Oraison
   and vicount of Cadenet (Ep 2049 n21).

2297
1 See Ep 2163 nn4 and 7.
2 Ep 2134
3 Ep 1970 n2
4 Alonso Fernández de Madrid (Ep 1904), the translator of Erasmus' *Enchiridion*
   into Spanish (Ep 1814 n21)
5 Luis Núñes Coronel; see Ep 1274.

your other friends who live here. The bishop of Zamora, president of the empress's council, to whom I act as secretary, is a great supporter of yours, especially after you became better known to him through me.[6] Believe me, it would be to your advantage to remember your friends now and then. One of these,[7] who is most devoted to you, on seeing that you had treated the ravings of Carvajal with contempt,[8] refuted several passages in his *Apologia*, and Echo has stored this away.[9]

Farewell. Madrid, 28 March

2298 / From Simon Riquinus   Cologne, 29 March 1530

The autograph of this letter (= Ep 121 in Förstemann / Günther) was in the Burscher Collection of the University Library at Leipzig (Ep 1254 introduction). It was carried as far as Strasbourg by Peter Medmann; see Ep 2304:1–4. On Riquinus, see Ep 2246.

Cordial greetings. Here, dear Erasmus, is a cup,[1] sent as a gift from our young prince;[2] it should be judged not by its value, but by the feeling behind it. The prince is still under the supervision of his guardians and trustees; however, he does not lack the will to become more worthy of the friendship of our Erasmus, which this noble youth considers superior to the greatest blessings of fortune. The leading men in the court, even those who sit at the helm of the ship of state, ardently desire to see you in the service of our prince.[3] Vlatten, scholaster of Aachen, a most charming man, is now

* * * * *

6 Francisco de Mendoza y Córdoba (d 29 March 1536), formerly bishop of Oviedo (1525–7), was now bishop of Zamora (1527–34), and would eventually become bishop of Palencia (1534–6). He presided over the royal treasury and, according to Gracián's testimony here, was chief counsellor to Empress Isabella in the emperor's absence as well as a great admirer of Erasmus. Mendoza is not known to have had any direct relations with Erasmus.

7 Possibly one of the two mentioned in Ep 2198:7–14, who wrote refutations but were persuaded not to publish them

8 See Ep 2110 n10, and cf Ep 2275 introduction.

9 This phrase is a puzzle. Echo, in ancient myth, was doomed never to speak except by echoing what she had heard. If the identification in the preceding note is accurate, the most likely meaning is that the refutations were kept secret and unreported.

2298
1 See Epp 2234:17–20, 2246:33–6.
2 William v of Cleves (Ep 2234)
3 Ie the reigning duke, John III

in the service of the court[4] – for this was the wish of the elder prince. Johann Gogreve, our chancellor, a man deserving of your good will and dis-   10
tinguished equally by the line of his ancestors and his interest in learning,[5]
brought this about so that, in carrying out his important duties, he might
have Vlatten as his faithful Achates.[6] You see that there are brilliant men
in our court – they are our jewelled necklaces. But what a wonderful pearl
would be added to it if among our councillors shone Erasmus in all his bril-   15
liance. I have observed at first hand that this is the dream not just of our
councillors but of both our princes also.

In reference to that ecclesiastical appointment,[7] I shall keep my eyes
open so as not to betray your expectations of me in anything. You know that
in a princely court one must watch patiently for the right moment. If you   20
were here, this business would already have been settled to your satisfaction. As God is my witness, there is no one for whom I shall more willingly
carry out whatever can possibly be achieved through my service, loyalty,
and influence.

Beatus Rhenanus made a good guess when he said that Riquinus had   25
once been a schoolmaster. I had accepted as pupils the two counts of Isenburg,[8] even though my father was pushing me in a different direction – he
had destined me for the court at Trier. At that time I was somewhat reluctant
to go to court, thinking it did not fit well with the studies I was pursuing.

* * * * *

4 See Epp 1390, 1948, and cf Ep 2246:37–9.
5 In the decade 1514–24 Johann Gogreve (d 1554) studied law at Cologne,
Orléans, and Bologna. It was probably in Cologne that he made the acquaintance of his later friends and colleagues Konrad Heresbach (Ep 1316) and Johann von Vlatten (Ep 2222). In 1524 he entered the service of Duke John III
of the the United Duchies of Jülich-Cleves-Berg and in 1528 was made chancellor, an office he held until his death. He lent his able support to the reform
programme of Heresbach and Vlatten, which made the United Duchies for
half a century a showcase of political government based on Erasmian principles. Gogreve's personal contribution to this achievement was the many diplomatic missions on which he not only promoted the political interests of the
United Duchies but also sought recognition for the dukes' Erasmian church
policies. Melanchthon and Bucer correctly saw in Gogreve and his collabo-
rators the chief obstacle to the advance of Lutheranism in the Lower Rhine
region. While much of Erasmus' correspondence with Vlatten and Heresbach
survives, that with Gogreve does not.
6 'Faithful Achates' was the companion of Aeneas in Virgil's *Aeneid*. Vlatten was
vice-chancellor.
7 For Quirinus; see Ep 2246:36–7.
8 Anton and Salentin von Isenburg (documented 1520–31) matriculated at Cologne in 1520. Their first tutor was Johannes Caesarius (Ep 374), who in 1523
dedicated to them an edition of Horace's *Epistles*.

When my pupils grew up and did not seem very interested in learning,   30
I began to feel dissatisfied with the role I was playing. So I turned my
thoughts towards other things, but always avoided my homeland, though it
kept offering me quite tempting prospects.

Meanwhile one of the presiding magistrates and the town clerk of
Diest approached me, attracted perhaps by my reputation (for so they said   35
themselves) and offered me one hundred Philippus florins from the public treasury as well as any additional fees I could scrape together from my
pupils if I would move there to take charge of a school that they had established specifically for liberal studies.[9] I liked the terms, which were sweet-
ened by many benefits, and I stayed there a little under three years,[10] not,   40
I think, without general approbation. In the end I tired of the meanness of
the situation and took myself off to Louvain.

My story, if I am not mistaken, is hardly commonplace. I have told it
at greater length because of the astonishment it provoked in those people.[11]
Really, I am not inventing anything. I had the impression that this was what   45
you were hinting at in your earlier letter, before I received the later one.[12]
I beg you to continue to love me and protect me against those who would
blacken my name. Farewell, Erasmus, my delightful friend.

Cologne, 29 March 1530

Simon Riquinus, physician, wrote this.   50

To the celebrated Master Erasmus of Rotterdam, theologian. At Freiburg im Breisgau

2299 / To Cristóbal Mexía   Freiburg, 30 March 1530

This letter, which responds to one now lost that was sent from Seville and
dated 6 January 1530 (line 154), was first published in the *Epistolae floridae*. The

* * * * *

9 Diest is in Brabant, north and east of Louvain. The Philippus florin in 1530 was
   evidently still worth only 50d groot, its official value before the issue of new
   gold coinages in February 1521; see Ep 2270 n3. This sum was therefore worth
   £20 16s 8d groot Flemish, equivalent in value to 552.5 days' wages for Antwerp master masons/carpenters in 1526–30 (2.6 years' money wage income;
   see CWE 12 649 Table 3C, 690–1 Tables 12 and 13 (for wage data).
10 1525–8
11 'Those people' (*illi*) has no identifiable antecedent in the letter. But it is probably a reference to 'those who would blacken my name' (lines 47–8). Cf Ep
   2246, where Riquinus complains that he is the victim of unfounded suspicions
   about his past.
12 Neither letter is extant.

manuscript, an autograph rough draft, is in the Royal Library at Copenhagen (MS GKS 95 Fol, folio 207). For the likely route of delivery to Spain, see Ep 2294 n8. Cristóbal Mexía of Seville is known only as the brother of Pero Mexía, for whom see Ep 2300.

ERASMUS OF ROTTERDAM TO CRISTÓBAL MEXÍA OF SPAIN,
GREETING

There is nothing about me, most honourable Cristóbal Mexía, that can in any way be compared with the divine excellences of Marcus Tullius.[1] Yet, what-ever my position may be among those who devote all their powers to the 5 cause of liberal studies, your warm heart, good sense, and fine judgment set you in my estimation above any petty ruler of Asia.[2] To receive a letter from an unknown and distant correspondent is nothing new to me – in fact it is an almost daily occurrence. Letters arrive regularly from scholars, grandees, bishops, and abbots of whose existence I was not aware; and kings, princes, 10 and prelates, men of such high rank that everyone knows of them, send not just letters, but splendid gifts as well.

I possess many letters from the emperor Charles written in such a flattering and affectionate manner that I value them more highly than the generosity he shows me, although it is to him that I owe a good part of 15 my modest assets.[3] Letters, no less frequent and no less friendly, arrive from King Ferdinand, and not without a gift, which is an honour in it-self.[4] How many invitations have I received from the king of France, and on what splendid terms![5] The king of England, by his frequent letters and spontaneous gifts, demonstrates his support for me and his exceptional 20 good will.[6] Nor does Catherine, his queen, who stands preeminent among women of our time, readily take second place to him.[7] Sigismund, king of Poland, sent me a letter that was a match for the truly regal gift that

* * * * *

2299
1 Cicero
2 Allen says 'evidently Deiotarus.' A satrap of western Galatia who, having man-aged to survive the fluctuations of Roman policy in the Middle East, Deiotarus was defended by Cicero in a famous case in Rome. This hardly suffices to make the identification self-evident. In the absence of Mexía's letter, Erasmus' mean-ing here remains unclear.
3 See Epp 1270, 1731, 1920.
4 See Ep 2005.
5 See Epp 522, 1375.
6 See Ep 1878.
7 Cf Ep 2312A:136–51.

accompanied it.[8] Duke George of Saxony addresses me frequently by letter
– he too is not without a gift.[9]   25

Need I mention William, archbishop of Canterbury,[10] or Cuthbert,[11]
lately bishop of London, now of Durham, or John, bishop of Lincoln?[12] These
men, besides writing letters that are more precious to me than any precious
stone, send me each year a sort of friendly tribute, something I neither seek
nor expect. From Albert, cardinal of Mainz, I have received, in addition to   30
his letters, a splendid reminder of his good will,[13] as I have also from Philip
of Burgundy, bishop of Utrecht, who died recently,[14] and likewise from Jean,
cardinal of Lorraine, brother of the duke.[15] Bernhard, bishop and cardinal of
Trent, besides honouring me with a gift – and not a small gift at that[16] – has
frequently sent such friendly and comforting letters that they could always   35
raise my spirits however low I felt. On top of all this he invited me to live
with him, offering the most generous conditions.[17] Just today I received a
letter from him, promising the same terms as he had offered before.[18] In
view of the way things are now, I shall perhaps take up his offer.[19] I believe
you have seen the letter sent me by the archbishop of Toledo, since it has   40
already been printed.[20] Could one imagine or wish for anything more affectionate and complimentary than this? Nor did he hold back either his fortune
or his characteristic generosity.[21] Lately prince William, the young duke of
Cleves and Jülich, a youth with a natural propensity to virtue, wrote me a
letter that was from beginning to end a tribute to his warm feelings, along   45
with which he sent a magnificent cup.[22] Anton Fugger, on hearing that I was
planning to leave Basel, sent me a hundred gold florins as travel expenses,

* * * * *

8 See Ep 1952.
9 See Ep 1691:28–9.
10 Warham
11 Tunstall
12 Longland
13 See Epp 986:41n, 1341A:1711–13.
14 In 1524; on the gift see Ep 1341A:1706–11.
15 Jean de Guise, cardinal of Lorraine (Epp 1841, 1911, 2009) was the brother of
   Antoine, duke of Lorraine. On the cardinal's gift to Erasmus, see Ep 1962 n7.
16 Epp 1771, 1793.
17 Since 1525 Bernhard von Cles had repeatedly invited Erasmus to come live at
   Trent; see Ep 2097:13–20 with n4.
18 Not extant
19 Cf Ep 2334:5–6.
20 Ep 2003, from Alonso de Fonseca, published in 1529 in the *Opus Epistolarum*
21 See Ep 2003:94–6.
22 Ep 2234

promising the same or more each year if I decided to move to Augsburg.[23]
When I replied that this would not suit me, he sent me a most elegant cup
as a pledge of the friendship between us.[24] A few days earlier Christoph   50
von Stadion, bishop of Augsburg, a man of high standing and deep learning, came here, a journey of seven days – and not a safe journey at that – for
no other reason, as he said himself, than to see Erasmus, who is, you know,
a mere shadow of a man. I say this to illustrate his generosity, not my merits. He brought with him two princely cups and two hundred gold florins,   55
offering also to share with me all that he possesses.[25]

While I was writing this, a letter arrived from Jacopo Sadoleto, bishop
of Carpentras,[26] a man of remarkable learning, integrity, and authority. He
too used to send me from time to time the most erudite letters. I might have
overlooked him, had not his letter arrived providentially to jog my memory.   60
No doubt more will now come to mind.

Meanwhile I recall the name of Piotr, bishop of Cracow, a man of great
learning and great authority, and chancellor of his realm.[27] He has shown his
devotion to me by writing the most affectionate letters and sending magnificent gifts.[28] Also in Poland there is Andrzej Krzycki, bishop of Płock, whose   65
courteous letters and learned poems have often cheered me up and raised
my spirits. He too is not without a gift.[29]

I have a room stuffed with letters from scholars, grandees, princes,
kings, cardinals, and bishops. I have a chest full of gifts, cups, flasks, spoons,
clocks, several of which are made of pure gold. There is a great number   70
of rings, and the number would be greater, had not several been given
away to others who are making a contribution to learning.[30] Among my
benefactors are many who excel not just in learning, but in holiness of
life, like the archbishop of Canterbury, the bishop of London, the bishop of
Augsburg, and most of all John, bishop of Rochester.[31] He had slipped my   75

* * * * *

23 Cf Ep 2222:7–9.
24 See Ep 2192:59–61.
25 See Ep 2277:2–6.
26 Ep 2272
27 Tomicki (Ep 1919) was really vice-chancellor.
28 See Ep 2035:30–1.
29 On Krzycki, see Ep 1629. Of his letters to Erasmus only Ep 1652 survives. The
   promised gift was much delayed; see Ep 2351:92–4, and cf Ep 2174 n9.
30 For the inventory of Easmus' cache of valuable coins and rings (9 April 1534)
   see Major 38–40; for the inventory of the rest of his valuables (10 April 1534)
   see Major 41–7, Sieber.
31 John Fisher (Ep 229)

memory,[32] as had also the bishop of Wrocław, Johannes Thurzo, who sent a box stuffed with the most elegant things to Antwerp, my place of residence at the time, although I had never heard or even dreamed of Wrocław or Thurzo.[33] His place was taken by his brother, the bishop of Olomouc.[34] Every day the number of such benefactors increases, although I have courted 80 no one's generosity and have always frankly declared that I have enough to support the sober life that I lead. Far from regretting my standard of living, I would more readily reduce it than add to it. And yet such is the spontaneous liberality of those men that, even if I lost all my income (and there are other sources beyond my imperial pension), what I have already been given 85 would be enough to support my studies. I have always refused gifts from men of moderate means whenever it was possible to do so without damaging our friendship, or I have accepted the gift out of courtesy while seeing that I made a generous return for it.

As you write in your letter, there are those who say that I have con- 90 tributed nothing to learning, and some who call me a seedbed of heresies. How then are we to explain the attitude of so many distinguished persons, persons generally agreed to be men of keen judgment and wholehearted supporters of true religion? But these jackdaws,[35] with deliberate malice, have been making every effort for the past ten years, and are still doing so 95 today, to undermine my standing with the courts of princes, and with bishops, the pope, and the emperor – in a word, with the very great and the very small. Everywhere they have discovered men ready to defend Erasmus, unexpected champions, in many cases even unknown. Who are these people who are on the side of impiety? Who are these supporters of a man 100 who has contributed nothing to learning? Or could they be sensible people who understand the malicious gabble of these potbellies?[36] I admit there are many who surpass me in the scale of popularity; but this is hardly surprising, since I was the first to attract hostility when I began to clear the land and pave the way. My only regret is that there are not more who surpass 105 me. For this was my aim when I began my sweated labour. If anyone compares the world as it was thirty-six years ago with the world of today, he

* * * * *

32 Ie in the list of English bishops in lines 26–7 above
33 For Thurzo see Ep 850. For the gift, see Ep 1047:37–44. Thurzo's letter, dated 1 December 1519, took six months to reach Erasmus (Ep 1137:5), arriving while Erasmus was visiting Antwerp following a period of ill health (Ep 1117 introduction). By the time Erasmus acknowledged the gift, Thurzo had been dead for several weeks (Ep 1137 introduction).
34 Stanislaus Thurzo (Ep 1242)
35 See Ep 2275 introduction.
36 See Ep 2275 n14.

will learn whether Erasmus contributed anything to learning. Twenty years
ago there was no prince who would spend a cent on the education of his
son. Now there is none who does not hire a private tutor at considerable ex-   110
pense. At the start theologians protested, but only the older ones and not
all of these. The younger ones are embracing my ideas; even greybeards are
becoming more moderate. A number of monks are beginning to accept what
they previously condemned. Two young Franciscans, as arrogant as they are
ignorant,[37] are now mounting the stage without understanding how much   115
they are harming their own order with (as the saying goes) their own horse
and cart.[38]

But I shall write more fully on this matter to your brother.[39] For the
moment I need only express the thanks I owe you for your readiness to do
battle with the Franciscans and with several powerful figures as well, not so   120
much on my behalf as for the sake of learning. I believe, my sensible friend,
that it is not helpful to fight with the monks. They are like the cauldrons of
Dodona: if you strike one, you will have struck them all.[40] But the magistrates ought to punish that printer, who, in contravention of the emperor's
edict and in opposition to the wishes of the Right Reverend archbishop of   125
Seville,[41] published an ignorant and libellous book without appending his
name.[42] If he had been duly punished on the first occasion, he would not
have added a second offence.[43] If they do not regard this as a debt they owe

* * * * *

37 Carvajal and Titelmans; see Ep 2275.
38 *Adagia* 1 i 50
39 Ep 2300
40 The great brass cauldrons in the oracle of Zeus at Dodona were so positioned
   that when one was struck, the reverberation caused all the others to ring out;
   see *Adagia* 1 i 7.
41 Alonso Manrique de Lara (Ep 1846); cf Ep 2301.
42 The book in question is clearly the 1528 Salamanca edition of Luis de Carvajal's *Apologia monasticae religionis*, in which the printer is not named (Ep 2110
   n10). Publication of the book was not, however, a contravention of 'the emperor's edict,' if by that is meant, as Allen assumes in his note, Charles v's
   injunction to the theologians of Louvain to abstain from publishing attacks on
   Erasmus (see Epp 1690 n11, 1747 introduction). On the other hand, Erasmus
   was well aware that Spain had governmental censorship of books on religion
   (Ep 1785:34–7 with n4) and that the emperor and his court were just as hostile to attacks on Erasmus in Spain as they were to those in the Netherlands
   (Epp 1784A, 1785).
43 If the 'he' of this sentence is the printer, it is difficult to see what his second offence was, since Carvajal's second attack on Erasmus, the *Dulcoratio
   amarulentiarum Erasmicae responsionis*, was published in Paris (Ep 2110 n10).
   Only if 'he' is Carvajal himself does the sentence make sense.

to the merits of Erasmus, let them do it for the sake of peace in Spain. Such
libellous works do nothing for religion or learning; they are effective only   130
in stirring up controversy. Genuine princes may sometimes be lured into
error by the wiles of people like these, especially when they do not read my
works, but, being courteous and experienced men, they can be influenced by
suitable arguments to adopt a better view. If that cannot happen, we should
still not abandon the path of virtue. Even these days to have found favour   135
with a few men (though men of the highest excellence) means something.
The judgments of posterity will be more sympathetic.

How I wish that some day I might welcome my dear Cristóbal and talk

It hurts me to see that band of Observants (for so they like to be called)
abandoning the simplicity of Francis and sinking back into worldliness.[44]
Those two young windbags would not dare to act so boldly if they were   140
not encouraged by the applause of the fathers and brothers.[45] The task now
is to settle this deadly conflict by moderate means, without spilling a lot
of blood, but these men by their seditious writings are trying to stir up
new hostility against us. They attack anyone in any place, inventing lies to
their hearts' content. They rant and roar among the ignorant in a way that is   145
completely alien to Francis, in whose name they glory. So far, however, they
have achieved nothing except to stir up or increase the hatred of good and
learned men against themselves. Since I see they are incurable, they should
be abandoned to their own distemper.

How I wish that some day I might welcome my dear Cristóbal and talk   150
with him face to face. If Fate denies us this good fortune, at any rate from
now on we shall always be closely joined in spirit. We shall converse by
letter from time to time despite the long distance that separates us.[46] Your
letter, dated 6 January from Seville, I received on March 28. Farewell.

Freiburg im Breisgau, 30 March AD 1530   155

2300 / To Pero Mexía   Freiburg, 30 March 1530

First published in the *Epistolae floridae*, this is Erasmus' response to a letter
now lost that presumably arrived at the same time as the one from Cristóbal
Mexía (Ep 2299:151–2). The manuscript, an autograph rough draft, is in the
Royal Library at Copenhagen (MS GKS 95 Fol, folio 228).

Pero Mexía of Seville (1499–1551) studied law at Salamanca and then held
various positions in the administration of his native city. He is remembered

* * * * *

44 Cf the salutation in Ep 2275.
45 On 'fathers and brothers,' see Ep 2275 n1.
46 The correspondence persisted (see Ep 2892), but no letters from either of the
    Mexía brothers has survived.

dedit ei Deus
ut sciret stellarū
dispositiones. Sap7.

ELDOCTO CAVALLERO PEDRO MEXIA

Si alguna duda uviera en el origen i Patria del Sapientissimo varon Pedro Mexia, i oi estuvieran en su antigua prosperidad la docta Atenas ila triumfan-
te Roma, no dudo que contendieran entresi, atribuyendoselo cada una por suyo: i
fuera no menos justa la causa, que en las Siete ciudades de Grecia por Home

10.

Pero Mexía
Biblioteca Digital Juridica, University of Seville

primarily for works published in Spanish in the 1540s. These included *Coloquios o diálogos nuevamente compuestos* (Seville: D. de Robertis 1547), inspired by the *Colloquies* of Erasmus, and *Historia imperial y cesárea* (Seville: J. de León 1545), a history of the emperors from Julius Caesar to Maximilian I. His *Historia de Carlos Quinto* remained unpublished until 1918 (*Revue hispanique* 44 1–556).

ERASMUS OF ROTTERDAM TO PERO MEXÍA, GREETING

As always, when the Frankfurt fair approaches, I am swamped with work, partly because of my scholarly activities, since at that time the presses are frenetically busy (in Froben's shop no fewer than six presses are constantly humming with activity), and partly from an accumulation of letters that 5 have floated in from every quarter of the world, sometimes calling for a reply. At such times I am hardly able to pay much attention to my health. But I have never been more burdened than at present, indeed during the past fortnight it has scarcely been possible to devote an hour to the weakened state of my health. Just when I was panting up to the finish line, your parcel 10 arrived containing the book by that jackdaw,[1] and on the following day an even larger parcel came from Italy. So I can only discuss matters with you briefly, dear Pero Mexía, though you are a man after my own heart.

Your letter is ample testimony to your devotion to me; it breathes throughout a heavenly spirit of affection, which I gladly embrace and will 15 reciprocate in so far as I can. But as for your urging that I respond to that drivel from Carvajal, even if there had been lots of time – and your letter arrived late – I would not have written one word of reply. I realize what a humiliating mistake I made when I dignified that bumptious young man with a reply.[2] In my heart I knew this would happen, and 20 a good friend, Alfonso de Valdés, had warned me in a letter not to give this blathering fool the satisfaction of a single word of reply.[3] But the man to whom he entrusted the letter was slow in delivering it to me, and the book,[4] which was sent from Paris, had reached me somewhat earlier. It had been secretly printed there through the efforts of the Seraphic Franciscans, 25 contrary to the edict of the Parlement and with the name of the printer

* * * * *

2300
1 Carvajal's *Dulcoratio*; see n20 below.
2 His *Responsio* (March 1529) to Carvajal's *Apologia monasticae religionis*; see Ep 2110 n10, and cf n20 below.
3 See Ep 2126:2.
4 The Paris edition of Carvajal's *Apologia monasticae religionis*; see Ep 2110 n10.

suppressed,[5] which made me all the more suspicious that the author's name was a pseudonym. So I have no intention of adding one sin to another.

There is at Louvain a certain Titelmans, a young man belonging to the same order.[6] He is somewhat more accomplished in the study of Scripture than your wretched countryman, and more moderate too, despite his monstrous vanity and insolent loquacity; but, as is characteristic of these people, he covers himself with a veneer of piety that is so false that anyone can see through it. He annotated the annotations of Valla, Lefèvre, and myself on the Epistle to the Romans,[7] but I was the real target of his pen. I replied briefly without mentioning him by name[8] or indulging in polemics except that I pointed out that since he was no expert in either Greek or Latin nor well read in a range of different authors, he was not equal to the task. I sent my book to friends at Louvain and asked them to consider if it would be wise to publish.[9] I was afraid that it might immediately raise the hackles of this vain young man. They printed it – with disastrous results. It seems that the fellow had got what he wanted, for at once he began to produce a flood of books, full of the most long-winded rubbish. He is laughed at by all men of learning but is content with the applause of his brothers. You will say, 'What then? Shall we allow these people to enjoy their triumph with impunity?' They cannot be defeated; even if defeated and crushed, they keep on at their opponent and draw him in, like persistent and inexperienced wrestlers. Whatever the outcome, to have extorted a reply from Erasmus is for them a sufficient trophy. They will certainly be deprived of much of the glory if they create a fuss and I am silent.

Here are the remedies that it would be preferable to employ in dealing with these people. The printer should be brought before the imperial magistrates,[10] since, contrary to the edict of the emperor, he has had the effrontery

* * * * *

5 For the decree of the Parlement of Paris (1521) authorizing the faculty of theology to licence or prohibit the publication of all books on religion, see Ep 1815 n16. Carvajal's work contains no indication that its publication was duly authorized.
6 See Ep 2261 n31.
7 In his *Collationes quinque super epistolam ad Romanos* of May 1529; see Ep 2206 introduction.
8 In his *Responsio ad collationes* Erasmus refers to Titelmans only as *iuvenis gerontodidascalus* 'a young teacher of old men'; cf Ep 2206.
9 See Ep 2260:135–54. The book was printed at Antwerp.
10 The Latin is *magistratus Caesareus*, which does not appear to be the designation of any specific body. The sense is simply that the printer should be made to answer in court for his violation of a decree of Charles v; see the following note.

to publish this sort of nonsense, suppressing his own name.[11] The Most Reverend archbishop of Seville had also imposed silence on the monks;[12] he too 55 should be advised to use his authority to restrain those of the fathers who encourage such clowns. He is a serious and godly man who, even if he were not favourably disposed towards me, could not possibly have approved such books. There are others who wish me well, the archbishop of Toledo and Don Juan Manuel.[13] A heavy fine imposed on one printer will be a warning 60 to the others. The prior himself[14] should be approached and asked where in the rule of St Francis he finds a warrant for disobeying the edicts of princes and, by libellous and seditious writings, attacking the reputation of one to whose qualities so many princes of the church bear ample testimony. I mentioned several of these in my letter to your brother, which was perhaps too 65 much in the style of a Thraso,[15] but it was less than the truth. The most recent letter sent me by the emperor contains these words: 'We wish therefore that you be of good heart, and be assured that we will do everything in our power to safeguard your honour and reputation,'[16] and in another letter he puts the same sentiment much more affectionately, promising to defend the 70 dignity and reputation of my name with no less zeal than his own.[17] Do you

* * * * *

11 Titelmans did not suppress his name in any of his works, though Erasmus seems initially to have become acquainted with the *Collationes* in the form of a manuscript that may have circulated anonymously; see Ep 2089 n2. In any case, Titelmans' published attack on Erasmus did violate injunctions of the imperial court and the papal curia to the theologians of Louvain to abstain from attacks on Erasmus; see Epp 1690 n11, 1747. For that reason the faculty of theology had tried unsuccessfully to prevent publication; see Epp 2063:59–61, 2089:1–5.

12 In 1527, in his capacity as inquisitor-general of Spain, Archbishop Alonso Manrique de Lara reminded the superiors of the religious orders in Spain that he had ordered their members to abstain from attacks on Erasmus unless they could produce documented charges of heresy against him. When the orders complied by filing such charges, Manrique summoned a conference of theologians that met at Valladolid in the summer of 1527 but was unable to reach a conclusion for or against Erasmus. See Ep 1846 introduction.

13 The archbishop of Toledo was Alonso de Fonseca (Ep 1748). For Don Juan Manuel, see Ep 1970 n2.

14 Allen identifies this as a reference to the prior 'of Carvajal's house at Seville,' but offers no evidence that Carvajal had moved to Seville from Salamanca, where he was living in July 1529 (see Ep 2198:16–17). Carvajal became warden of the Franciscan convent in Jerez in 1535, and of that in Seville in 1541.

15 The crude and boastful soldier in Terence's *Eunuchus*

16 Ep 1920:25–7

17 A paraphrase of Ep 1731:12–14.

think, then, that such a prince is going to approve libellous books of that sort?

It will also help to remedy the situation if good men are quietly advised not to donate to those who support such writings. They have no shame, much less any sense of guilt. They believe that they are free to do anything they wish. If they hear about a shortage in the kitchen, this is something they understand, for their ears are fixed to their bellies, not their heads.[18] I shall make sure that the emperor and his chancellor[19] understand the offensive commotion that these people have stirred up. In short, I am ready to do or suffer anything rather than respond to the drivel put out by these young fools.

I have not read the *Dulcoratio* of that man, as you call it,[20] nor do I intend to do so. I did, however, scan the headings on several pages. He dedicates this striking work to some grandee or other,[21] and at the beginning he sings a song in praise of peace, with much stolen from my *Querela pacis*.[22] He moves off from there to paint Erasmus as a behemoth, who, like all heretics, makes war on Christ under the banner of peace.[23] In fact, I would not wish to live to the end of this day if I had not a sincere and wholehearted

* * * * *

18 See Ep 2275 n14.
19 Mercurino Gattinara (Ep 1150)
20 *Dulcoratio amarulentiarum Erasmicae responsionis* (Sweetening of the Bitter Contents of Erasmus' *Responsio*), Carvajal's rejoinder to Erasmus' *Responsio adversus febricitantis cuiusdam libellum*; see Ep 2110 n10. The Latin of the text – 'Dulcorationem illius, ut vocas, non legi' – contains an ambiguity that cannot be reproduced in English. Mexía had evidently made reference to 'Dulcoratio Carvajalis,' which can be read either as 'the *Sweetening* of Carvajal,' or as 'the *Sweetening of Carvajal*. 'It was the sort of jest that neo-Latin authors enjoyed making.
21 The dedicatory letter is addressed to 'Clarissimo Principi Lodovico Cordovae demarcho Comariensis' (*Dulcoratio* folio 2 recto). From the references to him and his father further on in the letter (folio 6 recto), he can be identified as Luis Fernández de Córdoba y Pacheco, second marquis of Comares (1482–1564). He was the only son of the more famous first marquis, Diego Fernándes de Córdoba y Arellano (1463–1518), who played an important role in the Spanish conquest of Granada as well as of Mazalquivir and Oran in North Africa. Like his father before him, Luis served two terms as governor of Oran, 1518–20, 1523–31. (The credit for this identification goes to William J. Callahan of the University of Toronto.) In this case, 'grandee' is a more appropriate translation for *princeps* than 'prince,' which indicates a status loftier than the one Luis occupied.
22 *Dulcoratio* folio 2 recto and verso
23 *Dulcoratio* folio 4 recto

desire to promote the glory of Christ. Then he reports a speech that someone   90
had made at the conference,[24] listing all my horrendous errors. Some people
had written to me about this man, and if the report of his speech is accurate,
then he stated his case clearly enough, but it was a pack of lies; at the time he
was considered by the learned as a mad monk, which indeed he was. After
this our author launches into praise of the grandee, begging him to settle   95
the war against the monks that I and my friends have stirred up by our
seditious writings, and to compel me to recant.[25] What seditious writings is
he talking about? My *Apologia* contains nothing that is seditious,[26] and it was
approved by Mercurino the chancellor.[27] Who drove Carvajal to such folly?
I made fun of him not as a monk but as I thought him to be – a stand-in in   100
someone else's play.

   So much for his preface. Then, to demonstrate his erudition, he cites
for our benefit several passages from letters by people from whom perhaps
he had wrung out some little word of commendation.[28] This is a frequent
practice with these people (they are mendicants in this sense too). But none   105
of these letter writers, so far as I know, is a theologian, certainly not Vives
or Lee. If the case is to be prosecuted on such evidence, just think of the
piles of letters I could produce and the sort of people who wrote them!
As for his quibble about Terminus,[29] this was exceedingly silly, and yet he
refuses to accept my justification, as if I have ever been foolish enough to   110
claim preeminence in any single discipline, much less in all. And yet he
brings up the example of *Plus ultra* along with other silly irrelevancies.[30] No
need to say more – Carvajal has won his case. Somewhere in the course of
an argument I say, 'By this way of thinking it could appear that there was
some weakness in Christ.'[31] He concludes 'There was weakness in Christ: 115
that is blasphemy.'[32]

* * * * *

24 At Valladolid in 1527 (Ep 1791); *Dulcoratio* folio 4 verso
25 *Dulcoratio* folio 6 recto and verso
26 Ie Erasmus' *Responsio*; see n20 above.
27 Gattinara (Epp 1150, 1643, 2013), who would die in Innsbruck on 5 June 1530
   on his way to Augsburg with the emperor, must have expressed his approval
   in a letter now lost.
28 Juan Luis Vives (Ep 2208), Edward Lee (Ep 2094 n8), Francisco Castillo (Franciscan theologian of Salamanca, participant in the conference at Valladolid in
   1527), Pedro Carvajal (unidentified); *Dulcoratio* folios 18 verso–20 recto
29 On the importance of Terminus to Erasmus, see Ep 2018.
30 *Dulcoratio* folio 68 recto. *Plus ultra* was the motto of Charles v.
31 *Apologia adversus Stunicae Blasphemiae* (1522); see LB IX 362E–F.
32 *Dulcoratio* folio 66 verso

He collects many passages of this sort from hither and yon in my works and with no particular system. One thing I have learned from him: I now know what he meant by 'my harlot,' for I never could guess his meaning. There is a colloquy about a harlot and a young man. This he 120 refers to as 'Erasmus' harlot.'[33] I wish there were no worse harlots among those who think this colloquy obscene! We also learn that the emperor and several Spanish princes are monks with a white cowl[34] and that the emperor is an abbot.[35] This ought not to appear out of place since he makes Christ an abbot and the apostles monks and the Virgin Mother a nun.[36] I 125 had said, 'As a man approaches most closely the piety of Francis, so he is, has been, and always will be most dear to me.'[37] From this he makes the following inference: 'Francis was poor: extol poverty. Francis was celibate and chaste: extol celibacy.'[38] He ought rather to have made this inference, 'So whoever wishes to be loved by Erasmus should model his life 130 on that of Francis.' Such people I have always truly loved and I still love them.

At Louvain I enjoyed a Christian friendship with the Franciscans.[39] Lee was the first to scatter a few bad seeds surreptitiously.[40] Afterwards others brought the seeds to life until this impostor, whom the common 135

* * * * *

33 In his *Apologia monasticae religionis* (folio 25 verso) Carvajal had observed that 'in order to leave no stone unturned against those who love chastity, he [Erasmus] invents a thousand lies. Erasmus' harlot [*scortum Erasmi*] indicates as much.' In his *Responsio* to the *Apologia* (LB X 1681A–B), Erasmus professed to be baffled by the reference to his 'harlot.' In the *Dulcoratio* (83 verso) Carvajal explained that he was referring to the colloquy *Adolescentis et scorti* 'The Young Man and the Harlot' (CWE 39 381–9). In the colloquy, the harlot Lucretia, in the process of being talked into abandoning her wicked life and embracing piety, reveals that 'a sizable share' of her income had come from 'reverend gentlemen' of the mendicant orders, who had told her that Erasmus was 'a heretic and a half'; see CWE 39 384:33–385:19.
34 Ie 'monks of the Cistercian Order [who have] the cowl and are called monks and friars'; *Dulcoratio* folio 74 recto. They would have been so described as members of the military Order of Calatrava, founded in the twelfth century as a branch of the Cistercian Order and subject to a modified version of its rule.
35 In his capacity as general of the three great military orders of Santiago, Calatrava, and Alcantara; see *Dulcoratio* folio 72 verso.
36 *Dulcoratio* folios 87 verso, 88 recto
37 *Responsio adversus febricitantis cuiusdam libellum* LB X 1683B
38 *Dulcoratio* folios 93 verso, 94 recto
39 See Ep 1174 n5.
40 See Ep 1074:13–17 with n1.

people call 'God's crow,' came on the scene.[41] In Basel I was very close to the Franciscans as long as they held to the right course. Here the Franciscans are such close neighbours that, when I am in bed, I hear their chanting just as if I were among them in church.[42] We are on very friendly terms because there is no malice among them. They have an honest and mild-   140
mannered preacher, who sometimes even quotes Erasmus approvingly in his sermons.

Let them be poor as Francis was: everyone will love them. But these men are poor in name only and rich in reality. They have their chests, their procurators, and their allotments.[43] I am not quarrelling, however, with these   145
things: no one begrudges them their food and clothing, providing they do not jump on other people. Francis was celibate: does he also think that to be celibate and to be chaste is the same thing? Has anyone ever condemned chastity? I could hardly help laughing when I read: 'Francis was modest, humble, meek, long-suffering, an unrivalled follower of the crucified Christ,   150
a most fervent preacher, always obedient to the church. Praise, commend, extol not just Francis, but those who in the footsteps of Francis follow Christ their prince.'[44] I have always thought Francis a good man and I would willingly love those whom I saw following Christ as their leader in the footsteps of Francis. So let such men come forward and challenge me if I do not praise   155
them. However, if Francis were alive today, I doubt if he would recognize Carvajal as a true son of his or wish to be praised by him, any more than

* * * * *

41 Titelmans
42 In Freiburg the church of the Franciscan cloister (now St Martin's Church) is directly across the Franziskanergasse from the house 'zum Walfisch' (Ep 2112 4n).
43 The Franciscan rule forbade the ownership of private property or the possession of money, but the great expansion of the order and its devotion to the cause of higher learning meant that friars needed books and buildings as well as food and clothing for the exercise of their ministry. The solution to this difficulty was to arrange to have the use of property without actually owning it. The title to all property donated to the order was vested in the papacy; all money from alms or other sources was held in trust for the friars by 'spiritual friends'; and the purchase of goods and services was handled by procurators acting as agents for the pope. The 'chests' (scrinia) mentioned here were probably boxes with deeds and other records of properties held, and perhaps money as well. The word 'allotments' (assignationes) generally refers to grants of land. For a detailed discussion of Franciscan poverty, see the note by Craig Thompson in CWE 40 1026–32.
44 Dulcoratio folio 94 recto

Paul wanted to be praised by the girl with a Pythonical spirit.[45] But I would
be readier still to praise those who follow Christ in the footsteps of Paul,
who wished his gospel to be free of charge.[46]   160

Finally, he terrifies us with a thunderbolt from the pope.[47] It is they
themselves who are harming their order by the evil of their lives and their
foolish and libellous books. It is an outrageous lie to say that many have
pronounced me a heretic and have done so in print. So far as I know, Béda
did not do this, nor did Hoogstraten, or Latomus, or Lee, or Cousturier,[48]   165
and if anyone had done it, that would simply be a charge, not a conviction. No book of mine has ever been pronounced heretical in any legitimate
proceeding.

But I have gone on too long, dear Pero, about the absurdities of this
young man, who has nothing to offer but shameless ignorance and un-   170
bounded prolixity. Try the remedies I have suggested or anything better
you can think of. If there is something I can do, I shall not be found asleep.
From now on I shall not be drawn into an argumentative tit for tat unless
they write differently, which I do not expect from the Franciscans. Those
Franciscans who are learned and pious won't reply, and I care nothing for . 175
the vain and stupid. Meanwhile I shall continue to the best of my ability to
work for piety and learning. May you and your like-minded brother enjoy
a happy life in the gardens of the Muses.

Freiburg im Breisgau, 30 March 1530

2301 / To Alonso Manrique de Lara   Freiburg, 31 March 1530

Clearly contemporary with Epp 2299 and 2300, this letter was first published
in the *Epistolae floridae*. The autograph rough draft is in the Royal Library at
Copenhagen (MS GKS 95 Fol, folio 209). On Manrique, see Ep 1748.

* * * * *

45 Acts 16:16 (Vulgate and Douay); the meaning of 'Pythonical spirit' is given in
   the King James Version: 'possessed with a spirit of divination.'
46 1 Cor 9:18
47 The thunderbolt is found in *Dulcoratio* folio 94A (ie the folio which, thanks to
   Colines' faulty pagination, is the second one numbered 94). It is a composite of
   selected passages from the bull *Exiit qui seminat* (1279) in which Pope Nicholas
   III affirms that the way of life of the friars minor has been approved by God,
   the pope, and the church, and threatens with excommunication any who assert
   the contrary.
48 Epp 2213 n8 (Noël Béda), 1006 (Jacob of Hoogstraten), 934 introduction (Jacobus Latomus), 2094 n8 (Edward Lee), 2082 n24 (Pierre Cousturier)

TO ALONSO MANRIQUE, ARCHBISHOP OF SEVILLE

Most Reverend Archbishop, some time ago a book was sent here from Paris
with the name Luis de Carvajal on the title-page.[1] It was published there secretly with the name of the printer and the place of publication suppressed;
for according to an edict of the Parlement it is not permitted there to publish   5
anything that has not been approved.[2] Since I did not recognize the name,
and the book gave an impression of remarkable levity and scurrility, I suspected it was a joke and that the comedy was the work of a young man
who had been put up to it. My response was light-hearted rather than argumentative.[3] A little later there arrived the Spanish book,[4] along with a letter   10
from friends advising me not to dignify the fellow with a reply.[5] I have bitterly regretted that this advice arrived too late. Now this same young man
is sending me a much more scurrilous book,[6] printed in the same manner
without reference to place or printer, an evident infraction of the emperor's
edict.[7]   15

It is not my intention to engage with such fatuous publications, even if
a thousand were to appear. But I am surprised that such writing comes from
the great community of Observants,[8] since the rule (which many carry under
their robes and few in their hearts) prohibits defamation of any kind.[9] As for
myself, I have a clear conscience; moreover there are so many princes, kings,   20
cardinals, bishops, and scholars who show their appreciation of my work not
just by their letters but also by the gifts that they spontaneously offer me that

* * * * *

2301
1 The Paris edition of Carvajal's *Apologia monasticae religionis* (March 1529); see
   Epp 2110 n10, 2126:4–9, 2300:23–7.
2 See Ep 2300 n5.
3 *Responsio adversus febricitantis cuiusdam libellum* (Ep 2110 n10), which was full
   of sarcasm and ridicule.
4 The 1528 Salamanca edition of Carvajal's *Apologia*; see Epp 2110 n10, 2126:9–10.
5 See Ep 2126:2–4.
6 The *Dulcoratio*; see Epp 2110 n10, 2275, 2300:83–167.
7 Erasmus, no doubt writing in haste, has got things mixed up here. Carvajal's
   Dulcoratio was published with place and printer clearly named. Moreover, because the place was Paris, the only edict that could be infracted was that of the
   Parlement (see lines 5–6 above). Despite this, Allen's note is a cross-reference
   to his note in Ep 1690 concerning the edict of Charles v prohibiting attacks on
   Erasmus by the theologians of Louvain.
8 Cf the salutation in Ep 2275.
9 See §11 of the First Rule of the Friars Minor (1209): 'And let all the brothers
   take care not to calumniate anyone, nor to contend in words ...' *The Writings
   of St. Francis of Assisi* trans Paschal Robinson (Philadelphia 1905) 45.

I can easily disregard these shady conspirators.[10] But it would be conducive to peace in your beloved Spain if that clandestine printer were punished so that he would not commit more serious offences in the future when he   25 finds that his effrontery has paid off.[11] Nothing can be expected from these young men except what is stupid and seditious. If the older men have any interest in the defence of truth, let the youngsters show their writings to them before they publish.

I shall not impose upon you further, distinguished prelate. Even if   30 you think Erasmus deserves this kind of abuse, I am sure that, given your concern for justice, you will not neglect your responsibility for the public peace. May the Lord keep your Highness safe and well and abounding in all good things. Give my most cordial greetings to my friend, Master Luis Coronel.[12]   35

Freiburg im Breisgau, 31 March AD 1530

2302 / To Giambattista Egnazio   Freiburg, 31 March 1530

First published in the *Epistolae floridae*, this letter is Erasmus' reply to a letter from Egnazio written in response to Ep 2249.

ERASMUS OF ROTTERDAM TO BATTISTA EGNAZIO, GREETING
My ill will towards Budé and my bitter hatred of the man are such that, even if he openly turned the point of his pen against me, I could not help admiring him for the brilliant contribution he has made to scholarship! I am sending you a letter that deals with the comparison that some suspect   5 caused him offence.[1] If this puts your mind at ease, there is no need to say more. In any case the embarrassing comparison was removed in the later edition.[2] The furthest thing from my mind was to hurt Budé. But for the moment I shall not say another word about Budé or the *Ciceronianus*.

On the lamentable and almost hopeless dissension within the Chris-   10 tian faith, I see that our minds are as one. This is clear from my letter to

* * * * *

10 Cf Ep 2299.
11 The only relevant 'clandestine printer' in Spain would be the one who produced the Salamanca edition of Carvajal's *Apologia* in 1528.
12 See Ep 1274.

2302
1 Ie the comparison with Josse Bade in the *Ciceronianus*; see Epp 1948, 2021 introduction. The letter sent to Egnazio may have been a copy of Ep 2046.
2 The second edition of March 1529

Vulturius, which I am sending you herewith.[3] I place some hope, however, in the emperor – not just in his authority and power, his godliness and wisdom, and that gentleness of his that is a fitting accompaniment to sovereign rule, but also because he seems to possess a certain genius.[4] I hope this matter can be settled without much spilling of human blood and that in the end Christ will have the victory. A man of your good sense can guess what I am hinting at. But we must change our lives for the better and weary a merciful God with our fervent prayers.

I offer my hearty congratulations on your success, dear Egnazio; you have certainly earned it by your outstanding virtues. As for me, I must die in the gladiatorial arena,[5] for this is my fate. I shall try, however, to secure for myself a measure of peace by maintaining a stubborn silence in the face of all provocation.

Karel Uutenhove, a young man who in his own country enjoys a privileged situation and comes from a distinguished family, does not stand much in need of your assistance.[6] If at any time you will honour the man with your friendly encouragement, this will spur him on in his love of learning. Herwagen speaks highly of your courteous and generous disposition.[7] Please do what you can to see that the Chrysostom is published in full.[8] He is among the most pious of authors, and the enterprise is very costly.[9] I get nothing from it except hard work. Thank Heaven, I have enough to live on. Zasius returns your greetings;[10] he is a man of old-fashioned ways, a rare example of ancient virtue. Rhenanus is away in his homeland.[11] Henricus Glareanus, a perpetual tower of strength for all humane learning, moved here with me

* * * * *

3 The *Epistola contra pseudoevangelicos*, which was addressed to 'Vulturius Neocomus,' ie Gerard Geldenhouwer; see Epp 2219 n5, 2238 n1.
4 Cf Ep 2312A:294–5. The Latin word *genius* can mean 'attendant or guiding spirit' (cf Ep 2216 n1). More relevant here is the meaning 'inborn qualities,' 'natural cast of mind.' No one ever accused Charles V of exceptional intelligence or talent (a rare meaning of *genius* in classical Latin in any case), but he was commonly credited with inborn nobility of spirit and good intentions.
5 On Erasmus' fondness for gladiatorial imagery in describing battles with his critics, see Ep 2250 n9.
6 Cf Ep 2249:1–2.
7 Cf Ep 2249:44–9.
8 Ie by sending manuscripts; see Ep 1623:11–14.
9 The Latin Chrysostom published by Froben in the summer of 1530 (Ep 2359)
10 See Ep 2209 n8.
11 His correspondence places Beatus in his hometown of Sélestat in September 1529 and March 1530; see BRE Epp 267, 270.

when everything changed in Basel. He has a teaching post here on a public
salary.[12] I think he is not unknown to you.[13] Farewell.

Freiburg im Breisgau, 31 March AD 1530

2303 / To Konrad von Thüngen   Freiburg, 2 April 1530

This letter was first published in the *Epistolae floridae*. On Bishop Konrad, see
Ep 1124. His reply is Ep 2314.

ERASMUS OF ROTTERDAM TO KONRAD, BISHOP OF THE CHURCH
AT WÜRZBURG AND DUKE OF EASTERN FRANCONIA, GREETING
From what I hear, my presumption in approaching your Highness through
the Right Reverend Bishop Marius has not turned out badly.[1] So I am not
afraid to do the same now, particularly as I have found in Daniel Stiebar the   5
most suitable courier one could possibly hope for. In the past he shared my
home in Basel,[2] and now he has been with me again for several months in
Freiburg. For a considerable time we were brought together by sharing the
same table, something that was once regarded as a special mark of friendship. Never before have I encountered a young man with a more virtuous,   10
pure, and agreeable nature. Just as his company when he was my only companion was a very great comfort to me amid all the vexations of study, has-
sles, and advancing years, so his departure has saddened me greatly. However, I bear my sorrow all the more easily because it is for his own good
that he is being recalled to his own country.[3]   15

I must congratulate your celebrated chapter most warmly on acquiring
my young friend, who is endowed with such outstanding qualities of mind.
If he were free to devote another year or two to the study of the humane
disciplines, he would bring that much more honour and profit both to the

* * * * *

12 On the move to Freiburg, see Ep 2098 n1. On the reasons for the move, see Ep
2097 n1.
13 Cf Ep 2105:24–6.

2303
1 See Ep 2164, and for Augustinus Marius see Ep 2321.
2 In 1528; see Epp 2036, 2069 introductions.
3 Stiebar, who had been on leave from the cathedral chapter at Würzburg to
pursue his studies, was about to return home, where he received a canonry
and pursued a successful career in the administration of the imperial bishopric
of Würzburg.

chapter and to your Lordship, for whom, as is only proper, he has the most 20
affectionate and respectful regard. I shall not trouble to commend him to
you, for no one commends fine gems to a connoisseur of precious things.
Such outstanding virtue needs no commendation to one who has so great a
love for all that is fine. To draw attention to him is to commend him. If there
is anything in which my assistance would be welcome to your Lordship, 25
you will find me most willingly at your service. May the Lord keep your
Highness safe and well.

Freiburg im Breisgau, 2 April AD 1530

2304 / From Peter Medmann   Strasbourg, 2 April 1530

This letter was first published as Ep 122 in Förstemann / Günther. The autograph was part of the Burscher Collection in the University Library at Leipzig
(Ep 1254 introduction).

Peter Medmann of Cologne (1507–84) studied there (1522–6) and in Wittenberg (1526–8), and then became a tutor in the family of Anton von Isenburg
(cf Ep 2298 n8). He subsequently became a tutor in the family of Johann von
Wied, brother of Hermann von Wied, archbishop of Cologne. His duties as
family tutor soon gave way to those of adviser and diplomat to Archbishop
Hermann. From 1539 he was in close and friendly contact with Martin Bucer
and Philippus Melanchthon and was instrumental in securing their involvement in Hermann's unsuccessful attempt (1543–7) to transform the imperial
archbishopric and electorate of Cologne into a secularized Lutheran principal-
ity. From 1548 the geographical focus of Medmann's career was East Friesland,
and from 1553 until his death he was burgomaster of Emden.

Greetings. I was planning to deliver these letters personally from Master
Caesarius[1] and Master Riquinus,[2] two enthusiastic supporters of yours; at
any rate that was my intention when I left Cologne. But many things intervened to make that impossible. Meanwhile, most learned sir, if I may appeal to that great generosity of yours, which I seem to recognize in all your 5
learned writings, may I beg you to make my excuses to Master Riquinus,
when you write to him, for not delivering his letter to you. I cannot say how
sorry I am that it did not prove possible for me to visit you. But I bear my
disappointment more easily since I still have great hopes that some day you

* * * * *

2304
1 Johannes Caesarius (Ep 374). The letter is not extant.
2 Ep 2298

will come to us.[3] Master Johann von Riedt,[4] who is a great ornament to our   10
city, sends you his good wishes. He certainly deserves to have his name
passed on to posterity in your most elegant writings.

The people of Strasbourg are very cross with you on account of your
letter to Nijmegen.[5] I have heard much on this topic here. I would most
happily have written you a full account, if time had permitted. Farewell,   15
most learned of men. Be assured that I am devoted to you with all my heart.

Strasbourg, 2 April 1530. Farewell, again. In haste

Sincerely yours, Peter Medmann of Cologne

Please excuse this discourteous brevity. It could not be otherwise.

Greetings in Christ to Master Erasmus of Rotterdam, great high priest   20
of learning, from his friend

2305 / To Johannes Alexander Brassicanus   Freiburg, 4 April 1530

First published in the *Epistolae floridae*, this letter responds to one delivered by a
servant of Brassicanus who carried a text of Salvian of Marseille to Froben (line
18). On Brassicanus, since 1524 professor of rhetoric at Vienna, see Ep 1146.

ERASMUS OF ROTTERDAM TO JOHANNES ALEXANDER BRASSICANUS,
JURIST, GREETING

Your book of proverbs was delivered some time ago without your letter; I
found it delightful. [1] I also liked very much the letter that your servant delivered,[2] except that you never tire of jokes about the living dead. In my *Cicero-*   5
nianus I had not intended to mention all those who had gained fame through
their writing.[3] Otherwise, where would the volume have ended? Could you
possibly imagine anything more utterly silly? Ursinus mentioned you to me,
but it was too late.[4] I had not seen anything of yours except a few verses,
nor had I heard anything about you for several years. Perish the thought   10

* * * * *

3 In response to invitations to settle in Cologne; see Ep 2159:22–4.
4 Ep 2058
5 The *Epistola contra pseudevangelicos*; see Ep 2219 n5.

2305
1 *Proverbiorum Symmicta* (Vienna: H. Victor, March 1529)
2 Not extant
3 Cf Ep 2008:15–33. From the context here, it is clear that the joke was that the
   men of letters whom Erasmus did not mention in his survey of Latin authors
   in the *Ciceronianus* (Ep 1948) might as well be dead.
4 In a letter of 1528; see Ep 2008:30–1.

that all who are not mentioned there are dead! Beatus Rhenanus was passed over, so was Bonifacius Amerbach, whose style, in my opinion, hardly takes second place to Poliziano's. I know that you are joking, but throughout the letter you are unable to let go of the joke, which suggests to me some disgruntlement on your part. But, as I said already, I did not compile a full list of writers. In any case, if someone had been left out from the list, the omission should have been put down to ignorance or forgetfulness rather than malice. Your servant did not show me the Salvian,[5] although Froben will not act on it without my judgment.

I congratulate you most warmly on having made such excellent progress in acquiring a command of both languages. Your Greek translations are very accurate and not without style, and there is nothing in your diction to vex the reader. It seems to me that you put yourself to unnecessary trouble when in the preface you excuse yourself for dealing with proverbs after me. Surely no one has ever been so unfair as to prescribe a law forbidding anyone to treat a subject that has been treated by others? And would it not be even more unfair to prescribe such a law in this field, which is by its very nature boundless, especially at present when previously forgotten writers in both languages are coming to light every day? But when you add that I too was following others when I wrote proverbs, if you are speaking about Greek, I do not deny it. However, no one writing in Latin dealt with this subject before me. How I wish that the collections produced by the Greek paroemiologists had survived! When I first began, there was no help to be had from the Greeks except for a manuscript of the commentaries of Diogenianus, which was both mutilated and seriously corrupt. Later I obtained the collections of Zenobius,[6] which were in a not much happier state. Polidoro's attempt to claim priority is clearly not serious,[7] since I have shown that my first edition antedated his

* * * * *

5 A text of the surviving works of the fifth-century ecclesiastical writer Salvian of Marseille, based on a manuscript from the library of King Matthias Corvinus of Hungary that had been given to Brassicanus by King Louis II. The text was published by Froben in August 1530 with a preface by Brassicanus dated at Vienna on 1 March 1530.
6 Diogenianus and Zenobius, who lived in the reign of Hadrian in the second century, compiled the first known collections of Greek proverbs. Erasmus not only took many examples from them, but followed their precedent in arranging his material by centuries (hundreds) and chiliads (thousands). See E.L. von Leutsch and F.G. Schneidewin *Corpus paroemiographorum Graecorum* (Gottingen 1830–51).
7 On this quarrel between Erasmus and his friend Polidoro Virgilio, see Ep 1175 introduction.

by three months;[8] at that time neither of us was known to the other. I would like to think, my dearest Brassicanus, that your work will outdo my *Chiliads*[9] and put the name of Erasmus in the shade.[10] However, you describe some proverbs as new that are in fact in my collection, for example, 'If it is not disagreeable to you, it is agreeable to me' is cited by me in chiliad 2, century 1, proverb 33;[11] similarly 'The urchin giving birth' is chiliad 2, century 4, proverb 82;[12] 'Then the swans will sing, etc' is chiliad 3, century 3, proverb 97.[13] There are also others that are cited incidentally in my *Chiliads*.

I do not mention this to discourage you in your splendid undertaking – among friends everything is in common – but so that you may avoid captious criticism from others. I am not writing to Velius,[14] for I am not now in the best of health. Pass on my affectionate and respectful greetings to him and to any others who do not wish me ill.

Freiburg, 4 April AD 1530

2306 / From Johann Lotzer   Heidelberg, 4 April 1530

The autograph of this awkwardly verbose letter, first published as Ep 82 in Enthoven, is in the Rehdiger Collection of the University Library at Wrocław (MS Rehd 254.98). On Johann (I) Lotzer, personal physician to Louis V, elector Palatine, see Ep 2116.

Cordial greetings. Although I might have been afraid to obtrude myself upon you with a letter, especially since you are so fully occupied with serious and important business, nevertheless that generosity which has done as much as even your great learning for the high regard in which you are held has encouraged me to produce this token (such as it is) of my good will towards you. The letter that I am writing to you has no other purpose, I do assure you, than to acquaint you with my willingness and desire to serve and be of use to you and to let you know of my ardent devotion. Indeed there is no one among the scholars of this age whom I respect more or think of admiringly almost every day.

* * * * *

8 See Ep 1175:57–64.
9 The *Adagia*; see Ep 2210 n7 and cf n6 above.
10 Cf Ep 1107:9–10 with n1.
11 *Adagia* II i 33
12 *Adagia* II iv 82
13 *Adagia* III iii 97
14 Ursinus Velius, referred to as 'Ursinus' in line 8 above; see Ep 2313.

This was, if not my only reason, certainly my most important reason for sending my son (whom I love with a unique affection as befits an only son) to you in Freiburg.[1] I parted with him so that he could be near you, and could see, and get to know, and even at times hear the celebrated Erasmus (and I say 'the celebrated Erasmus' advisedly). It seems to me to be the highest felicity to be acquainted for a time with a man whose inspired and imperishable works are read with the greatest delight in every part of the world. If this were the moment at which you were free and willing to put yourself at the service of others, I would most readily have spared no expense so that he would return to me an educated man, the pupil of such a teacher. But even the present alternative I consider important enough to have him away from me for several years.

But I am detaining you too long, most courteous Erasmus, with these petty concerns of mine – perhaps you are already weary of them. So farewell, my most excellent sir, and know that you must now count and number Lotzer among your special friends.

It has just now occurred to me, illustrious sir, that I should ask you one further favour: if by your most effective intervention you could assist these young men, my son and his companion, Johann Fichard,[2] to acquire some modest appointment, I hope you would be kind enough to do so for my sake. This is especially important to Fichard, who needs this assistance so as to have free time for his studies, and is not unqualified for some such appointment. By this you would perform a most gratifying service to me etc. Farewell, again.

Heidelberg, 4 April in the year of our salvation 1530

Johann Lotzer, doctor of medicine, physician to the illustrious count Palatine, the archprince Louis

To Desiderius Erasmus of Rotterdam, a man greatly distinguished for piety and learning, his most respected master and friend

* * * * *

2306
1 Johann (II) Lotzer matriculated at Freiburg on 20 June 1530. Nothing is known of his subsequent career.
2 Johann Fichard of Frankfurt (1512–81) matriculated at Heidelberg on 17 May 1528. In the spring of 1530 he moved on to Freiburg, along with Johann (II) Lotzer, to study law under Udalricus Zasius (Ep 2209 n8). Not long after obtaining his doctorate in law (November 1531) he was appointed syndic in Frankfurt, where he also established himself as a well-known practising lawyer and published treatises on legal subjects. An able diplomat, Fichard played an important role in preventing reprisals against Frankfurt following the defeat of the Protestant League of Schmalkalden in 1546–7.

2307 / From Anton Fugger Augsburg, 7 April 1530

First published in LB III/2 1746 *Appendix epistolarum* no 357, this is Fugger's answer to Ep 2273. The manuscript is in the Rehdiger Collection of the University Library at Wrocław (MS Rehd 254.67).

Cordial greetings, Erasmus, most learned of the learned. Today, just when I had replied to your lengthy and delightful letter by writing at even greater length,[1] your secretary Lieven Panagathus[2] arrived, bringing a letter from you and a most delightful little gift, namely Xenophon's *Tyrant* with a dedication to me.[3] For such a courteous gesture towards me I send you my profound thanks and the gratitude that such a gift deserves, particularly because you did of your own free will what I could scarcely have dared to ask from you without blushing. I happily acknowledge your devotion and I welcome it; it is all the more gratifying since it comes from you spontaneously. At first glance, I like these little volumes of yours very much.[4] Nothing that does not merit praise and nothing that anyone could disapprove of can come from your study. For this reason I judge those men peculiarly blessed whom your Muse had commended to posterity, for they will never be forgotten.

In the other letter that I wrote you today[5] I gave you a full account of how things stand with us. Nothing new has come to mind since, except that they say the emperor will arrive in Trent tomorrow. Shortly after that he will reach Bressanone, where it is said he will remain through Holy Week until the Easter celebration. When he will reach us here in Augsburg is still uncertain.[6] We are told that the situation in Italy is quite calm except that the Florentines, who are still encircled in a desperate siege, have decided

* * * * *

2307
1 Neither Erasmus' letter nor Fugger's response is extant; cf Ep 2269:87–90 with n14.
2 From the Greek *panagathos* 'all-good,' a play on Lieven Algoet's surname; see Ep 2294 n8.
3 See Ep 2273.
4 Evidently another book was sent with the Xenophon. Allen conjectured that it might have been the *Ennaratio* on Psalm 22 (Ep 2266), which was published at about the same time. Cf Ep 2310:1–7.
5 See n1 above.
6 Easter in 1530 was on 17 April. The emperor was in Trent 24–8 April, and in Bressanone (Brixen) 30 April–2 May. He arrived in Augsburg on 15 June; see Ep 2294 n7.

to face any extremity rather than relinquish their ideal of liberty, to which
they are so strongly committed.[7] These, dear Erasmus, are the matters that
seemed worth adding to my previous letter. It is our fervent prayer that you
stay well for our sakes and for the sake of the Muses. May Christ keep you 25
safe and well for a long, long time to come, my dearest friend.

Augsburg, 7 April 1530

Yours most sincerely, Anton Fugger

To the celebrated theologian Doctor Desiderius Erasmus of Rotterdam,
his very special friend 30

2308 / To Johann Koler   Freiburg, 13 April 1530

This letter, Erasmus' response to Ep 2269, was first published as Ep 15 in vol 1
of *Erasmiana* ed Adalbert Horawitz 4 vols (Vienna 1878–84). The autograph is
in the Austrian National Library at Vienna (Cod 9737c folio 7). On the manuscript Koler noted that he had replied on 5 May 1530, but that letter is not
extant.

Cordial greetings. I received the letter you sent me on your return from
Italy. Nothing could have been more welcome, so great was the pleasure and
solace that it brought me. I wish that in drawing a picture of the honourable
Anton [1] I could surpass Apelles himself![2] But, unhappily, it is his bad luck
to be saddled with a virtual Choerilus.[3] I touched on this in my last letter,[4] 5
which I entrusted recently to the public courier from this city. Unless I am
mistaken, it was he who delivered your letter too.

May is said to be unlucky for entering on a marriage, hence the proverb
'Bad women marry in May.'[5] But I hope it will be a propitious month for
restoring peace to Germany. The emperor is dallying too long in Italy, and 10

* * * * *

7 The Florentines held out until 10 August in their struggle to prevent the
restoration by imperial forces of Pope Clement VII's family, the Medici, whom
they had expelled in May 1527; see Pastor 10 chapter 3.

2308
1 Fugger
2 Apelles (fourth century BC) was the most respected Greek painter of antiquity.
3 Choerilus, a proverbially bad epic poet, who attached himself to Alexander
the Great; see Horace *Ars poetica* 357 and *Epistles* 2.1.232–4.
4 Not extant; cf line 40.
5 *Adagia* I iv 9

seems too ready to accommodate the pope. To please him, he is pressing hard on the most flourishing city in Italy.[6] I see no turning point in the German tragedy unless some deus ex machina suddenly appears. Have you read my letter to Vulturius? I showed there how one could put an end to these upheavals.[7] That letter, however, provoked a great outcry against me 15 in Strasbourg,[8] although I did not mention the city or even that particular sect, only certain people whose lives, for all their flaunting of the gospel, damage the cause they wish to be seen as championing. Nor am I any less blunt in my admonition of the other side.

I come now to your other letter.[9] If my man Lieven told you the true 20 story,[10] then you have heard my tale of woe.[11] The Right Reverend Bishop Christoph of Augsburg came here a short time ago for no other reason, he said, than to see Erasmus. He brought me two most valuable cups, in which were placed two hundred florins.[12] I wonder if the man is not now regretting his journey and his generosity. At any rate I can say that I have not seen a 25 more courteous or affable man than he is.

I agree with you about Italy,[13] except that I would like to move from here to a bigger city elsewhere. Something will be decided when the printers return from the Frankfurt fair. As for going to Augsburg,[14] no decision can be made until the diet is concluded. But when will that be?[15] I do not know 30 if in the meantime it will be possible to remain here safely, particularly if the emperor begins to adopt sterner remedies, as people ominously predict.

* * * * *

6 See Ep 2307 n8.
7 The letter to Vulturius (Gerard Geldenhouwer) is the *Epistola contra pseudevangelicos* (Epp 2219 n5, 2238 n1). Erasmus is doubtless referring to the final section (CWE 78 245–52), which is an appeal for unity based on moderation, the removal of abuses, agreement on things conducive to piety, mutual toleration of conflicting opinions that are not obstacles to piety, and postponement to a later time of difficult matters that require further discussion.
8 Cf Ep 2304:13–14.
9 Not extant; probably contemporary with Ep 2307
10 Lieven Algoet; see Ep 2294 n8.
11 Doubtless a reference to his current illness; see introduction.
12 For the visit and the cups, see Ep 2277:2–6.
13 Possibly a reference to the dangerously unsettled conditions in Italy resulting from decades of warfare there (cf Ep 2269:1–2); or perhaps to Koler's comments on the emperor's efforts to restore peace there (Ep 2269:47–59).
14 Ie in response to Fugger's invitation to settle there; see Ep 2222:7–10.
15 The diet had been summoned to meet on 8 April, but the emperor himself did not arrive in Augsburg until 15 June. The diet lasted until 22 September.

On the other hand, the priests are as fearful of the emperor as they are of the Lutherans.[16]

I am glad that our friend Anton was so delighted by my little gesture 35 of respect.[17] I shall try to respond as best I can to his most generous friendship. His exceptional integrity deserves our love and our celebration even when there is no expectation of a return.

I thought I had detected in your character something not very different from my own; so in my last letter[18] I confided certain thoughts to you with 40 unusual frankness. You will realize that these were inspired not by malice of any kind but by a genuine affection for both Nachtgall[19] and Anton. Farewell, my kind and warm-hearted friend.

Freiburg, 13 April 1530

Yours truly, Erasmus. In his own hand 45

I have not reread this: pardon me if my pen has gone off the track at some point.

To the distinguished Master Johann Koler, provost of Chur. In Augsburg

2309 / From Johann Henckel   Linz, 13 April 1530

This letter, first published as Ep 123 in Förstemann / Günther, is Henckel's answer to Ep 2230. The autograph was in the Burscher Collection in the University Library at Leipzig (Ep 1254 introduction). The letter, accompanied by a gift cup (line 29), arrived on 7 July, along with one from Queen Mary of Hungary (n3); see Ep 2345:14–15. Erasmus' reply (Ep 2350:16) is not extant. On Henckel, Queen Mary's confessor, see Ep 2110, and cf Ep 2313:47–56.

For almost a whole year it has not been possible for me to write to you, most excellent Erasmus, for I was driven from my homeland and could find no permanent location in which to settle. I wandered from one place to another. Finally I have settled on alien soil, but must leave this place too in a few

* * * * *

16 They doubtless feared that the emperor, who had made clear his determination to restore religious peace and unity to the Empire, might do so at the cost of major concessions to the Lutherans.
17 See Epp 2273, 2307:3–8.
18 See line 5 above.
19 Cf Ep 2310:39–41, where it appears that the quarrel with Ottmar Nachtgall arising out of their joint occupancy of the house 'zum Walfisch' in Freiburg erupted at this time; see Ep 2166 n3.

days. We are setting out to pay our respects to Charles on his arrival in   5
Germany.[1]

Your letter caught up with me here in Linz. I received it from the hands
of my sovereign lady, for it was delivered to her, along with other letters,
by the post (as it is called).[2] When she discovered that it came from you, she
asked me if she could read it. She was very gratified that you mentioned her   10
in the letter. Here is a letter from her to you; from it you can better appreciate the singular regard that this excellent princess has for you. She wrote
it in her own hand, something that she does not usually do except when
writing to great princes and those who are especially dear to her. I have no
doubt that you will cherish it, considering from whom it comes and the de-   15
voted heart that inspired it.[3] Before long she will, I hope, send you another
letter. Or – and this is what I would prefer – she will talk to you in person
at the coming diet and express her heartfelt gratitude to you. If any of your
books has been gratefully received and held in high esteem, it is surely the
work that you presented and dedicated to our widowed queen. It is so loved   20
and cherished by her that many are surprised that she never tires of reading
it again and again. Indeed the young women in the queen's service, distinguished for their beauty, wealth, family, and chastity, are influenced by her
example, and even if they do not understand Latin, they delight to possess
the book and hold it in their hands. And now they are pressing me urgently   25
to have it translated into German, which I have undertaken to do.[4] Such, to
be sure, is the captivating brilliance of your writings that, as Plutarch says
of Homer,[5] no one ever wearies of reading what you have written.

I am sending you a cup,[6] a small thing to be sure, but something that
was once very precious to a great prince (I refer to the father of the present   30

* * * * *

2309
1 Henckel was with Queen Mary's court, which as late as May 1529 had been
  resident in Znojmo in Moravia. Since then the court had made the long journey to Linz, where in January 1530 Mary represented King Ferdinand at an
  assembly of the Austrian estates that was summoned to vote subsidies for the
  struggle against the Turks.
2 The reference is doubtless to the postal service that had been established in
  the Hapsburg lands by Johann Baptista von Taxis, Charles' postmaster general.
  See Ep 2089 n5.
3 The letter does not survive. It was delivered to Erasmus on the evening of 7
  July; see Ep 2345:14–15. He replied with Ep 2350.
4 If the translation of De vidua christiana was made, it has not survived.
5 Plutarch De garrulitate 3.5
6 Listed in the inventory of 10 April 1534; see Sieber 7, Major 42. For its delivery,
  see the introduction above.

margraves of Brandenburg).[7] I beg you to receive it graciously. Our friend Antonin, as I learn from his letter, has recovered totally from the mental illness with which he was seriously afflicted, and is now as well as he ever was.[8] This news, I am sure, will please you greatly. May the Lord God free you too from the stone and keep you safe for a long time to come, and may he bring you success in your studies and in all good things! This year my gout has laid me low for only three or four days. I have taken the part of the husband, but she follows close behind me, reminding me of my pledge, whereas I would like to hand her a bill of divorce and tear up my commitment.[9] I hope you will keep well. May you have every blessing!

Linz, 13 April AD 1530

Yours, Johann Henckel

To the erudite and most excellent Master Erasmus of Rotterdam, the leading exponent of a purer theology, his estimable and respected champion

2310 / From Johann von Botzheim   Überlingen, 13 April 1530

First published as Ep 124 in Förstemann / Günther, the manuscript of this letter was in the Burscher Collection of the University Library at Leipzig (Ep 1254 introduction). For Botzheim, see Epp 1285, 2205.

Greetings. I received from you, dear master, two literary packages. The first contained your *Responsiones Erasmi ad Collationes cuiusdam* together with the *Epistola contra quosdam qui se falso evangelicos iactant*.[1] The latter I read carefully once or twice, looking for that admixture of aconite which certain people find in the letter, and quickly reaching the conclusion that what offends them is the free expression of the truth. The second package contained the *Enarrationes in psalmum 22 of David*, a divine work and vintage Erasmus.[2] I lent it to a good scholar, a great supporter of yours and a man with a genuine love for the humanities. When he returned your *Enarrationes*, he wrote me this letter,[3] which I am sending on to you so that you will see that there

* * * * *

7 See Ep 1297 n10.

8 For Jan Antonin and his illness, see Ep 2011:10–22.

9 Since *podagra* (gout) is a feminine noun, a 'she,' it can be represented, as here, as a disagreeable wife from whom one would like to be divorced.

2310

1 For the *Responsio* to Titelmans see Ep 2206; for the *Epistola* to Geldenhouwer see Ep 2219 n5.

2 See Ep 2266.

3 The scholar has not been identified, and the letter is not extant.

are people here who appreciate you as you deserve. He presses me for a letter from Erasmus to mitigate in some measure his separation from his hero. On the other hand there are those here who in public pronouncements from the pulpit try to dissuade students from reading your translation of the New Testament, most recently on the occasion of the feast of the Annunciation of Mary, at which the angel's salutation had to be explained to the people. You could hardly imagine the abhorrence he expressed for your translation of that word in *Ave gratiosa, Dominus tecum.*[4] He repeatedly warned his hearers to be on their guard against new translations that perverted and corrupted the whole of Holy Scripture. I have not seen Nijmegen's notes on your *Epistola.*[5] Your man Lieven[6] had written to say he was sending them on your behalf, but he did not do so. I imagine that something has gone wrong: he sent your *Epistola* exactly as it was published at Freiburg (which I had received from you earlier) but without the notes.[7]

In your last letter you wrote that the Paris theologians were becoming milder.[8] Now you write that they have published an attack on

* * * * *

4 The preacher has not been identified. In translating the angel's greeting to Mary in Luke 1:28, Erasmus had changed the Vulgate's *Ave [Maria] gratia plena, Dominus tecum* 'Hail [Mary], full of grace, the Lord is with you' to *Ave [Maria] gratiosa, Dominus tecum* 'Hail [Mary] O gracious one, the Lord is with you,' arguing that this was a better translation of the Greek κεχαριτωμένη. This could be read as undermining the traditional understanding of *gratia plena* as 'full of divine grace.' Moreover, it made the angel's greeting, as Erasmus put it in his Annotations, akin to the 'loving' (*amatorius*) words of a suitor (which helped to explain why the virgin was initially perturbed by the greeting). Edward Lee and Pierre Cousturier were quick to object on two grounds: first, that Erasmus had cast doubt on the belief that the virgin had remained free of sin by virtue of a unique dispensation of grace, and second, that he had impiously characterized the encounter between the virgin and the angel as something amorous. In the notes for the 1527 edition of the New Testament, Erasmus retreated on the second point, eliminating all reference to 'loving' and 'suitor,' though not without expressing his disdain for his critics and their arguments. See Erika Rummel *Erasmus' Annotations on the New Testament: From Philologist to Theologian* (Toronto 1986) 167–9.
5 Ie Geldenhouwer's annotated edition of the *Epistola contra pseudevangelicos;* see Epp 2289 n2, 2293.
6 Algoet (Ep 2278 n2)
7 See lines 2–3 above.
8 Allen suggests that Botzheim is probably referring to Ep 2277, where Erasmus states (lines 11–12) that the theologians of Louvain were becoming more moderate in their attitude towards him. There was, or at any rate there had been, some basis for saying that (see Ep 2033 n12), but Erasmus had no known reason to suspect the Paris theologians of a similar lapse into moderation.

you.[9] The envious mind is never at peace. New works like the *Dulcoratio* are being hatched in Spain;[10] similar effusions are appearing in France and even worse in Germany. But I take comfort in the thought that the more praiseworthy a man's virtue may be, the more liable it is to attack by evil   30 men. The surest measure of true virtue is its greater exposure to the slanders of the wicked. Yet virtue, after many a battering, is likely to emerge all the more resplendent and triumphant.

Every day we are expecting Balthasar, who has now been elected and consecrated our bishop.[11] They say the emperor is in Innsbruck.[12] We are   35 all pinning our hopes on him, looking for the redemption of Israel,[13] not, I hope, in vain.

I have made up my mind to tear myself away from the treadmill and pay you a visit,[14] unless I am disappointed despite all my efforts. It surprises me that Nachtgall is not the man I thought he was.[15] Let me know   40 sometime what lies behind this business if you can guess the reasons. At court your enemies are not silent. Eck has summoned all the Lutherans to the assembly of princes at Augsburg; he intends to defend there the articles of faith and the Catholic church.[16] The duke of Saxony and the landgrave of Hessen,[17] I am told, have arranged accommodation for themselves at Augs-   45 burg at great expense, for they are planning to bring there all their theo-

* * * * *

9 The letter is not extant. It is not clear what 'new attack' could be laid at the door of the Louvain theologians as a group. Erasmus was aware that the faculty at Louvain had tried to prevent the publication of Titelmans' *Collationes*; see Ep 2089:1–6.

10 On Carvajal's *Dulcoratio*, see Ep 2110 n10.

11 After many years spent in the diplomatic service of the Hapsburgs, Balthasar Merklin (Epp 1342 n8, 2123 introduction) had become bishop of Constance on 9 March 1529. He was now preparing to attend the Diet of Augsburg in the retinue of the emperor.

12 He would not in fact reach Innsbruck until 4 May; see Ep 2294 n7.

13 Ps 130 (129 Vulgate):8, Luke 2:38

14 Ep 2316 shows that the visit took place.

15 See Ep 2308 n19.

16 Johann Maier of Eck, who called himself Johann Eck (Epp 386:95n, 769), was professor of theology at Ingolstadt and Luther's most vociferous Catholic antagonist. He had prepared for use at the coming diet 404 articles (published in April 1530) enumerating the heresies of the reformers. Erasmus, who had always disliked and distrusted Eck, would perceive in some of those articles an underhanded attack on himself (Epp 2371, 2387).

17 Elector John of Saxony (Ep 1670) and Landgrave Philip of Hessen (Ep 2141 n6) were the foremost members of the still small group of Protestant princes.

logical experts. They say that Michael, the leading light among the preachers in Augsburg, has fled to Zürich, fearing the arrival of the emperor.[18]
I am told that the people of Nürnberg and Ulm have at long last agreed
to and signed the imperial decree that was worked out several months ago   50
in Speyer.[19] There are many reports of this sort here; I don't need to tell
you if it is safe to believe them or not. The outcome will show what is true.
Many princes and cities will fudge and fabricate until the emperor returns
to Spain, leaving graver dangers behind him than existed before. May God
grant the emperor and the princes grace and wisdom to act circumspectly in   55
all things for the glory of God and the salvation of the whole of Christendom.
Amen.

I send you my very best wishes, dearest master. May Christ long keep
you safe and well for our sake.

Überlingen, 13 April 1530. Written in haste in a spicery because the   60
courier was pressing to be on his way

With all my heart, your friend, Johann von Botzheim

To Master Erasmus of Rotterdam, the incomparable champion of true
theology and sound learning, his greatly respected mentor and patron. In
Freiburg im Breisgau   65

2311 / From Gerard Morrhy   Frankfurt, 16 April 1530

The autograph of this letter, first published as Ep 125 in Förstemann / Günther,
was in the Burscher Collection of the University Library at Leipzig (Ep 1254
introduction).

* * * * *

18 Michael Cellarius (d 1548), a Bavarian priest who went over to the reformers,
visited Wittenberg in 1524 and was then appointed preacher at the Franciscan
church in Augsburg. A popular and influential preacher, he had by 1526 become a Zwinglian and did much to hinder the progress of Lutheranism in the
city. There appears to be no substance to the rumour reported here.
19 The 'imperial decree' in question was presumably the recess of the Diet of
Speyer in 1529, which was so hostile to the evangelical estates that they submitted a solemn protest against it (see Ep 2107 n1) and, on the day after it
had been formally adopted (25 April), agreed to send an appeal against it
to the emperor. Ulm and Nürnberg signed both the protest and the appeal
and did not subsequently change their minds. In the spring of 1530, on the
other hand, as the opening of the Diet of Augsburg drew near, both Ulm and
Nürnberg sent special delegations to the emperor at Bologna and Innsbruck
to seek reassurance of his good will; see *Deutsche Reichstagsakten jüngere Reihe*
8/1 ed Wolfgang Steglich (Göttingen 1970) 581–617 (Nürnberg), 647–93 (Ulm).
Botzheim may have heard misleading reports about that.

After obtaining his BA at Paris, Gerard Morrhy of Kampen (documented 1525–56) set himself up as a printer in that city, publishing more than fifty books in the period 1530–2, most of them Greek and Latin classics. He later returned to Kampen, where he was a member of the town council from 1536 to 1548. He and Erasmus were apparently old friends, although the only surviving record of their association is this letter, written from Frankfurt during the spring book fair, and Ep 2633.

Cordial greetings. Some days ago Polidoro Virgilio sent to Cyprianus, principal of the Italian college in Paris,[1] Saint John Chrysostom's little volume 'on the comparison of a prince and a Christian monk,' which he has translated into Latin, following, as he says, your suggestion;[2] he has dedicated it to you. When, as a mark of our friendship, he had shown it to me, I had it   5
printed as elegantly as possible at my own expense in the hope that, after circulating in a thousand copies, it would be sure to get eventually into the hands of Hieronymus Froben, for I had heard that he has reissued, under the imprint of his press, all the works of Chrysostom that have been translated.[3] I have greatly admired the careful attention that Cyprianus paid to   10
this task, for he did not think it a burden to strain his old and watery eyes on this work in the interests of greater accuracy and to meet as best he could all the obligations of friendship. In case the work has not yet reached you, I am sending you a copy with the bookseller who is delivering this letter. I sent another copy to Hieronymus Froben, which may surprise you, but at   15
that time I had not decided to go to Frankfurt for the current fair.

The count of Carpi is attempting to reconstitute his line of battle, which was routed by you not so long ago, and to attack you with a determination that would put a gladiator to shame.[4] I cannot guess what the outcome will be. He has his minions, hired to use their eyes on his behalf;[5] their role is   20
to assess your writings minutely, not with the lamp of Aristophanes but

* * * * *

2311
1 Cyprianus Taleus (Ep 768:2n). The 'Italian college' was the Collège des Lombards. On Virgilio, see Ep 1175.
2 See Epp 1734:11–12, 2019:3–4.
3 The five-volume Froben edition of Chrysostom in Latin was published later in the year; see Ep 2359. Virgilio's translation was not used.
4 Alberto Pio, prince of Carpi, was now writing his *Tres et viginti libri in locos lucubrationum variarum D. Erasmi Roterodami*, the bulky rejoinder to Erasmus' *Responsio ad epistolam Alberti Pii*; see Epp 1634 introduction.
5 Literally 'has his eye-slaves, and hired ones at that.' Morrhy uses here the unusual Greek word ὀφθαλμόδουλος 'eye-slave' in the sense of a research assistant, a slave hired to use his eyes.

with that of Momus,[6] and to search diligently for anything that could be demolished or, you may prefer to say, twisted into a false accusation. There
is something else: you are acquainted with that line from the satirists: 'You
know how to fob off a shivering dependent with a worn-out cloak.'[7] Well,   25
I was told the following story by a certain Gerard, a Frisian, a young man
of considerable promise.[8] He had spent several months at the home of the
count, who had courted him with glittering promises, hoping to use his intellectual abilities against you, principally in collating the New Testament.
No mention was made of this at the start, but the man quickly realized that   30
he would displease the count if he did not carry out his assignment with the
proper severity, whether this was justified or not; so he took the first opportunity to leave as soon as he found an honourable pretext for extricating
himself from the count's ménage. As he informed me later in a letter, he
had received a tolerably satisfactory appointment with someone at Tournai.   35

I found here by the merest chance your *Epistola* to Gerard of Nijmegen.[9]
I felt very sorry when I read it, for I remember that he was a great fan of
yours when he was living with Philip of Burgundy of pious memory.[10] It
would really be better, my dear Erasmus, if the initiates in the cult of the
Muses joined forces against the sworn enemies of the republic of letters,   40
who will leave no stone unturned in their determination to make the world
abandon the use of grain and return to gathering acorns.[11] Ah, how deeply
this tragic conflict distresses me!

Gervasius, a theologian at the Sorbonne, sends you his best wishes.[12]
He would have written you quite a long letter, had not my decision   45
to make this journey been so sudden. No less disappointed on that
score were Philippus Montanus,[13] Jacobus Omphalius,[14] and Joachim of

* * * * *

6 Aristophanes of Byzantium (c 275–180 BC) was a brilliant literary critic and
philologist. Momus was the god of carping criticism and mockery.
7 Persius 1.54
8 Unidentified; hardly the author of Ep 2232
9 The *Epistola contra pseudevangelicos*; see Ep 2219 n5.
10 Philip (I) of Burgundy, bishop of Utrecht, dedicatee of the *Querela pacis*; see
Ep 603.
11 Ie return to the life of primitive man. Morrhy probably borrowed the image
from Cicero *Orator* 31. There was an old legend that primitive man lived on
acorns until the discovery of grain by Triptolemus.
12 Gervasius Wain (Ep 1884)
13 See Ep 2065.
14 Omphalius (1500–67), native of Andernach near Koblenz on the Rhine, studied Latin and Greek at Louvain before going to Paris, where he taught Latin
authors at the Collège de Lisieux (1529–35), associating with Erasmus' friends
Philippus Montanus and Gerard Morrhy. In 1535 he took a doctorate in both

Ghent,[15] who would also have written letters. Joachim has recently published a translation by himself of Galen's work *On Foodstuffs*.[16] Philippus is a busy teacher of Greek, Omphalius of Latin. As for myself, I shall be 50 working with a German who has set up a new press in the area of the Sorbonne to ensure that what emerges from the press is as accurate as possible.[17] Chrétien Wechel commends himself to you and ardently prays that you be pleased some day to spare a thought for him.[18] Farewell, most learned Erasmus, and if you ever need my help in anything, please use me as though I 55 were your servant.

Frankfurt, on the eve of Easter 1530[19]

Yours to command, Gerard Morrhy of Kampen

To the most learned Master Erasmus of Rotterdam, his deeply respected mentor. In Freiburg 60

2312 / From Bonifacius Amerbach [Basel, c 16 April 1530]

There are two hastily written and much corrected autograph drafts of this letter (= Ep 1426 in AK) in the Öffentlich Bibliothek of the University of Basel: MS C VIa 73 174 (A) and MS C VIa 54 32 (B). The first published version was

* * * * *

laws at Toulouse and then returned to Germany, where in 1537 he entered the service of Hermann von Wied, archbishop-elector of Cologne, becoming his chancellor in 1545. Following the archbishop's unsuccessful attempt to introduce the Reformation into his electoral territory, Omphalius for a time served the new archbishop, Adolf von Schaumburg, and then in 1551 entered the service of William V, duke of Cleves, undertaking several diplomatic missions on his behalf. He also served as legal adviser to the city of Cologne, where he continued to reside, and was briefly (before 1565) a member of the Cologne faculty of law.

15 Joachim Martens (Ep 2049)
16 *De alimentorum facultatibus* (Paris: S. de Colines 1530)
17 Whoever he was, this German collaborator did not get his name mentioned in any of the books published by Morrhy.
18 Chrétien Wechel (d before 18 April 1554) of Herentals, near Antwerp, moved to Paris in 1518 or 1519 and went to work for the bookseller Konrad Resch, who had close connections with Basel. In 1529, having bought Resch's shop and stock (1526) as well as the press of Simon du Bois, he became simultaneously a bookseller, publisher, and printer, specializing in textbooks, classical works, and Greek medical authors. He maintained close commercial ties with Germany and the Low Countries and was a regular visitor to the Frankfurt fairs. He was an important publisher of works by Erasmus, and in 1534 was prosecuted for selling *De esu carnium*, which had been banned by the faculty of theology.
19 Easter was 17 April in 1530.

that of Burckhardt (Ep 57), based on B. Allen based his text on A, which he
judged to be closer to the letter actually sent, but recorded a few variants in
the apparatus. Allen assigned the approximate date largely on the basis of the
news concerning Oecolampadius, which is repeated by Erasmus in a letter of
22 May (Ep 2321).

Greetings, most illustrious Erasmus. I was told by Bebel[1] that Bucer is planning an attack on you and that the text has already been submitted for publication to the press of the printer Georg of Strasbourg.[2] It will be up to
you in your wisdom to consider what needs to be done to limit the damage caused by such an unconscionable act.[3] Are there any lengths to which a   5
shameless spirit will not go? Our Oecolampadius has left no stone unturned
(as the saying goes) to ensure by threats and terror that all Basel be present
at his celebration of the Lord's Supper. He consigns all non-participants to
hell, claiming that they should be treated like dogs and considered ineligi-
ble for any public office or distinction, or, if they hold an office, that they be   10
dismissed – in fact, expelled from the city.[4]
    Where in God's name is this fellow's piety? Is this the gentleness of the
gospel? He has compelled many to keep silent, contrary to their consciences,
for fear of exile. On the day of the Supper he tried,[5] by marshalling a host of

* * * * *

2312
1 Johann Bebel, a native of Strasbourg who operated a small press at Basel; see
  Ep 1477A n8.
2 The attack was the *Epistola apologetica ad sincerioris christianismi sectatores per
  Frisiam orientalem et alias Inferioris Germaniae regiones*, published in the name of
  all the Strasbourg reformers without attribution to any one of them (Strasbourg: Petrus Schaefer and Johannes Apronianus, May 1530). The printer
  'Georg' was apparently Georg Ulricher von Andlau (documented 1525–36),
  who published a number of works by Strasbourg reformers, but evidently not
  this one. The author of the *Epistola* was Martin Bucer, but Erasmus at first believed that Gerard Geldenhouwer (Epp 2219 nn4–5, 2238, 2293) was responsible for it; see Epp 2321:26–42, 2324:1–8, and cf Allen 2365:18–20, where Erasmus names Bucer and Geldenhouwer the joint authors. For a summary of
  Bucer's arguments in the *Epistola*, see CWE 78 256–62.
3 Erasmus responded to the *Epistola apologetica* with his *Epistola ad fratres Inferioris
  Germaniae*: see Ep 2324 n2.
4 On 18 June 1530 non-conforming members of the city council were informed
  that they could not stand for re-election; see Ep 2248 n6.
5 The 'day of the [Lord's] Supper' (*dies Coenae* [*Domini*]) is the Thursday before
  Good Friday (known in the English-speaking world as Maundy Thursday),
  when Jesus held the Last Supper with his disciples before his crucifixion on
  the following day. In 1530 it fell on 14 April.

EPISTOLA

APOLOGETICA AD SYNCE=
RIORIS CHRISTIANISMI SECTA
tores per Frisiam orientalem, & alias infe=
rioris Germaniæ regiones, in qua Euangelij
Christi uere studiosi, non qui se falso Euangeli=
cos iactant, ijs defenduntur criminibus, quæ
in illos ERASMI ROTERODAMI
epistola ad Vulturium Neocomum,
intendit.

Per ministros Euangelij, ecclesiæ
ARGENTORATEN.

Act. XXV.
Multa & grauia crimina intendebant
aduersus Paulum, quæ non pote=
rant probare.

M. D. XXX.

Title-page of the *Epistola apologetica* (1530)
Martin Bucer (see 000 n2)

arguments, to defend his doctrine of the Eucharist, finally ending up with   15
this peroration: 'Neither Luther, nor Erasmus, nor the whole world will have
an answer to this.' What a triumph! The fellow is invincible! Farewell.

2312A / To Jacopo Sadoleto   Freiburg, [c 16 April 1530]

First published in the *Epistolae floridae*, this is Erasmus' tardy reply to Ep 2272,
which reached him on 30 March (see Ep 2299:57–8). Although obviously written in 1530, the letter is dated 'M.D.XXIX' (with no month- or day-date) in the
Epistolae floridae. Dismissing this as an error, Allen numbered the letter Ep 2315
and assigned the date c 14 May 1530 on the ground that on 17 May Bonifacius
Amerbach wrote to Sadoleto that Erasmus had given him a packet of letters to
be sent on to him; see AK Ep 1435:1–2. If, however, one assumes that Erasmus
was observing the Freiburg custom of beginning the new year at Easter, as is
the case with several other letters (cf Ep 2268 introduction), it follows that the
letter has to have been written before 17 April, which was Easter Sunday in
1530. This is rendered more likely by the fact that on 18 April Erasmus was
laid low by a debilitating illness that lasted until near the end of June (see
Epp 2322:2–12, 2328:5–10). It seems unlikely that he would have written such
a long and elegant letter under such circumstances. By the same token, the dispatch of a letter written shortly before the onset of a serious illness might well
have been delayed until mid-May. For these reasons we have substituted the
conjectural date of 'c 16 April 1530' for Allen's conjecture of 'c 14 May 1530.'
If this redating is correct, it means that no letters written by Erasmus have
survived for the period c 16 April–20 May 1530 (Ep 2320), and that this can
be taken as further indication of the seriousness of his illness. There would
be a similar period without surviving letters between 6 and 24 June, that is,
between Epp 2327 and 2328.

Delays en route prevented the letters of Erasmus and Bonifacius from reaching Sadoleto until 8 September. He replied to both on 17 September; see Ep
2385 and AK Ep 1466.

ERASMUS OF ROTTERDAM TO JACOPO SADOLETO, GREETING
Great piles of letters are sent to me from every quarter of the world, especially at two times in the year: before the Frankfurt fair in the spring and
again before the autumn fair. So, in trying to reply to most of them (for
how could I reply to all?) I can hardly, at such times, take proper care of   5
my health. Some of these letters are trivial, full of windy rhetoric, some are
acrimonious, and some bring me great pleasure and comfort. In this latter
class there was scarcely any (believe me!) that was more gratifying than the
letter that came from you, dear Bishop, you who bring great honour to the

prelates of our time. So I set the letter aside somewhere, intending to an-   10
swer it carefully at leisure. But as often happens to me, by trying so hard
to prevent it from going astray, I managed to lose it. Sometime, I suppose,
when I am not searching for it, it will come to hand, and what no search can
now recover will reappear.

I thought it best to begin in this way so that you will feel more kindly   15
towards me if my answer does not quite come up to the standard of your
most elegant letter. I can hardly say how much I love you for that Psalm of
yours.[1] When I read it, it affected me so strongly that once I had begun, I
did not rest until I had reached the end, hardly stopping to catch my breath.
The effect that the reading had on me was first to pique my interest, then   20
to make me more determined in my opposition to the shameless ranting
of certain people, and finally to make me more ardent in the pursuit of
piety, in a word, to make me a better person. I clearly felt the power of the
Spirit speaking through you. You would not set me on fire in this way if
you were not on fire yourself, or carry me away as you have done if you   25
were not carried away yourself by the breath of the Spirit. I do not say this,
most honoured Bishop, merely to please the ear, for I do not praise you
for yourself: rather what I venerate and cherish in you is the consummate
goodness of God. Indeed, now that bishops like you are appearing on the
scene, I am emboldened to hope that Christ will some day have mercy on   30
us and restore his badly shattered church to her former vigour.

It is my opinion that if anyone were to read this commentary of yours
carefully and learn from it, it would suffice by itself to set out a true and
holy direction for the whole of his life. Is there any part of Christian philosophy that you do not treat there with the utmost care? What a strong battery   35
of arguments you advance to confound the impious who say there is no God
and those who deny that God takes any interest in the affairs of men! How
terrifying is your thunder against those who spurn the will of God and suc-
cumb to the evil desires of the heart! How I admire the moderate balance
that you strike in praising the teachings of the philosophers on how to lead   40
a happy life without allowing us to drop the anchor of our happiness in
those waters! Then, when you have explained what was missing even in the
Jewish faith, you lead us to Christ as the sole author of true felicity. How
vividly you show us that those who have given themselves over entirely
to godlessness are deeply unhappy, even in the moments of their greatest   45
happiness, while those who have placed their total confidence in Christ find

* * * * *

2312A
1 See Ep 2272 n4.

blessedness even amid the most painful tortures and deaths! With what a
true Christian spirit you root out from the hearts of men all longing for revenge! And what a forgiving spirit you have that will not deprive anyone,
however wicked, of the hope of forgiveness! You prefer to point the way by   50
which even the most desperate may regain God's favour. Then how I admire
the frank yet diplomatic honesty with which you point out the dreadful danger that princes and bishops fall into if, turning away from devotion to God
and neglecting the welfare of their people, they set their hearts on tyranny!
Surely the whole stem and stern (as the saying goes)² of the Christian faith   55
lies in these teachings, which you set forth, expound, and drive home with
such clarity, eloquence, and passionate intensity that any reader who is not
half asleep will quickly recognize that this is a lesson that comes not from
the surface of your lips but from the inmost recesses of your heart. Moreover, your frequent citations of Scripture, always apt and relevant, convince   60
me that you are familiar with the inner sanctum of the celestial philosophy
and that your devotion to it is neither casual nor half-hearted.

What now am I to say about that truly Ciceronian flow of language,
always pure, clear, rich, and beautiful? How often have I wished that that
heavenly philosophy would find an artist of the stature of Cicero as he was   65
when he pleaded cases before the courts or expounded Greek philosophy,
someone whose genuine piety was matched by the power of his eloquence.
You, if anyone, are beginning to fill that role with great success, and seem
likely to continue to do so. There was a special reason why the apostles
passed on to us the mysteries of Christ wrapped in a somewhat uncouth   70
cover: it was to ensure that the praise that belongs only to God was not
given to the powers of men. Now the argument is different. Some have
almost submerged theology beneath a heavy blanket of secular philosophy
and have besmirched it somewhat by the meanness of their language. From
time to time you sprinkle over your work a few ideas from the writings of   75
the philosophers, but in such a way as to serve religion, not to master it,
to season it rather than spoil it, to clarify, not to obfuscate. You apply the
fertile splendour of your prose to serve religion as the obliging handmaid
of religion, not to parade herself, but by her service to commend the majesty
of her queen.   80

What deep religious feeling lies in those frequent apostrophes of yours,
now to God, and now to the holy laws! I was impressed, too, by the marvellous skill with which you introduce quotations from Scripture, which you

* * * * *

2 *Adagia* 1 i 8

do so smoothly that you do not seem (as the saying goes) to be joining one
thread to another,[3] but the whole text coheres in a smooth and continuous   85
flow. What delighted me most of all was your intellectual consistency, which
never admits anything abrupt or disconnected or clumsy or any pointless
repetition or misplaced phrase. This is the special gift of a virtuous mind,
undisturbed by the turmoil of base desires. In such minds the celestial spirit
rejoices to exercise its powers.   90

So, eminent prelate, I do not doubt that others who are in a better position to observe the bounteous kindness of Christ towards you will express
their thanks to you more fully. I, for my part, can at least acknowledge,
and will always continue to acknowledge, the vast extent of my indebted-
ness to you. Agamemnon wished for ten Nestors;[4] I offer a more fervent   95
prayer for ten Sadoletos to assist the church of Christ. I do not despair that
this will come about, for the Lord's hand is not shortened,[5] and he has not
lost completely his heart of mercy, however much it may appear that he has
abandoned us for the time being in order to test and strengthen his elect.

As for your approval of my little effort on Psalm 85,[6] I am touched   100
by your exceptional kindness as much as I admire your incomparable erudition. Before this I was completely dissatisfied with it. When I compare my
clumsy babble with your wise and eloquent words, if I were not the kind
of person who delights to be outrun by as many people as possible in any
honourable and useful contest, I would feel like hanging myself. I only wish   105
that the world of learning were in such a happy state that Erasmus would
be laughed at as the last of the Mysians or classed, like the Megarians, as
a man of no consequence or account.[7] If I produce anything of this kind, I
do it, as a rule, to oblige someone else; and it is always incidental, like an
exercise to restore the vigour of one's mind after more taxing efforts.   110

No one could easily imagine the effort I put into revising and aug-
menting the *Adages*;[8] or into cleaning up the edition of Seneca, which had
dishonoured my name when, in my absence, some friends of mine published

* * * * *

3 Ie coupling together opposite and incompatible things; see *Adagia* I viii 59.
4 See Homer *Iliad* 2.372–3, where Agamemnon says that if he had ten counsellors
  like Nestor, the city of Troy would soon be captured.
5 Isa 59:1
6 See Ep 2017.
7 'The last of the Mysians [on a voyage]' was someone who had 'laboured in
  vain' (*Adagia* I vi 78); 'Megarians' was a scornful name for 'exceptionally idle
  and worthless people who had no claims to respect at all' (*Adagia* II i 78).
8 See Epp 2022–3.

an earlier edition without giving it proper attention;[9] or the labour I devoted
to my Augustine, or recently to my Chrysostom,[10] or to translating Greek   115
texts and comparing my versions with the originals. Imagine, too, the te-
dium involved in revising my works, when, as often happens, reprints are
demanded – and I say nothing of those minor pieces that friends are constantly wringing out of me.[11] Indeed, there is no task too menial for the
Froben press to thrust upon me, taking advantage in too cavalier a manner   120
of my good nature. It is my worst fault, for which I am unable to excuse
myself, that I bring nothing to full term but produce all the offspring of
my mind prematurely. I spent scarcely seven days on that little commentary that you were kind enough to read,[12] not full days either, and I was
not working when I was fresh, but in a state of exhaustion. When six or   125
seven presses are running at full speed, it is not possible to concentrate on
a single activity. And works of this sort generally come due just before the
fairs, when the press is in a state of total confusion. This explains why what
emerges is often marred by many errors. I escaped from Basel, but the business of the press follows me like a man's shadow. It is part of my nature to   130
find it difficult to deny anything to my friends, though for some time now
my mind has been longing for rest, and age and health are also demanding
peace and quiet.

    I am sending my poor commentary on Psalm 22 in exchange for your
little gem of a book, truly, to borrow your modest expression, an exchange   135
of bronze for gold.[13] I was requested to do this by a man of exceptional
learning, especially in philosophy, something that is rare among the nobility.[14] He is the father of the girl whom the king of England is said to have
marked out to take the place of the queen. I do not know why he asked me.
I had reluctantly obliged the queen with the *Christian Marriage*,[15] being to-   140
tally unaware of what was happening. Later I got wind of the news that
divorce was already being discussed, though in secret. Although I was completely in the dark about this, nevertheless in the book I stress the indissoluble bond of marriage from so many points of view that it seems as though

* * * * *

9 See Epp 2091–2.
10 See Epp 2157 (Augustine), 2359 (Chrysostom).
11 See Epp 2266, 2273–4, 2282, 2284–5.
12 See line 100 above.
13 For the 'poor commentary' see Ep 2266; for the 'modest expression' see Ep
   2272:15–18 with n5.
14 Thomas Boleyn; see Ep 2266 introduction.
15 See Ep 1727.

I had made up my mind to argue against the divorce. It is possible that the   145
other side, in seeking this work from me, has taken a leaf out of their opponent's book. This made me hesitate for a long time whether to comply with
the request, and I would certainly not have done so, had I not noticed that
the psalm is short and that its subject has nothing to do with divorce. For
I could never bring myself to get involved in that matter, although I was   150
asked to do so more than once.[16] Things that are beyond us are no concern
of ours. Now I have both parties equally well disposed to me. I only wish
that this excellent king and his saintly wife were equally of one mind about
everything else.

You cite a certain Hesychius,[17] to whom you seem to assign priority in   155
this genre. He was previously a complete unknown to me.[18] We have Hilary,
although in mutilated form; I think that he derived almost all that he handed
on to us from the commentaries of Origen.[19] I do not understand how I failed
to think of him (and of Pomerianus, too)[20] when I was expounding Psalm
85, not that I totally trust writers of this sort, but any chance encounter may   160
make a wise man wiser. We have the psalm commentaries of Jerome, seriously corrupted by some wretched impostor, whose drivel can be seen also
on that Psalm of yours. Augustine worked in this field with some care, but
he is compelled to adapt his words to the ears of the people he was instructing, and so introduces many matters that are not particularly necessary to   165
the busy and learned reader and are sometimes tiresome. For certain psalms
he wrote only the briefest of notes, not a commentary, as is the case with
this psalm that I am sending now. Cassiodorus preferred to cover everything in one way or another rather than treat a few carefully.[21] There are
brief commentaries on the Psalms by Bruno that are to be commended more   170

* * * * *

16 Cf Epp 2256, 2267.
17 In the commentary on Psalm 93 (Vulgate), at verse 20.
18 This would appear to be Hesychius of Jerusalem, a fifth-century Greek ex-
    egete. Sadoleto in Allen Ep 2385:86–92 explains that, although he had read
    an essay of Hesychius purporting to show that all of the Psalms were writ-
    ten by David, what he knew about Hesychius' commentary on the Psalms was
    derived from citations in other writers.
19 The second volume of Erasmus' edition of Hilary (Ep 1334) is devoted to
    Hilary's commentary on about fifty of the Psalms.
20 Ie Luther's colleague in Wittenberg, Johann Bugenhagen. Erasmus calls him
    'Pomerianus,' but he was known as 'Pomeranus.' His Latin commentary on the
    Psalms had been published in Basel by Adam Petri in 1524. Cf Ep 1539:79–81.
21 Cf Ep 2143:14–34.

Johann Bugenhagen and Erasmus
Detail from a painting (now lost) by Lucas Cranach the Younger
formerly in the Church of St Blasius, Nordhausen

for piety than learning.[22] Arnobius' explication is sometimes shorter than
the psalm itself.[23] Indeed, such a varied bibliography sometimes stands in
the way of the commentator on Scripture. In this psalm I have borrowed
nothing from any source except Jerome and the notes of Augustine. I noticed
that, in the earlier psalm you sent us,[24] you drew not a little from the works   175
of Ambrose.

I have been asked more than once, by the king of England among others, to produce a commentary on all of the Psalms, but many things have
held me back, two in particular: First, I realized that the subject could not
be treated as it deserved unless one had a sound knowledge of Hebrew and   180
also of Jewish antiquities, and second, I was afraid that the prophetic message was more likely to be obscured than elucidated by a plethora of commentaries. For who has not written on the Psalms? And who has not treated
the fiftieth Psalm, in which you first gave us an example of your godly
eloquence?[25] You, however, have left all your predecessors far behind.   185

Now to turn to something else: although, in view of your authority,
rank, and godliness, I could cheerfully accept from you not just friendly admonition but even a box on the ears, yet, when you are about to fulfil the
first duty of friendship, you take great pains to soften the blow, not accepting the right to criticize except with the stipulation that the same right be   190
granted to me. But I, my incomparable friend, am accustomed to looking up
to such heroic figures as you, not to admonishing them. It seems to upset
you that in my writings I criticize monastic orders and men of high rank
– though perhaps my memory is letting me down, for I do not remember
your exact words, which I read rapidly at the time.[26] It is possible that I may   195
have allowed something to slip out somewhere, but it was certainly not my
intention to hurt any group or any order in my writing, unless showing
how an order may acquire for itself, and increase, its authority and prestige
counts as 'hurting an order.' Just as the dignity of the profession of theology lies in eschewing pointless wrangling, treating Holy Scripture soberly   200
and reverently, and acting in such a way that one's behaviour is worthy of
one's profession, so for a monastic order, dignity consists in truly mortify-
ing human desires and showing that monks surpass ordinary folk in genuine godliness; for princes, dignity lies in keeping as far away as possible

* * * * *

22 See Ep 2143 n7.
23 See Ep 1304.
24 See lines 183–5 below.
25 See Ep 1586.
26 Cf lines 10–11 above.

from tyranny; for bishops, it is to approximate as closely as possible to the   205
merits of Christ and the apostles.

Anyone who gives such advice and criticizes those who are a disgrace
to their profession is not, at least in my opinion, injuring an order, but showing a serious concern for its honour and welfare. And so, in an effort to prevent anyone from misconstruing anything I said against certain degenerate   210
members as a insult directed against all, I beg the reader time after time not
to think that what is said about a few evil men applies to all. But perhaps I err
in making the point either too frequently or too strongly. I could put part of
the blame on Holy Scripture, which constantly provides an opening for such
warnings. And if I am at fault in being too persistent and too severe a critic,   215
these men are much more at fault who, despite such warnings, do not mend
their ways but become worse every day, and are less concerned with puri-
fying themselves than with besmirching their counsellor. However, I never
mention those intimate scandals that the people are always talking about.

Furthermore, if I attempted to rehearse all the tricks, the false accusa-   220
tions, the shameless lies, and the scurrilous pamphlets that they never cease
to launch against me, the tale would be a shock to your chaste ears, and
I am only glad enough to forget it. I see that the church is everywhere in
ruins, which saddens me, as it saddens you too, but it is an admitted fact
that today no class of men is more corrupt than the monks. Augustine says   225
that in a monastery one either lives most virtuously or sins most dangerously.[27] It is this latter case that the world now sees – and sighs. But the
monks, far from hastening to amend their lives, resort to subterfuge and
bullying. Many are so blind that, even though they realize that their actions
are getting them nowhere except to make them more and more hated by   230
all decent people, nevertheless they never stop stirring up trouble. I have
written many *apologiae*, I admit, but, I am proud to say, I have never written an invective. I have not responded to the outrageous attacks that many
have made on me, and when I have responded, I have shown myself many
leagues ahead of all my accusers in moderation and civility, although, as a   235
rule, one is more indulgent towards the party that has been provoked than
towards the provoker.

When, as a young man, I immersed myself in good literature, I greatly
admired in Naso the fact that he never soaked his pen in another's blood,[28]

* * * * *

27 Ep 78.9; cf Ep 2037:220–1.
28 Ovid (Naso) frequently claims, especially in his apologetic poems from exile,
    that he never injured anyone by his pen; see eg *Tristia* 2.563–8, *Ex Ponto* 4.14.44,
    and cf *Ibis* 1–6.

and I decided to imitate his example. For a long time I stood by this resolve,   240
although bitterly provoked on many occasions, until it came to a slanderous attack on my religious views. At that point I could not be silent, nor
should I have been. Nothing annoyed certain monks so much as the fact
that I refused to become a heretic to please them!

    If I were to describe all the acrimonious attacks on me from those who   245
hide under the false banner of the gospel, neither you nor anyone else would
believe me, but I, who experience these attacks, think that even death itself
would not be more bitter. And although there are many on the other side
who repay me for my efforts with hostility, I have never wanted to depart from the right path, always looking to Christ alone. I was ready to   250
die ten deaths rather than join any of the sects and turn away from the
fellowship of the church.[29] I admit that among the monks there are some
godly men, but it is obvious that this pitiful tragedy in which the world
is the victim had its opening scene and second act in the scandalous conduct of some members of that order, and I am much afraid that these same   255
people will preclude the ending that we long to see. Some time ago certain
Dominicans preached on indulgences in an intolerably impudent manner.
Luther countered in characteristic fashion.[30] This was the opening scene of
the drama. Prierias then produced an offensive reply,[31] to which the other
responded more offensively still.[32] Jacob of Hoogstraten, thinking he had   260
found a field for gain and glory, stirred up trouble everywhere.[33] Then in
Brabant came the seditious ranting of Nicolaas Egmondanus in his public
sermons.[34] Anyone who gave good advice was immediately branded 'a supporter of heretics.' This was the second act, where the plot of the tragedy
thickens.   265

                * * * * *

29 See Ep 2263 n3.
30 It was the hawking of indulgences by the Dominican Johann Tetzel in 1517
   that elicited from Luther his *Disputation on the Power and Efficacy of Indulgences*,
   commonly known as the Ninety-Five Theses (31 October 1517).
31 For Prierias (Silvestro Mazzolini of Priero) and his 'reply' (*In praesumptuosas
   Martini Lutheri conclusiones de potestate papae dialogus*, June 1518), see Ep 872
   n19.
32 *Ad dialogum Silvestri Prierati de potestate papae responsio* (August 1518); WA 1
   647–86.
33 In 1519 Hoogstraten (Epp 290:11n, 1006), visited Louvain, where he persuaded
   the Louvain theologians to follow the example of the theologians of Cologne
   in condemning Luther's writings. He also showed them (and others) Ep 980
   as evidence that Erasmus was friendly to Luther. See Ep 1030 n7.
34 For Nicolaas Baechem, known as Egmondanus, see Ep 1256 n6.

If at the start Martin had been left alone, the present conflagration would not have broken out, or at least would not have spread so widely. Now certain members of the Franciscan community who commend themselves to the people under the title of 'the Observance' are rushing into the arena.[35] Speaking for myself, I would be glad to see this scourge upon the church dealt with in some way or other, but when these people take action, I fear they only make matters worse. Think of the turmoil they caused in Spain, even holding great personages in contempt![36] Now two young men are writing books that are absolutely scurrilous, defying an edict of the emperor and the authority of the archbishop of Seville.[37] It is one's duty, they say, to obey God rather than men.[38] But that old refrain is an insult to the authority of bishops and the supreme pontiff. How often they have tried, in the Parlement of Paris, before the English bishops, at the emperor's court in Brabant, to prevent the books of Erasmus from being sold! Everywhere they have been met with deaf ears.[39] They have a young man, still beardless, in Louvain, who has the effrontery to commit to print any nonsense that falls from his lips during a meal with his friends, and every month he produces a new book.[40] Although he is laughed at by everyone, such is his egotism that he is incapable of any feeling of self-doubt. In the face of this sort of rubbish I have decided to preserve a stubborn silence in future. It would be easier to argue with a cardinal than with an ordinary member of that community.

I do not know what effect the emperor's arrival will have.[41] The Lord by a nod of his head can make a sudden change on the human stage. Unless he does so, I foresee nothing but a bloody uprising in Germany. The people and the peasants are in general either Lutherizers[42] or impatient for any chance to show their hatred of the priests. Nowadays sensible churchmen are

* * * * *

35 See Ep 2275.
36 For the turmoil in Spain, ie the charges of heresy against Erasmus that were heard at the conference of theologians at Valladolid in June–August 1527, and for developments since, see CWE 13 xii–xiii, 14 xiv–xvi, 15 xvi. Erasmus' word here for 'great personages' is *principes*, which in context cannot be translated simply as 'princes.' See Ep 2094 n5.
37 The two young men are Carvajal and Titelmans; see Epp 2299–2301.
38 Acts 5:29
39 See Epp 1721, 1902 introduction, 1905 (Parlement of Paris); Epp 1697:26–30, 90–7, and 124–6, 1704:24–46 (English bishops); Epp 1300:1–5, 1747 (emperor's court in Brabant).
40 Titelmans; see Ep 2261:71–5.
41 See Ep 2294 n7.
42 An invented, deliberately contemptuous term

as fearful of the princes and the soldiers as of heretics. In addition, hiding
under the name of the gospel are some desperately wicked people, who are
ready for any mischief. Two things give us some hope: one is the wonderful
genius of the emperor Charles,[43] and the second is that these people disagree   295
among themselves over their own doctrines.

As for me, standing here, as I do, between the altar and the knife,[44] I
place myself in the hands of the Lord. I see no quiet haven for myself, and
my poor body, almost broken under the weight of years,[45] has long dreaded
a change of residence. I note the care and circumspection with which you   300
pick your words whenever you give advice to kings and bishops on their
duty. This is the peculiar gift of that exceptional nature of yours; but although sensible and moderate advice delights the honest man who reads it,
it does not have the same effect on evil men, who are deeply oblivious of
their weaknesses.   305

However, in this matter I would not wish to be totally defensive. I
recognize that some of the fault is mine.[46] I misconstrued the tranquillity
of the age. I gave in to the wishes and the plaudits of my friends. If only
it were possible to unweave the past and begin again! I never suspected
that people could be so painfully sensitive to criticism. But now I am trying   310
as best I can to avoid offending anyone, especially in works that deal with
issues of faith and piety, and I take your moderation as a model for myself.
I imagine that these people have tried even your gentle patience with their
protests, for is there any place into which they do not poke their noses? Is
there anyone whose feelings they do not hurt, whose ears they do not weary   315
with their accusations, accusations that are generally without substance? I
pray the Lord will instil in them a better frame of mind so that they change
their behaviour and show themselves to the world as the sort of people they
would like to be thought to be.

I have already gone on too long about these matters. But I wanted to   320
assure your charitable self that your admonition was much more welcome
than your praise – although I am not unaware that both proceed from a
sincere and generous mind. Farewell.

I have noted a few printing errors on a separate sheet. It is up to you
to decide what is to be done about them.   325

Freiburg im Breisgau, 1529[47]

* * * * *

43 On Charles' 'genius,' see Ep 2302 n4.
44 See Ep 2253A n17.
45 But cf Ep 2275:24–37.
46 Cf Ep 1887:11–15.
47 The correct year-date is 1530; see introduction above.

2313 / From Caspar Ursinus Velius   Linz, 20 April 1530

> This letter was first published LB III/2 1290–1 *Epistolae* no 1109. For Ursinus
> Velius, holder of the chair of rhetoric at the University of Vienna and official
> historian to King Ferdinand, see Epp 1810 n35 and 2008 introduction.

It is true that I have written nothing in reply since your man Polyphemus
delivered your letter.[1] First, there was no one to whom I could properly
entrust a letter; then at the very time when I received your letter, I was acting
in the role of a suitor, a preoccupation that takes precedence over, and blots
out, everything else; later when it was time to marry, war was imminent,   5
and the enemy was on top of us, for he began pouring into Austria before
we expected him to arrive.[2] So instead of the music of the harp and all the
other tomfooleries that generally accompany a wedding,[3] I was serenaded
throughout the whole night by the rattling of Turkish arms almost under
the very walls of our historic and beautiful city. At the celebration of our   10
wedding we had none of those things that you strongly and, in my opinion,
rightly condemn in your little book dedicated to the British queen.[4] In fact,
far from any strong desire for them, I hated the charged eroticism and all
the trappings of a depraved and degrading sensuality. But – and this was
the most bitter pill of all – when I had been a husband for scarcely a single   15
night, I was forced, as soon as dawn appeared, to send my wife off with her
relatives. I followed her three days later, but it was only with difficulty that
I evaded the weapons of our grim enemy, who was laying waste everything
behind me with fire and sword.

After the siege was lifted and the enemy had departed, I found, on re-   20
turning to Vienna, that we had suffered a serious loss of property, both my
wife's and my own; outside the city the damage came from the depreda-
tions of the enemy and inside from the actions of our defenders. I do not
know which was more destructive, the savagery of the enemy in the country-
side or the greed, blatancy, and unparalleled brutishness inside the walls.   25
Among their own people, our defenders were edgy and violent, but faced

* * * * *

2313
1 The letter is not extant. Felix Rex, known as Polyphemus (Ep 2130 introduction)
  delivered it to Ursinus Velius in March 1529; see Ep 2130:87–8.
2 The Turkish advance from Hungary into Austria began in May 1529; the siege
  of Vienna began on 20 September and was lifted on 15–16 October.
3 Cf Ep 1756 n23.
4 The *Institutio christiani matrimonii*, dedicated to Catherine of Aragon; see Ep
  1727.

with the enemy, they became cowards and deserters; almost all of them, when tempted by the rich resources of the city, especially the wine, spread havoc everywhere with no sense of shame, destroying property both human and divine. Among them was a small band of Spaniards who, out of all proportion to their numbers, earned more genuine praise than those fine regiments that were sent to Vienna from the furthest regions of Germany. 30

On this subject I cannot write to you at present either freely or fully because I am afraid my letter may be published or circulated in some other way; moreover, there is hardly enough room in a letter to deal properly with a subject like this, which could scarcely be covered in a dozen books. I have asked you before not to publish any of my letters, for I often write things that could appear foolish or would be likely, if made public, to harm their author. Generally, I concentrate more on the subject I am writing about than on stylistic elegance or literary embellishment. So I have good reason to insist that you suppress any letters I have sent you in the past and any I shall send in future. I shall write at greater length when we get to Augsburg with the king.[5] Yesterday for the first time I returned here from Vienna, where I had spent three months of hard labour and effort on a description of the siege of that city,[6] which was once the most noble and beautiful of all but is now sadly disfigured by fire and plunder, the work of our enemies and our own soldiery. 35 40 45

I am enchanted by Henckel because of the gentleness of his character and the delight of his company, and my spirits are wonderfully raised and refreshed by his sermons.[7] He does not adopt the censorious and ill-tempered attitude taken by many German preachers, but is straight in teaching, brief in admonition, and modest and infrequent in rebuke; and since past faults cannot be put right, he concentrates on correcting present faults and dispelling future temptations from the minds of men. If only there were ten wise counsellors like him![8] Then we could easily storm the city and the defences of the ungodly, and conflicts among Christians would be less serious and less frequent. 50 55

Brassicanus showed me several epigrams by French writers,[9] including even Lascaris, in support of Budé and against you.[10] I am sure that you,

* * * * *

5 Ferdinand
6 His narrative of the siege is in book 6 of his *De bello Pannonico* (Vienna: Trattner 1762) 110–27.
7 Henckel was now residing in Linz; see Ep 2309.
8 See Ep 2312A n9.
9 For Brassicanus see Ep 2305.
10 For Lascaris et al and their epigrams see Epp 2021 introduction and 2027:27–30 with n14.

being a man of great good sense with a strong and self-confident mind, will
take no notice of them. Nor should you let it trouble you overmuch that   60
these squawking roosters of Frenchmen[11] are trying to drown out the song
of Philomela,[12] or be upset by Greeks criticizing a German. If they understand what you had in mind when you wrote your *Ciceronianus*,[13] then their
attacks are impious and unfair, whether they take the form of abusive language or foolish jests. Farewell, excellent and most learned Erasmus. Give   65
my greetings to my friend Bonifacius,[14] a most generous man, and also to
Beatus[15] and my other friends.

From Linz in Upper Austria, 20 April 1530

2314 / From Konrad von Thüngen   Würzburg, 9 May 1530

The manuscript of this letter, which was first published as Ep 126 in Förstemann / Günther, was in the Burscher Collection of the University Library at
Leipzig (Ep 1254 introduction). It is Thüngen's reply to Ep 2303. Erasmus'
response is Ep 2361. The translation is faithful to the constipated wordiness of
the original.

KONRAD, BISHOP OF WÜRZBURG, TO DESIDERIUS ERASMUS
OF ROTTERDAM, CORDIAL GREETINGS
Last year, when Master Augustinus Marius was moving from Freiburg to
Würzburg, you gave him a letter for me,[1] which contained, among other
things, your commendation of Marius. In the letter you said that you were   5
not commending him to us, since you knew that his merits were in themselves the best commendation; rather it was your hope and prayer that,
thanks to him, you yourself would be the more commended. Meanwhile
we have come to realize how closely the outcome has matched your wishes,
for by his integrity, character, and learning, in which he has so far given   10
an excellent account of himself, Marius has shown himself fully deserving of your commendation, and at the same time, by his frequent trum-
peting of Erasmus' praise, he has raised your status among us, although

* * * * *

11 Once again the pun on *galli* (roosters, cocks) and *Galli* (Frenchmen)
12 According to Ovid and other poets since, Philomena, the daughter of Pandion,
   was turned into a nightingale.
13 Ep 1948
14 Amerbach
15 Rhenanus

2314
1 Ep 2164

it is true that your own admirable erudition and eloquence have earned you the commendation and respect of the whole world. He has given us such a graphic account of your character, conversation, habits, intelligence, and all your kindly, affectionate, and pleasing ways, that we consider you as familiar to us as someone whom we have got to know, not by one or two meetings or conversations, but by a long and intimate association.

As for your present letter of commendation for Daniel Stiebar,[2] the same commendation has come from certain others, who have warmly praised the young man's intellect and avid interest in the humanities. But your encomium carries more weight with us, since you do not commend anyone lightly or you show us what a person has done to earn your commendation. So our hearty congratulations go not just to Stiebar, whom we admire for the quality of his mind, but also to our chapter for the honour it has gained by the addition of such a fine colleague. Both men are very dear to us, Marius and Stiebar, because they are the kind of men who earn their commendation on their merits, but also because it was on account of them that we have been fortunate enough to receive two learned and erudite letters from Erasmus, who is by far the most learned and erudite scholar in the world. So although we are greatly obliged to Erasmus himself, since of his own free will and without any provocation from us he has graciously agreed to enter into a pact of friendship with us, yet we readily admit that we owe something to both these men too, since it was through them that we had the chance to begin this friendship.

We are avidly reading the psalm that you sent us through Stiebar.[3] There is nothing in it that is not truly Erasmian, that is to say, it is elegant, brilliant, and timely. But so that you may have some appreciation of our good will in return, we are sending you with this letter a cup,[4] and we beg you most sincerely not to value this little gift by the cost of materials or workmanship, but by the mind of the donor; please accept it as a souvenir of your friend. Farewell, my most learned Erasmus, continue to hold us in your affection.

Würzburg, 9 May 1530

To the illustrious and erudite theologian Desiderius Erasmus of Rotterdam, his very dear friend

* * * * *

2 Ep 2303
3 The commentary on Psalm 22; see Ep 2266.
4 A large gold cup decorated with the bishop's arms; see Major 41, Sieber 5.

2315 / To Jacopo Sadoleto

This letter has been assigned the conjectural date 'c 16 April 1530' and now
appears as Ep 2312A.

2316 / From Johann von Botzheim   Überlingen, 18 May 1530

The autograph of this letter, which is in sequence with Ep 2310, was in the
Burscher Collection of the University Library at Leipzig (Ep 1254 introduction). It was first published as Ep 127 in Förstemann / Günther.

Greetings. I really do not know, my most learned mentor, by what fate it
came about that, when there was nothing I wanted more than to have a long
conversation with you, I was allowed only an unusually brief talk, without
our customary give and take, and in a low voice hardly above a murmur.
The serious illness from which you were suffering was the principal ob-   5
stacle in the way of that first talk, for it was evident that conversation was
very difficult for you.[1] However, when we talked the second time, God had
brought a considerable improvement to your health, though you were left
with a lingering fear that the old familiar pain would return at any moment and your body was so weakened and enfeebled that all conversation   10
seemed a burden to you. As a result, any possibility of a lengthy chat in
a free and easy manner disappeared. I wanted to thank you for the splendid letters addressed to me that you included in your *Opus epistolarum;*[2]
I also wanted to discuss several other matters, and of course to enjoy the
usual delights of conversation. All this was made impossible by your un-   15
fortunate illness, which had discomposed and depressed your spirits. So
there is no reason for you to suspect anything else. The same thing happened to our dear Bonifacius,[3] as we confessed to one another in a private
conversation.
      The emperor is having a busy time in Innsbruck, where he is sur-   20
rounded by a large number of ambassadors from kings and princes. The
Netherlandish cavalry, having suffered an intolerable affront from the
people of Kempten, have declared themselves public enemies of the little

* * * * *

2316
1 On the illness that befell Erasmus in March 1530 and became worse in April,
  see Ep 2320 n1.
2 Published in the summer of 1529; see Ep 2204 introduction.
3 Amerbach

town. Kempten, after seeking advice from all the surrounding cities, though
without success, finally dispatched envoys to the emperor, who sent a cool   25
response to their town council in terms that made clear his suppressed indignation. Two hundred horsemen have occupied the area round about, so
no one can safely move from Kempten. What this initial action means, I do
not know.[4]

Balthazar, our newly confirmed bishop,[5] has only one theme in his cor-   30
respondence with me, the intolerable and troubling storms that, he says, are
imminent, and so terrible as almost to take his breath away; he sees only
faint promises of hope. I foresee nothing good ahead, only empty gestures
and promises as insubstantial as a puff of smoke. May Christ make all things
work for our salvation! There is little to be hoped for in the protection of   35
princes. Farewell, my beloved master.

From Überlingen, 18 May 1530

Your humble and devoted friend, Johann Botzheim

To that true and most learned theologian and most eloquent of writers,
Master Desiderius Erasmus of Rotterdam, his respected mentor. In Freiburg   40

2317 / From Ferdinand to the Town Council of Freiburg

Innsbruck, 18 May 1530

The letter was first published by Allen. The original document, written in German in a secretary's hand and signed by the king himself, is in the Öffentliche
Bibliothek of the University of Basel (Erasmuslade Ba 2). There is a hastily written contemporary copy in the Rehdiger Collection of the University Library at
Wrocław, but Allen deemed it to be of no importance.

Erasmus had made his first will in 1527; see CWE 12 538–50. Now, evidently
motivated by the illness that was dogging him at this time (Ep 2320 n1) he was
contemplating making another; see Epp 2320:12–13, 2324:16–18. In the present
letter, doubtless requested of him by Erasmus, King Ferdinand wrote to the
city council of Freiburg to remove any legal obstacles they might put in the
way (cf Ep 2318).

* * * * *

4 Kempten was a free imperial city in the Allgäu, northwest of Innsbruck, on
the emperor's route to Augsburg. It had formally adopted the Reformation in
1527, though the bishop and the chapter remained loyal to the old church. We
have been unable to find further information about the incident referred to
here.
5 See Ep 2310 n11.

As far as is known, Erasmus did not in fact act on his intention at this time. He drew up a second will at Freiburg in 1533, but no copy of it survives. The following year he had an inventory of his possessions drawn up (Major 38–47, Sieber). But it was not until February 1536, after his return to Basel, that Erasmus made his final will (Allen XI 362–5).

FERDINAND, BY THE GRACE OF GOD KING OF HUNGARY AND BOHEMIA, ETC, INFANTE OF SPAIN, ARCHDUKE OF AUSTRIA, ETC

To our honourable, wise, especially cherished, and faithful councillors
It has come to our notice that the honourable and learned scholar, our beloved and pious Erasmus of Rotterdam, in view of his age and chronic ill health, 5
wishes to make a last will and testament and to direct how his books and other belongings are to be disposed of, and, consequently, that he wishes to designate and appoint executors for that purpose. He is, however, concerned that you might hinder him in this because of some privilege or municipal code or custom.   10

Since he has come to you as a guest and is eager to draw up a final testament respecting his property according to his own will and pleasure, and since we hold him in our special favour and deem his intentions to be good and Christian, it is therefore our desire that you be pleased, in accordance with our will and for the aforementioned reasons, to grant and 15
afford this favour to the said Erasmus of Rotterdam and also provide him with the documents with which he may draw up a will and allow him, for the administration of same, to appoint several executors of his choice. You will thereby do us a good favour in compliance with our intention.

Given in our city of Innsbruck on the eighteenth day of May in the 20
year etc [15]30, the fourth of our reign.[1]
Ferdinand
Seen by Bernhard, cardinal of Trent[2]
On the personal instructions of my lord the king
R. Wising[3]   25
To the honourable, wise, our especially cherished and faithful burgo-master and council of our city of Freiburg im Breisgau

* * * * *

2317
1 Ferdinand had been crowned king of Bohemia in February 1527, and of Hungary in the following October; cf Ep 2295 n8.
2 Bernhard von Cles, Ferdinand's chancellor (Epp 1357, 2007)
3 Presumably the secretary

2318 / Letter Patent of Charles V   Innsbruck, 20 May 1530

This letter was first published by Allen. The original document, written by secretary Schweiss (line 46) and signed by the emperor (line 44), is in the Öffentliche Bibliothek of the University of Basel (Erasmuslade A9).

CHARLES, BY THE BENEFICENT MERCY OF GOD THE EVER-AUGUST EMPEROR OF THE ROMANS AND KING OF GERMANY, THE SPAINS, BOTH SICILIES, JERUSALEM, HUNGARY, DALMATIA, CROATIA, ETC, ARCHDUKE OF AUSTRIA, DUKE OF BURGUNDY, BRABANT, ETC, COUNT OF HAPSBURG, FLANDERS, AND TYROL, ETC

5

By the tenor of these presents we make this known to all. Although it is our practice to attend with our grace and favour each and all of our faithful subjects, yet we regard as deserving of our special favour those who assist us and the common weal by their wise counsel, and who by their labours enrich the world. Hence it is that when our honourable, devoted, and beloved Desiderius Erasmus of Rotterdam, our councillor,[1] informed us that he desires to make testamentary provision for his property and seeks authorization from our Majesty so that the procedure will be sound and considered valid,[2] we, considering the justice of the request, and being desirous to oblige the aforementioned Erasmus in this, as we would in much more important matters, and acting on our own volition and with full knowledge, and by virtue of the plenitude of our absolute imperial authority and under any higher prerogative, grant and accord to Erasmus permission, licence, authority, and power to bequeath, will, and dispose of all his goods and effects, both during his lifetime and by his last will, or otherwise as may seem good and pleasing to himself. And acting now as in the past and and in the past as now, we, by virtue of our inclination, knowledge, and plenary authority, as aforementioned, approve all the arrangements and dispositions of the said Erasmus with regard to his possessions, notwithstanding, in all these cases, any laws, constitutions, ordinances, decrees or statutes whatsoever, and in particular any laws of the city of Freiburg im Breisgau, where he himself resides at present, that may mandate a contrary disposition. It is our wish and intent that, by virtue of the plenitude

10

15

20

25

* * * * *

2318
1 See Ep 370:18n.
2 Cf Ep 2317.

of our authority, each and all of such regulations be set aside to this end   30
and on this occasion, even if they are such as would require a special mention in these presents. We wish and intend that all the provisions of this letter be taken as a full and comprehensive statement, and we command each
and all of our dear and faithful subjects, whether of the Holy Empire or
of our hereditary lands, of whatever rank, status, and condition, to firmly   35
observe this our grace and concession and to see that it is carried out without violation, under pain of our displeasure and that of the Holy Empire
and of the payment of a fine of ten marks of pure gold, one part to our
imperial treasury and another to the victim of the injury.[3] By testimony of
this letter, signed in our own hand and provided with the stamp of our   40
seal. Dated Innsbruck, the twentieth day of the month of May in the year
of our Lord 1530, the tenth of our emperorship[4] and the fifteenth of our
reign.

> Charles
> On the personal instruction of his imperial and Catholic Majesty   45
> Alexander Schweis[5]

2319 / From Bonifacius Amerbach   Basel, [c 20 May 1530]

This short note (= AK Ep 1436) was first published by Allen. There are two
autograph rough drafts of it, both of them on the same sheet and the first
having only two lines, in the Öffentliche Bibliothek of the University of Basel
(MS C VIa 54 33 verso). Allen assigned the date on the ground that the note
was written shortly before Ep 2323.

* * * * *

3 This was a very heavy fine. The mark (*marc*) was a mint-weight unit widely
 used in late medieval and early modern Europe; here it undoubtedly refers to
 the mark of Cologne, used in the Rhineland and many other parts of imperial
 Hapsburg Germany. It weighed 233.856g. See CWE 1 324–5. In 1530, the value
 of that weight of fine gold on the Antwerp market was £22.569 groot Flemish, so that ten marks of fine gold were worth £225.69 (CWE 12 645 Table 2).
 That sum was equivalent to 5,981.7 days' wages (or 28 years' money wages at
 210 days per year) for Antwerp master masons/carpenters in 1526–30 (whose
 mean summer-winter daily wage was 9.05 d groot Flemish; CWE 12 691 Table
 13). That amount of money would have bought 15,686 litres of Rhine red wine
 in 1526–30 (CWE 12 661 Table 6A).
4 Charles dated the year of his emperorship from that of his coronation at
 Aachen on 23 October 1520.
5 Ep 1192

Cordial greetings. I am sending you, most distinguished Erasmus, a bundle of letters that I received from France;[1] they are later perhaps than you would wish, but you must put the blame on the shameless behaviour of the couriers. The day after I received them, I happened upon a courier who was starting off in your direction.   5

I am eager to know if you are now free from illness.[2] The courier who reports that you are strong again will deserve a splendid gratuity. No better or more welcome news could reach my ears. Farewell, most distinguished Erasmus.

In Basel   10

2320 / To Bonifacius Amerbach   [Freiburg], 20 May [1530]

This letter (= AK Ep 1437) was first published by Allen. The surviving manuscript, in the Öffentliche Bibliothek of the University of Basel, is a sixteenth-century copy in the hand of Basilius Amerbach, Bonifacius' older brother (MS G II 13a 50). Bonifacius' answer is Ep 2323.

Greetings. My stomach at any rate is getting better, my fatigue is diminishing, but the small lumps remain under my navel, and there are constant jabs of pain, sometimes rather mild, sometimes agonizing. I fear the problem is about to become chronic.[1] The doctor is very kind and not unlearned, but this poor body of mine is peculiar and the illness is unknown. If you know   5
of a doctor in Basel with more experience who could prepare an unguent or plaster or emollient that would be effective against such abscesses, send it by a courier hired at my expense, unless you happen to have a reliable man at hand. I shall settle with the doctor and the pharmacist. Tonight I am going

* * * * *

2319
1 None of them appear to have survived.
2 See Ep 2320 n1.

2320
1 This is the first indication in a letter of Erasmus himself that the disorder of the bowels first reported in March (Ep 2294:12–13) had subsequently developed into a serious and frightening illness featuring abdominal lumps. For earlier references to the illness by others, see Epp 2316:1–12, 2319:6; and for Erasmus' preoccupation with it see Epp 2321:2–4, 2322:2–12, 2326:5–10, 2328:6–10, 2329:62–75, 2332:2–28, 2341:3–5, 2343:7–23, 2349:6–9, 2353A:46–69, 2356:34–8. For an informed opinion concerning the identity of the illness, see the appendix, 'Erasmus' Illness in 1530,' 410–11 below.

to take an aperient to relieve the bowels, but I am wretchedly afraid that my   10
stomach will suffer a relapse. I would be happy to be rid of this wretched
body of mine. When Zasius returns from the thermal baths,[2] I shall work
on my will.[3]

Claudius is writing to you; he has now turned his mind seriously to
Greek.[4] I wish you and all your family the best of health. The plague is   15
breaking out sporadically in several places here; some people have come
down with the sweat.[5] Those winds that blew in the afternoons in April
were exceptionally cruel. They were the Etesian winds that blow in Italy
only in July and August, and only around three in the afternoon, when the
heat is intolerable. Farewell.   20

20 May

To the most learned Master Bonifacius Amerbach, jurist, his dearly
beloved friend

2321 / To Augustinus Marius   Freiburg, 22 May 1530

First published in the *Epistolae floridae*, this letter, clearly the answer to one no
longer extant, is the only one of the letters exchanged between Erasmus and
Marius to survive.

A native of Ulm, Augustinus Marius (1485–1543) studied at Vienna (1513–
19) and then spent a year in Padua, where he acquired a doctorate in theology. In 1521, after brief membership in the Vienna faculty of theology, he
moved to Regensburg as cathedral preacher and (from February 1522) suffragan bishop of Freising. In 1525 King Ferdinand's minister Johannes Fabri (Ep
2097) recommended Marius to the cathedral chapter at Basel, which was looking for a new cathedral preacher. Confirmed in office in April 1526 and made
suffragan bishop of Basel in March 1527, Marius soon established himself as
a vigorously polemical opponent of the reform party led by Oecolampadius.
Following the triumph of the reformers in the winter of 1528–9, Marius left
Basel for Freiburg, but in the summer of 1529 departed for Würzburg to take
up the post of cathedral preacher, bearing with him letters of recommendation

* * * * *

2 See Ep 2321:6. On Zasius see Ep 2209 n8.
3 See Ep 2317.
4 Not Claudius Janandus (Ep 2141), as Allen speculated, but Claudius Cantiuncula (Ep 2062 n18); see AK Ep 1452:11–12, where Bonifacius writes to Cantiuncula: 'Erasmus writes that you have now seriously turned your mind to
  Greek.'
5 See Ep 2209 n31 and cf Ep 2322:13–14.

from Erasmus to Bishop Konrad von Thüngen and Daniel Stiebar (Epp 2161, 2164). Although the present letter and others (eg 2303, 2314) are evidence of good relations between Erasmus and Marius, the latter was clearly one of the two 'monks' whom Erasmus charged with responsibility for stirring up religious passions in Basel and preventing a return to the kind of moderation that had made it possible for him to live in that city (Ep 2211:66–9). In 1536, Marius was made suffragan bishop of Würzburg.

ERASMUS OF ROTTERDAM TO AUGUSTINUS MARIUS, GREETING
For upwards of two months now I have been battling with a most persistent illness, stomach cramps. I got no help from the doctor, but one must never despair of the mercy of the Lord.[1] Baer has been ill too, but he is well again, although still so weak all over that he fears a relapse.[2] Glareanus triumphs.[3] 5
Zasius, before going to the baths,[4] cleaned out his bowels with an enema, which produced twelve very large stools, if the story the doctor told me is true. So purged, he is stuffing himself in the baths with strawberries, milk, and malmsey so that his belly will not be empty.

That commendation I wrote for you turned out most fortunately for 10
me, for, as a result of it, I have gained the acquaintance and the affection of so great a prince.[5] You owe me nothing for the commendation, for you possess in yourself all the magic that is needed to win the friendship of honest men. I am sending you several copies of my *Epistola ad gracculos*,[6] so that you will have something to interest your friends. I am against its being printed 15
in your town, if for no other reason than it might stir up people's interest in seeing the writings of the jackdaws, which would then become more marketable.[7] In fact, I regret myself having written that letter. In it I brag a great deal about my health.[8] Nemesis seems to have overheard my boasting and plunged me into my present trouble.[9] Nor do I see any good reason 20

* * * * *

2321
1 See Ep 2320 n1.
2 Cf Ep 2322:21–2. Baer (Ep 2225) had now moved from Thann to Freiburg.
3 Cf Ep 2302:34–7.
4 Cf Ep 2320:12 with n2.
5 The commendation is in lines 45–52 of Ep 2164, addressed to Bishop Konrad von Thüngen. For the development of friendly relations with the bishop, see Epp 2303, 2314.
6 Ep 2275
7 The plan to publish it at Würzburg was not carried out, nor was a similar plan at Louvain. Cf Ep 2352:311–14.
8 See Ep 2275:24–37.
9 See Ep 2209 n34.

why you should print my letter to you or to the Right Reverend bishop.[10]
If I am granted my health, you will find another subject more deserving of
print. I beg you most earnestly to continue commending me to your prince.
Please remember to give my fond greetings to the theologian whose name
you preferred to keep from me – could it perhaps be Usingus?[11]   25

Vulturius has had my *Epistola* secretly printed at Strasbourg with added
comments, in other words, with the addition of scurrilous abuse.[12] I reported
this by letter to the town council of Strasbourg.[13] Emmeus tells me that the
printer was thrown into jail on his return from the fair.[14] Now a load of
prosy trash has come out with the printer's name, but without mentioning   30
the city.[15] I have read none of it except the headings,[16] nor do I intend to
read it. He says that at Basel everything happened without any kind of dis-
turbance and in complete calm. With regard to the statues, he offers as an
excuse the fact that someone accidentally touched a statue with his spear and
soon after it crumbled. Then when one or two people tried the same thing   35
with a stick, the statues that were touched crumbled. They perceived in this
miracle the manifest will of God, and so demolished the rest of the statues

* * * * *

10 The letter to Marius is not extant, but it was probably contemporary with the
   one to the bishop, Ep 2303.
11 Erasmus writes 'Vemgus,' which is most likely a misreading of 'Usingus,'
   which would identify Bartholomaeus Arnoldi of Usingen; see CEBR III 360.
   Usingen (c 1465–1532) studied at Erfurt from 1484, taking his doctorate in
   1514, and taught scholastic philosophy and theology there until 1526. He
   was one of Martin Luther's teachers and belonged to the same house of Augustinian Eremites. Though sympathetic to humanism, Usingen strongly opposed the Reformation. In 1526 he left Erfurt to join the Augustinian house at
   Würzburg. He attended the Diet of Augsburg in the entourage of Bishop Konrad von Thüngen, which included also Daniel Stiebar and Augustinus Marius,
   to whom he appears to have been close.
12 For the unauthorized edition of Erasmus' *Epistola contra pseudevangelicos* by
   Gerard Geldenhouwer ('Vulturius') see Epp 2219 n5, 2238, 2289.
13 Ep 2293
14 Erasmus' informant was Johannes Faber Emmeus (d 1542), who had set up
   as printer at Basel in 1526. When the reformers gained control of Basel in
   1529, Faber joined the Catholic exodus and set up business in Freiburg, where
   he developed a close personal and working relationship with Erasmus. The
   most important of the works that he published for Erasmus was the *Epistolae
   palaeonaeoi* of 1532.
15 Bucer's *Epistola apologetica*, which Erasmus was still inclined to attribute, at
   least in large part, to Geldenhouwer, who is presumably the 'he' of line 32; cf
   Ep 2312 n2. While it is true that the colophon does not include the name of
   the city, it does name the Strasbourg firm that published the book.
16 Ie the topic headings, which are in the margins

too.[17] Almost everywhere one encounters this same arrant silliness. They
added to the title-page 'By ministers of the word,' since they need the services of two schoolmasters, one of whom, the rumour goes, is Scopegius.[18]   40
I suspect the work was printed outside the city to avoid a fine. So much for
the guileless simplicity of the gospel!

I would be happy to go on longer, if my health allowed it. On Holy
Thursday Oecolampadius, after setting out his case, added these words (I tell
you what I heard) 'Neither Luther, nor Erasmus, nor the whole world, will   45
be able to find an answer to this.'[19] He argued with great vehemence that
those who refused to come to his table should be expelled from the city.[20]
A great number have taken communion at neighbouring villages, some of
whom have been fined three pounds. Eight hundred have abstained completely from communion. These ominous reactions do not please Oecolam-   50
padius. Some, however, through fear, have set aside conscience and shared
his table. Farewell.

Freiburg im Breisgau, 22 May 1530

2322 / To Daniel Stiebar   Freiburg, 23 May 1530

This letter was first published in the *Epistolae floridae*. Stiebar, having spent
several months in Erasmus' household in Freiburg, was now back home in
Würzburg; see Ep 2303.

ERASMUS OF ROTTERDAM TO DANIEL STIEBAR, GREETING
After you left me, my dear Stiebar, all my good luck deserted me. My
strength has not yet returned after the illness with which March greeted
me.[1] On Easter Monday[2] treacherous breezes, which blew here during almost
the whole of April, though only in the afternoons (I imagine they were the   5
Etesians,[3] for north and east winds blew in the mornings) put their grip on

* * * * *

17 Folios I[8] verso–K verso. For Erasmus' own account of these events, see Ep
   2158:3–37.
18 Nothing is known of Scopegius (mentioned also in Allen Ep 2615:145–8), except that Erasmus thought he was one of the authors of the *Epistola apologetica*.
19 See Ep 2312:14–18.
20 Cf Epp 2248:16–18 with n5, 2281:9–10, 2312:6–11.

2322
1 See Ep 2320 n1.
2 18 April
3 See Ep 2320:17–20.

Moritz von Hutten
Bayerisches Landesamt für Denkmalpflege, Munich
Photo-Verlag Gundermann, Würzburg

my stomach below the navel, causing the most excruciating cramps. When the trouble persisted, I sent for the doctor, a kindly man and not without learning, but since he is unfamiliar both with my body and with the nature of this disease, he has so far brought no relief, in fact, what he administered 10 generally made things worse. I have been in this state now for upwards of a month, with no hope anywhere in sight except in the mercy of the Lord.[4] Many here have come down with the plague and with the sweating disease, and not a few with stomach cramps.[5]

If things go with you as you wish, that gives me great joy. As for recent 15 events, I think you people are better informed than I am. Best wishes, my dearest Stiebar.

Freiburg, 23 May 1530

Doctor Hieronymus – you know whom I mean – is dead.[6] You saw him from your horse when he invited us to a formal ceremony, and all of you, 20 dressed in green, and looking like locusts, paraded on horseback. Ludwig Baer has been ill too, but seems to have recovered.[7] Give my affectionate good wishes to Master Hutten.[8]

2323 / From Bonifacius Amerbach   Basel, [c 23 May 1530]

First published by Allen, this letter (= AK Ep 1438) is Bonifacius' answer to Ep 2320. The two autograph rough drafts in the Öffentliche Bibliothek of the University of Basel are in such close agreement that Allen deemed only one of the variants worthy of recording (MS C VIa 54 57 and 61). The letter was written shortly after the arrival of Andreas Karlstadt in Basel on 22 May (n5), and not long after 20 May, the date of Ep 2320.

* * * * *

4 See Ep 2320 n1.
5 Cf Ep 2320:15–17.
6 After studying with Udalricus Zasius at Freiburg, Hieronymus Jud of Pforzheim joined the Freiburg law faculty in 1528, serving as rector of the university for one term and thereafter twice as dean of the faculty. Payment for his funeral is recorded in the records of the faculty of law, 11 June 1530.
7 Cf Ep 2321:4–5.
8 Moritz von Hutten (1503–52), whose father was a magistrate of Würzburg and a cousin of Ulrich von Hutten, was Stiebar's fellow canon at Würzburg and had studied at Basel at the same time as Stiebar. In 1539 he was elected prince-bishop of Eichstätt. Among other things, he undertook the collection of the writings of his cousin Ulrich, many of which might otherwise have been lost to posterity.

Greetings. Recently I sent you a bundle of letters from France.[1] I would not like to think that it was not delivered, since the courier, whom I came upon by mere chance, promised faithfully to take it to you. I added a letter of my own, for I was eager to find out about your health – love, you know, is full of fear and anxiety.[2] But in the meantime I have just received your   5
letter,[3] from which I learned that your stomach is regaining its strength, your fatigue is departing, and, best of all, you have been brought back from death's door to good health. No news could have pleased or gratified me more than this. May Christ, our Saviour, grant that you continue to improve hour by hour.   10

I have diligently carried out your instructions about doctors. I approached Holzach, among others, to whom, some years ago, you did not hesitate to entrust your body.[4] Each was eager to show off his learning; yet while they differed astonishingly on the diagnosis, there was complete unanimity on this: that it would not be worthwhile to consult them except (to   15
employ a legal term in a medical context) 'in the presence of the subject,' where there would be an opportunity to interview the patient or to diagnose the problem from an examination of the urine. Otherwise, if they had made up some kind of plaster or poultice, I would have sent it at once.

Karlstadt arrived here recently with his wife and children.[5] If we take   20
Melanchthon's word for it, in doctrine he is a Judaizer and a revolutionary.[6] Nevertheless, Oecolampadius received him into his home with great

* * * * *

2323
1 Cf Ep 2319:1–2.
2 Ovid *Heroides* 1.12
3 Ep 2319
4 Eucharius Holzach (1486–1558), town physician at Basel and friend of the Amerbach family
5 By 1524 Andreas Karlstadt, one of Luther's earliest supporters at the University of Wittenberg, had incurred Luther's wrath by (among other things) his encouragement of iconoclasm and his opposition to infant baptism. Expelled from Saxony at Luther's behest, Karlstadt published at Basel a series of pamphlets in which he became the first of the reformers to deny the doctrine of the Real Presence; see Ep 1369 n7. In 1525 he sought and received reconciliation with Luther, but by 1529 he had fallen from favour once again and had to flee from Saxony; see Ep 1616 n6. He arrived in Strasbourg in February 1530 but, despite the hospitality and support offered him by Martin Bucer, was ordered to leave the city on 9 May. He went from there to Basel, arriving by 22 May; see Zw-Br Epp 1023, 1025, 1028.
6 Bonifacius is most likely referring to the letter of January/February 1530 that served as the preface to Melanchthon's *Sententiae veterum de coena domini*. In it

respect. Lucky Basel, to be constantly blessed with such fine men![7] As for
that buffoon of a Franciscan, Hieronymus will fill you in when he sees you.[8]
Farewell, Erasmus, my distinguished friend.   25

    Basel

    Your friend, Bonifacius Amerbach

2324 / To Bonifacius Amerbach   [Freiburg, c 25 May 1530]

> This letter (= AK Ep 1439) was first published in the *Epistolae familiares*. The
> autograph is in the Öffentliche Bibliothek of the University of Basel (MS AN
> III 15 21). Allen assigned the conjectural date on the basis of the receipt of Ep
> 2318 (lines 16–18).

Cordial greetings. If you have read that rubbish from the preachers of Strasbourg,[1] would you please note down their most blatant lies. For most of
the facts are unknown to me, especially what happened at Zürich or Bern
or St Gallen. That wretched man asserts that nothing happened in any of
those places as a result of violence. I have replied to his letter point by   5

* * * * *

    Melanchthon, who had a penchant for demonizing the 'impious' and 'bestial'
    Karlstadt, blamed him for the 'all the fanatical teachings of the Anabaptists'
    as well as the errors of the Zwinglians concerning the Real Presence (on the
    latter charge cf Ep 2204 n4). He also levelled the charge that Karlstadt was an
    advocate of the view that Mosaic law should replace Roman law as the basis
    for court decisions. See MBW Ep 868 T 4/1 48–9.

7 Oecolampadius received Karlstadt warmly but could not find him employ-
    ment. So Karlstadt departed for Zürich, where he spent most of the next four
    years as deacon at the hospital and corrector for the Froschauer press. In 1534
    he was called back to Basel, where he was to spend the rest of his life (d 1541)
    as a highly respected figure. He became preacher at St Peter's and professor
    of Old Testament at the university, where he served as dean of the faculty of
    theology (1536–41) and rector (1537–8).

8 Allen says that the Franciscan was perhaps Frans Titelmans (Ep 2206 intro-
    duction), which is possible. But 'buffoon' sounds more like Luis de Carva-
    jal, whom Erasmus had called 'Pantalabus,' the name of the buffoon in Ho-
    race's *Satires*; see Ep 2110 n10. Whichever Franciscan it was, it appears that
    Hieronymus Froben had brought back news of him from the Frankfurt book
    fair.

2324
1 Bucer's *Epistola apologetica*, which Erasmus still thought was largely the work
  of the 'wretched man' (line 4) Gerard Geldenhouwer (called 'Nijmegen' in line
  7); see Ep 2312 n2.

point,[2] except that the conclusion is missing in my copy. Perhaps they did that on purpose, for it is there that Nijmegen has a sting in his tail like a scorpion. I do not intend to publish it, but I shall send copies to several friends at court so that they will know what kind of schemers they are. However, I would not like them to get the slightest inkling that I dignified that trash of theirs with a reading. They had spread the rumour at Augsburg that the book affected me so badly that I had a breakdown and died. I have no doubt that Eppendorf spread that rumour through his agents.[3] Carlowitz wrote that for more than twenty days Eppendorf tried to get a meeting with the duke,[4] but without receiving an answer. I do not doubt that he is devising some ingenious plot under Nijmegen's instructions. The emperor sent me a carefully worded diploma, permitting me to make a will, free of all impediments whatsoever.[5]

To the most excellent Master Bonifacius Amerbach, doctor of laws. In Basel

2325 / To Erasmus Schets   Freiburg, 1 June 1530

> This letter was first published by Allen on the basis of the autograph in the
> British Museum (ms Add 38512 folio 44). Schets' reply is Ep 2364. On Schets,
> see Ep 2243 introduction.

Greetings, my special friend. Haio Cammingha of Friesland owes me forty crowns *soleil d'or*, which he borrowed from me, also twenty-six gold florins for board. He is to pay that sum in the same gold coins of proper weight, although, even so, I shall not come out of the transaction without a loss. I gave it to him on the understanding that if he did not happen to return here and he paid that sum to you, I would regard the debt as discharged.[1]

* * * * *

2 Apparently a draft of what was later to be published as the *Epistola ad fratres Inferioris Germaniae* (Freiburg: Johann Faber Emmeus, [September] 1530).
3 On the rumour and Eppendorf's supposed role in spreading it at Augsburg, cf Allen Ep 2400:29–31.
4 Duke George of Saxony. The letter from Carlowitz (for whom see Ep 2342) is not extant.
5 Ep 2318

2325
1 On Haio Cammingha and his debt to Erasmus, which was not repaid until 1531, see Epp 2073 introduction, 2352:305–10, 2356:46–9, 2364. The French *écu au soleil* was first struck in 1475, replacing the illustrious *écu à la couronne*,

The emperor and the princes have met;[2] I do not know yet what they are discussing. I am afraid there will be war; the pope and the priests are pressing for it. I hate the very idea of war. Everything here costs four times as much, and one can hardly obtain basic necessities. What will happen if war breaks out?

In England twenty pounds sterling of my pension, covering the period from last year to Easter just past, remain to be collected.[3] I wrote to the archbishop that he should hand the money to Luis de Castro.[4] So please see that the archbishop gets his letter.[5] Best wishes to you and yours.

Freiburg, 1 June 1530
Your friend, Erasmus of Rotterdam
To the honourable Erasmus Schets. In Antwerp

2326 / To Bernhard von Cles   Freiburg, 6 June [1530]

This letter was first published by Allen on the basis of the autograph rough draft in the Royal Library at Copenhagen (MS GKS 95 Fol, folio 235). On Bernhard von Cles, bishop of Trent and King Ferdinand's chancellor see Epp 1357, 2007.

TO BERNHARD, BISHOP AND CARDINAL OF TRENT
Greetings, Right Reverend Bishop. For this new honour, which is the just reward of your great virtues, my congratulations go not so much to you as to the church of God. [1] You will now be able to assist the church more effectively by reason of your increased authority. As for me, I have been afflicted by a most persistent illness that has lasted now for more than fifty days. At first I had cramps in the belly, now I am troubled by a huge abscess

* * * * *

first struck in 1385 (CWE 1 315–16). In 1530, it was the only French gold coin issued, with an official value of 40s *tournois*. See CWE 14 476 Table 3; CWE 12 354–5; Ep 1750 nn2–3.
2 At the diet in Augsburg. The emperor was in fact still on his way to Augsburg and would not arrive there until 15 June (cf Ep 2294 n7).
3 In 1530, Easter fell on 17 April. For the pension, see Ep 2332 n10. £20 was equivalent in value to 800 days' wages (3.81 years' money-wage income) for a Cambridge master mason.
4 Schets' agent in London (cf Ep 2270 n4)
5 The letter is not extant.

2326
1 Bernhard had been created cardinal on 19 March 1530.

below the navel.[2] Drugs have proved harmful. My poor body has been dehydrated. My digestion is wrecked. I was thinking of Italy. Perhaps God is
about to call me to his home. I only wish he would see fit to do so!   10

I beg your Highness now more urgently to do what you have most
generously done in the past and act as my friend and defender against my
slanderous attackers, who are to be found everywhere. In Spain there is a
young Franciscan whose audacity would make any gladiator look a weak-
ling; he has published a book full of intemperate and unscholarly drivel.[3]   15
The printer, however, has not dared to add his name or the place of publication. They are also planning other books. The emperor's absence had given
them courage to do so. But I remain firm in my decision that from now on I
shall not dignify such rubbish either by reading or refutation. The preachers
of Strasbourg have published two attacks on me that are so silly and fool-   20
ish that, far from thinking of answering them, I could not even bear to read
them.[4]

Heinrich, who carries this letter was, I think, once with you.[5] I would
not, however, want to put the least pressure on you by commending him.
There are many people with many needs. I am not particularly close to the   25
man.

May the Lord keep your Eminence well.
Freiburg, the morrow of Pentecost

2327 / To Cornelis de Schepper   Freiburg, 6 June [1530]

This letter was first published in *Vita Desiderii Erasmi Roterodami* ed Paul
Merula (Leiden: T. Basson 1607). Allen based his text on the original letter, an
autograph that in 1922 was in the private collection of D. Hudig of Rotterdam.
It is now in the Rotterdam City Library (Erasmuszaal 94D 5), which acquired
it from the Hudig family in 1974.

Cornelis de Schepper (Ep 1747 n23) was a trusted administrator and diplomat in the service of Charles v. It is doubtful that Erasmus and Schepper ever

* * * * *

2 See Ep 2320 n1.
3 Luis de Carvajal; see Ep 2110 n10.
4 One of these was Geldenhouwer's annotated edition of Erasmus' *Epistola contra
   pseudevangelicos* (Ep 2289 n2). The other was Martin Bucer's *Epistola apologetica*,
   which was published in the name of all the preachers at Strasbourg (Ep 2312
   n2). Erasmus would respond at length to the latter in the *Epistola ad fratres
   Inferioris Germaniae* (Ep 2324 n2).
5 On Heinrich, see Epp 1689 n3, 1690:164; and cf Epp 2331:2–3, 2344:2–4.

met, but they had many friends in common, including the imperial chancellor Mercurino Gattinara, which led Erasmus to regard Schepper as an influential ally. Schepper answered this letter from Augsburg on 28 June (Ep 2336).

Greetings. I have been battling a most persistent illness, not without danger to my life.[1] Do let me know what has happened to Alfonso de Valdés. For many months he has not written a word.[2] Either he is ill, or has been sent off somewhere, or has changed his attitude towards me. I would also like to have news of my friend Lieven.[3] This is the most I can write, dear Cornelis. 5

Freiburg, the morrow of Pentecost

Erasmus of Rotterdam

To the most learned Master Cornelis de Schepper, secretary to the emperor

2328 / To [Lorenzo Campeggi]   Freiburg, 24 June 1530

This letter was first published in the *Epistolae familiares*. The manuscript is a contemporary copy on two folio leaves that are bound with the collection of Erasmus' letters to Bonifacius Amerbach in the Öffentliche Bibliothek of the University of Basel (MS AN III 15 18a). On the second leaf the same hand has copied Ep 2341. Two letters to Bonifacius from Erasmus' servant Quirinus Talesius (6 and 11 January 1531) reveal that the two leaves containing this letter and Ep 2341 were written by Talesius for communication to Bonifacius and that both letters were addressed to Campeggi. See AK Epp 1488:1–18, 1491; and cf Allen's introduction to this letter.

Campeggi (cf Epp 2215 n17, 2256 n7), once again papal legate to Germany, had accompanied the emperor to Augsburg, where the imperial diet was now in session.

It seems to be your destiny to have the most difficult legations laid upon your shoulders.[1] Of course it is to outstanding leaders that the most burden-

* * * * *

2327
1 See Ep 2320 n1.
2 See Ep 2292.
3 Algoet had departed at end of March to the emperor's court and had found it at Trent; see Ep 2278 n2.

2328
1 The most difficult of all had been his legation to England to deal with the matter of the divorce; see Ep 2215 n17. His current mission was to prevent any concessions to the German Protestants at the Diet of Augsburg.

some tasks are usually assigned, and in your case the difficulty of these tasks is overcome by superb intelligence. It is a great pity that the force of that intelligence is impeded by poor physical health.   5

As for me, I have been battling now for a third month with a most persistent illness, so severe that I could not write or dictate or listen attentively to someone reading to me, while every day my poor body became more and more dehydrated. This was the Lord's will. Today the lancing of an abscess offers me some hope of recovery.[2]   10

Nothing compelled me to leave Basel except the open attack on the old religion and the constant revolutionary turmoil.[3] The Froben press depended on me almost totally. Even those who were ill disposed towards me because of our dogmatic differences wanted me to stay in Basel for fear that, by leaving, I might stir up hostility against them if it appeared I was   15 leaving out of hatred of their sect. First Oecolampadius, along with the tribune,[4] who was the force behind this whole business, pressed me strongly not to leave lest my departure bring odium upon the city. Finally they tried to find a pretext for detaining me on one excuse or another, but found none, for I was under obligation to no one on any account. Nor did I slink away   20 secretly: I left at noon from the bridge, a very busy place, after chatting for a long time with my friends. My departure did not pain me overmuch. I was glad to leave such a city, though it grieves me that a famous and elegant city, whose hospitality I have enjoyed for so long, has been brought to such a state. If only this were the only one whose fate we mourn!   25

The move meant a financial loss but turned out to be beneficial to my health.[5] How the world will receive me, I do not know. For a long time I have been looking for a place where I could await my final hour in peace and live to myself.[6] But nothing has turned up so far. This poor body of mine has many requirements, in particular it needs a good wine.[7] But not everything   30

* * * * *

2 In Ep 2332:24–8, also dated 24 June, the surgery is described as having taken place 'a few days ago' and Erasmus is already recovering. It follows that this letter to Campeggi was begun several days before the date given to it when it was dispatched. Cf lines 131–2.
3 For detailed narratives of Erasmus' departure from Basel in April 1529, see Epp 2158, 2196, 2328, and cf CWE 15 xi–xiii.
4 Jakob Meyer; see Ep 2158 n9.
5 See Ep 2209 n12.
6 'Live to myself' (*mecum vivere*); the phrase is borrowed from Cicero *De senectute* 14.49, where it refers to a quiet and independent old age free from the distractions of ordinary life; cf *Adagia* I vi 87.
7 On Erasmus' need for good Burgundy wine, see Epp 1342:504–41, 2057 n1, 2115:10–12, 2329:77–9, 2330:16–19, Allen Ep 2348:7–9.

I require is available everywhere. Moreover there is no shortage, on both sides, of people who wish me ill. Those who have given their allegiance to rejected doctrines hate no one more than me. In this group I have no more bitter enemies than those with whom I was once joined in the closest ties of friendship.[8] On the other side I have a number of griping critics who are trying to make me a Lutheran whether I want to be or not.[9] So on both sides I am lashed by bitter tongues and bombarded with the most virulent libels. But I consider it something of a distinction to be abused by men who are themselves condemned.

I find it easy to ignore all the silly nonsense that comes from the monks:[10] it is simply laughed at by every sensible person. But I wonder what motivates Alberto Pio, once prince of Carpi, to turn his pen against me.[11] He has already published a book in Paris,[12] to which I made a civil response.[13] Now, as I discover from the letters of my friends, he is working on another volume and, surprisingly, is using several paid assistants, in particular a Spaniard called Sepúlvela.[14] The gist of his argument is that I have been the cause, source, and leader of this whole ghastly tragedy. He collects passages that seem to be in line with Luther's teaching, although, if one is not bent on calumny, not a single idea of mine would be found to agree with Luther's. You would think it was a dark secret where this trouble first started! How much more useful it would have been if he had collected from my writings those passages that challenge Luther's teachings, of which the number is infinite. But if this is to be my fate, I shall find consolation in an easy conscience and in the judgment of good men.

Sometimes I think of Italy, but it is embarrassing for an old man to go travelling abroad. I found the climate of Padua congenial and I was charmed by the courtesy of the Italian people.[15] Although there are many things to

* * * * *

8 Ie the 'false evangelicals' of Strasbourg and elsewhere in southwestern Germany, with whom Erasmus was currently engaged in controversy; see Epp 2219 n4, 2238, 2312 n2, 2324, 2338:56–65, 2341:11–16.
9 Ie the Catholic critics who made Erasmus responsible for the Lutheran heresy; see Ep 1987 introduction.
10 Most recently the Franciscans Frans Titelmans and Luis de Carvajal; see Ep 2275 introduction.
11 See Ep 1634 introduction.
12 *Responsio accurata et paranaetica*, written in 1526 and circulated in manuscript but not published until January 1529 by Josse Bade in Paris
13 *Responsio ad epistolam paraeneticam Alberti Pii* (Froben: March 1529)
14 Cf Ep 2311:20–3. Again Erasmus misspells Sepúlveda; see Ep 2261:75–7.
15 See Ep 2209:31–5.

draw me to my native Brabant, there are as many to frighten me away, among them the weather, which I doubt my poor body could stand;[16] then there is the imperial court: if I attend it, that will be the end of me, and if 60 I fail to participate, I shall appear to be doing out of contempt what I am compelled to do from necessity.[17] But I shall think about this matter if my health happens to take a turn for the better.

Finally, I come to your request that I should indicate my hopes and my fears in the present state of the world,[18] though I see men who have far 65 more insight and a far deeper knowledge of German affairs, both public and private, than I have, who am only a visitor here. I can discern no way out of this enormous tragedy unless God suddenly appears like a deus ex machina and changes the hearts of men. I pray he may be pleased, in his mercy, to bring this about through the power and piety of the emperor. This, in my 70 opinion, is our only hope. Whenever I think of the plans and strategies of men, I see no hope at all. On the contrary, the more carefully I consider all aspects of this present evil, the more my mind trembles with foreboding when I ask myself what the world is bringing forth out of this appalling turmoil. It would be a happy outcome if this plague could be cured without 75 death and bloodshed, and there would be some hope of this if the factions would moderate their stubbornness. I fear, however, that if we resort to the knife, the face of Germany will be a pitiful sight, for not to mention the uncertain outcome of war, especially when the evil is so widespread, to look to cautery and surgery for a remedy would be to sacrifice almost the 80 whole body. So if one must make a choice from the worst of evils, it would perhaps be better to leave things in their present state of equilibrium until God takes pity on us and stretches out his healing hand.

In these circumstances, when there has been so much turmoil in the cities and when time and again people on both sides have rushed off to 85 arms, I have often wondered why not a single drop of blood has been shed so far and civil and peaceful relations have so far been preserved. There are many sore spots, many complaints by servants against their masters,

* * * * *

16 Ten years earlier Erasmus had nothing but praise for the climate of Brabant; see Ep1221 n4.
17 Erasmus had always been unwilling to compromise his own freedom by becoming a resident courtier to (and therefore partisan of) any of the warring monarchs of Europe. One of the principal attractions of Basel and Freiburg was that both were safely remote from royal and imperial courts.
18 A similar request reached him from Gattinara in Ep 2336:20–6. See also Epp 2339, 2341–4, 2346. Erasmus felt that he had already addressed the subject in his *Epistola ad pseudevangelicos*; see Ep 2308:13–15 with n7.

not always, it is said, unfounded. This was the spark that touched off the
peasant uprising,[19] whose ashes, I fear, are still smoldering. Then there are   90
complaints by the common people against the princes. Add to this the universal hatred of the clergy, which is not confined to Lutherans but common to almost all the laity. These bitter feelings have been inspired in no
small measure by our pride, extravagance, and blatant immorality. Yet we
see no one learning a lesson from these disasters and converting to a bet-   95
ter way of life. In Germany at present even those who detest the sects are
not much inclined to favour the pope – so much so that unless backed
up by the full force of authority, it would perhaps be better for the apostolic legate not to be there.[20] On top of all this there is the ferocity of the
Turks; I do not know how far it will go, for there is no doubt that they   100
fear the power of the two brothers, which is increasing every day.[21] Need
I mention not just the high cost but also the scarcity of everything? Finally,
supposing there was a meeting of wills among the princes of Germany,
how will a war be successful that is waged largely by an unwilling soldiery? For just as in those cities that profess the new doctrines there are a   105
number of Catholics, so in Catholic cities there are very many of a different persuasion. But once the signal for war is given, Erasmus will perish
like the proverbial bean at the end of the row.[22] For this place is far from
safe.

     I do not know if anyone but God could heal this spreading wound   110
that is now so badly inflamed, for it lies in his power to bring about a
sudden reversal in the human drama. We would have more hope that this
will happen if the princes of both estates,[23] in company with all other leaders, would, with a common purpose, turn their eyes towards Christ. But
if everyone looks to his own advantage, as they have done so far, we can   115
only pray that God in his mercy will bring something good out of the ill-

* * * * *

19 Of 1524–5
20 Ie at the diet in Augsburg
21 Cf Ep 2211 n12.
22 The Latin is *extrema faba*, literally 'a bean on the edge.' The expression, not
   found in the *Adagia*, refers to something or someone liable to be the first to
   perish, just as a bean at the end of a row is most likely to be stepped on or to
   be the first to be picked.
23 The language is imprecise, but Erasmus presumably means both the imperial bishops, who had princely rank and seats in the imperial diet, and the
   princes who ruled the secular principalities of the Empire. As Erasmus was
   fully aware, there was little hope of them acting in concert to resolve the
   religious divisions of Germany.

considered schemes of men, for it was he, and he alone, who was offended by man's sins and permitted this plague to invade his church, and he alone can remove it when he so chooses. What else can we see in this but evidence of the anger of Almighty God when such a huge defection has taken 120 place in so short a time through the efforts of humble and insignificant men. Think how quickly and how widely that ungodly error about the Eucharist spread![24] Think how blindly the hapless Anabaptists are rushing to their deaths![25] And the people of Germany are in such a mood that if someone came forth with an even sillier doctrine they would immediately embrace 125 it. May the Lord grant that all of us with one mind will turn to Christ our shepherd. I pray that the spirit of Christ will guide the minds of the emperor and the princes towards sound counsels for our deliverance. I shall be more willing to move from here if I see this dreadful tempest turned to calm. 130

I have dictated this with difficulty over several days because of the desperate state of my health.[26] I have written with exceptional frankness, trusting in your good nature. Please accept my most heartfelt and respectful greetings. May the Lord sustain and prosper you in all your doings.

Freiburg im Breisgau, the feast of St John[27] 1530 135

2329 / To Andrea Alciati   Freiburg, [c 24 June] 1530

This letter, Erasmus' reply to Ep 2276, was first published in the *Epistolae flori-dae*. The manuscript is an autograph rough draft, much corrected by Erasmus himself, in the Royal Library at Copenhagen (MS GKS 95 Fol, folio 210). The letter failed to reach Alciati, so a copy was dispatched to him in September; see Allen Ep 2378:10–11).

Allen found the dating of the letter difficult. Given that Erasmus' surgery (Ep 2328 n2) is behind him, it cannot be earlier than June. He speaks here (lines 72–3), as in Epp 2328:6–7 and 2330:7–8, of his illness being in its third month. In Ep 2326 it has passed the seventh week, and in Epp 2343 and 2348 it is in the fourth month. These considerations, and others cited by Allen in his introduction, support his conjecture that this letter is of the same date as Epp 2330–2, which follow it immediately in the Copenhagen manuscript.

* * * * *

24 Ie the denial of the Real Presence by Zwingli and his followers; cf Ep 2219 n12.
25 See Ep 1926 n9.
26 See Ep 2320 n1.
27 John the Baptist

TO ANDREA ALCIATI

Greetings. Because of the affection that I feel for you, which is a natural response to the outstanding qualities of your mind, you will not be surprised
that I was deeply pained by the utter ruin (or should I say, the complete
shipwreck) of your fortunes. Your last letter, however, gave me to under- 5
stand that my consolation was completely superfluous, since that Rhamnusian storm,[1] which was so awful as to make many a man into an atheistical
Diagoras,[2] not only failed to cast you down but turned you from a jurist
into a philosopher or, to be more precise, showed that, without changing,
you already are a philosopher. Evidently you possessed all along this great 10
force of character, but the cruelty of Fortune brought out what had previously lain hidden. It acts just like fire, which when it applies its force to gold
makes it finer and brighter. So it was with Fortune, which, in raging against
Alciati, did not make him despondent, but, through the loss of ordinary possessions, enriched and ennobled him in the true and lasting blessings of the 15
mind. For here was no creature made of figwood but a man, golden in the
purity of his heart, and adamantine in the strength of his spirit.[3] So, my dear
Alciati, I am delighted to change my tune and to send you, in place of a consolation, my congratulations on possessing these rare gifts from a beneficent
deity; with these you can rise above the universal despotism of Fortune. 20

It was a testament to your sense of duty that you wished above all
to be a good citizen to your homeland, but God wished your learning to
shine down on greater numbers. It seems somehow to be generally true that
the splendour of a man's genius is seen more dimly in his own country,
which, as the Lord points out in the gospel, is also attested by a Hebrew 25
proverb.[4] Zeno thought himself fortunate because, having lost his cargo by
being shipwrecked on his way to the Piraeus, he was thrust by this mishap

* * * * *

2329
1 Ie a storm sent by the goddess Nemesis, who had a shrine at Rhamnus in Attica and was often referred to as Rhamnusia. Nemesis, as goddess of retribution, is usually represented as bringing down the mighty because of their
   hubris; see *Adagia* II vi 38. But here there is no implication that the shipwreck
   of Alciati's fortunes had been a deserved punishment for hubris.
2 Diagoras of Melos, Greek philosopher and poet remembered for his spirited
   advocacy of atheism; see *Adagia* III iv 72.
3 Figwood was proverbially useless for any purpose; see Ep 2291 n4.
4 The sentiment is found in all four Gospels: Matt 13:57, Mark 6:4, Luke 4:24,
   John 4:44, but in none of these passages is there any reference to a Hebrew
   proverb.

into the study of philosophy. He lost his cargo of purple and found wisdom, which is more precious that all the wealth of the world.[5] I shall call you happy not, as you modestly suggest, because the loss of all your property   30 taught you that these transient things, which are given and taken away at the whim of Fortune, are of very little importance, but I give thanks to Fortune for revealing in a clearer light the greatness of your soul, something that I always suspected before. I first appreciated the loftiness of your mind when I observed that in all your writings there is never any trace of jealousy, nor   35 do you launch a bitter attack on anyone, although there has been no lack of provocation. I have no doubt that the radiance of your virtues will dispel all the mists of envy.

I am delighted that legal studies are flourishing in Bourges, even though, if what I am told is true, the city is not yet on good terms with the   40 Muses. I was particularly pleased that my efforts in commending Sucket and Viglius to you turned out to be totally superfluous.[6] Viglius, as I gather from his letter,[7] is thoroughly at home in the garden of the Muses; Sucket, although he too applies himself – and not without success – to polite letters, is more interested in legal studies.[8] I hope he will continue on this path   45 until he brings back to his native Flanders the laurel he has earned by his merits. He had a father and an uncle, both of whom were distinguished jurists and among the most popular and thoughtful members of the prince's court.[9] So the success that the son has in this branch of learning could appear to be part of his inheritance. I do not know Viglius by sight. But from his   50 writing I have abundant evidence of this young man's abilities, which hold the promise of considerable learning. Sucket has a most friendly and warmhearted nature. I love both of them very much, but you will give them the final polish, so that I shall love them more and more. Whatever distinction or influence they will ever acquire, they will attribute to Alciati. I congrat-   55 ulate both of them on not moving here: know that Sucket dallied with that question for a considerable time. Zasius teaches here, and he is certainly a great man – I doubt if Germany can boast of another like him – but already old age is pressing on him, and I do not yet see any successor who is ready

* * * * *

5 Zeno, the founder of Stoicism, was originally a merchant, but after his shipwreck and the loss of a valuable cargo of purple dye, he turned to philosophy.
6 For the commendations, see Epp 2210:8–14, 2213:24, 2276:31–4.
7 Ep 2210
8 See Ep 2191 introduction.
9 See Epp 1331 n11, 1556.

to match his reputation,[10] though there is no lack of scholars who teach the   60
law conscientiously and with some success.

My own Rhamnusian goddess[11] has treated me rather badly this summer. March launched the attack and April struck again while I was still
rather weak. The illness was caused by winds that were gentle enough, but
carried a deadly infection. At the beginning the only symptom was cramps   65
in the stomach. This was followed by an abscess, which affected different
places at first but soon settled around the navel. Nature would have rid
me of this completely if I had kept away from the doctors, who, by some
quirk of fate, have always spelled disaster for me. A surgeon was called
in too, a self-confident fellow who promised great things. Despite point-   70
less warnings, he tried to convert a hard abscess into an ulcer, and came
close to killing me with the pain from his powerful poultices. I spent three
months like this when I could neither eat, nor sleep, nor read, nor write –
hardly even talk with my close friends. Growing weary of the treatment,
we lanced the abscess with a knife. So I am gradually coming alive again,   75
and there would certainly be hope of recovery if only the fleas would allow
me to sleep[12] and I could get the kind of wine that was regularly supplied
to me during his lifetime by Ferry de Carondelet, archdeacon of the church
at Besançon.[13] The local wines here do not agree with me.

I am delighted that you and Budé have patched up your friendship.[14]   80
I still doubt if he is very well disposed to me, whatever certain people claim
or deny. I suspect there are some who are turning his mind against me.[15]
It is enough for me that I have given him no excuse to be any less friendly
towards me. So far none of the Lutherans has taken up his pen against me
except Luther himself, who, however, was satisfied with a single bout.[16]   85
Gerard of Nijmegen,[17] who was once a zealous supporter of Erasmus but

* * * * *

10 Born in 1461, Zasius (Ep 2209 n8) would live until November 1535.
.11 See n1 above.
12 Cf Allen Ep 2362:7–8.
13 See Ep 2328 n7.
14 In 1520–1 Alciati and Budé had become involved in a literary dispute; see Louis
    Delaruelle *Répertoire analytique et chronologique de la correspondence de Guillaume
    Budé* (Paris 1907; repr New York [1963?]) Epp 38, 55, 86. The dispute lasted for
    several years (Epp 2209:105–9, 2210:15–20, 2223:6–10); but a friendly exchange
    of letters initiated by Alciati in July 1529 restored good relations (Delaruelle
    Ep 164).
15 Cf Ep 2261:59–72.
16 See Epp 1419–20, 1481, 1667, 1853.
17 Geldenhouwer (Ep 2238)

is now an embittered enemy, moved to Strasbourg. Although within a few
months I had assisted him with my own money, he has now let fly against
me with four books;[18] a fifth has come out under the fictitious name of 'all
the preachers,' a remarkable medley of lies, insults, and hypocrisy.[19]   90

But I do not much care what heretics write about me. I wonder what
got into Alberto Pio, the former prince of Carpi, when a book that he wrote
in Italy was published in Paris,[20] presumably to please Béda and his like;[21]
not content with this, he then cobbled together a huge volume by collecting
from all of my works passages that might be construed as offering a toehold   95
to Luther. He did not do this work on his own, but had several handsomely
paid assistants, especially a Spaniard called Sepúlvela, a learned man, I
am told, who is the architect of this whole screed.[22] As a result Alberto is
not likely to earn much glory from this. The whole purpose of the work
is to demonstrate that I was the seedbed from which the entire Lutheran   100
tragedy developed. I wonder why a man who, I hear, is both learned and
cultivated should have decided to court fame from so odious a proposi-
tion. Unless I am wrong in my conjecture, Aleandro is pushing the project
and supplying the passages.[23] If this is to be my fate, then I must bear it
stoically.   105

I would have wished that Longueil had been spared to us longer,[24]
for what he has written so far has not contributed much to learning, unless we count the elegant gloss of his style. The fact that he mentions me
contemptuously several time does not bother me. There is among his letters
one addressed to Budé that is filled with enigmas and allegories, where, it is 110
said, you are the target.[25] I admire many men for their erudition, but I find
generosity in few, a special quality of yours, my dear Alciati, that I greatly
admire.

Farewell.

Freiburg, 1530   115

* * * * *

18 These would presumably be: the *Epistola Erasmi*; the *Annotationes*; the Latin
   edition of the *Antwort*; and Geldenhouwer's annotated edition of Erasmus'
   Epistola contra pseudevangelicos. See Epp 2219 n4, 2289 n2, and cf Augustijn
   153.
19 Bucer's *Epistola apologetica*; see Ep 2312 n2.
20 See Ep 2328:41–54.
21 Ep 2213 n8
22 Sepúlvela is Erasmus' habitual misspelling of Sepúlveda; see Ep 2261:75–7.
23 See Ep 1987 introduction, and cf Epp 2371, 2375, 2379.
24 See Ep 1706:4–6.
25 See Ep 1706:19–30

2330 / To Anton Fugger Freiburg, 24 June 1530

This letter was first published by Allen. The manuscript, an autograph rough draft with revisions in Erasmus' hand, is in the Royal Library at Copenhagen (MS GKS 95 Fol, folio 212). For Fugger, see Ep 2145.

TO ANTON FUGGER

Cordial greetings. I have never doubted your constancy, my distinguished friend. But a tiny little suspicion did cross my mind: the affairs of mortals being what they are, I feared that some little cloud was darkening the seren- ity of our friendship, and I would not like to see that friendship in any de- 5 gree impaired. I gladly accept your reassurance.[1] It is not that I lack courage, but for three months now I have been struggling with a very serious ill- ness.[2] It began with cramps in the stomach caused by the local winds which, though gentle enough, were thoroughly treacherous. After this came vom- iting and a badly upset stomach. From the doctors I got more trouble than 10 relief. In the end a great abscess covered the navel. We turned from the doc- tors to the surgeons, like descending from a horse to a donkey.[3] As a result I suffered for a long time with the excruciating pain from the vicious, thor- oughly German poultices that almost killed me. But as soon as the ulcer was lanced by the knife, I saw the first gleam of hope of recovery. I have now 15 made my peace with sleep and my stomach is returning to normal. I would have hopes of living if I had the kind of wine I want.[4] The Burgundy that was sent me most recently, though without it I would not be alive, is dry and does not dissolve in the body.

I think about leaving here, but do not know where to go. Many factors 20 hold me back from going to Brabant,[5] and even if there were no obstacles, I fear it would not be safe for me, since the emperor, as the rumour goes, is threatening the people of Strasbourg.[6] In Italy, even if it were at peace,

* * * * *

2330
1 Nothing in the surviving correspondence gives any clue to the nature of this 'little suspicion' or of the reassurance given.
2 See Ep 2320 n1.
3 *Adagia* I vii 29
4 See Ep 2328 n7.
5 See Ep 2222 n9.
6 Because of the religious changes introduced there: see *Correspondance des réformateurs dans les pays de langue française* ed Aimé Louis Herminjard 9 vols (Geneva 1866–97; repr Nieuwkoop 1965) Ep 289; *Briefwechsel der Brüder*

I would be embarrassed to find myself a stranger at my age. With regard to
the house, things are still up in the air. If I have to stay here, I would not   25
like to be thrown out during the winter.[7] There have been discussions about
buying a house, but although I am a poor wretched creature, I would prefer
to live in a large and crowded city. Here there is a great scarcity of things.
The place is more suited to the Muses than to Mercury.[8]

    Farewell, my most trusted friend.   30

    Freiburg, the birthday of John the Baptist 1530

2331 / To Johann Koler   Freiburg, 24 June 1530

> This letter was first published by Allen. The manuscript, an autograph rough
> draft, is in the Royal Library at Copenhagen (MS GKS 95 Fol, folio 212). For
> Koler, see Epp 2195 introduction, 2269.

TO JOHANN KOLER, PROVOST OF CHUR

Greetings. I sent you a letter recently when I was in very poor health and
gave it to a certain Heinrich to deliver.[1] There is no need to worry yourself
about that frank letter.[2] It was duly delivered. I would prefer to await the
conclusion of the diet in some other place, but illness ties me down.[3] Eck   5
continues to be Eck.[4] There are many reasons why I would like to leave here,
but I do not know where to go. If it is true that the emperor is threatening
Strasbourg, it would not even be safe to return to Brabant.[5]

    I wonder why you are interested in the letters of Ignatius.[6] If I had
them, I would make them available to you, but I have not heard of anyone   10

* * * * *

Ambrosius und Thomas Blaurer, 1509–1567 ed Traugott Schiess 3 vols (Freiburg
    im Breisgau 1908–12) Ep 162.
7 See Ep 2256:32–4.
8 Mercury was, among other things, the god of commerce.

2331
1 The letter, written c 6 June, is not extant. For Heinrich see Ep 2326 n5.
2 Perhaps Koler's reply to the unusually frank letter from Erasmus mentioned
    in Ep 2308:40–1.
3 The imperial diet was in session in Augsburg (Ep 2261 n7).
4 See Ep 2310 n16.
5 See Ep 2330 n6.
6 St Ignatius of Antioch. Lefèvre d'Etaples' Latin edition of the *Epistolae* had
    been published at Paris in 1498.

who possesses them. May I ask you to let me know periodically what is
happening in your part of the world, provided it is the sort of thing that
can safely be entrusted to a letter.

Farewell, my dearly beloved friend.

Freiburg, on the birthday of John the Baptist 1530   15

2332 / To Christoph von Stadion   Freiburg, 24 June 1530

This letter was first published in the *Epistolae floridae*. The manuscript, an autograph rough draft, is in the Royal Library at Copenhagen (MS GKS 95 Fol,
folio 212 verso). On Christoph von Stadion. bishop of Augsburg, see Ep 2029
introduction.

TO CHRISTOPH VON STADION, BISHOP OF AUGSBURG

Greetings, my Lord Bishop. For three months now I have been fighting a
battle with death.[1] This was the way March greeted me.[2] But I had scarcely
recovered from that when, lo and behold, on the day after Easter,[3] April
made a much more pitiless attack on me. The weather was at its most serene   5
and pleasant, a northeasterly wind was blowing in the upper air, but after
lunch soft winds, not dissimilar from the Etesians,[4] began to blow at a lower
level, deceptively gentle but extremely treacherous. I had realized the danger, and for some time I stayed home in the afternoons. But on the day after
Easter, since from the house I could observe no movement in the air, I ven-   10
tured forth and was immediately stricken. At first I had stomach cramps,
after that vomiting and an upset stomach, sleeplessness, and deep fatigue. I
got no help from the doctors, not because of their lack of skill, but this poor
body of mine cannot stand any stress. In the end, when the torture abated,
I developed a huge abscess, which was hard at first and then spread over   15
the navel.

A surgeon was called in, who, contrary to the opinion of the doctors,
promised that he could burst the abscess, which I did not believe would
happen. For several days he nearly killed me with his ulcerating fomentations, which made me weary of life. I was kept awake all night long and   20
suffered continuous and excruciating pain. All this time I was unable to

* * * * *

2332
1 On this prolonged illness, see Ep 2320 n1.
2 Cf Ep 2322:2–4.
3 18 April
4 See Ep 2320:17–19.

read or write or dictate or have a conversation or listen to someone reading. Meanwhile, my poor body was dehydrating and moving steadily towards death. A few days ago it was decided to lance the abscess. What a stinking quagmire burst forth from it! God in heaven! to think that a man can con-   25 ceal such a treasure in the body and yet survive! After this I am beginning to improve. I made my peace with sleep. My stomach is gradually returning to normal and my fatigue is lessening – but gradually.

During this dreadful illness the greatest consolation I received came from your Lordship's letter, which was so warm, so considerate, so full of   30 a deep devotion towards me.[5] If I deserved such respect, even if you alone thought so, I would count myself a fortunate man. Now whenever I think of your feelings for me and of your exceptional generosity, I blush with shame. Every day I pray fervently to God that by his Spirit he may be pleased to inspire the minds of the emperor and the princes with good counsels for   35 the salvation of Christendom, and that through the immense power of the emperor and his piety, which is as great as his power, God may calm this deadly storm, which cannot be stilled by human measures.

Cardinal Campeggi, the apostolic legate, is in your city now.[6] He has always been exceptionally well disposed towards me. He wrote to me from   40 Innsbruck.[7] I have been rather slow in replying to his letter because of my illness. I wanted your Lordship to know that this did not happen without reason.

The archbishop of Canterbury has now reached extreme old age. His next birthday will be at least his eightieth, if he has not got there already,   45 though I think he has passed that.[8] So far he has generally enjoyed excellent health, but now, it is said, he has taken to using a third leg.[9] I hope he will outlive me; but if it turns out otherwise, I intend to nominate you to take his place. From my two English pensions about two hundred florins are due every year,[10] but that sum comes to me through merchants after deductions,   50

* * * * *

5 The letter is not extant.
6 See Ep 2328 introduction.
7 The letter is not extant.
8 Born c 1456, Archbishop Warham was now in his mid-seventies.
9 Ie he now needs a walking stick, a reference to the riddle of the Sphinx: 'What walks on four legs, then two, then three?'
10 Cf Ep 2159:28–30. This is the clearest indication in the correspondence that Warham paid Erasmus pensions drawn from two livings in England, one at Aldington (Ep 255 introduction) and another that is unknown. The first indication of a second living is in Ep 1647:12–14, where the value of the two is given as £20 for the first and £10 for the second. By 1528, the combined value

which sometimes amount to as much as a quarter. Also from time to time
it is intercepted. If anything happened to the archbishop, as happens to all
men, nothing would be paid. I have only the official document from the
archbishop and the oath of those who are responsible for the payments.[11] I
do not know if the actual churches are under any obligation. Even if they   55
did have a binding obligation, they would give nothing to an absentee.

The Flanders pension,[12] which I received as a result of resigning a
prebend, was stolen from me by an act of unspeakable perfidy; the thief
was a person to whom I had entrusted all my affairs and would even have
entrusted my life.[13] Such a strong pull is exercised by the love of money.   60
From my imperial pension I have not received a cent since I left; even if I
returned I doubt if they would give me anything, for all their courting of
me with magnificent promises. So I think that within a short time Erasmus
will be reduced to a state of evangelical poverty, though (thank Heaven!) I
am still some way from that. If the situation requires it, I shall improve my   65
finances by living frugally, for up to now I have made many unnecessary
expenditures. You need not fear, however, that I shall become a burdensome
protégé.[14] In fact I was so far from being a nuisance to Canterbury that I
refused a generous offer that he made more than once.[15]

I wish I could be closer at hand to enjoy your civilized friendship and   70
extensive erudition. I would like to fly away from here to somewhere else,
not because anybody here is being tiresome, but because in a little town
with a small population those of us who have many requirements don't find
them here. If war breaks out, it would not be safe either to stay here or to
set out for somewhere else.[16] But I shall leave everything to the Lord. May   75
he defend your Reverence and prosper you in all things!

Freiburg, on the feast of John the Baptist 1530

* * * * *

of the two pensions appears to have risen to £35, the payment from the second living having been increased to £15 (Ep 2039:3–5, Allen Ep 2370:4–7). For
further details, see Allen Ep 2159:26n.

11 Since November 1514 Richard Master (1484–1552/8), rector of the parish at
   Aldington, had been responsible for the annual payment of £20.
12 From Courtrai; see Ep 436:6n.
13 Pierre Barbier; see Epp 2295:28–30, 2356:17–18.
14 Cf Allen Ep 2362:9.
15 Ie offers to settle in England on generous terms; see Epp 214, 1926:13–15,
   1955:10–11.
16 Erasmus feared both the outbreak of civil conflict in Switzerland, which could
   easily spill over the border into the Breisgau (Ep 2173:31–5), as well as armed
   conflict between the Catholic and Protestant estates of Germany (Ep 2219 n10).

2333 / From Simon Pistoris   Augsburg, 27 June 1530

This letter was first published as Ep 128 in Förstemann /Günther. The autograph was in the Burscher Collection at Leipzig (Ep1254 introduction). Erasmus' answer is Ep 2344. On Simon Pistoris (1489–1562), chancellor to Duke
George of Saxony and a trusted supporter of Erasmus, see Ep 1125 n6.

Greetings, most learned Erasmus. I have hesitated for a long time over
whether I should coax a letter out of you in reply to the one I sent you some
time ago.[1] I am certain it was delivered and, what is more, I know that in
the meantime you sent letters to other people here with which you could
conveniently have included a reply to me; so the only conclusion I could   5
readily draw was that the subject did not seem worthy of a reply. But since
the letter I sent was written in my own hand, and so in part, if I am not mistaken, was a letter from Duke George, containing a number of questions to
which he is still awaiting an answer,[2] I expect there is some other explanation for your failure to write. The courier is to return here shortly, so I beg   10
you not to let slip the opportunity to reply to both of us so that at least we
may know that you are fully restored to health, for a report reached us here
that your health had suffered as a result of a serious illness.[3]
    I do not doubt that you are kept informed of all that is happening here;
nevertheless I do not want to conceal from you that the day before yester-   15
day the elector of Saxony,[4] George, margrave of Brandenburg,[5] the dukes
of Lüneburg,[6] and the landgrave of Hessen[7] presented the emperor with a
document in both German and Latin, signed by themselves and their adherents, giving an account of their faith and their religious innovations. This
was read out at a public meeting with the other princes and is a summary of   20
the views that Luther has expressed and defended so far.[8] They did all this,

* * * * *

2333
1 The letter is not extant.
2 The most recent surviving letter from Duke George is Ep 2124 of 15 March
  1529.
3 On the illness, see Ep 2320 n1.
4 John, elector from 1525 to 1532; see Ep 1670 introduction.
5 George (1484–1543), ruler of the margraviate of Brandenburg-Ansbach in Franconia
6 Ernest I (1497–1546) and his brother Francis (1508–49), dukes of Braunschweig-
  Lüneburg
7 Philip (1504–67); cf Ep 2141 n6.
8 Drafted by Melanchthon in consultation with Luther and other theologians,

however, in a more moderate tone,[9] and with this stipulation, that if they could not reach agreement, and the bishops were unwilling to abandon the measures they had taken against those who followed their teaching, they felt that it was more important to obey God than man and wanted to abide   25 by the call that had been made earlier for an open and Christian general council.[10]

Three days ago, cardinal Campeggi,[11] in his role as legate of the apostolic see, offered his services to help resolve the dispute. So I think he will be invited to the diet and will be the first to pronounce the words 'May   30 God grant us the grace of reconciliation.' Many stick to the position that although, in their own opinion, several points could be accepted, it would nevertheless be impermissible without the authority and agreement of a general council to depart from the teaching of the Fathers even with the authority of the apostolic see. In this dilemma, if the larger party defeats the wiser, it   35 looks as though the gravest dissension lies ahead. Meanwhile on the orders of the emperor both sides are refraining from preaching, and the Gospel is read only by those who have not been involved in this affair. At first this

* * * * *

the Augsburg Confession (*Confessio Augustana*) had two parts: a lucid and succinct summary of the essential elements of the Lutheran faith (articles 1–21; and a defence of the changes in religious practice that had thus far been introduced (articles 22–8). It was offered as the basis on which the Lutherans would seek confessional unity with the Catholics. The text was read out before the emperor at a special session of the diet on 25 June 1530. Together with the more detailed Apology of the Augsburg Confession (1531), also by Melanchthon, the Confession remains the most important of the Lutheran confessional writings.

9 Because the Lutherans, particularly Saxony, were, for political as well as religious reasons, eager for reconciliation with the emperor and the Catholic estates, the Confession avoided fiery denunciations of 'popery' and instead emphasized those things that Lutherans and Catholics have in common (eg infant baptism and the Real Presence), while harshly condemning the views of Anabaptists and Zwinglians (cf lines 41–2 below). The later Apology (see n8 above) would be considerably less conciliatory towards the old church.

10 In the face of all attempts since 1521 by the Catholic majority in the imperial diet, led by Emperor Charles and King Ferdinand, to repress their movement, the evangelical princes and cities had taken the view that while in worldly matters (eg aid in defence against the Turks) they owed obedience to the emperor and cooperation with the majority, in matters of faith they were obligated to 'obey God rather than men' (Acts 5:29). At the same time, they repeatedly insisted that the competent authority for settling religious differences was 'a free, Christian council in German lands.'

11 Ep 2328

seemed very hard to the Lutherans, but now they understand that it was absolutely necessary, for the situation would have become more embittered 40
and hope of agreement more elusive. They refused to make common cause
with the Zwinglians. But it is said that the Zwinglians will also give an account of their faith.[12] I wish you were here and could count on people who
would follow your advice! For I am convinced that you could take on the
double role of Aristarchus and peacemaker.[13] So be all the more careful to 45
look after your health, so that if such a plan ever entered your head, you
would have the strength to carry it out.

Eppendorf is here.[14] If there is anything you would like me to discuss
with him, let me know. You can always count on my help, my concern, and
my energetic attention. All best wishes. 50

Augsburg, 27 June 1530

Yours, Simon Pistoris, doctor of canon and civil law etc

To the high priest of all the arts and a truly great theologian, Master
Erasmus of Rotterdam, his mentor and most worthy friend

2334 / From Bernhard von Cles   Augsburg, 27 June 1530

First published as Ep 129 in Förstemann / Günther, this is Bishop Bernhard's
answer to Ep 2326. The manuscript was in the Burscher Collection at Leipzig
(Ep 1254 introduction).

My venerable, estimable, and dearly beloved friend, I could not let
Polyphemus return to you without giving him some sort of note for

* * * * *

12 Unwilling to sign the Augsburg Confession, the four cities of Strasbourg,
Memmingen, Lindau, and Constance submitted at the diet their *Confessio
tetrapolitana* (Four Cities Confession), which attempted a moderate position
between Lutheranism and Zwinglianism. Written in great haste at the diet by
Martin Bucer with the help of Wolfgang Capito (Ep 459) and Caspar Hedio
(Ep 1459), it was presented to the emperor on 11 July, though it was not read
to him and received little attention. It is the oldest confessional writing of the
Reformed (ie Zwinglian, later Calvinist) tradition. As for Zwingli himself, in
the absence of a common confession of the Swiss evangelicals, he sent to Augsburg a personal account of his own faith, the *Ratio fidei ad Carolum Imperatorem*,
which was rejected by the emperor and not presented to the diet.
13 Aristarchus was a Greek critic of the first half of the second century BC whose
name Cicero made synonymous with 'demanding critic'; see *Adagia* I v 57. On
the wish of many that Erasmus would devise a plan that would serve as the
basis for the restoration of religious peace, cf Ep 2328.
14 Ep 1934 introduction

you;[1] he has always been, in my experience, most dependable and most attentive to me.[2] At present, however, there is little for me to say after the two long letters that I wrote from Trent in answer to that letter of 5 yours, in which, it appeared, you proposed coming to us towards autumn;[3] this is a possibility that has always been open to you. So I do not think there is any need to assure you repeatedly of our good will and of our desire to oblige you. It only remains for you to put us to the test, and meanwhile to beseech Almighty God in your prayers that now at last he 10 look upon his faithful Catholic people. Your prayers, I know, will be acceptable to his divine Majesty and truly helpful to a weakened Christian church.

I had just written this when a letter arrived from you, congratulating me on my elevated status,[4] though there was no need for congratulations 15 at this particular moment, when the world is in such turmoil. I hope that my new dignity will allow me to be of use to the universal church and to our tottering faith; but my inadequacies and my feeble powers work against this.

I am sincerely sorry about the illness that has overtaken you;[5] I found 20 the news deeply upsetting. So do all in your power to get well, and assure yourself that in everything you face I shall always be there to do whatever I can to maintain your distinguished reputation and physical well-being.

* * * * *

2334
1 After delivering the presentation copy of *De vidua christiana* to Mary of Hungary in the spring of 1529 (see Ep 2130:123–8), Erasmus' wayward servant Polyphemus (Felix Rex; Ep 2130 introduction) stayed on in Bohemia through the following winter, 'drinking valiantly' (Ep 2288:25). His intention to return to Erasmus at Freiburg at this point appears to have been frustrated by his obligations as a member of King Ferdinand's household; see Ep 2336:3–8. He is known to have paid a brief visit to Freiburg in January 1531 (AK Ep 1488), but he quickly returned to Augsburg, allegedly on his way once again to the service of King Ferdinand. After further wanderings, which included a sojourn at the court of Elector John of Saxony, he finally returned to Erasmus at Freiburg in February 1532.
2 Evidently worried by Erasmus' neglect of him during his long absence without leave (Ep 2288:24–5), Rex had now prompted friends to forward to Erasmus assurances of his loyalty; see Epp 2335:35–7; 2336:1–3, 77–80, 84–6; 2339:23–8.
3 This would have been Erasmus' letter in response to the one received from Bernhard on 30 March 1530 inviting him once again to settle in Trent (see Ep 2299:33–8). Neither Erasmus' letter nor Bernard's 'two long' replies are extant.
4 Ep 2326
5 See Ep 2320 n1.

Do not attach much importance to the slanderous abuse of your critics. They have no case, and you have given them no opening of any kind to stigmatize 25 you; moreover the princes and all Catholic people are only too aware of their honesty and integrity.[6] The rest of your letter does not call for a reply except that I would like to add what a difference it would make if you too were here during this stormy crisis, for you are someone whose good sense and learning could be of the greatest assistance and support to the faith and to 30 the church. I pray for your good health.

Augsburg, 27 June 1530

Bernhard, cardinal of Trent

To our venerable, estimable, and dearly beloved Master Erasmus of Rotterdam, doctor of sacred theology etc 35

2335 / From Johann von Vlatten   Augsburg, 28 June 1530

> This letter was first published as Ep 130 in Förstemann / Günther. The manuscript was in the Burscher Collection at Leipzig (Ep 1254 introduction). Erasmus' reply is Ep 2346. On Vlatten, see Ep 2222.

Greetings, Master Erasmus, my very dear friend. If I have written less frequently than usual to you, a man whom I respect and reverence in every way, it is not through indifference, but because of the malignancy of the treacherous times in which we live. My prince has been weighed down with various troublesome tasks,[1] so he wanted me to undertake certain mis- 5 sions on his behalf. I was sent to the emperor Charles in Italy,[2] then from Italy to our region of Lower Germany,[3] and from Germany back to Italy. When I returned, he sent me as his delegate to this distinguished assembly of states and princes. As a result for the past six months I have been flying hither and yon, with hardly time enough to draw my breath or to think 10 of those to whom I owe so much, or of my friends and relatives, and the companions of my studies.

* * * * *

6 The Latin is 'probitas et integritas *sua.*' Allen wondered if *sua* might not have been a slip for *vestra*, which would be '*your* honesty and integrity.'

2335
1 John III of Cleves-Mark-Jülich-Berg (Ep 829:14n)
2 Charles arrived in Italy from Spain in August 1529; see Ep 2208 n12.
3 The United Duchies of Cleves-Mark-Jülich-Berg were situated in what was commonly referred to as Lower Germany (*Niederdeutschland, Germania Inferior*); see Ep 1998 n6.

I am absolutely delighted that you have been restored to your former state of health.[4] I pray Almighty God that he will long keep you safe
and well for the benefit of our Christian commonwealth, so that by your   15
pious and profound teaching and your Christian gentleness and moderation you may be able to help the wretched and hapless land of Germany,
which (shame on it!), after abandoning its savagery and shedding its barbarous ways, is now not just divided over the Christian faith, but losing its
footing almost entirely. Amid the factiousness of our times, in this mael-   20
strom of feelings and emotions, without the wise counsel that you and men
like you provide, we risk losing much from lack of good advice, and many
things that call for clarification will remain unclear. Christendom is in peril
and struggling for its life; so come and help us by your presence, and do not
deny us your healing touch. The Christian world expects this of you, and   25
so do our invincible emperor and the most serene king of Hungary, along
with the most reverend prelates and all the other illustrious estates of the
Empire.

If I could be of any assistance to you or oblige you in any way, all you
have to do is say the word and I shall be at your service, dear Erasmus, for,   30
I swear, nothing would give me greater satisfaction. If you are still thinking
of moving, and if there is any place under the jurisdiction of my illustrious prince that would suit your requirements, just let me know; you will
find that in this matter I am ready to perform the role of a devoted friend.
I send my best wishes. Continue to love me and love our friend Polyphe-   35
mus, not because of my commendation, but for the man's faithfulness and
constancy.[5]

Augsburg, 28 June 1530

Yours affectionately, Johann von Vlatten, scholaster etc

To the erudite Master Erasmus of Rotterdam, his greatly respected   40
friend. In Freiburg

2336 / From Cornelis de Schepper   Augsburg, 28 June 1530

This letter was first published as Ep 131 in Förstemann / Günther. The autograph was in the Burscher Collection at Leipzig (Ep 1254 introduction). On
Cornelis de Schepper, who was currently attending the Diet of Augsburg in
the entourage of the emperor, see Ep 2327 introduction.

* * * * *

4 On Erasmus' recent illness see Ep 2320 n1.
5 See Ep 2334 n2.

Greetings. Your Polyphemus reached me in Innsbruck.[1] I was happy to make the man's acquaintance. Your commendation seems to me to have been perfectly justified, for he is indeed a faithful and devoted friend to you.[2] He planned to leave some weeks ago, and Doctor Fabri had obtained for him a leave of absence;[3] later he received some assistance from me too. But when 5 his royal Majesty, the king of Hungary, refused to allow members of his household to be absent when he was on his way to Augsburg, this imposed a further delay on Polyphemus.[4] Meanwhile God took from us our most revered grand chancellor.[5] I loved him deeply, both as a public figure, for he was a good man, and as a private person, because of the affection that 10 he had for me, not from any merits of my own, but from a natural empathy. So he has been taken from us – a loss that is perhaps irreparable, for we shall find no one like him who could match him in experience and administrative skill. There is no one alive today who possesses the qualities he had of loyalty and integrity. I speak of men who are engaged in affairs of state, 15 for we of the court are acquainted with men of every class and from every nation – a situation that is perhaps not without its embarrassments. I worshipped him when he was alive and I shall worship him no less now that he is dead, for I know what a great man he was.

When he arrived in Trent (where I met Lieven),[6] he inquired most graciously about you. And three days before he died, when Polyphemus said 20 that he would be leaving earlier than expected, he pressed me to write to you secretly on his behalf as well as my own and to ask you to suggest how this present storm could be calmed. He said that if you did not want it to be known that the suggestions had come from you, he would see to it that 25 no one would learn the identity of the author except himself and me. I was planning to write, when the Most Reverend bishop of Trent[7] informed me that Polyphemus could not decently set out before the arrival of his royal

* * * * *

2336
1 On Polyphemus (Felix Rex) see Ep 2334 n1.
2 Cf lines 77–80, 84–6 below, and see Ep 2334 n2.
3 Johannes Fabri (Ep 2097) was King Ferdinand's minister.
4 Cf lines 27–9 below. On Erasmus' recommendation, Rex had been appointed an archer in Ferdinand's household; see Ep 2130:58–75.
5 Mercurino Gattinara (Ep 2013), Erasmus' faithful friend and patron at the imperial court, had died in Innsbruck on 5 June, en route with the emperor to Augsburg.
6 The imperial court spent 24–8 April in Trent. On Lieven Algoet and his mission to the court, see Ep 2278 n2.
7 Bernhard von Cles (Ep 2326)

Majesty in Augsburg. So the whole plan was frustrated, and I was unwilling to risk sending the letter by anyone else. Then that great man left us, 30
and all our plans were turned upside down. As far as these external matters
are concerned, I am not much worried, and I do not know whether he could
have lived more happily than he died. He was especially fond of you, and
if God had wanted him to survive these times, you would have discovered
what I am telling you now. 35

You owe this relationship to Valdés,[8] who has always been a strong
supporter of yours. I have been able to do little to help my friends, though
I wish I could have done more, for I have little influence at court either
through my friendships or by persuasion – I am grateful to God, however, for the grace he has shown me. Before his death that great man,[9] on 40
my urging, read your *Consultatio de bello Turcico*,[10] your exposition of the
twenty-eighth psalm,[11] your *Hieron*,[12] and a few other pieces that Lieven
brought me. Lieven greeted me warmly on your behalf and brought me a
letter of recommendation for himself,[13] which pleased me very much, not
that I needed it, for I know your fondness for him, but because I was de- 45
lighted to see the confidence that you have in me. I assure you it is not
misplaced.

Lieven is staying with me now and will stay here until he has an offer of a better position. I shall continue to promote his career as best I can.
Meanwhile he lacks nothing. He may not be staying with some great per- 50
sonage, but he is with a man of middling fortune, and one whose affairs
are not in a desperate state. Given the tumultuous times in which we live,
I leave it to you to say in what way I could be of use. As for the bishop
of Seville,[14] Valdés has been instructed to look after that. Since I cannot
now discuss your situation with the chancellor, I have referred it to the em- 55
peror and to Ferdinand, who is strongly on your side, and I shall do so
again.

* * * * *

8 Alfonso de Valdés (Ep 2252), who was also a member of the imperial entourage
   at the Diet of Augsburg
9 Gattinara
10 Ep 2285
11 He means the exposition of Psalm 22 (Ep 2266). Psalm 28 was the basis of the
   De bello Turcico (see preceding note).
12 Ep 2273
13 Not extant
14 Alonso Manrique de Lara, whose support against his Spanish critics Erasmus
   was still actively cultivating; see Ep 2301.

Johannes Dantiscus, who is now bishop of Chełmno, returned to us a
couple of days ago.[15] He is a person of great integrity and common sense
without any obvious weakness. I have had a long association with him over 60
many years – as the saying goes, I have consumed a peck of salt with him.[16]
As a result I feel more free to speak about his integrity, of which I have personal knowledge, whereas in other circumstances I would be more hesitant.
When I was writing this letter, he told me that he also intended writing to
you, to plead with you, as a wise and learned man, not to allow yourself to 65
be upset by the libellous books that are written against you by men who are
responsible for the wrecking of Christendom, for it does not become you to
be put out by such behaviour. I too beg you not to let these tiresome tirades
add to the miseries of the stone;[17] you would do better to reserve yourself
for us. If there is anything you consider would be helpful in this situation, 70
or any matter you would like to be drawn discreetly to the attention of the
emperor or Ferdinand, you could mention it to Valdés or me. While I would
not wish to take second place to anyone in my regard and respect for you,
I would feel no resentment towards anyone for his devotion to you; on the
contrary I ask you to gather into your net as many men as possible, not for 75
your own sake, but for the sake of your immortal writings, which many evil
men are constantly dragging into the dust; their reward is laid up for them.
You can safely trust anything to Polyphemus, who is admired by many for
his honesty and his faithfulness to you and who, it seems to me, will not
swerve from this path. 80

There is no other news here. Valdés is in very good form. I am surprised that he has not written to you, but when I showed him the letter I
received from you, dated the day after Pentecost,[18] he promised me that he
would write to you today.[19] Polyphemus had already made all the necessary
preparations for leaving. Please keep him in your mind and commend him 85
to friends. If you ever get to Flanders, or if I am able to visit the area where
you and Glareanus live, nothing will please me more than to discuss with
you in person certain matters that I cannot put on paper. I would have done

* * * * *

15 Dantiscus (Ep 2163 n34) was the Polish ambassador to the imperial court,
   which he had accompanied on its journey to Italy and Augsburg in 1529–30.
16 Persons whose friendship had matured over a long time were said to have
   consumed a peck of salt together; see *Adagia* II i 14.
17 See Ep 2275 n9.
18 Ep 2327
19 The letter is not extant; Erasmus replied to it with Ep 2349.

so in any case, if our distinguished friend,[20] whom I cannot praise highly
enough, were still alive. Now that he has gone, I hope that you will not for-   90
get me if you wish to make suggestions about the present state of things.
Farewell, dearest master.

    Augsburg, the eve of the feast of Peter and Paul 1530

    Cornelis de Dobbele de Schepper

    Please remember me kindly to my old friend, Henricus Glareanus.[21]   95

    To Master Erasmus of Rotterdam, my most worthy mentor. In Freiburg

2337 / From Martinus Bovolinus   Venice, 29 June 1530

> This letter was first published as Ep 132 in Förstemann / Günther. The auto-
> graph was in the Burscher Collection at Leipzig (Ep 1254 introduction). Bo-
> volinus (Ep 2102) was at this time in Venice as diplomatic representative of the
> Three Leagues (later the Swiss canton of Grisons / Graubünden), and would
> shortly go on to Rome (line 30).

Cordial greetings. Just think, most distinguished Erasmus, of the exquisite
cunning of your slave, my poor humble self, in having contrived to make
the great Erasmus my letter carrier! My son is staying now with our friend
Glareanus.[1] Because I live in the remote mountains of Rhaetia,[2] I rarely or
never find a courier by whom to send him a letter. But when I was in Venice,   5
I fell in with a man who is a great admirer of yours (and is there any decent person who does not admire you, Erasmus?). I was about to hand him
a letter for Glareanus, when I realized that there would be a greater chance
of its being delivered if it was addressed to you. So it is in hope of your indulgence that I have saddled you with the task of having the attached letter   10
delivered to Glareanus. Some day Erasmus will make the acquaintance of

* * * * *

20 Gattinara
21 Ep 2290 n6

2337
1 The son, Lazarus Bovolinus (1514–50) had enrolled at the University of Basel
  in the winter term of 1526–7, becoming a student of Henricus Glareanus. Following the victory of the Reformation at Basel in 1529, Lazarus accompanied
  Glareanus on his emigration to Freiburg (Ep 2290 n6) and continued his studies there. In due course he followed in his father's footsteps by becoming a
  notary in his hometown of Mesocco.
2 His home was in the Mesolcina valley, in the southern part of Grisons, north
  of Bellinzona.

the person for whom he has done this. My dear son, in accordance with my wishes, is studying with Glareanus, because Glareanus, as well as being a distinguished man, has the added glamour of being a close friend of Erasmus; so the youth can boast that he is a pupil, if not of Erasmus, at least of an intimate of Erasmus. The splendour of your reputation makes me hesitant to write more about my boy; he himself knows what instructions he has received from me. It would be absurd for me to bore you with my foolish prattle; but is there anyone who, once an idea has entered his head, can resist? How I wish that Erasmus would consent to allow my son to join his household and serve him at my expense! If you agree to this, let his only recompense be the glory of your name. I shall consider I have made a good investment if you will kindly grant me this request. The lad's name is Lazarus.

I wrote to you on another occasion from the Valtelline.[3] When I got your reply,[4] I thought I was somebody, since I now possess a letter from Erasmus. If this happens again, I shall be highly gratified. So I ask you to write if this can be done without inconvenience to yourself. Pietro Bembo, the Venetian aristocrat, sends his greetings. He gave me a little book to be forwarded to you.[5] I promised to take care of this, and I shall do so when, God willing, I return from Rome. If you will honour me with a letter, give it to my boy, who will send it on.[6] My best wishes to you, who are the glory of this age. May the Lord direct your steps and ours. Amen.

Venice, 29 June 1530

Yours, Martinus Bovolinus of Mesocco

JESUS CHRIST

To the most famous and celebrated Desiderius Erasmus of Rotterdam, my master beyond compare. To Freiburg im Breisgau

2338 / To Duke George of Saxony   Freiburg, 30 June 1530

This letter was first published in the *Epistolae floridae*. The manuscript, an autograph rough draft in the Royal Library at Copenhagen (MS GKS 95 Fol, folio

* * * * *

3 Ep 2102
4 Not extant
5 Bembo (Ep 2106) published at Venice in 1530 a volume with two small dialogues: *De Virgilii culice* and *De Urbini ducibus* (Giovanni Antonio da Sabio and Brothers). Bembo dispatched a copy to Jacopo Sadoleto on 11 June (see Allen's note), and it is probably this same volume that he asked Bovolinus to send to Erasmus.
6 No such letter survives.

215), breaks off at line 74 in the middle of the phrase 'those who are true believers and those who are not.'

TO DUKE GEORGE OF SAXONY

Greetings. Illustrious prince, several days ago I wrote to Simon Pistoris, your Excellency's chancellor.[1] The parcel you entrusted to Walter of Leipzig[2] at the beginning of January was delivered to me at the end of April when I was very seriously ill.[3] The malady that struck me in March attacked me   5 again on Easter Monday in so violent a form that I could neither eat nor sleep nor read nor write nor listen to someone reading nor have a conversation with anyone. At first I suffered cramps in the belly, which were followed by a wicked abscess. As a result I am still very weak, and not yet out of the clutches of doctors and surgeon.   10

If the parcel had come before the fair, that would have been most welcome. It did not please me to see the names of Duke George and Martin Luther linked on the same page.[4] The fact that this arrogant impostor can get away with such an attack on a prince adds greatly to his conceit. I have never found him so offensive as in that apologia,[5] in which he makes a great   15 fuss about nothing, describing your conduct, if you please, as 'theft.'[6] There

* * * * *

2338
1 The letter, written c 6 June, is not extant; see Ep 2344 n2.
2 Unidentified; probably a carrier
3 See Ep 2320 n1.
4 Ie in the title of the 'apologia' identified in the following note
5 The work in question was *Von heimlichen vnd gestolen brieffen – widder Hertzog Georgen zu Sachsen*. Mart. Luth. 1529 (WA 30/2 25–48). It is clear, however, that the parcel from Duke George contained the Latin translation of the work published at the behest of the duke in a volume entitled *Epistolae atque libelli aliquot, continentes controversiam, quae inter ... Georgium Saxoniae Ducem ... & M. Lutherum ... versata est* (Leipzig: Melchior Lotter, December 1529). Luther's treatise bears the title *De privatis et furto surreptis literis ... contra Georgium Ducem Saxoniae* (folios G iii verso-M iii verso).
6 The acrimonious controversy between Luther and Duke George was a byproduct of the Pack Affair of 1528; see Ep 1934 n80 and cf Ep 2124 n9. George was infuriated by Luther's insulting refusal to take seriously his claim that Pack's fraud had been committed without his knowledge and that there had never been an alliance of Catholic princes planning to invade Electoral Saxony and Hessen. George somehow acquired a copy of a private letter to Wenzeslaus Linck in Nürnberg (21 June 1528) in which Luther interpreted George's 'preposterous' assertions of his innocence as tantamount to a confession that he had been plotting with his allies to 'eradicate the gospel.' George published the text of the letter as evidence that Luther was a liar and a demagogue,

is such bitterness in it, such chicanery, such shameless twisting of everything into a fault. He cites Jerome's complaint against those who broke into
his writing cases and stole several pages,[7] as if your Excellency ever did
anything like that, for what came into your possession was a letter that had   20
passed through many hands. What a dangerous exaggeration it is to claim
that you wanted to control Duke John of Saxony and the city council of
Nürnberg,[8] whereas in your letter there is not a single peremptory word!
And what a shabby trick it is to imply that saying something out loud or
writing it to someone else is the same as thinking it privately to oneself! No   25
one's reputation is injured by a simple thought, but scandal is created by a
letter or a conversation. How absurd it is to claim that the church does not
pass judgment on secret thoughts![9] On the contrary, the laws wring out se-
crets by torture, and the church demands that we reveal unholy thoughts
to a priest. Then after leaving no insult unsaid, he pretends to spare your   30
Excellency while threatening that unless you desist, he will smash over you
a whole barrel of acid.[10] How constantly he hammers away at the idea that

* * * * *

and demanded legal action against him. In *Von heimlichen vnd gestolen brieffen*,
Luther denounced George for the 'theft' and improper use of a letter that was
private and should have remained so. A detailed history of the controversy
can be found in WA 30/2 1–20. The relevant portion of the letter to Linck is
on pages 3–4.
7 WA 30/2 30:22–5. The reference, identified by the WA editors, is to Jerome
Contra Rufinum 2.24, 3.25.
8 Duke George had demanded the assistance of Luther's prince, Elector John of
Saxony, and the city council of Nürnberg in his efforts to find the original of
the letter to Linck. See WA 30/2 31, 17–27, 36:16–37:1.
9 In arguing that his letter to Linck and the thoughts expressed in it were things
done in secret that could therefore not legitimately be taken as evidence of
wrongdoing, Luther had cited the universally recognized legal maxim *De oc-
cultis non judicat ecclesia* 'The church does not judge secret things,' and added
multo minus judicat de eisdem magistratus 'much less does the magistrate judge
such things'; WA 30/2 32:26–8. Cf ibidem 38:33–4, where Luther cites one of
his favourite aphorisms, *Die Gedanken sind zollfrei* 'thoughts are duty free.'
10 What Luther actually said was that in the hope of achieving something with
Duke George by patience, he had restrained himself from responding to some
of the duke's attacks on him, but that if the duke did not now desist from his
current campaign of false accusations, he (Luther) might 'knock the bottom
out of the barrel, and render tit for tat,' ie shower the duke with a furious
denunciation of his own misdeeds; see WA 30/2 36:8–9 and folio K recto of the
Latin translation (n5 above). Luther makes no mention of acid, but the image
he uses is clearly one of dumping something unpleasant on one's opponent,
and in classical Latin *acidus* was often associated with bitter language.

you are his enemy, when you often address him in the most friendly manner, urging him to repent! Finally, with all the authority at his command
he consigns you to Satan along with all who support you in any way.[11] But   35
soon this merciful man loosened the knot he had tied even though you neither repent nor confess your sin.[12] God! how greatly this differs from the
spirit of the gospel! A hundred books attacking the man would not have
turned my mind against him so much as that tirade. Nowhere else does he
indulge so freely in exaggeration. It is nothing new for him to contradict   40
himself in his writings, and when learned men bring such instances to his
attention, this charming fellow is silent, as though their criticisms do not
deserve a reply.[13]

His palinode on the Turkish war made me laugh;[14] does he think that
Germany is now different from what it was, or God is no longer visiting   45
our sins upon us through the Turks? If he is right about this, it would not
be a godly act to resist any disaster, pestilence, or war, or pillage, or the

* * * * *

11 See WA 30/2 39:22–6, 43:9–22.
12 This is seemingly a reference to Luther's inclusion at the end of the work of
   a brief commentary on the seventh Psalm, designed as a summons to Duke
   George to repent; see WA 30/2 44–8
13 An apparent reference to Luther's failure to reply to either part of Erasmus'
   Hyperaspistes; cf Ep 2204 n5.
14 The 'palinode' (ie retraction; see *Adagia* I ix 59) was the treatise *On War Against
   the Turks* (Ep 2279 n1). Concerned by the misunderstanding that he opposed
   all resistance to the Turks (see Ep 2285 n35), Luther attempted to set the record
   straight in this new work, which was published just weeks before the com-
   mencement of the Turkish advance from Constantinople to Vienna in May–
   October 1529. While reaffirming his earlier assertion that it was improper for
   Christians as Christians to resist evil and that papal crusades against 'infidels' were a great blasphemy, Luther made perfectly clear that, as temporal
   sovereign, Emperor Charles had the divinely imposed obligation to defend
   his subjects against wrongful invasion by the Turks and that Christians should
   answer his call to arms. To hostile critics, however, this was evidence of de-
   plorable inconsistency. In his satire *Dialogus de bello contra Turcas, in Antilogias Lutheri* (Leipzig: Valentin Schumann, 30 June 1529), Johannes Cochlaeus
   put Luther's seemingly contradictory ideas into the mouths of two characters,
   Lutherus and Palinodus, who were pictured on the title page as two heads
   on one body. One suspects that it was Cochlaeus' rendition of Luther's 'palinode' that made Erasmus laugh. For a more detailed and nuanced summary of
   Luther's views than is possible here, see George W. Forell 'Luther and the War
   Against the Turks' *Church History* 14 (1945) 256–71; Martin Brecht 'Luther und
   die Türken' in *Europa und die Türken in der Renaissance* ed Bodo Guthmüller
   and Wilhelm Kühlmann (Tübingen 2000) 9–27, especially 10–18.

attacks of the peasants.[15] In his sermon on war against the Turks he makes
the dominion of the Turks unending and inviolable, and leaves us nothing
but fearful calamities and suffering.[16] As for me, despite what you call 'my   50
failing years,' I would not be deterred from joining battle with the fellow, if
experience had not taught us that we accomplish nothing by fighting except
to stir up a hornets' nest.[17] For a long time now I have of my own free will

* * * * *

15 Cf Ep 2285:135–7. Erasmus' point is that if it is true, as Luther had said in 1518,
that it was improper to resist the Turks because they are God's punishment for
sin, then neither should one resist any other plagues sent to punish them for
their sins. Whether the point is well made or not, it is strikingly irrelevant as a
comment about *On War Against the Turks* (see preceding note), in which Luther
vigorously affirmed the right of Christian rulers to take up arms against the
invading Turks. This failure to mention the essential point of Luther's treatise
(cf following note) was probably a deliberate tactic, applied for the reasons
outlined in n17 below.

16 The word 'sermon' (*concio* in Latin, *predigt* in German) indicates that Erasmus
might possibly be referring to Luther's *Heerpredigt widder den Türcken* (Ep 2279
n1) rather than to the treatise *On War Against the Turks*. On the other hand,
the sentence has no discernible connection with anything that Luther says in
the *Heerpredigt*. A *Heerpredigt* (or *Feldpredigt*) was a sermon preached to troops
on the eve of battle, and the treatise is Luther's most urgent statement of the
need to resist Turkish aggression.

17 In this paragraph Erasmus is studiously avoiding the uncomfortable truth that
he and Luther were in essential agreement on the subject of war against the
Turks. Both were inclined to see in the Turks a divine scourge upon Christendom for its sins, the most important response to which was repentance and
improvement of life; and both deemed it inappropriate for popes or other clergymen to summon crusades against infidels in defence of Christendom. On
the other hand, while both counselled against hasty resort to war under any
circumstances, both cautiously acknowledged the duty of secular rulers to defend their subjects against unlawful attack; see CWE 64 206–7. Even if, as seems
likely, Erasmus at this point knew Luther's *On War Against the Turks* only via
Cochlaeus' parody of it (see n14 above), he had to know from that source that
he and Luther shared not only their early opposition to crusades but also their
current affirmation of the justice of armed resistance to aggression. It is under-
standable, however, that Erasmus would be unwilling to advertise this agreement with Luther and thus provide ammunition for his conservative critics,
who did not take seriously his claim to be an opponent of Luther and were
waiting to pounce on any evidence that he was in agreement with Luther on
anything. They were the 'hornets' that he feared. In a work already written but
not published until 1531, Alberto Pio would accuse Erasmus (on the basis of
Ep 858:85–165) of having denounced war against the Turks absolutely; see CWE
84 350. The Paris theologians would surely follow suit if given any pretext for
doing so. So the prudent course was for Erasmus to emphasize his distance

kept away from vicious diatribes of this sort, comforting my old age with
reading the Holy Scriptures.   55

On the first of January I published an attack on those who falsely proclaim themselves to be evangelicals although they are nothing of the sort.[18]
Some were inspired by my book to issue two biting little works aimed at
me, which so far I have not even bothered to read, never mind to prepare
a response.[19] They have come out with a new dogma, that it is right to use   60
lies and deception for the propagation of 'the gospel' (for so they call their
sect),[20] and they claim that this is permitted by imperial law, as if anything
in the secular sphere that is permitted by human laws is also permissible
in the work of the gospel.[21] The laws do permit this, but only if no one is
harmed. Here innocent people are accused and unsuspecting victims have   65
their reputations blackened. I pray God continually that he will be pleased
to impart his Spirit to the emperor and to all other princes, so that if this appalling plague cannot be wiped out completely, it may at least be curbed,
and that this may be brought about in such a way that victory will go not
to one party, but to the truth. I have a horror of war, for its consequences   70
are unpredictable, and the good are harmed no less than the wicked. There
must be heresies, says Paul,[22] and in the past the impiety of heretics has
worked to the great advantage of the church by honing its teaching and dis-
tinguishing between those who are true believers and those who are not.

* * * * *

from Luther and conceal their fundamental agreement by finding fault with
Luther's alleged early position, which had been officially condemned, by referring (at least in this letter) to *On War Against the Turks* as a laughable 'palinode,' and by advancing a cautious argument justifying defensive war against
the Turks while ignoring Luther's similar justification of it (cf n15 above). In
De bello Turcico, therefore, he had announced that he 'would take issue with
two sets of opponents: those [the advocates of a crusade] who, wrongly, are
fired up for war on the Turks, and those [Luther] who, also wrongly, argue
against making war on the Turk'; see CWE 64 232, and for confirmation that he
was referring to Luther, see ibidem 234, 237. For a detailed discussion of these
matters, see Christoph J. Steppich 'Erasmus and the Alleged "Dogma Lutheri"
Concerning War Against the Turks' *Lutherjahrbuch* 78 (2011) 205–50.

18 The *Epistola contra pseudevangelicos*, which was actually published in December
   1529; see Ep 2219 n5.
19 See Ep 2326.
20 Ie the evangelicals (*evangelici*) claim to be the party of the gospel (*evangelium*)
21 This is a charge that Erasmus had levelled in the *Epistola contra pseudevangelicos* (see CWE 78 239–40) and would repeat in the *Epistola ad fratres Inferioris
   Germaniae* (see CWE 78 269–70).
22 1 Cor 11:19

The godly character of the emperor gives me good reason to hope that the 75
Lord will use the imperial power to cure much of this deadly affliction. I do
not see how it can be remedied by human plans or human measures.

In your Letter to Luther, on the first page of folio c,[23] there is a slip
made by the copyist or the printer: Augustine never belonged to the Arian
sect, but to the Manichaeans, and that only before his baptism, for he wrote 80
against the Manichaeans as a catechumen. So this reference has no bearing
on Luther.

May the Lord preserve your Excellency and prosper you in all your
doings.

Freiburg im Breisgau, on the morrow of the feast of Peter and Paul 85
1530

2339 / From Nicolaus Olahus   Augsburg, 1 July 1529

This letter was first published in *Oláh Miklós Levelezése* ed Arnold Ipolyi, Mon-
umenta Hungariae historica: Diplomataria xxv (Budapest 1875) page 69. The
manuscript is page 223 of the Olahus codex, a manuscript volume containing
copies of six hundred letters to and from Nicolaus Olahus and bearing the title *Epistolae familiares N. Olahi ad Amicos &c.* Sixteen of these are letters from
Erasmus and twenty-one are letters to him; all of them are from the period
1530–4. In 1922, when Allen examined the codex to collate it with the texts
in Ipolyi's edition, it was in the private possession of Prince Paul Esterhazy
and was catalogued as Repositorium 71, fascicle 23; see Allen VIII 500–1. It is
now part of the collection of the Hungarian National Archives in Budapest;
see Paul Oskar Kristeller *Iter Italicum: A Finding List of Uncatalogued or Incom-
pletely Catalogued Humanistic Manuscripts of the Renaissance in Italian and Other
Libraries* 6 vols (London 1963–96) IV 289.

Nicolaus Olahus (Miklós Oláh), 1493–1568, was born in Sibiu, Transylvania
into a family of Wallachian origin that had achieved the status of lesser nobility. In 1510 he was a page at the court of King Vladislav II in Buda, and on
the latter's death in 1516 he became secretary to the bishop of Pécs. That same
year he took holy orders and was subsequently made canon of Pécs (1518) and
of Esztergom (1522). While at the court in Buda, Olahus became a member
of the circle of Erasmians that included Queen Mary and her chaplain Johann
Henckel. In March 1526 Olahus was appointed secretary to both King Louis
II and Queen Mary, and later that year accompanied the king on the military

* * * * *

23 The reference is to folio c recto of the *Epistolae atque libelli aliquot*; see n5 above.

campaign that ended in the disaster at Mohács on 29 August. Olahus, who had been sent back to Buda three days before the battle, remained loyal to the queen and supported the claims to the Hungarian crown of her brother Ferdinand. In 1527 Ferdinand appointed Olahus canon of Székesfehérvár. For his loyalty to the Hapsburg cause, Olahus paid the price of exclusion from the greater part of his homeland, which was under the control of Ferdinand's rival John Zápolyai. Together with Henckel, Olahus accompanied Queen Mary to the imperial diet at Augsburg, and it was from there that he wrote this, the first letter in the correspondence with Erasmus that would continue until the latter's death. When Queen Mary was made regent of the Netherlands in 1531, Olahus accompanied her to Brussels and remained in her service. Despite the friendship of many of the leading humanists of the Netherlands, Olahus was homesick for his native land and could not understand why Erasmus, who was free to do so, did not return to his native Brabant. He consequently became the major promoter of the ultimately unsuccessful efforts to get Erasmus to come home. The same longing for his devastated homeland led Olahus to compose both a descriptive geography of it, called *Hungaria* (1536), and an account of its early history, entitled *Athila* (1537). In 1539 Olahus moved from Brussels to Vienna, and in 1542, following the death of John Zápolyai in 1540, he was able to return to Hungary in the service of King Ferdinand. Made a member of the royal council, he rose rapidly in the hierarchy of the Hungarian church, becoming bishop of Zagreb (1543), bishop of Eger (1548), and finally archbishop of Esztergom in 1553. Made chancellor of the realm as well as primate of the church, Olahus used his influence to further the cause of the Catholic Reformation in Hungary. He was instrumental in bringing the Jesuits to the country in 1561 and in the following year he founded their college at Trnava, the city where in due course he was buried.

NICOLAUS OLAHUS, TREASURER OF SZÉKESFEHÉRVÁR,
SECRETARY AND COUNCILLOR TO HER MOST SERENE MAJESTY
QUEEN MARY, TO ERASMUS OF ROTTERDAM, GREETING

Although I do not doubt that you have already been made aware by letters from your friends[1] how much pleasure and delight my most serene 5
sovereign, Queen Mary, and all of us derived from the publication of your
Christian Widow and its dedication to her;[2] I would nevertheless like you to

* * * * *

2339
1 Eg Ep 2309
2 Ep 2100

Nicolaus Olahus
Bild-Archiv und Porträt-sammlung
Österreichische Nationalbibliothek, Vienna

learn from me too, who am a stranger to you, though a friendly stranger, that nothing could have given her such unalloyed delight. For it brought great comfort to her mind, which had been deeply affected by the loss of   10 her most loving husband,[3] and at the same time it provided her with a most erudite lesson in how a widow should conduct and organize her life. As a result her affection and good will towards you were greatly increased. I believe that recently you had clear evidence of this from the letter she wrote to you in her own hand.[4]   15

I am possessed by a great desire to see you, for especially at this time when there is such disagreement over matters of faith, with danger-ous consequences for many people, your presence here would be critical, since it would permit you to offer helpful advice in the present confused state of things.[5] We hope therefore that you will come here, if not in re-   20 sponse to the urging of your friends, then for the sake of public peace,[6] and with this in mind, I say no more to you for the present. There is one matter, however, that I think ought not to be passed over: your friend Polyphemus, of the king's retinue, who presented to the queen in your name the book that you sent her, has omitted nothing that a good, faithful,   25 and diligent retainer ought to do and has faithfully carried out everything you asked of him both in relation to the queen and to your other devoted friends.[7]

It is true that I am unknown to you by sight; but I have gained such an affection for you, and you are so well known to me from your books, which   30 I take up frequently and read for hours on end, that in knowledge of you I shall not yield second place to those who are with you every day and enjoy the delights of your company. You have the best witnesses of my love and affection for you in Ursinus Velius, Henckel, and Polyphemus (who will

* * * * *

3 Louis II of Hungary, killed at the battle of Mohács in 1526
4 See Ep 2309:11–16.
5 On the desire in high places for Erasmus' advice on the current troubles, cf Ep 2328:64–7 with n18.
6 There was a rumour that Emperor Charles had invited Erasmus to the diet. Melanchthon reported it to Luther on 30 June; see MBW Ep 948 [2]. In July it was believed falsely that Erasmus had replied to the emperor; see Allen Ep 2358:3. At this time Erasmus was indeed expecting the emperor to summon him to the diet and was already pleading illness as his excuse for declining the invitation; see Epp 2344:20–1, 2353A:44–7. But no invitation came; see Epp 2350A:1, 2353A:44–5, Allen Ep 2365:14.
7 See Ep 2334 nn1 and 2.

deliver this letter to you),[8] and many others who are close friends of yours   35
and mine. If, as I hope, Almighty God brings you here safely, or I am given
some other opportunity to see you, you will discover this for yourself and
will have first-hand knowledge of the regard I have formed for you on account of your powers of intellect and your excellent accomplishments. I beg
you earnestly to accept my devotion and to count me among your friends.   40
Farewell, and think well of me, for I am your true and affectionate admirer.

Augsburg, 1 July 1530

2340 / From Germain de Brie   [?], 6 July 1530

First published in the *Epistolae floridae*, this is Brie's answer to Ep 2291. It is
liberally sprinkled with passages in Greek. Erasmus' reply to Brie is Ep 2379.

GERMAIN DE BRIE TO ERASMUS OF ROTTERDAM, GREETING

So I am about to receive, at almost one and the same time, a Chrysostom in
Latin from your own Germany and a Chrysostom in Greek from Italy; visi-
tors from Verona tell me that Gian Matteo,[1] the bishop of that city, is sparing
no expense to provide us with a Chrysostom speaking in his own tongue,   5
and a text that is as correct as it is possible to make it.[2] For this purpose he
is using manuscripts unearthed in Venice from the library of the cardinal
of Nicaea,[3] and has also consulted several other manuscripts, for which he
made a thorough search in many places. The work itself had already been
printed, but because it was found to be faulty by the Aristarchan critics to   10
whom the bishop had assigned this responsibility,[4] it was sent back to the
press on the bishop's orders and at his expense.

* * * * *

8 See Epp 2313 (Ursinus Velius), 2309 (Henckel), and preceding note (Polyphemus).

2340
1 Gian Matteo Giberti (Ep 1443A)
2 The complete edition of Chrysostom in Greek designed by Giberti did not get
   beyond the first three volumes, which were devoted to the Pauline epistles
   (Verona: Sabii, 28 June 1529).
3 Basilius (Johannes) Cardinal Bessarion (Ep 554:79n), one of the leading champions of Greek scholarship in his day. In 1485 gave his library to the republic
   of Venice, where it became the nucleus of the Biblioteca Marciana, the National
   Library of St Mark's.
4 On Aristarchan critics, see Ep 2333 n13.

Since I am waiting for that Greek text of Chrysostom, I have not contributed to your Latin edition by any further translations of my own beyond
the two pieces that I sent you earlier; these were done at your suggestion   15
and with your encouragement, and are now in circulation.[5] For surely no
one, even with the best will in the world, could commit himself to producing a translation without a text on which to base it? The lack of Greek copies
is the reason why, for the present, I cannot be of any further assistance to
you in this strenuous and exacting task. This makes me all the more pleased   20
to learn that there are people in your part of the world who can help you
in your labours. 'When two walk together . . .'[6]

If my *Monk* reached you late,[7] you should not blame my negligence but
that of your courier. I handed the work to him immediately on receiving
your letter, and I was hopeful that it could be delivered in time. As for the   25
cardinal chancellor, I see that you remember what you wrote to me in your
other letter.[8]

About Toussain,[9] believe me, he is a good friend of yours and as respectful of you as anyone. He is no less concerned with your reputation than
with Budé's, even if it is principally to Budé that he credits his initiation   30
into Greek learning. At a time when the sea itself was raging on all sides,
you should blame the violence of the storm and not the weakness of the man
if, along with the other passengers who had thoughtlessly embarked on the
same ship (as people are wont to do), he allowed himself for a very few
hours not just to be carried on his way, but to be swept headlong wherever   35
wind and wave impelled him. Upon my soul, that was such a fierce hurri-
cane that despite my firm resolve to hold the rudder steady, I was forced
to veer a little from my course in order to withstand more easily the force
of the waves and the rough waters that were coming thick and fast against
me, so that eventually I might reach our destined harbour, even though by   40
a somewhat altered course.

The wind that ruffled the sea at that time came from foreign parts and
from a foreign people.[10] You were not blind to this, Erasmus, for, in the long

* * * * *

5 *De Sacerdotio* (Ep 1733), *De Babyla martyre* (Ep 2052 n2)
6 Cited here in Greek, the phrase is from Homer *Iliad* 10.224, where Diomedes
    asks for a companion to make his mission more agreeable and safer. For its
    use as a proverb, see *Adagia* III 1 51.
7 Ep 2291:5–6
8 Ep 2291:22–6
9 Ep 2291:31–53
10 Allen read this sentence as a reference to Erasmus' old adversary Girolamo
    Aleandro (Ep 1553 n9) and his alleged Jewish ancestry (Ep 1166:93–4 with

letter you sent me some time ago, it was clear that you had cleverly sniffed
out the truth.[11] Now that the halcyon birds have brought us calm again and   45
tempers among us have cooled,[12] if, my dear Erasmus, your feelings have
been hurt, I sincerely hope that you too will be lenient and, either because
of your own generous nature or out of respect for me, admit Toussain back
into the friendship he earlier enjoyed, burying all the past in oblivion. There
is an old saying that friendships should be immortal and quarrels mortal.[13]   50
I can assure you that it never entered Toussain's head that he would meet
with your hostility. This is all the more reason why you should take him
back as a friend, especially since I am interceding on his behalf. Moreover,
it is only fitting that Erasmus, who has such a superb intellect and such a
fluent command of language, should match these qualities with a compa-   55
rable magnanimity. You should not allow your anger to mount because of
verses written by wretched scribblers who have absolutely no interest in the
Muses and Graces; such things should bother you no more than an Indian
elephant is bothered by a gnat's bite.[14] You know the proverb 'a heavy anvil
does not fear the noise.'[15] Believe me, the majesty of your fame and glory   60
is too great to be overturned by such pitiful and tasteless squibs as these.
Gods exist at a higher level than men.[16]

Moreover, those epigrams, which have much of the Carian muse about
them,[17] do not sound at all like the work of Toussain, who is celebrated as
one of the most eloquent writers in Greek and Latin, a man commended   65
by the integrity of his character and totally averse to scurrility of any kind.

* * * * *

n24). But Brie is clearly referring to 'a foreign people' (ie the Italians), not a
foreign individual, and the real reference is to the Italian origins of the excessive Ciceronianism that was the butt of Erasmus' satire in the *Ciceronianus*;
see n11 below. In his reply, however, Erasmus will wonder what 'foreigner'
is being referred to, and then identify Aleandro, though not by name, as the
culprit who deliberately sowed dissension between him and Budé; see Allen
Ep 2379:102–22.

11 See Ep 2046:49–53, 324–31.
12 In classical myth there was a seabird, called *halcyon* in Greek, that was said to
   nest on the open sea during periods of calm, known as 'halcyon days,' a term
   that became proverbial for periods of tranquillity and quiet; see *Adagia* II vi
   52.
13 *Adagia* IV v 26
14 *Adagia* I x 66
15 *Adagia* III i 29
16 Cited in Greek from Homer *Iliad* 11.264
17 The Carian Muse or Carian music was proverbial for its loud, rustic sound;
   see *Adagia* I viii 79.

Admittedly, he confesses that in the general excitement he improvised (he would not say 'composed') a single couplet. This he recited to a friend, who then published it along with some additional nonsense from other people. So it appeared in print, to the great embarrassment of the author. Moreover, I always imagined you were too magnanimous to attach any importance to windy trifles of this sort; I thought you were concerned only with matters that contributed to learning.

You remember, I am sure, what was once said by Alexander when he was told that someone had come forward and spoken ill of him: 'It is the lot of a king to be maligned when he has acted well.'[18] I would like you to imitate Alexander, at least in this particular, especially since, in my opinion and in that of many people (and I mean no flattery), your literary labours, your works, and your victories have earned you the right to be known to posterity as 'Erasmus the Great,' just as Alexander earned the same distinction from his actions, his exertions in battle, and his triumphs.

But enough on this subject. With regard to Budé,[19] clear your mind, I beg you, of whatever suspicions you may have. Indeed people who spread that sort of gossip seem to me to be quarrelsome troublemakers who do a disservice to both of you and to humane studies. Unless the mind of Budé is an absolutely closed book to me, there is nothing further from his thoughts than the story that, you say, was reported to you. In your previous letter you indicated your suspicions about him when he was preparing to publish his *Commentary on the Greek Language*. That book has now been published: tell me honestly, have you found any part of the work where your reputation has been injured or damaged? Is Budé not always Budé to you? Does he not show throughout that work a consistently modest respect for you? He is by nature and training so inclined towards generosity, so practised in modesty, that nothing ungenerous or intemperate could ever come from his mind or pen – unless by chance (and this is a conclusion no one will ever, or could ever, persuade me to accept) he has decided to betray his own nature and take on a different self and a different character. Even this volume of letters will prove the truth of what I am saying. I eagerly await a letter from you, but a letter that will be both an announcement and a permanent assurance that my friend Toussain, through my efforts, has been truly reconciled with you. Farewell and continue to love me.

6 July 1530

* * * * *

18 Plutarch *Alexander* 41; cited by Erasmus in the *Apophthegmata* CWE 37 357 no 67 (LB IV 199E).
19 Ep 2291:61–74

2341 / To [Lorenzo Campeggi]　　　　　Freiburg, 7 July 1530

This letter was first published by Allen. For the manuscript and the identity
of the addressee, see Ep 2328 introduction.

Four days ago I wrote to you and sent my letter with von Reinach, a canon
of Basel.[1] I am now sending a second copy of the letter, which I made for
that purpose. After a long and serious illness I am still dragging myself
around in a weakened state, and am not yet out of the clutches of doctors
and surgeon.[2]　　　　　5

If only the Lord would reveal to me some plan by which this present
storm might be calmed![3] But I trust that the spirit of Christ, working through
the piety and might of the emperor and through persons like yourself, will
cause something good to happen to the church. I would not like to see Luther
involved in this business. If any concessions or reforms are to be made, I　　10
would prefer this to happen on the initiative of others. At the present time
Zwingli's domain is more extensive than Luther's.[4] What upsets me is not
so much their teaching, especially Luther's, as the fact that, under the pretext of the gospel, I see a class of men emerging whom I find repugnant
from every point of view.[5] If we could get rid of their preachers, espe-　　15
cially Zwingli, Oecolampadius, and Capito, there would be hope of healing the people. I feel sorry for the Anabaptists; they could be helped if
baptism were the only issue, but they introduce confusion into everything.
They are possessed by a kind of madness; yet I am told that some members of this sect are not at all evil people.[6] Could I ask you to be kind　　20

* * * * *

2341
1 It appears that the dispatch of Epp 2328 (to Campeggi, dated 6 June) and
　2338 (to Duke George, dated 30 June) was delayed until this messenger be-
　came available; see Epp 2342:16–17, 2344:24–5. He has been identified as Jost
　von Reinach (documented 1486–1536), member of the second generation of a
　branch of the family von Reinach that had settled in Basel.
2 See Ep 2320 n1.
3 Cf Ep 2328:64–5 with n18.
4 At this point, Lutheranism was still confined largely to Electoral Saxony,
　the landgraviate of Hessen, and Franconia (the margraviate of Brandenburg-
　Ansbach and the city of Nürnberg), while Zwinglianism, established in the
　cities of Switzerland and southwestern Germany, seemed to cover a much
　larger geographical area.
5 A repugnance soon to reach its fullest expression in the *Epistola ad fratres
　Inferioris Germaniae*, which would be published in September (Ep 2324 n2)
6 Cf CWE 78 71–2 (*Epistola ad fratres Inferioris Germaniae*).

enough to read the extract from the *Epistola* that I wrote to Vulturius of
Nijmegen.[7]

When I gather more strength, I shall write you in greater detail. May
the Lord prosper what all of you are doing.

Freiburg, 7 July 1530   25

2342 / To Christoph von Carlowitz   Freiburg, 7 July 1530

This letter was first published in the *Epistolae floridae*. On Carlowitz, who had
now been in the service of Duke George of Saxony for about a year, see Epp
1951 n7, 2085 introduction.

ERASMUS OF ROTTERDAM TO CHRISTOPH VON CARLOWITZ,
GREETING

You are wrong, my dear Carlowitz, if you think anything would be more
welcome to me than a letter from you. I am happy that you have entered
upon that vast theatre of the world,[1] where you will be able to give some   5
proof of your learning and your good sense before such a large and distinguished audience.

I am truly sorry about that friend of mine who, by giving what you call
'salutary and necessary advice,' brought on himself considerable hostility,
most of which devolves on me.[2] Again and again I am invited to impart my   10
prescription for the restoration of peace.[3] This is the reward one gets for
suggesting anything that is just and fair! He was here with me, it is true,
and spoke with me for about three hours, but no word has passed between
us on that subject, not even by letter.

I do not much care to be defended by the Cyclops;[4] I fear that an in-   15
experienced and untimely defender may do more harm than good. I sent
a letter to your prince by von Reinach, a canon of Basel.[5] When I have an

* * * * *

7 Quite possibly a reference to the section of the *Epistola contra pseudevangelicos*
  in which Erasmus felt he had pointed out how the religious conflict should be
  dealt with; see Ep 2308:13–15 with n7.

2342
1 Ie the diet then meeting at Augsburg
2 Allen could not identify the friend, and neither can we.
3 See Ep 2328 n18.
4 Erasmus' derisive nickname for his servant Felix Rex, also known as Polyphemus (Ep 2130). For his recent whereabouts, see Ep 2334 n1.
5 The letter was Ep 2338. For the canon, see Ep 2341 n1.

opportunity to write again, I shall gladly and carefully carry out what you
advise. Do interrupt me frequently, my dear Carlowitz, with your letters. I
pray that the court will turn out well for you.   20

Freiburg im Breisgau, 7 July 1530

2343 / To Philippus Melanchthon   Freiburg, 7 July 1530

This letter (= MBW Ep 956) was first printed by Georg Coelestin in his *Historia Comitiorum anno M.D.XXX Augustae celebratorum* (Frankfurt and der Oder:
Eichorn 1577) II 207 verso, 302 verso (corrigenda). Allen based his text on the
manuscript in the University Library at Rostock (MS Theol 62² 2° folios 108
verso–109 recto), which was made around 1550 by Johann Aurifaber, the first
editor of Luther's letters. In so doing, Allen took account of collations that
were supplied to him by Bruno Claussen on the basis of the text printed in
F.W. Schirrmacher *Briefe und Akten zu der Geschichte des Religionsgespräches zu
Marburg 1529 und des Reichstages zu Augsburg 1530* (Gotha 1876) 105.

LETTER OF ERASMUS OF ROTTERDAM TO PHILIPPUS MELANCHTHON
Cordial greetings. Dearest Philippus, there is no possibility that I can resolve the tragic conflict that is now troubling the whole world: no one but
God will resolve it, even if ten diets were to assemble.[1] Anyone who pro-
poses a fair settlement is immediately met with cries of 'Lutheranism'; that   5
is the only reward he receives.

I have been ill now for four months.[2] First, I had cramps in the stomach, then vomiting, and after vomiting the ruin of my whole digestive system. This poor body of mine does not respond well to doctors. Everything
they prescribed proved harmful. The cramps were followed by an abscess   10
or, to be more precise, a scleroma, which at first spread widely over the left
side above the pubic region and the groin. Then it restricted itself to the middle of the belly, taking on the appearance of a serpent with its head biting
the navel, its body twisting this way and that, and its tail turned towards the
pubic regions; later with its head remaining where it was, it wound its way   15
around the navel on the left side so that its tail almost surrounded the navel.
It produced constant jabs of pain, which were at times intolerable. I could
neither eat nor sleep, nor read, nor write, nor dictate, nor listen to someone
reading; I could not even endure to converse with my friends. A surgeon was

* * * * *

2343
1 Cf Ep 2328:64–5 with n18.
2 On this illness, see Ep 2320 n1.

called in, who nearly killed me with his powerful plasters. At last we lanced   20
it with a knife. As soon as that was done, I was reconciled with sleep, and the
excruciating pain lessened. I drag myself around, since I am still very weak
and not yet free of the surgeon. In the middle of my illness my servant Quirinus was suddenly taken with the deadly sweat;[3] my other servant had been
called back to his homeland.[4] It was thus that the Lord saw fit to visit me.   25

I cannot find words to say how much Luther disgusted me by that
letter of his directed against Duke George, in which he makes a great fuss
over nothing with his accusation of theft.[5] Farewell.

Freiburg, 7 July 1530

2344 / To Simon Pistoris   Freiburg, 7 July 1530

This letter, Erasmus' answer to Ep 2333, was first published in the *Epistolae
floridae*.

ERASMUS OF ROTTERDAM TO SIMON PISTORIS, GREETING
When my illness was raging at its height,[1] I sent you a letter by a certain
Heinrich,[2] who seems to have carried out his duties most unsatisfactorily: it
appears that he only delivered the letter commending himself. Your most illustrious prince included no questions in his last letter,[3] but yours dealt with   5
some doubtful issues. To reply to these would require a long letter; it seems
to me that to take steps without public authority only leads to revolution.

I was gravely ill for several months,[4] first with cramps in the belly,
which led to vomiting as a result of the ruin of the digestive system, and
then to an extreme debility. This was followed by a wicked abscess around   10
the navel. It was lanced with the knife, but the hardness remains, which
makes me fear a new outbreak. The surgeon, acting contrary to nature,

* * * * *

3 On 'the sweat' see Ep 2209 n31. For Quirinus Talesius' non-fatal bout with it,
  see Epp 2348:19–20, 2349:9–10, 2353A:70–2, 2356:35–7.
4 Nicolaas Kan; see Ep 2261 n34.
5 See Ep 2338 nn5–6.

2344
1 See lines 8–16 below.
2 Cf Ep 2331:2–3. The letter, which is not extant, was presumably dated c 6 June,
  the date of Ep 2326, which Heinrich also carried; see Ep 2326 n5.
3 This letter from Duke George is not extant; it was probably contemporary with
  Ep 2333.
4 See Ep 2320 n1.

Philippus Melanchthon
Lucas Cranach, 1532
Bayerische Staatsgemäldesammlungen, Munich

applied hot and stinging poultices to the abscess, which ought to be have been treated with something cold; the result was that he produced an ulcer. I am still dragging myself around; my recovery is slow, and I am not yet 15 out of the clutches of doctors and surgeon.

Perish the thought that I should take on the role of Aristarchus in this intractable crisis – and win the ill will of both sides.[5] I wish that God would see fit to be an Aristarchus, for he alone can put an end to this deadly tragedy. But if the emperor is commanding me to come to Augsburg, he 20 must first exercise his authority over this wretched illness of mine.[6]

I do not know what can be done with such a Thraso.[7] You know the whole story. Quietly observe what he is plotting and if he bombards the duke with lies, see that he learns the truth. I recently sent a letter to the duke by a canon named von Reinach.[8] Farewell, patron par excellence. 25

Freiburg, 7 July 1530

2345 / To Nicolaus Olahus   Freiburg, 7 July 1530

First published in the *Epistolae floridae*, this is Erasmus' reply to Ep 2339. The manuscript is page 224 of the Olahus codex in the Hungarian National Archives at Budapest (see Ep 2339 introduction).

DESIDERIUS ERASMUS OF ROTTERDAM TO NICOLAUS OLAHUS,
TREASURER OF SZÉKESFEHÉRVÁR, SECRETARY AND
GRAND COUNCILLOR, GREETING

I welcome, most generous Nicolaus, the sentiments you expressed in your letter, and I shall add your name to the list of my special friends. The godly char- 5 acter and exceptional kindliness of your excellent queen have often been mentioned by Henckel in his letters,[1] and his authority carries very great weight with me. But no letter has come to me from the queen, either in her own hand

* * * * *

5 Although the name Aristarchus was synonymous with 'demanding critic' (see Ep 2333 n13), Aristarchus' work on the Greek poets was also restorative: he identified errors in the Greek texts and corrected them; see CWE 31 435–6, 44–51 (*Adagia* I v 57). On the desire of many that Erasmus should provide a plan for the restoration of religious unity, cf Ep 2328 n18.
6 See Ep 2339 n6.
7 Erasmus' usual nickname for Heinrich Eppendorf; see Ep 2216 n9.
8 See Ep 2341 n1.

2345
1 On both Queen Mary of Hungary and her chaplain, Johann Henckel, see Ep 2309.

or written in her name by someone else. If a letter had come, it would have
been a great comfort to me during the miseries of my illness.[2] Excuse this   10
short note: I am still rather fragile, and have many letters to write. I pray that
her most serene Majesty will have every success and happiness. Farewell.

Freiburg, 7 July 1530

After dinner, before I sealed this letter, I received letters from the
queen and from Henckel, who also sent a cup.[3]   15

2346 / To Johann von Vlatten   Freiburg, 9 July 1530

This letter, first published in the *Epistolae floridae*, is Erasmus' reply to Ep 2335.
Vlatten's reply to Erasmus is Ep 2360.

ERASMUS OF ROTTERDAM TO JOHANN VON VLATTEN, GREETING
Whether you write or not, I know that Vlatten is Vlatten. To have taken part
in so many legations and negotiations will prove an advantage to you one
day. The young duke of Jülich has sent me a cup with a letter.[1]

I do not see what I would do there considering my present state of   5
health, which makes me flee the courts 'on horseback,' as the saying is.[2]
I am gradually recovering from a long illness.[3] It is true that I have been
thinking of moving, but I see no very tranquil harbour. Without me the Lord
will provide the emperor and the other princes with helpful counsel.[4] It is
not safe for a humble person like me to become involved in such matters,   10
in which anyone who says anything that leans on the side of honesty and
fairness is immediately dubbed a Lutheran. I send you my very best wishes,
my dear and much loved friend.

Freiburg, 9 July 1530

2347 / To Luca Bonfiglio   Freiburg, 9 July 1530

This letter was first published in the *Epistolae floridae*, where Johannes Dantiscus
(Ep 2163 n34) was named as the addressee. When the letter was republished

* * * * *

2 On the illness, see Ep 2320 n1.
3 The letter from the queen is not extant; that from Henckel is Ep 2309. On the
  cup, see Ep 2309 n6.

2346
1 See Ep 2234.
2 Literally 'with sails and horses'; see *Adagia* I iv 17.
3 See Ep 2320 n1.
4 On requests for such counsel, see Ep 2328 n18.

in the *Epistolae palaeonaeoi*, Dantiscus was replaced by Luca Bonfiglio as the addressee, a correction that Allen accepted as having been the work of Erasmus himself. For that reason he accepted the new address as correct, even though he found it impossible to account for the original ascription to Dantiscus.

Not a great deal is known about Luca Bonfiglio (also known as Luca Bonfio) of Padua, c 1470–1540. Presumably educated as a humanist, he embarked on an ecclesiastical career in his home city. Around 1515 he entered the service of Pope Leo x on the recommendation of Pietro Bembo. In 1526 he was made canon of the cathedral at Padua and in 1529 he was made first dean of the chapter. That same year he became the secretary to Lorenzo Cardinal Campeggi, whom he accompanied to the Diet of Augsburg in 1530. The following year Bonfiglio accompanied Campeggi to the imperial court at Brussels. Returning to Italy in 1532 or 1533, he resigned his canonry at Padua to a nephew and, after unsuccessful efforts to secure a position in Rome, spent the rest of his life in Venice and Padua.

ERASMUS OF ROTTERDAM TO LUCA BONFIGLIO, GREETING

I shall be glad to read the little book of Leonico's,[1] for I know that nothing comes from the pen of an erudite and pious man that is not learned and pious. As for your urging me to attend the diet, I can only answer with that saying of Cato's: 'Come not to offer counsel before you are called.'[2] And 5 even if I were to receive a pressing call, my health ties me here.[3] Moreover I do not see what a man of humble station like me could do in such a complicated business, which an ecumenical council that sat for three years would hardly suffice to resolve. Then it is not safe for me to open my mouth here. If I were to make any fair proposal, I would immediately be dubbed 10 a Lutheran.[4] Unless the matter is taken in hand by the magnates with the complete agreement of the territories, they will achieve nothing; but from such a council all human ambitions must be set aside.[5]

* * * * *

2347
1 If one assumes that the reference is to a newly published 'little book' by Niccolò Leonico Tomeo, the work in question was perhaps the dialogue *De animorum essentia* (Venice: Sabii 1530).
2 *Adagia* I ii 90. There is word-play here. The Latin of Cato's saying as quoted by Erasmus (*Ad consilium ne accesseris priusquam voceris*) can also be read as 'Do not come to the diet before you are called.' On *consilium* (= *concilium*) as a word for 'diet,' see n5 below.
3 See Ep 2339 n6.
4 Cf Ep 2343:4–5.
5 This passage is rendered difficult by Erasmus' use of the word *synodus* 'assembly' to refer both to a church council and to an imperial diet. The

I thank you for your kind sentiments towards me. I promise in all
sincerity to reciprocate them. Farewell.   15
    Freiburg, 9 July 1530

2348 / To Frans van der Dilft   Freiburg, 9 July 1530

This letter was first published in the *Epistolae floridae*. Dilft (Ep 2222 n15) was
now in Spain, where he had entered the service of Alonso de Fonseca, archbishop of Toledo.

ERASMUS OF ROTTERDAM TO FRANS VAN DER DILFT
You are leaning on a straw, my dear Frans, when you set such store by my
letters.[1] I have already received a large enough reward from the archbishop
of Toledo, so there is no reason for you to be anxious on that account.[2] When
will the letters you are sending to Goclenius reach us here?[3] They would   5
arrive more quickly if you sent them to Anton Fugger in Augsburg. Many

* * * * *

religious situation, he says, is so complicated that even an ecumenical council (*Synodus οἰκουμενική*) of three years' duration (lines 8–9) could not be expected to deal with it. But it is not a church council that has taken the matter in hand; it is, rather, a meeting of the imperial diet, which is proposing to negotiate a national settlement of the religious question that will
be valid pending a general council. Addressing this situation, Erasmus ob-
serves (lines 11–12) that unless those with power, the magnates (*magnos*),
ie the emperor and the most powerful princes, take the lead and secure
the cooperation of all the imperial estates (*provinciae*), ie the principalities
and free cities with votes in the diet, nothing will be accomplished. Then
he adds, in the same sentence (lines 12–13) and still referring to the diet,
that such a *Synodus* must be free of all ambition. Cf Epp 2196:165, 2331:5,
2343:3, 2348:7, where Erasmus refers to the Diet of Augsburg as a *Consilium*,
a word often used as the equivalent of *concilium*. In the absence of a much
demanded but not delivered general council, Germans, to the distress of cu-
rialists and canonists in Rome, were more than ready to treat an imperial
diet or a meeting of provincial estates as the functional equivalent of a national church council or a provincial synod. Erasmus had no difficulty with
that.

2348
1 The letters of recommendation (Epp 2251–3) that Erasmus had provided for
  Dilft's second journey to Spain in search of employment. The letters provided
  for his first visit had failed of their purpose; see Ep 2109:3–24.
2 For Fonseca's gift, see Epp 2003:94–5, 2004:38–41. It reached Erasmus in March
  1529; see Ep 2126 n45.
3 On Conradus Goclenius, who lived in Louvain, see Ep 2352.

delegations will doubtless be going to the diet,[4] and couriers will be running to and fro.

I was badly fooled by the wine you brought me,[5] for although it pleased me greatly at the first sampling, as soon as I began to drink it seriously, it changed its colour, taste, and bouquet. For this reason Marcin the Pole[6] set out for Besançon with twenty crowns, but he did not bring back a drop.[7] The official and the treasurer were away on an embassy to the king of France.[8] The Pole stated bluntly that all the rest were mere nonentities. So I have been very ill for almost four months and have not yet regained my strength.[9]

This is in reply to your letter of the first of April,[10] which you sent by courier. In future do what they do in the courts and send two copies, and advise your friends to do the same. When I was very sick, my man Quirinus was suddenly seized with the British sweat,[11] and I did not have anyone else, for Kan, wanting to have his freedom, had returned to his homeland.[12] He has now become a priest and will pray for my success and happiness. Haio has gone back to Friesland.[13] Farewell, my dearest Dilft.

Freiburg, 9 July 1530

2349 / To Alfonso de Valdés   Freiburg, 9 July 1530

First published in the *Epistolae floridae*, this is Erasmus answer to the letter that Valdés promised to write on 28 June (Ep 2336:81–4).

ERASMUS OF ROTTERDAM TO ALFONSO DE VALDÉS, GREETING
I cannot but be deeply affected by the sad blow that has befallen you, my

* * * * *

4 Ie the imperial diet at Augsburg. Erasmus uses the word *Consilium* (= *Concilium*) to refer to the diet.
5 See Ep 2225 n7.
6 Marcin Słap Dąbrówski (Ep 2351)
7 The errand presumably took place in April or May, since Słap arrived in Louvain on 31 May (Ep 2351:114).
8 Leonard de Gruyères (the official; Epp 1534, 2139); François Bonvalot (the treasurer; Ep 2142). Bonvalot resided in France from April 1530 to March 1532; Gruyères' visit took place sometime in 1530. See *Actes de François I* IX 110.
9 See Ep 2320 n1.
10 Not extant
11 See Ep 2343 n3.
12 See Ep 2261 n34.
13 Haio Cammingha (Ep 2073), whose period of residence with Erasmus at Basel overlapped with that of Dilft

dear Valdés, in losing at the same time your excellent father[1] and your patron
Mercurino Gattinara,[2] who was as dear to you as a father. But one must be
strong in mind against all the misfortunes of our human lot.   5

The Lord has been pleased to visit me too. I am gradually recovering,
but the surgeon, by applying brutal poultices, turned a hard abscess into an
ulcer, which has healed in such a manner that the hardness remains; so I
am afraid the trouble will recur.[3] In the middle of my illness my servant,
the only one I had (for the other was recalled to his homeland),[4] came down 10
with the sweat.[5] He had shared with me both bedroom and table. But 'He
is the Lord, let him do what is good in his eyes.'[6]

Farewell, my very dear Valdés. After this storm through which you
are now going expect the calm. Nothing that has yet happened to you is
unusual. You have lost a father, but that happens every day. Gattinara could 15
not have lived long; you were leaning on a crumbling wall. Remember that
I am here to help you, such as I am. Farewell again.

Freiburg, 9 July 1530

2350 / To Mary of Austria   Freiburg, 9 July 1530

First published in the *Epistolae floridae*, this is Erasmus' reply to a brief, handwritten note received on 7 July; see Ep 2345:14–15.

ERASMUS OF ROTTERDAM TO MARY, FORMER QUEEN OF HUNGARY,
GREETING
Most serene queen, I am overjoyed that your Majesty has thought so kindly
of my *Widow*,[1] which I worked on as best I could, given the extent of my
obligations and my modest abilities. What pains me and makes me blush   5
with embarrassment is that this little work does poor justice to your greatness and your godly nature. I see that you are offended by any expression

* * * * *

2349
1 Fernando de Valdés, hereditary *regidor* of Cuenca in Castile. The date of his
  death is known only from this letter.
2 See Ep 2336 n5.
3 On this illness, see Ep 2320 n1.
4 Nicolaas Kan; see Ep 2259A n3.
5 Quirinus Talesius; see Ep 2343 n3.
6 1 Sam 3:18

2350
1 Ep 2100

of praise, although in treating such matters I have deliberately held back. But this makes you all the more deserving of praise, since you have now added modesty, the fairest gem of all, to your other outstanding virtues. May the Lord in his goodness be pleased to make you grow constantly in godliness, and bring you joy in place of sorrow. Sometimes he uses adversity to cleanse and strengthen us; but he knows how to temper bitterness with the abundant sweetness of his consolation. May he keep your Majesty safe and bring success to all your actions.

You will learn about my health from Henckel.[2] The little letter that you wrote me in your own hand will be preserved among my most valued possessions as a treasured pledge of your sentiments towards me.

Freiburg im Breisgau, 9 July 1530

2350A / To Christoph Truchsess von Waldburg   Freiburg, 9 July 1530

This letter, unknown to Allen, was discovered by Erika Rummel in a copy of the *Opus epistolarum* that once belonged to the addressee and is now in the Herzog August Bibliothek at Wolfenbüttel (P 528c. 2 Helmst). The text is found, in a sixteenth-century hand, on the recto of the last page of the volume (Froben's colophon is on the verso). See *Wolfenbütteler Renaissancemitteilungen* 12 (1988) 101–2.

After studying at Tübingen and Padua and attracting the favourable attention of Erasmus, Christoph Truchsess von Waldburg (Ep 1625) chose a military career in the service of Charles V and Ferdinand of Austria. In 1529 and again in 1532 he was one of Ferdinand's commanders against the Turks. In 1535 he accompanied Emperor Charles on his expedition to Tunis and died on the trip home, still in his twenties. Where he was at this point is not clear. The reference to his being 'so close at hand' (line 7) suggests the family castle at Waldburg, near Ravensburg on the north shore of Lake Constance. But the request to greet his father (line 9) suggests Augsburg.

TO BARON CHRISTOPH VON WALDBURG, HIS LORD AND MUCH RESPECTED FRIEND, FROM ERASMUS OF ROTTERDAM, GREETING
That I have been summoned by the emperor is an empty rumour.[1] Even if I were called, I could not go, because I have been seriously ill now for four

* * * * *

2 Erasmus' reply to Ep 2309 is not extant.

2350A
1 See Ep 2339 n6.

months;[2] I am gradually improving, but still have no strength. And even if   5
I were in good health, I would not dare trust my poor body to the journey.
I remember our exchange of letters;[3] I am glad that you are so close at hand
and am most grateful for the kindness that you and your father show me.
Please give my best wishes to your father.[4] I pray that you are flourishing,
my most distinguished young friend.   10

    Freiburg, 9 July 1530

2351 / From Marcin Słap Dąbrówski   Louvain, 12 July 1530

This letter was first published by Casimir von Miaskowski in the *Jahrbuch
für Theologie und spekulative Theologie* 15 (1901) 210. The manuscript, autograph
throughout, is in the Rehdiger Collection of the University Library at Wrocław
(MS Rehd 254.138).

    Marcin Słap (d 1550) was born to a family of gentry that owned the estate
of Dąbrówka (Dambrowska), near Poznań. His first appearance in the historical record is as a member of the clergy of the collegiate church of Our Lady
in Poznań (1525, 1526) and then as a priest in nearby Skórzewo. By 1528 he
had become a client of Andrzej Krzycki, bishop of Płock (Ep 1629), who in that
year sent him abroad as a companion to Andrzej Zebrzydowski (Ep 2078:30–1).
After spending some time together in Erasmus' household, Słap and Zebrzydowski left for Paris but soon returned to Erasmus and then parted company.
Zebrzydowski departed for Padua while Słap remained with Erasmus, moved
with him to Freiburg, and earned his warm praise. See Ep 2201:11–35, 64–
80. The separation from Zebrzydowski had been caused by disagreements of
some sort, and it appears from this letter (lines 96–7) that Erasmus wrote to
Krzycki defending Słap against charges levelled by Zebrzydowski. In October 1529 Słap returned briefly to Poland and the entourage of Krzycki at Cracow before journeying once again to western Europe. In the spring of 1530
he visited Erasmus at Freiburg, bringing with him letters (answered by Epp
2375–7) as well a gift from Krzycki (see lines 93–4). While in Freiburg, Słap
did Erasmus the favour of going to Besançon to fetch him a new supply of
wine (Ep 2348). Soon thereafter he departed for the University of Louvain,
arriving there on 31 May (line 114). In later years, following legal studies
in Padua (matriculated August 1534) and equipped with a doctorate in both

* * * * *

2 See Ep 2320 n1.
3 Epp 1625, 1649
4 Wilhelm Truchsess von Waldburg-Trauchburg (1469–1557), councillor of Ferdinand I and present with him at the diet in Augsburg

laws, Słap returned to Poland and had a successful career as an ecclesiastical
administrator in the diocese of Poznań.

Cordial greetings. Before the courier could depart, excellent sir, I began to
plan this letter, since I felt overwhelmed by your kindness, and I thought I
would let myself down if I did not, even once, thank your Honour for the
splendid commendations you gave me, especially since I seem to have no
chance of reciprocating your kindness. But as I thought about it, the words   5
slipped away; I was hampered by my ignorance, which does not allow me
to write a single word of Latin that would not offend the ears of even the
most unlearned person; what chance was there, therefore, that I could reveal
my thoughts in Latin to the greatest scholar of our age without causing you
disgust. However, I rely on your courtesy, hoping that you will receive this   10
barbarous letter from your friend Marcin in the same spirit in which you
receive the letters of your other well-wishers. If I had the eloquence of a
Cicero, I would scarcely ever be able to enumerate all your kindnesses to me
as they deserve, for they are very numerous and very great, and the more I
go over them in my mind, the more I discover other and greater examples.   15
    Your most recent letter to Master Conradus Goclenius was certainly a
godsend to me.[1] I soon found out how much weight it carried, for it was
on your account that he received me most courteously, and then showed
me such kindness and was so helpful to me that he could not have done
more if he had been my natural father. If he had not helped me, there is   20
no doubt I would have been compelled to return to Germany – not without
a small loss both of time and money. No one would have received me, a
stranger, into his home, for you know how often people have been deceived
in the past by the perfidy of others. His influence was so effective that I
have been admitted into the house of an eminent citizen, where I have the   25
benefit of excellent fare and a pleasant bedroom. All this was the result of
that most friendly recommendation that you were kind enough to insert at
the beginning of your letter (I know this because I saw what you wrote). For
this I offer you my most grateful thanks. I can think of no greater praise that
could have come my way than to be praised by one who is himself the most   30
highly praised and the most learned scholar of our time. The realization that
I do not deserve such praise makes me all the more anxious to try to live up
to it as far as I can.

* * * * *

2351
1 The letter is not extant. Carried by Słap (lines 80–1), it began with Erasmus'
  commendation of him to Goclenius; see lines 26–8.

But should I also mention the other compliments that I received when I returned recently to Poland to such a grand welcome? I would certainly 35 mention them, were I not afraid of appearing to act out of vanity rather than necessity. For when I returned home on previous occasions, I was scarcely noticed by anyone apart from my mother, but now I was received with great respect and applauded even by men whom I did not know – you might imagine I had never lived in this country until I returned from my visit to Eras- 40 mus. It was Erasmus, I tell you, who made me appear in their eyes as a distinguished and accomplished person and (can you believe it?) a great scholar; in every gathering (if I may borrow an expression from Horace) people have pointed me out as 'that famous friend of Erasmus.'[2] Yet how much greater their praise would have been had they seen even one sentence 45 of that flattering recommendation that you sent on my behalf to the great nobles of Poland![3] And so, excellent sir, as a result of your testimonial and of the whispered comments of others I am now more determined to devote myself to learning, which earlier I cultivated without much success and, as the saying goes, without the backing of the Muses;[4] the fault lay perhaps in 50 my youth or perhaps in my Sarmatian temperament,[5] which had little capacity for study, for 'I was born in the dull air of a land of muttonheads.'[6] However, if anyone is surprised that I am now getting down to work without, as they say, the blessing of Minerva,[7] I shall reply: 'Is there anyone so lazy and stupid as not to be stirred, or rather compelled, by the eloquence 55 of Erasmus to cultivate the liberal arts?' For not only is he deservedly loved as a beacon of light and respected by all for his hard-earned erudition, his virtuous life, and his authority, which should be for everyone like the voice of an oracle, but he also endeavours to cast over his followers the radiance of his learning. 60

As often as I turn these things over in my mind, my heart jumps for joy: first, because it was my good fortune to be born in the age in which you live, and second, because it was given to me to know you, something I always greatly wanted. Even if it should be my destiny to die now, I would consider

* * * * *

2 This is a skilful melding of Horace *Odes* 4.3.21–2 with *Satires* 1.6.47, with a reminiscence also of Persius 1.28 and Martial 5.13.3.
3 As in Ep 2201:64–80, and doubtless in other letters written at the same time
4 See *Adagia* 1 i 72.
5 In antiquity the Sarmatians were a nomadic people who inhabited a region roughly between the Vistula and the Don. Słap uses the term to describe himself as a Pole.
6 Juvenal 10.50, and cf Horace *Epistles* 2.1.244.
7 *Adagia* 1 i 42

death less bitter because these eyes of mine had already looked upon one 65
who was the glory of our age. So there is much that ought to be said about
the debt of affection that I owe your noble self, if the feebleness of my pen
permitted; in any case, I think you are partly aware of my affection for you
already, and I am conscious that your kindness to me has far outweighed
anything I could do. Even though I know that I can never repay you, I would 70
not want you to think that your help was given to an ingrate, and I hope
you will always realize that I am totally dedicated to you for the reasons
given and am most ready to assist you in anything you may be pleased to
ask of your devoted Marcin.

You cannot imagine how wretchedly I suffered for having left you in 75
Freiburg when you were ill.[8] Perhaps at that time I could have been of some
use to you – how I wish the idea had entered my head before I left! Time
and again I thought of returning and (as God is my witness) I was about to
do so, if I had not been frightened off by the fear of getting a reputation
for indecision; I also reckoned that I was under a greater obligation to de- 80
liver the letter you gave me for Master Goclenius.[9] I had resolved to stay
in Freiburg until you had fully recovered even if it meant a considerable
loss to myself – if an act that would have been both honourable and useful
could ever be counted as a loss. But when someone gave me the news that
you were feeling better, you can imagine how wonderfully happy I felt that 85
the originator and author of my good fortune, to whom I owe my present
life, has recovered. If it is true, and I fervently hope it is true, then I am delighted, and all my fears have gone. I was of course afraid that God would
take you before your time when the world still needed you. However, I feel
certain that the courier will bring me the happiest of news, that you are in 90
good health and out of danger.

I have another request to make: if you have occasion to write to Poland,[10] would you be kind enough to assure the bishop of Płock of my
good faith with regard to the ring,[11] for I fear that Master Andrzej[12] may

* * * * *

8 Given that he arrived in Louvain on 31 May (line 114), the date of his departure must be placed sometime in April or early May, well after the onset of
Erasmus' illness in March, and perhaps after it took a turn for the worse on
18 April; see Ep 2320 n1.
9 See lines 26–8 above.
10 See Epp 2375–7.
11 On the ring that Słap delivered to Erasmus on behalf of Bishop Krzycki, see
Ep 2174 n9, Allen Ep 2375:16–18.
12 Zebrzydowski

form an even graver suspicion about me when he realizes that I am be- 95
holden to him,[13] although the defence that your Honour made in clearing
my name will do much to remedy this difficulty. I do not doubt you will
write to the bishop of Cracow,[14] to whom I spoke only a word or two,
for his poor health would not permit more;[15] please let him know that
I delivered the letter to you.[16] The chancellor of the kingdom had given 100
me many assurances of his affection for you;[17] I thought they were not
important enough to bother you with at a time when you were so seriously ill, for they were the kind of ordinary greeting that you regularly receive from friends. He wished you a long and happy life and confirmed
his good wishes by raising a glass to your good health according to the 105
custom of the country. These and similar greetings he had entrusted me
to convey to you. It would please me very much if he was given to understand that I had passed on his messages of good will. This you could
do if your feelings for me have not been changed in some way by my
thoughtlessness. But if you will put off writing until the Frankfurt fair, I 110
shall write to Froben, whom the chancellor has commissioned to send securely to Poland certain pages of your Honour's work. Farewell, glory of
our age.

I reached Louvain on May 31. This city pleases me greatly for many
reasons, or perhaps I should say for this one reason, that it has much to en- 115
courage learning and very few distractions. Master Haio the Frisian is well.[18]
You will learn more of him from Master Goclenius.[19] These things I have
written, most learned sir, less in fear than with pleasure, for just as your
immense erudition made me fearful, so on the other side your exceptional
courtesy encouraged me greatly. Farewell again. 120

Louvain, 12 July AD 1530

Your most devoted friend, Marcin Słap of Dąbrówka the Pole

To the greatest and most learned of theologians, Master Erasmus of
Rotterdam

* * * * *

13 'I am beholden to him' is a literal translation of the Latin *me apud eum in gratia*
esse. The meaning is obscure.
14 Piotr Tomicki (Ep 2173)
15 On Tomicki's poor health, cf Allen Ep 2377:1–7.
16 Not extant; probably dated in March and possibly answering Ep 2173
17 The chancellor was Krzysztof Szydłowiecki (Ep 2177).
18 Cammingha (Epp 2262)
19 Ep 2352:305–10

2352 / From Conradus Goclenius   Louvain, 14 July [1530]

This letter was first published by Allen, using the autograph in the Öffentliche Bibliothek of the University of Basel (MS Goclenii epistolae 17). On Goclenius, professor of Latin at the Collegium Trilingue in Louvain, see Ep 1994A.

Although much of the content of this long letter consists of the routine stuff of friendly correspondence, its primary purpose was to clear up an embarrassing misunderstanding over money that had been caused by confusion on Erasmus' part. Before leaving Louvain in October 1521, Erasmus had deposited a sum of money with Jan de Neve, regent of the College of the Lily (Ep 298). In May 1522 he instructed Hilarius Bertolph (Ep 1712) to transfer that sum to Goclenius, to be added to a sum already on deposit with the latter. In the interim, the money deposited with Neve had declined in value, and he, not having kept the original coins, proposed to pay the sum at current value, arguing that since the sum was a deposit rather than a loan, the loss should be borne by Erasmus. Bertolph, fearful of Erasmus' anger, was reluctant to accept the diminished sum and suggested that Neve repay with the same kinds of coins that Erasmus had deposited. Neve replied that it would take him some time to acquire the coins. Goclenius then advised Bertolph to accept payment at current value and to make a list of the coins that Neve had received, in case Erasmus were to prefer to wait for the exact equivalent of the deposit. Bertolph agreed; Goclenius received the reduced sum, along with a list of the original coins made by Neve's secretary and signed by Bertolph. Goclenius retained this copy but, at Bertolph's request, made and signed a copy that was sent to Erasmus. Goclenius also sent to Erasmus a combined receipt for the sums that had come to him directly from Erasmus and indirectly from Neve. To these two deposits with Goclenius were subsequently added a third, made by Erasmus' famulus Quirinus Talesius (lines 61–2).

From this letter it emerges that now, after a lapse of eight years, Erasmus had, in an effort to keep things up to date, written to Goclenius, sending copies of all the documents in question (prepared by Quirinus Talesius) and asking for new receipts for the sums deposited. Concerning one document, the receipt for the later deposit by Quirinus, there was no disagreement. But Erasmus had sent with it the combined receipt for the first two deposits, together with the list of the coins deposited with Neve (lines 180–5), treating the latter as though it were documentation of an additional sum owed to him. Dismayed, Goclenius replies that the list of coins originally given to Neve was not a receipt, but only a detailed description of the coins received, for which Goclenius had accepted, as agreed, the equivalent at current value.

Cordial greetings. Kan wrote to me from Amsterdam about the first of March[1] to say that when he had reached Nijmegen a serious haemorrhage from the nose, which came on him suddenly, developed into a crisis that almost threatened to end his life. Because of the illness, which continued to dog him, he was forced to stay in Nijmegen for several days; how- 5 ever, being very anxious to carry out the mission you had given him, he handed the letter that you intended for me to a man from Antwerp who was well known to him and had proved his trustworthiness. He added that, if I did not receive it, he would bring it himself at Easter.[2] I imme- diately sent off a message to Erasmus Schets to inquire if any letters from 10 Erasmus of Rotterdam were held up at his place;[3] I acted expeditiously, for if your letter called for a response, I wanted to send my reply in time for the Lenten fair.[4] My effort, however, was ill timed, for at that point Schets had gone off to Liège on account of the death of his brother, who was archdeacon there. As a result it was not possible for me to send you 15 a letter by the merchants who were travelling to Frankfurt.[5] In the end Karl,[6] who had gone to Mechelen on business, happened, by the merest chance, to fall in with Erasmus van der Dilft's accountant,[7] from whom he learned that Dilft had a bundle of letters, but he said that he did not know to whom they should be sent. So it was necessary to go there to 20 look for your letter, and I did not get my hands on it before 13 April. It is only fair, therefore, that you pardon Kan for his misfortune and take a generous view of the lapse in my correspondence, for in both cases the fault lay with the vagaries of fortune rather than any lack of interest on our part.   25

* * * * *

2352
1 Nicolaas Kan (Ep 2261 n34) had left Erasmus in January, carrying with him a letter to Goclenius (see line 7) that was delivered on 13 April (lines 20–1 below).
2 This can only mean that Erasmus has followed his usual custom at this period of sending letters in duplicate, one of which Kan had retained. In 1530, Easter fell on 17 April.
3 For Erasmus Schets, through whose hands much of Erasmus' correspondence with England and the Netherlands passed, see Ep 2243.
4 In March
5 The location of the spring fair
6 Karl Harst (Ep 2231 n4)
7 Erasmus van der Dilft (d 1540) was the younger brother of Frans van der Dilft (Ep 2348). This is the only reference to him in Erasmus' correspondence. Concerning him little is known other than that he matriculated at Louvain along with his brother in 1519 and that he died at Padua.

I was more deeply upset than I can say by your letter or, to be more
precise, by the pages transcribed by your man Quirinus,[8] which you refer
to in your letter as 'copies of my receipts.'[9] One of these, dealing with
the money received by Hilarius from Neve, is not a copy of a receipt
from me: it simply lists the various currencies, both those that you de-   30
posited with Neve and those into which he exchanged your deposit. This
was sent to you not as a receipt but as an account of the sum handed
over by you as well as the sum received from Neve by Hilarius. For the
whole amount owed you by Neve is included in that comprehensive receipt,[10] which antedates the latest receipt given to Quirinus. The compre-   35
hensive receipt packages together, so to speak, both what remained of that
first deposit that you made with me when setting out for Germany and
the amount that Hilarius Bertholf extracted from Neve in the following
year. To help you to remember, I shall rehearse the whole matter from the
beginning.   40
    Three times in all you deposited money with me, first in the year 1521
when you were making for Germany at the onset of winter.[11]
    Then, when Neve returned the money,[12] you got Hilarius to deposit

* * * * *

8 Talesius (Ep 1966)
9 The letter is that of January 1530; see n1 above. The Latin for 'receipts' is *syn-
   graphae*. The word *syngrapha* is used in Erasmus correspondence for a variety of financial documents: receipts, promissory notes, and so forth. The basic
   sense is that of a written document in which one of two parties agrees to pay
   the other a stated sum. It is translated in various ways in this letter according
   to the context. Cf Ep 2109 n9.
10 Ie the combined receipt for the first two deposits with Goclenius. The Latin
   for 'comprehensive receipt' is *generalis syngrapha*.
11 Erasmus set out from Louvain for Basel on 28 October 1521; see Ep 1242 introduction. There was no receipt for this initial deposit; see lines 75–81 below.
12 Neve gave the coins enumerated to Hilarius Bertolph to deposit with Goclenius in 1522. In what follows, Goclenius explains to Erasmus that their current
   value is less than 'the old standard' in effect at that time.
   From about 1516 to the mid-1520s, various international economic factors had
   led to a rise in the market value of gold coins relative to the value of silver coins; see CWE 14 444–5. Francis I was the first to respond, with debasements (or revaluations) of his gold coins in May and July 1519. In the Hapsburg Netherlands, Emperor Charles V introduced entirely new gold coins in
   February 1521: the Carolus florin, at 40d groot (3s 4d); the réal, at 120d (10s
   od); and the demi-réal at 60d (5s od). Since these changes proved to be un-
   satisfactory, he subsequently raised the value of his gold coins by another 5
   per cent (equivalent to a debasement of 5.80 per cent) in August 1521: this increased the rate of his new Carolus florin to 42d groot; of the réal to 127d; of

with me 140 coins of the emperor,[13] each then having the value of 31½
stuivers; these, if placed in relation to the old standard, are now worth only   45
30 stuivers. In addition to this you deposited another 30 Carolus florins
worth 21 stuivers, now valued at only 20 stuivers; likewise, 53 Philippus
florins, now valued at 25 stuivers, but at that time paid back by Neve at a
rate of 26. Added to this were 5 angelets [angelati] in exchange for 15 Rhenish florins [Renenses], which at present are worth 15 stuivers short of that   50
amount. The last deposit in gold was for 7 gold coins [aurea], whose price is
now 28, but valued by Neve at 29. Finally, there was the addition in silver of
9 stuivers.[14] This made a total, reckoned in a single denomination, of 346½
Brabant florins. Today this sum, if the currency is related to its previous val-
uation, is considerably less, namely 330 Rhenish [florins] and 12 stuivers.[15]   55

* * * * *

the demi-réal to 63d (CWE 8 348–50 with Tables A and B). Though the intention
was to adjust the bimetallic ratio in favour of gold, complaints led to com-
pensatory (but even greater, at 12.5 per cent) debasements of the Hapsburg
silver coinages in November 1525 and again in December 1526. These monetary changes, however, failed to win approval from the market, so that the
coinage rates set in February 1521 were restored on 1 March 1527. See CWE 12
576–91 with Tables 2–3 (644–51).
13 The Latin for 'coins of the emperor' is nummos Caesaris. This rather vague
reference is clarified in a notarized document, written by Goclenius on 17
September 1533, acknowledging various sums deposited with him by Erasmus
(see Allen x Appendix 23, A 1). In that document these nummi are identified
as medii regales Caroli Caesaris, ie demi-réals of the emperor Charles v.
14 On 1 March 1527, the official values of legal-tender gold coins were restored to
those established in February 1521; see n12 above. The value of the demi-réal
was reduced from 63d to 60d groot (31.5 to 30 stuivers); that of the Carolus
florin, from 42d to 40d groot (21 to 20 stuivers); and that of the Philippus
florin, from 52d to 50d groot (26 stuivers to 25 stuivers). The stuiver, also
known as the patard and double groot, was a silver coin worth 2d groot (see
CWE 1 327, 331). The statement that 5 angelets (quinque angelati) were given
in exchange for fifteen Rhenish florins (pro quindecim Renensibus) must be an
error, because half angel-nobles, valued at 45d sterling (59½ d groot), were
then worth only slightly more than the Rhenish florins in England, about 40d
sterling (59d groot); see Ep 2222 n4. The seven gold coins currently valued
at 28 stuivers (56d groot) were almost certainly Rhenish florins. See CWE 8
348–50 with Tables A–B; CWE 12 649–50 Table 3.
15 Goclenius reckons the total as 346½ 'Brabant florins,' a sum worth 330 Rhenish florins and 12 stuivers at the current rate. The 'Brabant florins,' evidently
worth about 5 per cent more than Rhenish florins (ie about 58–59d groot),
cannot readily be identified (the current Philippus gold florin was worth only
50d, the Carolus florin and the Burgundian-Hapsburg florin money-of-account
only 40d groot). The sum of 330 Rhenish florins and 12 stuivers would have

If I show that this sum has been accounted for long ago and backed up by receipts, and you can show that nothing else has been received from Neve, it follows that you should not demand anything from me except that I return to you in good faith what I received in good faith. You may put me to the test on this at any time. 60

The third deposit was made by Quirinus Talesius, about which there is no disagreement between us. It was provided with its own separate receipt. But the two previous sums, both that which you entrusted to my good faith and that which we later got back from Neve, are covered by only one statement, as even a brief glance at the wording of the document will show, if 65 you take the trouble to examine it. A copy of it should have been sent to me if you wanted a single receipt to be made from the two,[16] rather than a copy of the pages from Neve, as I shall show presently. They were sent solely for the purpose of letting you know the kinds of currency in which Neve paid back your deposit. 70

Please recall the facts of the case with me so that if you have formed a false opinion about me or about the transaction itself, you may dismiss it from your mind. I am sure you will do this as soon as you understand the circumstances in which that sheet, which listed the various moneys that Neve handed to Hilarius, reached you. If you believe that this was a receipt, 75 you are completely mistaken, as you will presently understand, for at the beginning, when we were alone together and you were preparing to entrust your money to me on your departure for Germany, I asked you to accept a receipt from me and you refused absolutely, adding, what you repeated also in a letter,[17] that the strongest bond of all was good faith: 'honest dealings 80 among honest men.'[18]

But in the summer following your journey – here I beg you to pay particular attention, for I am coming to the nub of the matter – in that summer when we were still conducting our business without providing receipts, you made a request through Hilarius for Neve to repay your money. But since, 85 as it seems, he had converted to his own use your Edwardian rose-nobles

* * * * *

been worth (at the now reduced rate of 56d groot) £77 2s 0d groot Flemish (the equivalent value of 2,000 days' wages, or 9.53 years' money-wage income, for an Antwerp master mason).
16 The meaning here is presumably: 'if you wished me to provide a new comprehensive receipt, combining the earlier receipt for the first two deposits with the receipt for the third deposit made by Quirinus . . .'
17 Not extant
18 Cicero De officiis 3.61

and lions d'or,[19] and could not rapidly get his hands on this type of currency, he offered to pay in different currencies, which are listed by name
in what you have taken for a receipt. But Hilarius, either because he was
not offered the same currency as that in which you had made the deposit,   90
or because the price of money had recently gone up, as I pointed out earlier, rejected the terms offered by Neve. Neve then begged Hilarius not to
force him to pay back the money at a considerable loss to himself, for he
was sure that that was contrary to your intention. He suggested that Hilarius should go back to you, while he himself, within the next few months,   95
would look out for similar coinage and in the interval would change what
he had at his convenience. If I had not intervened, Hilarius would have offered no resistance to this proposal. But when I saw that the situation had
reached a turning point,[20] I suggested to Hilarius, when he asked me what I
thought it best to do, that he should certainly take what was offered. Hilar-   100
ius was reluctant to do this on the grounds that he was afraid of your anger,
but I replied that I would take the whole blame on myself. You thanked
me most warmly for this and praised me for acting in such a sensible and
friendly manner. Events proved the wisdom of my intervention, for a short

* * * * *

19 The 'Edwardian rose-nobles' (*Eduardici*) were, according to Allen (86n), 'rose-
   nobles of Edward IV.' One such coin is listed in the 1534 inventory of Erasmus'
   valuables (Major 38–9, 54, 64, picture on 47). This noble is better known as the
   'ryal' (royal) first struck on 6 March 1465, with a value of 10s 0d (120d) sterling (CWE 1 329). That value was retained until Henry VIII's first debasement
   of 24 July 1526, when its value was enhanced by 10 per cent, to 132d or 11s 0d
   sterling; on 5 November, its official value was raised again to 135d (11s 3d),
   for an overall increase of 12.5 per cent.
   The 'lions d'or' (*Leonati*) were, according to Allen's informant, Dr J.G. Milne
   (Keeper of Coinage at the Ashmolean Museum), 'French lions d'or = ²/₅ of a
   noble: first struck by Philip VI, and afterwards frequently in Burgundy and
   Flanders.' But Philip VI struck these coins only once, in October 1338, and they
   were not struck again by any of his royal successors. In the Low Countries,
   Duke Philip the Good of Burgundy struck a *lion d'or*, with an official value
   of 5s 0d (60d) groot Flemish, in January 1454; no coins of that name were
   struck by any of his Burgundian or Hapsburg successors. *Lions d'or* may, how-
   ever, have survived in circulation into the sixteenth century. See Christopher
   Challis 'Appendix II : Mint Contracts' in *A New History of the Royal Mint* ed
   Christopher Challis (Cambridge 1992) 712–25; Adrian Blanchet and Alphons
   Dieudonné *Manuel de numismatique française* 2 vols (Paris 1916) I 247; John
   Munro *Wool, Cloth and Gold: The Struggle for Bullion in Anglo-Burgundian Trade,
   ca. 1340–1478* (Brussels 1973) 149–50, 202–3 (Table F), 209–10 (Table J); Munro
   'The Coinages and Monetary Policies of Henry VIII' in CWE 14 423–76.
20 Literally 'the matter turned on this hinge'; see *Adagia* I i 19.

time afterwards Hondschoote died,[21] heavily in debt and with his affairs   105
in such disorder that I think not a cent would have been paid back to you.
As for the cups, I am sure that the executors often regretted that they had
delivered them.[22]

It is not difficult to imagine what would have happened to a large sum
like that when Neve was so heavily in debt. Indeed I thought that Neve was   110
using that excuse[23] to hold on to your money longer. So to make Hilarius
less apprehensive about you and to give you a better picture of the whole
affair so that you could make up your mind freely about it, I strongly urged
Hilarius to add the following stipulation, that Hondschoote should solemnly
promise that, if you did not approve of our action, he would take back the   115
moneys offered so that you would still be free to act, and at the same time
he should testify in writing what currency exchanges he had made and at
what price. So to fix the agreement on both sides, Hondschoote gave Hilarius
the document which you seem to have taken as a receipt from me, although
the original, from which I made the copy that was sent to you, was written   120
at Neve's suggestion by his secretary in Hilarius' presence; Hilarius also
signed his name to it, testifying that he had received the statement from
Neve.

Fortunately, as I now discover to my surprise, I had preserved the
statement in question. It was written with the sole purpose of explaining the   125
nature of the currency exchanges and preventing any quarrel from breaking out between you and Neve over that affair. I sent you a copy, written
in my own hand, of the original, which, as I have said, is still in my possession. It was not a receipt of any sort, but was produced, like the added
stipulation, to enable you to make a more accurate judgment of the whole   130
transaction. I did so at Hilarius' request as further evidence of good faith
– this was Hilarius' idea. As for the original itself, it seemed preferable to
leave it with me so that it would be available to anyone here who needed it
if you disapproved of Neve's action, for there is no one at your end, I feel
sure, who would not be equally satisfied with a copy. If you wonder why   135
the copy is written in my hand (for I had left this task to Hilarius), I wrote it
at Hilarius' request, for he insisted on having stronger testimony to present
to you than a document written by himself. So it is not some sort of receipt,
as you think, but a record of actions taken by Hilarius and Neve, which I

* * * * *

21 Another name for Neve (taken from his birthplace), who died on 25 November
   1522
22 See Ep 1355:23–9, and cf line 235 below.
23 Ie that he could not provide the appropriate currency

transmitted to you. I signed the document in my own hand not as a debtor   140
owing such an amount but as a witness to the transaction.

Hilarius is still available; the original which Hilarius signed survives;
Neve's secretary, who wrote the document at his master's bidding, is still
alive – not to mention that the document is not in the style of a receipt,
the day and the year (as the lawyers say) being missing.[24] Even if all these   145
things were not wanting, it would still have been inconsistent with your
fine reputation and moral character to demand twice what I admitted having received once, unless you had in mind to recover two payments for one
deposit, which I know to be completely foreign to your sense of justice. I do
not deny that the money recovered from Neve is included in that document;   150
I do not deny that it bears my signature; I do not deny that afterwards Hilarius deposited the money with me in your name. But if I prove that it was
not received by me but by Hilarius, and show that I issued a single receipt
covering the whole deposit from Neve, which is the truth, I would have to
be thought mad even by you to bind myself to pay the same amount a sec-   155
ond time, unless it was my wish to pay it twice. There is no question of another sum of money besides that which was retrieved from Neve, and that
was completely covered once, in the earlier of the receipts.

If you thought that the copy that describes the arrangement made by
Neve and Hilarius was the equivalent of a receipt, why, several years after   160
Neve's death, did you demand a receipt for all your deposits,[25] both the sum
that you entrusted to me and that which I received from Hilarius, since all
this took place when Neve was still alive? Had you changed your policy
of 'honest dealings among honest men'? The request seemed to me sensible
enough at that time, given, among other perils, the unpredictable destinies   165
of men, evidence of which we see every day. At that time I would have been
more afraid that the sky would fall than that any harm would come to me
from that earlier document dealing with the negotiations between Neve and
Hilarius. I was convinced in my own mind that I had not broken in any way
the bond of trust that existed between us. Indeed I could more readily have   170
conceived of robbing my father than cheating you even out of a penny, for
I have always regarded you as a father.[26] So either you did not consider as a
receipt the document that listed the various currencies deposited with Neve
and recovered by Hilarius, or if it did look to you like a regular receipt, you

* * * * *

24 The expression is literally 'the day and the consul [are missing],' referring to
   the Roman practice of identifying the year by the names of the consuls.
25 Ie the combined receipt for the first two deposits
26 Cf Ep 1437:161–3.

now possess two receipts from me in connection with a single deposit: what   175
need is there for a third?

When I reflect on these things, it is evident to me that you take an even
less than superficial interest in matters of this kind. This is only natural,
since the divine studies with which you bless our age occupy your mind
too completely to allow you time for trifling affairs of this kind. Possibly   180
the problem was caused by a mistake on the part of Quirinus, who, when
asked to make a copy of the receipt, wrote out this document, though this is
not at all relevant to the matter that interested you, or if it is relevant, it is
now completely superfluous since in another handwritten document I have
clearly included the money from Neve.   185

I fear that this detailed accounting will vex you. I could not write it
down myself without a feeling of vexation, but at the same time I could
not pretend that the problem did not exist. I wanted to explain to you why
I, who wish to oblige Erasmus above any other man, have not complied
with your wishes and sent a new receipt; at the same time I wanted you   190
to understand the reasonable fears that I am beginning to have about the
future as a result of this incident. After receiving your letter,[27] the danger
kept revolving in my mind. If, after all the letters and enclosures that have
travelled back and forth between us, and while both of us are still living,
something could still arise to make you ask for more than is actually owed,   195
can you imagine the confusion there could be if one of us were removed
from the scene. If I had happened to die recently (and death could not have
come closer),[28] what disgrace would have followed me to the grave if, in my
will, it appeared that I had given a false account of the deposit, or if I had left
you a certain sum as evidence of my feelings towards you, when you could   200
claim it as a matter of right (unless of course this provision could be satisfied
from elsewhere in my estate). Erasmus by virtue of his position would have
been credited with good faith. But no one would have been able to defend
me against an unjust claim. What is now being sought mistakenly from me
when I am alive might also have been sought when I was dead. It would   205
not trouble me if the greater part of my estate went to you, to whom I have
always professed that I owe all my fortune, but if this occurred without any
indication of my feelings for you, indeed in a situation where I would be
disgraced, that would truly be more bitter to me than death itself.

So I beg and beseech you, to consider what, in your judgment, will   210
be most advantageous for both of us, for I would not like my friendship

* * * * *

27 See line 7 above.
28 See lines 335–6 below.

with Erasmus, which I have always regarded as the greatest of my blessings, and which I have found beneficial in so many ways, to turn out in
the end to be disastrous for me. The best way to avoid this is to return to
me the document that reports the agreement between Hilarius and Neve so   215
that nothing could flow from it that would be injurious to me and to my
financial situation. If it could mislead a clear-sighted person like yourself,
it could certainly mislead others who are ignorant of what passed between
us. Secondly, if you will request the return of the money deposited with
me, you will relieve me of much anxiety. But if you leave it with me, I con-   220
sider that any trouble over your affairs, or indeed any anxiety I feel about
them, is a very light burden. If you want me to produce other receipts, I
think I have a right to demand that you return to me not just copies of the
two receipts you have, one concerning the deposits made by you and by
Neve, and a second made recently concerning the Quirinus deposit, but the   225
actual originals, for I fear that the duplication of receipts is beset with serious perils for me. How great a problem that could become for me is well
illustrated by the present case, in which, after payment had been made, a
second payment is requested even without a receipt. I have already made
it very clear what the purpose was in sending you a copy of the transaction   230
with Neve. But this is now being used, so to speak, to stab me with my own
sword.

Furthermore, it is very important for me to know if you made a record
that you received the things that Nicolaas Kan carried off from me at your
request, namely all the double ducats, the six silver cups,[29] three gold rings,   235
and several clasps with a box covered in silk. The same problem could arise
with these, for if it happens that you have not documented this, or if (a
common enough occurrence) your daybook should be lost, there is no doubt
that, because of the receipt, questions would be asked of me and I would
not be able to give any plausible explanation, since no one would believe   240
that I returned what I had formally acknowledged receiving unless you sent
back a receipt; and if I protested my innocence, I would gain nothing but
scorn for my stupidity, even if I appeared to be speaking the truth. So I
think it would be much the better course if you produced a handwritten
statement of everything that you received and everything that you planned   245
to recover later so that there would be agreement between us; this would
avoid any danger of misunderstanding on either side regarding the amount
of the deposit remaining with me.

* * * * *

29 These may be Venetian ducats. In 1530, a single ducat was worth 8od groot
Flemish (CWE 12 650 Table 3D). On the cups, cf line 108 above.

I have another similar request to make: there is a possibility that when you ask for the return of the whole deposit, Hilarius or Lieven[30] or Talesius or others who are privy to these matters might allow some information to leak out to those who expect some spoils from you, and if something should happen to you, as it does to all human beings (and I should rather see it happen to your enemies than to you, though it is the condition of our human existence that some day we must all bow to fate) – if, I say, those vultures should catch the scent of spoils, what a weak position I would be in if I denied their claims amid such overwhelming evidence. At least I would not be able to rid people's minds of suspicion. There is certainly nothing whose loss I would regret more than that of my good name. You, however, by a word or two, can save me from this embarrassment if you wish. I am certain you will not fail me in this. It will cost you nothing to do this for the honour and peace of mind of one of your most devoted friends.

I would ask you to pardon my long-windedness if you yourself were not clearly aware that the matter is too important to be glossed over, considering the middling state of my fortune, especially since I know how little your great rivers stand in need of my little streams – and may it always be so! But if things should turn out otherwise and you wished to estimate the extent of my affection by the size of my gifts, then I shall outdo Socrates' Phaedon and the other Socratics by as much as Phaedon outdid all his fellow students by giving himself to Socrates.[31] They brought huge gifts, each according to his means, while keeping the larger share for themselves. Phaedon, since he had nothing else, gave himself. I now place myself and all that is mine in the hands of Erasmus. Here is my pledge of total surrender: you may, when you wish, claim everything I have, down even to my private savings; even slave-owners who wish to make some claim to liberality generously permit their slaves to keep such savings.

Karl Harst has grown tired of the teacher's life and several months ago moved to the court of the duke of Jülich.[32] He was invited there by the chancellor and the leading figures of the court on what I hear are most respectable terms.[33] So when he changed his residence, and I saw that your

* * * * *

30 Algoet (Ep 2278 n2)
31 Phaedon was one of Socrates' closest friends. On his career see Diogenes Laertius 2.105, Martianus Capella 1.11.41. According to Diogenes Laertius 2.34 the poor man who offered himself to Socrates was the Socratic Aeschines.
32 William v (Ep 2234); for Harst see n6 above.
33 For the chancellor, Johann Gogreve, and the other 'leading figures,' see Ep 2298 n5.

Erasmius was left on his own,[34] I acted on your recommendation and invited him to come and live with me.

Now I almost regret my action for two reasons. First, because your more recent letter,[35] which I received after the Frankfurt fair, seems to plead   285
Erasmius' case with a limp hand,[36] rather suggesting that I should not take him in; indeed to speak plainly, I got the impression that the letter was simply a palinode for your previous recommendation.[37] If I had had any inkling of this before he moved here, I could certainly have invited others in his place who would pay forty florins and more per year. But your favour and   290
authority have always been stronger with me than any profit I might gain.

Second, I was no less disturbed by the fact that the young man himself is hopelessly weak in grammar. He is merely a listener – if you ask him to repeat what you have just taught, you realize that you are pouring your words into a broken pot.[38] However, when spurred on by embarrass-   295
ment before his fellows, he makes a bigger effort. I do not know what I can promise to achieve with him. At least his association with the respectable young men who are his fellow students will rid him of his rustic air, and by hearing and speaking Latin every day, he may learn the language properly. There are no French schools here. So there is no prospect of learning   300
French in this place. They say that he learned to speak Brabantian[39] fairly well when he lived in Karl's house, though this was spoiled by his stuttering, a problem that, I fear, is irremediable. However, I shall do my best, now that he has been entrusted to my care.

Just before the arrival of Marcin the Pole,[40] Haio Cammingha deliv-   305
ered your short note,[41] while carefully avoiding any reference to his debt. But when I got the letter that you sent with the Pole and in which I first became aware of Cammingha's debt,[42] I though it best to challenge the man in your name. He replied that he had long since satisfied you through the bankers.[43]   310

* * * * *

34 Erasmius Froben; see Ep 2229 introduction and n3.
35 Not extant
36 Ie 'very half-heartedly.' The phrase was often used of a lukewarm recommendation; see *Adagia* IV iv 2.
37 A palinode is a retraction; see *Adagia* I ix 59.
38 *Adagia* I iv 60
39 Ie Dutch as spoken in Brabant
40 Marcin Słap Dąbrówski, who arrived in Louvain on 31 May: see Ep 2351:114.
41 Not extant; doubtless dated c 31 January, like Ep 2261–2, also carried by Cammingha
42 See Ep 2351 n1.
43 The debt was not in fact paid until November 1531; see Ep 2325 n1.

The *Letter to the Friars Minor* I thought too old hat to be reproduced,[44] and I did not see that you would achieve anything by it except to provide an opening to those who are spoiling for a fight – though, I think, they have now tired themselves out and have gone silent on their own. As for the Pole whom you recommended to me so highly, I shall do what I can to see that no 315 door is closed to him that might be to his advantage. I have been unable to find a young man who wants to live in Germany in these troubled times.[45] The name of Germany is now so highly regarded that I would even find it easier to get ten men who would be willing to serve you in Scythia than one who would think of moving to Germany! 320

The bearer of this letter[46] was for about ten years in the exacting service of Dirk of Aalst.[47] If he thought he could satisfy you, perhaps he would not refuse an offer. He is ready to put up with hard work – and even sharp correction. His lettering in Greek and Latin is better than that of anyone else, certainly anyone in this university. If you like the idea, discuss the 325 matter with him yourself. In the meantime you will have no obligations to him for travel costs, since I have paid him handsomely from my own purse.

He should discuss with you whether he should go on to Basel to deliver the commentaries on Chrysostom that Nicolaus Episcopius left with me, not 330 because I had undertaken the task of translation,[48] but so that I could discuss the matter with Levinus Ammonius,[49] Frans van Cranevelt,[50] and Nicolaus Clenardus, who teaches Greek and Hebrew here privately.[51] He preferred

* * * * *

44 Ie the *Epistola ad gracculos*; see Epp 2275 and 2321:14–16.
45 The word here translated as 'young man' is *puer*, meaning a young person or, in classical Latin, a slave. Goclenius is talking about a replacement for Kan as a famulus for Erasmus.
46 In Allen Ep 2369:16 his name is given as Jacobus. He also carried Ep 2353; see lines 380–1 below and Ep 2353:2–5.
47 The printer Dirk Martens; see Epp 263:10n, 1899 n16.
48 See Ep 2258 n6. Episcopius (Ep 2233A n4) had also delivered a letter from Erasmus of c 11 November 1529; see Epp 2235 nn3–4, 2236 n5.
49 Ep 2258
50 Ep 1145
51 Clenardus (1495–1542) studied arts and theology at Louvain, taking his licence in theology in 1527. Meanwhile, in 1522 he became president for ten years of Houterlee's College, a position that allowed him to continue his humanistic studies with the help of Goclenius and others at the Collegium Trilingue. He taught privately and published successful textbooks for students of Hebrew and Greek. In 1531, disappointed in his hopes for a position in the faculty of arts or at the Collegium Trilingue, he entered the service of Hernando Colón (son of Christopher Columbus), whom he accompanied to Spain. He taught

that I do the translation, but I was prevented by business, which keeps over-
taking me like a succession of hurricanes and time after time interrupts the   335
progress of my work. Then some allowance had to be made for my health,
which has not yet sufficiently recovered from the recent plague.[52] But since
no one could be induced to do the work, I am returning the book at my own
expense, so that Froben will have no reason to find fault.

Gilles de Busleyden's tightfistedness is well known.[53] He does not dare   340
to be liberal with other people's money in case at some time he might learn
to be liberal with his own. Yet I confess that your support is worth as much
to me as if I had obtained a princely increase in salary.

I have not yet lost out on the Antwerp prize,[54] as you think. Even if I
should decide to give up my claim, there is available to me a far from con-   345
temptible pension. But it is my intention to pursue my rights however much
trouble it may be. If I get the shadow for the substance, I have something
with which to console myself, for by the goodness of God I have enough
to live on without falling into poverty. Also, better prospects are not ruled
out, if I wish to embrace them.   350

This courier would have gone to you earlier, but I held him back because of Pieter de Corte, who is about to receive his degree in theology on
12 July; he is receiving his degree at a time when he holds the highest office
in the university.[55] I was told that Vives,[56] Laurinus,[57] and several other of

* * * * *

Greek and Latin at Salamanca until 1533, when he entered the service of Prince
Henry of Portugal, archbishop of Braga. Clenardus founded a humanist college at Braga and directed it until 1538. Thereafter, with the support of Prince
Henry, Clenardus devoted himself to the study of Arabic in Granada, and for
a time also at Fez in Morocco, evidently in the belief that Muslims could be
converted to Christianity by force of persuasion in their own language. He
died in Granada.

52 Possibly the English sweat; see Epp 2209 n31, 2223:13–33.
53 Gilles de Busleyden (Ep 686), brother of Jérôme de Busleyden, founder of the
Collegium Trilingue at Louvain. After the death of Jérôme in 1517, Gilles was
instrumental in carrying out his plan for the foundation of the college, which
continued to benefit from Gilles' advice, protection, and close attention to the
budget. He had cordial relations with Erasmus, whom he consulted on appointments to the college (Epp 686, 691, 699) and helped in his efforts to
collect his imperial annuity (Ep 1461) and silence his critics in Louvain (Ep
1802).
54 See Ep 1994A n17.
55 Corte (Ep 1347 n66), regent of the College of the Lily, had been elected rector
of the university on 27 February 1530. Cf Ep 2353:16–17.
56 Juan Luis Vives (Ep 2208), now living at Bruges
57 Marcus Laurinus (Ep 1342), dean of St Donatian's at Bruges; cf Ep 2353:23–4.

your friends will be present on the day of the celebration. I met Vives; he 355
told me that if anything occurred to him that he wanted Erasmus to know,
he would send me a letter in good time, so I need not be anxious. If he
sends it to me, I shall include it with this. He is planning to give several
lectures and protreptic addresses here to make his books more saleable.[58]
At the same time he is negotiating with Rutgerus Rescius about printing a 360
treatise on the causes of the corruption of all disciplines and how they can
be restored to their proper state.[59] Such an ambitious project arouses the
highest expectations. Rutgerus, however, is not prepared to accept the job
except at the author's own risk. The outcome is still uncertain.[60] We expect
Laurinus any hour now. 365

I wrote this on the tenth of July. About two months ago I was visited
by a certain Willem of Haarlem, a brother from Liège,[61] who complained
bitterly of malicious reports by certain people accusing him falsely of being
an enemy of Erasmus. He swore by everything both sacred and profane
that he was innocent and that he would now be more careful that such a 370
suspicion did not stick to him in the future. He did everything but fall on his
knees to entreat me to clear his name with you. I do not know what his sin
was. I gathered that he was very afraid of your pen. I promised to intercede
on his behalf provided he could assure me that the accusation against him
was false. I ask you now to pardon this importunate suppliant, if his offence 375
is not monstrous. Whatever happens after this is not my business. You do
what you think is right.

Laurinus has arrived at last, but he says he has nothing that is important for you to know. I had the same response from Luis Vives and Barlandus.[62] I have asked the courier to visit Pieter Gillis also to see if there is 380
anything he wants to say or if he has received anything from Britain.[63]

Maarten Davidts, a former host of yours, complains much about being neglected, for he has received no letters from you for such a long

* * * * *

58 He delivered two; see lines 384–5 below and Ep 2353:1. A protreptic address
would be one exhorting people to study philosophy and humane letters.
59 The treatise was *De disciplinis libri* xx. Rescius, professor of Greek at the
Trilingue since 1518, had founded a press at Louvain in 1529.
60 The treatise was eventually published by Michaël Hillen at Antwerp (July
1531).
61 Unknown to Allen; he has been identified as Willem of Haarlem (documented
1508–36), a Brother of the Common Life attached to the school of the Brethren
at Liège. He may be the unnamed messenger in Allen Ep 2369:25–64, and the
Guilhelmus in Allen Ep 2566:62–6. See CEBR III 446–7.
62 Adrianus Cornelii Barlandus (Ep 492)
63 For Gillis see Ep 2260.

time.[64] After delivering two public lectures,[65] Vives has ended up by offering to give a private reading of his commentaries for a fee. He seems to 385
have come to a standstill.[66] Haio is still here. Farewell.

Louvain, 14 July

Yours with all my heart, Conradus Goclenius

2353 / From Jan of Heemstede   Louvain, 14 July 1530

This letter was first published in LB III/2 1746–7 *Appendix epistolarum* no 358. The autograph is in the Rehdiger Collection of the University Library at Wrocław (MS Rehd 254.88). On Jan of Heemstede, Carthusian of Louvain, see Epp 1646, 1900.

I attended Luis Vives' lecture to the young,[1] and just as I was leaving the university, I ran into my friend Goclenius, who told me that early in the morning he was sending a reliable courier to Erasmus,[2] and since I had not written to you for a long time, he asked me to give him at least a short note for you as an indication of my feelings towards you. I did so right away 5
with the greatest pleasure, for is there any greater pleasure than to avail oneself of a chance opportunity to let one's hand express the feelings of one's heart for an absent friend, whom, if present, I would venerate this side idolatry? Would that my greeting could prevail on Almighty God to keep you in good health! Would that I could bring back your youth for the 10
benefit of us all! But since I cannot do that, I may pray for something that is possible, namely that the Lord Jesus will long keep you safe and well for the good of his church.

I would have written at somewhat greater length if domestic concerns had not demanded my time elsewhere. One thing, however, I cannot pass 15
over: last Tuesday in the school of theology, when Pieter de Corte was promoted doctor of theology,[3] a Dominican named Eustachius,[4] in my hearing

* * * * *

64 For Davidts see Ep 1997A (c May 1528), which is Erasmus' last surviving letter
    to him.
65 See lines 358–9 above.
66 Ie to have been reduced to a state of extreme want; see *Adagia* IV vii 67.

2353
1 See Ep 2352:358–9, 384–5.
2 See Ep 2352:321–2.
3 See Ep 2352:352–4.
4 Eustachius van der Rivieren, who was currently dean of the faculty of theology; see Ep 2264 introduction.

and before a crowded assembly, delivered a silly and uncouth speech in which he made a most bitter attack on languages, though you, with the blessing of Heaven, have placed the study of languages almost beyond at- 20 tack, winning great glory for yourself. I nearly said 'To hell with silly donkeys who make such a vicious attack on things they know nothing about.'

Laurinus,[5] my friend and a great admirer of yours, left Louvain today. Languages are taught here valiantly, and especially Latin. Your heart would be filled with joy if you could see the young people running to class, 25 particularly when our friend Goclenius is teaching.[6] I shall never be able to forget you, and I shall continue to commend you to the Lord God as long as I live.

Louvain, at the Charterhouse, 14 July in the year 1530. All good wishes to my friend Quirinus.   30

Yours with all my heart, Jan of Heemstede, steward of the Carthusians at Louvain

To the most excellent doctor of theology, Master Erasmus of Rotterdam, my most worshipful mentor

2353A / To Johann Rinck   Freiburg, 14 July 1530

This letter was first published in the *Epistolae floridae*, where it is dated 'Freiburg, the eve of the feast of St Margaret, 1530' (see line 103). Allen, taking 20 July as the feast day in question, assigned 19 July 1530 as the date of the letter and numbered it Ep 2355. But while 20 July was the date of the feast of St Margaret in France (with exceptions), Italy, Scandinavia (except Finland), and England, in Germany it was otherwise. In the archdiocese of Mainz it was celebrated on 13 July except in a list of dioceses that included Constance, to which Freiburg belonged. There the date was 15 July, as was also the case in Basel (in the archdiocese of Besançon). See Hermann Grotefend *Zeitrechnung des deutschen Mittelalters und der Neuzeit* 2 vols (Hannover 1891–2; repr Aalen 1970) I 118. This means that the date of a letter written in Freiburg on the eve of the feast of St Margaret has to be 14 July 1530.

On Johann Rinck, see Ep 2285.

ERASMUS OF ROTTERDAM TO JOHANN RINCK, GREETING
Cordial greetings, kindliest of men. Even if your little gift had been as

* * * * *

5 See Ep 2352:354, 378–9.
6 Goclenius was professor of Latin at the Trilingue.

worthless as you modestly make it out to be,[1] yet your friendly sentiments, which are like gold or precious gems, and that letter of yours, which breathed throughout a spirit of genuine affection, could have added so much to it that   5 I would have welcomed it as a great treasure.[2] In fact, your gift could well have been given by a king; yet such is your modesty that you beg me to be gracious enough to accept it. I ought rather to have asked you to be gracious enough to accept my little book, which was hurried into the world, a sort of premature birth. But in this matter I realize I am competing with   10 Hercules, whom I see depicted on your cup. Just as he was indomitable in strength and in wielding the club, so Rinck cannot be outdone in courtesy and generosity. The symbol of the eagle, which is found on your shield, is not inappropriate to you. No one could be prompt enough in doing a good turn to get ahead of you. Mutual friendship, and that alone, would have   15 been enough for me. Such a friendly letter as that which you sent would have qualified as a great gift. But not content with that, you were generous enough to add the cup, whose workmanship and material value make it no ordinary gift. I put my hands up[3] to Hercules and shall continue the contest no further – except in this one point, that I would not like to be thought   20 inferior in affection.

So far my friends have written me a full account of what is happening at the diet.[4] The most important propositions have been set out: first, that the Germans should lend support in combatting the fury of the Turks; second, that an end should be put to the dissension of the sects, if possible   25 without bloodshed; third, that some consideration should be given to those who believe themselves oppressed. To achieve all this an ecumenical council sitting for three years would hardly be enough.[5] I do not know what will happen: unless God intervenes in the drama, I see no happy ending. And unless the thing is done with the consent of all the territories,[6] it will   30 end in revolution. Some people hope that an accommodation can be worked out with the Lutherans, since their demands are not extreme and the pope

* * * * *

2353A
1 For the gift, see Ep 2277 n5.
2 The letter is not extant; it acknowledged receipt of the *De bello Turcico* (Ep 2285).
3 To 'put one's hands up' was to acknowledge oneself beaten; see *Adagia* I ix 79.
4 Ie at the Diet of Augsburg
5 Cf Ep 2347:8–9.
6 Erasmus word here is 'provinces' (*provinciae*), by which he means the imperial estates, ie the imperial principalities and cities with votes in the diet; cf Ep 2347:11–13 with n5.

is prepared to make even large concessions. He has Cardinal Campeggi in
Augsburg, a most humane man, who has written to me twice.[7] The bishop
of Augsburg thinks it appropriate to make some concessions for the sake of   35
peace; as a result, I am told, some are calling him a Lutheran, although no
one is more devout and upright than he.[8] The Lutherans have presented a
summary of their faith.[9] Melanchthon, who is in charge of this, states in a
letter to me that he has not given up hope entirely.[10] As for the Zwinglians,
the emperor at first would not hear them; now, they say, it has been con-   40
ceded that they too may present an account of their faith. Hedio has been
sent for this purpose, since, as I hear, Capito has persistently refused the
assignment.[11]

Many are urging me by letter to attend the diet;[12] the emperor, however, has not yet summoned me,[13] and if he did, I have a better excuse than   45
I would like. This is now the fourth month since I fell ill and I have not
yet been able to regain my strength.[14] First, deceptively gentle winds that
turned out to be very treacherous brought on an attack of cramps in the
belly such as I had never experienced before. These led to vomiting, which,
as Hippocrates says, is hard for a person who is thin.[15] Vomiting caused the   50
ruin of my digestion, and the pain and the lack of food led to sleeplessness. The doctors too added considerably to my problems. The cramps were
followed by a hard abscess, which continued to spread until it covered the

* * * * *

7 The first letter was written from Innsbruck; see Ep 2332:40–1. The second may
  have been in response to Ep 2328 or 2341.
8 A view perhaps expressed in the letter from Christoph von Stadion mentioned
  in Ep 2332:29–31
9 The Augsburg Confession; see Ep 2333 n8.
10 The letter is not extant. The redating of the present letter from 19 to 14 July
   means that Melanchthon's letter can scarcely have been his response to Ep
   2343 (7 July 1530), which Allen thought possible. Ep 2365 (17 August 1530)
   may in part be Erasmus' response to it.
11 The account of faith in question was the *Confessio tetrapolitana*, written at the
   diet by Martin Bucer with the assistance of Wolfgang Capito (who was indeed
   there) and Caspar Hedio; see Ep 2333 n12.
12 See Epp 2333–5, 2339; in Epp 2331–2, 2347 Erasmus replies directly to invitations.
13 See Ep 2339 n6.
14 See Ep 2320 n1.
15 Erasmus is apparently thinking of Hippocrates *Aphorisms* 4.6, though in fact
   what is said there is that thin people find it easy to vomit. The following
   aphorism (4.7) says that stout people have difficulty vomiting. Erasmus seems
   to have confused the two passages.

left side of the belly. Soon afterwards it jumped across to the navel, taking
the appearance of a snake with its mouth fastened on the navel, the mid- 55
dle of its body twisted in a curve, and its tail pointed towards the genitals.
A little later it turned towards my left side, almost surrounding the navel.
Excruciating stabs of pain gave me no rest either night or day.

A surgeon was called, a man of some reputation by local standards. He
recognized no difference between an infection and a hard abscess (which 60
should have been treated and dissolved by gentle and cold remedies), and
so, despite protests from all sides, he applied strong plasters, which nearly
killed me. I think that those who suffer the fires of Purgatory are in less
torment. He caused ulcers to develop on certain tender spots and only succeeded in cooking the abscess, all the while promising great results. When 65
the ulcer had been lanced with a knife, a mixture of blood and pus flowed
from the soft part; from the hard lump through which he had pushed the
knife there was nothing but blood. Two days later I dismissed the man,
treated but not healed. The abscess still remains, though the pain is less.
The doctors had to be called in again. When my illness was at its most se- 70
vere, my one servant (the other had gone home) was suddenly seized with
the English sweat.[16] In this way the Lord has been pleased to visit me.

For some time I have wanted to move from here to somewhere else.
The town, though attractive, is not correspondingly well populated, since it
is some distance from the river;[17] it is a place more suited to the scholarly 75
life. Everything here is incredibly dear. The people are not very hospitable,
or so it is said, for thus far no one has troubled me much. But I cannot
see a quiet haven anywhere. I must stay here until we see the direction in
which things will move after the diet. Some are guessing that it will come
down principally to a demand for money,[18] that the issue of heresy will 80
be put off to an ecumenical council,[19] and that comforting words will be

* * * * *

16 Nicolaas Kan had returned to the Netherlands (Ep 2261 n34) when Quirinus
   Talesius fell ill with the sweat (Ep 2343 n3).
17 Ie from the Rhine, not from the Dreisam, which runs through the town
18 For aid against the Turks. It would take negotiations with the Protestants following the Diet of Augsburg, and concessions to them in the Religious Peace
   of Nürnberg (July 1532), to secure that money from them.
19 The recess of the diet (19 November) included a harsh condemnation of the
   Protestants as outlaws and rebels who had until 15 April 1531 to conform to
   the Edict of Worms (1521), which had outlawed Luther, his works, and his
   followers. But the recess also included the emperor's promise that within six
   months he would arrange for the convocation of a general council that would
   produce a settlement of the religious conflict.

said to priests, bishops, monks, and abbots who have been thrown out and dispossessed.[20]

I imagine you have already seen the books that have been lately hurled at my head. The person behind this campaign is, unless I am mistaken, 85 known to you.[21] Some time ago, as the cheerleader among my most dedicated friends, he would scarcely allow anyone to mention Erasmus without prefacing the name with some mark of honour. Now he is worse than a deadly enemy. Could anyone have believed that such venom lay hidden in this loud-mouthed tippler? It is many incidents of this sort that turn me 90 away from the professed beliefs of these people. They hate anyone with whom they disagree – and yet they deny the existence of free will. If God has not yet granted me the grace of which they boast, that is a reason for interceding with the Lord on my behalf, not for pursuing me with their hatred. My friends vary in their opinions: some think I should not even read 95 the rubbish that these people produce – so far my inclination has been to agree with them; on the other hand, those who move in princely circles urge me to respond vigorously. I do not know what I shall do.[22] Certainly my temper, my age, and my health all call for quiet.

This has been a weary letter, from a weary man. If the Lord gives 100 me back my strength, I hope that some day we may embrace one another. Meantime see that you keep well.

Freiburg, the eve of the feast of St Margaret[23] 1530

2354 / From Cornelis Croock   Amsterdam, July 1530

First published as Ep 86 in Enthoven, this is Croock's reply to Ep 2259A. The autograph is in the Rehdiger Collection of the University Library at Wrocław (ms Rehd 254.55).

Cordial greetings. Indeed, thrice beloved Erasmus, now that you have honoured me with a letter – and one in your own hand at that – I feel myself more fortunate than Fortune herself.

* * * * *

20 Disputes over the title to church properties seized by Protestant rulers for their own use and that of their churches and schools remained the subject of bitter dispute and prolonged litigation until the Peace of Westphalia in 1648.
21 Gerard Geldenhouwer; see Ep 2329:86–90.
22 He would publish his *Epistola ad fratres Inferioris Germaniae* in September; see Ep 2324 n2.
23 Margaret of Antioch, also known as Margaret the Virgin

I always hoped to see the day when I would be lucky enough to have some place among your friends. Even to be known to eminent men, to say 5 nothing of finding favour with them, is no small distinction,[1] although I think that a man may justly be said to 'have found favour' when he has received from you a most affectionate letter, and a little later has been the recipient of your good wishes. But that is only a small part of it, for you are also offering your love, in which you say you will take second place 10 to no one – and all this through no merit of my own. Although it is your exceptional learning that commends you to men of distinction, what you show to the whole world is a person who deserves to be embraced and admired for his kindness and civility. I have always wanted to be accepted by you and, if it is right to say so, I have often hoped for it; but to have 15 you offer yourself in this way has surpassed all my hopes and prayers. God forbid that I should be like those who hate and detest everything that has not yet passed from the earth and ended its days. These people are so attached to the past that they condemn indiscriminately anything that is recent – no, not just condemn it, but utterly abominate it. So they detest 20 you too, though you, like a second Prometheus,[2] have brought down from heaven the resplendent light of wisdom to illumine the black darkness of our mortal life. It is an old story, and thus hardly remarkable, that light is detested by owlish eyes.

You urge me to continue to run my race in the splendid arena of learn- 25 ing, and I am challenged to pursue the same goal by the example set by all great men. But I have now less need of the counsel of others since I have the example of your outstanding excellence, for you alone have risen above the contaminating influence of our native soil,[3] and shine like a beacon from the high point on Hesiod's path.[4] So what I could admire before in others, 30 and only admire, I now dare to promise to myself as something near and available, because I see that you, raised under the same sky and on the same soil, have attained such eminence. I am, therefore, determined to continue on the path on which I have begun, though now with a more sprightly step because of the encouragement your letter has given me. I shall not let you 35 think that you wrote to me in vain.

* * * * *

2354
1 Horace *Epistles* 1.17.35
2 Prometheus stole fire from heaven to give it to mankind; he was also the benefactor of mankind by teaching all arts and crafts.
3 For the proverbial dullness of the inhabitants of Batavia see *Adagia* IV vi 35.
4 Hesiod described the steep, high path to virtue in *Works and Days* 287–90.

As for the addition of my *Farrago of Inelegant Expressions* to the *Paraphrase on Valla*, I have only this to say.[5] I permitted the publication of the first part of it (in alphabetical order), partly because of persistent pressure and partly with the intention of testing, where the stakes were less high, whether such a subject would be acceptable for the general public – though I had been earnestly discouraged from publication of the *Paraphrase*. The later part had been hurriedly annotated by me at Louvain at a time when I possessed hardly more than a nodding acquaintance with polite letters (as the result shows all too clearly), and without my knowledge it was added to my *Farrago*, causing ridicule among the more learned. But Master Alaard has convinced me of his honest intentions. However, like the fisherman, once bitten, I shall know better.[6] May Christ keep you safe and well, for you are the acknowledged glory of the Christian world.

From Amsterdam, July 1530

Cornelis Croock of Amsterdam, your most devoted friend

To that great champion of learning and true religion, Desiderius Erasmus of Rotterdam. At Freiburg im Breisgau or at Augsburg

2355 / To Johann Rinck

This letter has been redated and appears as Ep 2353A.

2356 / To Viglius Zuichemus and Karel Sucket   Freiburg, 31 July 1530

This letter was first published in LB III/2 1747–8 *Appendix epistolarum* no 359. The manuscript, autograph throughout but with the address-sheet missing, is in the Papenbroek Collection of the University Library at Leiden (PAP 2).

Viglius Zuichemus (Ep 2210) and his friend Karel Sucket (Ep 2191) were at this time studying law with Andrea Alciati (Ep 1250) at Bourges.

Greetings. It is no use pursuing Kan with your letters. He left me in the month of January, if I am not mistaken,[1] and we have not yet been able

* * * * *

5 Erasmus did not mention this matter in Ep 2259A, but Croock had doubtless seen the letter to Pieter Gillis (Ep 2260:70–134) that was published with the *Hieron* of Xenophon (Ep 2273).
6 *Adagia* I i 29

2356
1 He seems to have departed on or before 23 January; see Ep 2259A:12, and cf Ep 2261:83–4, where he is said to have departed 'a few days' before 31 January 1530.

to discover where in the world he is. For several days he enjoyed himself at Strasbourg at the home of Gerard of Nijmegen, who was once a good friend of mine and has now become a deadly enemy.[2] He stirred up all 5 of Strasbourg and all the preachers against me. A fifth book has now been launched at my head.[3] If only he were with the duke of Gelderland![4] After enjoying Gerard's company, Kan set off for Cologne.[5] He has spent almost two months on this journey; this I have found out from the letters of friends, for he himself has not written a syllable to anyone. I suspect he has gone to 10 visit the evangelical churches in Saxony and Hessen.[6]

An incredible desire to leave me had taken hold of him, so much so that he was ready to depart at his own expense, and when I released him, he departed without eating, although the table had been set for lunch. He gave me as a reason that he was being called to the priesthood by his uncle; he 15 gave different excuses to different people. A more shifty rascal I have never seen. Pierre Barbier, who has long been burdened with debt, has misappropriated my Courtrai pension with a more than Punic perfidy.[7] After I had written several long letters on the subject, I entrusted them to Kan, but not before I had inquired if he was going to Flanders. He said he was. I asked if 20 he had enough money for the journey. 'Enough,' he said, 'to take me as far as Antwerp; I shall obtain all I need there.' 'Is it your wish,' I said, 'to undertake this task at your own expense?' He replied with an eager expression on his face 'Why not? I owe you more than that.' Believing him to be sincere in what he said, I gave him seven gold crowns. He has been away now for six 25 months, and no one has been able to find out where this fine fellow has betaken himself. I wonder how he has contrived to cast a spell over you and make you think him such a fine person. And you want this man to provide you with a commendation to me! He himself has always been in need of someone to recommend him. Bebel has published Greek epigrams, trans- 30 lated by various hands, including several by Kan, which, however, contain

* * * * *

2 Gerard Geldenhouwer (Ep 2219 n5)
3 Erasmus appears to be adding Bucer's *Epistola apologetica* (Ep 2312 n2) to the four works of Geldenhouwer listed in Ep 2329 n18.
4 Ie if only Geldenhouwer were in his hometown of Nijmegen, which is in the duchy of Gelderland
5 As the balance of this letter shows, the news of Kan's visit to Geldenhouwer completely soured Erasmus' opinion of him. Kan later wrote a letter of apology, but Erasmus never really forgave him; see Epp 2284, 3037, 3061.
6 Kan had in fact gone on to Amsterdam, arriving there before 1 March, having been seriously ill for several days at Nijmegen on the way; see Ep 2352:1–5.
7 On Barbier's 'perfidy,' cf Ep 2239 n1; on the proverbial perfidy of the Carthaginians, see *Adagia* I viii 28.

a fair sprinkling of childish errors. But he was so satisfied with himself that he did not think fit to show them to me.

In the month of March I began to be seriously ill; even now I have scarcely regained my strength.[8] When the illness was at its height, Quirinus, 35 who was the only servant with me at the time, suddenly came down with the English sweat and took to his bed.[9] I was compelled to engage someone else from the town.

I congratulate both of you on winning such a good name from Alciati, Sucket particularly for the praise he has earned by his lectures on civil law, 40 which drew a large audience.[10] I would be urging both of you to continue strongly on the course on which you have begun until you finish the race, if I were not deterred by that line of Homer 'you are urging on one who is himself running hard.'[11] Farewell, my very dear young friends.

Freiburg, 31 July 1530   45

Cammingha left me a little earlier than Kan:[12] friends had sent their own messenger specifically for this purpose. He promised to return in May. However, he left me a souvenir of himself to the tune of sixty crowns.[13] Farewell again.

If that very erudite young man, Pierre Du Chastel,[14] is there with you, 50 be sure to give him my greetings.

Yours, Erasmus of Rotterdam

* * * * *

8 See Ep 2320 n1.
9 See Ep 2343 n3.
10 Cf Ep 2276:31–43.
11 Ie urging someone to do what he is already eager to do; Homer *Iliad* 8.293–4. Cf *Adagia* I ii 46 and 47.
12 On Haio Cammingha and his debt to Erasmus, see Epp 2073 introduction, 2286:11–12, 2325:1–6.
13 'Souvenir' in the ironical sense of an unpaid debt
14 Ep 2213

ERASMUS' ILLNESS IN 1530

For over three months in the late winter and spring of 1530 Erasmus suffered from an illness the virulence, duration, and disruptiveness of which
were without precedent in his experience and caused him to fear for his life.
He describes the symptoms and the course of the illness, often in considerable detail, in a number of letters written in the period 23 May–31 July. His
vocabulary is not entirely consistent, and it is impossible to establish a precise chronology. Nevertheless, the available information is sufficiently clear
to permit a fairly confident conclusion concerning the nature of the illness.[1]

The trouble began sometime in March. At first, Erasmus suffered excruciating cramps in the belly, which were followed by vomiting, sleeplessness, and deep fatigue. This first stage, which turned suddenly worse on
Easter Monday (18 April), was followed by the development of 'a huge abscess' that began to spread in the region between the navel and the pubes.
The abscess consisted of a series of hard lumps, which Erasmus calls *mo-
lae* (literally 'millstones'). The array of lumps kept moving, and eventually took the form of a snake curling around the navel. The doctors at
first brought no relief. A surgeon, who claimed that he could burst the
abscess, was called. He applied 'powerful poultices' intended to 'turn the
abscess into an ulcer.' These 'ulcerating fomentations' caused pain and suffering, but the lumps remained and the infection did not go away. Eventually, on 24 June, 'the huge abscess' was lanced, whereupon a 'stinking quagmire' of blood and pus streamed out of it. This was the turning point. Erasmus' 'poor body,' which had hitherto been 'dehydrating
and moving steadily towards death,' began slowly to recover: pain abated,
sleep returned, stomach returned to normal, and fatigue lessened. There is
no evidence of any recurrence of the malady during Erasmus' remaining
years.

In the past, Erasmus had often complained of digestive problems, but
they had been the sort of thing that he could deal with simply by avoiding
food and drink that did not agree with him.[2] In 1530, by contrast, he had

* * * * *

1 For the complete list of references to the illness in this volume, see Ep 2320
  n1. The most detailed accounts of it are found in Epp 2329:62–79, 2343:7–23,
  and 2353A:46–70. There are further brief references in letters that will appear
  in CWE 17, but they throw no new light on the nature of the illness.
2 Convinced that his digestion had been ruined by college food during his years
  in Paris, and believing in particular that the eating of fish was detrimental to
  his health, Erasmus in 1525 procured from Pope Clement VII a dispensation
  to eat meat and dairy products during Lent and other times of fasting; see Ep
  1542. Finding, moreover, that the wines of Basel and Freiburg were harmful
  to his digestion and aggravated his attacks of the stone, Erasmus made special

evidently fallen victim to a severe and debilitating gastrointestinal infection that was soon accompanied by a frightening abdominal 'abscess.' Moreover, while Erasmus had never allowed any kind of pain or illness to interrupt his scholarly work for very long, this illness laid him low. He lamented that for weeks on end he could not write, dictate, listen attentively to someone reading to him, or enjoy the conversation of friends who came to visit him. And it is noteworthy that for the period between c 16 April and 20 May, and then again for that between 6 and 24 June, no letters by him survive.[3]

Some of these symptoms – abdominal pain and vomiting, chronic skin infection – might possibly be consistent with a diagnosis of tertiary syphilis. But this appears to be ruled out by the absence of any other evidence that Erasmus suffered from the disease, as well as by the abundant evidence that his mental faculties remained unimpaired until the very end.[4] This being so, the best explanation of his symptoms in 1530 is that the lumps making up the 'abscess' were carbuncles (lumps deep in the skin that may contain pus and are caused by staphylococcal infection of a group of hair follicles). When, as in Erasmus' case, carbuncles occur in groups, they constitute a condition that physicians describe as carbunculosis. Persons with weakened immune systems are more prone than those in robust health to develop carbunculosis. In Erasmus' case, it was most likely the debilitation caused by the gastrointestinal infection that triggered the development of the 'huge abscess' that caused him such fear and distress.

Thanks are due to Michael A. Hutcheon, MD, FRCP(C), professor of medicine at the University of Toronto, who examined the evidence summarized above, asked searching questions about it, and suggested the diagnosis offered here.

JME

* * * * *

efforts to be supplied with wine from Burgundy, the only kind he knew of that agreed with him; see Ep 2328 n7.

3 See Ep 2312A introduction.

4 At one time it was seriously argued, on the basis of the medical examination of what was mistakenly taken to be Erasmus' skeleton, that he had suffered from syphilis. For a careful demolition of this argument, see John B. Gleason 'The Allegation of Erasmus' Syphilis and the Question of His Burial Site' *Erasmus of Rotterdam Society Yearbook* 10 (1990) 122–39.

TABLE OF CORRESPONDENTS

WORKS FREQUENTLY CITED

SHORT-TITLE FORMS
FOR ERASMUS' WORKS

CORRIGENDA FOR CWE 15

INDEX

TABLE OF CORRESPONDENTS

2204   **To Janus Cornarius** Freiburg, 9 August 1529   2
2205   **To Johann von Botzheim** Freiburg, 13 August 1529   4
2206   **To Johann von Botzheim** Freiburg, 19 August 1529   14
2207   **From Johann von Botzheim** Überlingen, 20 August 1529   20
2208   **From Juan Luis Vives** Bruges, 30 August 1529   21
2209   **To Karel Uutenhove** Freiburg, 1 September 1529   24
2210   **From Viglius Zuichemus** Bourges, 1 September 1529   31
2211   **To Thomas More** Freiburg, 5 September 1529   35
2212   **To Margaret Roper** Freiburg, 6 September 1529   42
2213   **To Pierre Du Chastel** Freiburg, 7 September 1529   45
2214   **To Willibald Pirckheimer** Freiburg, 7 September 1529   46
2215   **To William Blount, Lord Mountjoy** Freiburg, 8 September 1529   46
2216   **From Petrus Plateanus** Jáchymov, 8 September 1529   48
2217   **To Jean de Lorraine** [Freiburg, September 1529]   51
2218   **To Bonifacius Amerbach** [Freiburg, c 25 September 1529]   54
2219   **From Bonifacius Amerbach** Basel, 27 September 1529   55
2220   **To Bonifacius Amerbach** Freiburg, 27 September 1529   59
2221   **From Bonifacius Amerbach** Basel, 30 September [1529]   60
2222   **To Johann von Vlatten** Freiburg, 2 October 1529   61
2223   **To Bonifacius Amerbach** Freiburg, 4 October 1529   65
2224   **From Bonifacius Amerbach** Basel, 18 October [1529]   66
2225   **To Ludwig Baer** Freiburg, 22 October 1529   68
2226   **From Cuthbert Tunstall** London, 24 October 1529   71
2227   **From John Longland** London, 28 October [1529]   74
2228   **From Thomas More** [Chelsea], 28 October [1529]   77
2229   **To Johannes Erasmius Froben** Freiburg, 2 November 1529   77
2230   **To Johann Henckel** Freiburg, 2 November 1529   79
2231   **To Bonifacius Amerbach** Freiburg, 4 November 1529   81
2232   **From Gerard of Friesland** [Westminster], 4 November 1529   85
2233   **From Margaret Roper** [Chelsea], 4 November [1529]   87
2233A **To Bonifacius Amerbach** Freiburg, 6 November 1529   89
2234   **From Duke William of Cleves** Büderich, 10 November 1529   90
2235   **From Bonifacius Amerbach** [Basel, November 1529]   91
2236   **To Bonifacius Amerbach** Freiburg, 18 November 1529   92
2237   **From Zacharias Deiotarus** London, 21 November 1529   93
2238   **To Gerard Geldenhouwer** Freiburg, 3 December 1529   94
2239   **From Pierre Barbier** Tournai, 7 December 1529   95
2240   **From Claudius Cantiuncula** [Vic-sur-Seille], 7 December [1529]   99
2241   **To François Bonvalot** Freiburg, 10 December 1529   102
2242   **To François Bonvalot [?]** Freiburg, 10 December 1529   103
2243   **From Erasmus Schets** Antwerp, 13 December 1529   104
2244   **From Adriaan van der Kammen** Mechelen, 26 December 1529   106
2245   **From Frans Titelmans** Louvain, December 1529   107
2246   **From Simon Riquinus** [?], 1 January 1530   110
2247   **From Jan Horák** Leipzig, 6 January 1530   112
2248   **From Bonifacius Amerbach** Basel, 9 January 1530   116

2249 **To Giambattista Egnazio** [Freiburg, c January] 1530   118
2250 **To Juan Maldonado** Freiburg, 13 January [1530]   120
2251 **To [Juan] de Valdés** Freiburg, 13 January 1530   122
2252 **To [Alfonso] de Valdés** Freiburg, 13 January 1530   123
2253 **To Juan de Vergara** [Freiburg, c 13 January 1530]   125
2253A **To [Alonso de Fonseca]** Freiburg, 13 January 1530   128
2254 **To Francisco de Vergara** Freiburg, 13 January [1530]   131
2255 **To Giovanni and Bernardo Boerio** Freiburg, 13 January [1530]   132
2256 **To Bonifacius Amerbach** Freiburg, 16 January [1530]   134
2257 **To Nicolaus Episcopius** Freiburg, 17 January 1530   138
2258 **From Levinus Ammonius** St Maartensbos, 17 January 1530   139
2259 This letter has been redated and will appear as Ep 2873A in cwe 20.   143
2259A **To Cornelis Croock** Freiburg, 23 January [1530]   143
2260 **To Pieter Gillis** Freiburg, 28 January 1530   145
2261 **To Haio Herman** Freiburg, 31 January 1530   159
2262 **To Gerard van Herema** Freiburg, 31 January 1530   164
2263 **To Cuthbert Tunstall** Freiburg, 31 January 1530   165
2264 **To a Theologian** [Freiburg, January 1530]   170
2265 **From Theodoricus Cortehoevius** Antwerp, 1 February 1530   171
2266 **To Thomas Boleyn** [Freiburg, February 1530]   174
2267 **From Bonifacius Amerbach** [Basel], 2 February 1530   176
2268 **To Erasmus Schets** Freiburg, 2 February [1530]   182
2269 **From Johann Koler** Augsburg, 3 February 1530   183
2270 **From Erasmus Schets** Antwerp, 4 February 1530   187
2271 **To Bonifacius Amerbach** [Freiburg, February 1530]   188
2272 **From Jacopo Sadoleto** Carpentras, 12 February 1530   189
2273 **To Anton Fugger** Freiburg, 13 February 1530   192
2274 **To Andreas and Christoph von Könneritz**
        Freiburg, 18 February [1530]   194
2275 **To the Franciscans** [Freiburg, February 1530]   195
2276 **From Andrea Alciati** Bourges, 1 March 1530   199
2277 **To Johann von Botzheim** Freiburg, 3 March [1530]   202
2278 **From Jan van Fevijn** Bruges, 6 March [1530]   203
2279 **To Bonifacius Amerbach** [Freiburg, March 1530]   205
2280 **From Bonifacius Amerbach** [Basel, March 1530]   206
2281 **To Bonifacius Amerbach** [Freiburg, March 1530]   208
2282 **To Henry of Burgundy** Freiburg, March 1530   208
2283 **To Hector Boece** Freiburg, 15 March 1530   210
2284 **To Balthasar Merklin** Freiburg, 15 March 1530   218
2285 **To Johann Rinck** Freiburg, 17 March 1530   226
2286 **To Erasmus Schets** Freiburg, 19 March 1530   232
2287 **To Richard Pace** Freiburg, 22 March 1530   233
2288 **To Karel Uutenhove** Freiburg, 23 March 1530   234
2289 **From Bonifacius Amerbach** [Basel], 24 March 1530   236
2290 **To Pietro Bembo** Freiburg, 25 March 1530   236
2291 **To Germain de Brie** Freiburg, 27 March 1530   241
2292 **To Alfonso de Valdés** Freiburg, 27 March [1530]   245
2293 **To the Magistrates of Strasbourg** Freiburg, 28 March 1530   245

2294 **To Bonifacius Amerbach** [Freiburg, c 28 March 1530] 247
2295 **To William Blount, Lord Mountjoy** Freiburg, 28 March [1530] 248
2296 **To Franciscus Cassander** Freiburg, 28 March 1530 251
2297 **From Diego Gracián de Alderete** Madrid, 28 March [1530] 253
2298 **From Simon Riquinus** Cologne, 29 March 1530 254
2299 **To Cristóbal Mexía** Freiburg, 30 March 1530 256
2300 **To Pero Mexía** Freiburg, 30 March 1530 262
2301 **To Alonso Manrique de Lara** Freiburg, 31 March 1530 271
2302 **To Giambattista Egnazio** Freiburg, 31 March 1530 273
2303 **To Konrad von Thüngen** Freiburg, 2 April 1530 275
2304 **From Peter Medmann** Strasbourg, 2 April 1530 276
2305 **To Johannes Alexander Brassicanus** Freiburg, 4 April 1530 277
2306 **From Johann Lotzer** Heidelberg, 4 April 1530 279
2307 **From Anton Fugger** Augsburg, 7 April 1530 281
2308 **To Johann Koler** Freiburg, 13 April 1530 282
2309 **From Johann Henckel** Linz, 13 April 1530 284
2310 **From Johann von Botzheim** Überlingen, 13 April 1530 286
2311 **From Gerard Morrhy** Frankfurt, 16 April 1530 292
2312 **From Bonifacius Amerbach** [Basel, c 16 April 1530] 295
2312A **To Jacopo Sadoleto** Freiburg, [c 16 April 1530] 307
2313 **From Caspar Ursinus Velius** Linz, 20 April 1530 309
2314 **From Konrad von Thüngen** Würzburg, 9 May 1530 311
2315 This letter has been redated and appears as Ep 2312A. 311
2316 **From Johann von Botzheim** Überlingen, 18 May 1530 311
2317 **From Ferdinand to the Town Council of Freiburg**
    Innsbruck, 18 May 1530 312
2318 **Letter Patent of Charles V** Innsbruck, 20 May 1530 314
2319 **From Bonifacius Amerbach** Basel, [c 20 May 1530] 315
2320 **To Bonifacius Amerbach** [Freiburg], 20 May [1530] 316
2321 **To Augustinus Marius** Freiburg, 22 May 1530 317
2322 **To Daniel Stiebar** Freiburg, 23 May 1530 320
2323 **From Bonifacius Amerbach** Basel, [c 23 May 1530] 322
2324 **To Bonifacius Amerbach** [Freiburg, c 25 May 1530] 324
2325 **To Erasmus Schets** Freiburg, 1 June 1530 325
2326 **To Bernhard von Cles** Freiburg, 6 June [1530] 326
2327 **To Cornelis de Schepper** Freiburg, 6 June [1530] 327
2328 **To [Lorenzo Campeggi]** Freiburg, 24 June 1530 328
2329 **To Andrea Alciati** Freiburg, [c 24 June] 1530 333
2330 **To Anton Fugger** Freiburg, 24 June 1530 338
2331 **To Johann Koler** Freiburg, 24 June 1530 339
2332 **To Christoph von Stadion** Freiburg, 24 June 1530 340
2333 **From Simon Pistoris** Augsburg, 27 June 1530 343
2334 **From Bernhard von Cles** Augsburg, 27 June 1530 345
2335 **From Johann von Vlatten** Augsburg, 28 June 1530 347
2336 **From Cornelis de Schepper** Augsburg, 28 June 1530 348
2337 **From Martinus Bovolinus** Venice, 29 June 1530 352
2338 **To Duke George of Saxony** Freiburg, 30 June 1530 353
2339 **From Nicolaus Olahus** Augsburg, 1 July 1530 359

2340 **From Germain de Brie** [?], 6 July 1530 363
2341 **To [Lorenzo Campeggi]** Freiburg, 7 July 1530 367
2342 **To Christoph von Carlowitz** Freiburg, 7 July 1530 368
2343 **To Philippus Melanchthon** Freiburg, 7 July 1530 369
2344 **To Simon Pistoris** Freiburg, 7 July 1530 371
2345 **To Nicolaus Olahus** Freiburg, 7 July 1530 372
2346 **To Johann von Vlatten** Freiburg, 9 July 1530 373
2347 **To Luca Bonfiglio** Freiburg, 9 July 1530 373
2348 **To Frans van der Dilft** Freiburg, 9 July 1530 375
2349 **To Alfonso de Valdés** Freiburg, 9 July 1530 376
2350 **To Mary of Austria** Freiburg, 9 July 1530 377
2350A **To Christoph Truchsess von Waldburg** Freiburg, 9 July 1530 378
2351 **From Marcin Słap Dąbrówski** Louvain, 12 July 1530 379
2352 **From Conradus Goclenius** Louvain, 14 July [1530] 384
2353 **From Jan of Heemstede** Louvain, 14 July 1530 399
2353A **To Johann Rinck** Freiburg, 14 July 1530 400
2354 **From Cornelis Croock** Amsterdam, July 1530 404
2355 This letter has been renumbered and appears as Ep 2353A. 406
2356 **To Viglius Zuichemus and Karel Sucket** Freiburg, 31 July 1530 406

WORKS FREQUENTLY CITED

Actes de François I
Catalogue des actes de François Ier (Paris 1887–1908) 10 vols

AK
Die Amerbach Korrespondenz ed Alfred Hartmann and B.R. Jenny (Basel 1942–)

Allen
Opus epistolarum Des. Erasmi Roterodami ed P.S. Allen, H.M. Allen, and H.W. Garrod (Oxford 1906–58) 11 vols and index

Analecta Belgica
C.P. Hoynck van Papendrecht *Analecta Belgica* 3 vols in 6 (The Hague 1743)

ASD
Opera omnia Desiderii Erasmi Roterodami (Amsterdam 1969–)

Augustijn
Cornelis Augustijn 'Gerard Geldenhouwer und die religiöse Toleranz' *Archiv für Reformationsgeschichte/Archive for Reformation History* 69 (1978) 132–56

Burckhardt
Theophilus Burckhardt-Biedermann *Bonifacius Amerbach und die Reformation* (Basel 1894)

CEBR
Contemporaries of Erasmus: A Biographical Register of the Renaissance and Reformation ed Peter G. Bietenholz and Thomas B. Deutscher (Toronto 1985–7) 3 vols

CWE
Collected Works of Erasmus (Toronto 1974–)

Enthoven
Briefe an Desiderius Erasmus von Rotterdam ed L.K. Enthoven (Strasbourg 1906)

Epistolae familiares
Epistolae familiares Des. Erasmi Roterodami ad Bonif. Amerbachium: cum nonnullis aliis ad Erasmum spectantibus (Basel: Sereni 1779)

Epistolae floridae
Des. Erasmi Roterodami epistolarum floridarum liber unus antehac nunquam excusus (Basel: J. Herwagen, September 1531)

Förstemann / Günther
Briefe an Desiderius Erasmus von Rotterdam ed J. Förstemann and O. Günther, XXVII. Beiheft zum *Zentralblatt für Bibliothekwesen* (Leipzig 1904)

Knecht
R. J. Knecht *Francis I* (Cambridge 1982)

LB

Desiderii Erasmi opera omnia ed J. Leclerc (Leiden 1703–6; repr 1961–2) 10 vols

LP

Letters and Papers, Foreign and Domestic, of the Reign of Henry VIII ed J.S. Brewer, J. Gairdner, and R.H. Brodie (London 1862–1932) 36 vols

LW

Luther's Works ed Jaroslav Pelikan, Helmut T. Lehmann et al (St Louis/Philadelphia 1955–86) 55 vols

Major

Emil Major *Erasmus von Rotterdam*, no 1 in the series *Virorum illustrium reliquiae* (Basel 1927)

MBW

Melanchthons Briefwechsel, kritische und kommentierte Gesamtausgabe ed Heinz Scheible et al (Stuttgart-Bad Canstatt 1977–   ) 26 vols to date. The edition is published in two series: *Regesten* (vols 1–13 in print); and *Texte* (vols T 1–T 12 in print). The letter numbers and bracketed section numbers are the same in both series. Only the *Texte* volumes have line numbers.

Opus epistolarum

Opus epistolarum Des. Erasmi Roterodami per autorem diligenter recognitum et adjectis innumeris novis fere ad trientem auctum (Basel: Froben, Herwagen, and Episcopius 1529)

Pastor

Ludwig von Pastor *The History of the Popes from the Close of the Middle Ages* ed and trans R.F. Kerr et al, 6th ed (London 1938–53) 40 vols

Pirckheimeri opera

Billibaldi Pirckheimeri – opera politica, historica, philologica et epistolica ed Melchior Goldast (Frankfurt 1610; repr Hildesheim / New York 1969)

PL

Patrologiae cursus completus – series Latina ed J.-P. Migne, 1st ed (Paris 1844–55, 1862–5; repr Turnhout) 217 vols plus 4 vols indexes. In the notes, references to volumes of PL in which column numbers in the first edition are different from those in later editions or reprints include the date of the edition cited.

Rémy

Ferdinand Rémy *Les grandes indulgences pontificales aux Pays-Bas à la fin du moyen age (1300–1531): Essai sur leur histoire et leur importance financière* (Uystpruyst 1928)

Rummel

Erika Rummel *Erasmus and his Catholic Critics* (Nieuwkoop 1989) 2 vols

Scarisbrick

J.J. Scarisbrick *Henry VIII* (Berkeley and Los Angeles 1968)

Sieber   Ludwig Sieber *Das Mobiliar des Erasmus: Verzeichnis vom 10. April 1534* (Basel 1891)

Staehelin   *Oekolampad-Bibliographie* ed Ernst Staehelin 2nd ed (Nieuwkoop 1963)

WA   *D. Martin Luthers Werke, Kritische Gesamtausgabe* (Weimar 1930–80) 60 vols

WA-DB   *D. Martin Luthers Werke: Deutsche Bibel* (Weimar 1906–61) 12 vols

WPB   *Willibald Pirckheimers Briefwechsel* ed Emil Reicke, Helga Scheible, et al (Munich 1940–2009) 7 vols

Zw-Br   *Huldreich Zwinglis Sämtliche Werke 7–11: Zwinglis Briefwechsel* ed Emil Egli et al, Corpus Reformatorum 94–8 (Leipzig 1911–35) 5 vols

Titles following colons are longer versions of the short-titles, or are alternative titles. Items entirely enclosed in square brackets are of doubtful authorship. For abbreviations see Works Frequently Cited.

Acta: Acta Academiae Lovaniensis contra Lutherum *Opuscula* / CWE 71

Adagia: Adagiorum chiliades 1508, etc (Adagiorum collectanea for the primitive form, when required) LB II / ASD II-1–9 / CWE 30–6

Admonitio adversus mendacium: Admonitio adversus mendacium et obtrectationem LB X / CWE 78

Annotationes in Novum Testamentum LB VI / ASD VI-5–10 / CWE 51–60

Antibarbari LB X / ASD I-1 / CWE 23

Apologia ad annotationes Stunicae: Apologia respondens ad ea quae Iacobus Lopis Stunica taxaverat in prima duntaxat Novi Testamenti aeditione LB IX / ASD IX-2

Apologia ad Caranzam: Apologia ad Sanctium Caranzam, or Apologia de tribus locis, or Responsio ad annotationem Stunicae . . . a Sanctio Caranza defensam LB IX

Apologia ad Fabrum: Apologia ad Iacobum Fabrum Stapulensem LB IX / ASD IX-3 / CWE 83

Apologia ad prodromon Stunicae LB IX

Apologia ad Stunicae conclusiones LB IX

Apologia adversus monachos: Apologia adversus monachos quosdam Hispanos LB IX

Apologia adversus Petrum Sutorem: Apologia adversus debacchationes Petri Sutoris LB IX

Apologia adversus rhapsodias Alberti Pii: Apologia ad viginti et quattuor libros A. Pii LB IX / CWE 84

Apologia adversus Stunicae Blasphemiae: Apologia adversus libellum Stunicae cui titulum fecit Blasphemiae et impietates Erasmi LB IX

Apologia contra Latomi dialogum: Apologia contra Iacobi Latomi dialogum de tribus linguis LB IX / CWE 71

Apologia de 'In principio erat sermo' LB IX

Apologia de laude matrimonii: Apologia pro declamatione de laude matrimonii LB IX / CWE 71

Apologia de loco 'Omnes quidem': Apologia de loco 'Omnes quidem resurgemus' LB IX

Apologia qua respondet invectivis Lei: Apologia qua respondet duabus invectivis Eduardi Lei *Opuscula* / ASD IX-4 / CWE 72

Apophthegmata LB IV / ASD IV-4 / CWE 37–8

Appendix de scriptis Clithovei LB IX / CWE 83

Appendix respondens ad Sutorem: Appendix respondens ad quaedam Antapologiae Petri Sutoris LB IX

Argumenta: Argumenta in omnes epistolas apostolicas nova (with Paraphrases)

Axiomata pro causa Lutheri: Axiomata pro causa Martini Lutheri *Opuscula* / CWE 71

Brevissima scholia: In Elenchum Alberti Pii brevissima scholia per eundem Erasmum Roterodamum CWE 84

Carmina LB I, IV, V, VIII / ASD I-7 / CWE 85–6
Catalogus lucubrationum LB I / CWE 9 (Ep 1341A)
Ciceronianus: Dialogus Ciceronianus LB I / ASD I-2 / CWE 28
Colloquia LB I / ASD I-3 / CWE 39–40
Compendium vitae Allen I / CWE 4
Conflictus: Conflictus Thaliae et Barbariei LB I / ASD I-8
[Consilium: Consilium cuiusdam ex animo cupientis esse consultum] *Opuscula* /
     CWE 71

De bello Turcico: Utilissima consultatio de bello Turcis inferendo, et obiter enarratus
     psalmus 28 LB V / ASD V-3 / CWE 64
De civilitate: De civilitate morum puerilium LB I / ASD I-8 / CWE 25
Declamatio de morte LB IV
Declamatiuncula LB IV
Declarationes ad censuras Lutetiae vulgatas: Declarationes ad censuras Lutetiae
     vulgatas sub nomine facultatis theologiae Parisiensis LB IX / CWE 82
De concordia: De sarcienda ecclesiae concordia, or De amabili ecclesiae concordia
     [on Psalm 83] LB V / ASD V-3 / CWE 65
De conscribendis epistolis LB I / ASD I-2 / CWE 25
De constructione: De constructione octo partium orationis, or Syntaxis LB I / ASD I-4
De contemptu mundi: Epistola de contemptu mundi LB V / ASD V-1 / CWE 66
De copia: De duplici copia verborum ac rerum LB I / ASD I-6 / CWE 24
De esu carnium: Epistola apologetica ad Christophorum episcopum Basiliensem de
     interdicto esu carnium LB IX / ASD IX-1
De immensa Dei misericordia: Concio de immensa Dei misericordia LB V / ASD V-7 /
     CWE 70
De libero arbitrio: De libero arbitrio diatribe LB IX / CWE 76
De philosophia evangelica LB VI
De praeparatione: De praeparatione ad mortem LB V / ASD V-1 / CWE 70
De pueris instituendis: De pueris statim ac liberaliter instituendis LB I / ASD I-2 /
     CWE 26
De puero Iesu: Concio de puero Iesu LB V / ASD V-7 / CWE 29
De puritate tabernaculi: Enarratio psalmi 14 qui est de puritate tabernaculi sive
     ecclesiae christianae LB V / ASD V-2 / CWE 65
De ratione studii LB I / ASD I-2 / CWE 24
De recta pronuntiatione: De recta latini graecique sermonis pronuntiatione LB I /
     ASD I-4 / CWE 26
De taedio Iesu: Disputatiuncula de taedio, pavore, tristicia Iesu LB V / ASD V-7 /
     CWE 70
Detectio praestigiarum: Detectio praestigiarum cuiusdam libelli Germanice scripti
     LB X / ASD IX-1 / CWE 78
De vidua christiana LB V / ASD V-6 / CWE 66
De virtute amplectenda: Oratio de virtute amplectenda LB V / CWE 29
[Dialogus bilinguium ac trilinguium: Chonradi Nastadiensis dialogus bilinguium
     ac trilinguium] *Opuscula* / CWE 7
Dilutio: Dilutio eorum quae Iodocus Clithoveus scripsit adversus declamationem
     suasoriam matrimonii / *Dilutio eorum quae Iodocus Clithoveus scripsit* ed Émile V.
     Telle (Paris 1968) / CWE 83

Divinationes ad notata Bedae: Divinationes ad notata per Bedam de Paraphrasi
    Erasmi in Matthaeum, et primo de duabus praemissis epistolis LB IX / ASD IX-5

Ecclesiastes: Ecclesiastes sive de ratione concionandi LB V / ASD V-4, 5
Elenchus in censuras Bedae: In N. Bedae censuras erroneas elenchus LB IX / ASD IX-5
Enchiridion: Enchiridion militis christiani LB V / CWE 66
Encomium matrimonii (in De conscribendis epistolis)
Encomium medicinae: Declamatio in laudem artis medicae LB I / ASD I-4 /
    CWE 29
Epistola ad Dorpium LB IX / CWE 3 (Ep 337) / CWE 71
Epistola ad fratres Inferioris Germaniae: Responsio ad fratres Germaniae In-
    ferioris ad epistolam apologeticam incerto autore proditam LB X / ASD IX-1 /
    CWE 78
Epistola ad gracculos: Epistola ad quosdam impudentissimos gracculos LB X /
    Ep 2275
Epistola apologetica adversus Stunicam LB IX / Ep 2172
Epistola apologetica de Termino LB X / Ep 2018
Epistola consolatoria: Epistola consolatoria virginibus sacris, or Epistola consolatoria
    in adversis LB V / CWE 69
Epistola contra pseudevangelicos: Epistola contra quosdam qui se falso iactant
    evangelicos LB X / ASD IX-1 / CWE 78
Euripidis Hecuba LB I / ASD I-1
Euripidis Iphigenia in Aulide LB I / ASD I-1
Exomologesis: Exomologesis sive modus confitendi LB V
Explanatio symboli: Explanatio symboli apostolorum sive catechismus LB V /
    ASD V-1 / CWE 70
Ex Plutarcho versa LB IV / ASD IV-2

Formula: Conficiendarum epistolarum formula (see De conscribendis epistolis)

Hyperaspistes LB X / CWE 76-7

In Nucem Ovidii commentarius LB I / ASD I-1 / CWE 29
In Prudentium: Commentarius in duos hymnos Prudentii LB V / ASD V-7 / CWE 29
In psalmum 1: Enarratio primi psalmi, 'Beatus vir,' iuxta tropologiam potissimum
    LB V / ASD V-2 / CWE 63
In psalmum 2: Commentarius in psalmum 2, 'Quare fremuerunt gentes?' LB V /
    ASD V-2 / CWE 63
In psalmum 3: Paraphrasis in tertium psalmum, 'Domine quid multiplicate' LB V /
    ASD V-2 / CWE 63
In psalmum 4: In psalmum quartum concio LB V / ASD V-2 / CWE 63
In psalmum 22: In psalmum 22 enarratio triplex LB V / ASD V-2 / CWE 64
In psalmum 33: Enarratio psalmi 33 LB V / ASD V-3 / CWE 64
In psalmum 38: Enarratio psalmi 38 LB V / ASD V-3 / CWE 65
In psalmum 85: Concionalis interpretatio, plena pietatis, in psalmum 85 LB V /
    ASD V-3 / CWE 64
Institutio christiani matrimonii LB V / ASD V-6 / CWE 69
Institutio principis christiani LB IV / ASD IV-1 / CWE 27

[Julius exclusus: Dialogus Julius exclusus e coelis] *Opuscula* ASD I-8 / CWE 27

Lingua LB IV / ASD IV-1A / CWE 29
Liturgia Virginis Matris: Virginis Matris apud Lauretum cultae liturgia LB V /
ASD V-1 / CWE 69
Luciani dialogi LB I / ASD I-1

Manifesta mendacia ASD IX-4 / CWE 71
Methodus (see Ratio)
Modus orandi Deum LB V / ASD V-1 / CWE 70
Moria: Moriae encomium LB IV / ASD IV-3 / CWE 27

Notatiunculae: Notatiunculae quaedam extemporales ad naenias Bedaicas, or
Responsio ad notulas Bedaicas LB IX / ASD IX-5
Novum Testamentum: Novum Testamentum 1519 and later (Novum instrumentum
for the first edition, 1516, when required) LB VI / ASD VI-2, 3, 4

Obsecratio ad Virginem Mariam: Obsecratio sive oratio ad Virginem Mariam in
rebus adversis, or Obsecratio ad Virginem Matrem Mariam in rebus adversis
LB V / CWE 69
Oratio de pace: Oratio de pace et discordia LB VIII
Oratio funebris: Oratio funebris in funere Bertae de Heyen LB VIII / CWE 29

Paean Virgini Matri: Paean Virgini Matri dicendus LB V / CWE 69
Panegyricus: Panegyricus ad Philippum Austriae ducem LB IV / ASD IV-1 /
CWE 27
Parabolae: Parabolae sive similia LB I / ASD I-5 / CWE 23
Paraclesis LB V, VI / ASD V-7
Paraphrasis in Elegantias Vallae: Paraphrasis in Elegantias Laurentii Vallae LB I /
ASD I-4
Paraphrasis in Matthaeum, etc LB VII / ASD VII-6 / CWE 42–50
Peregrinatio apostolorum: Peregrinatio apostolorum Petri et Pauli LB VI, VII
Precatio ad Virginis filium Iesum LB V / CWE 69
Precatio dominica LB V / CWE 69
Precationes: Precationes aliquot novae LB V / CWE 69
Precatio pro pace ecclesiae: Precatio ad Dominum Iesum pro pace ecclesiae LB IV,
V / CWE 69
Prologus supputationis: Prologus in supputationem calumniarum Natalis Bedae
(1526), or Prologus supputationis errorum in censuris Bedae (1527) LB IX /
ASD IX-5
Purgatio adversus epistolam Lutheri: Purgatio adversus epistolam non sobriam
Lutheri LB X / ASD IX-1 / CWE 78

Querela pacis LB IV / ASD IV-2 / CWE 27

Ratio: Ratio seu Methodus compendio perveniendi ad veram theologiam (Methodus
for the shorter version originally published in the Novum instrumentum of 1516)
LB V, VI

Responsio ad annotationes Lei: Responsio ad annotationes Eduardi Lei LB IX /
    ASD IX-4 / CWE 72
Responsio ad Collationes: Responsio ad Collationes cuiusdam iuvenis geronto-
    didascali LB IX
Responsio ad disputationem de divortio: Responsio ad disputationem cuiusdam
    Phimostomi de divortio LB IX / ASD IX-4 / CWE 83
Responsio ad epistolam Alberti Pii: Responsio ad epistolam paraeneticam Alberti
    Pii, or Responsio ad exhortationem Pii LB IX / CWE 84
Responsio ad notulas Bedaicas (*see* Notatiunculae)
Responsio ad Petri Cursii defensionem: Epistola de apologia Cursii LB X /
    Ep 3032
Responsio adversus febricitantis cuiusdam libellum LB X

Spongia: Spongia adversus aspergines Hutteni LB X / ASD IX-1 / CWE 78
Supputatio: Supputatio errorum in censuris Bedae LB IX
Supputationes: Supputationes errorum in censuris Natalis Bedae: contains Sup-
    putatio and reprints of Prologus supputationis; Divinationes ad notata Bedae;
    Elenchus in censuras Bedae; Appendix respondens ad Sutorem; Appendix de
    scriptis Clithovei LB IX / ASD IX-5

Tyrannicida: Tyrannicida, declamatio Lucianicae respondens LB I / ASD I-1 / CWE 29

Virginis et martyris comparatio LB V / ASD V-7 / CWE 69
Vita Hieronymi: Vita divi Hieronymi Stridonensis *Opuscula* / CWE 61

CORRIGENDA FOR CWE 15

Page 87 Ep 2100 introduction, last line: for 'Nicholaus' read 'Nicolaus.'

Page 107 Ep 2108 at lines 15–16, between the sentence ending 'from others' and that beginning 'Your friend,' insert the following: 'We live here in very great danger; I pray God will grant us a happy outcome.'

Page 129 Ep 2120 note 14: *duabus sellis sedere* is in fact found in *Adagia* I vii 2.

Page 135 Ep 2123 note 3: Thraso is a character in Terence's play *Eunuchus*.

Page 211 Ep 2151 note 1, line 3: for '2161:334' read '2161:33–4.'

Index

Agricola, Georgius 49–50, 51n, 194n, 195n; works: *Bermannus sive de re metallica* 49n, 194–5

Alaard of Amsterdam, publishes unauthorized edition of Erasmus' *Paraphrasis in Elegantias Vallae* xxiii, 144n, 149n, 406

Albert of Brandenburg, cardinal-archbishop-elector of Mainz 130, 134, 258

Alciati, Andrea, professor of law at Bourges 26–7, 28, 31n, 32–3, 43n, 44, 55, 59, 60, 65, 406n, 408
– letter from 199–202
– letter to 333–7

Aldington, Erasmus' living at xxiii, 341

Aldridge, Robert 75

Alexander the Great 366

Alexander vi, pope 230

Alger of Liège xx, 218n, 221, 222n, 224n, 225. *See also under* Erasmus, editions and translations

Algoet, Lieven, Erasmus' messenger 204, 245n, 248n, 281, 283, 287, 328, 349, 394

Alvarez de Toledo, Fadrique 22n

Ambrose, St 17, 19, 51n, 64n, 170, 218, 221, 302

Amerbach, Basilius 66, 89n, 206, 207, 236n, 316n

Amerbach, Bonifacius, professor of law at Basel xi, 2n, 25n, 32n, 44n, 78, 192n, 202n, 245n, 278, 295n, 309, 311, 328n

– letters from 55–9, 60–1, 66–8, 91–2, 116–18, 143, 176–82, 206–7, 236, 292–5, 315–16, 322–4
– letters to 54–5, 59–60, 65–6, 81–5, 89, 92–3, 134–8, 188–9, 205–6, 208, 247–8, 316–17, 324–5

Ammonio, Andrea 30

Ammonius, Levinus 26, 45n, 64n, 91n, 188, 233n, 235, 396
– letter from 139–43

Anabaptists 58n, 89n, 324n, 333, 344n, 367

Antonin, Jan 286

Antwerp xvi, xxii, xxv, 11, 13, 15n, 21, 22n, 62n, 84n, 96n, 104n, 105n, 107, 108n, 109, 117n, 141n, 145, 151n, 170n, 171n, 202n, 256n, 260, 265n, 292n, 315n, 385, 388n, 397, 398n, 407

Aretino, Francesco 74, 167, 242

Aristarchus 345, 372

Aristotle xx, 193n, 221

Arnobius the Younger 175, 302

Augsburg xxii, 11, 56n, 62, 114n, 171, 183n, 184–5, 192n, 202, 235, 259, 268n, 281, 283, 289, 308, 312n, 325, 328n, 340n, 346n, 349, 350, 351, 375, 378, 406; Diet of xiii–xiv, 113n, 119, 160, 204n, 248n, 283n, 288–9, 319n, 326n, 328n, 332n, 360n, 368n, 372, 374n, 375n, 376n, 379n, 401–2, 403n

Augsburg Confession (*Confessio Augustana*) xiv, 343–4n, 345n, 402n

Augustine of Hippo, St 17, 18, 19, 51n, 72, 98n, 155, 165, 170, 175, 221, 251–3,

300, 302, 303, 359. *See also under*
Erasmus, editions and translations
Augustinians 12, 109n, 319n
Austria xiii, 20n, 25n, 37n, 47, 63n, 97n,
116n, 135n, 161, 177n, 185n, 194n,
204n, 206n, 228n, 229, 249, 250n,
285n, 307, 378n

Bade, Josse, Paris printer and bookseller
32n, 60n, 67n, 118, 152n, 162, 163n,
243n, 273n, 330n
Baechem, Nicolaas, Carmelite of Louvain 10n, 304n
Baer, Ludwig 318, 322
– letter to 68–71
Barbier, Pierre 250, 342n, 407
– letter from 95–9
Barcelona 23; treaty of xii, xiii, 37–8n,
186n
Barlandus, Adrianus Cornelii 144n,
398
Basel xi, xii, xiv, xvii, xviii, 2n, 32n,
43n, 44n, 49, 53n, 56n, 58n, 60n, 65n,
67n, 78, 82n, 83, 84n, 85n, 89n, 92,
95n, 99n, 101n, 109n, 110, 116n, 120n,
129, 134n, 135n, 161, 176, 177n, 196n,
207n, 212n, 215, 217, 228n, 235n, 240,
270, 275, 292n, 300n, 313n, 316, 317–
18n, 322n, 323n, 324, 331n, 352n,
367, 368, 376n, 386n, 396, 400n, 410n;
course of Reformation in xi, 117–18,
293–5, 319–20; Erasmus' decision to
leave and move to Freiburg xi, xviii,
21, 25, 26, 38, 47, 54, 62, 63n, 69n, 71,
104, 119, 121, 171, 258, 299, 329
Basil, St 139, 140n, 143, 188, 195, 221
Beatus Rhenanus 206n, 208, 255, 274,
278, 309
Bebel, Johann, Basel printer 67, 85, 293,
407
Béda, Noël, syndic of the Paris faculty
of theology xvi, 44, 57n, 71, 168–9,
170–1, 197, 207, 271, 337
Bembo, Pietro 24, 186n, 353, 374n
– letter to 236–41
Berengar of Tours 218n, 220, 223
Bern 161, 324

Bernard of Clairvaux, St 231
Berquin, Louis de 10, 243
Bertholf, Hilarius 386
Besançon 64n, 69n, 97, 102, 103n, 116n,
336, 376, 379n, 400n
Bessarion, Basilius Cardinal 231, 363n
Birckmann, Franz, Antwerp bookseller
21–2n, 76
Bletz, Anton 43n
Blount, Charles 251n
Blount, William, Baron Mountjoy
– letters to 46–8, 248–51
Boece, Hector xxiii
– letter to 210–18 (includes 'List of All
the Works of Erasmus of Rotterdam,'
212–18)
Boerio, Giovanni and Bernardo, of
Genoa
– letter to 132–3
Bohemia 37n, 49n, 112n, 114, 194n, 235,
249n, 313n, 346n
Boleyn, Anne xxii, 174n
Boleyn, Thomas, Viscount Rochford
xxii, 86, 299n
– letter to 174–6
Bologna 100, 135n, 160, 178n, 179n,
194n, 248n, 255n, 289n
Bonfiglio, Luca
– letter to 373–5
Bonvalot, François, canon of Besançon
376n
– letters to 102–3, 103–4
Botzheim, Johann von, humanist and
canon of Constance xvii
– letters from 20–1, 286–90, 311–12
– letters to 4–14, 14–19, 202–3
Bourges 26, 31n, 32, 43n, 44, 55, 59,
61n, 68, 200n, 335, 406
Bovolinus, Martinus
– letter from 352–3
Brabant 63, 69, 110n, 112, 135, 138, 197,
256n, 304, 305, 331, 338, 339, 360n,
387, 395; 'tyranny' and 'villainy' of
monks in 118n, 119, 130, 134, 136,
169
Brandão, João 105
Brassicanus, Johannes Alexander 308

– letter to 277–9

Brie, Germain de 248n; contribution
to the Froben edition of Chrysostom
xxi, 140n, 166, 241–2, 363–4
– letter from 363–6
– letter to 241–5

British plague. *See* English sweat

Brunfels, Otto xvii, 246n, 247

Bucer, Martin, leader of the Reformation in Strasbourg xvii, xviii-xix,
56–7n, 58–9n, 117n, 255n, 276n, 293n,
323n; works: *Confessio tetrapolitana*
345n, 402n; *Epistola apologetica* xvii,
57n, 293n, 294 illustration, 319n,
320n, 324n, 327n, 337n, 345n, 402n,
407n

Buda 36n, 161, 359n, 360n

Budé, Guillaume, French humanist
xv, 28n, 32, 43n, 60–1, 65, 67, 118–
19, 162, 163n, 197, 243, 244–5, 248,
250, 273, 308–9, 336, 337, 364, 366;
works: *Altera aeditio annotationum in
Pandectas* 243n; *Annotationes in* XXIV
Pandectarum libros 32n; *Commentarii
linguae graecae* 60, 67, 85n, 162, 244

Bugenhagen, Johann 300n, 301 illustration

Burgundy 20n, 64n, 329n, 338, 389n,
411n

Burgundy, Adolf of, lord of Veere xxii,
209n

Burgundy, Henry of, son of Adolf xxii
– letter to 208–9

Burgundy, Maximilian of, elder brother
of Henry 209

Burgundy, Philip of, bishop of Utrecht
258, 291

Busleyden, Gilles de 397

Caesarius, Johannes 255n, 276

Cajetanus. *See* Vio, Tommaso de

Cambrai, Peace of ('Ladies Peace') xii,
xiii, 20–1n, 25n, 35n, 47n, 51n, 63n,
81n, 186n, 249n

Cammingha, Haio, of Friesland 78n,
159, 163, 164, 233n, 325, 376n, 383n,
395, 408

Campeggi, Lorenzo Cardinal, papal
legate to England and Germany xiv,
48, 134, 136, 341, 344, 374n
– letters to 328–33, 367–8

Campen, Jan van, professor of Hebrew at the Collegium Trilingue in
Louvain 111n

Cantiuncula, Claudius 317n
– letter from 99–101

Capito, Wolfgang, Strasbourg reformer
345n, 367, 402

Carinus, Ludovicus 84

Carlowitz, Christoph von 325
– letter to 368–9

Carmelites xvii, 10, 12

Carondelet, Ferry de, archdeacon of
Besançon 97, 366

Carvajal, Luis de, Spanish Franciscan
xvi, xvii, 13, 196n, 197n, 254, 261n,
264–5, 266n, 267–9, 270–1, 272–
3, 305n, 324n, 327n, 330n; works:
*Apologia monasticae religionis diluens
nugas Erasmi* xvi, 13n, 261n, 264n,
269n, 272n; *Dulcoratio amarulentiarum
Erasmicae responsionis* xvi, 195–7,
199n, 261n, 264n, 267–71, 272n, 288

Cassander, Franciscus
– letter to 251–3

Cassiodorus 175–6, 300

Castro, Luis de, Erasmus Schets' agent
in London 182, 188, 326

Catherine of Aragon, queen of England
xxii, 21n, 36n, 38n, 46n, 48n, 94n,
134n, 136n, 137 illustration, 174n,
215, 257, 307n. *See also* Henry VIII,
king of England: divorce of

Ceratinus, Jacobus 27, 208n, 209n

Charles V, Holy Roman emperor, king
of Spain, duke of Burgundy xii, xiii,
xviii, 9, 13, 20, 22n, 23, 25n, 36n,
37–8n, 42, 47n, 53, 58n, 62n, 63n,
69, 81n, 93n, 100n, 103, 119, 120n,
122n, 129n, 130, 134, 135, 160, 169,
177, 181, 184n, 185–6, 187n, 197, 198,
204n, 214, 215, 228n, 231n, 232n,
235n, 245, 248n, 249, 250n, 254n, 257,
260, 261, 264n, 265, 266, 267, 268n,

269, 272, 274, 281, 282–3, 284, 285, 288, 289, 305–6, 311–12, 325, 326, 327, 328n, 331, 333, 338, 339, 341, 343, 344, 345n, 347, 348, 349n, 351, 356n, 358–9, 362n, 367, 372, 373, 378n, 386n, 387n, 402, 403n; Erasmus' income from 63n, 96–7n, 109n, 260, 342. See also Augsburg: Diet of; Barcelona: Treaty of; Cambrai, Peace of
– Letter Patent of 314–15
Cicero 42n, 118, 156, 215, 257n, 297, 380
Clava, Antonius 145n, 148
Clement VII, pope xii, 9, 11, 20–1n, 37–8, 39 illustration, 48n, 70–1, 100n, 119, 134, 135n, 160, 181, 185–6, 260, 282n, 283, 326, 401–2, 410n
Clenardus, Nicolaus 396–7
Cles, Bernhard von, bishop of Trent 100n, 249n, 258n, 313n, 349n
– letter from 345–7
– letter to 326–7
Cleves, William v, duke of. See William v
Cochlaeus, Johannes, humanist and chaplain to Duke George of Saxony 98n, 113, 114n, 115, 206n, 357n; works: Dialogus de bello contra Turcas, in Antilogias Lutheri 356n; Septiceps Lutherus 115n
Colet, John 29
Cologne 28, 63, 98, 110n, 111n, 112n, 148, 149n, 150n, 215, 226n, 255n, 276, 277n, 292n, 304n, 315n, 407
Constance 4n, 58n, 101n, 218n, 288n, 345n, 378n, 400n
Constantinople 43n, 177, 331n, 356n
Cornarius, Janus 2n, 110–11; edits and translates Hippocrates 3; works: Hippocratis Coi De aere, aquis, & locis libellus. Eiusdem de flatibus graece et latine ... 3n; Hippocratis Coi medici vetustissimi ... libri omnes 3n; Hippocratis Coi ... Opera quae ad nos extant omnia 3n; In divi Hippocratis laudem praefatio ante eiusdem prognostica, per Ianum Cornarium Zuiccauien habita Basiliae 3n; Quarum artium, ac linguarum cog-

nitione medico opus sit. Praefatio ante Hippocratis Aphorismorum initium ... Aphorismi Hippocratis, graece 3n
– letter to 2–4
Cornibus, Petrus de 12
Coronel, Luis Núñes 253, 273
Corte, Pieter de 397, 399
Cortehoevius, Theodoricus, of Antwerp, publishes collection of Erasmus' Adagia xxii, 171n; works: Adagiorum aureum flumen xxii
– letter from 171–4
Courtrai, Erasmus' annuity from 96n, 105, 233n, 250, 342, 407
Cousturier, Pierre 271, 287n
Cranevelt, Frans von 140n, 396
Croock, Cornelis, of Amsterdam 149; works: Farrago sordidorum verborum 144n, 149n, 406
– letter from 404–6
– letter to 143–5
Cruyce, Jan van der 208n, 209
Cyprian, St 17, 19, 155, 198, 218, 221, 290

Dantiscus, Johannes 184, 351, 373–4n
Davidts, Maarten 398–9
Decius, Justus Lodovicus 206n
Deiotarus, Zacharius
– letter from 93–4
Diagoras of Milos 200, 334
Diest 110n, 256
Dilft, Erasmus van der 385
Dilft, Frans van der, Erasmus' famulus and courier 64, 69, 102, 103, 106, 116, 120–1n, 123–4, 125–7, 128n, 131, 132, 133, 134, 139n, 385
Diogenianus 278
Dôle 26, 33, 44n, 61, 159n
Dominicans xvii, 10, 11, 12, 38, 84n, 92n, 170n, 304, 300
Dorp, Maarten van 27, 217
Du Chastel, Emeric 43n
Du Chastel, Pierre
– letter to 42–5
Duprat, Antoine, chancellor of France 242n

Eck, Johann Maier of 288, 339
Edingen, Omaar van, of Ghent 26n,
64n, 140, 188, 233n, 235
Egenolff, Christian, Strasbourg printer
55n, 236n, 246n
Egnazio, Giambattista 24
– letters to 118–20, 273–5
Emser, Hieronymus 113
England 2n, 9, 13, 20, 35, 38n, 48n,
64n, 73n, 85n, 86n, 123, 125, 131, 134,
136, 178, 187n, 188, 189n, 203, 211n,
214, 215, 216, 251, 257, 299, 302, 326,
328n, 341n, 342n, 385n, 400n. *See also*
Catherine of Aragon; English sweat;
Henry VIII
English sweat (British plague, sweating
sickness) 28–30, 59, 61, 65–6, 69,
101n, 120, 131, 132
Episcopius, Nicolaus, Basel printer
21n, 89, 91, 93n, 396
– letter to 138–9
Eppendorf, Heinrich xv, 2n, 38, 50n,
247–8, 325, 345, 372n
Erasmus: complete list of his own works
(*see under* Boece, Hector); portraits of
frontispiece, 301 illustration
Erasmus, original works
– *Adagia* xxii, 3, 6, 10, 13, 20, 29, 31, 32,
33, 42, 43, 47, 53, 63, 72, 76, 79, 81,
86, 90, 107, 110, 111, 115, 120, 121,
122, 124, 131, 134, 140, 141, 142, 144,
151, 152, 158, 163, 166, 167, 169, 172,
173, 174, 176, 179, 180, 182, 190, 193,
195, 196, 198, 199, 200, 201, 210, 211,
214, 222, 229, 235, 239, 242, 244, 250,
261, 279, 282, 297, 298, 329, 332, 334,
338, 345, 351, 356, 364, 365, 372, 373,
374, 381, 389, 395, 399, 401, 405, 406,
407, 408
– *Admonitio adversus mendacium* 247n
– *Apologia adversus monachos quosdam
Hispanos* xvi, 8n, 56n
– *Apologia adversus rhapsodias Alberti Pii*
207
– *Apologia adversus Stunicae Blasphemiae*
268n
– *Apopthegmata* 162

– *Catalogus lucubrationum* 210n
– *Ciceronianus* xv, 24n, 28n, 44n, 60n,
118–19, 212, 241n, 273, 277n, 309,
365n
– *Colloquia* 50, 73, 78, 151, 162, 168,
207n, 214, 230n, 264n, 269
– *Consilium cuiusdam* (with Johannes
Faber) 11n
– *De bello Turcico* xx, 205n, 206n, 210n,
216, 226–32, 245n, 350, 358n, 401n
– *De civilitate* xxii, 208–9
– *De libero arbitrio* 4n, 217
– *De pueris instituendis* 64n, 90n, 212
– *De recta pronuntiatione* 24n, 209n
– *De sarcienda ecclesiae concordia* 224n
– *De vidua christiana* 37, 42, 46, 48,
62–3, 79, 161, 215, 285, 346, 360, 377
– *Detectio praestigiarum* 168n
– *Ecclesiastes* 70n
– *Enchiridion militis christiani* 64n, 215,
253n
– *Epistola ad fratres Inferioris Germaniae*
xix, 293n, 325n, 327n, 358n, 367n,
404n
– *Epistola ad gracculos* xvii, 15n, 195–9,
318, 396n
– *Epistola contra pseudevangelicos* xivn,
xviii, 56n, 57n, 94n, 95, 217, 234n,
236n, 237–8 illustration, 246n, 274n,
277n, 283n, 286, 287, 291, 319, 327,
331n, 337n, 358n, 368
– *Exomologesis* 8n, 215
– *Hyperaspistes* 4n, 217, 356
– *In psalmum* 22 *enarratio triplex* xii,
174–6, 281n
– *Institutio christiani matrimonii* 46n,
174n, 307n
– *Institutio principis christiani* 211n
– *Moriae encomium* 10, 229n
– *Opus epistolarum* xvii, 2n, 15n, 16n,
45n, 115, 128n, 140n, 234n, 258n, 311,
378
– *Paraphrases*: on Ephesians 7n; on
John 36n
– *Paraphrasis in Elegantias Vallae* xxiii,
144n, 148–51, 406
– *Responsio ad annotationes Lei* 178n

– *Responsio ad Collationes cuiusdam iuvenis gerontodidascali* xvii, 15n, 107, 151, 265n, 286
– *Responsio ad epistolam Alberti Pii* 163n, 290n, 330n
– *Responsio adversus febricitantis cuiusdam libellum* xvi, 31n, 197n, 264n, 267n, 269n, 272n
Erasmus, editions and translations
– Alger of Liège *De veritate corporis et sanguinis Dominici in Eucharistia* xx, 218–25
– Augustine *Opera omnia* xxi, xxiin, 21n, 22, 23n, 48, 64n, 74, 75–6, 124, 127, 129, 155, 162, 198, 203n, 204, 243, 299
– John Chrysostom *Opera* xxi–xxii, 73–4, 83, 99n, 121n, 125, 129–30, 139–41, 161, 166–7, 198, 242n, 274, 290n, 299, 364
– *Novum instrumentum* 119n, 152n
– Seneca *Opera omnia* 76, 298–9
– Valla, Lorenzo *Adnotationes in latinam Novi Testamenti interpretationem* 152n
– Xenophon *Hieron* xvii, xxii, 145, 192–4, 350, 406n
Euripides 214, 244
Evangelicals ('false evangelicals') 17n, 57, 115, 117, 234, 246, 255n, 330n, 345, 358

Faber, Johannes 11
Faber Emmeus, Johann, Freiburg printer 319
Faustus of Riez 97–8
Ferdinand of Hapsburg, archduke of Austria, king of Bohemia and Hungary, king of the Romans xi, xii, xiii, 25, 36–7, 46, 47, 57n, 62, 69, 70, 79n, 81, 100n, 103, 113n, 120n, 128n, 130, 135n, 161, 177n, 194n, 206, 210, 228n, 249, 250, 257, 285n, 307n, 308n, 317n, 326n, 344n, 346n, 348, 349n, 350, 351, 360n, 378n, 379n
– letter of to town council of Freiburg 312–13

Fernández de Madrid, Alonso, archdeacon of Alcor 253
Fevijn, Jan van, canon of St Donation's at Bruges
– letter from 203–5
Fichard, Johann 280
Flanders 26, 69, 205n, 230, 231n, 239, 335, 342, 351, 389n, 407
Florence, restoration of Medici rule by imperial troops in 38n, 134n, 160, 281–2
Fonseca, Alonso de, archbishop of Toledo 22, 23n, 124n, 127, 253, 258, 266, 375
– letter to 128–31
France, the French 2n, 7n, 9, 13, 17, 20, 28, 37, 44n, 65n, 69n, 71, 73n, 81, 93, 138, 177, 201, 211n, 230, 242n, 250, 257, 288, 316, 323, 376, 400n; Erasmus and 32, 118, 162, 241n, 244, 308–9; French language 17, 395; and the war in Italy 25, 37, 200n. *See also* Francis I, king of France; French disease
Francis, St 13–14, 26n, 262, 266, 269, 270
Franciscans (Observants, Conventuals) xvii, 4n, 10, 12–14, 15n, 72, 108n, 162n, 169, 196n, 261, 262, 264–5, 269–70, 271, 272, 330n
– open letter to 195–9
Francis I, king of France xii, xvi, 20, 25n, 37, 43n, 44n, 47n, 51n, 53, 63n, 81n, 93n, 138, 200n, 249n, 250n, 257, 376, 386. *See also* Cambrai, Peace of; France
Frankfurt am Main 2n, 246n, 280n; book fairs at 15n, 44n, 59n, 114, 174n, 187, 196n, 236, 283, 290, 292n, 295, 324n, 383, 385, 395
Frankfurt an der Oder 113n, 114
Freiburg im Breisgau xi, xii, xiv, 2n, 20, 21, 43, 49n, 56n, 57n, 64n, 66n, 69n, 77n, 84, 91, 92n, 101n, 116n, 121n, 134n, 135n, 139n, 176, 182n, 187n, 194n, 196n, 203n, 204n, 205n, 207n, 210, 218n, 221n, 224n, 240n, 245n, 248n, 270n, 275, 280, 284n, 287, 295n,

309, 312n, 313n, 314, 317n, 318n, 319n, 320n, 322n, 325n, 331n, 339n, 346n, 352n, 379n, 382, 400n, 410n; Erasmus moves to xi–xii, 25, 26, 47, 62n, 71, 104, 119

French disease (French pox) 30–1n, 148, 227

Friesland 10, 93n, 159n, 163n, 164n, 231n, 276n, 325, 376

Friesland, Gerard of
– letter from 85–6

Froben, Hieronymus, publisher at Basel 44, 45n, 78, 81, 84–5n, 89n, 91, 138n, 195, 208, 277n, 278, 290, 324n, 383, 397. *See also* Froben press

Froben, Johann, publisher at Basel 82n, 83–4, 120n, 138n

Froben, Johannes Erasmius 81n, 82, 83, 84, 85n, 395
– letter to 77–8

Froben press xi, xxi, 3n, 13n, 21n, 22, 24n, 32n, 43n, 47, 49n, 60n, 64n, 74, 78n, 82n, 83n, 121n, 124n, 140n, 162n, 166n, 174n, 192n, 194n, 206n, 208n, 226n, 242, 264, 274, 278, 290, 299, 329, 330n, 378n

Fuchs, Leonhard, mayor of Neuenburg am Rhein and father-in-law of Bonifacius Amerbach 135n, 207n

Fuchs, Martha, wife of Bonifacius Amerbach 66n, 207

Fugger, Anton, head of banking house of Fugger xxii, 62, 183n, 184, 186, 188, 233, 248n, 258–9, 282, 283n, 375
– letter from 281–2
– letters to 192–4, 338–9

Fulgentius, St 98

Gachi, Jean 12
Galen 50, 292
Gattinara, Mercurino, imperial chancellor 103n, 129n, 267n, 268n, 328n, 331n, 349n, 350n, 352n, 377

Gaza, Theodorus 244
Gelasius, pope 220
Geldenhouwer, Gerard, of Nijmegen, Dutch humanist and Strasbourg reformer xviii–xix, 55–7, 95n, 161, 236, 246n, 247n, 250n, 274, 283, 286n, 287n, 293n, 319, 324n, 327n, 336n, 337n, 368, 404n, 407n; publishes unauthorized edition of Erasmus' *Epistola contra pseudevangelicos* xviii, 57n, 94–5, 236n, 237–8 illustration, 246n, 287, 319, 327n, 337n; works: *D. Erasmi Roterodami Annotationes in leges pontificias et caesareas de haereticis. Epistolae aliquot Gerardi Noviomagi* 56n, 337n; *Ejn Antwort des D. Erasmi von Roterdam, die ersuchung und verfolgung der Ketzer betreffend, disser zeyt allen Flursten, Herren, Ratherren, Richter und allen gewalthabern fast nötig zu wissen* 56n, 337n; *Epistolae Erasmi* (lost work) 56n, 337n; *Verzeychnung Erasmi Roterodami über Bäpstliche vnnd Kaiserliche Recht von den Ketzern. Etlich Sendtbrieff Gerardi Noviomagi* 56n.
– letter to 94–5, 238 illustration

Gellius, Aulus 33
Genoa 20, 133n, 184n
George, duke of Saxony xiv, 38, 113n, 114n, 258, 325n, 343, 367n, 368n, 370; works: *Epistolae atque libelli aliquot, continentes controversiam, quae inter ... Georgium Saxoniae Ducem ... & M. Lutherum ... versata est* 354n

George, margrave of Brandenburg 343
George, messenger 83, 84
George of Masevaux, abbot of Murbach 101n

George of Trebizond 244n
Germany (Holy Roman Empire) xi, xii, xiii, xv, xvii, xviii, 2, 20n, 21, 57n, 58n, 59, 63n, 65, 71, 86, 100n, 101, 116n, 118n, 119, 122n, 125, 130n, 135n, 160n, 169n, 171, 174, 183n, 185, 186, 203n, 205, 226n, 229, 230, 240, 241, 248n, 249n, 282, 284n, 285, 288, 292n, 305, 308, 315, 328n, 330n, 331–3, 335, 342n, 347, 348, 356, 363, 367n, 380, 386, 388, 396, 400n

Giberti, Gian Matteo, bishop of Verona 363

Gillis, Pieter, town clerk of Antwerp 105, 147 illustration, 395, 406
– letter to 145–59
Glareanus, Henricus, eminent Swiss humanist 53n, 54, 101, 240, 274, 318, 351, 352–3
Goclenius, Conradus, professor of Latin at the Collegium Trilingue in Louvain 62n, 78n, 90n, 91n, 93, 111, 140n, 187n, 196n, 375, 380, 382, 383, 300, 400; and Erasmus' finances xxii, 354, 386–94
– letter from 384–99
Gogreve, Johann, chancellor of Cleves 112n, 255, 394n
Gracián de Alderete, Diego
– letter from 253–4
Gratian 207, 220n
Griffolini, Francesco, of Arezzo. See Aretino, Francesco
Gruyères, Leonard de, canon of Besançon 102n, 103n, 376n
Grynaeus, Simon, professor of Greek at Basel 83n, 85n, 242n
Guise, Antoine de, duke of Lorraine 52 illustration, 53, 258n
Guise, Jean de, bishop of Metz and cardinal of Lorraine 99n, 258n
– letter to 51–4
Guitmund 221, 222n

Haio Herman, of Friesland
– letter to 159–63
Harst, Karl, councillor to the duke of Cleves 78n, 82, 385n, 394
Heemstede, Jan of
– letter from 399–400
Heinrich, messenger 329, 339, 370
Henckel, Johann, court preacher to Mary of Hungary 42n, 308, 359–60n, 362, 363n, 372, 373, 378
– letter from 284–6
– letter to 79–81
Henry VIII, king of England 20, 21n, 35, 47n, 86, 133n, 174n, 235n, 250, 389n; divorce of xxii, 36n, 38n, 48n, 94n, 134n, 136–8, 178–82

Henry of Portugal, archbishop of Braga 397
Herema, Gerard van
– letter to 164–5
Heresbach, Konrad, counsellor to the duke of Cleves 90, 11, 255n
Herman, Haio. See Haio Herman
's-Hertogenbosch 49n, 51
Herwagen, Johann, Basel printer 82n, 83n, 84–5n, 92, 93, 120, 235, 274
Hessen xiii, 47n, 58n, 354n, 367n, 407. See also Philip, landgrave of Hessen
Hesychius of Jerusalem 135, 300
Hilary of Poitiers, St 97n, 162, 221, 300
Hippocrates 3, 50, 402. See also Cornarius, Janus
Holbein, Hans, the Younger 40–1
Holzach, Eucharius 323
Hondt, Jan de 105
Hoogstraten, Jacob of, Dominican of Cologne 63n, 271, 304
Horace 241, 381
Horák, Jan
– letter from 112–15
Hormisdas, pope 98
Hungary xii, 14, 36–7, 42, 46, 47, 53n, 62n, 69, 71, 79n, 81n, 93, 97n, 135n, 161n, 194n, 206n, 215, 228–9, 249, 250n, 278n, 284n, 307n, 313, 346n, 348, 349, 360n, 363n, 372n, 377
Hutten, Moritz von 321 illustration, 322
Hutten, Ulrich von xvii, 217, 246n, 322n

Ignatius of Antioch, St 339–40
Innsbruck 160, 248n, 268n, 288, 289n, 311, 312n, 313, 315, 341, 349, 402n
Isabella of Portugal, empress (wife of Charles v) 22n, 254n
Isenburg, Anton and Salentin von, counts 255
Italy xii, 14, 17, 20, 24, 25, 26, 28, 30, 38, 43n, 47, 50n, 93, 100n, 103, 105, 119n, 122n, 129, 133n, 135, 136, 159n, 160n, 164n, 177, 179n, 183, 184, 185, 200n, 211n, 228, 229n, 235n, 239, 244, 249, 253,

264, 281, 282–3, 290, 317, 327, 330, 337, 338, 347, 351n, 363, 365n, 374n, 400n

James IV, king of Scotland 211
James V, king of Scotland 211
Jerome, St 16n, 17, 18, 19, 72, 101n, 108, 152n, 154, 155, 162, 170, 175, 198, 221, 251, 300, 302, 355
John, elector of Saxony 288n, 343n, 346n, 355
John Chrysostom, St 91n, 105n, 188, 216, 221, 232–3, 241n, 252, 290, 363, 396. *See also under* Erasmus, editions and translations
John III, duke of Cleves 110n, 254n, 347n
Jud, Hieronymus 322n

Kammen, Adriaan van der, of Mechelen
– letter from 106–7
Kan, Nicolaas, Erasmus' servant-messenger 78, 92n, 97, 144, 163, 370n, 376, 377n, 385, 393, 396n, 403n, 406, 407, 408
Kappel: First Kappel War 59n, 60n, 241n; First Peace of Kappel 60n
Karlstadt, Andreas 322n, 323–4
Keck, Georg 21n
Kempten 311–12
Koler, Johann, canon of St Moritz in Augsburg 193, 235
– letter from 183–7
– letters to 282–4, 339–40
Könneritz, Andreas and Christoph
– letter to 194–5
Krzycki, Andrzej, bishop of Płock 259, 379n, 382

Laelius 34
Lascaris, Janus 28n, 118n, 243, 308
Łaski, Hieronim 206n
Łaski, Jan (II) 205–6, 208
Latomus, Jacobus 14n, 197, 271
Laurensen, Laurens 10n, 11n
Laurinus, Marcus, canon of St Donation's at Bruges 204–5, 233, 397, 398, 400

Lee, Edward 178, 180n, 268, 269, 271, 287n
Lefèvre d'Etaples, Jacques xvi, 15n, 19, 152, 265, 339n
Leipzig 2n, 112n, 113n, 114n, 115, 194n, 354, 356n
Leonico Tomeo, Niccolò 374n
Leo X, pope 10n, 20n, 230n, 231, 374n
Linz 285
Listrius, Gerardus 85n, 86
Longland, John, bishop of Lincoln 64n, 168, 258
– letter from 74–6
López Zúñiga, Diego 184
Lorraine, Antoine. *See* Guise, Antoine de
Lorraine, Jean. *See* Guise, Jean de
Lotzer, Johann
– letter from 279–80
Louis II, king of Hungary and Bohemia 37, 228n, 278n, 359n, 362n
Louis V, elector Palatine 130–4, 279n, 280
Louvain xvi, xxiii, 2n, 10, 11n, 13, 14–15n, 16n, 27n, 62n, 63n, 78n, 82, 83n, 91, 92, 106n, 110, 112n, 140, 144n, 163, 164n, 170n, 196n, 203, 209n, 233, 242, 256, 261n, 265, 266n, 269, 272, 287n, 288n, 291n, 304n, 305, 318n, 375n, 379n, 382n, 383, 384n, 385n, 386n, 395n, 396n, 399n, 400, 406; College of the Lily at 384n, 397n; Collegium Trilingue at 49n, 110n, 111n, 397n, 398n
Luther, Martin xii, xv, xvii, xix–xx, 3–4, 9, 11n, 12, 13n, 38, 44n, 57n, 58, 61, 82n, 109n, 113n, 114, 115n, 117n, 170n, 182, 204, 205, 207, 218n, 230n, 231–2, 288n, 295, 300n, 304, 319n, 320, 323n, 330, 336, 337, 343, 354–8, 359, 362n, 367, 369n, 370, 403n; revises the Vulgate New Testament 61n; works: *Ad dialogum Silvestri Prierati de potestate papae responsio* 304n; *Declamationes in Genesin* 182n; *De servo arbitrio* 4n; *Eine Heerpredigt widder den Türcken* 205–6n, 357n;

Explanations of the Ninety-Five Theses
231–2n; *New Zeittung von Leyptzig*
115n; *Ninety-Five Theses on the Power*
and Efficacy of Indulgences 230n, 304n;
Von heimlichen vnd gestolen brieffen –
widder Hertzog Georgen zu Sachsen.
Mart. Luth. 354–6, 370; *Vom kriege*
widder die Türcken 205–6n, 207, 356n,
357n, 358n
Lutherans xiii, xiv, 58–9n, 74, 101n,
119n, 249, 255n, 276n, 284, 288, 289n,
305, 330, 332, 336, 337, 344n, 345,
367n, 369, 373, 374, 401, 402
Lyon 31, 60n, 78n, 82, 179n, 189n

Mainz. *See* Albert of Brandenburg
Maldonado, Juan, vicar-general at
Burgos
– letter to 120–2
Manrique de Lara, Alonso, archbishop
of Seville 129, 261, 266, 350
– letter to 271–3
Manuel, Don Juan 253, 266
Marburg 2n, 49, 58
Marburg Colloquy 3n, 58–9n, 60n, 67n
Marck, Erard de la, cardinal of Liège
63
Margaret of Angoulême, queen of
Navarre 44
Marius, Augustinus, cathedral preacher
at Würzburg 38n, 221n, 275, 309, 310
– letter to 317–20
Marseille 23
Martens, Dirk, of Aalst, printer at
Louvain 396
Martens, Joachim, of Ghent 195, 291–2
Mary, princess, future queen of Eng-
land 136, 180
Mary of Austria, queen of Hungary 37,
42, 46, 62, 79n, 97n, 204n, 215, 228,
284n, 285n, 346n, 359n, 360, 372n
– letter to 377–8
Maxentius, Joannes 98
Maximilian I, Holy Roman emperor 40
Mechelen 64n, 97n, 106, 163n, 185
Medmann, Peter 254n
– letter from 276–7

Melanchthon, Philippus 3, 49n, 58–
9n, 61n, 117n, 255n, 276n, 323, 324n,
343–4n, 362n, 371 illustration
– letter to 369–70
Mendoza y Córdoba, Francisco de,
bishop of Zamora 254
Merklin, Balthasar, bishop of Constance
101n, 219 illustration, 298n
– letter to 218–25
Mexía, Cristóbal, brother of Pero xvii,
256–7n
– letter to 256–62
Mexía, Pero, of Seville xvii, 15n, 261,
262–4n, 263 illustration
– letter to 262–71
Middleton, Alice, wife of Thomas More
42n
Monaco 20
Montanus, Philippus 291, 292
Moravia 37, 63, 79n, 228n, 285n
More, Cecily 42n
More, Elizabeth 42n
More, John 42
More, Margaret. *See* Roper, Margaret
More, Thomas, lord chancellor of
England 27n, 40n, 41 illustration,
42n, 66, 94n, 125, 126 illustration,
166, 169n, 203
– letter from 77
– letter to 35–40
More family 41 illustration
Morrhy, Gerard
– letter from 289–92

Nachtgall, Ottmar 171, 187, 284, 288
Naerden, Maerten van 163
Neocomus, Vulturius. *See* Geldenhouwer, Gerard
Nesen, Wilhelm 76n
Netherlands xxii, 2n, 31n, 63n, 97n,
104n, 106n, 119n, 164n, 187n, 204n,
261n, 360n, 385n, 386n, 403n
Neuenahr, Hermann von, count,
archdeacon of the Cologne cathedral chapter 110n, 111; works: (co-
author with Simon Riquinus) *De*
novo hactenusque Germaniae inaudito

*morbo sudatoria febri, quem vulgo su-
dorem Britannicum vocant ... iudicium
doctissimum* 112n, 138n
Neve, Jean de, and Erasmus' finances
384, 386–92, 393
Nicolai, Everardus 163, 164n
Nijmegen, Gerard of. *See* Geldenhouwer, Gerard
Novimagus, Gerardus. *See* Geldenhouwer, Gerard
Nürnberg 289, 355, 367n, 402n

Oecolampadius, Johannes, leader of
the Reformation in Basel xvii, xviii,
26n, 38n, 58, 67n, 83, 85n, 117, 205n,
208, 293, 317n, 320, 323–4, 329, 367;
translates St John Chrysostom and
Theophylact xxi, 74, 83n, 99, 141n,
166–7, 242n
Offenburg, Johann Egli 53n, 54n
Olahus, Nicolaus, chief minister to
Mary of Hungary 204n, 361 illustration
– letter from 359–63
– letter to 372–3
Omphalius, Jacobus 291, 292
Origen 72, 73n, 167–8, 216
Orléans 32, 43n, 164n, 255n
Ovid 117, 303n

Pace, Richard 125
– letter to 233–4
Padua 24, 136, 179n, 186, 235, 239–40,
317n, 330, 374n, 378n, 379n, 385n
Palatinate. *See* Louis v, elector Palatine
Paris 12n, 13, 22n, 43–4, 60n, 65n, 67,
71n, 78n, 83, 91, 92, 148, 149–50,
152n, 162, 166n, 196n, 210, 242n,
243n, 244, 261n, 264, 272, 290, 291n,
292n, 330, 337, 339n, 379n, 410;
Collège des Lombards at 290n;
faculty of theology at 10n, 44n, 51,
207n, 232n, 287, 357n (*see also* Béda,
Noël); Parlement of 264–5, 272n, 305;
trilingual college at 162–3
Paul, St 27, 72, 153, 156, 165, 168, 188,
209, 222, 271, 358

Paulinus, St, bishop of Nola 51
Persius 34
Phaedon 394
Philip, landgrave of Hessen xiii, 58n,
130, 134, 288–9, 343
Pimpinella, Vincenzo, archbishop of
Rossano 70n
Pio, Alberto, prince of Carpi xvi,
57n, 85n, 207n, 243, 290, 330, 337,
357n; works: *Responsio accurata et
paranaetica* 330n; *Tres et viginti libri
in locos lucubrationum Erasmi* 163n,
290n
Pirckheimer, Willibald, Nürnberg
humanist 98n, 140n
– letter to 45–6
Pistoris, Simon, chancellor of the duchy
of Saxony 354
– letter from 343–5
– letter to 370–2
Pius II, pope 231
Plateanus, Petrus 194n
– letter from 48–51
Plato 174
Pliny 30, 34n, 43n, 206n
Plutarch 162, 214, 244, 285
Poland 14, 17, 184, 206n, 250, 257, 259,
379–80n, 381, 382, 383
Polyphemus. *See* Rex, Felix
Proost, Jacob 109

Quiñones, Cardinal Francisco de 13n,
184n

Reinach, Jost von, canon of Basel 367,
368, 372
Rem, Wolfgang 183, 187
Resch, Konrad 65n, 292n
Rescius, Rutgerus, professor of Greek
at the Collegium Trilingue in Lou-
vain 111, 398
Rex, Felix (nicknamed Polyphemus),
Erasmus' famulus and letter-carrier
36n, 79n, 235n, 345, 349, 351, 362,
368n
Rhenanus, Beatus. *See* Beatus Rhenanus
Riedt, Johann von 277

Rievieren, Eustachius van der, Dominican of Cologne 64n, 170n, 397n
– letter to (?) 170–1
Rinck, Johann, of Cologne 203
– letters to 226–32, 400–4
Riquinus, Simon, physician at the court of Jülich-Cleves 2n, 64n, 195, 276; works (co-author with Hermann von Neuenahr) *De novo hactenusque Germaniae inaudito morbo sudatoria febri, quem vulgo sudorem Britannicum vocant ... iudicium doctissimum* 112n, 138n
– letters from 110–12, 254–6
Rome 11n, 12, 37–8n, 43n, 48n, 58, 69, 70n, 135n, 144n, 160, 179n, 211n, 223n, 229n, 230n, 244, 257n, 352n, 353, 374n, 375n
Roper, Margaret, *née* More 46, 88 illustration
– letter from 87–9
– letter to 40–2
Roper, William 42, 88 illustration
Rotterdam 51

Sadoleto, Jacopo, bishop of Carpentras 191 illustration, 239–40, 259; works: *In Psalmum 93 interpretatio* 189–90, 296–8, 300n
– letter from 189–92
– letter to 295–306
Salamanca xvi, 12n, 13, 196, 261n, 262n, 266n, 268n, 272n, 273n, 397n
Salvian of Marseille 277n, 278
Santiago de Compostela 230
Savona 23
Saxony, duchy of. *See* George, duke of Saxony
Saxony, electorate of 47n, 49n, 58n, 113n, 115n, 288, 323n, 344n, 354n, 376n, 407. *See also* John, elector of Saxony
Schabler, Johann, known as Wattenschnee 60, 65n
Schepper, Cornelis de, diplomat in the service of Charles v 204n, 205n, 248n

– letter from 327–8
– letter to 348–52
Schets, Erasmus, Antwerp banker and manager of Erasmus' financial affairs in the Netherlands and England xxiii, 64n, 96n, 139n, 140, 165, 385
– letters from 104–6, 187–8
– letters to 182–3, 232–3, 325–6
Schott, Johann, Strasbourg printer 246n
Schmalkalden, Protestant League of 58n, 59n, 113n, 280n
Schweis, Alexander 314n, 315
Scuppegius, Lucas 51
Sedulius Scottus, ninth-century biblical scholar 19
Seneca. *See under* Erasmus, editions and translations
Sepúlveda, Juan Ginés de 163n, 330n, 337n
Sigismund i, king of Poland 250, 257–8
Słap Dąbrówski, Marcin 376n, 395
– letter from 379–83
Socrates 27n, 172, 394
Spain xvi, 7, 12, 13, 17, 22, 23, 64n, 103, 116n, 120n, 123–4, 127–9, 132, 133, 134n, 196n, 197, 214, 230n, 231n, 248n, 249, 257n, 261n, 262, 266n, 273, 288, 289, 305, 327, 347n, 375n, 396n
Speyer 25, 62, 79n, 194n; Diet of xiii, 36–7, 47–8n, 57–8n, 61n, 100n, 119n, 289
Stadion, Christoph von, bishop of Augsburg 162n, 183n, 185, 202, 259, 402
– letter to 340–2
Standish, Henry, bishop of St Asaph 13
Stella, Petrus 32
Stewart, Alexander, archbishop of St Andrew's 211
Stewart, James, early of Moray 211n
St Gallen 324
Stiebar, Daniel 275, 310, 318n, 319n
– letter to 320–2
Strasbourg xvii, xviii–xix, 2n, 28, 55, 56n, 58n, 69, 82n, 89n, 95n, 138n, 161, 194n, 236n, 247, 250n, 254n, 277, 283, 293, 319, 323n, 324, 327, 330n, 337, 338, 339, 345n, 407

– letter to magistrates of 245–7

Stromer, Heinrich, of Auerbach 114

Sucket, Karel, law student at Bourges 26, 33, 44, 201, 335
– letter to 406–8

Swabian League 183

sweating sickness. *See* English sweat

Switzerland xi, xv, xvii, 57n, 58n, 59n, 60n, 73n, 116n, 135n, 177n, 249n, 342n, 352n, 367n

Szydłowiecki, Krzysztof, chancellor of Poland 383n

Talesius, Quirinus, Erasmus' famulus and messenger 64, 69n, 71n, 75, 76, 77, 85n, 87, 93–4, 99, 102n, 104–5, 106n, 110, 111, 112, 125n, 139n, 143, 170, 187–8, 233, 234, 255, 328n, 370, 376, 377n, 384n, 386, 388, 392, 393, 400, 403n, 408

Taxander, Godefridus Ruysius, pseudonymous author of *Apologia in eum librum quem ab anno Erasmus Roterodamus de confessione edidit* 11n. *See also* Theoderici, Vincentius

Terence 154, 155, 172

Theoderici, Vincentius 10n, 11n. *See also* Taxander, Godefridus Ruysius

Theophylact 98

Thüngen, Konrad von, bishop of Würzburg 318n, 319n
– letter from 309–10
– letter to 275–6

Thurzo, Johannes, bishop of Wrocław 260

Thurzo, Stanislaus, bishop of Olomouc 260

Titelmans, Frans, Franciscan at Louvain xvi–xvii, 4n, 13n, 14–15n, 130n, 145n, 151–2, 163, 169n, 196n, 197n, 203n, 261n, 265–6, 270n, 286n, 305n, 324n, 330n; works: *Collationes quinque super epistolam ad Romanos* 15–19, 107–8, 152–8, 265–6, 288n; *De authoritate libri Apocalypsis* 15n, 109; *Epistola apologetica pro opere Collationum* 15n, 107–9

– letter from 107–9

Tomicki, Piotr, bishop of Cracow 259, 383

Tournai 64n, 95n, 96n, 291

Tournon, François de, bishop of Bourges 44

Toussaint, Jacques 28n, 65, 118n, 162n, 243–4, 364, 365, 366

Trechsel, Melchior, Lyon printer 82n

Trent 20, 36, 100, 113, 204n, 248n, 249, 258, 281, 313, 326n, 328n, 346, 349

Truchsess von Waldburg, Christoph
– letter to 378–9

Tunstall, Cuthbert, bishop of London 64n, 182, 258
– letter from 71–4
– letter to 165–9

Turks xii, xiii, xix-xx, 36–7, 47, 53, 62n, 63, 69, 71n, 79, 81n, 93, 101n, 103n, 120, 130, 135, 148, 160, 161n, 177, 205–6, 207, 226n, 228, 344n, 356–7, 378n, 401, 403n. *See also* Vienna: siege of

Überlingen 4

Ulm 289

Ursinus Velius, Caspar 277, 279, 362
– letter from 307–9

Uutenhove, Karel, of Ghent 118, 239, 241, 274
– letters to 24–31, 234–6

Valdés, Alfonso de, Latin secretary to Charles v 121, 128, 129, 253, 264, 328, 350, 351
– letters to 123–4, 245, 376–7

Valdés, Fernando de 377n

Valdés, Juan de
– letter to 122–3

Valla, Lorenzo xvi, 15n, 19n, 32n, 74n, 45n, 152, 207, 265; Erasmus publishes paraphrase of his *Elegantiae linguae latinae* xxiii, 144n, 148–51, 406; other works (*see under* Erasmus, editions and translations)

Valladolid, conference of theologians at 12n, 198n, 266n, 268n, 305n

Venice 50, 118, 120n, 136, 160n, 179n, 352, 353n, 363, 374n
Vergara, Francisco de, professor of Greek at Alcalá
– letter to 131–2
Vergara, Juan de, secretary to Alonso de Fonseca, archbishop of Toledo 129, 131
– letter to 124–8
Vienna 25, 36, 37, 62, 277n, 278n, 307n, 317n, 360n; siege of xii, xiii, 36n, 53n, 62n, 71n, 80 illustration, 81n, 161, 307–8, 356n
Vio, Tommaso de (Cajetanus) 12
Virgilio, Polidoro 278n, 290
Vitoria, Francisco de 12n
Vitoria, Pedro de 12n
Vives, Juan Luis 268, 397–8, 399; edits Augustine's *City of God* 21–2n, 75–6
– letter from 21–3
Vlatten, Johann von, councillor to the duke of Cleves 112n, 254–5
– letter from 347–8
– letters to 61–4, 373
Vulturius. *See* Geldenhouwer, Gerard

Wain, Gervasius 60n, 291n
Wakefield, Robert 234n
Walther, Hieronymus, Leipzig agent of the Welser bank of Augsburg 114
Warham, William, archbishop of Canterbury 93n, 105, 125, 250, 258, 259, 341; and Erasmus' income from England xxiii, 250n, 341–2n
Wattenschnee. *See* Schabler, Johann
Wechel, Chrétien 292
Weynsen, Matthias 13n, 108n, 109n
Willem of Haarlem 398
William v, duke of Cleves 64n, 111n, 162n, 254n, 258, 292n

– letter from 90–1
Wimpina, Conradus Coci de, professor of theology at Frankfurt an der Oder 113, 114–15
Wittenberg 3
Wolsey, Thomas Cardinal 48n, 77n, 86n, 94, 99n, 100n, 104, 125, 208n, 234n, 250n
Worms, Edict of xiii, 403n

Xenophon, ancient Greek historian, *Hieron. See under* Erasmus, editions and translations.

Zápolyai, John, rival of Ferdinand of Austria for the kingship of Hungary 36n, 37n, 161n, 206n, 250n, 360n
Zasius, Udalricus, professor of law at Freiburg 2n, 25, 32n, 135n, 176, 194n, 240, 274, 280n, 317, 318, 322n, 335, 336n
Zeeland 27, 231n
Zeno 334
Zenobius 278
Ziegler, Paul, bishop of Chur 185
Znojmo 37, 79n, 285n
Zuichemus, Viglius, student of law at Bourges 55, 65, 201, 335
– letter from 31–5
– letter to 406–8
Zúñiga, Diego López. *See* López Zúñiga, Diego
Zúñiga, Francesco de 22n
Zürich xvii, 3n, 58–9n, 67, 89n, 161, 289, 324
Zwingli, Huldrych xvii, xx, 3–4n, 58–9n, 60n, 67–8n, 218n, 221n, 333n, 345n, 367; works: *Ratio fidei ad Carolum Imperatorem* 345n
Zwinglians xiii, 3n, 58–9n, 101n, 289n, 324n, 344n, 345, 367n, 402

The design of
THE COLLECTED WORKS
OF ERASMUS
was created
by
ALLAN FLEMING
1929–1977
for
the University
of Toronto
Press